MORAL PHILOSOPHY
Selected Readings

GEORGE SHER
University of Vermont

Under the general editorship of
Robert J. Fogelin
Dartmouth College

HARCOURT BRACE JOVANOVICH, PUBLISHERS
San Diego   New York   Chicago   Austin
London   Sydney   Tokyo   Toronto

ISBN: 0–15–564070–4
Library of Congress Catalog Card Number: 85-82629
Printed in the United States of America

Copyrights and Acknowledgments

The author is grateful to the following publishers and copyright holders for permission to use the selections reprinted in this book:

BASIC BOOKS   For "The Experience Machine," from *Anarchy, State, and Utopia* by Robert Nozick. © 1974 by Basic Books, Inc., Publishers. Reprinted by permission of the publisher.

CAMBRIDGE UNIVERSITY PRESS   For "Goodness as Simple and Indefinable," from *Principia Ethica,* by G. E. Moore; for "Moral Luck," from *Mortal Questions* by Thomas Nagel; for "Desire, Choice, and the Good," from *Liberalism and the Limits of Justice* by Michael J. Sandel; for "Why Act Morally," from *Practical Ethics,* by Peter Singer. All reprinted by permission of the publisher, Cambridge University Press.

CORNELL UNIVERSITY PRESS   For "The Moral Point of View," from *The Moral Point of View: A Rational Basis of Ethics.* © 1958 by Cornell University Press. Used by permission of the publisher, Cornell University Press.

DOVER PUBLICATIONS   For "The Emotive Theory of Ethics," from *Language, Truth, and Logic,* by A. J. Ayer. Reprinted by permission of the publisher.

FOOT, PHILIPPA   For "Morality as a System of Hypothetical Imperative." Reprinted by permission of the author.

GEWIRTH, ALAN   For "The Is-Ought Problem Resolved," from *Proceedings and Addresses of The American Philosophical Association 1973–74* (vol. XLVII). Reprinted by permission of the author.

HACKETT PUBLISHING COMPANY   For "Euthyphro," from *The Trial and Death of Socrates,* by Plato, translated by G. M. A. Grube; for "The ring of Gyges," from *The Republic of Plato,* translated by G. M. A. Grube. Reprinted by permission of Hackett Publishing Co., Inc., Indianapolis, Indiana.

HARPER & ROW   For "Indoctrination Versus Relativity in Value Education," from *The Philosophy of Moral Development,* vol. 1, by Lawrence Kohlberg. Copyright © 1971 Joint Publication Board of Zygon and the University of Chicago. Reprinted by permission of Harper & Row, Publishers, Inc.

HARVARD UNIVERSITY PRESS   For "Imposing Risks Upon Others," excerpted by permission of the author and publisher from *An Anatomy of Values,* by Charles Fried, Cambridge, MA: Harvard University Press. Copyright © 1970 by The President and Fellows of Harvard College; for "Intention, Harm, and Personal Discretion," reprinted by permission of the author and publishers from *Right and Wrong,* by Charles Fried, Cambridge, MA: Harvard University Press. Copyright © 1978 by the President and Fellows of Harvard College; for "A Theory of Justice," "Classical Utilitarianism," and "Rational Life Plans," reprinted by permission of the publisher from *A Theory of Justice,* by John Rawls, Cambridge, MA: The Belknap Press of Harvard University Press, © 1971 by the President and Fellows of Harvard College.

continued on page 711

Preface

Moral Philosophy: Selected Readings introduces the reader to the full range of problems of moral philosophy, from metaethics to applied ethics. It combines substantial chunks of the classics, which everyone should read, with some of the best of the extremely interesting work of the recent past and the present. In general, my principle of selection has been simply to include as much as possible of what seems to be best and most important. However, in Part VI, Applications, I have purposely included none of the fine recent work on social policy and the justice of institutions. Essays on these topics would not mesh well with the preceding selections, which focus mostly on individual behavior.

There is no need for lengthy introductory discussion; the essays speak for themselves. But two pedagogical matters do require brief mention. There is, first, the matter of the book's organization. To provide the student with some structure, I have followed the convention of grouping the readings into sections. But I am as aware as anyone that the divisions thus imposed are largely spurious. We cannot fully understand why someone ought to be moral without understanding what it is to have a reason, and neither can we fully understand what it is to have a reason without understanding how reasons can engage the will. Because of this, the issues raised in the first three sections flow back and forth into one another. Things are somewhat—but only somewhat—more orderly when we come to the next three sections. Thus, I bequeath to the instructor the problem of imparting a sense of multiple connectedness without allowing the inquiry to degenerate into formless free-for-all.

The second pedagogical issue concerns the readings' level of difficulty. Some very important positions in moral philosophy are inherently complex, while others presuppose sophisticated views from other areas of philosophy. As a result, any collection of this type must strike some balance between comprehensiveness and comprehensibility. In establishing my own balance, I have included a few essays that seem too difficult to assign to beginning students. But I think the great majority of the book's essays—far more than can be taught in any single semester—fall well within the grasp of the beginning student. Thus, the anthology is compatible with a variety of styles of introductory ethics courses. At the same time, it should be suitable for an intermediate or even an advanced course in moral theory.

In compiling and editing the book, I have received help from a variety of friends and colleagues, and I am pleased to acknowledge their contributions. While choosing the readings, I received many helpful suggestions from Hilary Kornblith, Arthur Kuflik, A. John Simmons, Robert Simon, Richard Werner, and William Wilcox. When writing the introductory material, I received valuable criticism from Hilary Kornblith, Arthur Kuflik, William Mann, and William Wilcox, none of whom should be held responsible for any errors the introductory material may now contain. At both stages, Robert Fogelin, Philosophy Series Editor for Harcourt Brace Jovanovich, was extremely helpful. In addition, I benefited from the highly professional skills of Bill McLane, Eleanor Garner, and Rick Roehrich at Harcourt Brace Jovanovich, and—as always—of Leslie Weiger at the University of Vermont. To all these people, I am very grateful.

George Sher

Contents

I

MORAL PSYCHOLOGY
AND MORAL
EDUCATION

MORALITY IS ACTION-GUIDING. When we ask which acts are right and wrong, we are, in part, trying to discover how to act. Moreover, our beliefs about morality often affect the ways in which we *do* act. In many cases, people seem to do things precisely because they believe them to be right. The study of such moral behavior is known as *moral psychology*.

Perhaps the most basic question of moral psychology is *how* moral reasons move us to act. When people do what they have promised to do, or support worthy causes out of duty, are they influenced by the rightness of the acts themselves? Or is it because they expect to receive some benefit by doing what is right? The view that we always pursue our own benefit—that our ultimate motive in acting is always self-interest—is known as *psychological egoism*. Because there are different views about what is in a person's interest, there are also different versions of psychological egoism. In one common view, our interest consists entirely of pleasure and the avoidance of pain. If a psychological egoist believes this, he accepts *psychological hedonism*.

Because it is obvious that we do care about what affects us, psychological egoism has an immediate plausibility. Versions of this view can be found in the thoughts of Thomas Hobbes (reading 18), Jeremy Bentham (reading 34), and, although less consistently, John Stuart Mill (reading 26). Yet despite its attractiveness, psychological egoism is far from obviously correct. Indeed, when we are given arguments such as those presented by Joel Feinberg (reading 1), the case for it seems far weaker than many believe.

What are the alternatives? One possibility, often associated with Immanuel Kant (reading 29), is that moral reasons can themselves move us to act. On this view, appreciating why we ought to do something can by itself provide us with the impetus to do it. Indeed, there are places where Kant appears to go further. He sometimes suggests that unless moral rightness can be demonstrated by reason alone, the motivation it provides is too contingent, too accidental, to confer genuine moral worth upon acts. As Kant himself describes it, "[t]he practical necessity of acting according to this principle, i.e. duty, does not rest at all on feelings, impulses, and inclinations; it rests merely on the relation of rational beings to one another, in which the will of a rational being must always be regarded as legislative. . . ." In short, reason itself can be practical, and thus supply guidance to agents.

Kant's view of moral motivation is elevated and inspiring. But it is also obscure. For how, exactly, can moral reasons (or our awareness of them) provide an impulse to do something if the desire to act on such reasons is not already present? The view that this cannot occur—that reason can show us how to achieve our ends, but cannot supply those ends themselves—is defended by David Hume in reading 20. If we accept Hume's argument, we may be attracted to yet another account of moral motivation. In that account, developed by Philippa Foot in reading 21, the moral person is moved not by a bare awareness of moral reasons, but by that awareness plus an independent desire to act on such reasons. This alternative appears to assimilate moral motivation to a familiar pattern. However, the Kantian might reply that it leaves open the question of why persons *have* the desire to act morally, and thus also leaves room for the answer that moral reasons have intrinsic appeal.

Whatever we say about this, the desire to act morally is clearly not our *only* desire. We care about much else besides doing what is right. Thus, any theory of morality must elucidate the relationship between moral and nonmoral desires. On many theories, persons are only permitted to act on nonmoral desires if they can do so within the constraints of morality. But in reading 2, Bernard Williams contests this ordering. He argues that when our fundamental desires conflict with moral principles, it is unrealistic to expect us to subordinate those desires. In addition, our personal relationships may demand a kind of partiality that rules out the impersonal perspective of morality. For example, our devotion to our children may require that we favor them over others. In a similar vein, Susan Wolf argues in reading 3 that nonmoral values and ideals provide reasons that are just as compelling, and just as valid, as moral reasons. If Williams and Wolf are right, the person who always assigns the highest priority to moral duty may be alienated from other worthwhile goals and relationships. But Marcia Baron argues in reading 4 that acting from duty does not alienate us either from others or from our own fundamental commitments. The idea that it does reflects a number of mistaken assumptions. Once these are exposed, we see that duty leaves ample room for other valuable motives.

So far, we have focused on the moral agent's responsiveness to moral reasons, and on the relation between those reasons and other motives. But further questions concern the ways in which people *become* moral agents. In his classic discussion (reading 5), Aristotle construes moral education as the acquisition of virtuous character traits. These are acquired in the same way as other habits—through repeated performance of the relevant acts. In Aristotle's view, we learn to be good by being good. But according to Lawrence Kohlberg (reading 6), moral education is less practical and more cognitive than this. In his view, the learner moves through a series of developmental stages until he reaches a maximally articulated moral sensibility. At the highest stage, the learner has transcended his earlier desires merely to please others or obey conventional norms, and is committed to respect for persons as determined by fully universal principles of right. By presenting hypothetical examples that make the learner aware of the inadequacies of his present stage, the moral educator stimulates him to move to a higher stage.

If Kohlberg is correct, moral educators need not use nonrational techniques to influence behavior. They need not resort to punishment, reward, exhortation, or the setting of examples. But many do favor such "directive" techniques. Thus, we must ask whether directive techniques can be distinguished from mere indoctrination. When a teacher goes beyond appeals to reason, and tries to instill good moral habits by voicing approval and disapproval or setting a personal example, isn't he interfering with the child's ability to recognize reasons? And isn't this a violation of the right to exercise moral autonomy by choosing for oneself? In reading 7, George Sher and William J. Bennett concede that directive techniques can be misused, but argue that they need not violate the autonomy of either the child or the adult he will later become. Sher and Bennett also argue that such techniques are compatible with the democratic values of pluralism and tolerance.

Most often, people perform the acts that they believe are supported by the strongest reasons. But sometimes a person will believe that it is best to perform one act, and yet perform another. Such a person exhibits weakness of will. Because people may exhibit weakness by eating or drinking too much as well as by acting wrongly, this is not exclusively a moral phenomenon. Still, weakness of will is clearly pertinent to moral psychology. In his dialogue *The Protagoras*, Plato represented his teacher Socrates as arguing that we never knowingly pursue evil. When we do something wrong, it is always because we are ignorant of what we should do. In the second part of reading 5, Plato's own student, Aristotle, disputes this Socratic view. According to Aristotle, the weak-willed person *does* know that he is acting wrongly or foolishly, but his knowledge is ineffective. It is not "worked into the living texture of the mind." Gary Watson takes up this theme in reading 8. Watson agrees that the weak-willed person knows he is acting wrongly or foolishly, but asks why, in that case, he acts as he does. Is it because he fails to resist impulses that he could resist, or is his will overborne by his impulses? Although the second alternative threatens to conflate weakness with compulsion, Watson regards it as the more plausible. In his view, we exhibit weakness when we are unable to resist impulses that the normal person could resist.

1

Psychological Egoism

JOEL FEINBERG

Joel Feinberg (b. 1926), Professor of Philosophy at the University of Arizona, has done influential work in social and legal philosophy. His books include Doing and Deserving, Social Philosophy, *and a recent quadrilogy with the overall title* The Moral Limits of the Criminal Law.

In this reading, Feinberg examines psychological egoism—the view that we never want or pursue anything except our own happiness or self-interest. Although this view claims to explain why we act as we do, Feinberg points out that it is rarely supported by empirical evidence. Instead, it trades on certain arguments that are seldom carefully examined. Psychological egoism is, for example, often thought to hold because each person is motivated by his own desires and no one else's. However, as Feinberg notes, the fact that my desires are my own implies nothing about what I desire. Thus, it does not imply that I desire only my own happiness or satisfaction. Again, defenders of the view sometimes note that we get pleasure from helping others (or feel pangs of conscience about not helping). Yet far from supporting psychological egoism, this fact actually tells against it. For why should we feel such pleasure, if not that helping others satisfies a desire to help them—a desire that is emphatically not aimed only at our own happiness?

These examples do not exhaust the arguments considered by Feinberg. Throughout his discussion, however, the main point is clear. When we consider the matter carefully, we find no good reason to accept psychological egoism. We are free, therefore, to accept the common-sense view that people often act not to increase their own happiness, but simply to help others or to do the right thing.

The Theory

1. "PSYCHOLOGICAL EGOISM" is the name given to a theory widely held by ordinary men, and at one time almost universally accepted by political economists, philosophers, and psychologists, according to which all human actions when properly understood can be seen to be motivated by selfish desires. More precisely, psychological egoism is the doctrine that the only thing anyone is capable of desiring or pursuing ultimately (as an end in itself) is his *own* self-interest. No psychological egoist denies that men sometimes do desire things other than their own welfare—the happiness of other people, for example; but all psychological egoists insist that men are capable of desiring the happiness of others only when they take it to be a *means* to their own happiness. In short,

purely altruistic and benevolent actions and desires do not exist; but people sometimes appear to be acting unselfishly and disinterestedly when they take the interests of others to be means to the promotion of their own self-interest.

2. This theory is called *psychological* egoism to indicate that it is not a theory about what *ought* to be the case, but rather about what, as a matter of fact, *is* the case. That is, the theory claims to be a description of psychological facts, not a prescription of ethical ideals. It asserts, however, not merely that all men do as a contingent matter of fact "put their own interests first," but also that they are capable of nothing else, human nature being what it is. Universal selfishness is not just an accident or a coincidence on this view; rather, it is an unavoidable consequence of psychological laws.

The theory is to be distinguished from another doctrine, so-called "ethical egoism," according to which all men *ought* to pursue their own well-being. This doctrine, being a prescription of what *ought* to be the case, makes no claim to be a psychological theory of human motives; hence the word "ethical" appears in its name to distinguish it from *psychological* egoism.

3. There are a number of types of motives and desires which might reasonably be called "egoistic" or "selfish," and corresponding to each of them is a possible version of psychological egoism. Perhaps the most common version of the theory is that apparently held by Jeremy Bentham.[1] According to this version, all persons have only one ultimate motive in all their voluntary behavior and that motive is a selfish one; more specifically, it is one particular kind of selfish motive—namely, a desire for one's own *pleasure*. According to this version of the theory, "the only kind of ultimate desire is the desire to get or to prolong pleasant experiences, and to avoid or to cut short unpleasant experiences for oneself."[2] This form of psychological egoism is often given the cumbersome name—*psychological egoistic hedonism*.

Prima Facie Reasons in Support of the Theory

4. Psychological egoism has seemed plausible to many people for a variety of reasons, of which the following are typical:

a. "Every action of mine is prompted by motives or desires or impulses which are *my* motives and not somebody else's. This fact might be expressed by saying that whenever I act I am always pursuing my own ends or trying to satisfy my own desires. And from this we might pass on to—'I am always pursuing something for myself or seeking my own satisfaction.' Here is what seems like a proper description of a man acting selfishly,

[1] See his *Introduction to the Principles of Morals and Legislation* (1789), Chap. I, first paragraph: "Nature has placed mankind under the governance of two sovereign masters, *pain* and *pleasure*. It is for them alone to point out what we ought to do, as well as to determine what we shall do. . . . They govern us in all we do, in all we say, in all we think: every effort we can make to throw off our subjection will serve but to demonstrate and confirm it."

[2] C. D. Broad, *Ethics and the History of Philosophy* (New York: The Humanities Press, 1952), Essay 10—"Egoism as a Theory of Human Motives," p. 218. This essay is highly recommended.

6

and if the description applies to all actions of all men, then it follows that all men in all their actions are selfish."[3]

b. It is a truism that when a person gets what he wants he characteristically feels pleasure. This has suggested to many people that what we really want in every case is our own pleasure, and that we pursue other things only as a means.

c. *Self-Deception.* Often we deceive ourselves into thinking that we desire something fine or noble when what we really want is to be thought well of by others or to be able to congratulate ourselves, or to be able to enjoy the pleasures of a good conscience. It is a well-known fact that people tend to conceal their true motives from themselves by camouflaging them with words like "virtue," "duty," etc. Since we are so often misled concerning both our own real motives and the real motives of others, is it not reasonable to suspect that we might *always* be deceived when we think motives disinterested and altruistic? . . .

d. *Moral education.* Morality, good manners, decency, and other virtues must be teachable. Psychological egoists often notice that moral education and the inculcation of manners usually utilize what Bentham calls the "sanctions of pleasure and pain." Children are made to acquire the civilizing virtues only by the method of enticing rewards and painful punishments. Much the same is true of the history of the race. People in general have been inclined to behave well only when it is made plain to them that there is "something in it for them." Is it not then highly probable that just such a mechanism of human motivation as Bentham describes must be presupposed by our methods of moral education?

Critique of Psychological Egoism: Confusions in the Arguments

5. *Non-Empirical Character of the Arguments.* If the arguments of the psychological egoist consisted for the most part of carefully acquired empirical evidence (well-documented reports of controlled experiments, surveys, interviews, laboratory data, and so on), then the critical philosopher would have no business carping at them. After all, since psychological egoism purports to be a scientific theory of human motives, it is the concern of the experimental psychologist, not the philosopher, to accept or reject it. But as a matter of fact, empirical evidence of the required sort is seldom presented in support of psychological egoism. Psychologists, on the whole, shy away from generalizations about human motives which are so sweeping and so vaguely formulated that they are virtually incapable of scientific testing. It is usually the "armchair scientist" who holds the theory of universal selfishness, and his usual arguments are either based simply on his "impressions" or else are largely of a nonempirical sort. The latter are often shot full of a very subtle kind of logical

---

[3] Austin Duncan-Jones, *Butler's Moral Philosophy* (London: Penguin Books, 1952), p. 96. Duncan-Jones goes on to reject this argument. See p. 512f.

confusion, and this makes their criticism a matter of special interest to the analytic philosopher.

6. The psychological egoist's first argument (see 4a) is a good example of logical confusion. It begins with a truism—namely, that all of my motives and desires are *my* motives and desires and not someone else's. (Who would deny this?) But from this simple tautology nothing whatever concerning the nature of my motives or the objective of my desires can possibly follow. The fallacy of this argument consists in its violation of the general logical rule that analytic statements (tautologies),* cannot entail synthetic (factual) ones.† That every voluntary act is prompted by the agent's own motives is a tautology; hence, it cannot be equivalent to "A person is always seeking something for himself" or "All of a person's motives are selfish," which are synthetic. What the egoist must prove is not merely:

(i) Every voluntary action is prompted by a motive of the agent's own.

but rather:

(ii) Every voluntary action is prompted by a motive of a quite particular kind, viz. a selfish one.

Statement (i) is obviously true, but it cannot all by itself give any logical support to statement (ii).

The source of the confusion in this argument is readily apparent. It is not the genesis of an action or the *origin* or its motives which makes it a "selfish" one, but rather the "purpose" of the act or the *objective* of its motives; *not where the motive comes from* (in voluntary actions it always comes from the agent) but *what it aims at* determines whether or not it is selfish. There is surely a valid distinction between voluntary behavior, in which the agent's action is motivated by purposes of his own, and *selfish* behavior in which the agent's motives are of one exclusive sort. The egoist's argument assimilates all voluntary action into the class of selfish action, by requiring, in effect, that an unselfish action be one which is not really motivated at all.

. . .

7. But if argument 4a fails to prove its point, argument 4b does no better. From the fact that all our successful actions (those in which we get what we were after) are accompanied or followed by pleasure it does not follow, as the egoist claims, that the *objective* of every action is to get pleasure for oneself. To begin with, the premise of the argument is not, strictly speaking, even true. Fulfillment of desire (simply getting what one was after) is no guarantee of satisfaction (pleasant feelings of gratification in the mind of the agent). Sometimes when we get what we want we *also* get, as a kind of extra dividend, a warm, glowing feeling of contentment; but often, far too often, we get no

---

* Traditionally, analytic statements have been taken to be statements that are true by virtue of the meanings of words, and hence convey no information about the world.

† Traditionally, statements that do convey information about the world.

dividend at all, or, even worse, the bitter taste of ashes. Indeed, it has been said that the characteristic psychological problem of our time is the *dissatisfaction* that attends the fulfillment of our very most powerful desires.

Even if we grant, however, for the sake of argument, that getting what one wants *usually* yields satisfaction, the egoist's conclusion does not follow. We can concede that we normally get pleasure (in the sense of satisfaction) when our desires are satisfied, *no matter what our desires are for;* but it does not follow from this roughly accurate generalization that the only thing we ever desire is our own satisfaction. Pleasure may well be the usual accompaniment of all actions in which the agent gets what he wants; but to infer from this that what the agent always wants is his own pleasure is like arguing, in William James's example,[4] that because an ocean liner constantly consumes coal on its trans-Atlantic passage that therefore the *purpose* of its voyage is to consume coal. The immediate inference from even constant accompaniment to purpose (or motive) is always a *non sequitur.*

Perhaps there is a sense of "satisfaction" (desire fulfillment) such that it is certainly and universally true that we get satisfaction whenever we get what we want. But satisfaction in this sense is simply the "coming into existence of that which is desired." Hence, to say that desire fulfillment always yields "satisfaction" in this sense is to say no more than that we always get what we want when we get what we want, which is to utter a tautology like "a rose is a rose." It can no more entail a synthetic truth in psychology (like the egoistic thesis) than "a rose is a rose" can entail significant information in botany.

8. *Disinterested Benevolence.* The fallacy in argument 4b then consists, as Garvin puts it, "in the supposition that the apparently unselfish desire to benefit others is transformed into a selfish one by the fact that we derive pleasure from carrying it out."[5] Not only is this argument fallacious; it also provides us with a suggestion of a counter-argument to show that its conclusion (psychological egoistic hedonism) is false. Not only is the presence of pleasure (satisfaction) as a by-product of an action no proof that the action was selfish; in some special cases it provides rather conclusive proof that the action was *unselfish.* For in those special cases the fact that we get pleasure from a particular action *presupposes that we desired something else*—something other than our own pleasure—as an end in itself and not merely as a means to our own pleasant state of mind.

This way of turning the egoistic hedonist's argument back on him can be illustrated by taking a typical egoist argument, one attributed (perhaps apocryphally) to Abraham Lincoln, and then examining it closely:

> Mr. Lincoln once remarked to a fellow-passenger on an old-time mud-coach that all men were prompted by selfishness in doing good. His fellow-passenger was antagonizing this position when they were passing over a corduroy bridge that

---

[4] *The Principles of Psychology* (New York: Henry Holt, 1890), Vol. II, p. 558.

[5] Lucius Garvin, *A Modern Introduction to Ethics* (Boston: Houghton Mifflin, 1953), p. 39.

spanned a slough. As they crossed this bridge they espied an old razor-backed sow on the bank making a terrible noise because her pigs had got into the slough and were in danger of drowning. As the old coach began to climb the hill, Mr. Lincoln called out, "Driver, can't you stop just a moment?" Then Mr. Lincoln jumped out, ran back and lifted the little pigs out of the mud and water and placed them on the bank. When he returned, his companion remarked: "Now Abe, where does selfishness come in on this little episode?" "Why, bless your soul Ed, that was the very essence of selfishness. I should have had no peace of mind all day had I gone on and left that suffering old sow worrying over those pigs. I did it to get peace of mind, don't you see?"[6]

If Lincoln had cared not a whit for the welfare of the little pigs and their "suffering" mother, but only for his own "peace of mind," it would be difficult to explain how he could have derived pleasure from helping them. The very fact that he did feel satisfaction as a result of helping the pigs presupposes that he had a preexisting desire for something other than his own happiness. Then when *that* desire was satisfied, Lincoln of course derived pleasure. The *object* of Lincoln's desire was not pleasure; rather pleasure was the *consequence* of his preexisting desire for something else. If Lincoln had been wholly indifferent to the plight of the little pigs as he claimed, how could he possibly have derived any pleasure from helping them? He could not have achieved peace of mind from rescuing the pigs, had he not a prior concern—on which his peace of mind depended—for the welfare of the pigs for its own sake.

In general, the psychological hedonist analyzes apparent benevolence into a desire for "benevolent pleasure." No doubt the benevolent man does get pleasure from his benevolence, but in most cases, this is only because he has previously desired the good of some person, or animal, or mankind at large. Where there is no such desire, benevolent conduct is not generally found to give pleasure to the agent.

9. *Malevolence.* Difficult cases for the psychological egoist include not only instances of disinterested benevolence, but also cases of "disinterested malevolence." Indeed, malice and hatred are generally no more "selfish" than benevolence. Both are motives likely to cause an agent to sacrifice his own interests—in the case of benevolence, in order to help someone else, in the case of malevolence in order to harm someone else. The selfish man is concerned ultimately only with his own pleasure, happiness, or power; the benevolent man is often equally concerned with the happiness of others; to the malevolent man, the *injury* of another is often an end in itself—an end to be pursued sometimes with no thought for his own interests. There is reason to think that men have as often sacrificed themselves to injure or kill others as to help or to save others, and with as much "heroism" in the one case as in the other. The unselfish nature of malevolence was first noticed by the Anglican Bishop and

---

[6] Quoted from the *Springfield* (Illinois) *Monitor,* by F. C. Sharp in his *Ethics* (New York: Appleton-Century, 1928), p. 75.

moral philosopher Joseph Butler (1692–1752), who regretted that men are no more selfish than they are.[7]

10. *Lack of Evidence for Universal Self-Deception.* The more cynical sort of psychological egoist who is impressed by the widespread phenomenon of self-deception (see 4c) cannot be so quickly disposed of, for he has committed no *logical* mistakes. We can only argue that the acknowledged frequency of self-deception is insufficient evidence for his universal generalization. His argument is not fallacious, but inconclusive.

No one but the agent himself can ever be certain what conscious motives really prompted his action, and where motives are disreputable, even the agent may not admit to himself the true nature of his desires. Thus, for every apparent case of altruistic behavior, the psychological egoist can argue, with some plausibility, that the true motivation *might* be selfish, appearance to the contrary. Philanthropic acts are really motivated by the desire to receive gratitude; acts of self-sacrifice, when truly understood, are seen to be motivated by the desire to feel self-esteem; and so on. We must concede to the egoist that all apparent altruism might be deceptive in this way; but such a sweeping generalization requires considerable empirical evidence, and such evidence is not presently available.

11. *The "Paradox of Hedonism" and Its Consequences for Education.* The psychological egoistic Hedonist (e.g., Jeremy Bentham) has the simplest possible theory of human motivation. According to this variety of egoistic theory, all human motives without exception can be reduced to one—namely, the desire for one's own pleasure. But this theory, despite its attractive simplicity, or perhaps because of it, involves one immediately in a paradox. Astute observers of human affairs from the time of the ancient Greeks have often noticed that pleasure, happiness, and satisfaction are states of mind which stand in a very peculiar relation to desire. An exclusive desire for happiness is the surest way to prevent happiness from coming into being. Happiness has a way of "sneaking up" on persons when they are preoccupied with other things; but when persons deliberately and single-mindedly set off in pursuit of happiness, it vanishes utterly from sight and cannot be captured. This is the famous "paradox of hedonism": the single-minded pursuit of happiness is necessarily self-defeating, for *the way to get happiness is to forget it;* then perhaps it will come to you. If you aim exclusively at pleasure itself, with no concern for the things that bring pleasure, then pleasure will never come. To derive satisfaction, one must ordinarily first desire something other than satisfaction, and then find the means to get what one desires.

To feel the full force of the paradox of hedonism the reader should conduct an experiment in his imagination. Imagine a person (let's call him "Jones") who is, first of all, devoid of intellectual curiosity. He has no desire to acquire

---

[7] See his *Fifteen Sermons on Human Nature Preached at the Rolls Chapel* (1726), especially the first and eleventh.

any kind of knowledge for its own sake, and thus is utterly indifferent to questions of science, mathematics, and philosophy. Imagine further that the beauties of nature leave Jones cold: he is unimpressed by the autumn foliage, the snow-capped mountains, and the rolling oceans. Long walks in the country on spring mornings and skiing forays in the winter are to him equally a bore. Moreover, let us suppose that Jones can find no appeal in art. Novels are dull, poetry a pain, paintings nonsense and music just noise. Suppose further that Jones has neither the participant's nor the spectator's passion for baseball, football, tennis, or any other sport. Swimming to him is a cruel aquatic form of calisthenics, the sun only a cause of sunburn. Dancing is coeducational idiocy, conversation a waste of time, the other sex an unappealing mystery. Politics is a fraud, religion mere superstition; and the misery of millions of underprivileged human beings is nothing to be concerned with or excited about. Suppose finally that Jones has no talent for any kind of handicraft, industry, or commerce, and that he does not regret that fact.

What then is Jones interested in? He must desire something. To be sure, he does. Jones has an overwhelming passion for, a complete preoccupation with, his own happiness. The one exclusive desire of his life is *to be happy*. It takes little imagination at this point to see that Jones's one desire is bound to be frustrated. People who—like Jones—most hotly pursue their own happiness are the least likely to find it. Happy people are those who successfully pursue such things as aesthetic or religious experience, self-expression, service to others, victory in competitions, knowledge, power, and so on. If none of these things in themselves and for their own sakes mean anything to a person, if they are valued at all then only as a means to one's own pleasant states of mind—then that pleasure can never come. The way to achieve happiness is to pursue something else.

Almost all people at one time or another in their lives feel pleasure. Some people (though perhaps not many) really do live lives which are on the whole happy. But if pleasure and happiness presuppose desires for something other than pleasure and happiness, then the existence of pleasure and happiness in the experience of some people proves that those people have strong desires for something other than their own happiness—egoistic hedonism to the contrary.

The implications of the "paradox of hedonism" for educational theory should be obvious. The parents least likely to raise a happy child are those who, even with the best intentions, train their child to seek happiness directly. How often have we heard parents say:

> I don't care if my child does not become an intellectual, or a football star, or a great artist. I just want him to be a plain average sort of person. Happiness does not require great ambitions and great frustrations; it's not worth it to suffer and become neurotic for the sake of science, art, or do-goodism. I just want my child to be happy.

This can be a dangerous mistake, for it is the child (and the adult for that matter) without "outer-directed" interests who is the most likely to be unhappy. The pure egoist would be the most wretched of persons.

The educator might well beware of "life adjustment" as the conscious goal of the educational process for similar reasons. "Life adjustment" can be achieved only as a by-product of other pursuits. A whole curriculum of "life adjustment courses" unsupplemented by courses designed to incite an interest in things other than life adjustment would be tragically self-defeating.

As for moral education, it is probably true that punishment and reward are indispensable means of inculcation. But if the child comes to believe that the *sole* reasons for being moral are that he will escape the pain of punishment thereby and/or that he will gain the pleasure of a good reputation, then what is to prevent him from doing the immoral thing whenever he is sure that he will not be found out? While punishment and reward then are important tools for the moral educator, they obviously have their limitations. Beware of the man who does the moral thing only out of fear of pain or love of pleasure. He is not likely to be wholly trustworthy. Moral education is truly successful when it produces persons who are willing to do the right thing *simply because it is right,* and not merely because it is popular or safe.

12. *Pleasure as Sensation.* One final argument against psychological hedonism should suffice to put that form of the egoistic psychology to rest once and for all. The egoistic hedonist claims that all desires can be reduced to the single desire for one's own *pleasure*. Now the word "pleasure" is ambiguous. On the one hand, it can stand for a certain indefinable, but very familiar and specific kind of sensation, or more accurately, a property of sensations; and it is generally, if not exclusively, associated with the senses. For example, certain taste sensations such as sweetness, thermal sensations of the sort derived from a hot bath or the feel of the August sun while one lies on a sandy beach, erotic sensations, olfactory sensations (say) of the fragrance of flowers or perfume, and tactual and kinesthetic sensations from a good massage, are all pleasant in this sense. Let us call this sense of "pleasure," which is the converse of "physical pain," pleasure$_1$.

On the other hand, the word "pleasure" is often used simply as a synonym for "satisfaction" (in the sense of gratification, not mere desire fulfillment). In this sense, the existence of pleasure presupposes the prior existence of desire. Knowledge, religious experience, aesthetic expression, and other so-called "spiritual activities" often give pleasure in this sense. In fact, as we have seen, we tend to get pleasure in this sense whenever we get what we desire, no matter what we desire. The masochist even derives pleasure (in the sense of "satisfaction") from his own physically painful sensations. Let us call the sense of "pleasure" which means "satisfaction"—pleasure$_2$.

Now we can evaluate the psychological hedonist's claim that the sole human motive is a desire for one's own pleasure, bearing in mind (as he often does not) the ambiguity of the word "pleasure." First, let us take the hedonist to be saying that it is the desire for pleasure$_1$ (pleasant sensation) which is the sole ultimate desire of all people and the sole desire capable of providing a motive for action. Now I have little doubt that all (or most) people desire their own pleasure, *sometimes*. But even this familiar kind of desire occurs, I think, rather rarely. When I am hungry, I often desire to eat, or, more specifically, to eat this piece of steak and these potatoes. Much less often do I desire to eat certain morsels simply for the sake of the pleasant gustatory sensations they might cause. I have, on the other hand, been motivated in the latter way when I have gone to especially exotic (and expensive) French or Chinese restaurants; but normally, pleasant gastronomic sensations are simply a happy consequence or by-product of my eating, not the antecedently desired objective of my eating. There are, of course, others who take gustatory sensations far more seriously: the *gourmet* who eats only to savor the textures and flavors of fine foods, and the wine fancier who "collects" the exquisitely subtle and very pleasant tastes of rare old wines. Such men are truly absorbed in their taste sensations when they eat and drink, and there may even be some (rich) persons whose desire for such sensations is the sole motive for eating and drinking. It should take little argument, however, to convince the reader that such persons are extremely rare.

Similarly, I usually derive pleasure from taking a hot bath, and on occasion (though not very often) I even decide to bathe simply for the sake of such sensations. Even if this is equally true of everyone, however, it hardly provides grounds for inferring that *no one ever* bathes for *any* other motive. It should be empirically obvious that we sometimes bathe simply in order to get clean, or to please others, or simply from habit.

The view then that we are never after anything in our actions but our own pleasure—that all men are complete "gourmets" of one sort or another—is not only morally cynical; it is also contrary to common sense and everyday experience. In fact, the view that pleasant sensations play such an enormous role in human affairs is so patently false, on the available evidence, that we must conclude that the psychological hedonist has the other sense of "pleasure"—satisfaction—in mind when he states his thesis. If, on the other hand, he really does try to reduce the apparent multitude of human motives to the one desire for pleasant sensations, then the abundance of historical counter-examples justifies our rejection out of hand of his thesis. It surely seems incredible that the Christian martyrs were ardently pursuing their own pleasure when they marched off to face the lions, or that what the Russian soldiers at Stalingrad "really" wanted when they doused themselves with gasoline, ignited themselves, and then threw the flaming torches of their own bodies on German tanks, was simply the experience of pleasant physical sensations.

13. *Pleasure as Satisfaction.* Let us consider now the other interpretation of the hedonist's thesis, that according to which it is one's own pleasure$_2$ (satisfaction) and not merely pleasure$_1$ (pleasant sensation) which is the sole ultimate objective of all voluntary behavior. In one respect, the "satisfaction thesis" is even less plausible than the "physical sensation thesis"; for the latter at least is a genuine empirical hypothesis, testable in experience, though contrary to the facts which experience discloses. The former, however, is so confused that it cannot even be completely stated without paradox. It is, so to speak, defeated in its own formulation. Any attempted explication of the theory that all men at all times desire only their own satisfaction leads to an *infinite regress* in the following way:

> "All men desire only satisfaction."
> "Satisfaction of what?"
> "Satisfaction of their desires."
> "Their desires for what?"
> "Their desires for satisfaction."
> "Satisfaction of what?"
> "Their desires."
> "For what?"
> "For satisfaction."—etc., *ad infinitum*.

In short, psychological hedonism interpreted in this way attributes to all people as their sole motive a wholly vacuous and infinitely self-defeating desire. The source of this absurdity is in the notion that satisfaction can, so to speak, feed on itself, and perform the miracle of perpetual self-regeneration in the absence of desires for anything other than itself.

To summarize the argument of sections 11 and 12: The word "pleasure" is ambiguous. Pleasure$_1$ means a certain indefinable characteristic of physical sensation. Pleasure$_2$ refers to the feeling of satisfaction that often comes when one gets what one desires whatever be the nature of that which one desires. Now, if the hedonist means pleasure$_1$ when he says that one's own pleasure is the ultimate objective of all of one's behavior, then his view is not supported by the facts. On the other hand, if he means pleasure$_2$, then his theory cannot even be clearly formulated, since it leads to the following infinite regress: "I desire only satisfaction of my desire for satisfaction of my desire for satisfaction . . . etc., *ad infinitum*." I conclude then that psychological hedonism (the most common form of psychological egoism), however interpreted, is untenable.

. . .

2
Persons, Character, and Morality

BERNARD WILLIAMS

Bernard Williams (b. 1929) is Knightbridge Professor of Philosophy at
Cambridge University. He has made important contributions to ethics and
the philosophy of mind. Two collections of his papers are entitled Problems
of the Self *and* Moral Luck. *His most recent book is* Ethics and the Limits
of Philosophy.

In this essay, taken from Moral Luck, *Williams mounts an important*
criticism of two very familiar moral theories, utilitarianism and Kantianism.
(For presentation of these theories, see readings 26, 27, and 29.) Although
the two theories differ in many respects, Williams argues that they share an
overly abstract conception of the person. More particularly, they both tend
to ignore the basic commitments that are central to people's characters.
These commitments, or "ground projects," may range from artistic
endeavors to attempts to bring social justice. They give meaning to people's
lives and provide reasons for wanting to continue to live. In Williams's view,
inattention to the commitments has led some utilitarians to underestimate
the strength of the connections between the different stages of people's lives.
In addition, inattention to the demands of personal relationships has led
both utilitarians and Kantians to overestimate the force of impersonal
morality. According to Williams, impartial principles provide neither the
only nor the ultimate reason for acting.

I

MUCH OF THE MOST interesting recent work in moral philosophy has
been of basically Kantian inspiration; Rawls' own work[1] and those to varying
degrees influenced by him such as Richards[2] and Nagel[3] are very evidently in
the debt of Kant, while it is interesting that a writer such as Fried[4] who gives
evident signs of being pulled away from some characteristic features of this
way of looking at morality nevertheless, I shall suggest later, tends to get pulled
back into it. This is not of course a very pure Kantianism, and still less is it an

[1] John Rawls, *A Theory of Justice* (Oxford, 1972).

[2] D. A. J. Richards, *A Theory of Reasons for Action* (Oxford, 1971).

[3] Thomas Nagel, *The Possibility of Altruism* (Oxford, 1970).

[4] Charles Fried, *An Anatomy of Values* (Cambridge, Mass., 1970).

16

expository or subservient one. It differs from Kant among other things in making no demands on a theory of noumenal freedom, and also, importantly, in admitting considerations of a general empirical character in determining fundamental moral demands, which Kant at least supposed himself not to be doing. But allowing for those and many other important differences, the inspiration is there and the similarities both significant and acknowledged. They extend far beyond the evident point that both the extent and the nature of opposition to Utilitarianism resembles Kant's: though it is interesting that in this respect they are more Kantian than a philosophy which bears an obvious but superficial formal resemblance to Kantianism, namely Hare's. Indeed, Hare now supposes that when a substantial moral theory is elicited from his philosophical premises, it turns out to be a version of Utilitarianism. This is not merely because the universal and prescriptive character of moral judgements lays on the agent, according to Hare, a requirement of hypothetical identification with each person affected by a given decision—so much is a purely Kantian element. It is rather that each identification is treated just as yielding 'acceptance' or 'rejection' of a certain prescription, and they in turn are construed solely in terms of satisfactions, so that the outputs of the various identifications can, under the usual Utilitarian assumptions, be regarded additively.

Among Kantian elements in these outlooks are, in particular, these: that the moral point of view is basically different from a non-moral, and in particular self-interested, point of view, and by a difference of kind; that the moral point of view is specially characterized by its impartiality and its indifference to any particular relations to particular persons, and that moral thought requires abstraction from particular circumstances and particular characteristics of the parties, including the agent, except in so far as these can be treated as universal features of any morally similar situation; and that the motivations of a moral agent, correspondingly, involve a rational application of impartial principle and are thus different in kind from the sorts of motivations that he might have for treating some particular persons (for instance, though not exclusively, himself) differently because he happened to have some particular interest towards them. Of course, it is not intended that these demands should exclude other and more intimate relations nor prevent someone from acting in ways demanded by and appropriate to them: that is a matter of the relations of the moral point of view to other points of view. But I think it is fair to say that included among the similarities of these views to Kant's is the point that like his they do not make the question of the relations between those points of view at all easy to answer. The deeply disparate character of moral and of non-moral motivation, together with the special dignity or supremacy attached to the moral, make it very difficult to assign to those other relations and motivations the significance or structural importance in life which some of them are capable of possessing.

It is worth remarking that this detachment of moral motivations and the moral point of view from the level of particular relations to particular persons, and more generally from the level of all motivations and perceptions other than those of an impartial character, obtains even when the moral point of view is itself explained in terms of the self-interest under conditions of ignorance of some abstractly conceived contracting parties, as it is by Rawls, and by Richards, who is particularly concerned with applying directly to the characterization of the moral interest, the structure used by Rawls chiefly to characterize social justice. For while the contracting parties are pictured as making some kind of self-interested or prudential choice of a set of rules, they are entirely abstract persons making this choice in ignorance of their own particular properties, tastes, and so forth; and the self-interested choice of an abstract agent is intended to model precisely the moral choice of a concrete agent, by representing what he would choose granted that he made just the kinds of abstraction from his actual personality, situation and relations which the Kantian picture of moral experience requires.

Some elements in this very general picture serve already to distinguish the outlook in question from Utilitarianism. Choices made in deliberate abstraction from empirical information which actually exists are necessarily from a Utilitarian point of view irrational, and to that extent the formal structure of the outlook, even allowing the admission of *general* empirical information, is counter-Utilitarian. There is a further point of difference with Utilitarianism, which comes out if one starts from the fact that there is one respect at least in which Utilitarianism itself requires a notable abstraction in moral thought, an abstraction which in this respect goes even further than the Kantians': if Kantianism abstracts in moral thought from the identity of persons, Utilitarianism strikingly abstracts from their separateness. This is true in more than one way. First, as the Kantian theorists have themselves emphasized, persons lose their separateness as beneficiaries of the Utilitarian provisions, since in the form which maximizes total utility, and even in that which maximizes average utility, there is an agglomeration of satisfactions which is basically indifferent to the separateness of those who have the satisfactions; this is evidently so in the total maximization system, and it is only superficially not so in the average maximization system, where the agglomeration occurs before the division. Richards,[5] following Rawls, has suggested that the device of the ideal observer serves to model the agglomeration of these satisfactions: equivalent to the world could be one person, with an indefinite capacity for happiness and pain. The Kantian view stands opposed to this; the idea of the contractual element, even between these shadowy and abstract participants, is in part to make the point that there are limitations built in at the bottom to permissible trade-offs between the satisfactions of individuals.

A second aspect of the Utilitarian abstraction from separateness involves agency.[6] It turns on the point that the basic bearer of value for Utilitarianism

---

[5] Richards, op. cit., p. 87 al; cf. Rawls, op. cit., p. 27; also Nagel, op. cit., p. 134. This is not the only, nor perhaps historically the soundest, interpretation of the device: cf. Derek Parfit, 'Later Selves and Moral Principles', in A. Montefiore, ed., *Philosophy and Personal Relations* (London, 1973), pp. 149–50 and nn. 30–4.

[6] For a more detailed account, see 'A Critique of Utilitarianism', in J. J. C. Smart and B. Williams, *Utilitarianism: For and Against* (Cambridge, 1973).

is the *state of affairs,* and hence, when the relevant causal differences have been allowed for, it cannot make any further difference who produces a given state of affairs: if S1 consists of my doing something, together with consequences, and S2 consists of someone else doing something, with consequences, and S2 comes about just in case S1 does not, and S1 is better than S2, then I should bring about S1, however *prima facie* nasty S1 is. Thus, unsurprisingly, the doctrine of negative responsibility has its roots at the foundation of Utilitarianism; and whatever projects, desires, ideals, or whatever I may have as a particular individual, as a Utilitarian agent my action has to be the output of *all* relevant causal items bearing on the situation, including all projects and desires within causal reach, my own and others. As a Utilitarian agent, I am just the representative of the satisfaction system who happens to be near certain causal levers at a certain time. At this level, there is abstraction not merely from the identity of agents, but, once more, from their separateness, since a conceivable extension or restriction of the causal powers of a given agent could always replace the activities of some other agent, so far as Utilitarian outcomes are concerned, and an outcome allocated to two agents as things are could equivalently be the product of one agent, or three, under a conceivable redistribution of causal powers.

In this latter respect also the Kantian outlook can be expected to disagree. For since we are concerned not just with outcomes, but at a basic level with actions and policies, *who* acts in a given situation makes a difference, and in particular I have a particular responsibility for *my* actions. Thus in more than one way the Kantian outlook emphasizes something like the separateness of agents, and in that sense makes less of an abstraction than Utilitarianism does (though, as we have seen, there are other respects, with regard to causally relevant empirical facts, in which its abstraction is greater). But now the question arises, of whether the honourable instincts of Kantianism to defend the individuality of individuals against the agglomerative indifference of Utilitarianism can in fact be effective granted the impoverished and abstract character of persons as moral agents which the Kantian view seems to impose. Findlay has said 'the separateness of persons . . . is . . . the basic fact for morals',[7] and Richards hopes to have respected that fact.[8] Similarly Rawls claims that impartiality does not mean impersonality.[9] But it is a real question, whether the conception of the individual provided by the Kantian theories is in fact enough to yield what is wanted, even by the Kantians; let alone enough for others who, while equally rejecting Utilitarianism, want to allow more room than Kantianism can allow for the importance of individual character and personal relations in moral experience.

---

[7] Findlay, *Values and Intentions* (London, 1961), pp. 235–6.

[8] Richards, op. cit., p. 87.

[9] Rawls, op. cit., p. 190.

II

I am going to take up two aspects of this large subject. They both involve the idea that an individual person has a set of desires, concerns or, as I shall often call them, projects, which help to constitute a *character*. The first issue concerns the connection between that fact and the man's having a reason for living at all. I approach this through a discussion of some work by Derek Parfit; though I touch on a variety of points in this, my overriding aim is to emphasize the basic importance for our thought of the ordinary idea of a self or person which undergoes changes of character, as opposed to an approach which, even if only metaphorically, would dissolve the person, under changes of character, into a series of 'selves'.

In this section I am concerned just with the point that each person has a character, not with the point that different people have different characters. That latter point comes more to the fore on the second issue, which I take up in part III, and which concerns personal relations. Both issues suggest that the Kantian view contains an important misrepresentation.

First, then, I should like to comment on some arguments of Parfit which explore connections between moral issues and a certain view of personal identity: a view which, he thinks, might offer, among other things, '*some* defence'[10] of the Utilitarian neglect of the separateness of persons. This view Parfit calls the 'Complex View'. This view takes seriously the idea that relations of psychological connectedness (such as memory and persistence of character and motivation) are what really matter with regard to most questions which have been discussed in relation to personal identity. The suggestion is that morality should take this seriously as well, and that there is more than one way of its doing so. Psychological connectedness (unlike the surface logic of personal identity) admits of degrees. Let us call the relevant properties and relations which admit of degrees, *scalar* items. One of Parfit's aims is to make moral thought reflect more directly the scalar character of phenomena which underlie personal identity. In particular, in those cases in which the scalar relations hold in reduced degree, this fact should receive recognition in moral thought.

Another, and more general, consequence of taking the Complex View is that the matter of personal identity may appear altogether less deep, as Parfit puts it, than if one takes the Simple View, as he calls that alternative view which sees as basically significant the all-or-nothing logic of personal identity. If the matter of personal identity appears less deep, the *separateness* of persons, also, may come to seem less an ultimate and specially significant consideration for morality. The connection between those two thoughts is not direct, but there is more than one indirect connection between them.[11]

---

[10] Parfit, op. cit., p. 160, his emphasis. In what follows and elsewhere in this chapter I am grateful to Parfit for valuable criticisms of an earlier draft.

[11] Parfit develops one such connection in the matter of distributive justice: pp. 148ff. In general it can be said that one very natural correlate of being impressed by the separateness of several persons' lives is being impressed by the particular unity of one person's life.

So far as the problems of *agency* are concerned, Parfit's treatment is not going to help Utilitarianism. His loosening of identity is diachronic, by reference to the weakening of psychological connectedness over time: where there is such weakening to a sufficient degree, he is prepared to speak of 'successive selves', though this is intended only as a *façon de parler*.[12] But the problems that face Utilitarianism about agency can arise with any agent whose projects stretch over enough time, and are sufficiently grounded in character, to be in any substantial sense *his* projects, and that condition will be satisfied by something that is, for Parfit, even *one* self. Thus there is nothing in this degree of dissolution of the traditional self which can help over agency.

In discussing the issues involved in making moral thought reflect more directly the scalar nature of what underlies personal identity, it is important to keep in mind that the talk of 'past selves', 'future selves' and generally 'several selves' is only a convenient fiction. Neglect of this may make the transpositions in moral thought required by the Complex View seem simpler and perhaps more inviting than they are, since they may glide along on what seems to be a mere multiplication, in the case of these new 'selves', of familiar interpersonal relations. We must concentrate on the scalar facts. But many moral notions show a notable resistance to reflecting the scalar: or, rather, to reflecting it in the right way. We may take the case of promising, which Parfit has discussed.[13] Suppose that I promise to A that I will help him in certain ways in three years time. In three years time a person appears, let us say A*, whose memories, character etc., bear some, but a rather low, degree of connectedness to A's. How am I to mirror these scalar facts in my thought about whether, or how, I am to carry out my promise?

Something, first, should be said about the promise itself. '*You*' was the expression it used: 'I will help *you*', and it used that expression in such a way that it covered both the recipient of these words and the potential recipient of the help. This was not a promise that could be carried out (or, more generally, honoured) by helping anyone else, or indeed by doing anything except helping that person I addressed when I said 'you'—thus the situation is not like that with some promises to the dead (those where there is still something one can do about it).[14] If there is to be any action of mine which is to count as honouring that promise, it will have to be action which consists in now helping A*. How am I to mirror, in my action and my thought about it, A*'s scalar relations to A?

There seem to be only three ways in which they could be so mirrored, and none seems satisfactory. First, the action promised might itself have some significant scalar dimension, and it might be suggested that this should vary with my sense of the proximity or remoteness of A* from A. But this will not do: it is clearly a lunatic idea that if I promised to pay A a sum of money, then my

---

[12] Ibid., n. 14, pp. 161–2.

[13] Ibid., pp. 144ff.

[14] Ibid., p. 144 fin.

obligation is to pay A^* some money, but a smaller sum. A more serious suggestion would be that what varies with the degree of connectedness of A^* to A is the degree of stringency of the obligation to do what was promised. While less evidently dotty, it is still, on reflection, dotty; thus, to take a perhaps unfair example, it seems hard to believe that if someone had promised to marry A, they would have an obligation to marry A^*, only an obligation which came lower down the queue.

What, in contrast, is an entirely familiar sort of thought is, last of all, one that embodies degrees of doubt or obscurity whether a given obligation (of fixed stringency) applies or not. Thus a secret agent might think that he was obliged to kill the man in front of him if and only if that man was Martin Bormann; and be in doubt whether he should kill this man, because he was in doubt whether it was Bormann. (Contrast the two analogously dotty types of solution to this case: that, at any rate, he is obliged to wound him; or, that he is obliged to kill him, but it has a lower priority than it would have otherwise.) But this type of thought is familiar at the cost of not really embodying the scalar facts; it is a style of thought appropriate to uncertainty about a matter of all-or-nothing and so embodies in effect what Parfit calls the Simple View, that which does not take seriously the scalar facts to which the Complex View addresses itself.

These considerations do not, of course show that there are no ways of mirroring the Complex View in these areas of moral thought, but they do suggest that the displacements required are fairly radical. It is significant that by far the easiest place in which to find the influence of the scalar considerations is in certain *sentiments,* which themselves have a scalar dimension—here we can see a place where the Complex View and Utilitarianism easily fit together. But the structure of such sentiments is not adequate to produce the structure of all moral thought. The rest of it will have to be more radically adapted, or abandoned, if the Complex View is really to have its effect.

One vitally important item which is in part (though only in part) scalar is a man's concern for (what commonsense would call) his own future. That a man should have some interest now in what he will do or undergo later, requires that he have some desires or projects or concerns now which relate to those doings or happenings later; or, as a special case of that, that some very general desire or project or concern of his now relate to desires or projects which he will have then. The limiting case, at the basic physical level, is that in which he is merely concerned with future pain, and it may be that that concern can properly reach through any degree of psychological discontinuity.[15] But even if so, it is not our present concern, since the mere desire to avoid physical pain is not adequate to constitute a character. We are here concerned with more distinctive and structured patterns of desire and project, and there are possible psychological changes in these which could be predicted for a person and which would put his future after such changes beyond his present interest. Such a

[15] Cf. 'The Self and the Future', in *Problems of the Self* (Cambridge, 1973).

future would be, so to speak, over the horizon of his interest, though of course if the future picture could be filled in as a *series* of changes leading from here to there, he might recapture an interest in the outcome.

. . .

It might be wondered why, unless we believe in a possibly hostile after-life, or else are in a muddle which the Epicureans claimed to expose, we should regard death as an evil.[16] One answer to that is that we desire certain things: if one desires something, then to that extent one has reason to resist the happening of anything which prevents one getting it, and death certainly does that, for a large range of desires. Some desires are admittedly contingent on the prospect of one's being alive, but not all desires can be in that sense conditional, since it is possible to imagine a person rationally contemplating suicide, in the face of some predicted evil, and if he decides to go on in life, then he is propelled forward into it by some desire (however general or inchoate) which cannot operate conditionally on his being alive, since it settles the question of whether he is going to be alive. Such a desire we may call a categorical desire. Most people have many categorical desires, which do not depend on the assumption of the person's existence, since they serve to prevent that assumption's being questioned, or to answer the question if it is raised. Thus one's pattern of interests, desires and projects not only provide the reason for an interest in what happens within the horizon of one's future, but also constitute the conditions of there being such a future at all.

Here, once more, to deal in terms of later selves who were like descendants would be to misplace the heart of the problem. Whether to commit suicide, and whether to leave descendants, are two separate decisions: one can produce children before committing suicide. A person might even choose deliberately to do that, for comprehensible sorts of reasons; or again one could be deterred, as by the thought that one would not be there to look after them. Later selves, however, evade all these thoughts by having the strange property that while they come into existence only with the death of their ancestor, the physical death of their ancestor will abort them entirely. The analogy seems unhelpfully strained, when we are forced to the conclusion that the failure of all my projects, and my consequent suicide, would take with me all my 'descendants', although they are in any case a kind of descendants who arise only with my ceasing to exist. More than unhelpfully, it runs together what are two quite different questions: whether, my projects having failed, I should cease to exist, and whether I shall have descendants whose projects may be quite different from mine and are in any case largely unknown. The analogy makes every question of the first kind involve a question of the second kind, and thus obscures the peculiar significance of the first question to the theory of the self. If, on the other hand, a man's future self is not another self, but the future of his self, then it is unproblematic why it should be eliminated with the failure of that which might propel him into it. The primacy of one's ordinary self is

---

[16] The argument is developed in more detail in *Problems of the Self*, pp. 82ff.

given, once more, by the thought that it is precisely what will not be in the world if one commits suicide.

The language of 'later selves', too literally taken, could exaggerate in one direction the degree to which my relation to some of my own projects resembles my relation to the projects of others. The Kantian emphasis on moral impartiality exaggerates it in quite another, by providing ultimately too slim a sense in which any projects are mine at all. This point once more involves the idea that my present projects are the condition of my existence,[17] in the sense that unless I am propelled forward by the conatus of desire, project and interest, it is unclear why I should go on at all: the world, certainly, as a kingdom of moral agents, has no particular claim on my presence or, indeed, interest in it. (That kingdom, like others, has to respect the natural right to emigration.) Now the categorical desires which propel one on do not have to be even very evident to consciousness, let alone grand or large; one good testimony to one's existence having a point is that the question of its point does not arise, and the propelling concerns may be of a relatively everyday kind such as certainly provide the ground of many sorts of happiness. Equally, while these projects may present *some* conflicts with the demands of morality, as Kantianly conceived, these conflicts may be fairly minor; after all—and I do not want to deny or forget it—these projects, in a normally socialized individual, have in good part been formed within, and formed by, dispositions which constitute a commitment to morality. But, on the other hand, the possibility of radical conflict is also there. A man may have, for a lot of his life or even just for some part of it, a *ground* project or set of projects which are closely related to his existence and which to a significant degree give a meaning to his life.

I do not mean by that they provide him with a life-plan, in Rawls' sense. On the contrary, Rawls' conception, and the conception of practical rationality, shared by Nagel, which goes with it, seems to me rather to imply an external view of one's own life, as something like a given rectangle that has to be optimally filled in.[18] This perspective omits the vital consideration already mentioned, that the continuation and size of this rectangle is up to me; so, slightly less drastically, is the question of how much of it I care to cultivate. The correct perspective on one's life is *from now*. The consequences of that

---

[17] We can note the consequence that present projects are the condition of future ones. This view stands in opposition to Nagel's: as do the formulations used above, p. 10. But while, as Nagel says, taking a rational interest in preparing for the realization of my later projects does not require that they be my present projects, it seems nevertheless true that it presupposes my having some present projects which directly or indirectly reach out to a time when those later projects will be my projects.

[18] It is of course a separate question what the criteria of optimality are, but it is not surprising that a view which presupposes that no risks are taken with the useful area of the rectangle should also favour a very low risk strategy in filling it: cf. Rawls (on prudential rationality in general), op. cit., p. 422: 'we have the guiding principle that a rational individual is always to act so that he need never blame himself no matter how things finally transpire.' Cf. also the passages cited in Rawls' footnote. For more on this and the relations of ground projects to rationality, see chapter 2, below.

for practical reasoning (particularly with regard to the relevance of proximity or remoteness in time of one's objective), is a large question which cannot be pursued here; here we need only the idea of a man's ground projects providing the motive force which propels him into the future, and gives him a reason for living.

For a project to play this ground role, it does not have to be true that if it were frustrated or in any of various ways he lost it, he would have to commit suicide, nor does he have to think that. Other things, or the mere hope of other things, may keep him going. But he may feel in those circumstances that he might as well have died. Of course, in general a man does not have one separable project which plays this ground role: rather, there is a nexus of projects, related to his conditions of life, and it would be the loss of all or most of them that would remove meaning.

Ground projects do not have to be selfish, in the sense that they are just concerned with things for the agent. Nor do they have to be self-centred, in the sense that the creative projects of a Romantic artist could be considered self-centred (where it has to be *him,* but not *for* him). They may certainly be altruistic, and in a very evident sense moral, projects; thus he may be working for reform, or justice, or general improvement. There is no contradiction in the idea of a man's dying for a ground project—quite the reverse, since if death really is necessary for the project, then to live would be to live with it unsatisfied, something which, if it really is his ground project, he has no reason to do.

That a man's projects were altruistic or moral would not make them immune to conflict with impartial morality, any more than the artist's projects are immune. Admittedly *some* conflicts are ruled out by the projects sincerely being *those* projects; thus a man devoted to the cause of curing injustice in a certain place, cannot just insist on his plan for doing that over others', if convinced that theirs will be as effective as his (something it may be hard to convince him of). For if he does insist on that, then we learn that his concern is not merely that injustice be removed, but that *he* remove it—not necessarily a dishonourable concern, but a different one. Thus some conflicts are ruled out by the project being not self-centred. But not all conflicts: thus his selfless concern for justice may do havoc to quite other commitments.

A man who has such a ground project will be required by Utilitarianism to give up what it requires in a given case just if that conflicts with what he is required to do as an impersonal utility-maximizer when all the causally relevant considerations are in. That is a quite absurd requirement.[19] But the Kantian, who can do rather better than that, still cannot do well enough. For impartial morality, if the conflict really does arise, must be required to win; and that cannot necessarily be a reasonable demand on the agent. There can come a point at which it is quite unreasonable for a man to give up, in the name of the impartial good ordering of the world of moral agents, something which is a condition of his having any interest in being around in that world

---

[19] Cf. 'A Critique of Utilitarianism', sections 3–5.

at all. Once one thinks about what is involved in having a character, one can see that the Kantians' omission of character is a condition of their ultimate insistence on the demands of impartial morality, just as it is a reason for finding inadequate their account of the individual.

III

All this argument depends on the idea of one person's having a character, in the sense of having projects and categorical desires with which that person is identified; nothing has yet been said about different persons having different characters. It is perhaps important, in order to avoid misunderstanding, to make clear a way in which difference of character does *not* come into the previous argument. It does not come in by way of the man's thinking that only if he affirms these projects will they be affirmed, while (by contrast) the aims of Kantian morality can be affirmed by anyone. Though that thought could be present in some cases, it is not the point of the argument. The man is not pictured as thinking that he will have earned his place in the world, if his project is affirmed: that a distinctive contribution to the world will have been made, if his distinctive project is carried forward. The point is that he wants these things, finds his life bound up with them, and that they propel him forward, and thus they give him a reason for living his life. But that is compatible with these drives, and this life, being much like others'. They give him, distinctively, a reason for living this life, in the sense that he has no desire to give up and make room for others, but they do not require him to lead a *distinctive* life. While this is so, and the point has some importance, nevertheless the interest and substance of most of the discussion depends on its in fact being the case that people have dissimilar characters and projects. Our *general* view of these matters, and the significance given to individuality in our own and others' lives, would certainly change if there were not between persons indefinitely many differences which are important to us. The level of description is of course also vital for determining what is the same or different. A similar description can be given of two people's dispositions, but the concrete detail be perceived very differently—and it is a feature of our experience of persons that we can perceive and be conscious of an indefinitely fine degree of difference in concrete detail (though it is only in certain connections and certain cultures that one spends much time rehearsing it).

One area in which *difference* of character directly plays a role in the concept of moral individuality is that of personal relations, and I shall close with some remarks in this connection. Differences of character give substance to the idea that individuals are not inter-substitutable. As I have just argued, a particular man so long as he is propelled forward does not need to assure himself that he is unlike others, in order not to feel substitutable, but in his personal relations to others the idea of difference can certainly make a contribution, in more than one way. To the thought that his friend cannot just be equivalently replaced by another friend, is added both the thought that he cannot just be replaced himself, and also the thought that he and his friend are different from each other. This last thought is important to us as part of our view of friendship, a view thus set apart from Aristotle's opinion that a good man's friend was a duplication of himself. This I suspect to have been an Aristotelian, and not generally a Greek, opinion. It is connected with another feature of his views which seems even stranger to us, at least with regard to any deeply commited friendship, namely that friendship for him has to be minimally *risky*—one of his problems is indeed to reconcile the role of friendship with his unappetizing ideal of self-sufficiency. Once one agrees that a three-dimensional mirror would not represent the ideal of friendship, one can begin to see both how some degree of difference can play an essential role, and, also, how a commitment or involvement with a particular other person might be one of the kinds of project which figured basically in a man's life in the ways already sketched— something which would be mysterious or even sinister on an Aristotelian account.

For Kantians, personal relations at least presuppose moral relations, and some are rather disposed to go further and regard them as a *species* of moral relations, as in the richly moralistic account given by Richards[20] of one of the four main principles of supererogation which would be accepted in 'the Original Position' (that is to say, adopted as a moral limitation):

> a principle of mutual love requiring that people should not show personal affection and love to others on the basis of arbitrary physical characteristics alone, but rather on the basis of traits of personality and character related to acting on moral principles.

This righteous absurdity is no doubt to be traced to a feeling that love, even love based on 'arbitrary physical characteristics', is something which has enough power and even authority to conflict badly with morality unless it can be brought within it from the beginning, and evidently that is a sound feeling, though it is an optimistic Kantian who thinks that much will be done about that by the adoption of this principle in the Original Position. The weaker view, that love and similar relations presuppose moral relations, in the sense that one could love someone only if one also had to them the moral relations one has to all people, is less absurd, but also wrong. It is of course true that loving someone involves some relations of the kind that morality requires or imports more generally, but it does not follow from that that one cannot have them in a particular case unless one has them generally in the way the moral person does. Someone might be concerned about the interests of someone else, and even about carrying out promises he made to that person, while not very concerned about these things with other persons. To the extent (whatever it may be) that loving someone involves showing some of the same concerns in relation to them that the moral person shows, or at least thinks he ought to show, elsewhere, the lover's relations will be examples of moral relations, or at least resemble them, but this does not have to be because they are *applications*

[20] Richards, op. cit., p. 94.

to this case of relations which the lover, *qua* moral person, more generally enters into. (That might not be the best description of the situation even if he *is* a moral person who enters into such relations more generally.)

However, once morality is there, and also personal relations to be taken seriously, so is the possibility of conflict. This of course does not mean that if there is some friendship with which his life is much involved, then a man must prefer any possible demand of that over other, impartial, moral demands. That would be absurd, and also a pathological kind of friendship, since both parties exist in the world and it is part of the sense of their friendship that it exists in the world. But the possibility of conflict with substantial moral claims of others is there, and it is not only in the outcome. There can also be conflict with moral demands on how the outcome is arrived at: the situation may not have been subjected to an impartial process of resolution, and this fact itself may cause unease to the impartial moral consciousness. There is an example of such unease in a passage by Fried. After an illuminating discussion of the question why, if at all, we should give priority of resources to actual and present sufferers over absent or future ones, he writes:[21]

> surely it would be absurd to insist that if a man could, at no risk or cost to himself, save one or two persons in equal peril, and one of those in peril was, say, his wife, he must treat both equally, perhaps by flipping a coin. One answer is that where the potential rescuer occupies no office such as that of captain of a ship, public health official or the like, the occurrence of the accident may itself stand as a sufficient randomizing event to meet the dictates of fairness, so he may prefer his friend, or loved one. Where the rescuer does occupy an official position, the argument that he must overlook personal ties is not unacceptable.

The most striking feature of this passage is the direction in which Fried implicitly places the onus of proof: the fact that coin-flipping would be inappropriate raises some question to which an 'answer' is required, while the resolution of the question by the rescuer's occupying an official position is met with what sounds like relief (though it remains unclear what that rescuer does when he 'overlooks personal ties'—does *he* flip a coin?). The thought here seems to be that it is unfair to the second victim that, the first being the rescuer's wife, they never even get a chance of being rescued; and the answer (as I read the reference to the 'sufficient randomizing event') is that at another level it is sufficiently fair—although in this disaster this rescuer has a special reason for saving the other person, it might have been another disaster in which another rescuer had a special reason for saving them. But, apart from anything else, that 'might have been' is far too slim to sustain a reintroduction of the notion of fairness. The 'random' element in such events, as in certain events of tragedy, should be seen not so much as affording a justification, in terms of an appro-

---

[21] Fried, op. cit., p. 227. [Note 1981] Fried has perhaps now modified the view criticised here. He has himself used the idea of friendship as creating special moral relations, but in a connexion where, it seems to me, it is out of place: for criticism, see chapter 4, below.

priate application of a lottery, as being a reminder that some situations lie beyond justifications.

But has anything yet shown that? For even if we leave behind thoughts of higher-order randomization, surely *this* is a justification on behalf of the rescuer, that the person he chose to rescue was his wife? It depends on how much weight is carried by 'justification': the consideration that it was his wife is certainly, for instance, an explanation which should silence comment. But something more ambitious than this is usually intended, essentially involving the idea that moral principle can legitimate his preference, yielding the conclusion that in situations of this kind it is at least all right (morally permissible) to save one's wife. (This could be combined with a variety of higher-order thoughts to give it a rationale; rule-Utilitarians might favour the idea that in matters of this kind it is best for each to look after his own, like house insurance.) But this construction provides the agent with one thought too many: it might have been hoped by some (for instance, by his wife) that his motivating thought, fully spelled out, would be the thought that it was his wife, not that it was his wife and that in situations of this kind it is permissible to save one's wife.

Perhaps others will have other feelings about this case. But the point is that somewhere (and if not in this case, where?) one reaches the necessity that such things as deep attachments to other persons will express themselves in the world in ways which cannot at the same time embody the impartial view, and that they also run the risk of offending against it.

They run that risk if they exist at all; yet unless such things exist, there will not be enough substance or conviction in a man's life to compel his allegiance to life itself. Life has to have substance if anything is to have sense, including adherence to the impartial system; but if it has substance, then it cannot grant supreme importance to the impartial system, and that system's hold on it will be, at the limit, insecure.

It follows that moral philosophy's habit, particularly in its Kantian forms, of treating persons in abstraction from character is not so much a legitimate device for dealing with one aspect of thought, but is rather a misrepresentation, since it leaves out what both limits and helps to define that aspect of thought. Nor can it be judged solely as a theoretical device: this is one of the areas in which one's conception of the self, and of oneself, most importantly meet.

3

Moral Saints

SUSAN WOLF[*]

Susan Wolf (b. 1952) is Associate Professor of Philosophy at the University of Maryland. She has published essays in ethics and on the problem of free will.

In this selection, Wolf asks whether moral perfection is a desirable ideal toward which to strive. Although many would answer affirmatively, Wolf does not agree. Instead, she contends that a perfectly moral person—a "moral saint"—would be deficient in important ways. Such a person would be bland and uninteresting. More importantly, being always committed to furthering the good of others, this person could not be deeply interested in intellectual inquiry, sports, art, or the other activities that enrich human life. If one is wholeheartedly committed to some such activity, one cannot be fully responsive to the needs of others. Thus, we must choose between moral and non-moral ideals.

This may not seem surprising. It has always been clear that being moral requires restrictions on self-interested action. But Wolf's insight is that it requires more. The moral person must forego aspects of life that are of genuine value, even apart from the perspective of the agent. Moreover, Wolf argues that this problem is raised not only by the inchoate moral ideals of common sense, but also by such more formal theories as utilitarianism and Kantianism. Like Bernard Williams (reading 2), she denies that morality is the highest source of ideals or reasons for acting. But if morality does not dominate, then neither do ideals of personal perfection. At some point, we must "raise normative questions from a perspective that is unattached to a commitment to any particular well-ordered system of values."

I DON'T KNOW whether there are any moral saints. But if there are, I am glad that neither I nor those about whom I care most are among them. By *moral saint* I mean a person whose every action is as morally good as possible, a person, that is, who is as morally worthy as can be. Though I shall in a moment acknowledge the variety of types of person that might be thought to satisfy this description, it seems to me that none of these types serve as unequivocally compelling personal ideals. In other words, I believe that moral perfection, in the sense of moral saintliness, does not constitute a model of

[*] I have benefited from the comments of many people who have heard or read an earlier draft of this paper. I wish particularly to thank Douglas MacLean, Robert Nozick, Martha Nussbaum, and the Society for Ethics and Legal Philosophy.

personal well-being toward which it would be particularly rational or good or desirable for a human being to strive.

Outside the context of moral discussion, this will strike many as an obvious point. But, within that context, the point, if it be granted, will be granted with some discomfort. For within that context it is generally assumed that one ought to be as morally good as possible and that what limits there are to morality's hold on us are set by features of human nature of which we ought not to be proud. If, as I believe, the ideals that are derivable from common sense and philosophically popular moral theories do not support these assumptions, then something has to change. Either we must change our moral theories in ways that will make them yield more palatable ideals, or, as I shall argue, we must change our conception of what is involved in affirming a moral theory.

In this paper, I wish to examine the notion of a moral saint, first, to understand what a moral saint would be like and why such a being would be unattractive, and second, to raise some questions about the significance of this paradoxical figure for moral philosophy. I shall look first at the model(s) of moral sainthood that might be extrapolated from the morality or moralities of common sense. Then I shall consider what relations these have to conclusions that can be drawn from utilitarian and Kantian moral theories. Finally, I shall speculate on the implications of these considerations for moral philosophy.

Moral Saints and Common Sense

Consider first what, pretheoretically, would count for us—contemporary members of Western culture—as a moral saint. A necessary condition of moral sainthood would be that one's life be dominated by a commitment to improving the welfare of others or of society as a whole. As to what role this commitment must play in the individual's motivational system, two contrasting accounts suggest themselves to me which might equally be thought to qualify a person for moral sainthood.

First, a moral saint might be someone whose concern for others plays the role that is played in most of our lives by more selfish, or, at any rate, less morally worthy concerns. For the moral saint, the promotion of the welfare of others might play the role that is played for most of us by the enjoyment of material comforts, the opportunity to engage in the intellectual and physical activities of our choice, and the love, respect, and companionship of people whom we love, respect, and enjoy. The happiness of the moral saint, then, would truly lie in the happiness of others, and so he would devote himself to others gladly, and with a whole and open heart.

On the other hand, a moral saint might be someone for whom the basic ingredients of happiness are not unlike those of most of the rest of us. What makes him a moral saint is rather that he pays little or no attention to his own happiness in light of the overriding importance he gives to the wider concerns of morality. In other words, this person sacrifices his own interests to the interests of others, and feels the sacrifice as such.

Roughly, these two models may be distinguished according to whether one thinks of the moral saint as being a saint out of love or one thinks of the moral saint as being a saint out of duty (or some other intellectual appreciation and recognition of moral principles). We may refer to the first model as the model of the Loving Saint; to the second, as the model of the Rational Saint.

The two models differ considerably with respect to the qualities of the motives of the individuals who conform to them. But this difference would have limited effect on the saints' respective public personalities. The shared content of what these individuals are motivated to be—namely, as morally good as possible—would play the dominant role in the determination of their characters. Of course, just as a variety of large-scale projects, from tending the sick to political campaigning, may be equally and maximally morally worthy, so a variety of characters are compatible with the ideal of moral sainthood. One moral saint may be more or less jovial, more or less garrulous, more or less athletic than another. But above all, a moral saint must have and cultivate those qualities which are apt to allow him to treat others as justly and kindly as possible. He will have the standard moral virtues to a nonstandard degree. He will be patient, considerate, even-tempered, hospitable, charitable in thought as well as in deed. He will be very reluctant to make negative judgments of other people. He will be careful not to favor some people over others on the basis of properties they could not help but have.

Perhaps what I have already said is enough to make some people begin to regard the absence of moral saints in their lives as a blessing. For there comes a point in the listing of virtues that a moral saint is likely to have where one might naturally begin to wonder whether the moral saint isn't after all, too good—if not too good for his own good, at least too good for his own well-being. For the moral virtues, given that they are, by hypothesis, *all* present in the same individual, and to an extreme degree, are apt to crowd out the non-moral virtues, as well as many of the interests and personal characteristics that we generally think contribute to a healthy, well-rounded, richly developed character.

In other words, if the moral saint is devoting all his time to feeding the hungry or healing the sick or raising money for Oxfam, then necessarily he is not reading Victorian novels, playing the oboe, or improving his backhand. Although no one of the interests or tastes in the category containing these latter activities could be claimed to be a necessary element in a life well lived, a life in which *none* of these possible aspects of character are developed may seem to be a life strangely barren.

The reasons why a moral saint cannot, in general, encourage the discovery and development of significant nonmoral interests and skills are not logical but practical reasons. There are, in addition, a class of nonmoral characteristics that a moral saint cannot encourage in himself for reasons that are not just practical. There is a more substantial tension between having any of these qualities unashamedly and being a moral saint. These qualities might be described as going against the moral grain. For example, a cynical or sarcastic wit, or a sense of humor that appreciates this kind of wit in others, requires that one take an attitude of resignation and pessimism toward the flaws and vices to be found in the world. A moral saint, on the other hand, has reason to take an attitude in opposition to this—he should try to look for the best in people, give them the benefit of the doubt as long as possible, try to improve regrettable situations as long as there is any hope of success. This suggests that, although a moral saint might well enjoy a good episode of *Father Knows Best,* he may not in good conscience be able to laugh at a Marx Brothers movie or enjoy a play by George Bernard Shaw.

An interest in something like gourmet cooking will be, for different reasons, difficult for a moral saint to rest easy with. For it seems to me that no plausible argument can justify the use of human resources involved in producing a *paté de canard en croute* against possible alternative beneficent ends to which these resources might be put. If there is a justification for the institution of haute cuisine, it is one which rests on the decision *not* to justify every activity against morally beneficial alternatives, and this is a decision a moral saint will never make. Presumably, an interest in high fashion or interior design will fare much the same, as will, very possibly, a cultivation of the finer arts as well.

A moral saint will have to be very, very nice. It is important that he not be offensive. The worry is that, as a result, he will have to be dull-witted or humorless or bland.

This worry is confirmed when we consider what sorts of characters, taken and refined both from life and from fiction, typically form our ideals. One would hope they would be figures who are morally good—and by this I mean more than just not morally bad—but one would hope, too, that they are not *just* morally good, but talented or accomplished or attractive in nonmoral ways as well. We may make ideals out of athletes, scholars, artists—more frivolously, out of cowboys, private eyes, and rock stars. We may strive for Katharine Hepburn's grace, Paul Newman's "cool"; we are attracted to the high-spirited passionate nature of Natasha Rostov; we admire the keen perceptiveness of Lambert Strether. Though there is certainly nothing immoral about the ideal characters or traits I have in mind, they cannot be superimposed upon the ideal of a moral saint. For although it is a part of many of these ideals that the characters set high, and not merely acceptable, moral standards for themselves, it is also essential to their power and attractiveness that the moral strengths go, so to speak, alongside of specific, independently admirable, nonmoral ground projects and dominant personal traits.

When one does finally turn one's eyes toward lives that are dominated by explicitly moral commitments, moreover, one finds oneself relieved at the discovery of idiosyncrasies or eccentricities not quite in line with the picture of moral perfection. One prefers the blunt, tactless, and opinionated Betsy Trotwood to the unfailingly kind and patient Agnes Copperfield; one prefers the mischievousness and the sense of irony in Chesterton's Father Brown to the innocence and undiscriminating love of St. Francis.

It seems that, as we look in our ideals for people who achieve nonmoral varieties of personal excellence in conjunction with or colored by some version of high moral tone, we look in our paragons of moral excellence for people

whose moral achievements occur in conjunction with or colored by some interests or traits that have low moral tone. In other words, there seems to be a
limit to how much morality we can stand.

One might suspect that the essence of the problem is simply that there is a
limit to how much of *any* single value, or any single type of value, we can
stand. Our objection then would not be specific to a life in which one's dominant concern is morality, but would apply to any life that can be so completely
characterized by an extraordinarily dominant concern. The objection in that
case would reduce to the recognition that such a life is incompatible with well-
roundedness. If that were the objection, one could fairly reply that well-roundedness is no more supreme a virtue than the totality of moral virtues embodied
by the ideal it is being used to criticize. But I think this misidentifies the
objection. For the way in which a concern for morality may dominate a life,
or, more to the point, the way in which it may dominate an ideal of life, is not
easily imagined by analogy to the dominance an aspiration to become an
Olympic swimmer or a concert pianist might have.

A person who is passionately committed to one of these latter concerns might
decide that her attachment to it is strong enough to be worth the sacrifice of
her ability to maintain and pursue a significant portion of what else life might
offer which a proper devotion to her dominant passion would require. But a
desire to be as morally good as possible is not likely to take the form of one
desire among others which, because of its peculiar psychological strength, requires
one to forego the pursuit of other weaker and separately less demanding desires.
Rather, the desire to be as morally good as possible is apt to have the character
not just of a stronger, but of a higher desire, which does not merely successfully
compete with one's other desires but which rather subsumes or demotes them.
The sacrifice of other interests for the interest in morality, then, will have the
character, not of a choice, but of an imperative.

Moreover, there is something odd about the idea of morality itself, or moral
goodness, serving as the object of a dominant passion in the way that a more
concrete and specific vision of a goal (even a concrete *moral* goal) might be
imagined to serve. Morality itself does not seem to be a suitable object of
passion. Thus, when one reflects, for example, on the Loving Saint easily and
gladly giving up his fishing trip or his stereo or his hot fudge sundae at the
drop of the moral hat, one is apt to wonder not at how much he loves morality,
but at how little he loves these other things. One thinks that, if he can give
these up so easily, he does not know what it *is* to truly love them. There seems,
in other words, to be a kind of joy which the Loving Saint, either by nature
or by practice, is incapable of experiencing. The Rational Saint, on the other
hand, might retain strong nonmoral and concrete desires—he simply denies
himself the opportunity to act on them. But this is no less troubling. The Loving
Saint one might suspect of missing a piece of perceptual machinery, of being
blind to some of what the world has to offer. The Rational Saint, who sees it
but foregoes it, one suspects of having a different problem—a pathological fear
of damnation, perhaps, or an extreme form of self-hatred that interferes with
his ability to enjoy the enjoyable in life.

In other words, the ideal of a life of moral sainthood disturbs not simply because it is an ideal of a life in which morality unduly dominates. The normal person's direct and specific desires for objects, activities, and events that conflict with the attainment of moral perfection are not simply sacrificed but removed, suppressed, or subsumed. The way in which morality, unlike other possible goals, is apt to dominate is particularly disturbing, for it seems to require either the lack or the denial of the existence of an identifiable, personal self.

This distinctively troubling feature is not, I think, absolutely unique to the ideal of the moral saint, as I have been using that phrase. It is shared by the conception of the pure aesthete, by a certain kind of religious ideal, and, somewhat paradoxically, by the model of the thorough-going, self-conscious egoist. It is not a coincidence that the ways of comprehending the world of which these ideals are the extreme embodiments are sometimes described as "moralities" themselves. At any rate, they compete with what we ordinarily mean by 'morality'. Nor is it a coincidence that these ideals are naturally described as fanatical. But it is easy to see that these other types of perfection cannot serve as satisfactory personal ideals; for the realization of these ideals would be straightforwardly immoral. It may come as a surprise to some that there may in addition be such a thing as a *moral* fanatic.

Some will object that I am being unfair to "common-sense morality"—that it does not really require a moral saint to be either a disgusting goody-goody or an obsessive ascetic. Admittedly, there is no logical inconsistency between having any of the personal characteristics I have mentioned and being a moral saint. It is not morally wrong to notice the faults and shortcomings of others or to recognize and appreciate nonmoral talents and skills. Nor is it immoral to be an avid Celtics fan or to have a passion for caviar or to be an excellent cellist. With enough imagination, we can always contrive a suitable history and set of circumstances that will embrace such characteristics in one or another specific fictional story of a perfect moral saint.

If one turned onto the path of moral sainthood relatively late in life, one may have already developed interests that can be turned to moral purposes. It may be that a good golf game is just what is needed to secure that big donation to Oxfam. Perhaps the cultivation of one's exceptional artistic talent will turn out to be the way one can make one's greatest contribution to society. Furthermore, one might stumble upon joys and skills in the very service of morality. If, because the children are short a ninth player for the team, one's generous offer to serve reveals a natural fielding arm or if one's part in the campaign against nuclear power requires accepting a lobbyist's invitation to lunch at Le Lion d'Or, there is no moral gain in denying the satisfaction one gets from these activities. The moral saint, then, may, by happy accident, find himself with nonmoral virtues on which he can capitalize morally or which make psychological demands to which he has no choice but to attend. The point is that, for a moral saint, the existence of these interests and skills can be given at best the status of happy accidents—they cannot be encouraged for their own sakes as distinct, independent aspects of the realization of human good.

It must be remembered that from the fact that there is a tension between having any of these qualities and being a moral saint it does not follow that having any of these qualities is immoral. For it is not part of common-sense morality that one ought to be a moral saint. Still, if someone just happened to want to be a moral saint, he or she would not have or encourage these qualities, and, on the basis of our common-sense values, this counts as a reason *not* to want to be a moral saint.

One might still wonder what kind of reason this is, and what kind of conclusion this properly allows us to draw. For the fact that the models of moral saints are unattractive does not necessarily mean that they are unsuitable ideals. Perhaps they are unattractive because they make us feel uncomfortable—they highlight our own weaknesses, vices, and flaws. If so, the fault lies not in the characters of the saints, but in those of our unsaintly selves.

To be sure, some of the reasons behind the disaffection we feel for the model of moral sainthood have to do with a reluctance to criticize ourselves and a reluctance to committing ourselves to trying to give up activities and interests that we heartily enjoy. These considerations might provide an *excuse* for the fact that we are not moral saints, but they do not provide a basis for criticizing sainthood as a possible ideal. Since these considerations rely on an appeal to the egoistic, hedonistic side of our natures, to use them as a basis for criticizing the ideal of the moral saint would be at best to beg the question and at worst to glorify features of ourselves that ought to be condemned.

The fact that the moral saint would be without qualities which we have and which, indeed, we like to have, does not in itself provide reason to condemn the ideal of the moral saint. The fact that some of these qualities are good qualities, however, and that they are qualities we *ought* to like, does provide reason to discourage this ideal and to offer other ideals in its place. In other words, some of the qualities the moral saint necessarily lacks are virtues, albeit nonmoral virtues, in the unsaintly characters who have them. The feats of Groucho Marx, Reggie Jackson, and the head chef at Lutèce are impressive accomplishments that it is not only permissible but positively appropriate to recognize as such. In general, the admiration of and striving toward achieving any of a great variety of forms of personal excellence are character traits it is valuable and desirable for people to have. In advocating the development of these varieties of excellence, we advocate nonmoral reasons for acting, and in thinking that it is good for a person to strive for an ideal that gives a substantial role to the interests and values that correspond to these virtues, we implicitly acknowledge the goodness of ideals incompatible with that of the moral saint. Finally, if we think that it is *as* good, or even better for a person to strive for one of these ideals than it is for him or her to strive for and realize the ideal of the moral saint, we express a conviction that it is good not to be a moral saint.

Moral Saints and Moral Theories

I have tried so far to paint a picture—or rather, two pictures—of what a moral saint might be like, drawing on what I take to be the attitudes and beliefs about morality prevalent in contemporary, common-sense thought. To my suggestion that common-sense morality generates conceptions of moral saints that are unattractive or otherwise unacceptable, it is open to someone to reply, "so much the worse for common-sense morality." After all, it is often claimed that the goal of moral philosophy is to correct and improve upon common-sense morality, and I have as yet given no attention to the question of what conceptions of moral sainthood, if any, are generated from the leading moral theories of our time.

A quick, breezy reading of utilitarian and Kantian writings will suggest the images, respectively, of the Loving Saint and the Rational Saint. A utilitarian, with his emphasis on happiness, will certainly prefer the Loving Saint to the Rational one, since the Loving Saint will himself be a happier person than the Rational Saint. A Kantian, with his emphasis on reason, on the other hand, will find at least as much to praise in the latter as in the former. Still, both models, drawn as they are from common sense, appeal to an impure mixture of utilitarian and Kantian intuitions. A more careful examination of these moral theories raises questions about whether either model of moral sainthood would really be advocated by a believer in the explicit doctrines associated with either of these views.

Certainly, the utilitarian in no way denies the value of self-realization. He in no way disparages the development of interests, talents, and other personally attractive traits that I have claimed the moral saint would be without. Indeed, since just these features enhance the happiness both of the individuals who possess them and of those with whom they associate, the ability to promote these features both in oneself and in others will have considerable positive weight in utilitarian calculations.

This implies that the utilitarian would not support moral sainthood as a universal ideal. A world in which everyone, or even a large number of people, achieved moral sainthood—even a world in which they *strove* to achieve it— would probably contain less happiness than a world in which people realized a diversity of ideals involving a variety of personal and perfectionist values. More pragmatic considerations also suggest that, if the utilitarian wants to influence more people to achieve more good, then he would do better to encourage them to pursue happiness-producing goals that are more attractive and more within a normal person's reach.

These considerations still leave open, however, the question of what kind of an ideal the committed utilitarian should privately aspire to himself. Utilitarianism requires him to want to achieve the greatest general happiness, and this would seem to commit him to the ideal of the moral saint.

One might try to use the claims I made earlier as a basis for an argument that a utilitarian should choose to give up utilitarianism. If, as I have said, a moral saint would be a less happy person both to be and to be around than many other possible ideals, perhaps one could create more total happiness by not trying too hard to promote the total happiness. But this argument is simply unconvincing in light of the empirical circumstances of our world. The gain in happiness that would accrue to oneself and one's neighbors by a more well-rounded, richer life than that of the moral saint would be pathetically small in comparison to the amount by which one could increase the general happiness if one devoted oneself explicitly to the care of the sick, the downtrodden, the starving, and the homeless. Of course, there may be psychological limits to the extent to which a person can devote himself to such things without going crazy. But the utilitarian's individual limitations would not thereby become a positive feature of his personal ideals.

The unattractiveness of the moral saint, then, ought not rationally convince the utilitarian to abandon his utilitarianism. It may, however, convince him to take efforts not to wear his saintly moral aspirations on his sleeve. If it is not too difficult, the utilitarian will try not to make those around him uncomfortable. He will not want to appear "holier than thou"; he will not want to inhibit others' ability to enjoy themselves. In practice, this might make the perfect utilitarian a less nauseating companion than the moral saint I earlier portrayed. But insofar as this kind of reasoning produces a more bearable public personality, it is at the cost of giving him a personality that must be evaluated as hypocritical and condescending when his private thoughts and attitudes are taken into account.

Still, the criticisms I have raised against the saint of common-sense morality should make some difference to the utilitarian's conception of an ideal which neither requires him to abandon his utilitarian principles nor forces him to fake an interest he does not have or a judgment he does not make. For it may be that a limited and carefully monitored allotment of time and energy to be devoted to the pursuit of some nonmoral interests or to the development of some nonmoral talents would make a person a better contributor to the general welfare than he would be if he allowed himself no indulgences of this sort. The enjoyment of such activities in no way compromises a commitment to utilitarian principles as long as the involvement with these activities is conditioned by a willingness to give them up whenever it is recognized that they cease to be in the general interest.

This will go some way in mitigating the picture of the loving saint that an understanding of utilitarianism will on first impression suggest. But I think it will not go very far. For the limitations on time and energy will have to be rather severe, and the need to monitor will restrict not only the extent but also the quality of one's attachment to these interests and traits. They are only weak and somewhat peculiar sorts of passions to which one can consciously remain so conditionally committed. Moreover, the way in which the utilitarian can enjoy these "extra-curricular" aspects of his life is simply not the way in which these aspects are to be enjoyed insofar as they figure into our less saintly ideals.

The problem is not exactly that the utilitarian values these aspects of his life only as a means to an end, for the enjoyment he and others get from these aspects are not a means to, but a part of, the general happiness. Nonetheless, he values these things only because of and insofar as they *are* a part of the general happiness. He values them, as it were, under the description 'a contribution to the general happiness'. This is to be contrasted with the various ways in which these aspects of life may be valued by nonutilitarians. A person might love literature because of the insights into human nature literature affords. Another might love the cultivation of roses because roses are things of great beauty and delicacy. It may be true that these features of the respective activities also explain why these activities are happiness-producing. But, to the nonutilitarian, this may not be to the point. For if one values these activities in these more direct ways, one may not be willing to exchange them for others that produce an equal, or even a greater amount of happiness. From that point of view, it is not because they produce happiness that these activities are valuable; it is because these activities are valuable in more direct and specific ways that they produce happiness.

To adopt a phrase of Bernard Williams', the utilitarian's manner of valuing the not explicitly moral aspects of his life "provides (him) with one thought too many".[1] The requirement that the utilitarian have this thought—periodically, at least—is indicative of not only a weakness but a shallowness in his appreciation of the aspects in question. Thus, the ideals toward which a utilitarian could acceptably strive would remain too close to the model of the common-sense moral saint to escape the criticisms of that model which I earlier suggested. Whether a Kantian would be similarly committed to so restrictive and unattractive a range of possible ideals is a somewhat more difficult question.

The Kantian believes that being morally worthy consists in always acting from maxims that one could will to be universal law, and doing this not out of any pathological desire but out of reverence for the moral law as such. Or, to take a different formulation of the categorical imperative, the Kantian believes that moral action consists in treating other persons always as ends and never as means only. Presumably, and according to Kant himself, the Kantian thereby commits himself to some degree of benevolence as well as to the rules of fair play. But we surely would not will that *every* person become a moral saint, and treating others as ends hardly requires bending over backwards to protect and promote their interests. On one interpretation of Kantian doctrine, then, moral perfection would be achieved simply by unerring obedience to a limited set of side-constraints. On this interpretation, Kantian theory simply does not yield an ideal conception of a person of any fullness comparable to that of the moral saints I have so far been portraying.

On the other hand, Kant does say explicitly that we have a duty of benevolence, a duty not only to allow others to pursue their ends, but to take up their ends as our own. In addition, we have positive duties to ourselves, duties to increase our natural as well as our moral perfection. These duties are unlimited in the degree to which they *may* dominate a life. If action in accordance with and motivated by the thought of these duties is considered virtuous, it is natural to assume that the more one performs such actions, the more virtuous

---

[1] "Persons, Character and Morality" in Amelie Rorty, ed., *The Identities of Persons* (Berkeley: Univ. of California Press, 1976), p. 214. [Reprinted in this volume, reading 2.]

one is. Moreover, of virtue in general Kant says, "it is an ideal which is unattainable while yet our duty is constantly to approximate to it".[2] On this interpretation, then, the Kantian moral saint, like the other moral saints I have been considering, is dominated by the motivation to be moral.

Which of these interpretations of Kant one prefers will depend on the interpretation and the importance one gives to the role of the imperfect duties in Kant's over-all system. Rather than choose between them here, I shall consider each briefly in turn.

On the second interpretation of Kant, the Kantian moral saint is, not surprisingly, subject to many of the same objections I have been raising against other versions of moral sainthood. Though the Kantian saint may differ from the utilitarian saint as to *which* actions he is bound to perform and which he is bound to refrain from performing, I suspect that the range of activities acceptable to the Kantian saint will remain objectionably restrictive. Moreover, the manner in which the Kantian saint must think about and justify the activities he pursues and the character traits he develops will strike us, as it did with the utilitarian saint, as containing "one thought too many." As the utilitarian could value his activities and character traits only insofar as they fell under the description of 'contributions to the general happiness', the Kantian would have to value his activities and character traits insofar as they were manifestations of respect for the moral law. If the development of our powers to achieve physical, intellectual, or artistic excellence, or the activities directed toward making others happy are to have any moral worth, they must arise from a reverence for the dignity that members of our species have as a result of being endowed with pure practical reason. This is a good and noble motivation, to be sure. But it is hardly what one expects to be dominantly behind a person's aspirations to dance as well as Fred Astaire, to paint as well as Picasso, or to solve some outstanding problem in abstract algebra, and it is hardly what one hopes to find lying dominantly behind a father's action on behalf of his son or a lover's on behalf of her beloved.

Since the basic problem with any of the models of moral sainthood we have been considering is that they are dominated by a single, all-important value under which all other possible values must be subsumed, it may seem that the alternative interpretation of Kant, as providing a stringent but finite set of obligations and constraints, might provide a more acceptable morality. According to this interpretation of Kant, one is as morally good as can be so long as one devotes some limited portion of one's energies toward altruism and the maintenance of one's physical and spiritual health, and otherwise pursues one's independently motivated interests and values in such a way as to avoid overstepping certain bounds. Certainly, if it be a requirement of an acceptable moral theory that perfect obedience to its laws and maximal devotion to its interests and concerns be something we can wholeheartedly strive for in ourselves and wish for in those around us, it will count in favor of this brand of Kantianism

[2] Immanuel Kant, *The Doctrine of Virtue*, Mary J. Gregor, trans. (New York: Harper & Row, 1964), p. 71.

40

that its commands can be fulfilled without swallowing up the perfect moral agent's entire personality.

Even this more limited understanding of morality, if its connection to Kant's views is to be taken at all seriously, is not likely to give an unqualified seal of approval to the nonmorally directed ideals I have been advocating. For Kant is explicit about what he calls "duties of apathy and self-mastery" (69/70)—duties to ensure that our passions are never so strong as to interfere with calm, practical deliberation, or so deep as to wrest control from the more disinterested, rational part of ourselves. The tight and self-conscious rein we are thus obliged to keep on our commitments to specific individuals and causes will doubtless restrict our value in these things, assigning them a necessarily attenuated place.

A more interesting objection to this brand of Kantianism, however, comes when we consider the implications of placing the kind of upper bound on moral worthiness which seemed to count in favor of this conception of morality. For to put such a limit on one's capacity to be moral is effectively to deny, not just the moral necessity, but the moral goodness of a devotion to benevolence and the maintenance of justice that passes beyond a certain, required point. It is to deny the possibility of going morally above and beyond the call of a restricted set of duties. Despite my claim that all-consuming moral saintliness is not a particularly healthy and desirable ideal, it seems perverse to insist that, were moral saints to exist, they would not, in their way, be remarkably noble and admirable figures. Despite my conviction that it is as rational and as good for a person to take Katharine Hepburn or Jane Austen as her role model instead of Mother Theresa, it would be absurd to deny that Mother Theresa is a morally better person.

I can think of two ways of viewing morality as having an upper bound. First, we can think that altruism and impartiality are indeed positive moral interests, but that they are moral only if the degree to which these interests are actively pursued remains within certain fixed limits. Second, we can think that these positive interests are only incidentally related to morality and that the essence of morality lies elsewhere, in, say, an implicit social contract or in the recognition of our own dignified rationality. According to the first conception of morality, there is a cut-off line to the amount of altruism or to the extent of devotion to justice and fairness that is worthy of moral praise. But to draw this line earlier than the line that brings the altruist in question to a worse-off position than all those to whom he devotes himself seems unacceptably artificial and gratuitous. According to the second conception, these positive interests are not essentially related to morality at all. But then we are unable to regard a more affectionate and generous expression of good will toward others as a natural and reasonable extension of morality, and we encourage a cold and unduly self-centered approach to the development and evaluation of our motivations and concerns.

A moral theory that does not contain the seeds of an all-consuming ideal of moral sainthood thus seems to place false and unnatural limits on our opportunity to do moral good and our potential to deserve moral praise. Yet the main thrust of the arguments of this paper has been leading to the conclusion that, when such ideals are present, they are not ideals to which it is particularly reasonable or healthy or desirable for human beings to aspire. These claims, taken together, have the appearance of a dilemma from which there is no obvious escape. In a moment, I shall argue that, despite appearances, these claims should not be understood as constituting a dilemma. But, before I do, let me briefly describe another path which those who are convinced by my above remarks may feel inclined to take.

If the above remarks are understood to be implicitly critical of the views on the content of morality which seem most popular today, an alternative that naturally suggests itself is that we revise our views about the content of morality. More specifically, my remarks may be taken to support a more Aristotelian, or even a more Nietzschean, approach to moral philosophy. Such a change in approach involves substantially broadening or replacing our contemporary intuitions about which character traits constitute moral virtues and vices and which interests constitute moral interests. If, for example, we include personal bearing, or creativity, or sense of style, as features that contribute to one's *moral* personality, then we can create moral ideals which are incompatible with and probably more attractive than the Kantian and utilitarian ideals I have discussed. Given such an alteration of our conception of morality, the figures with which I have been concerned above might, far from being considered to be moral saints, be seen as morally inferior to other more appealing or more interesting models of individuals.

This approach seems unlikely to succeed, if for no other reason, because it is doubtful that any single, or even any reasonably small number of substantial personal ideals could capture the full range of possible ways of realizing human potential or achieving human good which deserve encouragement and praise. Even if we could provide a sufficiently broad characterization of the range of positive ways for human beings to live, however, I think there are strong reasons not to want to incorporate such a characterization more centrally into the framework of morality itself. For, in claiming that a character trait or activity is morally good, one claims that there is a certain kind of reason for developing that trait or engaging in that activity. Yet, lying behind our criticism of more conventional conceptions of moral sainthood, there seems to be a recognition that among the immensely valuable traits and activities that a human life might positively embrace are some of which we hope that, if a person does embrace them, he does so *not* for moral reasons. In other words, no matter how flexible we make the guide to conduct which we choose to label "morality," no matter how rich we make the life in which perfect obedience to this guide would result, we will have reason to hope that a person does not wholly rule and direct his life by the abstract and impersonal consideration that such a life would be morally good.

Once it is recognized that morality itself should not serve as a comprehensive guide to conduct, moreover, we can see reasons to retain the admittedly vague contemporary intuitions about what the classification of moral and nonmoral virtues, interests, and the like should be. That is, there seem to be important differences between the aspects of a person's life which are currently considered appropriate objects of moral evaluation and the aspects that might be included under the altered conception of morality we are now considering, which the latter approach would tend wrongly to blur or to neglect. Moral evaluation now is focused primarily on features of a person's life over which that person has control; it is largely restricted to aspects of his life which are likely to have considerable effect on other people. These restrictions seem as they should be. Even if responsible people could reach agreement as to what constituted good taste or a healthy degree of well-roundedness, for example, it seems wrong to insist that everyone try to achieve these things or to blame someone who fails or refuses to conform.

If we are not to respond to the unattractiveness of the moral ideals that contemporary theories yield either by offering alternative theories with more palatable ideals or by understanding these theories in such a way as to prevent them from yielding ideals at all, how, then, are we to respond? Simply, I think, by admitting that moral ideals do not, and need not, make the best personal ideals. Earlier, I mentioned one of the consequences of regarding as a test of an adequate moral theory that perfect obedience to its laws and maximal devotion to its interests be something we can wholeheartedly strive for in ourselves and wish for in those around us. Drawing out the consequences somewhat further should, I think, make us more doubtful of the proposed test than of the theories which, on this test, would fail. Given the empirical circumstances of our world, it seems to be an ethical fact that we have unlimited potential to be morally good, and endless opportunity to promote moral interests. But this is not incompatible with the not-so-ethical fact that we have sound, compelling, and not particularly selfish reasons to choose not to devote ourselves univocally to realizing this potential or to taking up this opportunity.

Thus, in one sense at least, I am not really criticizing either Kantianism or utilitarianism. Insofar as the point of view I am offering bears directly on recent work in moral philosophy, in fact, it bears on critics of these theories who, in a spirit not unlike the spirit of most of this paper, point out that the perfect utilitarian would be flawed in this way or the perfect Kantian flawed in that.[3] The assumption lying behind these claims, implicitly or explicitly, has been that the recognition of these flaws shows us something wrong with utilitarianism, as opposed to Kantianism, or something wrong with Kantianism as opposed to utilitarianism, or something wrong with both of these theories as opposed to some nameless third alternative. The claims of this paper suggest, however, that this assumption is unwarranted. The flaws of a perfect master of a moral theory need not reflect flaws in the intramoral content of the theory itself.

[3] See, e.g., Williams, op. cit. and J. J. C. Smart and Bernard Williams, *Utilitarianism: For and Against* (New York: Cambridge, 1973). Also, Michael Stocker, "The Schizophrenia of Modern Ethical Theories," this JOURNAL, LXIII, 14 (Aug. 12, 1976): 453–466.

Moral Saints and Moral Philosophy

In pointing out the regrettable features and the necessary absence of some desirable features in a moral saint, I have not meant to condemn the moral saint or the person who aspires to become one. Rather, I have meant to insist that the ideal of moral sainthood should not be held as a standard against which any other ideal must be judged or justified, and that the posture we take in response to the recognition that our lives are not as morally good as they might be need not be defensive.[4] It is misleading to insist that one is *permitted* to live a life in which the goals, relationships, activities, and interests that one pursues are not maximally morally good. For our lives are not so comprehensively subject to the requirement that we apply for permission, and our nonmoral reasons for the goals we set ourselves are not excuses, but may rather be positive, good reasons which do not exist *despite* any reasons that might threaten to outweigh them. In other words, a person may be *perfectly wonderful* without being *perfectly moral.*

Recognizing this requires a perspective which contemporary moral philosophy has generally ignored. This perspective yields judgments of a type that is neither moral nor egoistic. Like moral judgments, judgments about what it would be good for a person to be are made from a point of view outside the limits set by the values, interests, and desires that the person might actually have. And, like moral judgments, these judgments claim for themselves a kind of objectivity or a grounding in a perspective which any rational and perceptive being can take up. Unlike moral judgments, however, the good with which these judgments are concerned is not the good of anyone or any group other than the individual himself.

Nonetheless, it would be equally misleading to say that these judgments are made for the sake of the individual himself. For these judgments are not concerned with what kind of life it is in a person's interest to lead, but with what kind of interests it would be good for a person to have, and it need not be in a person's interest that he acquire or maintain objectively good interests. Indeed, the model of the Loving Saint, whose interests are identified with the interests of morality, is a model of a person for whom the dictates of rational self-interest and the dictates of morality coincide. Yet, I have urged that we have reason not to aspire to this ideal and that some of us would have reason to be sorry if our children aspired to and achieved it.

---

[4] George Orwell makes a similar point in "Reflections on Gandhi," in *A Collection of Essays by George Orwell* (New York: Harcourt Brace Jovanovich, 1945), p. 176: "sainthood is . . . a thing that human beings must avoid . . . It is too readily assumed that . . . the ordinary man only rejects it because it is too difficult; in other words, that the average human being is a failed saint. It is doubtful whether this is true. Many people genuinely do not wish to be saints, and it is probable that some who achieve or aspire to sainthood have never felt much temptation to be human beings."

The moral point of view, we might say, is the point of view one takes up insofar as one takes the recognition of the fact that one is just one person among others equally real and deserving of the good things in life as a fact with practical consequences, a fact the recognition of which demands expression in one's actions and in the form of one's practical deliberations. Competing moral theories offer alternative answers to the question of what the most correct or the best way to express this fact is. In doing so, they offer alternative ways to evaluate and to compare the variety of actions, states of affairs, and so on that appear good and bad to agents from other, nonmoral points of view. But it seems that alternative interpretations of the moral point of view do not exhaust the ways in which our actions, characters, and their consequences can be comprehensively and objectively evaluated. Let us call the point of view from which we consider what kinds of lives are good lives, and what kinds of persons it would be good for ourselves and others to be, the *point of view of individual perfection*.

Since either point of view provides a way of comprehensively evaluating a person's life, each point of view takes account of, and, in a sense, subsumes the other. From the moral point of view, the perfection of an individual life will have some, but limited, value—for each individual remains, after all, just one person among others. From the perfectionist point of view, the moral worth of an individual's relation to his world will likewise have some, but limited, value—for, as I have argued, the (perfectionist) goodness of an individual's life does not vary proportionally with the degree to which it exemplifies moral goodness.

It may not be the case that the perfectionist point of view is like the moral point of view in being a point of view we are ever *obliged* to take up and express in our actions. Nonetheless, it provides us with reasons that are independent of moral reasons for wanting ourselves and others to develop our characters and live our lives in certain ways. When we take up this point of view and ask how much it would be good for an individual to act from the moral point of view, we do not find an obvious answer.[5]

The considerations of this paper suggest, at any rate, that the answer is not "as much as possible." This has implications both for the continued development of moral theories and for the development of metamoral views and for our conception of moral philosophy more generally. From the moral point of view, we have reasons to want people to live lives that seem good from outside

---

[5] A similar view, which has strongly influenced mine, is expressed by Thomas Nagel in "The Fragmentation of Value," in *Mortal Questions* (New York: Cambridge, 1979), pp. 128-141. Nagel focuses on the difficulties such apparently incommensurable points of view create for specific, isolable practical decisions that must be made both by individuals and by societies. In focusing on the way in which these points of view figure into the development of individual personal ideals, the questions with which I am concerned are more likely to lurk in the background of any individual's life.

that point of view. If, as I have argued, this means that we have reason to want people to live lives that are not morally perfect, then any plausible moral theory must make use of some conception of supererogation.[6]

If moral philosophers are to address themselves at the most basic level to the question of how people should live, however, they must do more than adjust the content of their moral theories in ways that leave room for the affirmation of nonmoral values. They must examine explicitly the range and nature of these nonmoral values, and, in light of this examination, they must ask how the acceptance of a moral theory is to be understood and acted upon. For the claims of this paper do not so much conflict with the content of any particular currently popular moral theory as they call into question a metamoral assumption that implicitly surrounds discussions of moral theory more generally. Specifically, they call into question the assumption that it is always better to be morally better.

The role morality plays in the development of our characters and the shape of our practical deliberations need be neither that of a universal medium into which all other values must be translated nor that of an ever-present filter through which all other values must pass. This is not to say that moral value should not be an important, even the most important, kind of value we attend to in evaluating and improving ourselves and our world. It is to say that our values cannot be fully comprehended on the model of a hierarchical system with morality at the top.

The philosophical temperament will naturally incline, at this point, toward asking, "What, then, *is* at the top—or, if there is no top, how *are* we to decide when and how much to be moral?" In other words, there is a temptation to seek a metamoral—though not, in the standard sense, metaethical—theory that will give us principles, or, at least, informal directives on the basis of which we can develop and evaluate more comprehensive personal ideals. Perhaps a theory that distinguishes among the various roles a person is expected to play within a life—as professional, as citizen, as friend, and so on—might give us some rules that would offer us, if nothing else, a better framework in which to think about and discuss these questions. I am pessimistic, however, about the chances of such a theory to yield substantial and satisfying results. For I do not see how a metamoral theory could be constructed which would not be subject to considerations parallel to those which seem inherently to limit

---

[6] The variety of forms that a conception of supererogation might take, however, has not generally been noticed. Moral theories that make use of this notion typically do so by identifying some specific set of principles as universal moral requirements and supplement this list with a further set of directives which it is morally praiseworthy but not required for an agent to follow. [See, e.g., Charles Fried, *Right and Wrong* (Cambridge, Mass.: Harvard, 1979).] But it is possible that the ability to live a morally blameless life cannot be so easily or definitely secured as this type of theory would suggest. The fact that there are some situations in which an agent is morally required to do something and other situations in which it would be good but not required for an agent to do something does not imply that there are specific principles such that, in any situation, an agent is required to act in accordance with these principles and other specific principles such that, in any situation, it would be good but not required for an agent to act in accordance with those principles.

the appropriateness of regarding moral theories as ultimate comprehensive guides for action.

This suggests that, at some point, both in our philosophizing and in our lives, we must be willing to raise normative questions from a perspective that is unattached to a commitment to any particular well-ordered system of values. It must be admitted that, in doing so, we run the risk of finding normative answers that diverge from the answers given by whatever moral theory one accepts. This, I take it, is the grain of truth in G. E. Moore's "open question" argument. In the background of this paper, then, there lurks a commitment to what seems to me to be a healthy form of intuitionism. It is a form of intuitionism which is not intended to take the place of more rigorous, systematically developed, moral theories—rather, it is intended to put these more rigorous and systematic moral theories in their place.

4

The Alleged Moral Repugnance of Acting From Duty*

MARCIA BARON

Marcia Baron (b. 1955) is Assistant Professor of Philosophy at the University of Illinois at Urbana. She has published a number of essays on moral philosophy.

In recent years, some philosophers have argued that impersonal moral duties are not decisive when they conflict with deep desires or commitments. (For versions of this claim, see Bernard Williams and Susan Wolf, readings 2 and 3.) Here Marcia Baron defends the more traditional view that a morally good person does act from a sense of duty. To establish this, she carefully examines two examples in which acting from duty seems to rule out responses of care or affection. These examples, which include a case in which someone visits a sick friend merely out of duty, are said to show that acting from duty is "morally repugnant." But Baron argues that they show no such thing. If the actions seem repugnant, it is partly because we assume that the agents have motives that are repugnant, but have little to do with duty. In addition, we may go wrong by regarding duty as an independent source of motivation. Instead, Baron suggests that we should regard it as a potential restraint on other motives. Duty is, in her view, a filter through which our desires and responses must pass.

FRIENDS AS WELL AS FOES of Kant have long been uneasy over his emphasis on duty, but lately the view that there is something morally repugnant about acting from duty seems to be gaining in popularity. More and more philosophers indicate their readiness to jettison duty and the moral 'ought' and to conceive of the perfectly moral person as someone who has all the right

*My paper was improved by incisive comments from Thomas Carson, Nancy Davis, Thomas Hill, Jr., Joan Leguard, Robert McKim, Peter Railton, Frederick Schmitt, Holly Smith, Susan Wolf, and the members of colloquia at Ohio State University (November, 1982) and the NEH Summer Institute on Kantian Ethics (July, 1983) to whom earlier versions of this paper were presented. I would also like to thank Peter Railton for sharing with me some years ago a rough draft of a long manuscript on moral alienation, a manuscript which deepened my appreciation of Williams's and Stocker's worries.

desires and acts accordingly *without* any notion that (s)he *ought* to act in this way. Elsewhere[1] I have argued that such a picture of the perfectly moral person is flawed. In this paper I examine the claim that acting from duty is morally repugnant. There is some truth to this charge, but, I argue, the repugnance attaches not to acting from duty as such, but only to certain ways of acting from duty. In isolating the objectionable elements of acting from duty, I hope not only to vindicate the skeletal concept but also to offer illumination on the question of just how we should understand morally good conduct.

My aim to vindicate acting from duty should not be construed as an aim to vindicate Kant. Indeed, part of the motivation for this paper is the belief that acting from duty can be understood in a number of different ways, some more and some less closely related to Kant's conception of morally good conduct.[2] Nor should my aim be thought to include defending the Kantian thesis that only acts done from duty have moral worth. The reason I wish to vindicate acting from duty is simply (or not so simply) that acting from duty seems to me to be crucial to morally good conduct.[3]

---

[1] In my "On De-Kantianizing the Perfectly Moral Person," *Journal of Value Inquiry*, xvii, 4 (December 1983): 281–293, and "Varieties of Ethics of Virtue," *American Philosophical Quarterly* XXI, 1 (January 1985): 47–53.

[2] Since writing this paper I have become convinced, through reading Barbara Herman's excellent papers on Kant's ethics, that my account of acting from duty is even closer to Kant's view than I had thought. See Herman, "On the Value of Acting from the Motive of Duty," *Philosophical Review* XC, 3 (July 1981): 359–82; and "Integrity and Impartiality," *Monist* LXVI, 2 (April 1983): 233–50. Parenthetical page references to Herman are to the first paper.

[3] Or, in other words, that one necessary condition for perfectly moral personhood is that one act from duty. When it is put this way, we see that it is in fact not simple at all. For what is meant by 'perfectly moral personhood'? What is at issue when it is asserted or denied that something is a necessary condition for perfectly moral personhood? Briefly, I take the point of asking what constitutes perfectly moral personhood to be that of trying to determine what types of people we should aspire and endeavor to be, and with what aims we should bring up and educate children. If this *is* the point, then to say that it is a necessary condition of perfectly moral personhood that one act from duty is to say only that we should aim in (self-)education to bring it about that the persons in question will act from duty—which, given the account of acting from duty that I present in this paper, is to say, very roughly, that they will be committed to doing whatever is right and to striving to determine what is right. This two-pronged commitment will govern their conduct. It is *not* to say that someone with a sense of duty but corrupt desires is (or is not) better than someone with "perfect" desires but no sense of duty. Nor is it claimed that, for any given person, that person is morally better if he is governed by a sense of duty than if he isn't. People who are exceptionally flawed, morally, and flawed in the relevant sorts of ways, may be morally better if they do not act from a sense of duty. [Suppose, for instance, that their sense of what is right is like that of Heinrich Himmler (as discussed in Jonathan Bennett's paper, cited in fn 7, below).] Finally, the order in which these things are taught may be important: a sense of duty may well be of great value *only* once the person has learned to distinguish morality from convention, honor, power, etc. For a further discussion of these points, see my "The Ethics of Duty/Ethics of Virtue Debate and its Relevance to Educational Theory," *Educational Theory* XXXV, 2 (Spring 1985): 135–49.

My position should not be taken to commit me to any stand as to whether ethical theories should be couched in aretaic rather than deontic terms. It is important to clarify that nothing hangs on my use of deontic terms. I use 'duty' and 'ought' repeatedly, partly in the hope of convincing readers that much of the opposition to acting from duty is nothing but dislike for the word 'duty'. See section II.

One last preliminary. My project is to examine the formal details of acting from duty in light of contemporary objections, in particular, those raised via examples offered by Michael Stocker[4] and Bernard Williams,[5] and to suggest forms of acting from duty that steer clear of the problems that those examples depict. A different but related question concerns the content of the agent's conception of duty. This question will not be addressed, though it does bear on the issue, since certain normative conceptions of what one's duty is and certain metaethical conceptions of what morality is may make acting from duty, as explicated and defended below, morally undesirable. Hence, a caveat: My defense of acting from duty may not hold across all possible metaethical and normative views. If, for instance, one takes an especially stern view about what people's duties are, one may be inclined to say, "Well, it's better if people don't feel *too* compelled invariably to do what one morally ought to do." Or again, someone who takes morality to be strictly other-regarding is likely to say, "A commitment to act morally can go too far: after all, people need to think about themselves, too."[6]

I

The allegation that acting from duty is morally repugnant can be broken down into three charges: first, that to act from duty is to act just minimally morally; second, that acting from duty is alienating; and third, that thinking in terms of what one ought to do or what morality directs one to do is at least as likely to yield the wrong answer as the right one. The third objection is quite different from the others, for it centers on the problem of the fallibility of conscience.[7] I do not address that objection in this paper. Here I am concerned with something more elusive: an alleged flaw in the way that someone who acts from duty regards other people. The first objection is that someone who acts from duty does not really care about others, but fulfills his duties toward them just in order to meet a minimum requirement: to do the boy-scout-good-deed-of-the-day. The second objection is more complex and harder, at least initially, to make explicit; here the worry is that action done from duty expresses

---

[4] "The Schizophrenia of Modern Ethical Theories," this JOURNAL, LXIII, 4 (Aug. 12, 1976): 453–466. Parenthetical page references to Stocker will be to this article.

[5] "Persons, Character and Morality," in Amelie O. Rorty, ed., *The Identities of Persons* (Berkeley: Univ. of California Press, 1976), pp. 214/5. Parenthetical page references to Williams will be to this book. [Reprinted in this volume, reading 2.]

[6] This would, I think, be Susan Wolf's reaction. See her "Moral Saints," this JOURNAL, LXXIX, 8 (August 1982): 419–439. [Reprinted in this volume, reading 3.]

[7] For an intriguing discussion of this problem, illustrated by reference to Huck Finn, Heinrich Himmler, and Jonathan Edwards, see Jonathan Bennett, "The Conscience of Huckleberry Finn," *Philosophy*, LXIX, 110 (April 1974): 123–134.

and perhaps nurtures the wrong sorts of attitude toward others. I begin with the first objection, which will turn out to be easy to get out of the way. The bulk of the paper focuses on the second charge.

II

Given the many pejorative associations that we have with the word 'duty', it is no surprise that many people think of a concern to do one's duty as a concern to do only what one *has* to do. We sometimes associate 'duty' with unconditional demands placed on us from without, and especially by social institutions or norms that are themselves morally dubious.[8] Someone who is deeply concerned to do his duty in *that* sense seems unreflective, cowardly, or both. Karenin's concern with duty (in *Anna Karenina*) hardly inspires us with respect, but that is, I think, because we are thinking of duty in this more colloquial sense, which contrasts sharply with the Kantian notion of duty as what one (truly!) morally ought to do.

Those who are motivated by duty in this pejorative sense of 'duty' may seem not to be morally motivated at all, but moved instead to do what they have to do in order to be off the hook, where the danger of the "hook" might be, say, social ostracism. But one may think of the hook and the motivation to avoid it as moral, where the agent is seen to act morally, but only minimally so. The thought is that someone who acts from duty is concerned only with what morality demands, not with what morality recommends. Thus, in defense of his claim that it is better to perform altruistic acts from "direct altruism" than from a sense of duty, Lawrence Blum argues that "most altruistic acts are not . . . duties."[9] Giving someone directions, letting someone with few groceries ahead of you in the checkout line, and pressing the desired floor button for a blind person in an elevator are, he thinks, examples of altruistic acts that are not duties (*loc. cit.*).

Now, if one thinks of duty (or duties) as what morality *requires* and only that, then, arguably, the first two examples are *not* duties—though the third, I think, clearly is. And thus the charge of minimal morality would have some force, since one would have reason to worry that the person who acts from duty, in this sense, would not be concerned to give directions, etc., and might just not bother to do so.

---

[8] Consider, for instance, the following inscription on a statue on the campus of the University of North Carolina at Chapel Hill: "To the sons of the University, who entered the war of 1861–1865 in answer to the call of their country and whose lives taught the lesson of the great commander that duty [sic] is the sublimest word in the English language."

[9] *Friendship, Altruism and Morality* (London: Routledge & Kegan Paul, 1980), p. 92.

To obviate the charge of minimal morality, we need only to explain that the person who acts from duty, *in the sense in which acting from duty is being advocated,* is moved *both* by considerations that *x* is morally required and by considerations that *x* is morally recommended. Moreover, she is committed to being moved by both.

III

I turn now to the more complex charge that acting from duty is alienating; or, in long form, that it is alienating and, as such, morally repugnant, and that it is, therefore, morally preferable that one not act from duty. Vaguely—and it must remain so for now—the idea is that acting in a certain way, from a certain type of motivation betrays (and perhaps further entrenches) attitudes toward others and toward one's relations with others which are, morally and otherwise, regrettable.

The objection has been pressed forcefully and yet elusively by both Michael Stocker and Bernard Williams. They have made their points largely by way of examples—one example each—with less commentary than one would like. Susan Wolf[10] has made considerable headway in clarifying the objection, and I shall make use of her comments—although it would be unfair to assume that, thus clarified, the objection is precisely what either Stocker or Williams had in mind. My strategy will be to analyze their examples with the interlocking aims of determining exactly what it is that makes the contents disturbing and then of using these findings to decide whether acting from duty is as such alienating or whether it is only certain modes of acting from duty that are objectionable in this way. If, as I suspect, the latter is the case, our scrutiny of Williams's and Stocker's examples should enable us to separate the good in acting from duty from the ill, and to suggest the type—or rather, the way—of acting from duty which is worthy of defense. I will proceed by first asking what it is about the behavior Stocker describes that is morally repugnant and then querying what conclusions concerning acting from duty can be drawn from the fact that those aspects of his behavior are morally repugnant. Because of the nature of the examples, I will focus on Stocker's example for the next several pages and only later discuss Williams's.

IV

Stocker's example is that of a hospitalized person who receives a visit from his friend, Smith:

> You are very bored and restless and at loose ends when Smith comes in once
> again. You are now convinced more than ever that he is a fine fellow and a real

---

[10] *The Failure of Autonomy.* Ph.D. dissertation, Princeton University, 1978, ch. 1. Unless otherwise noted, all references to Wolf will be to this work.

friend—taking so much time to cheer you up, travelling all the way across town, and so on. You are so effusive with your praise and thanks that he protests that he always tries to do what he thinks is his duty, what he thinks will be best. You at first think he is engaging in a polite form of self-deprecation, relieving the moral burden. But the more you two speak, the more clear it becomes that he was telling the literal truth: that it is not essentially because of you that he came to see you, not because you are friends, but because he thought it his duty, perhaps as a fellow Christian or Communist or whatever, or simply because he knows of no one more in need of cheering up and no one easier to cheer up (462).

Clearly there is something disturbing about Stocker's example. None of us would want to be treated by a friend the way Smith's friend is treated by Smith; moreover, we can see that there is something morally objectionable about Smith's conduct. But what?

There are a number of different ways in which (perhaps without knowing it) we may be filling in Stocker's sketch of Smith. We need to consider them separately in order to determine just what is disturbing about Smith's conduct and whether or not it impugns acting from duty.

The image that we have of Smith is something like this: he does not want to visit his friend, but believing it to be his duty to visit her, he forces himself to do so and, later, we fear, revels sanctimoniously in his goodness. The two features of this picture of Smith that contribute to the over-all repugnance of his conduct are his disinclination (or lack of inclination) to see his friend and his sanctimoniousness. I will shelve sanctimoniousness for now and concentrate on determining the relevance of disinclination to the moral repugnance of acting from duty. To do so it will be necessary to examine a number of different cases.

Consider the first case in which Smith is disinclined to visit the hospitalized friend—whom I'll call Thompson—and yet visits her because he believes it is his duty to visit fellow X's and she is, he believes, a fellow X. 'X' could be replaced by 'Christian', 'Communist', 'Republican', etc.[11] This case will be contrasted with those in which Smith thinks it his duty to visit her *as a friend*. Suppose that in Stocker's story Thompson thinks that Smith is coming to see her as a friend and then realizes, with a jolt, that it isn't friendship but a sense of (community and) special obligation to other Christians (or whatever) that brings him to her hospital room. She will feel alienated if she thinks he isn't coming to see *her*, but rather to see the member of his church who is in the hospital. All the worse if he misleadingly acts as if he is coming as a friend when he isn't. Even if he doesn't mislead, and she is clear from the outset that he is visiting her as a fellow Christian, the situation may still be alienating if she does not strongly identify herself as a Christian (especially if he had no reason to suppose that she did).

---

[11] The type and size of the group that gets covered by 'etc.' would make some difference to how one would feel about Smith's visiting him or her from a sense that he ought to pay a call on hospitalized fellow X's, but I ignore that here.

All the above are details that we may, more or less clearly, have in our various pictures of Smith, and any of them accounts for at least some of what bothers us about Smith's conduct. But none of them has anything to do with acting from duty. To see this, just note that what goes wrong would equally go wrong if Smith visited her simply from an inclination to visit a fellow Christian.

Once these features are pushed to one side, there is, I think, nothing objectionable in Smith's visiting Thompson because he thought it his duty as a fellow X. Thompson thought he was visiting her as a friend, but in fact he came in quite a different capacity; he was wrong to pretend to come qua friend, if indeed he did pretend this, and it was thoughtless of him to visit her as a fellow X if he had reason to think that she did not have a sense of community with X's. But barring these problems, there would be nothing expressive of or conducive to alienation or otherwise objectionable about one fellow Christian or Communist visiting another because he thought it right to do so.

V

Stocker's example becomes more compelling if we think of Smith as visiting Thompson because he thinks it is his duty *as a friend* to do so. This situation is interestingly different, for friendship, unlike a sense of community with fellow Christians, does not sit easily with one's not wanting to visit one's friend but doing so out of duty. Stocker's belief appears to be that insofar as one is motivated on a particular occasion to do something for a friend out of duty, one is not acting as a true friend. The point has considerable force. The fact that the agent acted from duty tends to suggest (as in Stocker's example) that he is not much of a friend—at least not much of a friend to the person in question.

We should note that much of the compellingness of Stocker's belief draws from the conception of the motive of duty as excluding inclination to do what one regards as one's duty—here visiting a hospitalized friend. As will be elaborated later, it is possible to do x from a sense of duty while wanting to do $x;$ and acting from duty plus inclination meshes better with friendship than does acting from duty without inclination, or in the face of a strong opposing inclination.[12] But to that shortly. Let us first examine whether visiting a friend from duty (or for that matter helping or trying to comfort a friend from duty) without the inclination to do so is morally undesirable. To put it differently, let us see whether acts of friendship, if done from duty, lose their status as acts of friendship.

Depending on how one interprets Stocker's example (and how one pictures other instances of friendly acts done from duty), there are a number of reasons one might have for supposing that this is the case. One might think of Smith as visiting Thompson grudgingly or resentfully. Thus understood, his conduct

---

[12] The last case is, tellingly, less at odds with friendship. See the examples in sec. VII below.

is morally objectionable on two counts. First, his attitude may show through, making the visit rather unpleasant for Thompson. If this is the case, then the problem lies primarily not with Smith's motives, but with what he did. He acted contrary to duty. His duty was not to make an appearance in Thompson's room, but to do her some good by visiting her—cheer her up, divert her, alleviate her boredom, let her see that at least one of her friends is thinking of her and is concerned about her. Of course if he fails to cheer her up because she is just too depressed, this would not impugn his conduct, but it is another matter if he conveys hostility toward her for having occasioned, as he sees it, the moral demand that he visit her, when he'd much prefer to be elsewhere. The important point here is that the flaw in his conduct lies not in his acting from duty, but in his acting from a misconception of what his duty is or perhaps failing to do what he sees to be his duty.

Visiting a friend grudgingly or resentfully is objectionable on a second count. Thompson may be unaware of Smith's resentment and may find his visit enjoyable, even gratifying. Yet there is something amiss in Smith's conduct if he harbors resentment toward Thompson, or even annoyance that takes no particular object. He ought not have such feelings, and although that isn't to say that he must be in control of whether or not he has those feelings and is at fault for having them, his conduct is morally deficient. Part of what one morally ought to do is cultivate certain attitudes and dispositions, e.g., sympathy rather than resentment or repulsion for the ailing; a cheerful readiness to help and to find ways in which one can help out.

If Smith's deficiency is that he lacks such attitudes and dispositions and feels resentful, then whether or not he successfully masks it, it does not indict acting from duty as such. It shows that there is something wrong with acting from a false conception of one's duty, a conception that overlooks the importance of the attitudes and dispositions one has when one performs certain acts, especially those which are intended to express affection or concern. Thus although it does not indict acting from duty as such, it points to certain parameters within which satisfactory ways of acting from duty must be located. Similarly, it highlights the fact that any ethical theory that dismissed such feelings as irrelevant as long as "outwardly" the agent did her duty (narrowly construed) and did it from the sense that she ought to, would be unacceptable.

So far, then, the problems we have uncovered in Smith's conduct do not signify any flaws in acting from duty as such. The same can be said of a number of other worrisome attitudes one might attribute to the man Stocker describes. One might, for instance, suspect that if Smith is disinclined to visit Thompson and goes solely from duty, he may persistently think of his visit under the description of *what morality requires or recommends* (or *what I ought to do,* or *what is right to do*). Here one might be worried that Smith will be reveling throughout the visit in his own goodness. And this, one may suspect, will render him cold, cut off from others, alienated from people by his preoccupation with morality (cf. Wolf, 52).

One's response to this, at least initially (cf. sec. VI, below) is that if he revels throughout the visit in his own goodness then again his flaw is that he is not conducting himself as he ought, i.e., not really doing his duty. This is the problem; there is no reason to pin it on his acting from duty. And so once again, no conclusions concerning the merits or hazards of acting from duty can be drawn from the phenomenon. For there is no reason to suppose that if one acts from duty, one must be preoccupied with morality.

One might object to Smith's conduct on different grounds. One might imagine that, since Smith is visiting Thompson out of duty and against his predominant inclinations, this must be the way he always is with the people he thinks of and speaks of as his friends. The inference is not warranted, but that isn't my concern. The objection is nonetheless instructive. For though once again there appears to be no reason to think that someone who acts from duty always needs the motive of duty to impel him to seek out his friends—I will return to this shortly—it is worth noting that any ethical theory would be seriously flawed if it held that someone who is so dependent on the motive of duty can still qualify as perfectly moral. A person S is morally deficient if S is so motivationally depleted that, for actions to which most of us would be moved by sympathy, fellow-feeling, or affection for a particular person (the list is not exhaustive), the only sufficient motive S has is his belief that morality recommends (or requires) this act.[13]

To sum up the foregoing: we have considered a number of different explanations of what it is that we find morally repugnant about Smith's conduct in Stocker's example. In each case the explanation could be exploited to point the way to conceptions of acting from duty which, typically because of misconceptions of what one's duty is, are of dubious merit. The explanations did not, however, provide any reason for thinking that acting from duty is by its very nature alienating or otherwise morally repugnant.

VI

One might object that I have not yet done justice to Stocker's worries. What if the problems we have detected are more deep-seated than I have supposed? What if Smith's failure to fulfill—indeed to recognize—certain of his duties is rooted in an inability to be a true friend to anyone, to care about others? Perhaps, in other words, the whole problem is that Smith is alienated from others by virtue of his commitment to doing whatever he morally ought to do. If so, the objectionable features enumerated above are mere symptoms of the real difficulty which, Stocker thinks, is that, insofar as one acts from duty, one is unable "to realize the great goods of love, friendship, affection, fellow-feeling and community" (461), for these goods "essentially contain certain motives and essentially preclude others," among those precluded being the motive to do what one believes one morally ought to do (461/2).

---

[13] This is not intended as a definition. I have merely stated a sufficient condition (and there are many) for being morally deficient.

If this is right, then the answer I have suggested will not suffice. It will not do to say that the problem lies not with acting from duty but with doing one's duty, if in fact there are certain duties that one cannot fulfill if one acts from duty.

As a preliminary to addressing this challenge, I will offer some positive suggestions as to how acting from duty can be understood. The suggestions will draw on a bit of conceptual machinery—three overlapping distinctions—concerning acting from duty.

The first distinction will be familiar. 'Duty' can be thought to refer only to moral requirements or to moral recommendations as well as to moral requirements.

The second distinction, which I borrow with some modification from Barbara Herman (372–376), is between primary and secondary motives. A primary motive supplies the agent with the motivation to do the act in question, whereas a secondary motive provides limiting conditions on what may be done from other motives. Although qua secondary motive it cannot by itself move one to act, a secondary motive is nonetheless a motive, for the agent would not proceed to perform the action without the "approval" of the secondary motive.[14]

Accordingly, the sense of duty can function in two very different ways if, for example, I help someone from duty. First, my sense of duty may prompt me to help the person, and it may motivate me without the aid of inclination and possibly, in the face of conflicting inclinations. Here, my sense of duty operates as a primary motive. But imagine instead that I want to help someone—for example, a student who is having trouble with an assignment—and do so in the conviction that I should help him (or, that I do not act wrongly in helping him). In this case, my sense of duty is a secondary motive.[15] It tells me that I may or that I should act as I wished. In different circumstances— suppose the assignment was such that students were not to get outside help of any sort—it would tell me that I should not do as I wished.[16]

[14] It remains to be worked out just what the proper level of generality is for secondary motives. "Never pick one's nose in public" would not qualify, but just what would qualify is not entirely clear. This is roughly the same as the generality problem that vexes Kant scholars who seek to explain what counts as a maxim in Kant's ethics.

[15] As I understand the distinction between primary and secondary motives (and here, I believe, I differ from Herman), a motive may initially operate as a secondary motive, but then, if it conflicts with and overpowers another motive, take on the function of a primary motive. Hence the distinction, as I see it, is not really between *types* of motives, but rather between functions that the motives assume.

[16] It should be noted that, when it operates as a primary motive, the sense of duty can prompt one to perform required or recommended actions, but it cannot suffice to motivate a merely permissible action. To choose to perform a particular permissible action, there must be something besides its permissibility that attracts one to it, for there are a great many permissible actions that one could perform in most given sets of circumstances, and thus mere permissibility would not pick out any one action from the range of possible actions. But when it operates as a secondary motive, the sense of duty can prompt one to perform any morally recommended, permissible, or required action. (Unfortunately, it can also prompt one to perform morally impermissible actions, but that misfortune is beyond the scope of this paper.)

Views on what it is to act from duty divide in yet a third way. Some may hold that to act from duty, the agent must think about x's rightness just before acting (and an assortment of views is available as to how reflective one's thought about x should be); others hold that one need not do so at that particular time. The latter view is difficult to spell out with precision, but I want to say something about it, for it seems clearly to be the correct view.

On this view, at least in the form I wish to defend, what is expected of the agent is first and foremost that she be committed to doing what is right and understand this commitment to carry with it a commitment to thinking about what is right. But there are right times and there are wrong times for reflecting on the moral status of various forms of conduct, and the period immediately prior to action will frequently be one of the wrong times. To the extent that we know what it would be to evaluate the rightness or wrongness of every action just before doing it, it would be as inappropriate for a responsible moral agent to do so as it would be for a responsible driver to think about the correctness or incorrectness of applying the brakes or quickly turning the steering wheel before performing each such action.[17] A responsible moral agent should think from time to time about the moral status not only of various actions, but also of acting from certain motives. She should also reflect on her character traits and be committed to changing her focus of attention in ways that will facilitate any changes that appear to be in order.

With these distinctions before us, I can clarify the form of acting from duty which can meet the challenge presented in the beginning of this section.

As explained earlier, I think that a concern to do what one morally ought to do should be understood as a concern to do the morally recommended as well as the morally required. Otherwise, a commitment to do one's duty is of limited importance in an agent morality and will not have the role of unifying and undergirding one's acts and one's conception of oneself which, for reasons yet to be adumbrated, I believe it should have.

It scarcely needs stating that acting from duty should *not* be thought to involve thinking just before every action about the moral status of the intended action. More important and more subtle is how this point interlocks with the distinction between primary and secondary motives of duty. On the conception that I am recommending, duty is seen as attaching primarily not to individual actions but to *conduct,* to how one lives, and only derivatively to isolated actions. The definitive feature of someone who acts from duty is her commit-

[17] The analogy between morally responsible agents and responsible drivers was drawn by W. D. Falk in an unpublished paper, "Morality: Form and Content." It is important to note that although the analogy is useful in that it brings out the fact that one can have certain principles in one's mind—be they moral or principles of driving—and be influenced by them without consciously thinking of them, the analogy breaks down at another point: whereas there is such a thing as having the rules and techniques of driving "down pat," there is no comparable stage in morality. My point is not that few of us reach such a stage, but rather that moral principles must be regarded as always open to revision. It *is* possible that someone could accept moral principles that are absolutely correct, leaving no room for improvement, but it is impossible that anyone (with the possible exception of a deity) could *know* that they were correct.

ment to doing what she really ought to do—and to determining what she ought to do—and this is significant as a long-term, wide-ranging commitment, governing all one does.

Once we break from the idea that acting from duty primarily concerns isolated actions, there is no temptation to suppose that one must ask before each action whether one ought to do what one is proposing to do. But once we break from *that* idea (and no longer ask the typical "How often is one supposed to act from duty? Is acting from duty being advocated only for a certain range of actions? If so, which?"), we see the vital role of the sense of duty as a *secondary* motive. On my view, one should (ideally) always act from duty, but this is only to say that all of one's conduct should be governed by one's unconditional commitment to doing what one morally ought to do. To say that one should always act from duty is not to say that one should always act from duty as a primary motive. One's sense of duty will serve generally as a limiting condition and at the same time as an impetus to think about one's conduct, to appraise one's goals, to be conscious of oneself as a self-determining being, and sometimes to give one the strength one needs to do what one sees one really should do.

VII

We are now in a position to return to the questions posed. First, does a commitment to doing whatever one morally ought to do alienate one from others? Does it either make one unable to care for or about other people or make the concern or affection that one has for others less deep or less genuine? Second, is it an expression or symptom of alienation?

It would seem that, in the form in which I have defended it, acting from duty would not involve any such difficulty, simply because it can operate together with sympathetic concern, deep attachment to the person, and so on. By 'together' I do not mean merely 'alongside'; the motives will typically be interwoven, and in more ways than one. To list just a few: first, one's awareness of how one ought to conduct oneself will not atypically be enriched by one's affective responses to fiction, the plight of others, etc. Second, since any materially adequate sense of duty will recognize that one has duties to be concerned about the welfare of others and that one has special duties as a friend, among one's duties will be those of cultivating certain attitudes and dispositions.[18] Third, and most important for present purposes, one's sense of duty will serve to strengthen other motives as the following examples illustrate.

Suppose, following our well-worn motif, that, on a raw, chilly Sunday when I am inclined to stay home and read, I push myself to visit a friend who is in

---

[18] Just what these other motives are that will motivate the agent whose actions are governed by a sense of duty remains to be worked out. It is beyond the scope of this paper to discuss them, since my project is to argue that acting from duty is not in all shapes and forms morally repugnant, and to suggest a form of acting from duty which leaves room for the other motives that are important to morally good conduct.

the hospital awaiting surgery the next day. I'd prefer to see her elsewhere (I dislike hospitals) and on a different day, but I really ought to visit her, since she would be especially anxious, as well as disappointed if I didn't (and helping out at times like this is part of friendship).[19] Or, to borrow an example from Richard Norman[20]

> Suppose that a friend of mine has come to grief, in a totally predictable way about which I had insistently warned him—yet another disastrous love-affair, perhaps—and now comes to me for sympathy; it has happened so often before, and was so obviously bound to turn out this way, that I have lost all patience with him and can feel no sympathy for him, but still I know that he needs my help and that I ought to do what I can for him (169).

These examples (and many others like them) illustrate that the motive of duty can supplement the motives that opponents of acting from duty prefer to see operate as the sole motive.[21] If it operates in this way, there appears to be no ground for regarding it as symptomatic of alienation.

VIII

Thus understood, acting from duty would seem to be unobjectionable. But it does not seem so to Susan Wolf and Bernard Williams. This is evident from

---

[19] Someone might protest that there would be something alienating about an agent who actually thought the parenthetical conclusion to him- or herself. "It's so distanced, so abstract; what purpose could it possibly serve? Why doesn't the agent leave things at 'she'd be very disappointed'?" My answer is that often it would not serve any purpose; hence the parentheses. But not infrequently it would: for the agent may recall a situation in which the fact that a friend would be very disappointed was not a sufficient reason for making plans accordingly, and may wonder why (or whether) this case is different. [Imagine, for instance, that a "suitor" pressed her to cancel her plans with a female friend so that he could go out with her (the agent). The fact that he would be very disappointed if she didn't cancel the plans (more, we suppose, than she expected her female friend would be) was not, she thought, sufficient reason to change her plans; for although she'd be at least as happy to spend the evening with him as with the other friend, she believed that women should strive to avoid the traditional pattern of putting romantic interests above their friendships with women.] The thought serves the purpose, in such circumstances, of clarifying to the agent the relevant difference between the two situations.

[20] "Critical Notice: Rodger Bechler, *Moral Life*," *Canadian Journal of Philosophy*, XI, 1 (March 1981): 157–183.

[21] In the examples, my affection and concern for my friend would not suffice to overcome my inclination to stay home or, in Norman's example, to tell my friend to handle his problems himself. An opponent might argue that the examples serve to demonstrate only that morally deficient people need a sense of duty (a point which is consistent with and probably strategically useful for the thesis I am opposing, viz. that acting from duty is morally repugnant). This would be to suppose that the fact that I was strongly inclined to stay home or that I lost all patience with my friend shows me to be morally flawed. I think that the supposition should be rejected, but to defend my claim would take us too far afield, since it would require (among other things) an evaluation of the view of morality according to which an agent's goodness is a function solely of his unselfishness and indeed selflessness. Unless one accepts that view of morality, one will grant, I think, that a sense of duty is important to the conduct of morally perfect persons.

their discussions of Williams's example. Indeed Wolf remarks that his example is particularly apt in that, unlike Stocker's, it reveals the flaws in acting from friendship or love that is governed or mediated by one's sense of duty—not just the flaws in acting from duty as a primary motive. The example, taken from Charles Fried's *An Anatomy of Values*,[22] describes a situation in which a man in a position to save one of two persons in equal peril chooses to save his wife. Fried explains that it is permissible for him to choose his wife rather than make the choice by a flip of a coin, because "the occurrence of the accident may itself stand as a sufficient randomizing event to meet the dictates of fairness" (27). Insisting that "surely this is a justification on behalf of the rescuer, that the person he chose to rescue was his wife," Williams objects to the "idea that moral principle can legitimate the man's preference." "This construction," he elaborates, "provides the agent with one thought too many: it might have been hoped by some (for instance, by his wife) that his motivating thought, fully spelled out, would be the thought that it was his wife, not that it was his wife and that in situations of this kind it is permissible to save one's wife."[23] Echoing Williams, Wolf adds, "Ideally, it seems, when one acts on behalf of a loved one, one acts plainly and simply *for his sake*. One's motivating thought, fully spelled out, is something like 'It's good for George' " (50).

The objection to the idea that the man should be thinking about fairness in such a situation can be dismissed, since we have seen that one's action can be governed by a belief that one is acting fairly without its being the case that one thinks about fairness at the time of action. But what about the claim that the agent should act "plainly and simply" for his wife's sake? Here the point seems to go beyond the suggestion that he shouldn't be thinking at that particular time about fairness; Williams objects, remember, "to the idea that moral principle can legitimate the man's preference."

Would it be preferable if the action of the man in Williams's example were motivated simply by love for his wife, i.e., if it were not governed by a belief that what he does is morally permissible? I think not, and the reason why can be gleaned if we revise the example slightly and imagine that his wife is badly shaken up, in terrible pain, but unlike the stranger, not in any life-threatening danger. Assuming that there is hope of saving the stranger's life but very little time, it would be wrong of the husband to devote his attention to his wife before attending to the stranger. It is difficult to turn away from the anguished cries of someone whom one loves dearly in order to administer mouth-to-mouth resuscitation to a stranger; but far from supporting Wolf's and Williams's claims, this underscores the importance of acting from affections that are informed by a sense of what is right and, if necessary, adjusted accordingly. Or, if one's affections are recalcitrant, one will need to act from one's

---

[22] Cambridge, Mass.: Harvard University Press, 1970.

[23] Williams, *op.cit.*, pp. 214/5.

recognition of what one's affections would be if they were not so unyielding—i.e., from one's sense of what is right.[24]

What about the argument that it might have been hoped by some (e.g., by his wife) that the thought that it was she would have been sufficient motivation for him? Several comments are in order here. First, the mere fact that she might have hoped this is in itself of no relevance. Many of us are insecure about the strength of our loved ones' affection for us; it might worry us that our spouse was not so overwhelmed by the sight of us in excruciating pain as to lack the presence of mind needed to see that the stranger was (or wasn't) in greater need. The spouse in the example as I revised it might be pained because she didn't receive any comfort or reassurance right away. She may realize that her husband was right to save (or try to save) the person whose life was imperiled before comforting her; but her pain may persist. If this is the situation, Williams's point is again of no relevance.

Someone might object, "But surely it is of relevance! After all, she feels alienated from her husband. She knows he did what was right, but it still hurts. And this goes to show the clash between morality and love." Now, if *this* is the force of the claim that acting from duty is alienating, then the difficulty lies not with acting from duty, but with doing what one morally ought to do, whether or not one does it *for the reason* that it is what one morally ought to do. The claim is thus not that acting from duty is morally repugnant, but rather that doing what one morally ought to do is morally repugnant, an interesting and curious claim, but not central to the focus of this paper.

To return to Williams's argument: it is true of both his example and my variation on it that there *might* be cause for worry. It's possible that the husband saw his wife's suffering just as *someone's suffering,* or the prospect of her death just as the prospect of *someone's* tragic death. But we would need to know more about the husband to determine this, since an alternative interpretation is available.

Of course his wife would have reason to be dismayed if it had not pained him to hear her moans and to be unable to comfort her while tending to the more severe case. There would be cause for worry if his sympathetic responses were naturally directly proportional to the severity of the case: equal anguish in Williams's example for his spouse and the stranger; in my example, greater for the stranger than for his wife. But it is one thing to claim that there is something wrong if a person's spontaneous affective responses aren't such and such in circumstances C; it is another matter to say that there is something wrong, in circumstances C, with putting one's affective responses through a filter rather than acting on them with no thought of what it is right to do or what one ought to do.

---

[24] It should be evident from my appeal to "adjusted affections" that my view of morally good conduct derives from Hume as well as from Kant. See Hume, *Treatise,* III.3.i. and the second *Enquiry,* pp. 228 and 239 of the Selby-Bigge and Nidditch edition.

Now it must be admitted that the conduct of the man in Williams's example is questionable. The man has curious moral intuitions if he thinks that, in the absence of "a sufficient randomizing event," he might be morally required to toss a coin to determine whom to aid. In the absence of reasons that weigh in favor of helping the stranger rather than his wife, the fact that she is this person whom he dearly loves is reason enough to choose her.[25] Of course, the fact that he has bizarre moral intuitions in no way implicates acting from duty, since there is no reason to think that people who act from duty necessarily or even generally have his intuitions.

Our scrutiny of Williams's and Stocker's examples discloses nothing that impugns acting from duty as such. It is true that there are instances in which someone may feel alienated or rejected if a friend puts some moral consideration above his needs or wishes, but to the extent that this is an instance where acting from duty is alienating, it hardly seems to support the claim that acting from duty is morally repugnant.

A more plausible objection concerns sanctimoniousness or, perhaps more accurately—since sanctimoniousness is sometimes thought to involve hypocrisy[26]—moral narcissism. Earlier I remarked that if someone who acts from duty is a moral narcissist, his flaw need not show that there is anything morally undesirable about acting from duty, since, in being a moral narcissist, the agent is actually failing to conduct himself as he morally ought to, i.e., failing to do his duty. I later acknowledged the objection that, if one who acts from duty is precluded from or even merely less able to fulfill certain duties, this fact does impugn acting from duty after all. Now, someone might argue that moral narcissism falls under this heading. The view seems initially plausible. It is true that someone who is committed to doing whatever she morally ought to do and to striving to determine just what she morally ought to do is, other things equal, more likely to be a moral narcissist than someone who pays no attention to the moral rectitude of his conduct. But though this is true, to conclude on that basis that acting from duty is morally undesirable would hardly be warranted. If, on the other hand, one could show that the individuals are very likely to be despicably obsessed with their own (individual) goodness and that proper moral education cannot ward off this malady, the case would be somewhat different. There appears, however, to be no reason to think this at all likely. It would seem perfectly feasible to bring children up to have, as adults, senses of duty without being excessively attentive to or smug about their moral characters.

Having addressed the objection that acting from duty is morally repugnant

---

[25] But this is not to say that no other thoughts or beliefs should influence his action. The agent does well to be alert to the possibility that there are reasons that weigh in favor of helping the stranger.

[26] Or so say *Webster's Seventh New Collegiate Dictionary* and *The American Heritage Dictionary of the English Language.*

because it involves moral narcissism, we may—barring the development of further objections along these lines—conclude that Stocker was wrong to suggest that the motive of duty drives out such morally significant motives as concern for the weal and woe of others.

IX

Someone might protest, however, that my analysis of Stocker's and Williams's examples minimizes the difficulties and misconstrues the charge. I have, my opponent might acknowledge, refuted the charge that the motive of duty *drives out* these other valuable motives; but maybe that is not what Stocker (and Williams and Wolf) meant. Their claim might be conceptual rather than empirical. They may be claiming this: one just is not acting as a friend if one acts from duty. Friendship is such that acts of friendship lose their status as acts of friendship if done from duty.[27] If *this* is the position, then the dispute is over the nature of friendship.

On the position in question, I am not a true friend to S unless I put S first, before all else. This is an exceptionally restrictive view of friendship. It entails that one cannot be friends with more than one person. This is surely an undesirable consequence, as well as counter-intuitive! There seems no reason for thinking that friendship is essentially exclusionary. It also seems to be the case that friendship is nonetheless friendship if it is not wholly conditional. Certain conditions are, to be sure, quite unreasonable; but to expect your friend to stick by you come what may, e.g., to lie for you on the witness stand or to assist you in a fraudulent business transaction, is hardly warranted. Yet it would be warranted if, by the very nature of friendship, one does not act as a friend if one's conduct vis-à-vis one's friend is governed by a sense of duty.

My criticism of the implicit definition of friendship can be made more crisply in the following manner. Susan Wolf remarks that the person who visits or otherwise aids another from duty sees that person "first as a possible object of moral concern and only second as a person whose comfort and happiness he naturally cares about increasing" (48). *Does* acting from duty mean that people are given a priority rating of 2: that morality counts for more than people? There is a sense in which the answer is "Yes, morality does come before people": what one morally ought to do imposes an ultimate constraint on one's conduct.[28] Part of what it is to act from duty is to act with a counterfactual condition always at hand (though not always in one's thoughts): one would not do this if it were morally counter-recommended.

If opponents insist that such a counterfactual condition gets in the way of friendship and love, then, I want to say, so much the worse for friendship and

---

[27] I am grateful to Holly Smith for pointing out this possible interpretation.

[28] This is not to deny that there is also a (much more obvious) sense in which the answer is 'No'.

love—thus conceived. Unless one buys into an extremely romantic notion of love and a similar notion of unconditional friendship, the conflict is bogus.

X

Some questions might arise concerning the nature of this counterfactual condition. The last section may give the impression that to act from duty is nothing more than acting with the counterfactual condition mentioned above always at hand. I want to emphasize that this is not my view, and to explain what else acting from duty involves.

First, part of one's motivation must be a commitment to doing what is right (and to seeking to determine what is right). The fact that had one believed it wrong to do X, one would not have done X—and would not have for the reason that one believed it wrong—does not suffice to show that one is acting from duty. Part of one's motivation must be a commitment to doing whatever is right.

Second, since the commitment—like all commitments—must persist over a period of time, the question of whether one acts from duty is a question about one's conduct over a stretch of time, not about discreet actions. As I use 'acts from duty', it would not make sense to say of someone that he had acted from duty on only one occasion; for one acts from duty only insofar as all of one's conduct is informed and governed by a commitment to do whatever one ought to do.

Just how is this commitment to be understood? Since my aim here is not to provide a full account of acting from duty, but rather to challenge the suggestion that acting from duty is morally repugnant, this is not the place to discuss the commitment at length. I will, however, briefly indicate how the commitment to doing whatever is right is manifested and in what sense one who acts from duty acts from this commitment. We should first observe that a "perfect record" in doing one's duty is not only not sufficient to acting from duty, but also not necessary. A certain amount of backsliding is consistent with having this commitment; one can correctly be said to act from duty even if one occasionally fails to do what one sees one should do.[29] But the commitment will have other manifestations besides conformity to one's sense of duty, most notably, reflection on how one should live, readiness to revise one's moral beliefs and one's plans and aims in light of one's reflections, willingness to entertain evidence that tells against one's moral beliefs. In addition, one who acts from duty will reflect on her conduct and not be left cold by thoughts about how she acted—nor will she feel only the retrospective emotions (e.g., regret, unlike remorse) which enable one to evade moral responsibility for the conduct in question. And, of course, the agent will sometimes evince *resolve* to act as she sees she ought to act.

---

[29] I see no way to spell out just how much backsliding is too much.

The sense in which one acts from this commitment, even in instances in which one gives no thought to the ethical nature of one's conduct before proceeding with the intended action, is roughly as follows: a very rich explanation of any nontrivial choice or action, e.g., the sort of explanation that a novelist might give, would make reference to some of the manifestations listed above.

My remarks in this section have, I hope, helped to clarify my position in two (not unrelated) respects. First, when one bears in mind the centrality of the agent's commitment to my account of acting from duty, it becomes clear why I never speak of acting from a *desire* to do one's duty: acting from duty, as I understand it, is altogether different from acting from a desire (simpliciter) to do one's duty, since the desire does not require that one's conduct be governed by a sense of duty. A desire to do one's duty is in the end a desire; a commitment to doing whatever one morally ought to do is not. A desire to do one's duty does not have the legislative powers that a sense of duty has. Second, acting from duty, as I have defended it, must be thought of not in terms of isolated actions, but as conduct viewed over a stretch of time, and governed by a commitment which unifies and directs the self.

5

The Nature of Moral Virtue

ARISTOTLE

Aristotle (384–322 B.C.) systematically explored virtually every branch of what is now thought of as philosophy. In addition, he did pioneering work in rhetoric, politics, astronomy, physics, biology, and other areas. The selection included here is from his Nicomachean Ethics.

In the first part of this selection, Aristotle discusses the way people acquire a virtuous disposition. One possible answer is that they are taught the correct principles or reasons for acting. However, Aristotle objects that merely theoretical knowledge of what is right makes us like invalids "who listen carefully to all the doctor says but do not carry out a single one of his orders." He proposes, instead, that we best learn virtue by actually practicing it. If we continually do what is right, we will eventually acquire the appropriate habits. These habits will enable us to strike the proper balance between extremes. Thus, the virtuous person is neither rash nor cowardly but brave, neither obsequious nor surly but friendly, and so on.

In the selection's second part, Aristotle addresses the difficult topic of incontinence, or weakness of will. Here the problem is whether, and how, a person who knows what he ought to do can nevertheless do something else. Aristotle rejects the straightforward Socratic view that all who act wrongly do so through ignorance. In its stead, he offers a number of subtle distinctions among types of incontinence and ways of lacking full knowledge.

FROM *NICOMACHEAN ETHICS*, BOOK TWO

Chapter I

VIRTUE, THEN, IS of two kinds, intellectual and moral. Of these the intellectual is in the main indebted to teaching for its production and growth, and this calls for time and experience. Moral goodness, on the other hand, is the child of habit, from which it has got its very name, ethics being derived from *ethos*, 'habit,' by a slight alteration in the quantity of the *e*. This is an indication that none of the moral virtues is implanted in us by nature, since nothing that nature creates can be taught by habit to change the direction of its development. For instance a stone, the natural tendency of which is to fall down, could never, however often you threw it up in the air, be trained to go in that direction. No more can you train fire to burn downwards. Nothing in fact, if the law of its being is to behave in one way, can be habituated to behave in another. The moral virtues, then, are produced in us neither *by* Nature nor *against* Nature. Nature, indeed, prepares in us the ground for their reception, but their complete formation is the product of habit.

Consider again these powers or faculties with which Nature endows us. We acquire the ability to use them before we do use them. The senses provide us with a good illustration of this truth. We have not acquired the sense of sight from repeated acts of seeing, or the sense of hearing from repeated acts of hearing. It is the other way round. We had these senses before we used them, we did not acquire them as a result of using them. But the moral virtues we do acquire by first exercising them. The same is true of the arts and crafts in general. The craftsman has to learn how to make things, but he learns in the process of making them. So men become builders by building, harp players by playing the harp. By a similar process we become just by performing just actions, temperate by performing temperate actions, brave by performing brave actions. Look at what happens in political societies—it confirms our view. We find legislators seeking to make good men of their fellows by making good behaviour habitual with them. That is the aim of every lawgiver, and when he is unable to carry it out effectively, he is a failure; nay, success or failure in this is what makes the difference between a good constitution and a bad.

Again, the creation and the destruction of any virtue are effected by identical causes and identical means; and this may be said, too, of every art. It is as a result of playing the harp that harpers become good or bad in their art. The same is true of builders and all other craftsmen. Men will become good builders as a result of building well, and bad builders as a result of building badly. Otherwise what would be the use of having anyone to teach a trade? Craftsmen would all be born either good or bad. Now this holds also of the virtues. It is in the course of our dealings with our fellow-men that we become just or unjust. It is our behaviour in a crisis and our habitual reactions to danger that make us brave or cowardly, as it may be. So with our desires and passions. Some men are made temperate and gentle, others profligate and passionate, the former by conducting themselves in one way, the latter by conducting themselves in another, in situations in which their feelings are involved. We may sum it all up in the generalization, 'Like activities produce like dispositions.' This makes it our duty to see that our activities have the right character, since the differences of quality in them are repeated in the dispositions that follow in their train. So it is a matter of real importance whether our early education confirms us in one set of habits or another. It would be nearer the truth to say that it makes a very great difference indeed, in fact all the difference in the world.

Chapter II

Since the branch of philosophy on which we are at present engaged differs from the others in not being a subject of merely intellectual interest—I mean we are not concerned to know what goodness essentially is, but how we are to become good men, for this alone gives the study its practical value—we must apply our minds to the solution of the problems of conduct. For, as I remarked, it is our actions that determine our dispositions.

Now that when we act we should do so according to the right principle, is common ground and I propose to take it as a basis of discussion.[1] But we must begin with the admission that any theory of conduct must be content with an outline without much precision in details. We noted this when I said at the beginning of our discussion of this part of our subject that the measure of exactness of statement in any field of study must be determined by the nature of the matter studied. Now matters of conduct and considerations of what is to our advantage have no fixity about them any more than matters affecting our health. And if this be true of moral philosophy as a whole, it is still more true that the discussion of particular problems in ethics admits of no exactitude. For they do not fall under any science or professional tradition, but those who are following some line of conduct are forced in every collocation of circumstances to think out for themselves what is suited to these circumstances, just as doctors and navigators have to do in their different *métiers*. We can do no more than give our arguments, inexact as they necessarily are, such support as is available.

Let us begin with the following observation. It is in the nature of moral qualities that they can be destroyed by deficiency on the one hand and excess on the other. We can see this in the instances of bodily health and strength.[2] Physical strength is destroyed by too much and also by too little exercise. Similarly health is ruined by eating and drinking either too much or too little, while it is produced, increased and preserved by taking the right quantity of drink and victuals. Well, it is the same with temperance, courage, and the other virtues. The man who shuns and fears everything and can stand up to nothing becomes a coward. The man who is afraid of nothing at all, but marches up to every danger, becomes foolhardy. In the same way the man who indulges in every pleasure without refraining from a single one becomes incontinent. If, on the other hand, a man behaves like the Boor in comedy and turns his back on every pleasure, he will find his sensibilities becoming blunted. So also temperance and courage are destroyed both by excess and deficiency, and they are kept alive by observance of the mean.

Let us go back to our statement that the virtues are produced and fostered as a result, and by the agency, of actions of the same quality as effect their destruction. It is also true that after the virtues have been formed they find expression in actions of that kind. We may see this in a concrete instance— bodily strength. It results from taking plenty of nourishment and going in for hard training, and it is the strong man who is best fitted to cope with such

---

[1] There will be an opportunity later of considering what is meant by this formula, in particular what is meant by 'the right principle' and how, in its ethical aspect, it is related to the moral virtues.

[2] If we are to illustrate the material, it must be by concrete images.

conditions. So with the virtues. It is by refraining from pleasures that we become temperate, and it is when we have become temperate that we are most able to abstain from pleasures. Or take courage. It is by habituating ourselves to make light of alarming situations and to confront them that we become brave, and it is when we have become brave that we shall be most able to face an alarming situation.

Chapter III

We may use the pleasure (or pain) that accompanies the exercise of our dispositions as an index of how far they have established themselves. A man is temperate who abstaining from bodily pleasures finds this abstinence pleasant; if he finds it irksome, he is intemperate. Again, it is the man who encounters danger gladly, or at least without painful sensations, who is brave; the man who has these sensations is a coward. In a word, moral virtue has to do with pains and pleasures. There are a number of reasons for believing this. (1) Pleasure has a way of making us do what is disgraceful; pain deters us from doing what is right and fine. Hence the importance—I quote Plato—of having been brought up to find pleasure and pain in the right things. True education is just such a training. (2) The virtues operate with actions and emotions, each of which is accompanied by pleasure or pain. This is only another way of saying that virtue has to do with pleasures and pains. (3) Pain is used as an instrument of punishment. For in her remedies Nature works by opposites, and pain can be remedial. (4) When any disposition finds its complete expression it is, as we noted, in dealing with just those things by which it is its nature to be made better or worse, and which constitute the sphere of its operations. Now when men become bad it is under the influence of pleasures and pains when they seek the wrong ones among them, or seek them at the wrong time, or in the wrong manner, or in any of the wrong forms which such offences may take; and in seeking the wrong pleasures and pains they shun the right. This has led some thinkers to identify the moral virtues with conditions of the soul in which passion is eliminated or reduced to a minimum. But this is to make too absolute a statement—it needs to be qualified by adding that such a condition must be attained 'in the right manner and at the right time' together with the other modifying circumstances.

So far, then, we have got this result. Moral goodness is a quality disposing us to act in the best way when we are dealing with pleasures and pains, while vice is one which leads us to act in the worst way when we deal with them.

The point may be brought out more clearly by some other considerations. There are three kinds of things that determine our choice in all our actions—the morally fine, the expedient, the pleasant; and three that we shun—the base, the harmful, the painful. Now in his dealings with all of these it is the good man who is most likely to go right, and the bad man who tends to go wrong, and that most notably in the matter of pleasure. The sensation of pleasure is felt by us in common with all animals, accompanying everything we choose, for even the fine and the expedient have a pleasurable effect upon us. (6) The capacity for experiencing pleasure has grown in us from infancy as part of our general development, and human life, being dyed in grain with it, receives therefrom a colour hard to scrape off. (7) Pleasure and pain are also the standards by which with greater or less strictness we regulate our considered actions. Since to feel pleasure and pain rightly or wrongly is an important factor in human behaviour, it follows that we are primarily concerned with these sensations. (8) Heraclitus says it is hard to fight against anger, but it is harder still to fight against pleasure. Yet to grapple with the harder has always been the business, as of art, so of goodness, success in a task being proportionate to its difficulty. This gives us another reason for believing that morality and statesmanship must concentrate on pleasures and pains, seeing it is the man who deals rightly with them who will be good, and the man who deals with them wrongly who will be bad.

Here, then, are our conclusions. (*a*) Virtue is concerned with pains and pleasures. (*b*) The actions which produce virtue are identical in character with those which increase it. (*c*) These actions differently performed destroy it. (*d*) The actions which produced it are identical with those in which it finds expression.

Chapter IV

A difficulty, however, may be raised as to what we mean when we say that we must perform just actions if we are to become just, and temperate actions if we are to be temperate. It may be argued that, if I do what is just and temperate, I am just and temperate already, exactly as, if I spell words or play music correctly, I must already be literate or musical. This I take to be a false analogy, even in the arts. It is possible to spell a word right by accident or because somebody tips you the answer. But you will be a scholar only if your spelling is done as a scholar does it, that is thanks to the scholarship in your own mind. Nor will the suggested analogy with the arts bear scrutiny. A work of art is good or bad in itself—let it possess a certain quality, and that is all we ask of it. But virtuous actions are not done in a virtuous—a just or temperate—way merely because *they* have the appropriate quality. The *doer* must be in a certain frame of mind when he does them. Three conditions are involved. (1) The agent must act in full consciousness of what he is doing. (2) He must 'will' his action, and will it for its own sake. (3) The act must proceed from a fixed and unchangeable disposition. Now these requirements, if we except mere knowledge, are not counted among the necessary qualifications of an artist. For the acquisition of virtue, on the other hand, knowledge is of little or no value, but the other requirements are of immense, of sovran, importance, since it is the repeated performance of just and temperate actions that produces virtue. Actions, to be sure, are *called* just and temperate when they are such as a just or temperate man would do. But the doer is just or temperate not because he does such things but when he does them in the way of just and temperate persons. It is therefore quite fair to say that a man becomes just by the performance of just, and temperate by the performance of temperate, actions; nor is there the smallest likelihood of a man's becoming good by any other course of conduct. It is not, however, a popular line to take, most men preferring theory to practice under the impression that arguing about morals proves them to be philosophers, and that in this way they will turn out to be fine characters. Herein they resemble invalids, who listen carefully to all the doctor says but do not carry out a single one of his orders. The bodies of such people will never respond to treatment—nor will the souls of such 'philosophers.'

Chapter V

We now come to the formal definition of virtue. Note first, however, that the human soul is conditioned in three ways. It may have (1) feelings, (2) capacities, (3) dispositions; so virtue must be one of these three. By 'feelings' I mean a desire, anger, fear, daring, envy, gratification, friendliness, hatred, longing, jealousy, pity and in general all states of mind that are attended by pleasure or pain. By 'capacities' I mean those faculties in virtue of which we may be described as capable of the feelings in question—anger, for instance, or pain, or pity. By 'dispositions' I mean states of mind in virtue of which we are well or ill disposed in respect of the feelings concerned. We have, for instance, a bad disposition where angry feelings are concerned if we are disposed to become excessively or insufficiently angry, and a good disposition in this respect if we consistently feel the due amount of anger, which comes between these extremes. So with the other feelings.

Now, neither the virtues nor the vices are feelings. We are not spoken of as good or bad in respect of our feelings but of our virtues and vices. Neither are we praised or blamed for the way we feel. A man is not praised for being frightened or angry, nor is he blamed just for being angry; it is for being angry in a particular way. But we *are* praised and blamed for our virtues and vices. Again, feeling angry or frightened is something we can't help, but our virtues are in a manner expressions of our will; at any rate there is an element of will in their formation. Finally, we are said to be 'moved' when our feelings are affected, but when it is a question of moral goodness or badness we are not said to be 'moved' but to be 'disposed' in a particular way. A similar line of reasoning will prove that the virtues and vices are not capacities either. We are not spoken of as good or bad, nor are we praised or blamed, merely because we are *capable* of feeling. Again, what capacities we have, we have by nature; but it is not nature that makes us good or bad. . . . So, if the virtues are neither feelings nor capacities, it remains that they must be dispositions. . . .

Chapter VI

It is not, however, enough to give this account of the *genus* of virtue—that it is a disposition; we must describe its *species*. Let us begin, then, with this proposition. Excellence of whatever kind affects that of which it is the excellence in two ways. (1) It produces a good state in it. (2) It enables it to perform its function well. Take eyesight. The goodness of your eye is not only that which makes your eye good, it is also that which makes it function well. Or take the case of a horse. The goodness of a horse makes him a good horse, but it also makes him good at running, carrying a rider and facing the enemy. Our proposition, then, seems to be true, and it enables us to say that virtue in a man will be the disposition which (a) makes him a good man, (b) enables him to perform his function well. We have already touched on this point, but more light will be thrown upon it if we consider what is the specific nature of virtue.

In anything continuous and divisible it is possible to take the half, or more than the half, or less than the half. Now these parts may be larger, smaller and equal either in relation to the thing divided or in relation to us. The equal part may be described as a mean between too much and too little. By the mean of the thing I understand a point equidistant from the extremes; and this is one and the same for everybody. Let me give an illustration. Ten, let us say, is 'many' and two is 'few' of something. We get the mean of the thing if we take six;[3] that is, six exceeds and is exceeded by an equal number. This is the rule which gives us the arithmetical mean. But such a method will not give us the mean in relation to ourselves. Let ten pounds of food be a large, and two pounds a small, allowance for an athlete. It does not follow that the trainer will prescribe six pounds. That might be a large or it might be a small allowance for the particular athlete who is to get it. It would be little for Milo but a lot for a man who has just begun his training.[4] It is the same in all walks of life. The man who knows his business avoids both too much and too little. It is the mean he seeks and adopts—not the mean of the thing but the relative mean.

Every form, then, of applied knowledge, when it performs its function well, looks to the mean and works to the standard set by that. It is because people feel this that they apply the *cliché*, 'You couldn't add anything to it or take anything from it' to an artistic masterpiece, the implication being that too much and too little alike destroy perfection, while the mean preserves it. Now if this be so, and if it be true, as we say, that good craftsmen work to the standard of the mean, then, since goodness like nature is more exact and of a higher character than any art, it follows that goodness is the quality that hits the mean. By 'goodness' I mean goodness of moral character, since it is moral goodness that deals with feelings and actions, and it is in them that we find excess, deficiency and a mean. It is possible, for example, to experience fear, boldness, desire, anger, pity, and pleasures and pains generally, too much or too little or to the right amount. If we feel them too much or too little, we are wrong. But to have these feelings at the right times on the right occasions towards the right people for the right motive and in the right way is to have them in the right measure, that is somewhere between the extremes; and this is what characterizes goodness. The same may be said of the mean and extremes in actions. Now it is in the field of actions and feelings that goodness operates; in them we find excess, deficiency and, between them, the mean, the first two

---

[3] $6 - 2 = 10 - 6$.

[4] What applies to gymnastics applies also to running and wrestling.

being wrong, the mean right and praised as such.[5] Goodness, then, is a mean condition in the sense that it aims at and hits the mean.

Consider, too, that it is possible to go wrong in more ways than one. (In Pythagorean terminology evil is a form of the Unlimited, good of the Limited.) But there is only one way of being right. That is why going wrong is easy, and going right difficult; it is easy to miss the bull's eye and difficult to hit it. Here, then, is another explanation of why the too much and the too little are connected with evil and the mean with good. As the poet says,

Goodness is one, evil is multiform.

We may now define virtue as a disposition of the soul in which, when it has to choose among actions and feelings, it observes the mean relative to us, this being determined by such a rule or principle as would take shape in the mind of a man of sense or practical wisdom. We call it a mean condition as lying between two forms of badness, one being excess and the other deficiency; and also for this reason, that, whereas badness either falls short of or exceeds the right measure in feelings and actions, virtue discovers the mean and deliberately chooses it. Thus, looked at from the point of view of its essence as embodied in its definition, virtue no doubt is a mean; judged by the standard of what is right and best, it is an extreme.

But choice of a mean is not possible in every action or every feeling. The very names of some have an immediate connotation of evil. Such are malice, shamelessness, envy among feelings, and among actions adultery, theft, murder. All these and more like them have a bad name as being evil in themselves; it is not merely the excess or deficiency of them that we censure. In their case, then, it is impossible to act rightly; whatever we do is wrong. Nor do circumstances make any difference in the rightness or wrongness of them. When a man commits adultery there is no point in asking whether it is with the right woman or at the right time or in the right way, for to do anything like that is simply wrong. It would amount to claiming that there is a mean and excess and defect in unjust or cowardly or intemperate actions. If such a thing were possible, we should find ourselves with a mean quantity of excess, a mean of deficiency, an excess of excess and a deficiency of deficiency. But just as in temperance and justice there can be no mean or excess or deficiency, because the mean in a sense *is* an extreme, so there can be no mean or excess or deficiency in those vicious actions—however done, they are wrong. Putting the matter into general language, we may say that there is no mean in the extremes, and no extreme in the mean, to be observed by anybody.

Chapter VII

But a generalization of this kind is not enough; we must show that our definition fits particular cases. When we are discussing actions particular state-

---

[5] Being right or successful and being praised are both indicative of excellence.

ments come nearer the heart of the matter, though general statements cover a wider field. The reason is that human behaviour consists in the performance of particular acts, and our theories must be brought into harmony with them.

You see here a diagram of the virtues. Let us take our particular instances from that.

In the section confined to the feelings inspired by danger you will observe that the mean state is 'courage.' Of those who go to extremes in one direction or the other the man who shows an excess of fearlessness has no name to describe him, the man who exceeds in confidence or daring is called 'rash' or 'foolhardy,' the man who shows an excess of fear and a deficiency of confidence is called a 'coward.' In the pleasures and pains—though not all pleasures and pains, especially pains—the virtue which observes the mean is 'temperance,' the excess is the vice of 'intemperance.' Persons defective in the power to enjoy pleasures are a somewhat rare class, and so have not had a name assigned to them: suppose we call them 'unimpressionable.' Coming to the giving and acquiring of money, we find that the mean is 'liberality,' the excess 'prodigality,' the deficiency 'meanness.' But here we meet a complication. The prodigal man and the mean man exceed and fall short in opposite ways. The prodigal exceeds in giving and falls short in getting money, whereas the mean man exceeds in getting and falls short in giving it away. Of course this is but a summary account of the matter—a bare outline. But it meets our immediate requirements. Later on these types of character will be more accurately delineated.

. . .

Chapter IX

I have said enough to show that moral excellence is a mean, and I have shown in what sense it is so. It is, namely, a mean between two forms of badness, one of excess and the other of defect, and is so described because it aims at hitting the mean point in feelings and in actions. This makes virtue hard of achievement, because finding the middle point is never easy. It is not everybody, for instance, who can find the centre of a circle—that calls for a geometrician. Thus, too, it is easy to fly into a passion—anybody can do that— but to be angry with the right person and to the right extent and at the right time and with the right object and in the right way—that is not easy, and it is not everyone who can do it. This is equally true of giving or spending money. Hence we infer that to do these things properly is rare, laudable and fine.

In view of this we shall find it useful when aiming at the mean to observe these rules (1) *Keep away from that extreme which is the more opposed to the mean.* It is Calypso's advice:

'Swing round the ship clear of this surf and surge.'

For one of the extremes is always a more dangerous error than the other; and—since it is hard to hit the bull's-eye—we must take the next best course and choose the least of the evils. And it will be easiest for us to do this if we follow the rule I have suggested. (2) *Note the errors into which we personally are most liable to fall.* (Each of us has his natural bias in one direction or another.) We shall find out what ours are by noting what gives us pleasure and pain. After that we must drag ourselves in the opposite direction. For our best way of reaching the middle is by giving a wide berth to our darling sin. It is the method used by a carpenter when he is straightening a warped board. (3) *Always be particularly on your guard against pleasure and pleasant things.* When Pleasure is at the bar the jury is not impartial. So it will be best for us if we feel towards her as the Trojan elders felt towards Helen, and regularly apply their words to her. If we are for packing her off, as they were with Helen, we shall be the less likely to go wrong.

To sum up. These are the rules by observation of which we have the best chance of hitting the mean. But of course difficulties spring up, especially when we are confronted with an exceptional case. For example, it is not easy to say precisely what is the right way to be angry and with whom and on what grounds and for how long. In fact we are inconsistent on this point, sometimes praising people who are deficient in the capacity for anger and calling them 'gentle,' sometimes praising the choleric and calling them 'stout fellows.' To be sure we are not hard on a man who goes off the straight path in the direction of too much or too little, if he goes off only a little way. We reserve our censure for the man who swerves widely from the course, because then we are bound to notice it. Yet it is not easy to find a formula by which we may determine how far and up to what point a man may go wrong before he incurs blame. But this difficulty of definition is inherent in every object of perception; such questions of degree are bound up with the circumstances of the individual case, where our only criterion *is* the perception.

So much, then, has become clear. In all our conduct it is the mean state that is to be praised. But one should lean sometimes in the direction of the more, sometimes in that of the less, because that is the readiest way of attaining to goodness and the mean.

FROM *NICOMACHEAN ETHICS*, BOOK SEVEN

Chapter I

. . .

I cannot, however, omit here some account of incontinence and softness of luxuriousness, as well as of continence and fortitude or endurance. We should not think of either of those dispositions—the good and the bad—as identical with virtue and vice respectively. Neither must we think of them as different in kind.

The true method for us to follow, here and elsewhere, is to set forth the views which are held on the subject and then, after discussing the problems involved in these, to indicate what truth lies in all or—if that proves impossible—in the greatest in number and importance of the beliefs generally entertained about these states of mind. I am convinced that, if the difficulties can be resolved and we are left with certain of these beliefs—those, namely, which have stood our test—we shall have reached as satisfactory a conclusion as is possible in cases of the kind. In the present case the general beliefs are these. (*a*) Continence and endurance are good and commendable qualities, whereas their opposites, incontinence and softness, are bad and blameworthy. (*b*) The continent man has the characteristic of sticking by the conclusions he has been led to draw, whereas the incontinent man tends to give his up. (*c*) The incontinent or morally weak man does wrong, knowing it to be wrong, because he cannot control his passions, whereas the continent man, knowing that his lusts are evil, refuses to follow them, because his principles forbid it. (*d*) The temperate man is always continent and enduring, though whether the continent man is always temperate is an open question, some asserting and others denying that it is so, the former distinguishing between the intemperate and the incontinent man, the latter confounding all distinction between them. (*e*) It is sometimes maintained that it is impossible for the prudent man to be incontinent, sometimes that *some* prudent and clever men are guilty of incontinence. (*f*) Some men are described as 'incontinent' in their anger and in their pursuit of honour or gain.—Such are the views that have found expression.

Chapter II

Now for the difficulties that may be raised. To take the third (*c*) of our opinions first, how can a man be said to show incontinence, if he has a correct apprehension of the fact that he is acting wrongly? Some thinkers maintain that he cannot, if he has full knowledge that the action is wrong. It is, as Socrates thought, hard to believe that, if a man really *knows*, and has this knowledge in his soul, it should be mastered by something else which, in Plato's phrase, 'hauls it about like a slave.' Socrates to be sure was out and out opposed to the view we are now criticizing, on the ground that there is no such thing as this moral weakness we call 'incontinence.' For, said he, nobody acts in opposition to what is best—and the best is the goal of all our endeavours—if he has a clear idea of what he is doing. He can only go wrong out of ignorance. This reasoning, however, is in glaring contrast with notorious facts; and that obliges us to look more closely into the frame of mind on which it is based. Conceding that ignorance is the cause of moral weakness, let us consider what form of ignorance. For it is clear that the man who succumbs to temptation is not ignorant of the wrongness of his action *before* he is involved in the temptation.

. . .

Chapter III

We have then to consider these points. (1) When men show moral weakness (or incontinence) do they or do they not know the wrongness of their actions? If they know it, in what sense do they know it? (2) What are we to posit as the objects to which continence and incontinence are directed? I mean, are they concerned with every kind of pleasures and pains or only with a special division of them? (3) Is continence the same or not the same as endurance? (4) Other questions germane to the subject.

We may begin our enquiry by asking whether it is the objects or the dispositions of the continent and incontinent man that enter into the definition of these types as their differentiating qualities. Put it this way. Is a man to be described as incontinent merely because he cannot restrain his desires for certain things, or is it because he has a certain disposition, or do both causes operate? Here is a second question. Can incontinence and continence be exercised towards everything? Yes or no? One is aware that when a man is described as "incontinent" without further qualification it is not implied that he is incontinent in everything, but only in those things in which a man can show intemperance; nor is it implied merely that he is concerned with those things,[6] but that he is concerned with them in a certain way. The intemperate man deliberately chooses to follow in the train of his lusts from a belief that he ought always to pursue the pleasure of the moment. The incontinent man pursues it too, but has no such belief.

(1) The theory that when men behave incontinently they are not acting against knowledge but against true opinion contributes nothing of value to our discussion. It never occurs to some people to question the truth of their opinions; indeed, they do not regard them as opinions but as ascertained truths. Consequently, if we base an argument on lack of conviction in some men, and say that this is the reason why those who shall be found to act against their conception of what is right must be said to have an opinion rather than knowledge, the difference between opinion and knowledge will vanish. For some men are just as sure of the truth of their opinions as are others of what they know. Heraclitus alone proves that. And if we say a man 'knows' something, we may be using the word in one of two senses. We may mean that he has the knowledge and acts upon it, or that he has the knowledge but makes no use of it. This being so, it will make a difference whether a man who is doing wrong knows that what he is doing is wrong but has this knowledge only in a latent or subconscious form, or whether, having the knowledge, he has it in an active form. If the latter, his doing wrong may well surprise us; but it will not, if his knowledge is not fully realized.

(2) When logical reasoning is applied to actions, the premises will assume two forms.[7] Now a man who is acting against knowledge may very well know both premises, yet put into practice only his knowledge of the universal or major premise and not his knowledge of the particular or minor premise. Yet it is this minor premise that is decisive for action, because acts are particulars. We have also to note that in reasoning about actions there are two universals involved. One is predicated of the *man*, the other of the *thing*. For example,

---

[6] For if that were so, incontinence would be identical with intemperance.

[7] In other words the application of a 'practical syllogism' involves two syllogisms.

he may know, and be in a position to act on the knowledge, that (*a*) dry food is good for all men,[8] and (*b*) he is himself a man. But he may not know, or may not be prepared to act on his knowledge, whether the particular food before him is that sort of food. It will be found then that there is an immeasurable distance between these two ways of knowing, so that we cannot think it odd that the incontinent man should know in one and not the other. The truly strange thing would be if he *did* know in the other.

(3) Moreover, it is possible for men to have knowledge—I use the word without prejudice—in another way besides those described. We have noted the distinction between actual and potential knowledge. But even in the second case, which is a condition of having knowledge without allowing it to operate, we can see a distinction. For there is a sense in which a man can both have and not have knowledge—he might, for instance, be asleep or out of his mind, or drunk. And what better are people when their feelings are too much for them? Doesn't everybody know that rage and lust and some other passions actually produce physiological changes, in some cases even insanity? It is evident then that, if we must say that the incontinent have knowledge, it can only be like that possessed by the persons to whom I have referred. The moral weakling may *say* he has knowledge, but that is no proof that he has it. People suffering from the disabilities I have mentioned will repeat to you the proof of some problem in geometry or a passage from Empedocles. In the same way people who have begun the study of a subject reel off a string of propositions which they do not as yet understand. For knowledge must be worked into the living texture of the mind, and this takes time. So we should think of incontinent men as like actors—mouthpieces of the sentiments of other people.

(4) It is also possible to study the cause of incontinence from the point of view of the scientist. This involves what we call the practical syllogism. In this the major premise is an opinion, while the minor premise is a statement about particulars, the objects of sense-perception. When the two premises are combined to form the syllogism, we have a result analogous to what we have in pure ratiocination. As in the latter the mind is forced to *affirm* the conclusion, so in the practical syllogism we are forced straight-way to *do* it. Suppose you have these premises: 'All sweet things ought to be tasted,' and 'That thing is sweet.'[9] When these premises are brought into relation you are bound, if nothing prevents you and you can do it, to go and taste the thing. Now there may be simultaneously present in the mind two universal judgments, one saying, 'You must not taste,' the other, 'Every sweet thing is pleasant.' When this happens, and then the minor premise, 'That thing is sweet,' presents itself,[10] while at the same time desire is present, then in spite of the fact that the first

---

[8] He may even know that such and such a food is dry.

[9] Here the minor premise is a particular instance of the class of things about which the major premise makes a general statement.

[10] Remember that it is the minor premise that introduces the possibility of action.

universal bids you avoid the thing in question, the desire leads you to it.[11] It is therefore, we conclude, to some extent an intellectual principle or opinion which influences the incontinent man to behave as he does—an opinion not in itself contradictory of the right principle but only opposed to it by an accidental conjunction of circumstances.[12] This is the reason why the lower animals are not incontinent. They are incapable of understanding a generalization; all they have is mental images and the memory of particular objects.

We may ask how the ignorance of the incontinent man is overcome and knowledge restored to him. The explanation which accounts for the so-called knowledge of the drunk or sleeping man will serve in this case also; it applies to more than continence. But on this point it is for the physiologist to instruct us.

There are then these points to be considered. (a) The last—that is the minor—premise, that which can influence action, is an opinion which is related to some object of sense-perception. (b) This opinion the incontinent man, when he abandons himself to his emotions, does not possess or possesses only in such a way as does not entitle it to be regarded as knowledge, but only enables him to quote its tenor as a drunk man quotes Empedocles. (c) The ultimate term—that is the particular proposition which forms the minor premise—is not a universal and is not regarded as an object of knowledge in the way that a universal judgment is. Since these three statements are evidently true, it does appear that our conclusions must be that which Socrates directed his questions to prove. For the knowledge which accompanies the collapse of moral resistance is not what is thought to be knowledge properly speaking. Neither is it true knowledge that is dragged about by passion, but only such as can be supplied by the senses. . . .

Chapter VII

. . .

Opposed to incontinence is continence, opposed to softness is hardness or endurance. The difference between endurance and continence is this. Endurance consists in holding out, continence in preserving mastery. They are two very different things, as different as the avoidance of defeat from victory. We are bound therefore to prefer continence. A man who fails to withstand such pains as most people can and do support is soft or luxury-loving; for luxury is a kind of softness. He is the sort of man to let his cloak trail on the ground rather than have the bother of lifting it, or to affect the languor of sickness without reflecting that an assumed distress is a real distress. It is much the same with continence and incontinence. If a man gives way to violent or exces-

---

[11] This is because only desire can set the various limbs in motion—the body corresponding to the potential major premise, and the desire to the active minor.

[12] It is the desire, not the opinion, that is the true opposite.

sive pleasure or pain, that can surprise nobody. Indeed, he may be forgiven for succumbing, if he does not do it without a struggle. One thinks of Philoctetes when he is bitten by the viper in the play of Theodectes, or of Cercyon in the *Alope* of Carcinus. Or—to take an example of resistance to pleasure—think of a man trying his best to hold in a laugh who bursts out at last into a stentorian guffaw.[13] But it does surprise us to see a man give way to pleasures and pains which most of us are capable of withstanding. It is different of course if his weakness is due to disease or some hereditary taint, such as the congenital impotence of the Scythian royal family, or the less hardy constitution of the female, as compared with the male, sex.

It is a popular notion that a love of amusement is a sign of intemperance. In reality it is a sign of softness. For amusement is a way of enjoying one's leisure by relaxation. You may say, then, that the devotee of amusement indulges too much in relaxation. But relaxation is not pleasure, and it is the man who is insatiable in his pursuit of pleasure that is intemperate.

Incontinence is found in two forms, which we may call (*a*) impulsiveness and (*b*) weakness. The weak do form a resolution, but they are prevented by their sensibilities from keeping to it. The impulsive or headstrong are carried away by their feelings, because they have not thought about the matter that excites them at all. If they had, their behaviour might be different. For some people can hold out against strong emotion, whether painful or pleasurable, if they feel or see it coming and have time to rouse themselves—by which I mean their reasoning faculty—beforehand, just as a man can't tickle you if you have tickled him first. It is high-strung and excitable people who are most prone to the impulsive form of incontinence. The high-strung are too hasty, and the excitable too vehement, to wait for reason, since they instinctively follow the suggestions of their own imaginations.

Chapter VIII

It is different with the intemperate man, who, as I said, does not repent or feel remorse, since he abides by his choice. The incontinent man on the other hand is always capable of remorse. Consequently the objection we mentioned—that the intemperate man might be cured—is refuted by the fact. It is just the intemperate man who is incurable; the incontinent man is not. Vice such as is shown by the intemperate man is like dropsy or tuberculosis, whereas incontinence is like epilepsy. For vice is a chronic, incontinence an intermittent, ill. More than that, vice and incontinence are totally different in kind. The vicious man does not realize that he is vicious, but the incontinent man is aware of his incontinence.

With regard to the incontinent themselves, the impulsive among them are morally superior to the weak, who are in possession of the right principle but do not hold fast to it. These are worse, because they yield to a feebler impulse

---

[13] This actually happened to Xenophantus.

and after deliberation. Such men resemble dipsomaniacs, who get drunk quickly and on a small amount of wine or less than most people. It is obvious in fact that incontinence is not a vice, at least in the strict sense of that word. For vice is deliberate, and incontinence is not. Yet there is a similarity in the actions which result from them. Something of the kind is noted in the epigram of Demodocus upon the citizens of Miletus.

> Milesians are no fools, you'd swear,
> And yet they act as if they were.

To parody Demodocus: The incontinent are not bad, but they act badly.

To resume. While pursuing bodily pleasures of an excessive kind and contrary to right principle, the incontinent man is so constituted that he pursues them without the conviction that he is right, whereas the intemperate man has this conviction, which he has come to feel because it is now second nature with him to seek these gratifications. Hence the incontinent man can readily be persuaded to change his mode of behaviour—but not the other. For virtue preserves, while vice destroys, that intuitive perception of the true end of life which is the starting point in conduct. We may compare the propositions which the geometer sets out to prove and which are *his* starting-point. In moral as in mathematical science the knowledge of its first principles is not reached by a process of reasoning. The good man has it in virtue of his goodness, whether innate or acquired by the habit of thinking rightly about the first principle. Such a man is temperate, while the man who does not know the primary assumptions of all ethics is intemperate. But there is another type—the man who is driven from his considered course of action by a flood of emotion contrary to right principle. He is prevented by overmastering passion from acting in accordance with that principle, yet not so completely as to make him the kind of man to believe that it is right to abandon himself to such pleasures as he seeks. Such is the incontinent man. He is morally superior to the intemperate man and is not to be called bad without qualification, for he preserves his noblest element—that conviction on which all morality is founded. Different and at the opposite pole from him is the man who having made his choice holds fast by that, unshaken by the storms of passion. These considerations prove that continence is a good, and incontinence a bad, quality.

6

Indoctrination Versus Relativity in Value Education

LAWRENCE KOHLBERG

Lawrence Kohlberg (b. 1927) is Professor of Educational and Social Psychology at Harvard University. He has done pioneering research in the psychology of moral development. His publications include The Philosophy of Moral Development, *a collection of papers from which this selection is taken.*

In this selection, Kohlberg summarizes his theory of moral development. On that theory, people pass through three levels of moral thought as they mature. At the first or preconventional level, they base their moral judgments on what benefits them. At the conventional level, people appeal to the norms of their family, group, or nation. And at the postconventional level, they appeal to independent moral standards. Each level has two distinct substages, and each advance brings an increase in ability to make relevant distinctions, to order values hierarchically, and to generalize one's views. Nobody occupies any stage without passing through all lower stages.

According to Kohlberg, this theory has important implications for moral education. In the eyes of many, such education poses a dilemma. If teachers do impart moral standards, then they indoctrinate students; if they don't they imply that "anything goes." But Kohlberg argues that on his theory the dilemma does not arise. Since moral development always follows a single path, educators who stimulate children to move along that path neither indoctrinate nor embrace relativism.

THE FIRST POINT I want to make is that the problem raised by my title, "Indoctrination Versus Relativity in Value Education," requires coming to grips with morality and moral education. I hope I will be able to make moral education a somewhat less forbidding term by presenting my own approach to it. My basic task, however, is not to convince you of my approach to moral education but to convince you that the only way to solve the problems of relativity and indoctrination in value education is to formulate a notion of *moral development* that is justified philosophically and psychologically.

Although *moral education* has a forbidding sound to teachers, they constantly practice it. They tell children what to do, make evaluations of children's behavior, and direct children's relations in the classrooms. Sometimes teachers do these things without being aware that they are engaging in moral education, but the children are aware of it. For example, my second-grade son told me that he did not want to be one of the bad boys. Asked "Who were the bad boys?" he replied, "The ones who don't put their books back where they belong and get yelled at." His teacher would have been surprised to know that her concerns with classroom management defined for her children what she and her school thought were basic moral values or that she was engaged in value indoctrination.

Most teachers are aware that they are teaching values, like it or not, and are very concerned as to whether this teaching is unjustified indoctrination. In particular, they are uncertain as to whether their own moral opinions should be presented as "moral truths," whether they should be expressed merely as personal opinion or should be omitted from classroom discussion entirely. As an example, an experienced junior high school teacher told us,

> My class deals with morality and right and wrong quite a bit. I don't expect all of them to agree with me; each has to satisfy himself according to his own convictions, as long as he is sincere and thinks he is pursuing what is right. I often discuss cheating this way but I always get *defeated*, because they still argue cheating is all right. After you accept the idea that kids have the right to build a position with logical arguments, you have to accept what they come out with, even though you drive at it ten times a year and they still come out with the same conclusion.

This teacher's confusion is apparent. She believes everyone should "have his own ideas," and yet she is most unhappy if this leads to a point where some of these ideas include the notion that "it's all right to cheat." In other words, she is smack up against the problem of relativity of values in moral education. Using this teacher as an example, I will attempt to demonstrate that moral education can be free from the charge of cultural relativity and arbitrary indoctrination that inhibits her when she talks about cheating.

Cop-Out Solutions to the Relativity Problem

To begin with, I want to reject a few cop-outs or false solutions sometimes suggested as solving the relativity problem. One is to call moral education *socialization*. Sociologists have sometimes claimed that moralization in the interests of classroom management and maintenance of the school as a social system is a hidden curriculum; that it performs hidden services in helping children adapt to society (Jackson, 1968). They have argued that, since praise and blame on the part of teachers is a necessary aspect of the socialization process, the teacher does not have to consider the psychological and philosophic issues of moral education. In learning to conform to the teacher's expectations and the school rules, children are becoming socialized, they are internalizing the norms and standards of society. I argue in Chapter 2 why this approach is a cop-out. In practice, it means that we call the teacher's yelling at her students for not putting their books away *socialization*. To label it *socialization* does not legitimate it as valid education, nor does it remove the charge of arbitrary indoctrination from it. Basically, this sociological argument implies that respect for social authority is a moral good in itself. Stated in different terms, the notion that it is valid for the teacher to have an unreflective hidden curriculum is based on the notion that the teacher is the agent of the state, the church, or the social system, rather than being a free moral agent dealing with children who are free moral agents. The notion that the teacher is the agent of the state is taken for granted in some educational systems, such as that of the Soviets. However, the moral curriculum is not hidden in Soviet education; it is done explicitly and well as straight indoctrination (Bronfenbrenner, 1968). For the moment, I will not argue what is wrong with indoctrination but will assume that it is incompatible with the conceptions of civil liberties that are central not only to American democracy but to any just social system.

Let us turn now to the second cop-out. This is to rely on vaguely positive and honorific-sounding terms such as "moral values" or "moral and spiritual values." We can see in the following statements how a program called "Teaching Children Values in the Upper Elementary School" (Carr and Wellenberg, 1966) relies on a vague usage of "moral and spiritual values":

> Many of our national leaders have expressed anxiety about an increasing lack of concern for personal moral and spiritual values. Throughout history, nations have sought value systems to help people live congenially. The Golden Rule and the Ten Commandments are examples of such value systems. Each pupil needs to acquire a foundation of sound values to help him act correctly and make proper choices between right and wrong, truth and untruth. The teacher can develop a sound value system in the following ways:
>
> 1. Be a good example.
> 2. Help young people to assess conflict situations and to gain insight into the development of constructive values and attitudes. Situations arise daily in which pupils can receive praise that will reinforce behavior that exemplified desired values.
> 3. Show young people how to make generalizations concerning experience through evaluation and expression of desirable values.
> 4. Help students acquire an understanding of the importance of values that society considers worthwhile.
> 5. Aid children to uphold and use positive values when confronted by adverse pressure from peers. [p. 11]

The problem, however, is to define these "positive values." We may agree that "positive values" are desirable, but the term conceals the fact that teachers, children, and societies have different ideas as to what constitutes "positive values." Although Carr and Wellenberg cite the Ten Commandments and the Golden Rule as "value systems sought by nations," they also could have used the code of the Hitler or of the communist youth as examples of "value systems sought by nations."

I raise the issue of the "relativity of values" in this context because the words *moral, positive,* and *values* are interpreted by each teacher in a different way, depending on the teacher's own values and standards.

This becomes clear when we consider our third cop-out. This is the cop-out of defining moral values in terms of what I call a "bag of virtues." By a "bag of virtues," I mean a set of personality traits generally considered to be positive. Defining the aims of moral education in terms of a set of "virtues" is as old as Aristotle, who said, "Virtue . . . [is] of two kinds, intellectual and moral. . . . [The moral] virtues we get by first exercising them . . . we become just by doing just acts, temperate by doing temperate acts, brave by doing brave acts."

The attraction of such an approach is evident. Although it is true that people often cannot agree on details of right and wrong or even on fundamental moral principles, we all think such "traits" as honesty and responsibility are good things. By adding enough traits to the virtue bag, we eventually get a list that contains something to suit everyone.

This approach to moral education was widely prevalent in the public schools in the 1920s and 1930s and was called "character education." The educators and psychologists, such as Havighurst and Taba (1949), who developed these approaches defined character as the sum total of a set of "those traits of personality which are subject to the moral sanctions of society."

One difficulty with this approach to moral character is that everyone has his own bag. However, the problem runs deeper than the composition of a given list of virtues and vices. Although it may be true that the notion of teaching virtues, such as honesty or integrity, arouses little controversy, it is also true that a vague consensus on the goodness of these virtues conceals a great deal of actual disagreement over their definitions. What is one person's "integrity" is another person's "stubbornness," what is one person's honesty in "expressing your true feelings" is another person's insensitivity to the feelings of others. This is evident in controversial fields of adult behavior. Student protestors view their behavior as reflecting the virtues of altruism, idealism, awareness, and courage. Those in opposition regard the same behavior as reflecting the vices of irresponsibility and disrespect for "law and order." Although this difficulty can be recognized clearly in college education, it is easier for teachers of younger children to think that their judgments in terms of the bag of virtues are objective and independent of their own value biases. However, a parent will not agree that a child's specific failure to obey an "unreasonable" request by the teacher was wrong, even if the teacher calls the act "uncooperative," as some teachers are prone to do.

I have summarized three cop-outs from the relativity problem and rejected them. Socialization, teaching positive values, and developing a bag of virtues all leave the teacher where she was—stuck with her own personal value standards and biases to be imposed on her students. There is one last cop-out to the relativity problem. That is to lie back and enjoy it or encourage it. In the new social studies, this is called *value clarification*.

As summarized by Engel (in Simon, 1971, p. 902), this position holds that

> In the consideration of values, there is no single correct answer, but value clari-
> fication is supremely important. One must contrast value clarification and value
> inculcation. Inculcation suggests that the learner has limited control and hence

limited responsibility in the development of his own values. He needs to be told what values are or what he should value.

This is not to suggest, however, that nothing is ever inculcated. As a matter of fact, in order to clarify values, at least one principle needs to be adopted by all concerned. Perhaps the only way the principle can be adopted is through some procedure which might best be termed *inculcation*. That principle might be stated as follows: in the consideration of values there is no single correct answer. More specifically it might be said that the adequate posture both for students and teachers in clarifying values is openness.

Although the basic premise of this value clarification approach is that "everyone has his own values," it is further advocated that children can and should learn (1) to be more aware of their own values and how they relate to their decisions, (2) to make their values consistent and to order them in hierarchies for decisions, (3) to be more aware of the divergencies between their value hierarchies and those of others, and (4) to learn to tolerate these divergencies. In other words, although values are regarded as arbitrary and relative, there may be universal, rational strategies for making decisions that maximize these values. Part of this rational strategy is to recognize that values are relative. Within this set of premises, it is quite logical to teach that values are relative as part of the overall program.

An elaboration of this approach can be found in *Decision Making: A Guide for Teachers Who Would Help Preadolescent Children Become Imaginative and Responsible Decision Makers* (Dodder and Dodder, 1968). In a portion of this book, modern social scientific perspectives are used to develop a curriculum unit entitled "Why Don't We All Make the Same Decisions?" A set of classroom materials and activities are then presented to demonstrate to children the following propositions: (1) we don't all make the same decisions because our values are different; (2) our values tend to originate outside ourselves; (3) our values are different because each of us has been influenced by different important others; and (4) our values are different because each of us has been influenced by a different cultural environment.

The teacher is told to have the children discuss moral dilemmas in such a way as to reveal those different values. As an example, one child might make a moral decision in terms of avoiding punishment, another in terms of the welfare of other people, another in terms of certain rules, another in terms of getting the most for himself. The children are then to be encouraged to discuss their values with each other and to recognize that everyone has different values. Whether or not "the welfare of others" is a more adequate value than "avoiding punishment" is not an issue to be raised by the teacher. Rather, the teacher is instructed to teach only that "our values are different."

Indeed, acceptance of the idea that *all* values are relative does, logically, lead to the conclusion that the teacher should not attempt to teach *any* particular moral values. This leaves the teacher in the quandary of our teacher who could not successfully argue against cheating. The students of a teacher who has been successful in communicating moral relativism will believe, like the teacher, that "everyone has his own bag" and that "everyone should keep doing his thing." If one of these students has learned his relativity lesson, when he is caught cheating he will argue that he did nothing wrong. The basis of his argument will be that his own hierarchy of values, which may be different from that of the teacher, made it right for him to cheat. Although recognizing that other people believe that cheating is wrong, he himself holds the "value" that one should cheat when the opportunity presents itself. If teachers want to be consistent and retain their relativistic beliefs, they would have to concede.

Now I am not criticizing the value clarification approach itself. It is a basic and valuable component of the new social studies curricula, as I have discussed (1973). My point is, rather, that value clarification is not a sufficient solution to the relativity problem. Furthermore, the actual teaching of relativism is itself an indoctrination or teaching of a fixed belief, a belief that we are going to show is not true scientifically or philosophically. . . .

A Typological Scheme on the Stages of Moral Thought

In other words, I am happy to report that I can propose a solution to the relativity problem that has plagued philosophers for three thousand years. I can say this with due modesty because it did not depend on being smart. It only happened that my colleagues and I were the first people in history to do detailed cross-cultural studies on the development of moral thinking.

The following dilemma should clarify the issue:

The Heinz Dilemma

> In Europe, a woman was near death from a very bad disease, a special kind of cancer. There was one drug that the doctors thought might save her. It was a form of radium that a druggist in the same town had recently discovered. The drug was expensive to make, but the druggist was charging ten times what the drug cost him to make. He paid $200 for the radium and charged $2,000 for a small dose of the drug. The sick woman's husband, Heinz, went to everyone he knew to borrow the money, but he could get together only about $1,000, which was half of what it cost. He told the druggist that his wife was dying and asked him to sell it cheaper or let him pay later. But the druggist said, "No, I discovered the drug and I'm going to make money from it." Heinz got desperate and broke into the man's store to steal the drug for his wife.

Should the husband have done that? Was it right or wrong? Is your decision that it is right (or wrong) objectively right, is it morally universal, or is it your personal opinion? If you think it is morally right to steal the drug, you must face the fact that it is legally wrong. What is the basis of your view that it is morally right, then, more than your personal opinion? Is it anything that can be agreed on? If you think so, let me report the results of a National Opinion Research Survey on the question, asked of a representative sample of adult Americans. Seventy-five percent said it was wrong to steal, though most said they might do it.

Can one take anything but a relativist position on the question? By a relativist position, I mean a position like that of Bob, a high school senior. He said, "There's a million ways to look at it. Heinz had a moral decision to make. Was it worse to steal or let his wife die? In my mind, I can either condemn him or condone him. In this case, I think it was fine. But possibly the druggist was working on a capitalist morality of supply and demand."

I went on to ask Bob, "Would it be wrong if he didn't steal it?"

Bob replied, "It depends on how he is oriented morally. If he thinks it's worse to steal than to let his wife die, then it would be wrong what he did. It's all relative; what I would do is steal the drug. I can't say that's right or wrong or that it's what everyone should do."

But even if you agree with Bob's relativism you may not want to go as far as he did. He started the interview by wondering if he could answer because he "questioned the whole terminology, the whole moral bag." He continued, "But then I'm also an incredible moralist, a real puritan in some sense and moods. My moral judgment and the way I perceive things morally changes very much when my mood changes. When I'm in a cynical mood, I take a cynical view of morals, but still, whether I like it or not, I'm terribly moral in the way I look at things. But I'm not too comfortable with it." Bob's moral perspective was well expressed in the late Joe Gould's poem called "My Religion." Brief and to the point, the poem said, "In winter I'm a Buddhist, in the summer I'm a nudist."

Now, Bob's relativism rests on a confusion. The confusion is that between relativity as the social science fact that different people *do* have different moral values and relativity as the philosophic claim that people *ought* to have different moral values, that no moral values are justified for all people.

To illustrate, I quote a not atypical response of one of my graduate students to the same moral dilemma. She said, "I think he should steal it because if there is any such thing as a universal human value, it is the value of life, and that would justify it."

I then asked her, "Is there any such thing as a universal human value?" and she answered, "No, all values are relative to your culture."

She began by claiming that one ought to act in terms of the universal value of human life, implying that human life is a universal value in the sense that it is logical and desirable for all people to respect all human life, that one can demonstrate to other people that it is logical and desirable to act in this way. If she were clear in her thinking, she would see that the fact that all people do not always act in terms of this value does not contradict the claim that all people ought to always act in accordance with it. Because she made this confusion, she ended in total confusion.

What I am going to claim is that if we distinguish the issues of universality as fact and the possibility of universal moral ideals we get a positive answer to both questions. As far as facts go, I claim just the opposite of what Dodder and Dodder (1968) claimed to be basic social science truths. I claim that

1. We often make different decisions and yet have the same basic moral values.

2. Our values tend to originate inside ourselves as we process our social experience.
3. In every culture and subculture of the world, both the same basic moral values and the same steps toward moral maturity are found. Although social environments directly produce different specific beliefs (for example, smoking is wrong, eating pork is wrong), they do not engender different basic moral principles (for example, "consider the welfare of others," "treat other people equally," and so on).
4. Basic values are different largely because we are at different levels of maturity in thinking about basic moral and social issues and concepts. Exposure to others more mature than ourselves helps stimulate maturity in our own value process.

All parents know that the basic values of their children do not come from the outside, from the parents, although many wish they did. For example, at the age of four my son joined the pacifist and vegetarian movement and refused to eat meat because, he said, it is bad to kill animals. In spite of his parents' attempts to dissuade him by arguing about the difference between justified and unjustified killing, he remained a vegetarian for six months. However, he did recognize that some forms of killing were "legitimate." One night I read to him from a book about Eskimo life that included a description of a seal-killing expedition. While listening to the story, he became very angry and said, "You know, there is one kind of meat I would eat, Eskimo meat. It's bad to kill animals so it's all right to eat Eskimos."

This episode illustrates (1) that children often generate their own moral values and maintain them in the face of cultural training, and (2) that these values have universal roots. Every child believes it is bad to kill because regard for the lives of others or pain at death is a natural empathic response, although it is not necessarily universally and consistently maintained. In this example, the value of life led both to vegetarianism and to the desire to kill Eskimos. This latter desire comes also from a universal value tendency: a belief in justice or reciprocity here expressed in terms of revenge or punishment (at higher levels, the belief that those who infringe on the rights of others cannot expect their own rights to be respected).

I quoted my son's response because it is shockingly different from the way you think and yet it has universal elements you will recognize. What is the shocking difference between my son's way of thinking and your own? If you are a psychoanalyst, you will start thinking about oral cannibalistic fantasies and defenses against them and all that. However, that is not really what the difference is at all. You do not have to be cannibalistic to wonder why it is right for humans to kill and eat animals but it is not right for animals or humans to kill and eat humans. The response really shows that my son was a philosopher, like every young child: he wondered about things that most grown-ups take for granted. If you want to study children, however, you have to be a bit of a philosopher yourself and ask the moral philosopher's question: "Why is it all right to kill and eat animals but not humans?" I wonder how many of you can give a good answer. In any case, Piaget started the modern study of child development by recognizing that the child, like the adult philosopher, was puzzled by the basic questions of life: by the meaning of space, time, causality, life, death, right and wrong, and so on. What he found was that the child asked all the great philosophic questions but answered them in a very different way from the adults. This way was so different that Piaget called the difference a difference in stage or quality of thinking, rather than a difference in amount of knowledge or accuracy of thinking. The difference in thinking between you and my son, then, is basically a difference in stage.

My own work on morality started from Piaget's notions of stages and Piaget's notion that the child was a philosopher. Inspired by Jean Piaget's (1948) pioneering effort to apply a structural approach to moral development, I have gradually elaborated over the years a typological scheme describing general stages of moral thought that can be defined independently of the specific content of particular moral decisions or actions. We studied seventy-five American boys from early adolescence on. These youths were continually presented with hypothetical moral dilemmas, all deliberately philosophical, some found in medieval works of casuistry. On the basis of their reasoning about these dilemmas at a given age, we constructed the typology of definite and universal levels of development in moral thought.

The typology contains three distinct levels of moral thinking, and within each of these levels are two related stages. These levels and stages may be considered separate moral philosophies, distinct views of the social-moral world.

We can speak of the children as having their own morality or series of moralities. Adults seldom listen to children's moralizing. If children throw back a few adult clichés and behave themselves, most parents—and many anthropologists and psychologists as well—think that the children have adopted or internalized the appropriate parental standards.

Actually, as soon as we talk with children about morality we find that they have many ways of making judgments that are not "internalized" from the outside and that do not come in any direct and obvious way from parents, teachers, or even peers.

The preconventional level is the first of three levels of moral thinking; the second level is conventional; and the third is postconventional or autonomous. Although preconventional children are often "well behaved" and responsive to cultural labels of good and bad, they interpret these labels in terms of their physical consequences (punishment, reward, exchange of favors) or in terms of the physical power of those who enunciate the rules and labels of good and bad.

This level is usually occupied by children aged four to ten, a fact well known to sensitive observers of children. The capacity of "properly behaved" children of this age to engage in cruel behavior when there are holes in the power structure is sometimes noted as tragic (*Lord of the Flies* and *High Wind in Jamaica*), sometimes as comic (Lucy in *Peanuts*).

The second or conventional level also can be described as *conformist*—but that is perhaps too smug a term. Maintaining the expectations and rules of the individual's family, group, or nation is perceived as valuable in its own right. There is a concern not only with conforming to the individual's social order but in maintaining, supporting, and justifying this order.

The postconventional level is characterized by a major thrust toward autonomous moral principles that have validity and application apart from authority of the groups or people who hold them and apart from the individual's identification with those people or groups.

Within each of these three levels, there are two discernible stages. The following paragraphs explain the dual moral stages of each level just described.

Definition of Moral Stages

Preconventional Level

At this level, the child is responsive to cultural rules and labels of good and bad, right or wrong, but interprets these labels in terms of either the physical or the hedonistic consequences of action (punishment, reward, exchange of favors) or in terms of the physical power of those who enunciate the rules and labels. The level is divided into the following two stages:

Stage 1.   The Punishment and Obedience Orientation

The physical consequences of action determine its goodness or badness regardless of the human meaning or value of these consequences. Avoidance of punishment and unquestioning deference to power are valued in their own right.

Stage 2.   The Instrumental Relativist Orientation

Right action consists of that which instrumentally satisfies one's needs and occasionally the needs of others. Human relations are viewed in terms like those of the marketplace. Elements of fairness, reciprocity, and equal sharing are present, but they are always interpreted in a physical, pragmatic way. Reciprocity is a matter of "You scratch my back and I'll scratch yours."

Conventional Level

At this level, maintaining the expectations of the individual's family, group, or nation is perceived as valuable in its own right, regardless of immediate and obvious consequences. The attitude is not only one of conformity to personal expectations and social order, but of loyalty to it, of actively maintaining, supporting, and justifying the order and of identifying with the people or group involved in it. At this level, there are the following two stages:

Stage 3.   The Interpersonal Concordance or "Good Boy–Nice Girl" Orientation

Good behavior is that which pleases or helps others and is approved by them. There is much conformity to stereotypical images of what is majority or "natural" behavior. Behavior is frequently judged by intention—the judgment "he means well" becomes important for the first time. One earns approval by being "nice."

Stage 4. Society Maintaining Orientation

There is an orientation toward authority, fixed rules, and the maintenance of the social order. Right behavior consists of doing one's duty, showing respect for authority, and maintaining the given social order for its own sake.

Postconventional, Autonomous, or Principled Level

At this level, there is a clear effort to define moral values and principles that have validity and application apart from the authority of the groups or people holding these principles and apart from the individual's own identification with these groups. This level again has two stages:

Stage 5. The Social Contract Orientation

Right action tends to be defined in terms of general individual rights and in terms of standards that have been critically examined and agreed on by the whole society. There is a clear awareness of the relativism of personal values and opinions and a corresponding emphasis on procedural rules for reaching consensus. Aside from what is constitutionally and democratically agreed on, the right is a matter of personal "values" and "opinion." The result is an emphasis on the "legal point of view," but with an emphasis on the possibility of changing law in terms of rational considerations of social utility (rather than freezing it in terms of Stage 4 "law and order"). Outside the legal realm, free agreement and contract are the binding elements of obligation. This is the "official" morality of the American government and Constitution.

Stage 6. The Universal Ethical Principle Orientation

Right is defined by the decision of conscience in accord with self-chosen ethical principles appealing to logical comprehensiveness, universality, and consistency. These principles are abstract and ethical (the Golden Rule, the categorical imperative); they are not concrete moral rules such as the Ten Commandments. At heart, these are universal principles of justice, of the reciprocity and equality of human rights, and of respect for the dignity of human beings as individuals.

To understand what these stages mean concretely, let us look at them with regard to two of twenty-five basic moral concepts or aspects used to form the dilemmas we used in our research. One such aspect, for instance, is "motive given for rule obedience or moral action." In this instance, the six stages look like this:

1. Obey rules to avoid punishment.
2. Conform to obtain rewards, have favors returned, and so on.
3. Conform to avoid disapproval and dislike by others.

4. Conform to avoid censure by legitimate authorities and resultant guilt.
5. Conform to maintain the respect of the impartial spectator judging in terms of community welfare.
6. Conform to avoid self-condemnation.

In another of these twenty-five moral aspects, the value of human life, the six stages can be defined thus:

1. The value of human life is confused with the value of physical objects and is based on the social status or physical attributes of the possessor.
2. The value of human life is seen as instrumental to the satisfaction of the needs of its possessor or of other people.
3. The value of human life is based on the empathy and affection of family members and others toward its possessor.
4. Life is conceived as sacred in terms of its place in a categorical moral or religious order of rights and duties.
5. Life is valued both in terms of its relation to community welfare and in terms of life being a universal human right.
6. Human life is sacred—a universal human value of respect for the individual.

I have called this scheme a *typology*. This is because about 67 percent of most people's thinking is at a single stage, regardless of the moral dilemma involved. We call our types *stages* because they seem to represent an invariant development sequence. "True" stages come one at a time and always in the same order.

In our stages, all movement is forward in sequence and does not skip steps. Children may move through these stages at varying speeds, of course, and may be found half in and half out of a particular stage. Individuals may stop at any given stage and at any age, but if they continue to move, they must move in accord with these steps. Moral reasoning of the conventional kind or Stages 3–4, never occurs before the preconventional Stage 1 and Stage 2 thought has taken place. No adult in Stage 4 has gone through Stage 5, but all Stage 5 adults have gone through Stage 4.

Although the evidence is not complete, my study strongly suggests that moral change fits the stage pattern just described.

As a single example of our findings of stage sequence, take the progress of two boys on the aspect "the value of human life." The first boy, Tommy, who had suggested that one should perhaps steal for an important person, is asked, "Is it better to save the life of one important person or a lot of unimportant people?" At age ten, he answers, "All the people that aren't important because one man just has one house, maybe a lot of furniture, but a whole bunch of people have an awful lot of furniture, and some of these poor people might have a lot of money and it doesn't look it."

Clearly Tommy is Stage 1: he confuses the value of a human being with the value of the property he possesses. Three years later (age thirteen), Tommy's conceptions of life's values are most clearly elicited by the question "Should the doctor 'mercy kill' a fatally ill woman requesting death because of her pain?" He answers, "Maybe it would be good to put her out of pain, she'd be better off that way. But the husband wouldn't want it, it's not like an animal. If a pet dies you can get along without it—it isn't something you really need. Well, you can get a new wife, but it's not really the same."

Here his answer is Stage 2: the value of the woman's life is partly contingent on its instrumental value to her husband, who cannot replace her as easily as he can a pet.

Three years later still (age sixteen), Tommy's conception of life's value is elicited by the same question, to which he replies, "It might be best for her, but her husband—it's human life—not like an animal; it just doesn't have the same relationship that a human being does to a family. You can become attached to a dog, but nothing like a human, you know."

Now Tommy has moved from a Stage 2 instrumental view of the woman's value to a Stage 3 view based on the husband's distinctively human empathy and love for someone in his family. Equally clearly, it lacks any basis for a universal human value of the woman's life, which would hold if she had no husband or if her husband did not love her. Tommy, then, has moved step by step through three stages during the age ten to sixteen. Although bright (IQ 120), he is a slow developer in moral judgment.

Let us take another boy, Richard, to show us sequential movement through the remaining three steps. At age thirteen, Richard said about the mercy killing, "If she requests it, it's really up to her. She is in such terrible pain, just the same as people are always putting animals out of their pain," and in general showed a mixture of Stage 2 and Stage 3 responses concerning the value of life. At sixteen, he said, "I don't know. In one way, it's murder, it's not right or privilege of man to decide who shall live and who should die. God put life into everybody on earth and you're taking away something from that person that came directly from God, and you're destroying something that is very sacred, it's in a way part of God and it's almost destroying a part of God when you kill a person. There's something of God in everyone."

Here Richard clearly displays a Stage 4 concept of life as sacred in terms of its place in a categorical moral or religious order. The value of human life is universal; it is true for all humans. It still, however, depends on something else—on respect for God and God's authority; it is not an autonomous human value. Presumably if God told Richard to murder, as God commanded Abraham to murder Isaac, he would do so.

At age twenty, Richard said to the same question, "There are more and more people in the medical profession who think it is a hardship on everyone, the person, the family, when you know they are going to die. When a person is kept alive by an artificial lung or kidney, it's more like being a vegetable than being a human. If it's her own choice, I think there are certain rights and privileges that go along with being a human being. I am a human being, and I have certain desires for life, and I think everybody else does too. You have a world of which you are the center, and everybody else does too, and in that sense we're all equal."

Richard's response is clearly Stage 5, in that the value of life is defined in terms of equal and universal human rights in a context of relativity ("You have a world of which you are the center, and in that sense we're all equal") and of concern for utility or welfare consequences.

At twenty-four, Richard says, "A human life, whoever it is, takes precedence over any other moral or legal value. A human life has inherent value whether or not it is valued by a particular individual. The worth of the individual human being is central where the principles of justice and love are normative for all human relationships."

This young man is at Stage 6 in seeing the value of human life as absolute in representing a universal and equal respect for the human as an individual. He has moved step by step through a sequence culminating in a definition of human life as centrally valuable rather than derived from or dependent on social or divine authority.

In a genuine and culturally universal sense, these steps lead toward an increased morality of value judgment, where morality is considered as a form of judging, as it has been in a philosophic tradition running from the analyses of Kant to those of the modern analytic or "ordinary language" philosophers. At Stage 6 people have disentangled judgments of—or language about—human life from status and property values (Stage 1); from its uses to others (Stage 2); from interpersonal affection (Stage 3); and so on; they have a means of moral judgment that is universal and impersonal. Stage 6 people answer in moral words such as *duty* or *morally right* and use them in a way implying universality, ideals and impersonality. They think and speak in phrases such as "regardless of who it was" or "I would do it in spite of punishment."

Universal Invariant Sequence of Moral Development

When I first decided to explore moral development in other cultures, I was told by anthropologist friends that I would have to throw away my culture-bound moral concepts and stories and start from scratch learning a whole new set of values for each new culture. My first try consisted of a brace of villages, one Atayal (Malaysian aboriginal) and the other Taiwanese.

My guide was a young Chinese ethnographer who had written an account of the moral and religious patterns of the Atayal and Taiwanese villages. Taiwanese boys in the ten to thirteen age group were asked about a story involving theft of food: A man's wife is starving to death but the store owner would not give the man any food unless he could pay, and he cannot. Should he break in and steal some food? Why? Many of the boys said, "He should steal the food for his wife because if she dies he'll have to pay for her funeral, and that costs a lot."

My guide was amused by these responses, but I was relieved: they were, of course, "classic" Stage 2 responses. In the Atayal village, funerals were not such a big thing, so the Stage 2 boys said, "He should steal the food because he needs his wife to cook for him."

This means that we have to consult our anthropologists to know what content Stage 2 children will include in instrumental exchange calculations, or what Stage 4 adults will identify as the proper social order. But one certainly does not have to start from scratch. What made my guide laugh was the difference in form between the children's Stage 2 thought and his own, a difference definable independently of particular cultures.

Figures 1.1 and 1.2 indicate the cultural universality of the sequence of stages we have found. Figure 1.1 presents the age trends for middle-class urban boys in the United States, Taiwan, and Mexico. At age ten in each country, the order of use of each stage is the same as the order of its difficulty or maturity.

In the United States, by age sixteen the order is the reverse, from the highest to the lowest, except that Stage 6 is still little used. At age thirteen, the good-boy middle stage (Stage 3) is most used.

The results in Mexico and Taiwan are the same, except that development is a little slower. The most conspicuous feature is that, at the age of sixteen, Stage 5 thinking is much more salient in the United States than in Mexico or Taiwan. Nevertheless, it is present in the other countries, so we know that this is not purely an American democratic construct.

Figure 1.2 shows strikingly similar results from two isolated villages, one in Yucatan, one in Turkey, Although conventional moral thought increases steadily from ages ten to sixteen, it still has not achieved a clear ascendancy over preconventional thought.

Trends for lower-class urban groups are intermediate in the rate of development between those for the middle-class and for the village boys. In the three divergent cultures that I studied, middle-class children were found to be more advanced in moral judgment than matched lower-class children. This was not due to the fact that the middle-class children heavily favored some one type of thought that could be seen as corresponding to the prevailing middle-class pattern. Instead, middle-class and working-class children move through the same sequences, but the middle-class children move faster and farther.

This sequence is not dependent on a particular religion or on any religion at all in the usual sense. I found no important differences in the development of moral thinking among Catholics, Protestants, Jews, Buddhists, Moslems, and atheists.

In summary, the nature of our sequence is not significantly affected by widely varying social, cultural, or religious conditions. The only thing that is affected is the rate at which individuals progress through this sequence.

Why should there be such a universal invariant sequence of development? In answering this question, we need first to analyze these developing social concepts in terms of their internal logical structure. At each stage, the same basic moral concept or aspect is defined, but at each higher stage this definition is more differentiated, more integrated, and more general or universal. When one's concept of human life moves from Stage 1 to Stage 2, the value of life becomes more differentiated from the value of property, more integrated (the value of life enters an organizational hierarchy where it is "higher" than property so that one steals property in order to save life), and more universalized

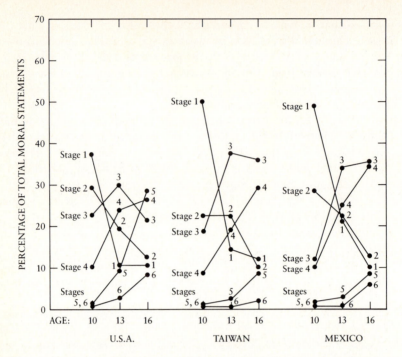

Figure 1.1 Moral development of middle-class urban boys in the United States, Taiwan, and Mexico. At age ten, the stages are used according to difficulty. At age thirteen, Stage 3 is most used by all three groups. At age sixteen, U.S. boys have reversed the order of age ten stages (with the exception of 6). In Taiwan and Mexico, conventional (3–4) stages prevail at age sixteen, with Stage 5 also little used (Kohlberg, 1968a).

(the life of any sentient being is valuable regardless of status or property). The same advance is true at each stage in the hierarchy. Each step of development, then, is a better cognitive organization than the one before it, one that takes account of everything present in the previous stage but making new distinctions and organizes them into a more comprehensive or more equilibrated structure. The fact that this is the case has been demonstrated by a series of studies indicating that children and adolescents comprehend all stages up to their own, but not more than one stage beyond their own (Rest, 1973). And, importantly, they prefer this next stage.

Moral thought, then, seems to behave like all other kinds of thought. Progress through the moral levels and stages is characterized by increasing differentiation and increasing integration, and hence is the same kind of progress that scientific theory represents. Like acceptable scientific theory—or like any theory or structure of knowledge—moral thought may be considered partially to generate its own data as it goes along, or at least to expand so as to contain in a balanced, self-consistent way a wider and wider experiential field. The raw data in the case of our ethical philosophies may be considered as conflicts between roles, or values, or as the social order in which people live.

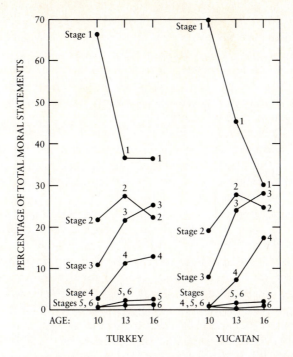

Figure 1.2 Two isolated villages, one in Turkey, the other in Yucatan, show similar patterns in moral thinking. There is no reversal of order, and conventional (stages 3–4) thought does not gain in a clear ascendancy over preconventional stages at age sixteen (Kohlberg, 1968a).

The social worlds of all people seem to contain the same basic structures. All the societies we have studied have the same basic institutions—family, economy, law, government. In addition, however, all societies are alike because they are societies—systems of defined complementary roles. In order to play a social role in the family, school, or society, children must implicitly take the role of others toward themselves and toward others in the group. These role-taking tendencies form the basis of all social institutions. They represent various patternings of shared or complementary expectations.

In the preconventional and conventional levels (Stages 1–4), moral content or value is largely accidental or culture bound. Anything from "honesty" to "courage in battle" can be the central value. But in the higher postconventional levels, Socrates, Lincoln, Thoreau, and Martin Luther King tend to speak without confusion of tongues, as it were. This is because the ideal principles of any social structure are basically alike, if only because there simply are not that many principles that are articulate, comprehensive, and integrated enough to be satisfying to the human intellect. And most of these principles have gone by the name of justice.

I have discussed at some length the culturally universal sequences of stages of moral judgment. I have not entirely clarified how such a sequence helps to resolve relativistic questioning of moral principles, a task taken up in our Chapter 4, "From *Is* to *Ought*." It is easier to clarify how such a sequence helps resolve the dilemma of relativity versus indoctrination in values education. The sequence provides us with a concept of moral development that can be stimulated by education without indoctrination and yet that helps to move student judgment toward more adequate principles.

The way to stimulate stage growth is to pose real or hypothetical dilemmas to students in such a way as to arouse disagreement and uncertainty as to what is right. The teacher's primary role is to present such dilemmas and to ask Socratic questions that arouse student reasoning and focus student listening on one another's reasons.

I noted research by Rest (1973) showing that students prefer the highest stage of reasoning they comprehend but that they do not comprehend more than one stage above their own. As a result, assimilation of reasoning occurs primarily when it is the next stage up from the student's level. Developmental moral discussion thus arouses cognitive-moral conflict and exposes students to reasoning by other students at the next stage above their own.

Using this approach, Blatt and Kohlberg (1975) were able to stimulate one-third of experimental classes of students to advance one stage in a time period in which control classes remained unchanged in moral stage. One year later, the experimental classes retained their relative advance over the control classes.

The developmental approach, first experimentally elaborated by Blatt, is one that any thoughtful classroom teacher may practice. Unlike values clarification, its assumptions are not relativistic but, rather, are based on universal goals and principles. It asks the student for reasons, on the assumption that some reasons are more adequate than others.

The approach differs from indoctrinative approaches because it tries to move student's thinking in a direction that is natural for the student rather than moving the student in the direction of accepting the teacher's moral assumptions. It avoids preaching or didacticism linked to the teacher's authority.

As I have characterized developmental moral education, it is neither an indoctrinative or relativistic classroom discussion process. . . .

References

Blatt, M., and L. Kohlberg. "The Effects of Classroom Moral Discussion upon Children's Level of Moral Judgment." *Journal of Moral Education* 4 (1975): 129–61.

Bronfenbrenner, U. "Soviet Methods of Upbringing and Their Effects: A Social-Psychological Analysis." Paper read at conference on Studies of the Acquisition and Development of Values, National Institute of Child Health and Human Development, Washington, D.C., May 23, 1968.

Carr, D. B., and E. P. Wellenberg. *Teaching Children Values*. Freeport, Calif.: Honor Your Partner Records, 1966.

Dodder, C., and B. Dodder. *Decision Making: A Guide for Teachers Who Would Help Preadolescent Children Become Imaginative and Responsible Decision Makers*. Boston: Beacon Press, 1968.

Havighurst, R. J., and H. Taba. *Adolescent Character and Personality*. New York: Wiley, 1949.

Jackson, P. W. *Life in the Classroom*. New York: Holt, Rinehart and Winston, 1968.

Kohlberg, L. "Moral Development and the New Social Studies." *Social Education* 37 (1973): 368–75.

Piaget, J. *The Moral Judgment of the Child*. New York: Free Press, 1948. (Originally published 1932.)

Rest, J. "The Hierarchical Nature of Moral Judgment." *Journal of Personality* 41 (1973): 86–109.

Simon, S. "Value-Clarification vs. Indoctrination." *Social Education* 35 (1971): 902.

7

Moral Education and Indoctrination

GEORGE SHER and WILLIAM J. BENNETT

George Sher (b. 1942) is Professor of Philosophy at the University of Vermont. He has published numerous articles on ethics, social philosophy, and metaphysics. William J. Bennett (b. 1943) has served as chairman of the National Endowment for the Humanities, and is now United States Secretary of Education. He is coauthor of Counting by Race. *This selection was written before he assumed his current position.*

In the selection, Sher and Bennett discuss the teaching of morality. When teachers try to impart moral values through exhortation and by personal example, they are often criticized for indoctrinating students. Their actions are held both to violate students' autonomy and to conflict with society's commitment to tolerate diversity. (For relevant discussion, see Kohlberg's criticism in reading 6 of the "bag of virtues" approach.) But Sher and Bennett argue that such charges are unfounded. In their view, "directive" moral education need not diminish one's later capacity to make autonomous moral decisions. In fact, when practiced properly, it actually enhances that capacity. In addition, such education need not violate defensible norms of tolerance or discourage criticism of existing practices.

IT IS NOW widely agreed that educators have no business inculcating moral views in the classroom. According to many philosophers and educational theorists, all attempts to influence students' moral behavior through exhortation and personal example are indoctrinative and should give way to more discursive efforts to guide children in developing their own values.[1] Yet although the nondirective approach to moral education has become the new orthodoxy,

---

[1] Thus, for example: "[I]t is . . . wrong to teach ethics by presenting and attempting to inculcate a number of rules or precepts of conduct so as to improve, or at least to alter character, dispositions, or responses. The most effective means for altering responses, and possibly character as well, are those of advertising, propaganda (is there any difference?), indoctrination and brainwashing. These are all objectionable on moral grounds, so one cannot possibly improve character by these means" [Marcus Singer, "The Teaching of Introductory Ethics," *The Monist*, LVIII, 4 (October 1974), p. 617]. "If moral education promotes a definite moral perspective, it tends to be toward indoctrination and the denial of moral autonomy. . . . The problem and the challenge of moral education in our age is to find a middle way which neither indoctrinates young people into one set of moral rules nor gives them the impression that decision making is all a matter of personal opinion" [Robert Hall, "Moral Education Today: Progress, Prospects and Problems of a Field Come of Age," *The Humanist* (November/December 1978), p. 12].

its philosophical underpinnings remain largely unexplored. In particular, the familiar charge that all directive moral education is indoctrinative has not been carefully defended. In this paper, we will argue that no plausible version of it *can* be defended and that adequate moral education must include both directive *and* discursive elements. Because the charge of indoctrination is so unclear, we will not confront it directly. Instead, we will address two closely related claims: that directive moral education (1) violates a student's autonomy, and (2) involves sectarian teaching inappropriate to a pluralistic society. If these complaints can be shown to lack substance, then the charge of indoctrination will carry little weight.

I

Before discussing the major objections to directive moral education, we must make clearer what such education involves. In particular, we must specify (a) the traits and principles to be taught, and (b) the relevant methods of teaching them, and (c) the positive reasons for adopting such methods.

The traits and principles we have in mind are best illustrated by example. In Talawanda, Ohio, the local school district recently took the position that "the schools should help students realize the importance" of principles and traits including:

— Achieving self-discipline, defined as the strength to do what we believe we should do, even when we would rather not do it.
— Being trustworthy, so that when we say we will or will not do something, we can be believed.
— Telling the truth, especially when it hurts us to do so.
— Having the courage to resist group pressures to do what we believe, when alone, that we should not do.
— Using honorable means, those that respect the rights of others, in seeking our individual and collective ends.
— Conducting ourselves, where significant moral behavior is involved, in a manner which does not fear exposure.
— Having the courage to say, "I'm sorry, I was wrong."
— Treating others as we would wish to be treated; recognizing that this principle applies to persons of every class, race, nationality, and religion.
— Doing work well, whatever that work may be.
— Respecting the democratic values of free speech, a free press, freedom of assembly, freedom of religion, and due process of law. Recognizing that this principle applies to speech we abhor, groups we dislike, persons we despise.

Later, we will discuss the degree to which the Talawanda list embodies moral or ideological bias. For now, it suffices to note that the items just listed are close to noncontroversial within our society. They illustrate, but do not exhaust, the traits and principles whose directive teaching we will discuss.

What, exactly, does such teaching involve? Although a full account is again impossible, certain elements stand out. Of these, perhaps the most important is a teacher or administrator's willingness to demonstrate that he himself endorses certain principles—that he accepts them as guides in his own conduct and expects his students to do likewise. This requires that he act as an intentional model of behavior in accordance with the favored principles. It also requires that he explicitly urge his students to develop habits of acting in similar ways and that he express his disapproval, both verbally and through punishment, when his expectations are not met. It is often desirable to explain *why* one should act in the relevant ways, but efforts to influence behavior should not be confined to such explanations. Both encouragement and expressions of disapproval may persist when the proffered reasons are not grasped.

Why should morality be taught in these ways? Quite obviously, any rationale for adopting directive methods must be an instrumental one. The claim must be that, at elementary levels of development, such methods are effective ways of getting children to internalize desirable habits and behave in desirable ways and that, at more advanced levels, the previous application of these methods is necessary for the success of more discursive methods. We believe these claims are supported by recent studies of child and adolescent development and "moral psychology."[2] However, even if all empirical issues remained open, the permissibility of directive moral education would still be worth ascertaining. Even those who are not convinced that such methods work must be interested in learning whether we would be morally permitted to employ them if they did.

II

Consider, first, the objection that directive moral education violates autonomy. At the core of this objection is a distinction between actions produced by nonrational causes and actions motivated by an awareness of the reasons for performing them. When a child acts to imitate a respected model or in response to exhortation or threat, he is said to be motivated only in the former way. Even if there are good reasons for his action, the very same techniques that have motivated his act could just as well have been used to motivate behavior unsupported by such reasons. Thus, his behavior is evidently *not* produced simply by his appreciation of the reasons for it. Hence, it is said to be neither fully his own nor an appropriate object of moral appraisal.

There is plainly something right about this objection. On any plausible account, an adequate moral education must produce not only a tendency to act rightly, but also a tendency to do so for the right reasons. But, despite its superficial clarity, the objection as stated is both ambiguous and incomplete. It is ambiguous because it does not specify whether the person whose autonomy is violated

<hr/>

[2] See especially Norman T. Feather, "Values in Adolescence," and Martin L. Hoffman, "Moral Development in Adolescence," in Joseph Adelson, ed., *The Handbook of Adolescent Psychology* (New York: Wiley, 1980), pp. 247-344.

is the child to whom directive education is administered or the adult whom the child will later become. It is incomplete because it does not explain *how* autonomy is violated in either case.

Whose autonomy is violated by directive moral education? Of the two possible answers, the more straightforward is "the child's." But to this answer, there is a quick rejoinder. However desirable it is to appeal to a person's appreciation of reasons, it surely need not be wrong to influence his behavior in other ways when he cannot respond to reasons alone. But this is manifestly true of young children. With them, appeals to principle simply fail. We must ascend the developmental scale quite far before such appeals promise much success. According to the leading proponent of nondirective moral education, Lawrence Kohlberg, the most common motive for moral action among 13-year-olds is still a desire to avoid disapproval and dislike by others.[3] In Kohlberg's typology, this motive is three full stages away from conscientious aversion to self-reproach. Moreover, in Kohlberg's view, one cannot reach a given stage of moral development without first traversing all the lower stages. Thus, even Kohlberg must acknowledge that, before middle adolescence, most children cannot respond to unadorned appeals to moral reasons. But if so, we do not violate their autonomy when we supplement such appeals with more efficacious influences.

This reply may appear inconclusive; for the opponent of directive moral education can respond by weakening his requirements for autonomy. Instead of contending that moral autonomy requires that one act from moral reasons, he can assert that it requires only that one's motives be those of the highest Kohlbergian level available to one. If so, even a child who acts to satisfy an impersonally construed authority (Kohlberg's level 4) may act significantly more autonomously than one who seeks to imitate a respected elder or to avoid punishment. However, considered by itself, such denatured "autonomy" has little value. Its main significance is pretty clearly to pave the way for further moral development. Thus, the response does not really save the claim that directive techniques violate a child's autonomy. If anything, it reinforces the claim that what is violated is the autonomy of the adult whom the child will become.

Put in this second form, the objection no longer presupposes an obviously impossible ideal of autonomy. Unlike children, mature adults often do seem to respond to moral reasons. But why should the previous application of directive techniques be thought to prevent this? It is true that directive techniques use nonrational means to produce desires and character traits that will eventually influence one's adult actions. However, even if an adult *is* motivated by a desire that was originally produced by nonrational means, it still seems possible for his action to be done for good moral reasons. In particular, this still seems possible if his nonrationally produced desire is precisely to act *in accordance*

---

[3] For elaboration, see Kohlberg, *The Philosophy of Moral Development* (New York: Harper & Row, 1981).

with such reasons. But it is surely just this desire which the sensitive practitioner of directive moral education seeks to instill.

If moral autonomy required only action in accordance with moral reasons, this response would be decisive. However, another strain of thought construes the requirements for autonomy more strictly. On this view, genuine moral autonomy requires not only that an agent act *in accordance with* moral reasons, but also that he *be motivated by* his awareness of them. In Kantian terms, the autonomous agent must be "self-legislating." On this expanded account the effectiveness of a past directive education may again seem threatening to current autonomy. If without his past directive education the agent would not now act as he does, then it is apparently just the desires produced by that education which supply the motivational energy for his current act. But if so, that motivational energy is evidently *not* supplied by his recognition of reasons themselves. His recognition of reasons may *trigger* the motivational energy for his act; but what is triggered is still energy with an independent source. Hence, the requirements for moral autonomy still seem unsatisfied.

With this refinement, we approach the heart of the objection that directive moral education violates autonomy. But although the refinement is familiar, the resulting argument is problematical. Most obviously, it rests on both the obscure metaphor of motivational energy and the undefended requirement that autonomous acts must draw such energy from reasons themselves. But the difficulty goes deeper. Even if its premises were both intelligible and defensible, the argument would be a non sequitur. Although it purports to demonstrate that directive moral education *violates* moral autonomy, it really shows only that such education does not *contribute* to moral autonomy. Far from establishing that directive techniques are pernicious, it at best establishes that they are morally neutral.

For why *should* desires produced by nonrational techniques be thought to prevent one from being motivated by an appreciation of reasons? Is the point merely that anyone subject to nonrationally produced desires would perform his act even if he were *not* motivated by an appreciation of the moral reasons for it? If so, then the most that follows is that his act is motivationally overdetermined. Since this does not negate the motivating force of his appreciation of reasons, it does not undermine his autonomy. Is the point rather that, if one's directively induced desires are required to produce one's action, then the motivation supplied by one's appreciation of reasons is too *weak* to produce it—that the latter motivation requires supplementation? If so, then, without his directive moral education, the agent would not have performed the act at all, and so *a fortiori* would not have performed it autonomously. Here again, nothing suggests that his directive moral education has reduced or violated his autonomy.

Given these considerations, even the strengthened analysis of autonomy does not establish that directive moral education violates one's later autonomy. To show this, one would need two yet stronger premises: that (1) a single act cannot simultaneously be motivated by both the agent's recognition of reasons and a nonrationally induced desire, and (2) when motivation from both sources

106

converges, the motivational energy supplied by the nonrationally induced desire always excludes that supplied by an appreciation of reasons. But although these premises would indeed save the argument, there is little independent basis for them. In ordinary contexts, energy from any number of sources can combine to produce a single result. Hence, given our working metaphor, we must also presume that *motivational* energy from different sources can combine. The presumption must be that the motivating force of reasons does *not* give way when other factors motivate the same act. Moreover, these presumptions are not defeated by any independent theoretical considerations; for no adequate theory of how reasons motivate has yet been proposed.

III

So far, we have argued that directive moral education need not violate any-one's present or future moral autonomy. This conclusion, if correct, suffices to rebut the first objection to directive education. But more can be said here. Even if autonomy does require motivation by moral reasons, one's past directive education may actually help such autonomy to develop and flourish.

To see how directive education can have this result, recall first that, even if one's grasp of a moral reason does supply one with some impulse to do the right thing, that impulse may be too weak to issue in action. Because of this, its effect may depend on other factors. In particular, that effect may well be increased by one's past directive education. Of course, the desires produced by such education will not contribute to one's moral autonomy if they merely add their weight to the motivation supplied by one's appreciation of reasons. How-ever, and crucially, a past directive education may also augment one's appre-ciation of reasons in another way. It may neutralize or eliminate what would otherwise be a competing motive, and so may enable one's appreciation of reasons to affect one more strongly. If directive education works this way, it will indeed render the agent more autonomous. Put in terms of our guiding metaphor, its function will be not to provide an additional source of motiva-tional energy, but rather to clear away obstacles so that the energy supplied by reasons can suffice.

How likely is it that directive moral education actually does work in this way? It is not likely to do so always or exclusively. That directive education does not *always* work by eliminating obstacles to moral reasons is shown by the fact that it motivates even very young children and can motivate adults to act immorally. That it rarely works *only* by eliminating such obstacles is sug-gested by the fact that one's prerational desires seem likely to persist as one matures. But even if a past directive education often affects adults in ways that do not enhance their autonomy, it may simultaneously affect them in other ways as well. Thus, the question is not whether our model is exclusively correct, but only whether it accurately reflects *one* way in which directive moral edu-cation often works.

When the question is put this way, we think its answer is clearly yes. It is a psychological commonplace that one's ability to respond to any reason depends on various external considerations. Hunger, anxiety, pain, and fear can all reduce the effect of reasons by diminishing attention to them and by supplying other motives. Thus, eliminating these distractions plainly does increase the motivating force of reasons. But if so, then eliminating other distractions seems likely to serve a similar function. Two considerations which most often distract us from moral obligations are preoccupation with our own interests and concern for our own comfort. Hence, one very natural way of increasing the motivating force of moral reasons is to reduce the impact of such distractions. But how better to prevent someone from being unduly distracted by self-interest than by causing him to acquire settled habits of honesty, fair play, and concern for others? Given these habits, one will automatically discount one's selfish interests when they conflict with one's duty. Hence, one will attach proper weight to one's moral obligations as a matter of course. Moreover, how better to ensure that someone will follow his decisions through than by causing him to acquire further habits of diligence, perseverance, and conscientiousness? Given *these* habits, one will not be sidetracked by the blandishments of comfort or inertia. Hence, one's appreciation of reasons will again be rendered more effective.

Given all of this, the traditional content of directive moral education acquires new significance. As the Talawanda list suggests, such education has long aimed at producing the habits just mentioned. These habits are often criticized as poor substitutes for self-conscious and reasoned morality, but we can now see that this criticism misses the point. Far from being alternatives to self-conscious morality, the habits are best understood as indispensible auxiliaries to it. They increase the impact of moral reasons by reducing one's tendency to be diverted. When the habits exist in persons who do not appreciate moral reasons, they may be mere facsimiles of virtue. However, when they exist in conjunction *with* an appreciation of reasons, they surely do contribute to moral autonomy.

IV

Until now, we have considered only the objection that directive moral education violates the ideal of the morally autonomous agent. However, one may also argue that it violates a related *social* ideal. There is wide agreement that our society should be both tolerant and pluralistic. Instead of stifling disagreements, it should accept and encourage diversity of opinion and should protect unpopular attitudes and beliefs. But a society that officially practices directive moral education seems not to do this. Instead of encouraging diversity, it instills in all children a single "approved" set of values. Far from being neutral, it is unabashedly partisan. Thus, such education may seem flatly incompatible with pluralism and tolerance.

This argument is narrower in scope than its predecessor; for it tells only against the use of directive techniques in public schools. Still, it does seem to animate many charges of indoctrination, and so we must examine it. To see the problems it raises, consider first the premise that society should tolerate and protect diverse values. This premise may mean either that (1) society should not coerce or persecute those who already hold unorthodox values, or (2) society should not try to induce people to acquire (or prevent people from acquiring) any values they do not yet hold. Whenever society coerces or persecutes those with unpopular values, it provides a disincentive for others to acquire those values. Hence, any violation of (1) is likely to violate (2). However, society may tolerate dissenters while trying to prevent others from acquiring their values. Hence, a violation of (2) does not necessarily violate (1).

Directive moral education neither persecutes anyone nor coerces any adults. When its techniques include punishment, it may be said to coerce children. However, (1) is generally not taken to apply to children, and punishment is in any case theoretically dispensable. Thus, directive moral education need not violate (1). It does violate (2); but that counts against it only if (2) is a proper interpretation of the pluralistic ideal. At first glance, (2) may appear to follow from a more general requirement that unorthodox views should receive a fair hearing. However, this would imply that we owe fair treatment to values as well as persons; and, as John Rawls has noted, such an obligation is highly unlikely.[4] Thus, the more promising strategy is to defend (2) less directly. To do that, one might appeal either to a societal obligation to allow persons to choose their own values or else to the undesirable consequences of inculcating official values. We will argue that neither defense succeeds.

The claim that societal attempts to inculcate values would violate an obligation to allow people to choose their own values is inherently problematical. In standard cases, people's choices are guided by their values, but here it is precisely one's basic values that are said to *be* chosen. Hence, the relevant choices cannot be grounded in any deeper values. But how, then, *are* such choices grounded? Shall we say they have no grounding, but are simply arbitrary? If so, they hardly warrant society's protection. Are they grounded in considerations outside the agent's value system, such as his recognition of independent moral reasons? If so, the complaint against inculcating values must be that it prevents people from *responding* to such reasons. But we already know this is false. The desires and habits produced by directive moral education need not diminish, but may actually enhance, the motivating force of moral reasons. Is the claim, finally, that societally induced desires and habits do allow rational choice of values when they coincide with moral reasons, but prevent it in cases of conflict? If so, the argument is not that it is wrong to inculcate values, but only that society may inculcate the wrong values. Thus construed, the argument appeals to consequences. Hence, having come this far, we may abandon the rubric of choice, and confront the consequentialist approach directly.

The *locus classicus* of consequentialist arguments for tolerance is John Stuart Mill's *On Liberty*.[5] It is true that Mill's main target is not the inculcation of values, but rather intolerance involving coercion and persecution. However,

---

[4] "Fairness to Goodness," *Philosophical Review,* LXXXIV, 4 (October 1975): p. 554.

[5] *On Liberty* (Indianapolis: Hackett, 1978).

there are also passages where Mill suggests that his arguments *do* extend to education, and presumably *a fortiori* to directive education (104-106). Moreover, whatever Mill's own views, any convincing consequentialist argument for (2) is likely to rest on precisely the familiar claims that society is fallible, that genuine challenges to belief enhance understanding, and that diverse practices provide people with a variety of models and "experiments of living." Thus, it is essentially the Millian arguments that we must now consider. Do they show that society should refrain from using nonrational techniques to instill values in its citizens?

We think not. Mill is right to insist that neither anyone's subjective feeling of certainty nor the agreement of society can guarantee the truth of an opinion or the utility of its adoption. However, the warrant for accepting the values of fairness, honesty, and consideration of others is no mere feeling of conviction. Instead, there is good independent reason to believe that, if any moral propositions are true, propositions enjoining such behavior are among them. Moreover, if the issue turns on social utility, then the warrant for inculcating these values is still more obvious. There is of course a danger that, once any inculcation of values is admitted, dogmatists and fanatics will seek to inculcate values that are *not* well-grounded or useful. However, this danger, though real, is far from decisive. If we can avoid the slippery slope by insisting that *no* values be inculcated, then we can also do so by insisting that society inculcate only values that satisfy high standards of justifiability. This will of course require some exercise of judgment; but that seems unavoidable in any case. As Mill himself remarks, "there is no difficulty in proving any ethical standard whatever to work ill, if we suppose universal idiocy to be conjoined with it."[6]

In view of this, (2) cannot be supported by appealing to human fallibility. But the other consequentialist arguments are no better. A person's comprehension of his beliefs and values may indeed be deepened by challenges posed by dissenters, but such challenges are generally not needed to promote either adequate comprehension or tenacious acceptance of moral values. The suggestion that they are is contradicted by common experience. Moreover, even if wide-spread challenges to moral values did bring real benefits, these would be trivial compared to the mischief done by large numbers of people uncommitted to honesty, integrity, or concern for others. Nor, similarly, is it likely that exposure to cruelty, dishonesty, and insensitivity will promote personal development or bring out traits beneficial to others.

These considerations show that directive moral education need not be condemned as incompatible with pluralism. But that point can also be made in another way. It would be self-defeating for pluralists to demand that society be completely neutral toward all values; for the general acceptance of some values is required by pluralism itself. This holds most obviously for the value of toleration, but it is no less true of other values on the Talawanda list. If people were not committed to fairness, cooperation, and trustworthiness, they

---

[6] *Utilitarianism* (Indianapolis: Hackett, 1979), p. 23.

could hardly maintain a framework within which the rights of the weak and unpopular were protected. This may or may not justify the coercive suppression of some views—intolerance in the name of tolerance remains a disputed question of liberalism—but it surely does call for something beyond mere neutrality. If we as a society value toleration, then we must also value the general acceptance of principles that support and further it. Hence, if there is an effective method of advancing such principles which is not otherwise objectionable, we must acknowledge a strong case for adopting it. But precisely this is true of directive moral education. Thus, at least some forms of it seem justified by our commitment to toleration itself.

V

We have now rejected several familiar arguments against directive moral education. However, in endorsing such education, we do not mean that it should be used to teach every widely accepted moral belief or that it should utilize every effective method of procuring assent. Despite the strong moral component in many issues of economic distribution, foreign policy, and religion, we believe that normative propositions about these matters should generally not be taught directively. And although we believe that fairness and honesty *should* be taught directively, we believe their teaching should not involve immoderate humiliation or pain. But if we are to make such distinctions, we face a difficult further question: why are some forms of directive moral education permissible but others not?

This question is too large for us to answer fully, but some considerations are obviously relevant. To warrant directive teaching, a moral principle must first be clearly and firmly grounded. In addition, it should be simple enough to be comprehended at an early developmental stage, general enough to apply in a variety of situations, and central rather than peripheral to our moral corpus. To be acceptable as a *method* of directive teaching, a practice must neither impair a child's later ability to respond to moral reasons nor violate his rights. In many instances, the satisfaction of these requirements is undisputed. However, if an otherwise eligible principle or method is unacceptable to a conscientious minority, then respect for that minority may itself dictate restraint in directive teaching.

With this we can confront a final objection. It is sometimes said that because directive moral education reflects the prevailing moral climate, it inevitably favors existing practices and institutions. Because it grows out of entrenched attitudes, it is said objectionably to perpetuate the status quo. But we can now see that such worries are overblown. If the principles and habits that are directively taught are strongly justified, central to our evaluative scheme, and of more than parochial application, they are not likely to ratify all aspects of the status quo. Instead, they may well generate considerable dissatisfaction with existing realities. If someone is fair, considers others' interests, and respects democratic values, then he will be highly critical of many existing practices. If he is unmoved by group pressures, he will press his criticism even when it is unpopular. If he respects the truth and disdains dishonorable means, he will abjure self-interested silence. All in all, such a person is unlikely to be passive and indiscriminately accepting. Instead, he is apt vigorously to oppose various existing practices.

This shows that directive moral education need not favor the status quo. But should it ever be used to teach principles that *do* have this effect? To see the problem here, consider some further Talawanda entries:

— Practicing good sportsmanship. Recognizing that although the will to win is important, winning is not all-important.
— Showing respect for the property of others—school property, business property, government property, everyone's property.
— Abstaining from premature sexual experience and developing sexual attitudes compatible with the values of family life.

We believe there is much to be said for each of these. However, each is closely associated with a contested social institution. The first presupposes the legitimacy of competition, the second assumes an economic system which distributes wealth unequally, and the third overtly favors marriage and the family. Alternatives to each institution have been proposed. Does this imply that these principles should not be directively taught?

We believe this question has no simple answer. To decide whether association with an existing institution disqualifies a principle, one must first clarify the nature of the association. Does the principle merely apply *only in the context of* the institution? Or does it, in addition, require that one *accept* it? If acceptance of (say) property or the family is required, must one accept only some form of the institution, or all its current details? If the details need not be accepted, the argument amounts to little. But even if a principle does require full acceptance of an existing institution, the question of its directive teaching is not settled. The main reasons for not directively teaching such principles are to permit full evaluation of alternative institutions and to display respect for persons proposing them. However, despite their relevance, these factors are not always decisive. We saw above that a major determinant of whether a principle should be directively taught is its degree of justification. But if so, then when a principle requires acceptance of a contested institution, we cannot avoid asking how reasonable it is to oppose that institution and how plausible the alternatives are. If these questions are asked, their answers may tip the balance. Hence, directive teaching of principles favoring existing institutions cannot be ruled out.

This of course says little of substance. To evaluate directive teaching about property, sexual behavior, or other matters of controversy, one must say more about a whole range of issues. But that much more must be said is precisely our point. Where directive moral education is concerned, we begin to make progress only when we abandon as sterile the notion of indoctrination and its cognates.

8

Skepticism About Weakness of Will*

GARY WATSON

> *Gary Watson (b. 1943) teaches philosophy at the University of California at Irvine. He has published a number of papers on aspects of the will.*
>
> *In this selection, Watson discusses weakness of will. Like Aristotle (reading 5), he rejects Socrates' view that what looks like weakness is really ignorance of what one ought to do. Instead, he argues that appetite and emotion may sway even correct judgment. But while this explains how people can act against their judgment, it also raises a further question. Since compulsives also surrender to emotion or impulse, what distinguishes weakness from psychological compulsion?*
>
> *One possibility is that the weak person can resist his impulse while the compulsive cannot. In compulsion, but not in weakness, the impulse to which one surrenders is irresistably strong. But Watson rejects this because it leaves us without an explanation of why the weak do not resist. Instead, he proposes that neither the weak nor the compulsive can resist their desires, but that when compulsives give in, they surrender to desires that no person of normal capacity could resist. By contrast, what makes people count as weak is that they "give in to desires which . . . the normal degree of self-control would enable them to resist."*

Two Kinds of Skepticism

ALTHOUGH IT OCCURS with deplorable frequency, weakness of will has seemed to many philosophers hard to understand. The motivation of weak behavior[1] is generally familiar and intelligible enough: the desire to remain in bed, or the desire for another drink are ordinary examples. Nevertheless, our common ways of describing and explaining this phenomenon have been thought to involve serious difficulties. These descriptions and explanations can, upon reflection, seem incoherent.

---

* Many people have contributed to my thinking on this topic. I am especially grateful to Robert Audi, Charles Kahn, Ruth Mattern, the editors of the *Philosophical Review*, and Michael Slote.

[1] Weakness of will occurs only if one knowingly does something contrary to one's better judgment. We will see that this condition does not distinguish between weakness and compulsion.

Accordingly, weakness of will has given rise to various forms of skepticism. The most notorious form is socratism, which denies the possibility of such behavior. Another form of skepticism admits its possibility but casts doubt upon a complex of distinctions and moral attitudes involved in the common view. Briefly, it argues that no one who acts contrary to his or her better judgment does so freely, that weakness of will cannot be significantly distinguished from psychological compulsion[2], and that therefore certain moral distinctions implicit in the common view cannot be justified.

My concern in this paper will be to explore and develop a version of non-socratic skepticism. In my view, socratism is incorrect, but like Socrates, I think that the common understanding of weakness of will raises serious problems. Contrary to socratism, it is possible for a person knowingly to act contrary to his or her better judgment. But this description does not exhaust the common view of weakness. Also implicit in this view is the belief that actions which are contrary to one's better judgment are free in the sense that the agent could have done otherwise. The grounds for skepticism about this belief will be my theme.

To clear the way and to introduce some important distinctions, it will be helpful to begin with a discussion of socratic skepticism. Then I will set out what I take to be the crucial elements in the common account of weakness, and consider the apparent emptiness of that account as an explanatory model; it is said that one takes the drink *because* one's will is weak, for example, and this explanation is supposed to contrast with the compulsive case in which one takes the drink because one's desire is too strong. Finally, I will discuss and compare the merits of an alternative way of drawing the distinction between weakness and compulsion.

Socrates' Position

. . .

[R]ecall the reasoning in Plato's *Protagoras* which led Socrates (or the early Plato) to deny the possibility of *akrasia*. In this work, Socrates denied the common account, according to which agents may knowingly fail to do what they believe best in the situation, because they yield to temptation, or short-term pleasure, or are overcome by appetite. Socrates denied this account because he believed that human beings always most desire, and hence pursue, what is (thought to be) best. On this supposition, in acting weakly they would have to be pursuing what they believe to be best, believing it not to be best.

Instead, Socrates insisted that what is called weakness of will (*akrasia*) is really a species of ignorance. The weak agent suffers from a kind of evaluation

---

[2] I shall assume throughout that if someone is psychologically compelled to do something, he or she is unable to refrain from doing it (though not necessarily conversely). The compulsive's motivation is literally irresistible. This concept is discussed further [below].

illusion, very like an optical illusion—the nearer, more immediate good looks the greater. The so-called weak agent lacks the art of measurement, the art of correctly weighing nearer and farther goods, and to have this art is to have knowledge of good and evil. (Hence the thesis that virtue is a kind of knowledge, to which I shall return.)

Despite the ingenuity of this appeal to evaluational illusions (which I think in fact occur), the later Plato came to see this matter differently. He came to realize that we are generally susceptible to motivation which is independent, in strength and origin, of our judgments concerning how it is best to act. Plato's distinction between the rational and nonrational parts of the soul may be taken as a distinction between sources of motivation. The rational part of the soul is the source of evaluations—judgments as to the value or worth of a particular course of action or state of affairs. The nonrational part of the soul is the source of such desires as arise from the appetites and emotions. These desires are blind in the sense that they do not depend fundamentally upon the agent's view of the good. Since these sources of motivation differ, they may conflict, and in certain cases, the desires of the nonrational soul may motivate the agent contrary to his or her "desires" for the good. In some such way, Plato tried to account for motivational conflict and for the possibility of both self-mastery and its opposite.[3]

On the basis of this distinction, then, Plato rejected Socrates' (or his own earlier) view that a person's desires are always desires for the "good" and that what a person most desires is what is (thought) best. Elementary as these points are, they suffice to show the possibility of weakness of will. The desires of hunger and sex, the desires of anger and fear, do not depend upon one's assessment of the value of doing what one is thereby inclined to do. But if such desires exist, as they surely do, then it is possible that they are strong enough to motivate one contrary to one's judgment of what is best; it is possible that one's evaluations and desires diverge in certain cases in such a way that one is led to do things which one does not think worth doing, or as much worth doing as some available option. Hence socratism is false. There are no good theoretical grounds for denying *akrasia*.

Self-Control and the Socratic Theory of Virtue

Consider the virtue of courage, and how this virtue is misconceived by the socratic view. Courage is a virtue which it is in the interest of everyone to have, and is in this respect like continence. Now for Socrates, courage is, as it should be, the virtue which applies to situations of danger. But for him it applies in

---

[3] I develop this distinction, and apply it to the concept of free action, in "Free Agency", *Journal of Philosophy*, April 24, 1975.

An interpretative point: Plato appears to have held that the distinction between knowledge and belief is relevant in some way I fail to appreciate. Hence he may still have denied the possibility of acting contrary to one's *knowledge*.

the following eccentric way: courage is the knowledge of what is really dangerous or not. Since Socrates thought that the only danger is evil, or doing evil, all that it takes to possess the virtue of courage, and to act courageously, in appropriate circumstances, is the knowledge of what is good and evil. (This is the keystone of his doctrine of the unity of the virtues: each virtue is a special case of wisdom (knowledge of good and evil) applied to particular contexts: courage is wisdom about danger, temperance is wisdom about what is really pleasant, justice is wisdom applied to social relationships and statecraft, and so on. If you have wisdom in general, then you will have the other virtues, and if you lack one of these, you will lack wisdom). Hence the coward is one who has a false view of what is really dangerous. The courageous person is one who is able to distinguish apparent from real dangers.

But surely courage is not like this. Courage is the capacity to deal with one's fear in contexts where one is thereby spontaneously inclined to actions which are contrary to one's view of what should be done. The virtue of courage has a role only because we are not as Socrates says we are; it is needed because of the irrational part of the soul, because our inclinations do not always harmonize with our judgments of the good. Socrates thinks that the courageous person's virtue is that he or she sees there is nothing really to fear, whereas the coward is benighted about this. But the truth appears to be that courage is needed precisely where there *is* something to fear, but where this emotion would lead one to act contrary to one's better judgment.

Courage is thus a special type of self-control; it is self-control in situations of personal danger. Consequently, self-control has a broader application than to pleasure and temptation. If human psychology were as Socrates assumes, such a virtue would have no use. Self-control is a virtue only for beings who are susceptible to motivation which is in potential conflict with their judgments of what is good to pursue; only to beings like ourselves who have appetites and emotions which may incline them contrary to their better judgments.[4]

In passing, it is worth noting that possessing the capacity to make one's practical judgments effective in action is generally in the interest of every being with some sort of view of how to live, and does not presuppose a particularly austere or "rationalistic" ethic. Even those who favor spontaneity and propose to follow their inclinations should want the virtue of self-control. To use an

---

[4] The appetites and emotions are not the only sources of such motivation. Perhaps appetites (like hunger, thirst, sex) may be distinguished from emotions (like anger, fear, resentment) in that the latter essentially involve beliefs (that something is dangerous, that one has been wronged, that another is obstructing one), whereas appetites do not. But the following examples do not seem to fit clearly into either category—the inclinations arising from pain, the inclination to excrete, the inclination to sleep (arising from sleepiness)—and these surely belong to the "non-rational" part of the soul. Why isn't sleepiness, like hunger, an appetite?

Let me hasten to add that, as Ruth Mattern has pointed out to me, self-control should not be conceived as a unified capacity, such that if one has it in one area, one will have it in all areas. A person may be "soft" with respect to pain, but never yield to temptation, or one may be perfectly courageous, but continually give in to the desire to drink.

example of Thomas Nagel,[5] even those who favor a spontaneous life will want to be able to resist the sudden urge to join the Marine Corps—or more generally, to resist those inclinations the satisfaction of which would render them unable to act impulsively in the future.

As I see it, then, the virtue of self-control is the capacity to counteract recalcitrant motivation, that is, motivation which is contrary to one's better judgment. It is this virtue that the weak agent lacks, or at least fails to exercise; and for this virtue, knowledge in the ordinary sense is clearly insufficient. Now both compulsion and weakness of will involve a failure of self-control. In the next section, I want to consider some common ways of distinguishing these types of failure.

Weakness and Compulsion

Suppose that a particular woman intentionally takes a drink. To provide an evaluative context, suppose also that we think she ought not to have another because she will then be unfit to fulfill some of her obligations. Preanalytically, most of us would insist on the possibility and significance of the following three descriptions of the case. (1) the reckless or self-indulgent case; (2) the weak case; and (3) the compulsive case. In (1), the woman knows what she is doing but accepts the consequences. Her choice is to get drunk or risk getting drunk. She acts in accordance with her judgment. In (2) the woman knowingly takes the drink contrary to her (conscious) better judgment; the explanation for this lack of self-control is that she is weak-willed. In (3), she knowingly takes the drink contrary to her better judgment, but she is a victim of a compulsive (irresistible) desire to drink.

These variations reveal the leading features of the common conception of weakness. On this model, the weak drinker is like the compulsive drinker in that she acts contrary to her better judgment,[6] but she is like the reckless drinker in that she is able to resist the drink. Accordingly, she is placed morally somewhere "in between" the others. Since she acted contrary to her judgment, she is not, like the reckless drinker, just morally "bad"—her values and judgment are not in question. But unlike the compulsive, she is not a victim of irresistible desires. She shares with the reckless the ability to resist, and for this reason we hold her responsible.

The common account, then, insists that the weak person has, but fails to exercise, the capacity of self-control. It is this requirement that nonsocratic skepticism challenges. Before posing the challenge, I will illustrate and clarify the concept of motivational compulsion, and then raise some preliminary dif-

---

[5] In *The Possibility of Altruism,* Oxford, The Clarendon Press, 1970.

[6] Acting contrary to one's better judgment is not, however, a necessary condition of compulsion; one's desire might be compulsive and happen to accord with one's judgment.

ficulties in distinguishing it from weakness. Subsequently, I will argue that this common way of making the distinction is untenable, and will propose an alternative way that does not rest upon this requirement.

The notion of psychological or motivational compulsion is probably an extension of the ordinary notion of interpersonal compulsion, in which one person is forced by another to act "against his will." Although psychological compulsion may not be widely recognized in ordinary life, I think that the concepts of mania, phobia, and addiction imply its possibility.[7] I shall assume that when an action is literally compelled motivationally, the agent is motivated by a desire (or "impulse" or "inclination") that he or she is unable to resist. In illustration, a man might have a dread fear of spiders or rats so overwhelmingly strong that, even when it is urgently important for him to do so, he is literally unable to handle one. Or a starving woman may be driven by her hunger to do such acts as she would rather die than perform. Or a drug addict, because of his or her unconquerable craving for the drug, may be unable (at least over a span of time) to refuse the opportunity to obtain and consume some heroin.

It is not true that manic and phobic actions are necessarily compulsive; the motivations may raise the cost of alternative actions prohibitively, and thus "coerce" rather than compel. If I give in to my fear of flying, recognizing all the while that this fear is baseless, it does not follow that I was compelled to remain grounded. It may rather be that the difficulties and anxieties involved in my overcoming my admittedly irrational fear make doing so too costly. (Nor would this be a case of weakness of will; here I act on my judgment that flying is not worth the suffering.) However, there may be circumstances in which I am unable to overcome my phobia, even when it is practically urgent for me to fly. Nevertheless, even though manic or phobic desires do not necessarily compel, they are potentially compulsive in that their strength is to a large degree independent of the person's will.

In what follows, I wish to exclude from consideration cases of unconscious or "semi-conscious" or self-deceptive actions. Where one deceives oneself about what is best, or about one's situation of action, one does not act contrary to one's better judgment, but rather in accordance with one's self-deceptive judgment. Or perhaps in such cases, it is radically unclear what the real judgment *is*. Self-deception is itself philosophically troublesome, and as a matter of fact many actions we call weak may involve self-deception of some sort. But no philosophical reasons drive us to redescribe the phenomenon in this way, and certainly the common view insists on the possibility of "clear-headed" action contrary to better judgment. Furthermore, the problems raised by weakness of will differ distinctively from the problems raised by self-deception. The former problem is how a judgment can fail to lead to appropriate action. The latter

---

[7] See the leading psychological study, *Fears and Phobias,* by Marks. In his discussion of "obsessive-compulsive" neuroses, Freud also speaks of being unable to resist certain "impulses."

problem concerns the way in which beliefs and judgments can be influenced by desires. Consequently, I will restrict my attention to actions involving failures of the former kind.[8]

Preliminary Difficulties

It is important to emphasize that "weakness of will," in ordinary usage, purports to be an explanatory concept; weakness of will is not just any sort of action contrary to the agent's judgment. To identify behavior in this way is to offer a minimal kind of explanation: one acts contrary to one's better judgment *because* one is weak; one *yields* to temptation, *allows* oneself to give in to appetite, and so forth.

Now the force of this explanation is quite unclear, especially if it is supposed to contrast with an explanation in terms of compulsion. For the present, the problem of distinguishing weakness from compulsion may be expressed in the following way. In those examples given earlier, what is most striking, and leads naturally to the invocation of the notion of compulsion, is that the agents' actual motivation is independent of any conception that they have of the worth of their actions. Their motivation is in this way "alien" to them. In some significant sense, they seem motivated contrary to their own wills. Clearly, the "will" here cannot be the *strongest* motive; for compulsives do not act contrary to their strongest motive. They act contrary to their judgments of the worth of their actions. It is plausible, then, to identify the "will" with practical judgment. This suggests that the mark of a compulsive desire is its capacity to motivate the agent contrary to practical judgment. But it follows that the weak agent acts contrary to his or her judgment in exactly the same the same sense, and therefore acts under compulsion.

This consequence is admittedly counterintuitive. Surely if it is plausible in some circumstances to say that a starving person is unable to resist taking the bread, that in general compulsives are driven ineluctably to acts beyond their control, it is quite implausible to say this of the well-nourished who capitulate to their fondness for bagels.

Similarly, we are inclined to contrast weakness and compulsion like so: in the case of compulsive acts, it is not so much that the will is too weak as that the contrary motivation is too strong; whereas, in weakness of will properly

---

[8] On a larger view, this distinction may prove to be superficial. If, as I suggest, self-control or strength of will is the capacity to ensure that one's practical judgment is effective in action, then presumably it would be part of this capacity to maintain clarity of judgment in the face of temptation. In a significant sense, one's practical judgment is ineffective in self-deceptive action, and one can yield to bad reasoning as well as directly to temptation. But I shall adhere in the text to this characterization of weakness as action contrary to one's conscious and immediate practical judgment, both for simplicity and because this case is conceptually most problematic for my concerns.

so-called, it is not that the contrary motivation is too strong, but that the will is too weak.

There is, I think, something correct in this contrast; but the following difficulty remains. This talk of strength of desires is obscure enough, but insofar as it has meaning, there does not appear to be any way of judging the strength of desires except as they result in action. For why is it said that the compulsive's desires are too strong? Isn't it just because these agents are motivated contrary to their wills? Isn't the only relatively clear measure of strength of desires the tendency of those desires to express themselves independently of the agent's will? If this is so, the desires which motivate the weak contrary to their judgments are "too strong" as well, and explanations of weakness and compulsion come to the same thing. We are left again with the conclusion that weakness is a case of compulsion.[9]

We have seen why socratism is to be rejected, but a real problem remains. If a sufficient condition of compulsive motivation is that the motivation be contrary to the agent's practical judgment, then weakness of will is a species of compulsion. And if compulsive behavior is involuntary and unfree, weak behavior is involuntary and unfree. In any case, weakness and compulsion are on a par. The intuition that the agent's will is too weak, whereas in the other case, the contrary motivation is too strong, appears to rest on an illusion.

One way to avoid this conclusion—that all weak actions are compulsive— would be to argue that no actions are compulsive, since no desires are irresistible. One philosopher who is skeptical about the idea of an irresistible desire is Joel Feinberg. "There is much obscurity in the notion of the strength of a desire," Feinberg writes, but he thinks several points are clear:

> The first is that strictly speaking no impulse is irresistible; for every case of giving in to a desire, I would argue, it will be true that, if the person had tried harder he would have resisted it successfully. . . . Nevertheless, it does make sense to say that some desires are stronger than others and that some have an intensity and power that are felt as overwhelming.[10]

Feinberg's confidence on these points puzzles me. One may well be dubious in practice about particular pleas of irresistibility. And, if one is in the dark about the notion of strength, one may well have blanket doubts about such claims. But if it is granted that desires may be *hard* to resist, on what grounds can it be denied that sometimes desires may be *too* hard to resist? Why must

[9] A few remarks on internalism may be in order here. I am supposing, as I think we ordinarily do, that when one acts weakly, one wants to some degree to do what one judges best. Weakness of will is marked by conflict and regret. However, this supposition does not entail a commitment to a general internalist view that a person necessarily wants what he or she judges best. . . . For even if it is possible not at all to want what one judges best, it would be a distortion to describe such a case as weakness of will. For such an externalist agent would have a strong and undivided will—and what he or she lacked certainly would not be self-control.

[10] "What is So Special about Mental Illness?", in *Doing and Deserving*, Princeton University Press, 1970, pp. 282-283.

the feeling that some desires are overwhelmingly "intense and powerful" be mistaken? What puzzles me is how the possibility of irresistible desires can be rejected a priori unless the notion of strength here is altogether empty.

Not only do many psychologists assume this possibility, the common view of weakness seems committed to it as well. For it insists that the weak person has but does not exercise the capacity to resist. This insistence presupposes the intelligibility of lacking this capacity. In any case, even if it is true, as Feinberg believes, that in all cases, "if the person had tried harder, he would have resisted," this does not show that no desires are irresistible. For a person may be unable to try harder and for this reason be unable to resist.

Therefore, it seems unjustified to hold that no desires are too strong for an agent to resist. In fact, we very frequently compare the strengths of desires, both when they are those of a particular individual at a given time, and when the desires belong to different persons or the same person at different times. (P's desire to lounge in bed is stronger than his desire to keep appointments; Q has stronger sexual desires than most, or than she herself had when she was fifteen.) It is not clear what criteria we invoke in such comparisons, but two obvious criteria are clearly unhelpful. Motivational efficacy will not do because on this measure any desire which motivates would thereby be the strongest.[11] And this measure would not allow for significant interpersonal comparisons. Nor, once again, will independence of the agent's will or better judgment do, for then the desires of the weak and the compulsive will be equally strong.

Strength and Resistibility

It might help at this point to return to my earlier description of self-control as the capacity to resist recalcitrant desires; such desires are strong to the extent to which they *need* to be resisted. For again, not all actual desires which one does not in the end act upon are therefore resisted. To resist cannot simply be to refrain from acting upon some desire one has. As Aristotle observed (*Nicomachean Ethics*, 1152a1 ff.), there is a difference between the "continent" and the "temperate" person which rests upon the notion of strength. For both types, "choice" regulates action—both act upon their evaluations—but while the temperate person has moderate appetites, the continent person acts rightly *despite* strong contrary inclinations. A person's desires are moderate to the degree to which they do not require resistance.

The important point is that practical conflict may assume both a decision-

---

[11] This needs some qualification. The motivational efficacy of desire could be understood counterfactually. For example, it may be that a woman is motivated by her thirst rather than her hunger, even though the latter is stronger than the former in this sense: if she had thought she could satisfy her hunger, that desire rather than her thirst would have motivated her. But the statement in the text seems to hold for *competing* desires, where two desires are competing if the agent believes it is now possible to satisfy either but not both. I owe this notion of a competing desire to Robert Audi.

theoretic and a psychological form. When the conflict takes the first form, it arises from the question of what to do. But motivational conflicts may persist after this question is settled. Here the strength of desires is revealed and the need for resistance emerges. The temperate are less susceptible than others to this motivational conflict. Their souls are harmonious. The continent are so susceptible, but manage to resist. The weak fail.

Why then do the continent manage successfully to resist, whereas the weak do not? The answer cannot be that the weak are subject to stronger desires than the continent, for this would not explain why they are weaker; nor would it enable us to distinguish weakness from compulsion. The proposal I now wish to entertain is the following. The weak and the strong may be subject to desires of exactly the same strength. What makes the former weak is that they give in to desires which the possession of the normal degree of self-control would enable them to resist. In contrast, compulsive desires are such that the normal capacities of resistance are or would be insufficient to enable the agent to resist. This fact about compulsive desires is what gives substance to the claim that they are too strong. The fact that weak agents' desires would be controlled by the exercise of the normal capacities of resistance gives point to the claim that these agents are weak.

Something like this distinction is suggested by a passage of Aristotle. He remarks that the difference between weakness and what we have called compulsion might depend on the fact that the desires which defeat the weak person are such that most people could have resisted:

> ... if a man is defeated by violent and excessive pleasures or pains, there is nothing wonderful in that; indeed we are ready to pardon him if he has resisted [is overcome while offering resistance—Ostwald] ... But it is surprising if a man is defeated by and cannot resist pleasures and pains which most men can hold out against, when this is not due to heredity and disease ... (*Nicomachean Ethics,* 1150b7 ff., Ross trans.).

This way of expressing the point is unfortunate; for it may suggest that desires are like barbells which most people can or cannot lift. Whatever the ontological status of desires, it does not seem intelligible to say of an inclination that a particular person has on a particular occasion, that most others would be able to hold out against that very inclination. It makes better sense to ask not whether other people could have resisted that particular motivation—but whether the individual would have been able to hold out had he or she possessed and exercised the kinds of capacity of self-control normally possessed by others, or whether persons of normal self-control would resist similar desires of the same strength. Such a counterfactual is no doubt formidable to establish, but at least it is intelligible. I suggest that when we believe it, or something like it, to be true of people who do not resist, we think them weak (the fault is with them, not with the opposing desires); when we believe that they could not have resisted even so, then we think of them as victims of compulsion (the fault is not with them, but rather their desires are too strong). (Perhaps this way of looking at the matter also presupposes that we believe weak persons both could and should possess and exercise those skills—otherwise it would not be their *fault*.) In this manner, we can distinguish among "temperance" and "continence" (in Aristotle's sense), weakness and compulsion. And we can avoid saying either that no desires are irresistible or that weakness is a case of compulsion.

In summary, then, there are capacities and skills of resistance which are generally acquired in the normal course of socialization and practice, and which we hold one another responsible for acquiring and maintaining. Weak agents fall short of standards of "reasonable and normal" self-control (for which we hold them responsible), whereas compulsive agents are motivated by desires which they could not resist even if they met those standards. That is why we focus on the weakness of the agent in the one case (it is the agent's fault), but on the power of the contrary motivation in the compulsive case. And this view allows explanations in terms of weakness of will to be significantly different from explanations in terms of compulsion. In the case of weakness, one acts contrary to one's better judgment *because one has failed* to meet standards of reasonable or normal self-control; whereas, this explanation does not hold of compulsive behavior.

Let us now note some of the implications of this proposal. One obvious point is that, on this account, a desire is compulsive (irresistible) or not only relative to certain norms of self-control; only relative to the capacities of the normal person, and this probably means the typical adult in our society. It may be true, for example, that having undergone from childhood an intensive program of discipline, such as yoga, would have enabled a person to resist certain desires now. But this fact would not incline us at all to withdraw the claim that the individual was suffering from compulsive desires. Hence the fact that one would be a weak person in a community of yogis does not mean that one would not be compulsive among us. (It does follow from this account, however, that weak agents are those with less self-control than most others in their society *in fact* have. Weakness is relative to expectations and norms, and it is conceivable that a whole community could fall short of these.)

The relativity of this viewpoint may conflict with our ordinary view of weakness; perhaps prior to reflection we think that a desire is either resistible or it isn't. Even so, it seems to me that this relativity is a desirable feature of the present account. We could define an absolute concept of compulsion in something like the following manner: an agent is motivated by a compulsive desire if *no* degree of training and discipline would have enabled him or her to resist. But it is an open question whether *any* desires are compulsive on this definition, and it does not seem to apply in the right way to the cases we think of as compulsive. Relativity is in any case a feature of the concept of weakness in general—for example, the concept of physical weakness. The possible existence of races of creatures who could lift 500-pound weights, or of training programs which would enable most of us to do so, would not mean that those of us who cannot lift this weight were physically weak.[12]

This doctrine accords fairly closely with typical moral attitudes toward weakness as well. In contrast to "bad characters," we do not criticize weak agents for their principles or values but for their failure to develop or maintain the capacities necessary to make those values effective in action. The appropriate blaming attitudes toward the weak, by themselves and others, are shame and (if one goes in for this sort of thing) contempt, not guilt and indignation. For the fault is not injustice, but lack of control. And since they have (or may have) the right values, they are as much an object of pity as reproach—from any point of view, *especially their own,*[13] they are in a bad way. Since shame characteristically involves falling short of shared standards of excellence in conduct, shame will often be appropriate in the case of weakness in a way in which it will not be for compulsion.[14]

The Proposed Account Versus the Common Account

The proposed account entails that the desires of weak agents are resistible in the sense that had they developed and maintained certain normal capacities of self-control, they would have resisted them. And to the degree to which we judge such agents blameworthy and responsible for their weak behavior, we believe they could and should have developed and maintained these capacities. So the weak must be constitutionally capable of meeting these standards. But these implications are consistent with their being unable at the time of action to resist. Hence, this account differs significantly from the common one. On the latter the ability to resist at the time of action is a distinguishing feature of weakness.

Morally, the proposed account likens weakness to negligence in its emphasis on the point that blameworthiness does not require that one be able to resist or that weak behavior be fully under voluntary control. For negligence is a paradigm case of blameworthy but nonvoluntary behavior. Engrossed in an interesting conversation, a man forgets to look both ways at the intersection and therefore collides with another vehicle. He does not do so voluntarily, or

---

[12] Note, however, that on this account I could easily be mistaken about whether my action was weak or compulsive, because I could be mistaken about what the relevant standards were. Indeed, in the absence of shared expectations and norms the distinction might come to lose its force altogether.

[13] For one's "point of view" includes preeminently the values which determine one's better judgment.

[14] To say that there is generally a moral contrast between weak and compulsive behavior is neither to deny that a compulsive may sometimes be blameworthy, nor to imply that a weak person always is. Just as compulsive agents may sometimes be responsible and blameworthy for having allowed themselves to become or remain compulsive, so the failure of the weak agent might be excusable, as Aristotle intimates, if it were due to "disease." Perhaps we would not or should not classify such a person as weak of will; we would not call a person negligent who was subnormally careless due to disease. If so, weakness of will differs in this respect from physical weakness, which carries no implication of responsibility.

even intentionally, and yet we may judge him blameworthy for failing to meet standards (or the "duty") of reasonable care. (To be sure, the man is engaged in numerous voluntary actions at the time of the collision, but colliding, for which he is blamed, is not among them.) Could he have remembered? It is not at all clear that he could have. Remembering is not in this case even an action. What we believe is that he should have remembered to look and because of this, that he falls short of standards of reasonable care. The accident is explained by his fault (just as weak behavior is explained by the agent's fault).[15]

Perhaps to think him blameworthy we must also believe that he could have been or become the kind of person who exercises reasonable care. But these beliefs do not entail that he was able, at the time of action, to avoid the accident. On the proposed account, the case of weak behavior is quite parallel. The weak person may be seen as negligent for failing to acquire the relevant capacities. And like the standard of normal self-control, the standard of reasonable care (and thus what counts as negligence) is relative to social norms and particular contexts. Moreover, like the weak person in the above example, the negligent person is not criticized for his values and judgments (he is not bad or unjust) but for failing to ensure that his behavior is informed by, and conforms to, those values and judgments. (However, unlike the negligent person, but like the compulsive, the weak person does of course act intentionally.)[16]

Therefore, the fact that on the proposed account weak agents may be no more able at the time of action to conform their behavior to their judgments than compulsives does not rob the distinction between weakness and compulsion of its moral significance. That distinction can be significantly drawn without requiring ability. I shall now argue that, furthermore, there are strong reasons for doubting that this requirement can be satisfied, and thus for rejecting this central feature of the common account. By the common account, the culpability of the drinker in our earlier example is located not in her failure to develop or maintain the normal capacity of resistance, but in her failure to exercise the capacity she possesses. The challenge to this account is to find a pertinent explanation of this failure.

---

[15] I do not suppose that the phenomenon of negligence is well understood; it poses some hard questions for the theory of responsibility. I would claim, however, that weakness resembles negligence in this respect, that both are nonvoluntary behavior thought to be open to blame. The important point is that the responsibility of weak agents is no more (or less) problematic than the responsibility of negligent agents.

[16] Some may wish to deny that compulsive behavior is, or can be, intentional if it is not free. This denial seems to me unjustified. For one thing, on leading views of intentionality, both compulsive and weak action will count as intentional. Both the compulsive and the weak person act on a "primary reason" (in Davidson's sense: "Actions, Reasons, and Causes", *Journal of Philosophy*, 1963.) Their behavior is consciously motivated; hence both may have "practical knowledge" and be able to answer a certain kind of question "Why?" (See E. Anscombe, *Intention.*) More decisively, compulsive and weak behavior both involve at least a minimal form of practical reasoning: the person with a dread fear of spiders may reason about how best to escape, a weak person about how best to obtain some cigarettes. To deny intentionality here is unjustifiably to conflate intentional with free action.

Generally, people fail to perform some action for a combination of the following kinds of reason: (*a*) they are unaware of the action as an option; (*b*) they do not want or choose to do it; or (*c*) they are unable to do it. Given awareness, nonperformance indicates lack of "power" or lack of "will" or both.[17] This is why inquiries into capacities and knowledge are relevant in contexts of moral appraisal. For instance, if you know that the curtains are burning, and you are able to extinguish the fire, I infer from your nonperformance that you did not want or choose to put the fire out. I thereby learn something important about your values and priorities. On the other hand, of course, if you did not choose to let the curtains burn, or did not even do it knowingly, you would not necessarily be exculpated, for your action or omission may be explained by your culpable ignorance or carelessness. Generally, then, culpable failures or omissions are explained either by lack of choice, or by culpable lack of care, knowledge, or ability.

The proposed account fits weakness into a scheme of this kind. Weak agents fail or neglect to meet certain standards of self-control, and their culpability does not require choice or ability at the time of action. The explanation of the weak agent's failure to act upon practical judgment involves attributing this failure to another culpable failure to develop or maintain the relevant capacities.

The challenge to the common account is to provide a similarly pertinent explanation of the weak person's failure. This failure is due neither to lack of knowledge nor, putatively, to lack of ability or negligence. To return to the case of the weak drinker, the woman judges that she should resist and therefore, by her own lights, has sufficient reason for exercising her alleged capacity. What might explain her not doing so?

There seem to me only two possible explanations. (1) She *chooses* not to. (2) Her *effort* to resist is culpably insufficient. Both of these explanations will be found inadequate.

(1) First, the notion of choice (and also decision) seems to me to involve the notion of applying one's values to the perceived practical options. (Aristotle is close when he speaks of choice as desire in accordance with deliberation.) In this sense, it is of course generally true that one may choose not to exercise some capacity that one has. But the capacity of self-control is special in this respect. For the capacity of self-control involves the capacity to counteract and resist the strength of desires which are contrary to what one has chosen or judged best to do. The weak drinker's failure to resist her desire to drink is a failure to implement her choice not to drink. To choose not to implement this choice would be to change her original judgment, and the case would no longer be a case of failure to implement judgment. Therefore, the weak agent's failure to resist the drink cannot intelligibly be explained by her choice.

Equally important, even if it made sense to explain her failure in this way, doing so would result in the moral assimilation of the weak case to the reckless

---

[17] This theme is pursued in Chapter 2 of Stuart Hampshire's *Freedom of the Individual*.

case. The common account rightly wishes to distinguish these, but the difference would collapse if both involved choice.

(2) Second, it might be supposed that the drinker's failure is to be explained by her culpably insufficient *effort*. Sometimes we attribute a person's failure, not to absence of ability or choice, but to lack of sufficient effort.[18] I may try and fail to throw a coin across the Schuylkill River even when I wanted very much to do so and was able to do so. The explanation may be that I misjudged either the amount of effort required or the distance across. Or in a basketball game, my failure to make a jump-shot from the free-throw line might be explained by insufficient concentration rather than lack of capability or will. Using "effort" to include both physical exertion and psychological factors such as concentration and "keeping one's head," in both cases, we may suppose, I not only would have succeeded with greater effort, but could have made the requisite effort.

Perhaps weakness of will is commonly viewed as involving insufficient effort. In order to help here, an explanation of this kind must be conjoined with the assumption that the weak person is able to make the requisite effort to resist. For obviously, if effort of a certain kind and degree is necessary to successful resistance, it will be true that the drinker is able to resist only if she has the capacity to make an effort of that kind and degree to resist. Our focus is thus shifted to her failure of effort, and everything now turns on why she does not make *it*. But it is far from clear what explanation is forthcoming.

The explanation cannot be that making the effort is not thought to be worth it. For once again, implicit in the judgment that it is best not to drink is the judgment that it is best to resist contrary desires. If the drinker really judges that it is not worth that much effort, she either changes her mind or originally only made a conditional judgment of the form: it is best not to drink unless not doing so requires too much effort.

The explanation cannot be that she misjudged the amount of effort required. I may have underestimated how much exertion would be required to throw the coin across the Schuylkill, or how much concentration was necessary to make the basket. But it is not clear what the analogue to this in the case of resisting a drink would be. And even if misjudgment were involved, that would be a different fault from weakness of will.

So we do not seem to have a pertinent explanation of why the weak drinker fails to exert adequate effort. No doubt her failure has something to do with the relative strengths of her desires to resist and to drink. But *this* is not enough for the common account, since it is consistent with her being unable to make the effort. Inasmuch as she has the same good reasons for making the effort to resist as for not drinking, we need an explanation which makes it clear that she is able to resist. For even if some (further) effort would enable her to resist, the desire to drink may generate desires not to make this effort (in the way

---

[18] I owe my appreciation of this point to the editors of *The Philosophical Review*.

that desires frequently cause other desires for the means to their fulfillment) and these may be irresistibly strong.

Given her strong motive for making an effort (namely, her considered practical judgment), and in the absence of a special explanation for her not making it (such as "I didn't think it was worth it," or "I didn't think it was necessary"), we are entitled to be skeptical about the common view, and to conclude that the person was unable to resist.

Conclusion

Socrates found the common conception of weakness of will to be confused. However, his reasons for rejecting that account are unsound. They deny the morally and psychologically important complexity of human motivation, and in particular the potential divergence between certain kinds of desire and judgments of the good. This divergence is what makes room for the virtue of self-control and, obversely, the vice of weakness of will.

Just the same, I have offered doubts of a nonsocratic sort about the common account of weakness. To take seriously the possibility of acting contrary to one's better judgment is at the same time to raise problems about the distinction between weakness and compulsion. I have argued that the common view, according to which the differentiating feature is that the weak are able to conform their behavior to their practical judgments, is unjustified. Instead, I have proposed that weakness of will involves the failure to develop certain normal capacities of self-control, whereas compulsion involves desires which even the possession of such capacities would not enable one to resist.

II

MORAL
EPISTEMOLOGY

OUR ATTITUDE TOWARD moral claims is not straightforward. On the one hand, we often deliberate, debate, and even agonize about what we morally ought to do. That we engage in these activities suggests that we believe there are correct answers to questions about right and wrong. It also suggests that we have some confidence in our ability to discover these answers. Yet many have doubted the objectivity of morals. For a variety of reasons, ethical judgments can seem to depend more on us, and less on external facts, than corresponding judgments about science or the everyday world. Obviously, there are questions about whether these attitudes can be reconciled, and, if not, about which of them should prevail. Because the branch of philosophy that studies knowledge is known as epistemology, these are questions of *moral epistemology*.

Can we coherently say that the world contains objective moral facts, and that these facts are accessible to human knowers? Both G. E. Moore and W. D. Ross believe that we can. In reading 9, Moore asks what ethical properties—goodness and (by extension) rightness—could be like. According to Moore, such properties cannot be identified with any combinations of "natural" properties such as color, shape, or the ability to produce sensation. For example, we cannot identify goodness with the tendency to produce happiness, or with the property of being an object that we wish to desire. Of any such tendency or property, it makes sense to ask, "but *is* it good?" Moreover, it is always conceivable that the answer might be "no." Thus, goodness must be a different sort of property altogether. To distinguish goodness from everything in the natural realm, Moore calls it a *nonnatural* property.

If nonnatural properties exist, how can we know that acts or states of affairs possess them? This question is addressed by W. D. Ross. In reading 10 (and again in reading 31), Ross compares our knowledge of moral truths with our knowledge of the truths of arithmetic. Although numbers are not constituents of the natural world like tables and chairs, we recognize (or can be led to recognize) the relations between them. And just as we immediately apprehend that $2 + 3 = 5$, we may recognize that a given act of charity is required, or that a certain lie is wrong. Having understood this, we may generalize our conclusion to apply to all similar acts. We might accept Ross's view that ethical truths are known through a kind of intuition without accepting Moore's view that ethical properties are nonnatural; but it is harder to see how we could accept Moore's nonnaturalism without also accepting Ross's intuitionism.

Should we accept either? Although Moore and Ross do capture one strand of our ethical thinking, their accounts raise many further questions. Is it legitimate to complicate our world picture by admitting such strange entities as nonnatural properties? If these properties exist, how do they interact with the natural world? How, in particular, can they bring us to do things that we would not otherwise be inclined to do? Why isn't there more agreement about which acts and occurrences possess them? And how much is really explained by saying that we simply recognize goodness or rightness?

The next four readings explore these challenges. Consider first the issue of disagreement. If what is right or wrong is independent of the attitudes of individuals or groups, it may seem that even people of widely differing backgrounds should agree about what is right. But anthropological data suggest that different cultures hold widely divergent values and norms. This has led some to hold that what one ought to do is just what is approved of or commanded by one's society. On this view, known as *normative relativism,* the members of societies that condone polygamy or ritual murder are morally permitted to practice these activities; but because our own society forbids such acts, we are not. According to normative relativism, there is no deeper truth about how everyone ought to act.

As we just saw, it is customary to defend normative relativism by appealing to anthropological evidence. Yet as Paul Taylor argues in reading 11, it is not clear that this evidence proves that societies disagree about the most basic values. It may be, instead, that most, or all, societies accept the same ultimate principles, but that differences of history, belief, and economic and geographic circumstance have led societies to embrace different secondary codes. Moreover, even if societies do hold differing ultimate principles, Taylor argues that this by itself does not establish normative relativism. Nor, we may add, do we clearly avoid commitment to independent moral facts by saying that what each person ought to do is what his society commands or approves.

Accepting normative relativism is one way of capturing the idea that right and wrong have some important connection to human attitudes. But other theories also capture this idea. In reading 12, A. J. Ayer advances the more extreme view that ethical utterances do not describe anything at all, but merely express the attitudes of speakers toward acts. For example, when we say that a cruel act is wrong, or that an agent should not have behaved cruelly, we express our disapproval and exhort others to refrain from similar acts. The difference between describing and expressing our attitudes is that only through description do we say what is true or false. A moan of pain, or a grunt of disgust, may vent one's feelings, but it has no truth-value. Because Ayer's theory denies that ethical utterances are true or false, it implies that there is literally nothing to know about ethics. Hence, it belongs to a type of theory known as *noncognitive*. Because it assimilates ethical discourse to the expression of emotion, Ayer's theory is often referred to as the *emotive theory*.

Noncognitivism implies that ethical utterances are not made true by moral facts; but we may reject noncognitivism without embracing moral facts. As Gilbert Harman and J. L. Mackie point out, there may simply be no good reason to accept such facts. In reading 13, Harman contends that although we need to postulate scientific facts to explain our observations of the world, we may not need to postulate moral facts to explain our moral observations or beliefs. When someone observes that an act such as setting a cat afire for fun is wrong, the explanation may lie solely in his psychological conditioning and other nonmoral facts. Although Harman ultimately defends a version of relativism, and so holds that moral facts can be reduced to natural facts, his position here is that introducing independent moral facts may be unreasonable. And to this, J. L. Mackie adds that various "patterns of objectification" would lead us to believe that the world contained objective moral values whether or not it really did. For example, all communities impose demands on their members for the common good; and these (merely social) demands are easily confused with the demands of an objective morality. Mackie also argues that independently existing moral values—what others call moral facts—would be such strange entities that their existence is implausible, and that the well-known variation among moral codes is most easily explained if we abandon objectivism. For these and other reasons, Mackie denies that there are objective values.

Can objectivists respond to these arguments? In the next two readings, two philosophers take up the challenge. In reading 15, Nicholas Sturgeon carefully criticizes Harman's position, arguing that Harman has not successfully made the case against moral facts. As we have seen, Harman's contention is that moral facts seem to play no role in explaining our observations. To establish this, Harman must assume, for purposes of argument, that such facts do exist. But Sturgeon argues that once we assume this, we find that moral facts "*do* appear relevant, by perfectly ordinary standards, to the explanation of moral beliefs and of a good deal else besides." If we discount their explanatory role, we must also discount the role of tables and chairs in explaining our observations of the world. Thus, Sturgeon concludes that the only remaining arguments against moral facts are general skeptical arguments.

By thus defending moral objectivity, Sturgeon appears to accept Harman's way of framing the problem. He seems to agree that the basic question is whether moral facts are needed to explain moral observations or judgments. Yet this assumption may itself be questioned. As Mackie reminds us in reading

14, the issue is not just the truth of moral judgments, but also their authority over action. This may lead us to be even more skeptical about the existence of independent moral values—that is Mackie's response—but it may also lead us to seek a different understanding of moral objectivity. In reading 16, John Rawls takes the latter tack. He proposes that moral objectivity is best understood in terms of a rationally defensible procedure for arriving at moral principles, and for settling conflicts among them. By sketching such a "decision procedure for ethics," Rawls defends its objectivity in the specified sense.

9

Goodness as Simple and Indefinable

G. E. MOORE

G. E. Moore (1873–1958) taught for many years at Cambridge University. An influential figure in twentieth-century philosophy, he made important contributions both in the theory of knowledge and in ethics. His major works include Principia Ethica, Ethics, *and* Philosophical Studies.

In this selection, taken from Principia Ethica, *Moore asks what sort of thing goodness is. His question has important implications for moral knowledge. If goodness is a property in the natural world—if, for instance, it is the tendency to make people happy—then we can discover its existence by using ordinary empirical methods. But if goodness is not a natural property, then our knowledge of it must take some other form.*

Moore believes that goodness is neither a simple nor a composite natural property. Rather than being definable in any simpler terms, goodness is one of the simple elements in terms of which other things may be defined. But it cannot be identified with any of the simple things that are found in nature. If goodness could be defined as pleasure, then the question, "Is pleasure good?" would boil down to the triviality, "Is pleasure pleasant?" But the two questions are not the same. In general, Moore is more explicit about what goodness is not than about what it is. However, the core of his view— that goodness differs from anything that is empirically discoverable, yet still has some sort of objective existence—is clear enough. According to many, this view contains an important element of truth.

. . .

THAT WHICH IS meant by 'good' is, in fact, except its converse 'bad,' the *only* simple object of thought which is peculiar to Ethics. Its definition is, therefore, the most essential point in the definition of Ethics; and moreover a mistake with regard to it entails a far larger number of erroneous ethical judgments than any other. Unless this first question be fully understood, and its true answer clearly recognised, the rest of Ethics is as good as useless from the point of view of systematic knowledge. True ethical judgments, of the two kinds last dealt with, may indeed be made by those who do not know the answer to this question as well as by those who do; and it goes without saying that the two classes of people may lead equally good lives. But it is extremely unlikely that the *most general* ethical judgments will be equally valid, in the absence of a true answer to this question: I shall presently try to shew that the gravest errors have been largely due to beliefs in a false answer. And, in any case, it is impossible that, till the answer to this question be known, any one should know *what is the evidence* for any ethical judgment whatsoever. But the main object of Ethics, as a systematic science, is to give correct *reasons* for thinking that this or that is good; and, unless this question be answered, such reasons cannot be given. Even, therefore, apart from the fact that a false answer leads to false conclusions, the present enquiry is a most necessary and important part of the science of Ethics.

6. What, then, is good? How is good to be defined? Now, it may be thought that this is a verbal question. A definition does indeed often mean the expressing of one word's meaning in other words. But this is not the sort of definition I am asking for. Such a definition can never be of ultimate importance in any study except lexicography. If I wanted that kind of definition I should have to consider in the first place how people generally used the word 'good'; but my business is not with its proper usage, as established by custom. I should, indeed, be foolish, if I tried to use it for something which it did not usually denote: if, for instance, I were to announce that, whenever I used the word 'good,' I must be understood to be thinking of that object which is usually denoted by the word 'table.' I shall, therefore, use the word in the sense in which I think it is ordinarily used; but at the same time I am not anxious to discuss whether I am right in thinking that it is so used. My business is solely with that object or idea, which I hold, rightly or wrongly, that the word is generally used to stand for. What I want to discover is the nature of that object or idea, and about this I am extremely anxious to arrive at an agreement.

But, if we understand the question in this sense, my answer to it may seem a very disappointing one. If I am asked 'What is good?' my answer is that good is good, and that is the end of the matter. Or if I am asked 'How is good to be defined?' my answer is that it cannot be defined, and that is all I have to say about it. But disappointing as these answers may appear, they are of the very last importance. To readers who are familiar with philosophic terminology, I can express their importance by saying that they amount to this: That propositions about the good are all of them synthetic and never analytic; and that is plainly no trivial matter. And the same thing may be expressed more popularly, by saying that, if I am right, then nobody can foist upon us such an axiom as that 'Pleasure is the only good' or that 'The good is the desired' on the pretence that this is 'the very meaning of the word.'

7. Let us, then, consider this position. My point is that 'good' is a simple notion, just as 'yellow' is a simple notion; that, just as you cannot, by any manner of means, explain to any one who does not already know it, what yellow is, so you cannot explain what good is. Definitions of the kind that I was asking for, definitions which describe the real nature of the object or notion denoted by a word, and which do not merely tell us what the word is used to mean, are only possible when the object or notion in question is something complex. You can give a definition of a horse, because a horse has many different properties and qualities, all of which you can enumerate. But when you

have enumerated them all, when you have reduced a horse to his simplest terms, then you can no longer define those terms. They are simply something which you think of or perceive, and to any one who cannot think of or perceive them, you can never, by any definition, make their nature known. It may perhaps be objected to this that we are able to describe to others, objects which they have never seen or thought of. We can, for instance, make a man understand what a chimaera is, although he has never heard of one or seen one. You can tell him that it is an animal with a lioness's head and body, with a goat's head growing from the middle of its back, and with a snake in place of a tail. But here the object which you are describing is a complex object; it is entirely composed of parts, with which we are all perfectly familiar—a snake, a goat, a lioness; and we know, too, the manner in which those parts are to be put together, because we know what is meant by the middle of a lioness's back, and where her tail is wont to grow. And so it is with all objects, not previously known, which we are able to define: they are all complex; all composed of parts, which may themselves, in the first instance, be capable of similar definition, but which must in the end be reducible to simplest parts, which can no longer be defined. But yellow and good, we say, are not complex: they are notions of that simple kind, out of which definitions are composed and with which the power of further defining ceases.

8. When we say, as Webster says, 'The definition of horse is "A hoofed quadruped of the genus Equus," ' we may, in fact, mean three different things. (1) We may mean merely: 'When I say "horse," you are to understand that I am talking about a hoofed quadruped of the genus Equus.' This might be called the arbitrary verbal definition: and I do not mean that good is indefinable in that sense. (2) We may mean, as Webster ought to mean: 'When most English people say "horse," they mean a hoofed quadruped of the genus Equus.' This may be called the verbal definition proper, and I do not say that good is indefinable in this sense either; for it is certainly possible to discover how people use a word: otherwise, we could never have known that 'good' may be translated by 'gut' in German and by 'bon' in French. But (3) we may, when we define horse, mean something much more important. We may mean that a certain object, which we all of us know, is composed in a certain manner: that it has four legs, a head, a heart, a liver, etc., etc., all of them arranged in definite relations to one another. It is in this sense that I deny good to be definable. I say that it is not composed of any parts, which we can substitute for it in our minds when we are thinking of it. We might think just as clearly and correctly about a horse, if we thought of all its parts and their arrangement instead of thinking of the whole; we could, I say, think how a horse differed from a donkey just as well, just as truly, in this way, as now we do, only not so easily; but there is nothing whatsoever which we could so substitute for good; and that is what I mean, when I say that good is indefinable.

9. But I am afraid I have still not removed the chief difficulty which may prevent acceptance of the proposition that good is indefinable. I do not mean to say that *the* good, that which is good, is thus indefinable; if I did think so, I should not be writing on Ethics, for my main object is to help towards

discovering that definition. It is just because I think there will be less risk of error in our search for a definition of 'the good,' that I am now insisting that *good* is indefinable. I must try to explain the difference between these two. I suppose it may be granted that 'good' is an adjective. Well 'the good, that which is good,' must therefore be the substantive to which the adjective 'good' will apply: it must be the whole of that to which the adjective will apply, and the adjective must *always* truly apply to it. But if it is that to which the adjective will apply, it must be something different from that adjective itself; and the whole of that something different, whatever it is, will be our definition of *the* good. Now it may be that this something will have other adjectives, beside 'good,' that will apply to it. It may be full of pleasure, for example: it may be intelligent: and if these two adjectives are really part of its definition, then it will certainly be true, that pleasure and intelligence are good. And many people appear to think that, if we say 'Pleasure and intelligence are good,' or if we say 'Only pleasure and intelligence are good,' we are defining 'good.' Well, I cannot deny that propositions of this nature may sometimes be called definitions; I do not know well enough how the word is generally used to decide upon this point. I only wish it to be understood that that is not what I mean when I say there is no possible definition of good, and that I shall not mean this if I use the word again. I do most fully believe that some true proposition of the form 'Intelligence is good and intelligence alone is good' can be found; if none could be found, our definition of *the* good would be impossible. As it is, I believe *the* good to be definable; and yet I still say that good itself is indefinable.

10. 'Good,' then, if we mean by it that quality which we assert to belong to a thing, when we say that the thing is good, is incapable of any definition, in the most important sense of that word. The most important sense of 'definition' is that in which a definition states what are the parts which invariably compose a certain whole; and in this sense 'good' has no definition because it is simple and has no parts. It is one of those innumerable objects of thought which are themselves incapable of definition, because they are the ultimate terms by reference to which whatever *is* capable of definition must be defined. That there must be an indefinite number of such terms is obvious, on reflection; since we cannot define anything except by an analysis, which, when carried as far as it will go, refers us to something, which is simply different from anything else, and which by that ultimate difference explains the peculiarity of the whole which we are defining: for every whole contains some parts which are common to other wholes also. There is, therefore, no intrinsic difficulty in the contention that 'good' denotes a simple and indefinable quality. There are many other instances of such qualities.

Consider yellow, for example. We may try to define it, by describing its physical equivalent; we may state what kind of light-vibrations must stimulate the normal eye, in order that we may perceive it. But a moment's reflection is sufficient to shew that those light-vibrations are not themselves what we mean by yellow. *They* are not what we perceive. Indeed we should never have been able to discover their existence, unless we had first been struck by the patent difference of quality between the different colours. The most we can be entitled to say of those vibrations is that they are what corresponds in space to the yellow which we actually perceive.

Yet a mistake of this simple kind has commonly been made about 'good.' It may be true that all things which are good are *also* something else, just as it is true that all things which are yellow produce a certain kind of vibration in the light. And it is a fact, that Ethics aims at discovering what are those other properties belonging to all things which are good. But far too many philosophers have thought that when they named those other properties they were actually defining good; that these properties, in fact, were simply not 'other,' but absolutely and entirely the same with goodness. This view I propose to call the 'naturalistic fallacy' and of it I shall now endeavour to dispose.

11. Let us consider what it is such philosophers say. And first it is to be noticed that they do not agree among themselves. They not only say that they are right as to what good is, but they endeavour to prove that other people who say that it is something else, are wrong. One, for instance, will affirm that good is pleasure, another, perhaps, that good is that which is desired; and each of these will argue eagerly to prove that the other is wrong. But how is that possible? One of them says that good is nothing but the object of desire, and at the same time tries to prove that it is not pleasure. But from his first assertion, that good just means the object of desire, one of two things must follow as regards his proof:

(1) He may be trying to prove that the object of desire is not pleasure. But, if this be all, where is his Ethics? The position he is maintaining is merely a psychological one. Desire is something which occurs in our minds, and pleasure is something else which so occurs; and our would-be ethical philosopher is merely holding that the latter is not the object of the former. But what has that to do with the question in dispute? His opponent held the ethical proposition that pleasure was the good, and although he should prove a million times over the psychological proposition that pleasure is not the object of desire, he is no nearer proving his opponent to be wrong. The position is like this. One man says a triangle is a circle: another replies 'A triangle is a straight line, and I will prove to you that I am right: *for*' (this is the only argument) 'a straight line is not a circle.' 'That is quite true,' the other may reply; 'but nevertheless a triangle is a circle, and you have said nothing whatever to prove the contrary. What is proved is that one of us is wrong, for we agree that a triangle cannot be both a straight line and a circle: but which is wrong, there can be no earthly means of proving, since you define triangle as straight line and I define it as circle.'—Well, that is one alternative which any naturalistic Ethics has to face; if good is *defined* as something else, it is then impossible either to prove that any other definition is wrong or even to deny such definition.

(2) The other alternative will scarcely be more welcome. It is that the discussion is after all a verbal one. When A says 'Good means pleasant' and B says 'Good means desired,' they may merely wish to assert that most people have used the word for what is pleasant and for what is desired respectively. And this is quite an interesting subject for discussion: only it is not a whit more

an ethical discussion than the last was. Nor do I think that any exponent of naturalistic Ethics would be willing to allow that this was all he meant. They are all so anxious to persuade us that what they call the good is what we really ought to do. 'Do, pray, act so, because the word "good" is generally used to denote actions of this nature': such, on this view, would be the substance of their teaching. And in so far as they tell us how we ought to act, their teaching is truly ethical, as they mean it to be. But how perfectly absurd is the reason they would give for it! 'You are to do this, because most people use a certain word to denote conduct such as this.' 'You are to say the thing which is not, because most people call it lying.' That is an argument just as good!—My dear sirs, what we want to know from you as ethical teachers, is not how people use a word; it is not even, what kind of actions they approve, which the use of this word 'good' may certainly imply: what we want to know is simply what *is* good. We may indeed agree that what most people do think good, is actually so; we shall at all events be glad to know their opinions: but when we say their opinions about what *is* good, we do mean what we say; we do not care whether they call that thing which they mean 'horse' or 'table' or 'chair,' 'gut' or 'bon' or 'ἀγαθός'; we want to know what it is that they so call. When they say 'Pleasure is good,' we cannot believe that they merely mean 'Pleasure is pleasure' and nothing more than that.

12. Suppose a man says 'I am pleased'; and suppose that is not a lie or a mistake but the truth. Well, if it is true, what does that mean? It means that his mind, a certain definite mind, distinguished by certain definite marks from all others, has at this moment a certain definite feeling called pleasure. 'Pleased' *means* nothing but having pleasure, and though we may be more pleased or less pleased, and even, we may admit for the present, have one or another kind of pleasure; yet in so far as it is pleasure we have, whether there be more or less of it, and whether it be of one kind or another, what we have is one definite thing, absolutely indefinable, some one thing that is the same in all the various degrees and all the various kinds of it that there may be. We may be able to say how it is related to other things: that, for example, it is in the mind, that it causes desire, that we are conscious of it, etc., etc. We can, I say, describe its relations to other things, but define it we can *not*. And if anybody tried to define pleasure for us as being any other natural object; if anybody were to say, for instance, that pleasure *means* the sensation of red, and were to proceed to deduce from that that pleasure is a colour, we should be entitled to laugh at him and to distrust his future statements about pleasure. Well, that would be the same fallacy which I have called the naturalistic fallacy. That 'pleased' does not mean 'having the sensation of red,' or anything else whatever, does not prevent us from understanding what it does mean. It is enough for us to know that 'pleased' does mean 'having the sensation of pleasure,' and though pleasure is absolutely indefinable, though pleasure is pleasure and nothing else whatever, yet we feel no difficulty in saying that we are pleased. The reason is, of course, that when I say 'I am pleased,' I do *not* mean that 'I' am the same thing as 'having pleasure.' And similarly no difficulty need be found in my saying that 'pleasure is good' and yet not meaning that 'pleasure' is the same

thing as 'good,' that pleasure *means* good, and that good *means* pleasure. If I were to imagine that when I said 'I am pleased,' I meant that I was exactly the same thing as 'pleased,' I should not indeed call that a naturalistic fallacy, although it would be the same fallacy as I have called naturalistic with reference to Ethics. The reason of this is obvious enough. When a man confuses two natural objects with one another, defining the one by the other, if for instance, he confuses himself, who is one natural object, with 'pleased' or with 'pleasure' which are others, then there is no reason to call the fallacy naturalistic. But if he confuses 'good,' which is not in the same sense a natural object, with any natural object whatever, then there is a reason for calling that a naturalistic fallacy; its being made with regard to 'good' marks it as something quite specific, and this specific mistake deserves a name because it is so common. As for the reasons why good is not to be considered a natural object, they may be reserved for discussion in another place. But, for the present, it is sufficient to notice this: Even if it were a natural object, that would not alter the nature of the fallacy nor diminish its importance one whit. All that I have said about it would remain quite equally true: only the name which I have called it would not be so appropriate as I think it is. And I do not care about the name: what I do care about is the fallacy. It does not matter what we call it, provided we recognise it when we meet with it. It is to be met with in almost every book on Ethics; and yet it is not recognised: and that is why it is necessary to multiply illustrations of it, and convenient to give it a name. It is a very simple fallacy indeed. When we say that an orange is yellow, we do not think our statement binds us to hold that 'orange' means nothing else than 'yellow,' or that nothing can be yellow but an orange. Supposing the orange is also sweet! Does that bind us to say that 'sweet' is exactly the same thing as 'yellow,' that 'sweet' must be defined as 'yellow'? And supposing it be recognised that 'yellow' just means 'yellow' and nothing else whatever, does that make it any more difficult to hold that oranges are yellow? Most certainly it does not: on the contrary, it would be absolutely meaningless to say that oranges were yellow, unless yellow did in the end mean just 'yellow' and nothing else whatever—unless it was absolutely indefinable. We should not get any very clear notion about things, which are yellow—we should not get very far with our science, if we were bound to hold that everything which was yellow, *meant* exactly the same thing as yellow. We should find we had to hold that an orange was exactly the same thing as a stool, a piece of paper, a lemon, anything you like. We could prove any number of absurdities; but should we be the nearer to the truth? Why, then, should it be different with 'good'? Why, if good is good and indefinable, should I be held to deny that pleasure is good? Is there any difficulty in holding both to be true at once? On the contrary, there is no meaning in saying that pleasure is good, unless good is something different from pleasure. It is absolutely useless, so far as Ethics is concerned, to prove, as Mr Spencer tries to do, that increase of pleasure coincides with increase of life, unless good *means* something different from either life or pleasure. He might just as well try to prove that an orange is yellow by shewing that it always is wrapped up in paper.

13. In fact, if it is not the case that 'good' denotes something simple and indefinable, only two alternatives are possible: either it is a complex, a given whole, about the correct analysis of which there may be disagreement; or else it means nothing at all, and there is no such subject as Ethics. In general, however, ethical philosophers have attempted to define good, without recognising what such an attempt must mean. They actually use arguments which involve one or both of the absurdities considered in § 11. We are, therefore, justified in concluding that the attempt to define good is chiefly due to want of clearness as to the possible nature of definition. There are, in fact, only two serious alternatives to be considered, in order to establish the conclusion that 'good' does denote a simple and indefinable notion. It might possibly denote a complex, as 'horse' does; or it might have no meaning at all. Neither of these possibilities has, however, been clearly conceived and seriously maintained, as such, by those who presume to define good; and both may be dismissed by a simple appeal to facts.

(1) The hypothesis that disagreement about the meaning of good is disagreement with regard to the correct analysis of a given whole, may be most plainly seen to be incorrect by consideration of the fact that, whatever definition be offered, it may be always asked, with significance, of the complex so defined, whether it is itself good. To take, for instance, one of the more plausible, because one of the more complicated, of such proposed definitions, it may easily be thought, at first sight, that to be good may mean to be that which we desire to desire. Thus if we apply this definition to a particular instance and say 'When we think that A is good, we are thinking that A is one of the things which we desire to desire,' our proposition may seem quite plausible. But, if we carry the investigation further, and ask ourselves 'Is it good to desire to desire A?' it is apparent, on a little reflection, that this question is itself as intelligible, as the original question 'Is A good?'—that we are in fact, now asking for exactly the same information about the desire to desire A, for which we formerly asked with regard to A itself. But it is also apparent that the meaning of this second question cannot be correctly analysed into 'Is the desire to desire A one of the things which we desire to desire?': we have not before our minds anything so complicated as the question 'Do we desire to desire to desire to desire A?' Moreover any one can easily convince himself by inspection that the predicate of this proposition—'good'—is positively different from the notion of 'desiring to desire' which enters into its subject: 'That we should desire to desire A is good' is *not* merely equivalent to 'That A should be good is good.' It may indeed be true that what we desire to desire is always also good; perhaps, even the converse may be true: but it is very doubtful whether this is the case, and the mere fact that we understand very well what is meant by doubting it, shews clearly that we have two different notions before our minds.

(2) And the same consideration is sufficient to dismiss the hypothesis that 'good' has no meaning whatsoever. It is very natural to make the mistake of supposing that what is universally true is of such a nature that its negation would be self-contradictory: the importance which has been assigned to analytic propositions in the history of philosophy shews how easy such a mistake

is. And thus it is very easy to conclude that what seems to be a universal ethical principle is in fact an identical proposition; that, if, for example, whatever is called 'good' seems to be pleasant, the proposition 'Pleasure is the good' does not assert a connection between two different notions, but involves only one, that of pleasure, which is easily recognised as a distinct entity. But whoever will attentively consider with himself what is actually before his mind when he asks the question 'Is pleasure (or whatever it may be) after all good?' can easily satisfy himself that he is not merely wondering whether pleasure is pleasant. And if he will try this experiment with each suggested definition in succession, he may become expert enough to recognise that in every case he has before his mind a unique object, with regard to the connection of which with any other object, a distinct question may be asked. Every one does in fact understand the question 'Is this good?' When he thinks of it, his state of mind is different from what it would be, were he asked 'Is this pleasant, or desired, or approved?' It has a distinct meaning for him, even though he may not recognise in what respect it is distinct. Whenever he thinks of 'intrinsic value,' or 'intrinsic worth,' or says that a thing 'ought to exist,' he has before his mind the unique object—the unique property of things—which I mean by 'good.' Everybody is constantly aware of this notion, although he may never become aware at all that it is different from other notions of which he is also aware. But, for correct ethical reasoning, it is extremely important that he should become aware of this fact; and, as soon as the nature of the problem is clearly understood, there should be little difficulty in advancing so far in analysis.

. . .

10

Our Intuitive Knowledge of Right and Wrong

W. D. ROSS

Sir William David Ross (1877–1971) was Provost of Oriel College, Oxford University. His views on ethics, set forth in The Right and the Good *and* Foundations of Ethics, *continue to command widespread attention. He also published influential translations of, and commentaries upon, the works of Aristotle.*

In this short excerpt from Foundations of Ethics, *Ross sketches his account of how we know what is right and wrong. According to him, we begin by directly recognizing that a particular act is right or wrong, and then go on to generalize our conclusion to encompass all similar acts. (In reading 31, Ross claims that the rightness of types of acts is self-evident, but the rightness of particular acts is not. Whether that is consistent with what he says in this reading is left for further thought.)*

When Ross says that we directly recognize that particular acts are right, he does not mean to say that rightness, like yellowness or loudness, can be perceived through sensory experience. Rather, he holds that rightness is "an attribute that an act has because it has another attribute." It is only this other attribute that may be perceived through sensory experience. Because Ross believes this, his view has important affinities to G. E. Moore's contention, advanced in reading 9, that goodness is a nonnatural property. It is also closely related to Sturgeon's claim, in reading 15, that "moral features supervene on more basic natural properties."

I TURN NEXT to the epistemological questions connected with duty. Can we be said to *know* our duty? And if we can, how do we acquire this knowledge? I will start with a simple case. I am walking along the street, and I see a blind man at a loss to get across the street through the stream of traffic. I probably do not ask myself what I ought to do, but more or less instinctively take him by the arm and pilot him across. But if afterwards I stop to ask whether I have done what I ought, I shall almost certainly say 'Yes'; and if for any reason I ask myself, before doing the act, whether I ought to do it, I shall give the same answer. Now it is clear that it is in virtue of my thinking the act to have some other character that I think I ought to do it. Rightness is always a resultant attribute, an attribute that an act has because it has another attribute. It is not an attribute that its subject is just directly perceived in experience to have, as I perceive a particular extended patch to be yellow, or a particular noise to be loud. No doubt there are causes which cause this patch to be yellow, or that noise to be loud; but I can perceive the one to be yellow, or the other to be loud, without knowing anything of the causes that account for this. I see the attributes in question to attach to the subjects merely as these subjects, not as subjects of such and such a character. On the other hand, it is only by knowing or thinking my act to have a particular character, out of the many that it in fact has, that I know or think it to be right. It is, among other things, the directing of a physical body in a certain direction, but I never dream that it is right in consequence of that. I think that it is right because it is the relieving of a human being from distress. Now it seems at first sight to follow from this that our perception of the particular duty follows from the perception of a general duty to relieve human beings in distress. And, generalizing, we might feel inclined to say that our perception of particular duties is always an act of inference, in which the major premiss is some general moral principle. And no doubt my grasp of the principle that I should relieve human beings in distress precedes my grasp of the fact that I should relieve this blind man, since up to this moment I may not have known of the existence of this man, and certainly did not know of his desire to cross this particular street; while I certainly had at least a latent awareness of the general principle, an awareness which the occurrence of *any* instance falling under the principle might call into activity— just as I have a latent knowledge of the laws of arithmetic or of English grammar before I proceed to make up my accounts or to write a letter.

Yet it will not do to make our perception of particular duties essentially inference from general principles. For it may, I suppose, be taken for granted that man was a practical being before he became a theoretical one, and that in particular he answered somehow the question how he ought to behave in particular circumstances, before he engaged in general speculation on the principles of duty. No doubt there was an earlier stage still, when men in fact did right acts without ever asking whether they were right, when, for instance, they helped one another in distress without thinking of any duty to do so. We see disinterested help being given by men to one another every day, without any thought of duty. Aristotle puts the point simply:

'Parent seems by nature to feel friendship for offspring and offspring for parent, not only among men but among birds and among most animals; it is felt mutually by members of the same race, and especially by men. . . . We may see even in our travels how near and dear every man is to every other.'

Butler puts the matter more eloquently:

'There is such a natural principle of attraction in man towards man, that having trod the same tract of land, having breathed in the same climate, barely having been born in the same artificial district or division, becomes the occasion of contracting acquaintances and familiarities many years after: for any thing may serve the purpose. Thus relations merely nominal are sought and invented, not by governors, but by the lowest of the people; which are found sufficient to hold mankind together in little fraternities and copartnerships: weak ties indeed, and what may afford fund enough for ridicule, if they are absurdly considered as the real principles of that union: but they are in truth merely the occasions, as any thing may be of any thing, upon which our nature carries us on according to its own previous bent and bias; which occasions therefore would be nothing at all, were there not this prior disposition and bias of nature.'[1]

Aristotle's reference is perhaps the more interesting, in two respects. In the first place, it takes the practice of disinterested aid further back in time, by asserting its existence not merely among men, but among animals. He opens up the vista of the development of disinterested action, as it exists in man, from the instinctive co-operation of the members of an animal community. And secondly, he points to what is much the most striking and universal example of disinterested action, the operation of parental love, from which perhaps all disinterested action may be supposed to have developed.

In such action, in its earliest form, there was no thought of duty. We must suppose that when a certain degree of mental maturity had been reached, and a certain amount of attention had been, for whatever reason, focused on acts which had hitherto been done without any thought of their rightness, they came to be recognized, first rather vaguely as *suitable* to the situation, and then, with more urgency, as *called for* by the situation. *Thus* first, as belonging to particular acts in virtue of a particular character they possessed, was rightness recognized. Their rightness was not deduced from any general principle; rather the general principle was later recognized by intuitive induction as being implied in the judgements already passed on particular acts.

The question may, however, be asked: 'Once the general principles have been reached, are particular acts recognized as right by deduction from general principles, or by direct reflection on the acts as particular acts having a certain character?' Do we, without seeing directly that the particular act is right, read off its rightness from the general principle, or do we directly see its rightness? Either would be a possible account of what happens. But when I reflect on my own attitude towards particular acts, I seem to find that it is not by deduction but by direct insight that I see them to be right, or wrong. I never seem to be in the position of not seeing directly the rightness of a particular act of kindness, for instance, and of having to read this off from a general principle—'all acts of kindness are right, and therefore this must be, though I cannot see its rightness directly'.

It appears to me that we apprehend individual facts by deduction from general principles in two kinds of situation, and in no more. (1) We may have no real insight that the attribute A implies the presence of the attribute B. But we may have accepted on what we believe to be good grounds the *belief* that A always implies B, and we then may say to ourselves, 'This is an instance of A,

[1] Sermon I (Gladstone's ed.), 38–9.

and therefore it must be an instance of *B*; I cannot see it for myself to be so, but I think it must be, because of a general principle which I have for good reason accepted'. Or (2) the general principle may be one that is not self-evident, but known as the consequence of a proof; and we may remember the principle while we have forgotten the proof. There again, we shall not see with self-evidence that the particular *A* is also a *B,* but we shall read this conclusion off from the remembered general principle 'all *A* is *B*'.

Both these situations actually occur in morals. (1) In most people's lives there is a stage at which they accept some moral principle on authority before they have really come to recognize its truth for themselves; and in such a case the rightness or wrongness of the particular act is not apprehended on its own merits but read off from the general principle. The suggestion is indeed sometimes made that we never pass beyond this stage of acceptance of moral principles on authority to a fresh original recognition of them. But the difficulty at once arises, that the reference to authority either lands us in an infinite regress, or leads back to *some one* who recognized the principle for himself. *A* may believe it because *B* said it was true, and *B* because *C* said it was true, but sooner or later we come to some one who believed it on its merit. Further, I think we can by careful introspection distinguish the acceptance of a moral principle on authority from its acceptance on its own merits, as we can distinguish the stage at which we accepted mathematical principles on our teacher's authority from that at which we came to recognize their truth for ourselves. It is probably the case that many people all through their lives remain in the condition of accepting most of their moral principles on authority, but we can hardly fail to recognize in the best and most enlightened of men an absolutely original and direct insight into moral principles, and in many others the power of seeing for themselves the truth of moral principles when these are pointed out to them. There is really no more reason to doubt this than to doubt that there are people who can grasp mathematical principles and proofs for themselves.

(2) The other situation in which we read off the rightness of particular acts from some general principle also arises. The general principle may have been accepted not on authority but on its merits, but it may have involved for its recognition a fairly elaborate consideration of the probable consequences of a certain type of act; this would be true of such a principle as the principle that indiscriminate charity is wrong. In such a case the rightness or wrongness of an individual act falling under such a description is by no means self-evident. It would involve for its recognition a tracing out of the probable consequences, which we in fact do not perform; but we remember the general principle, while we have forgotten, or do not take the time to recollect, the arguments for it; and so we read off the rightness or wrongness of the particular act from it.

Our insight into the basic principles of morality is not of this order. When we consider a particular act as a lie, or as the breaking of a promise, or as a gratuitous infliction of pain, we do not need to, and do not, fall back on a remembered general principle; we see the individual act to be by its very nature wrong.

. . .

11
Ethical Relativism

PAUL TAYLOR

*Paul Taylor (b. 1923) is Professor of Philosophy at Brooklyn College, City
University of New York. He is the author of* Normative Discourse, *and of
numerous articles on ethics.*

*In this selection, Taylor considers ethical relativism—the view that moral
rules or standards are somehow relative to the attitudes of one's society or
group. Although ethical relativism is accepted by many, those who accept it
are not always completely clear about what they mean. As Taylor notes, the
view may be taken to assert either that (1) different societies do, in fact,
accept different moral codes (descriptive relativism), that (2) each person
ought to do what is dictated by his society's code (normative ethical
relativism), or that (3) there is no standard of reasoning about morality that
is independent of the practices of particular societies (metaethical relativism).*

*Why should we accept ethical relativism in any form? As Taylor suggests,
normative and metaethical relativism are often grounded in descriptive
relativism. In other words, because different societies seem to disagree about
what is right or wrong, and about the standards for reasoning about such
matters, many people equate what one ought to do and the way one ought
to reason, with what one's society considers right or valid. Moreover,
descriptive relativism in turn seems to rest on the findings of anthropologists
and on our own observations of diverse attitudes and customs. However, as
Taylor notes, there are at least two problems here. First, diversity of behavior
does not necessarily show that different societies do disagree in their deepest
moral convictions. They may, instead, be in agreement on fundamental
principles (for example, that it is always best to maximize happiness), but
disagree about which practices will achieve this end. And, second, even if
different societies do disagree about what is right or wrong, it remains
possible that some views are correct while others are in error. Although
different societies disagree about the causes of disease, we do not say that all
views about this are equally correct. If values should be treated differently,
this must be shown by some further argument.*

ONE OF THE most commonly held opinions in ethics is that all moral
norms are *relative* to particular cultures. The rules of conduct that are applicable in one society, it is claimed, do not apply to the actions of people in
another society. Each community has its own norms, and morality is entirely
a matter of conforming to the standards and rules accepted in one's own culture. To put it simply: What is right is what my society approves of; what is
wrong is what my society disapproves of.

This view raises serious doubts about the whole enterprise of normative ethics. For if right and wrong are completely determined by the given moral code of a particular time and place, and if moral codes vary from time to time and place to place, it would seem that there are no unchanging cross-cultural principles that could constitute an ideal ethical system applicable to everyone. Since the purpose of normative ethics is to construct and defend just such a universal system of principles, belief in the relativity of moral norms denies the possibility of normative ethics. It is therefore important at the outset to examine the theory of ethical relativism.

The question raised by the ethical relativist may be expressed thus: Are moral values absolute, or are they relative? We may understand this question as asking, Are there any moral standards and rules of conduct that are universal (applicable to all mankind) or are they all culture-bound (applicable only to the members of a particular society or group)? Even when the question is interpreted in this way, however, it still remains unclear. For those who answer the question by claiming that all moral values are relative or culture-bound may be expressing any one of three different ideas. They may, first, be making an empirical or factual assertion. Or secondly, they may be making a normative claim. And thirdly, they may be understood to be uttering a metaethical principle. The term "ethical relativism" has been used to refer to any or all of these three positions. In order to keep clear the differences among them, the following terminology will be used. We shall call the first position "descriptive relativism," the second "normative ethical relativism," and the third "metaethical relativism." Let us consider each in turn.

Descriptive Relativism

Certain facts about the moral values of different societies and about the way an individual's values are dependent on those of his society have been taken as empirical evidence in support of the claim that all moral values are relative to the particular culture in which they are accepted. These facts are cited by the relativist as reasons for holding a general theory about moral norms, namely, that no such norms are universal. This theory is what we shall designate "descriptive relativism." It is a factual or empirical theory because it holds that, as a matter of historical and sociological fact, no moral standard or rule of conduct has been universally recognized to be the basis of moral obligation. According to the descriptive relativist there are no moral norms common to all cultures. Each society has its own view of what is morally right and wrong and these views vary from society to society because of the differences in their moral codes. Thus it is a mistake to think there are common norms that bind all mankind in one moral community.

Those who accept the position of descriptive relativism point to certain facts as supporting evidence for their theory. These facts may be conveniently summed up under the following headings:

(1) The facts of cultural variability.

(2) Facts about the origin of moral beliefs and moral codes.

(3) The fact of ethnocentrism.

(1) The facts of cultural variability are now so familiar to everyone that they need hardly be enumerated in detail. We all know from reading anthropologists' studies of primitive cultures how extreme is the variation in the customs and taboos, the religions and moralities, the daily habits and the general outlook on life to be found in the cultures of different peoples. But we need not go beyond our own culture to recognize the facts of variability. Historians of Western civilization have long pointed out the great differences in the beliefs and values of people living in different periods. Great differences have also been discovered among the various socioeconomic classes existing within the social structure at any one time. Finally, our own contemporary world reveals a tremendous variety of ways of living. No one who dwells in a modern city can escape the impact of this spectrum of different views on work and play, on family life and education, on what constitutes personal happiness, and on what is right and wrong.

(2) When we add to these facts of cultural and historical variability the recent psychological findings about how the individual's values reflect those of his own social group and his own time, we may begin to question the universal validity of our own values. For it is now a well-established fact that no moral values or beliefs are inborn. All our moral attitudes and judgments are learned from the social environment. Even our deepest convictions about justice and the rights of man are originally nothing but the "introjected" or "internalized" views of our culture, transmitted to us through our parents and teachers. Our very conscience itself is formed by the internalizing of the sanctions used by our society to support its moral norms. When we were told in childhood what we ought and ought not to do, and when our parents expressed their approval and disapproval of us for what we did, we were being taught the standards and rules of conduct accepted in our society. The result of this learning process (sometimes called "acculturation") was to ingrain in us a set of attitudes about our own conduct, so that even when our parents were no longer around to guide us or to blame us, we would guide or blame ourselves by thinking, "This is what I ought to do"; "That would be wrong to do"; and so on. If we then did something we believed was wrong we would feel guilty about it, whether or not anyone caught us at it or punished us for it.

It is this unconscious process of internalizing the norms of one's society through early childhood training that explains the origin of an individual's moral values. If we go beyond this and ask about the origin of society's values, we find a long and gradual development of traditions and customs which have given stability to the society's way of life and whose obscure beginnings lie in ritual magic, taboos, tribal ceremonies, and practices of religious worship. Whether we are dealing with the formation of an individual's conscience or the development of a society's moral code, then, the origin of a set of values seems to have little or nothing to do with rational, controlled thought. Neither individuals nor societies originally acquire their moral beliefs by means of logical reasoning or through the use of an objective method for gaining knowledge.

(3) Finally, the descriptive relativist points out another fact about people and their moralities that must be acknowledged. This is the fact that most people are ethnocentric (group centered). They think not only that there is but one true morality for all mankind, but that the one true morality is their own. They are convinced that the moral code under which they grew up and which formed their deepest feelings about right and wrong—namely, the moral code of their own society—is the only code for anyone to live by. Indeed, they often refuse even to entertain the possibility that their own values might be false or that another society's code might be more correct, more enlightened, or more advanced than their own. Thus ethnocentrism often leads to intolerance and dogmatism. It causes people to be extremely narrow-minded in their ethical outlook, afraid to admit any doubt about a moral issue, and unable to take a detached, objective stance regarding their own moral beliefs. Being absolutely certain that their beliefs are true, they can think only that those who disagree with them are in total error and ignorance on moral matters. Their attitude is: We are advanced, they are backward. We are civilized, they are savages.

It is but a short step from dogmatism to intolerance. Intolerance is simply dogmatism in action. Because the moral values of people directly affect their conduct, those who have divergent moral convictions will often come into active conflict with one another in the area of practical life. Each will believe he alone has the true morality and the other is living in the darkness of sin. Each will see the other as practicing moral abominations. Each will then try to force the other to accept the truth, or at least will not allow the other to live by his own values. The self-righteous person will not tolerate the presence of "shocking" acts which he views with outraged indignation. Thus it comes about that no differences of opinion on moral matters will be permitted within a society. The ethnocentric society will tend to be a closed society, as far as moral belief and practice are concerned.

The argument for descriptive relativism, then, may be summarized as follows. Since every culture varies with respect to its moral rules and standards, and since each individual's moral beliefs—including his inner conviction of their absolute truth—have been learned within the framework of his own culture's moral code, it follows that there are no universal moral norms. If a person believes there are such norms, this is to be explained by his ethnocentrism, which leads him to project his own culture's norms upon everyone else and to consider those who disagree with him either as innocent but "morally blind" people or as sinners who do not want to face the truth about their own evil ways.

In order to assess the soundness of this argument it is necesary to make a distinction between (a) specific moral standards and rules, and (b) ultimate moral principles. Both (a) and (b) can be called "norms," and it is because the descriptive relativist often overlooks this distinction that his argument is open to doubt. A specific moral standard (such as personal courage or trustworthiness) functions as a criterion for judging whether and to what degree a person's character is morally good or bad. A specific rule of conduct (such as "Help others in time of need" or "Do not tell lies for one's own advantage") is a prescription of how people ought or ought not to act. It functions as a criterion for judging whether an action is right or wrong. In contrast with specific standards and rules, an ultimate moral principle is a universal proposition or statement about the conditions that must hold if a standard or rule is to be used as a criterion for judging *any* person or action. Such a principle will be of the form: Standard S or rule R applies to a person or action if and only if condition C is fulfilled. An example of an ultimate moral principle is that of utility, which we shall be examining in detail in Chapter 4. The principle of utility may be expressed thus: A standard or rule applies to a person or action if, and only if, the use of the standard or rule in the actual guidance of people's conduct will result in an increase in everyone's happiness or a decrease in everyone's unhappiness.

Now it is perfectly possible for an ultimate moral principle to be consistent with a variety of specific standards and rules as found in the moral codes of different societies. For if we take into account the traditions of a culture, the beliefs about reality and the attitudes toward life that are part of each culture's world-outlook, and if we also take into account the physical or geographical setting of each culture, we will find that a standard or rule which increases people's happiness in one culture will not increase, but rather decrease people's happiness in another. In one society, for example, letting elderly people die when they can no longer contribute to economic production will be necessary for the survival of everyone else. But another society may have an abundant economy that can easily support people in their old age. Thus the principle of utility would require that in the first society the rule "Do not keep a person alive when he can no longer produce" be part of its moral code, and in the second society it would require a contrary rule. In this case the very same kind of action that is wrong in one society will be right in another. Yet there is a single principle that makes an action of that kind wrong (in one set of circumstances) and another action of that kind right (in a different set of circumstances). In other words, the reason why one action is wrong and the other right is based on one and the same principle, namely utility.

Having in mind this distinction between specific standards and rules on the one hand and ultimate moral principles on the other, what can we say about the argument for descriptive relativism given above? It will immediately be seen that the facts pointed out by the relativist as evidence in support of his theory do not show that ultimate moral principles are relative or culture-bound. They show only that specific standards and rules are relative or culture-bound. The fact that different societies accept different norms of good and bad, right and wrong, is a fact about the standards and rules that make up the various moral codes of those societies. Such a fact does not provide evidence that there is no single ultimate principle which, explicitly or implicitly, every society appeals to as the final justifying ground for its moral code. For if there were such a common ultimate principle, the actual variation in moral codes could be explained in terms of the different world-outlooks, traditions, and physical circumstances of the different societies.

Similarly, facts about ethnocentrism and the causal dependence of an individual's moral beliefs upon his society's moral code do not count as evidence against the view that there is a universal ultimate principle which everyone would refer to in giving a final justification for his society's standards and rules, if he were challenged to do so. Whether there is such a principle and if there is, what sort of conditions it specifies for the validity of specific standards and rules, are questions still to be explored. (In later chapters of this book we shall be considering some of the answers that philosophers have given to these questions.) But the facts cited by the descriptive relativist leave these questions open. We may accept those facts and still be consistent in affirming a single universal ultimate moral principle.

Normative Ethical Relativism

The statement, "What is right in one society may be wrong in another," is a popular way of explaining what is meant by the "relativity of morals." It is usually contrasted with "ethical universalism," taken as the view that "right and wrong do not vary from society to society." These statements are ambiguous, however, and it is important for us to be mindful of their ambiguity. For they may be understood either as factual claims or as normative claims, and it makes a great deal of difference which way they are understood. (They may also be taken as metaethical claims, but we shall postpone this way of considering them until later.)

When it is said that what is right in one society may be wrong in another, this may be understood to mean that what is *believed* to be right in one society is *believed* to be wrong in another. And when it is said that moral right and wrong vary from society to society, this may be understood to mean that different moral norms are adopted by different societies, so that an act which fulfills the norms of one society may violate the norms of another. If this is what is meant, then we are here being told merely of the cultural variability of specific standards and rules, which we have already considered in connection with descriptive relativism.

But the statement, "What is right in one society may be wrong in another," may be interpreted in quite a different way. It may be taken as a normative claim rather than as a factual assertion. Instead of asserting the unsurprising fact that what is believed to be right in one society is believed to be wrong in another, it expresses the far more radical and seemingly paradoxical claim that what *actually is* right in one society may *actually be* wrong in another. According to this view, moral norms are to be considered valid only within the society which has adopted them as part of its way of life. Such norms are not to be considered valid outside that society. The conclusion is then drawn that it is not legitimate to judge people in other societies by applying the norms of one's own society to their conduct. This is the view we shall designate "normative ethical relativism." In order to be perfectly clear about what it claims, we shall examine two ways in which it can be stated, one focusing our attention upon moral judgments, the other on moral norms.

With regard to moral judgments, normative ethical relativism holds that two *apparently* contradictory statements can both be true. The argument runs as follows. Consider the two statements:

(1) It is wrong for unmarried women to have their faces unveiled in front of strangers.

(2) It is not wrong for . . . (as above).

Here it seems as if there is a flat contradiction between two moral judgments, so that if one is true the other must be false. But the normative ethical relativist holds that they are both true, because the statements as given in (1) and (2) are incomplete. They should read as follows:

(3) It is wrong for unmarried women *who are members of society S* to have their faces unveiled in front of strangers.

(4) It is not wrong for unmarried women *outside of society S* to have their faces unveiled in front of strangers.

Statements (3) and (4) are not contradictories. To assert one is not to deny the other. The normative ethical relativist simply translates all moral judgments of the form "Doing act X is right" into statements of the form "Doing X is right when the agent is a member of society S." The latter statement can then be seen to be consistent with statements of the form "Doing X is wrong when the agent is not a member of society S."

The normative ethical relativist's view of moral norms accounts for the foregoing theory of moral judgments. A moral norm, we have seen, is either a standard used in a judgment of good and bad character or a rule used in a judgment of right and wrong conduct. Thus a person is judged to be good insofar as he fulfills the standard, and an action is judged to be right or wrong according to whether it conforms to or violates the rule. Now when a normative ethical relativist says that moral norms vary from society to society, he does not intend merely to assert the fact that different societies have adopted different norms. He is going beyond descriptive relativism and is making a normative claim. He is denying any universal validity to moral norms. He is saying that a moral standard or rule is correctly applicable only to the members of the particular society which has adopted the standard or rule as part of its actual moral code. He therefore thinks it is illegitimate to judge the character or conduct of those outside the society by such a standard or rule. Anyone who uses the norms of one society as the basis for judging the character or conduct of persons in another society is consequently in error.

It is not that a normative ethical relativist necessarily believes in *tolerance* of other people's norms. Nor does his position imply that he grants others the *right* to live by their own norms, for he would hold a relativist view even about tolerance itself. A society whose code included a rule of tolerance would be right in tolerating others, while one that denied tolerance would be right (relative to its own norm of intolerance) in prohibiting others from living by different norms. The normative ethical relativist would simply say that *we* should not judge the tolerant society to be any better than the intolerant one, for this would be applying our own norm of tolerance to other societies. Tolerance, like any other norm, is culture-bound. Anyone who claims that every society has a *right* to live by its own norms, provided that it respects a similar right in other societies, is an ethical universalist, since he holds at least one norm valid for all societies, namely, the right to practice a way of life without interference from others. And he deems this universal norm a valid one, whether or not every society does in fact accept it.

If the normative ethical relativist is challenged to prove his position, he may do either of two things. On the one hand, he may try to argue that his position follows from, or is based on the very same facts that are cited by the descriptive relativist as evidence for *his* position. Or, on the other hand, he may turn for support to metaethical considerations. Putting aside the second move for the moment, let us look more closely at the first.

The most frequent argument given in defense of normative ethical relativism is that, if the facts pointed out by the descriptive relativist are indeed true, then we must accept normative ethical relativism as the only position consistent with those facts. For it seems that if each person's moral judgments are formed within the framework of the norms of his own culture and historical epoch, and if such norms vary among cultures and epochs, it would follow necessarily that it is unwarranted for anyone to apply his own norms to conduct in other societies and times. To do so would be ethnocentrism, which is, as the descriptive relativist shows, a kind of blind, narrow-minded dogmatism. To escape the irrationality of being ethnocentric, we need but realize that the only norms one may legitimately apply to any given group are the ones accepted by that group. Since different peoples accept different norms, there are no universal norms applicable to everyone throughout the world. Now, to say that there are no universal norms applicable worldwide is to commit oneself to normative ethical relativism. Thus, the argument concludes, normative ethical relativism follows from the facts of descriptive relativism.

Is this a valid argument? Suppose one accepts the facts pointed out by the descriptive relativist. Must he then also accept normative ethical relativism? Let us examine some of the objections that have been raised to this argument. In the first place, it is claimed that the facts of cultural variability do not, *by themselves,* entail normative ethical relativism. The reason is that it is perfectly possible for someone to accept those facts and deny normative ethical relativism without contradicting himself. No matter how great may be the differences in the moral beliefs of different cultures and in the moral norms they accept, it is still possible to hold that some of these beliefs are true and others false, or that some of the norms are more correct, justified, or enlightened than others. The fact that societies differ about what is right and wrong does not mean that one society may not have better reasons for holding its views than does another. After all, just because two people (or two groups of people) disagree about whether a disease is caused by bacteria or by evil spirits does not lead to the conclusion that there is no correct or enlightened view about the cause of the disease. So it does not follow from the fact that two societies differ about whether genocide is right that there is no correct or enlightened view about this moral matter.

A similar argument can be used with regard to the second set of facts asserted by the descriptive relativist. No contradiction is involved in affirming that all moral beliefs come from the social environment and denying normative ethical relativism. The fact that a belief is learned from one's society does not mean that it is neither true nor false, or that if it is true, its truth is "relative" to the society in which it was learned. All of our beliefs, empirical ones no less than moral ones, are learned from our society. We are not born with any innate beliefs about chemistry or physics; we learn these only in our schools. Yet this does not make us skeptical about the universal validity of these sciences. So the fact that our moral beliefs come from our society and are learned in our homes and schools has no bearing on their universal validity. The origin or cause of a person's *acquiring* a belief does not determine whether the *content* of the belief is true or false, or even whether there are good grounds for his accepting that content to be true or false.

If it is claimed that our moral beliefs are based on attitudes or feelings culturally conditioned in us from childhood, the same point can still be made. Suppose, for example, that a person who believes slavery is wrong feels disapproval, dislike, or even abhorrence towards the institution of slavery. His negative attitude, which has undoubtedly been influenced by the value system of his culture, may be contrasted with a positive stance (approval, liking, admiring) of someone brought up in an environment where slave owning was accepted. Here are positive and negative attitudes toward slavery, each being causally conditioned by the given cultural environment. It does not follow from this that the two are equally justified, or that neither can be justified. The question of whether a certain attitude toward slavery is justified or unjustified depends on whether good reasons can be given *for* anyone taking the one attitude and *against* anyone taking the other. This question requires the exercise of our reasoning powers. Exactly how we can justify attitudes, or show them to be unjustified, is a complex problem that will be dealt with in later chapters of this book. But the mere fact that the attitudes which underlie moral beliefs are all learned from the social environment leaves open the question of what attitudes an intelligent, rational, and well-informed person would take toward a given action or social practice.

The same kind of argument also holds with respect to the third fact of descriptive relativism: ethnocentrism. People who are ethnocentric *believe* that the one true moral code is that of their own society. But this leaves open the question, Is their belief true or false? Two people of different cultures, both ethnocentric but with opposite moral beliefs, may each think his particular moral norms are valid for everyone; however, this has no bearing on whether either one—or neither one—is correct. We must inquire independently into the possibility of establishing the universal validity of a set of moral norms, regardless of who might or might not believe them to be universally true.

It should be noted that these various objections to the first argument for normative ethical relativism, even if sound, are not sufficient to show that normative ethical relativism is false. They only provide reasons for rejecting one argument in support of that position. To show that the position is false, it would be necessary to give a sound argument in defense of ethical universalism. The sorts of arguments set forth by philosophers to establish universalism will be disclosed in later chapters. It is only if one or more of these arguments proves acceptable that normative ethical relativism is refuted.

A second argument by which the normative ethical relativist defends his position was mentioned earlier. This argument is based on metaethical considerations, so it is appropriate now to examine the bearing of metaethics on the relativism-universalism controversy.

Metaethical Relativism

It will be convenient to distinguish between two forms of metaethical relativism, called "conceptual relativism" and "methodological relativism." Conceptual relativism is the view that moral concepts vary from culture to culture and therefore the moral judgments of one society are meaningless or unintelligible to the members of another. For example, the idea in our own society of individual freedom as a basic human right may not be understandable to a society lacking the concept of human rights or with a view of individual freedom different from ours. The conceptual relativist holds that the meaning of a moral idea can be understood only within the context of a given culture's ethical system as a whole. The conclusion drawn from this is that intercultural comparisons of moral judgments cannot be made. There is no standpoint outside of all cultures from which to decide whether the moral judgments of one society are more enlightened or correct than those of another. Such a comparison would require that both sets of judgments be intelligible to the same individual and this, the conceptual relativist claims, is impossible.

One logical consequence of this view is the following. Suppose a person from culture X utters the judgment "Polygamy is wrong," and a person from culture Y replies, "No, polygamy is not wrong." It would appear that the person from Y is contradicting the person from X. But according to the conceptual relativist this appearance is false; there is actually no contradiction at all between them. For the word "wrong" stands for a different idea—that is, has a different meaning—in each statement. The two persons are not talking about the same thing when they use the word "wrong" (even if they are talking about the same thing when they say "polygamy"—a point also open to doubt in the conceptual relativist's view). Thus in culture X "wrong" might mean "what is detrimental to the common good" while in culture Y it might mean "prohibited by the gods." It may be that polygamy is detrimental to the common good in culture X and is permitted by the gods of culture Y. In these circumstances both statements are true, and thus there can be no contradiction between them.

A further point is now made by the conceptual relativist. Not only do the *meanings* of words like "right" and "wrong," "good" and "bad" vary from culture to culture, but there is also great variation in what the words *refer to*.

In one culture, for instance, the term "a good man" will refer to anyone who is meek and forgiving. In another culture the same term will refer to one who is quick to avenge himself on others and is ruthless with his enemies. Similarly, in one society the statement "That act is right" will be applied to every case in which it is believed that the given act is necessary to uphold the honor of one's family. In another society the same statement will apply to all situations where the given act involves treating everyone concerned—friends and strangers alike—fairly and impartially.

On the basis of considerations like these, the conceptual relativist argues that what a particular word means and what it refers to in moral discourse depend on the specific system of moral norms accepted by the society in which the discourse takes place. He concludes that it makes no sense to talk, as the ethical universalist does, about a *true view* of right action or a *correct* conception of the good man. Such talk assumes that intercultural comparisons of moral concepts are possible. But, he asserts, this assumption is false, since the meaning and application of every moral concept must be relativized to a particular culture.

Is the conceptual relativist right? Can his theory stand up to critical scrutiny when it is examined with care? The answer depends on what analysis is made of the meaning and reference of words and statements used in moral discourse, a matter which will be of concern throughout the rest of this book. So the question must be left open at this juncture.

The second form of metaethical relativism, methodological relativism, maintains that different cultures use different methods of reasoning to justify moral judgments. The conclusion drawn is that the same judgment may be justified in one culture but not in another. Each method provides its own criteria for determining whether a reason given in a moral argument is a good or valid one. If such criteria vary from culture to culture, it may be possible to establish the truth of a moral belief in one social environment and to show it to be false in another. Moral knowledge, being based on different verification procedures, would then be culturally relative. Unless there were some uniform, cross-cultural method for gaining moral knowledge or a uniform, cross-cultural set of rules of reasoning that could tell us whether a person in *any* culture is thinking correctly, no claim could be made for the universal validity of moral norms. And the methodological relativist argues that there is no such method or set of rules of reasoning. Whether his argument is to be accepted is a question that must be considered in the light of those ways that have been proposed by moral philosophers for obtaining genuine moral knowledge. A number of such ways will be found in later chapters of this book.

It has been claimed that one serious implication of methodological relativism is ethical skepticism, or the complete denial of moral knowledge. The reasoning behind this claim is as follows. When the methodological relativist asserts that all moral knowledge is "relative" to a given culture, he is ruling out the very conditions that make it possible for such a thing as genuine moral knowledge to exist at all. In effect he is saying that, if we investigate the assumptions underlying the alleged universal methods adopted by different cultures, we find that in every case one procedure will define "valid" or "good" reasons in one way and another will define them differently. It follows that the question of which, if any, of these given procedures really does lead to moral knowledge is *logically undecidable*. For to choose between any two methods, a neutral third method must be used—one that would enable us to give reasons for accepting one method and rejecting the other. But any such third way will itself merely postulate its own criteria of "valid" reasons, and we would then have to justify our choice of *these* criteria. This however, would in turn also require our giving reasons for our choice, presupposing still another procedure. Since we cannot go to infinity in seeking methods for justifying other methods, we are left at some point with an arbitrary decision. But no claim to genuine moral knowledge can rest on an arbitrary decision, since a different decision— as unjustified as the first—might lead to opposite conclusions regarding a moral issue. This is precisely the kind of situation that the word "knowledge" precludes, if that word is to be understood in its ordinary sense. Therefore genuine moral knowledge is impossible.

Moral philosophers reply to this argument simply by constructing, clearly and systematically, a method of moral reasoning whose logical principles can be shown to be in fact presupposed by anyone, in any culture, who intends to think rationally about moral matters. By considering how any reasonable being would carry on his thinking when he understands clearly the meaning of moral concepts, the uses of moral language, and the function of moral norms in the guidance of conduct, the philosopher attempts to show that there *is* a valid way of determining whether any moral judgment is true or false and, hence, that there is a warranted method for obtaining genuine moral knowledge. In this book we shall become acquainted with some of the most important of these attempts.

Ethical Absolutism

When someone asks, "Are moral norms relative or absolute?" there is often an ambiguity in his question, not only with respect to the word "relative" but also with respect to the word "absolute." We have seen that "relative" can mean, among other things, "causally dependent on variable factors in different cultures" (descriptive relativism); *or* "validly applicable only within the culture which accepts the norm" (normative ethical relativism); *or* "impossible to justify on cross-cultural grounds" (methodological relativism). Let us now examine an important ambiguity in the term "absolute" as it is applied to moral norms. For unless this ambiguity is cleared up, we cannot give a straightforward answer to the question of whether moral norms are relative or absolute.

That moral norms (that is, specific moral rules and standards) are "absolute" can mean either of two things. It can mean that at least some moral norms are justifiable on grounds that can be established by a cross-cultural method of reasoning and that, consequently, these norms correctly apply to the conduct of all human beings. This, we have seen, is ethical universalism. It entails the denial of normative ethical relativism and also the denial of metaethical relativism. Hence, in this first sense of the term "absolute," ethical absolutism may simply be equated with ethical universalism.

The second meaning of the term "absolute" is entirely different from the first. According to the second meaning, to say that moral norms are "absolute" is to say that they *have no exceptions*. Thus, if the rule "It is wrong to break a promise" is an absolute moral norm in this second sense, then one must never break a promise no matter what the circumstances. It follows that it is our duty to keep a promise, even if doing so brings suffering to innocent people. It means, for example, that a hired gunman who promises his boss to murder someone should commit the murder. It signifies that, if we have promised a friend to go to a movie with him on Saturday night, we must do so even if our parents are injured in an automobile accident Saturday afternoon and desperately need our help. Extreme cases like these show that, at least in our ordinary unreflective moral judgments, the rule "Do not break promises" has exceptions and that, consequently, ethical absolutism in the second sense of the term is not true of that particular moral rule.

Are there *any* rules of conduct that are "absolute" in the second sense? The reader should try to work out his own answer to this question for himself. What is important for present purposes is to notice the *logical independence* of the two meanings of "ethical absolutism."

According to the first meaning, an ethical absolutist holds that there are moral norms that apply to everyone, no matter what norms are actually accepted in a given society. According to the second meaning, an ethical absolutist is one who claims that at least some moral norms allow for no legitimate or justifiable exceptions. It is clear that the first meaning of ethical absolutism does not necessarily entail the second. In other words, it is possible to be an ethical absolutist in the first sense but not in the second. For it may be that all moral norms valid for everyone in any society are norms that allow for legitimate exceptions in special circumstances, *whenever* those circumstances occur. Let us consider an example.

Suppose we think that in almost all situations of life it is wrong for one person to take the life of another. Suppose, further, that we hold the rule "Thou shalt not kill" to be a universal moral norm, believing that it applies to all persons in all societies (even if a certain group of people in a given society do not accept the rule). Thus, with respect to this rule we are ethical universalists. Now suppose that we also think that there are very unusual conditions which, when they occur, make it permissible for one person to kill another. For instance, we might think that if a person's only means of defending his life or the lives of his children against the attack of a madman is to kill him, then it is not wrong to kill him. Or we might think that killing is permissible when such an act is necessary to overthrow a totalitarian government carrying out a policy of systematic genocide. If we hold these cases to be legitimate exceptions to the rule "Thou shalt not kill," are we contradicting our position of ethical universalism with regard to that rule? The answer is no, since we may be willing to consider these exceptions universally legitimate whenever they occur, no matter whether a given society accepts them as legitimate exceptions or not. In this case the *full* statement of our rule against killing would be expressed thus: It is wrong for anyone, in any society, to take the life of another, except when such an act is necessary for self-defense or the prevention of systematic genocide.

When a moral rule is stated in this manner, it encompasses its own exceptions. In other words, the complete rule stipulates all the kinds of situations in which an action of the sort *generally* forbidden by the rule is right. If we then accept the rule in its complete form, *including the list of exceptions,* as validly applicable to all human beings, we are ethical universalists (and hence ethical absolutists in the first sense of the term) with respect to this rule. However, we are not ethical absolutists in the second sense of the term, since we hold that the simple rule "Thou shalt not kill" does have legitimate exceptions.

It is true that in this case we may not be willing to allow for exceptions to the whole rule in its *complete* form, since we may think our statement of the rule includes all the possible exceptions it could have. With regard to the rule in its complete form, we would then be ethical absolutists in both senses of the term. On the other hand, if we are not sure we have included all the exceptions that could possibly be legitimate, then with regard to such an *incomplete* rule we would not be ethical absolutists in the second sense. The rule as we have formulated it may still have legitimate exceptions which we have overlooked, but we can nevertheless be ethical universalists about such an incomplete rule. For we might believe that, even in its incomplete form, it correctly applies to all mankind.

The main point of this discussion may now be indicated. When an ethical universalist says that there are moral norms applicable to everyone everywhere, he does not mean that the application of these norms to particular circumstances must determine that one kind of action is always right (or that it is always wrong). He means only that, whenever the norms do apply, they apply regardless of whether a given society may have accepted them in its actual moral code and another society may have excluded them from *its* moral code. The (normative) ethical relativist, on the other hand, claims that what makes an act right is precisely its conformity to the accepted norms of the society in which it occurs, while its violation of such accepted norms makes it wrong. Consider, then, two acts of the very same kind done in the very same sort of circumstances, but each occurring in a different society. One can be right and the other wrong, according to the relativist, since the moral norms of the two societies may disagree concerning the behavior in question. The ethical universalist (or "absolutist" in the first sense), however, would say that if one act is right the other is too and if one is wrong so is the other. For both are acts of an identical kind performed in identical circumstances. Therefore a rule which required or prohibited the one would also require or prohibit the other, and only one rule validly applies to such actions performed in circumstances of that sort. Thus the universalist holds that the rightness and wrongness of actions do not change according to variations in the norms accepted by different societies, even though (contrary to what the "absolutist" in the second sense says) the rightness and wrongness of actions do vary with differences in the sorts of circumstances in which they are performed.

If we keep this distinction between the two meanings of ethical absolutism clearly in mind, we can then see that it is possible to be an absolutist in one sense and not in the other. Whether either sense of absolutism is a correct view is a matter that cannot be settled without further study of normative and analytic ethics. Perhaps the reader will be able to decide these questions for himself as he pursues his own ethical inquiry.

12

The Emotive Theory of Ethics

A. J. AYER

Alfred Jules Ayer (b. 1910) taught for many years at the University of London and at Oxford University. His book Language, Truth, and Logic, *first published in 1936, introduced the English-speaking world to the movement known as logical positivism. Ayer's other works include* Foundations of Empirical Knowledge, Philosophical Essays, *and* The Problem of Knowledge.*

In this selection, from Language, Truth, and Logic, *Ayer argues that ethical utterances are not attempts to state facts, and so are not capable of being either true or false. Since they thus lack cognitive meaning, they must play some other role. In Ayer's view, their function is roughly like that of cheers and boos. When we say something like "lying is wrong," we are merely expressing our disapproval of lying, and thus attempting to discourage others from lying.*

Why does Ayer hold that ethical utterances lack cognitive meaning? The lynchpin of his argument is his "verifiability principle." This principle asserts that any statement that is neither true by definition nor verifiable through the five senses is meaningless. Like Moore (reading 9), Ayer argues that "good" (and related terms such as "right") cannot be defined. But Ayer rejects Moore's alternative view that goodness is simple and indefinable. Moreover, he argues that claims to "see" or "intuit" what is good or right, such as those advanced by Ross in reading 10, cannot be verified by sense-observation. Thus, Ayer concludes that ethical utterances are, in the specified sense, meaningless.

THERE IS STILL one objection to be met before we can claim to have justified our view that all synthetic propositions are empirical hypotheses. This objection is based on the common supposition that our speculative knowledge is of two distinct kinds—that which relates to questions of empirical fact, and that which relates to questions of value. It will be said that "statements of value" are genuine synthetic propositions, but that they cannot with any show of justice be represented as hypotheses, which are used to predict the course of our sensations; and, accordingly, that the existence of ethics and aesthetics as branches of speculative knowledge presents an insuperable objection to our radical empiricist thesis.

In face of this objection, it is our business to give an account of "judgements of value" which is both satisfactory in itself and consistent with our general empiricist principles. We shall set ourselves to show that in so far as statements of value are significant, they are ordinary "scientific" statements; and that in so far as they are not scientific, they are not in the literal sense significant, but are simply expressions of emotion which can be neither true nor false. In maintaining this view, we may confine ourselves for the present to the case of ethical statements. What is said about them will be found to apply, *mutatis mutandis,* to the case of aesthetic statements also.

The ordinary system of ethics, as elaborated in the works of ethical philosophers, is very far from being a homogeneous whole. Not only is it apt to contain pieces of metaphysics, and analyses of non-ethical concepts: its actual ethical contents are themselves of very different kinds. We may divide them, indeed, into four main classes. There are, first of all, propositions which express definitions of ethical terms, or judgements about the legitimacy or possibility of certain definitions. Secondly, there are propositions describing the phenomena of moral experience, and their causes. Thirdly, there are exhortations to moral virtue. And, lastly, there are actual ethical judgements. It is unfortunately the case that the distinction between these four classes, plain as it is, is commonly ignored by ethical philosophers; with the result that it is often very difficult to tell from their works what it is that they are seeking to discover or prove.

In fact, it is easy to see that only the first of our four classes, namely that which comprises the propositions relating to the definitions of ethical terms, can be said to constitute ethical philosophy. The propositions which describe the phenomena of moral experience, and their causes, must be assigned to the science of psychology, or sociology. The exhortations to moral virtue are not propositions at all, but ejaculations or commands which are designed to provoke the reader to action of a certain sort. Accordingly, they do not belong to any branch of philosophy or science. As for the expressions of ethical judgements, we have not yet determined how they should be classified. But inasmuch as they are certainly neither definitions nor comments upon definitions, nor quotations, we may say decisively that they do not belong to ethical philosophy. A strictly philosophical treatise on ethics should therefore make no ethical pronouncements. But it should, by giving an analysis of ethical terms, show what is the category to which all such pronouncements belong. And this is what we are now about to do.

A question which is often discussed by ethical philosophers is whether it is possible to find definitions which would reduce all ethical terms to one or two fundamental terms. But this question, though it undeniably belongs to ethical philosophy, is not relevant to our present enquiry. We are not now concerned to discover which term, within the sphere of ethical terms, is to be taken as fundamental; whether, for example, "good" can be defined in terms of "right" or "right" in terms of "good," or both in terms of "value." What we are interested in is the possibility of reducing the whole sphere of ethical terms to non-ethical terms. We are enquiring whether statements of ethical value can be translated into statements of empirical fact.

That they can be so translated is the contention of those ethical philosophers who are commonly called subjectivists, and of those who are known as utilitarians. For the utilitarian defines the rightness of actions, and the goodness of ends, in terms of the pleasure, or happiness, or satisfaction, to which they give rise; the subjectivist, in terms of the feelings of approval which a certain person, or group of people, has towards them. Each of these types of definition makes moral judgements into a sub-class of psychological or sociological judgements; and for this reason they are very attractive to us. For, if either was correct, it would follow that ethical assertions were not generically different from the factual assertions which are ordinarily contrasted with them; and the account which we have already given of empirical hypotheses would apply to them also.

Nevertheless we shall not adopt either a subjectivist or a utilitarian analysis of ethical terms. We reject the subjectivist view that to call an action right, or a thing good, is to say that it is generally approved of, because it is not self-contradictory to assert that some actions which are generally approved of are not right, or that some things which are generally approved of are not good. And we reject the alternative subjectivist view that a man who asserts that a certain action is right, or that a certain thing is good, is saying that he himself approves of it, on the ground that a man who confessed that he sometimes approved of what was bad or wrong would not be contradicting himself. And a similar argument is fatal to utilitarianism. We cannot agree that to call an action right is to say that of all the actions possible in the circumstances it would cause, or be likely to cause, the greatest happiness, or the greatest balance of pleasure over pain, or the greatest balance of satisfied over unsatisfied desire, because we find that it is not self-contradictory to say that it is sometimes wrong to perform the action which would actually or probably cause the greatest happiness, or the greatest balance of pleasure over pain, or of satisfied over unsatisfied desire. And since it is not self-contradictory to say that some pleasant things are not good, or that some bad things are desired, it cannot be the case that the sentence "x is good" is equivalent to "x is pleasant," or to "x is desired." And to every other variant of utilitarianism with which I am acquainted the same objection can be made. And therefore we should, I think, conclude that the validity of ethical judgements is not determined by the felicific tendencies of actions, any more than by the nature of people's feelings; but that it must be regarded as "absolute" or "intrinsic," and not empirically calculable.

If we say this, we are not, of course, denying that it is possible to invent a language in which all ethical symbols are definable in non-ethical terms, or even that it is desirable to invent such a language and adopt it in place of our own; what we are denying is that the suggested reduction of ethical to non-ethical statements is consistent with the conventions of our actual language. That is, we reject utilitarianism and subjectivism, not as proposals to replace our existing ethical notions by new ones, but as analyses of our existing ethical notions. Our contention is simply that, in our language, sentences which contain normative ethical symbols are not equivalent to sentences which express psychological propositions, or indeed empirical propositions of any kind.

It is advisable here to make it plain that it is only normative ethical symbols, and not descriptive ethical symbols, that are held by us to be indefinable in factual terms. There is a danger of confusing these two types of symbols, because they are commonly constituted by signs of the same sensible form. Thus a complex sign of the form "x is wrong" may constitute a sentence which expresses a moral judgement concerning a certain type of conduct, or it may constitute a sentence which states that a certain type of conduct is repugnant to the moral sense of a particular society. In the latter case, the symbol "wrong" is a descriptive ethical symbol, and the sentence in which it occurs expresses an ordinary sociological proposition; in the former case, the symbol "wrong" is a normative ethical symbol, and the sentence in which it occurs does not, we maintain, express an empirical proposition at all. It is only with normative ethics that we are at present concerned; so that whenever ethical symbols are used in the course of this argument without qualification, they are always to be interpreted as symbols of the normative type.

In admitting that normative ethical concepts are irreducible to empirical concepts, we seem to be leaving the way clear for the "absolutist" view of ethics—that is, the view that statements of value are not controlled by observation, as ordinary empirical propositions are, but only by a mysterious "intellectual intuition." A feature of this theory, which is seldom recognized by its advocates, is that it makes statements of value unverifiable. For it is notorious that what seems intuitively certain to one person may seem doubtful, or even false, to another. So that unless it is possible to provide some criterion by which one may decide between conflicting intuitions, a mere appeal to intuition is worthless as a test of a proposition's validity. But in the case of moral judgements, no such criterion can be given. Some moralists claim to settle the matter by saying that they "know" that their own moral judgements are correct. But such an assertion is of purely psychological interest, and has not the slightest tendency to prove the validity of any moral judgement. For dissentient moralists may equally well "know" that their ethical views are correct. And, as far as subjective certainty goes, there will be nothing to choose between them. When such differences of opinion arise in connection with an ordinary empirical proposition, one may attempt to resolve them by referring to, or actually carrying out, some relevant empirical test. But with regard to ethical statements, there is, on the "absolutist" or "intuitionist" theory, no relevant empirical test. We are therefore justified in saying that on this theory ethical statements are held to be unverifiable. They are, of course, also held to be genuine synthetic propositions.

Considering the use which we have made of the principle that a synthetic proposition is significant only if it is empirically verifiable, it is clear that the acceptance of an "absolutist" theory of ethics would undermine the whole of our main argument. And as we have already rejected the "naturalistic" theories which are commonly supposed to provide the only alternative to "absolutism" in ethics, we seem to have reached a difficult position. We shall meet the difficulty by showing that the correct treatment of ethical statements is afforded by a third theory, which is wholly compatible with our radical empiricism.

We begin by admitting that the fundamental ethical concepts are unanalysable, inasmuch as there is no criterion by which one can test the validity of the judgements in which they occur. So far we are in agreement with the absolutists. But, unlike the absolutists, we are able to give an explanation of this fact about ethical concepts. We say that the reason why they are unanalysable is that they are mere pseudo-concepts. The presence of an ethical symbol in a proposition adds nothing to its factual content. Thus if I say to someone, "You acted wrongly in stealing that money," I am not stating anything more than if I had simply said, "You stole that money." In adding that this action is wrong I am not making any further statement about it. I am simply evincing my moral disapproval of it. It is as if I had said, "You stole that money," in a peculiar tone of horror, or written it with the addition of some special exclamation marks. The tone, or the exclamation marks, adds nothing to the literal meaning of the sentence. It merely serves to show that the expression of it is attended by certain feelings in the speaker.

If now I generalise my previous statement and say, "Stealing money is wrong," I produce a sentence which has no factual meaning—that is, expresses no proposition which can be either true or false. It is as if I had written "Stealing money!!"—where the shape and thickness of the exclamation marks show, by a suitable convention, that a special sort of moral disapproval is the feeling which is being expressed. It is clear that there is nothing said here which can be true or false. Another man may disagree with me about the wrongness of stealing, in the sense that he may not have the same feelings about stealing as I have, and he may quarrel with me on account of my moral sentiments. But he cannot, strictly speaking, contradict me. For in saying that a certain type of action is right or wrong, I am not making any factual statement, not even a statement about my own state of mind. I am merely expressing certain moral sentiments. And the man who is ostensibly contradicting me is merely expressing his moral sentiments. So that there is plainly no sense in asking which of us is in the right. For neither of us is asserting a genuine proposition.

What we have just been saying about the symbol "wrong" applies to all normative ethical symbols. Sometimes they occur in sentences which record ordinary empirical facts besides expressing ethical feeling about those facts: sometimes they occur in sentences which simply express ethical feeling about a certain type of action, or situation, without making any statement of fact. But in every case in which one would commonly be said to be making an ethical judgement, the function of the relevant ethical word is purely "emotive." It is used to express feeling about certain objects, but not to make any assertion about them.

It is worth mentioning that ethical terms do not serve only to express feeling. They are calculated also to arouse feeling, and so to stimulate action. Indeed some of them are used in such a way as to give the sentences in which they occur the effect of commands. Thus the sentence "It is your duty to tell the truth" may be regarded both as the expression of a certain sort of ethical feeling about truthfulness and as the expression of the command "Tell the truth." The sentence "You ought to tell the truth" also involves the command "Tell the truth," but here the tone of the command is less emphatic. In the sentence "It is good to tell the truth" the command has become little more than a suggestion. And thus the "meaning" of the word "good," in its ethical usage, is differentiated from that of the word "duty" or the word "ought." In fact we may define the meaning of the various ethical words in terms both of the different feelings they are ordinarily taken to express, and also the different responses which they are calculated to provoke.

We can now see why it is impossible to find a criterion for determining the validity of ethical judgements. It is not because they have an "absolute" validity which is mysteriously independent of ordinary sense-experience, but because they have no objective validity whatsoever. If a sentence makes no statement at all, there is obviously no sense in asking whether what it says is true or false. And we have seen that sentences which simply express moral judgements do not say anything. They are pure expressions of feeling and as such do not come under the category of truth and falsehood. They are unverifiable for the same reason as a cry of pain or a word of command is unverifiable—because they do not express genuine propositions.

Thus, although our theory of ethics might fairly be said to be radically subjectivist, it differs in a very important respect from the orthodox subjectivist theory. For the orthodox subjectivist does not deny, as we do, that the sentences of a moralizer express genuine propositions. All he denies is that they express propositions of a unique non-empirical character. His own view is that they express propositions about the speaker's feelings. If this were so, ethical judgements clearly would be capable of being true or false. They would be true if the speaker had the relevant feelings, and false if he had not. And this is a matter which is, in principle, empirically verifiable. Furthermore they could be significantly contradicted. For if I say, "Tolerance is a virtue," and someone answers, "You don't approve of it," he would, on the ordinary subjectivist theory, be contradicting me. On our theory, he would not be contradicting me, because, in saying that tolerance was a virtue, I should not be making any statement about my own feelings or about anything else. I should simply be evincing my feelings, which is not at all the same thing as saying that I have them.

The distinction between the expression of feeling and the assertion of feeling is complicated by the fact that the assertion that one has a certain feeling often accompanies the expression of that feeling, and is then, indeed, a factor in the expression of that feeling. Thus I may simultaneously express boredom and say that I am bored, and in that case my utterance of the words, "I am bored," is one of the circumstances which make it true to say that I am expressing or evincing boredom. But I can express boredom without actually saying that I am bored. I can express it by my tone and gestures, while making a statement about something wholly unconnected with it, or by an ejaculation, or without uttering any words at all. So that even if the assertion that one has a certain feeling always involves the expression of that feeling, the expression of a feeling assuredly does not always involve the assertion that one has it. And this is the important point to grasp in considering the distinction between our theory and the ordinary subjectivist theory. For whereas the subjectivist holds that ethical statements actually assert the existence of certain feelings, we hold that ethical statements are expressions and excitants of feeling which do not necessarily involve any assertions.

We have already remarked that the main objection to the ordinary subjectivist theory is that the validity of ethical judgements is not determined by the nature of their author's feelings. And this is an objection which our theory escapes. For it does not imply that the existence of any feelings is a necessary and sufficient condition of the validity of an ethical judgement. It implies, on the contrary, that ethical judgements have no validity.

There is , however, a celebrated argument against subjectivist theories which our theory does not escape. It has been pointed out by Moore that if ethical statements were simply statements about the speaker's feelings, it would be impossible to argue about questions of value. To take a typical example: if a man said that thrift was a virtue, and another replied that it was a vice, they would not, on this theory, be disputing with one another. One would be saying that he approved of thrift, and the other that *he* didn't; and there is no reason why both these statements should not be true. Now Moore held it to be obvious that we do dispute about questions of value, and accordingly concluded that the particular form of subjectivism which he was discussing was false.

It is plain that the conclusion that it is impossible to dispute about questions of value follows from our theory also. For as we hold that such sentences as "Thrift is a virtue" and "Thrift is a vice" do not express propositions at all, we clearly cannot hold that they express incompatible propositions. We must therefore admit that if Moore's argument really refutes the ordinary subjectivist theory, it also refutes ours. But, in fact, we deny that it does refute even the ordinary subjectivist theory. For we hold that one really never does dispute about questions of value.

This may seem, at first sight, to be a very paradoxical assertion. For we certainly do engage in disputes which are ordinarily regarded as disputes about questions of value. But, in all such cases, we find, if we consider the matter closely, that the dispute is not really about a question of value, but about a question of fact. When someone disagrees with us about the moral value of a certain action or type of action, we do admittedly resort to argument in order to win him over to our way of thinking. But we do not attempt to show by our arguments that he has the "wrong" ethical feeling towards a situation whose nature he has correctly apprehended. What we attempt to show is that he is mistaken about the facts of the case. We argue that he has misconceived the agent's motive: or that he has misjudged the effects of the action, or its probable effects in view of the agent's knowledge; or that he has failed to take into account the special circumstances in which the agent was placed. Or else we employ more general arguments about the effects which actions of a certain type tend to produce, or the qualities which are usually manifested in their performance. We do this in the hope that we have only to get our opponent to agree with us about the nature of the empirical facts for him to adopt the same moral attitude towards them as we do. And as the people with whom we argue have generally received the same moral education as ourselves, and live in the same social order, our expectation is usually justified. But if our opponent happens to have undergone a different process of moral "conditioning" from ourselves, so that, even when he acknowledges all the facts, he still disagrees with us about the moral value of the actions under discussion, then we abandon the attempt to convince him by argument. We say that it is impossible to argue with him because he has a distorted or undeveloped moral sense; which signifies merely that he employs a different set of values from our own. We feel that our own system of values is superior, and therefore speak in such derogatory terms of his. But we cannot bring forward any arguments to show that our system is superior. For our judgement that it is so is itself a judgement of value, and accordingly outside the scope of argument. It is because argument fails us when we come to deal with pure questions of value, as distinct from questions of fact, that we finally resort to mere abuse.

In short, we find that argument is possible on moral questions only if some system of values is presupposed. If our opponent concurs with us in expressing moral disapproval of all actions of a given type *t*, then we may get him to condemn a particular action A, by bringing forward arguments to show that A is of type *t*. For the question whether A does or does not belong to that type is a plain question of fact. Given that a man has certain moral principles, we argue that he must, in order to be consistent, react morally to certain things in a certain way. What we do not and cannot argue about is the validity of these moral principles. We merely praise or condemn them in the light of our own feelings.

If anyone doubts the accuracy of this account of moral disputes, let him try to construct even an imaginary argument on a question of value which does not reduce itself to an argument about a question of logic or about an empirical matter of fact. I am confident that he will not succeed in producing a single example. And if that is the case, he must allow that its involving the impossibility of purely ethical arguments is not, as Moore thought, a ground of objection to our theory, but rather a point in favour of it.

Having upheld our theory against the only criticism which appeared to threaten it, we may now use it to define the nature of all ethical enquiries. We find that ethical philosophy consists simply in saying that ethical concepts are pseudo-concepts and therefore unanalysable. The further task of describing the different feelings that the different ethical terms are used to express, and the different reactions that they customarily provoke, is a task for the psychologist. There cannot be such a thing as ethical science, if by ethical science one means the elaboration of a "true" system of morals. For we have seen that, as ethical judgements are mere expressions of feeling, there can be no way of determining the validity of any ethical system, and, indeed, no sense in asking whether any such system is true. All that one may legitimately enquire in this connection is, What are the moral habits of a given person or group of people, and what causes them to have precisely those habits and feelings? And this enquiry falls wholly within the scope of the existing social sciences.

It appears, then, that ethics, as a branch of knowledge, is nothing more than a department of psychology and sociology. And in case anyone thinks that we are overlooking the existence of casuistry, we may remark that casuistry is not a science, but is a purely analytical investigation of the structure of a given moral system. In other words, it is an exercise in formal logic.

When one comes to pursue the psychological enquiries which constitute ethical science, one is immediately enabled to account for the Kantian and hedonistic theories of morals. For one finds that one of the chief causes of moral behaviour is fear, both conscious and unconscious, of a god's displeasure, and fear of the enmity of society. And this, indeed, is the reason why moral precepts present themselves to some people as "categorical" commands. And one finds, also, that the moral code of a society is partly determined by the beliefs of that society concerning the conditions of its own happiness—or, in other words, that a society tends to encourage or discourage a given type of conduct by the use of moral sanctions according as it appears to promote or detract from the contentment of the society as a whole. And this is the reason why altruism is recommended in most moral codes and egotism condemned. It is from the observation of this connection between morality and happiness that hedonistic or eudaemonistic theories of morals ultimately spring, just as the moral theory of Kant is based on the fact, previously explained, that moral precepts have for some people the force of inexorable commands. As each of these theories ignores the fact which lies at the root of the other, both may be criticized as being one-sided; but this is not the main objection to either of them. Their essential defect is that they treat propositions which refer to the causes and attributes of our ethical feelings as if they were definitions of ethical concepts. And thus they fail to recognise that ethical concepts are pseudo-concepts and consequently indefinable.

13
Ethics and Observation

GILBERT HARMAN

Gilbert Harman (b. 1938) is Professor of Philosophy at Princeton University. In addition to his work in ethics, he has made major contributions in the theory of knowledge. He is the author of Thought, The Nature of Morality, *and of many articles.*

In this selection from The Nature of Morality, *Harman compares the principles of ethics to those of science. He argues that while observation and experiment can make it reasonable to accept or reject scientific principles, the principles of ethics do not appear similarly confirmable or testable. At first glance, his reason for saying this may seem to be simply that observation can tell us what happens, but cannot tell us whether what happens is right or wrong. But this is not quite Harman's position. On his account, an observation is any opinion that is formed as a direct result of perception without conscious inference. Because a given perception (say of some children setting fire to a cat) may directly cause us to believe that what is happening is wrong, Harman believes that there can be moral observation.*

If moral observations are possible, why should we doubt that they can confirm moral principles as laboratory observations confirm scientific principles? The answer, according to Harman, lies in the explanatory role of what is observed. When a physicist sees a vapor trail in a cloud chamber, and directly forms the opinion that he is confronted with a proton, the best explanation of his forming this opinion will include a reference to the fact that he has been confronted with a proton. By contrast, when a moralist sees a child torturing a cat, and directly forms the opinion that the child's activity is wrong, the best explanation of his forming this opinion seems to include no reference to the torture's wrongness. Instead, it appears to include only references to the moralist's upbringing, conditioning, and so on. Because moral facts do not seem to be needed to explain moral observations, those observations do not appear to confirm moral principles. This is not Harman's final position, but it is one he regards as worthy of serious consideration.

The Basic Issue

CAN MORAL PRINCIPLES be tested and confirmed in the way scientific principles can? Consider the principle that, if you are given a choice between five people alive and one dead or five people dead and one alive, you should always choose to have five people alive and one dead rather than the other way round. We can easily imagine examples that appear to confirm this principle. Here is one:

> You are a doctor in a hospital's emergency room when six accident victims are brought in. All six are in danger of dying but one is much worse off than the others. You can just barely save that person if you devote all of your resources to him and let the others die. Alternatively, you can save the other five if you are willing to ignore the most seriously injured person.

It would seem that in this case you, the doctor, would be right to save the five and let the other person die. So this example, taken by itself, confirms the principle under consideration. Next, consider the following case.

> You have five patients in the hospital who are dying, each in need of a separate organ. One needs a kidney, another a lung, a third a heart, and so forth. You can save all five if you take a single healthy person and remove his heart, lungs, kidneys, and so forth, to distribute to these five patients. Just such a healthy person is in room 306. He is in the hospital for routine tests. Having seen his test results, you know that he is perfectly healthy and of the right tissue compatibility. If you do nothing, he will survive without incident; the other patients will die, however. The other five patients can be saved only if the person in Room 306 is cut up and his organs distributed. In that case, there would be one dead but five saved.

The principle in question tells us that you should cut up the patient in Room 306. But in this case, surely you must not sacrifice this innocent bystander, even to save the five other patients. Here a moral principle has been tested and disconfirmed in what may seem to be a surprising way.

This, of course, was a "thought experiment." We did not really compare a hypothesis with the world. We compared an explicit principle with our feelings about certain imagined examples. In the same way, a physicist performs thought experiments in order to compare explicit hypotheses with his "sense" of what should happen in certain situations, a "sense" that he has acquired as a result of his long working familiarity with current theory. But scientific hypotheses can also be tested in real experiments, out in the world.

Can moral principles be tested in the same way, out in the world? You can observe someone do something, but can you ever perceive the rightness or wrongness of what he does? If you round a corner and see a group of young hoodlums pour gasoline on a cat and ignite it, you do not need to *conclude* that what they are doing is wrong; you do not need to figure anything out; you can *see* that it is wrong. But is your reaction due to the actual wrongness of what you see or is it simply a reflection of your moral "sense," a "sense" that you have acquired perhaps as a result of your moral upbringing?

Observation

The issue is complicated. There are no pure observations. Observations are always "theory laden." What you perceive depends to some extent on the theory you hold, consciously or unconsciously. You see some children pour gasoline on a cat and ignite it. To really see that, you have to possess a great deal of knowledge, know about a considerable number of objects, know about people: that people pass through the life stages infant, baby, child, adolescent, adult. You must know what flesh and blood animals are, and in particular, cats. You must have some idea of life. You must know what gasoline is, what burning is, and much more. In one sense, what you "see" is a pattern of light on your retina, a shifting array of splotches, although, even that is theory, and you could never adequately describe what you see in that sense. In another sense, you see what you do because of the theories you hold. Change those theories and you would see something else, given the same pattern of light.

Similarly, if you hold a moral view, whether it is held consciously or unconsciously, you will be able to perceive rightness or wrongness, goodness or badness, justice or injustice. There is no difference in this respect between moral propositions and other theoretical propositions. If there is a difference, it must be found elsewhere.

Observation depends on theory because perception involves forming a belief as a fairly direct result of observing something; you can form a belief only if you understand the relevant concepts and a concept is what it is by virtue of its role in some theory or system of beliefs. To recognize a child as a child is to employ, consciously or unconsciously, a concept that is defined by its place in a framework of the stages of human life. Similarly, burning is an empty concept apart from its theoretical connections to the concepts of heat, destruction, smoke, and fire.

Moral concepts—Right and Wrong, Good and Bad, Justice and Injustice—also have a place in your theory or system of beliefs and are the concepts they are because of their context. If we say that observation has occurred whenever an opinion is a direct result of perception, we must allow that there is moral observation, because such an opinion can be a moral opinion as easily as any other sort. In this sense, observation may be used to confirm or disconfirm moral theories. The observational opinions that, in this sense, you find yourself with can be in either agreement or conflict with your consciously explicit moral principles. When they are in conflict, you must choose between your explicit theory and observation. In ethics, as in science, you sometimes opt for theory, and say that you made an error in observation or were biased or whatever, or you sometimes opt for observation, and modify your theory.

In other words, in both science and ethics, general principles are invoked to explain particular cases and, therefore, in both science and ethics, the general principles you accept can be tested by appealing to particular judgments that certain things are right or wrong, just or unjust, and so forth; and these judgments are analogous to direct perceptual judgments about facts.

Observational Evidence

Nevertheless, observation plays a role in science that it does not seem to play in ethics. The difference is that you need to make assumptions about certain physical facts to explain the occurrence of the observations that support a scientific theory, but you do not seem to need to make assumptions about any moral facts to explain the occurrence of the so-called moral observations I have been talking about. In the moral case, it would seem that you need only make assumptions about the psychology or moral sensibility of the person making the moral observation. In the scientific case, theory is tested against the world.

The point is subtle but important. Consider a physicist making an observation to test a scientific theory. Seeing a vapor trail in a cloud chamber, he thinks, "There goes a proton." Let us suppose that this is an observation in the relevant sense, namely, an immediate judgment made in response to the situation without any conscious reasoning having taken place. Let us also suppose that his observation confirms his theory, a theory that helps give meaning to the very term "proton" as it occurs in his observational judgment. Such a confirmation rests on inferring an explanation. He can count his making the observation as confirming evidence for his theory only to the extent that it is reasonable to explain his making the observation by assuming that, not only is he in a certain psychological "set," given the theory he accepts and his beliefs about the experimental apparatus, but furthermore, there really was a proton going through the cloud chamber, causing the vapor trail, which he saw as a proton. (This is evidence for the theory to the extent that the theory can explain the proton's being there better than competing theories can.) But, if his having made that observation could have been equally well explained by his psychological set alone, without the need for any assumption about a proton, then the observation would not have been evidence for the existence of that proton and therefore would not have been evidence for the theory. His making the observation supports the theory only because, in order to explain his making the observation, it is reasonable to assume something about the world over and above the assumptions made about the observer's psychology. In particular, it is reasonable to assume that there was a proton going through the cloud chamber, causing the vapor trail.

Compare this case with one in which you make a moral judgment immediately and without conscious reasoning, say, that the children are wrong to set the cat on fire or that the doctor would be wrong to cut up one healthy patient to save five dying patients. In order to explain your making the first of these judgments, it would be reasonable to assume, perhaps, that the children really are pouring gasoline on a cat and you are seeing them do it. But, in neither case is there any obvious reason to assume anything about "moral facts," such as that it really is wrong to set the cat on fire or to cut up the patient in Room 306. Indeed, an assumption about moral facts would seem to be totally irrelevant to the explanation of your making the judgment you make. It would seem that all we need assume is that you have certain more or less well articulated moral principles that are reflected in the judgments you make, based on your moral sensibility. It seems to be completely irrelevant to our explanation whether your intuitive immediate judgment is true or false.

The observation of an event can provide observational evidence for or against a scientific theory in the sense that the truth of that observation can be relevant to a reasonable explanation of why that observation was made. A moral observation does not seem, in the same sense, to be observational evidence for or against any moral theory, since the truth or falsity of the moral observation seems to be completely irrelevant to any reasonable explanation of why that observation was made. The fact that an observation of an event was made at the time it was made is evidence not only about the observer but also about the physical facts. The fact that you made a particular moral observation when you did does not seem to be evidence about moral facts, only evidence about you and your moral sensibility. Facts about protons can affect what you observe, since a proton passing through the cloud chamber can cause a vapor trail that reflects light to your eye in a way that, given your scientific training and psychological set, leads you to judge that what you see is a proton. But there does not seem to be any way in which the actual rightness or wrongness of a given situation can have any effect on your perceptual apparatus. In this respect, ethics seems to differ from science.

In considering whether moral principles can help explain observations, it is therefore important to note an ambiguity in the word "observation." You see the children set the cat on fire and immediately think, "That's wrong." In one sense, your observation is that what the children are doing is wrong. In another sense, your observation is your thinking that thought. Moral observations might explain observations in the first sense but not in the second sense. Certain moral principles might help to explain why it was *wrong* of the children to set the cat on fire, but moral principles seem to be of no help in explaining *your thinking* that that is wrong. In the first sense of "observation," moral principles can be tested by observation—"That this act is wrong is evidence that causing unnecessary suffering is wrong." But in the second sense of "observation," moral principles cannot clearly be tested by observation, since they do not appear to help explain observations in this second sense of "observation." Moral principles do not seem to help explain your observing what you observe.

Of course, if you are already given the moral principle that it is wrong to cause unnecessary suffering, you can take your seeing the children setting the cat on fire as observational evidence that they are doing something wrong. Similarly, you can suppose that your seeing the vapor trail is observational evidence that a proton is going through the cloud chamber, if you are given the relevant physical theory. But there is an important apparent difference between the two cases. In the scientific case, your making that observation is itself evidence for the physical theory because the physical theory explains the proton, which explains the trail, which explains your observation. In the moral case, your making your observation does not seem to be evidence for the relevant moral principle because that principle does not seem to help explain your observation. The explanatory chain from principle to observation seems to be broken in morality. The moral principle may "explain" why it is wrong for the children to set the cat on fire. But the wrongness of that act does not appear to help explain the act, which you observe, itself. The explanatory chain appears to be broken in such a way that neither the moral principle nor the wrongness of the act can help explain why you observe what you observe.

A qualification may seem to be needed here. Perhaps the children perversely set the cat on fire simply "because it is wrong." Here it may seem at first that the actual wrongness of the act does help explain why they do it and therefore indirectly helps explain why you observe what you observe just as a physical theory, by explaining why the proton is producing a vapor trail, indirectly helps explain why the observer observes what he observes. But on reflection we must agree that this is probably an illusion. What explains the children's act is not clearly the actual wrongness of the act but, rather, their belief that the act is wrong. The actual rightness or wrongness of their act seems to have nothing to do with why they do it.

Observational evidence plays a part in science it does not appear to play in ethics, because scientific principles can be justified ultimately by their role in explaining observations, in the second sense of observation—by their explanatory role. Apparently, moral principles cannot be justified in the same way. It appears to be true that there can be no explanatory chain between moral principles and particular observings in the way that there can be such a chain between scientific principles and particular observings. Conceived as an explanatory theory, morality, unlike science, seems to be cut off from observation.

Not that every legitimate scientific hypothesis is susceptible to direct observational testing. Certain hypotheses about "black holes" in space cannot be directly tested, for example, because no signal is emitted from within a black hole. The connection with observation in such a case is indirect. And there are many similar examples. Nevertheless, seen in the large, there is the apparent difference between science and ethics we have noted. The scientific realm is accessible to observation in a way the moral realm is not.

Ethics and Mathematics

Perhaps ethics is to be compared, not with physics, but with mathematics. Perhaps such a moral principle as "You ought to keep your promises" is confirmed or disconfirmed in the way (whatever it is) in which such a mathematical principle as "$5 + 7 = 12$" is. Observation does not seem to play the role in mathematics it plays in physics. We do not and cannot perceive numbers, for example, since we cannot be in causal contact with them. We do not even understand what it would be like to be in causal contact with the number 12, say. Relations among numbers cannot have any more of an effect on our perceptual apparatus than moral facts can.

Observation, however, *is* relevant to mathematics. In explaining the observations that support a physical theory, scientists typically appeal to mathematical principles. On the other hand, one never seems to need to appeal in this way to moral principles. Since an observation is evidence for what best explains it, and since mathematics often figures in the explanations of scientific observations, there is indirect observational evidence for mathematics. There does not seem to be observational evidence, even indirectly, for basic moral principles. In explaining why certain observations have been made, we never seem to use purely moral assumptions. In this respect, then, ethics appears to differ not only from physics but also from mathematics.

. . .

14

The Subjectivity of Values

J. L. MACKIE

J. L. Mackie (1917–81) taught philosophy at various universities, and most recently at Oxford. He was a philosopher of impressive breadth. His works include The Cement of the Universe, The Miracle of Theism, Problems From Locke, *and* Ethics: Inventing Right and Wrong.

In this selection, taken from Ethics: Inventing Right and Wrong, *Mackie argues that there are no objective values. He begins by distinguishing his thesis from a number of others. For example, unlike Ayer (reading 12), Mackie is not maintaining that ethical utterances lack cognitive meaning. He is, instead, contending that such utterances are meaningful but false. In his view, the basic question is whether the world contains items such as values—entities at once external to persons and authoritative over their behavior. According to Mackie, it does not.*

Why does Mackie take this position? Although he says more than can easily be summarized, his main arguments include appeals to variations in actual moral codes and to the "queerness" of the entities that objectivists must postulate. (For relevant discussion, see, respectively, Paul Taylor, reading 11, and Gilbert Harman, reading 13.) In addition, Mackie tries to show how people could come to believe in objective values even if none existed. Taken together, his arguments constitute a formidable challenge to the objectivity of value.

1. Moral Scepticism

THERE ARE NO objective values. This is a bald statement of the thesis of this chapter, but before arguing for it I shall try to clarify and restrict it in ways that may meet some objections and prevent some misunderstanding.

The statement of this thesis is liable to provoke one of three very different reactions. Some will think it not merely false but pernicious; they will see it as a threat to morality and to everything else that is worthwhile, and they will find the presenting of such a thesis in what purports to be a book on ethics paradoxical or even outrageous. Others will regard it as a trivial truth, almost too obvious to be worth mentioning, and certainly too plain to be worth much argument. Others again will say that it is meaningless or empty, that no real issue is raised by the question whether values are or are not part of the fabric of the world. But, precisely because there can be these three different reactions, much more needs to be said.

The claim that values are not objective, are not part of the fabric of the world, is meant to include not only moral goodness, which might be most naturally equated with moral value, but also other things that could be more loosely called moral values or disvalues—rightness or wrongness, duty, obligation, an action's being rotten and contemptible, and so on. It also includes non-moral values, notably aesthetic ones, beauty and various kinds of artistic merit. I shall not discuss these explicitly, but clearly much the same considerations apply to aesthetic and to moral values, and there would be at least some initial implausibility in a view that gave the one a different status from the other.

Since it is with moral values that I am primarily concerned, the view I am adopting may be called moral scepticism. But this name is likely to be misunderstood: 'moral scepticism' might also be used as a name for either of two first order views, or perhaps for an incoherent mixture of the two. A moral sceptic might be the sort of person who says 'All this talk of morality is tripe,' who rejects morality and will take no notice of it. Such a person may be literally rejecting all moral judgements; he is more likely to be making moral judgements of his own, expressing a positive moral condemnation of all that conventionally passes for morality; or he may be confusing these two logically incompatible views, and saying that he rejects all morality, while he is in fact rejecting only a particular morality that is current in the society in which he has grown up. But I am not at present concerned with the merits or faults of such a position. These are first order moral views, positive or negative: the person who adopts either of them is taking a certain practical, normative, stand. By contrast, what I am discussing is a second order view, a view about the status of moral values and the nature of moral valuing, about where and how they fit into the world. These first and second order views are not merely distinct but completely independent: one could be a second order moral sceptic without being a first order one, or again the other way round. A man could hold strong moral views, and indeed ones whose content was thoroughly conventional, while believing that they were simply attitudes and policies with regard to conduct that he and other people held. Conversely, a man could reject all established morality while believing it to be an objective truth that it was evil or corrupt.

With another sort of misunderstanding moral scepticism would seem not so much pernicious as absurd. How could anyone deny that there is a difference between a kind action and a cruel one, or that a coward and a brave man behave differently in the face of danger? Of course, this is undeniable; but it is not to the point. The kinds of behaviour to which moral values and disvalues are ascribed are indeed part of the furniture of the world, and so are the natural, descriptive, differences between them; but not, perhaps, their differences in value. It is a hard fact that cruel actions differ from kind ones, and hence that we can learn, as in fact we all do, to distinguish them fairly well in practice, and to use the words 'cruel' and 'kind' with fairly clear descriptive meanings;

but is it an equally hard fact that actions which are cruel in such a descriptive sense are to be condemned? The present issue is with regard to the objectivity specifically of value, not with regard to the objectivity of those natural, factual, differences on the basis of which differing values are assigned.

2. Subjectivism

Another name often used, as an alternative to 'moral scepticism', for the view I am discussing is 'subjectivism'. But this too has more than one meaning. Moral subjectivism too could be a first order, normative, view, namely that everyone really ought to do whatever he thinks he should. This plainly is a (systematic) first order view; on examination it soon ceases to be plausible, but that is beside the point, for it is quite independent of the second order thesis at present under consideration. What is more confusing is that different second order views compete for the name 'subjectivism'. Several of these are doctrines about the meaning of moral terms and moral statements. What is often called moral subjectivism is the doctrine that, for example, 'This action is right' *means* 'I approve of this action', or more generally that moral judgements are equivalent to reports of the speaker's own feelings or attitudes. But the view I am now discussing is to be distinguished in two vital respects from any such doctrine as this. First, what I have called moral scepticism is a negative doctrine, not a positive one: it says what there isn't, not what there is. It says that there do not exist entities or relations of a certain kind, objective values or requirements, which many people have believed to exist. Of course, the moral sceptic cannot leave it at that. If his position is to be at all plausible, he must give some account of how other people have fallen into what he regards as an error, and this account will have to include some positive suggestions about how values fail to be objective, about what has been mistaken for, or has led to false beliefs about, objective values. But this will be a development of his theory, not its core: its core is the negation. Secondly, what I have called moral scepticism is an ontological thesis, not a linguistic or conceptual one. It is not, like the other doctrine often called moral subjectivism, a view about the meanings of moral statements. Again, no doubt, if it is to be at all plausible, it will have to give some account of their meanings, and I shall say something about this in Section 7 of this chapter and again in Chapters 2, 3, and 4. But this too will be a development of the theory, not its core.

It is true that those who have accepted the moral subjectivism which is the doctrine that moral judgements are equivalent to reports of the speaker's own feelings or attitudes have usually presupposed what I am calling moral scepticism. It is because they have assumed that there are no objective values that they have looked elsewhere for an analysis of what moral statements might mean, and have settled upon subjective reports. Indeed, if all our moral statements were such subjective reports, it would follow that, at least so far as we are aware, there are no objective moral values. If we were aware of them, we would say something about them. In this sense this sort of subjectivism entails moral scepticism. But the converse entailment does not hold. The denial that there are objective values does not commit one to any particular view about what moral statements mean, and certainly not to the view that they are equivalent to subjective reports. No doubt if moral values are not objective they are in some very broad sense subjective, and for this reason I would accept 'moral subjectivism' as an alternative name to 'moral scepticism'. But subjectivism in this broad sense must be distinguished from the specific doctrine about meaning referred to above. Neither name is altogether satisfactory: we simply have to guard against the (different) misinterpretations which each may suggest.

3. The Multiplicity of Second Order Questions

The distinctions drawn in the last two sections rest not only on the well-known and generally recognized difference between first and second order questions, but also on the more controversial claim that there are several kinds of second order moral question. Those most often mentioned are questions about the meaning and use of ethical terms, or the analysis of ethical concepts. With these go questions about the logic of moral statements: there may be special patterns of moral argument, licensed, perhaps, by aspects of the meanings of moral terms—for example, it may be part of the meaning of moral statements that they are universalizable. But there are also ontological, as contrasted with linguistic or conceptual, questions about the nature and status of goodness or rightness or whatever it is that first order moral statements are distinctively about. These are questions of factual rather than conceptual analysis: the problem of what goodness is cannot be settled conclusively or exhaustively by finding out what the word 'good' means, or what it is conventionally used to say or to do.

Recent philosophy, biased as it has been towards various kinds of linguistic inquiry, has tended to doubt this, but the distinction betwen conceptual and factual analysis in ethics can be supported by analogies with other areas. The question of what perception is, what goes on when someone perceives something, is not adequately answered by finding out what words like 'see' and 'hear' mean, or what someone is doing in saying 'I perceive . . .', by analysing, however fully and accurately, any established concept of perception. There is a still closer analogy with colours. Robert Boyle and John Locke called colours 'secondary qualities', meaning that colours as they occur in material things consist simply in patterns of arrangement and movement of minute particles on the surfaces of objects, which make them, as we would now say, reflect light of some frequencies better than others, and so enable these objects to produce colour sensations in us, but that colours as we see them do not literally belong to the surfaces of material things. Whether Boyle and Locke were right about this cannot be settled by finding out how we use colour words and what we mean in using them. Naïve realism about colours might be a correct analysis not only of our pre-scientific colour concepts but also of the conventional meanings of colour words, and even of the meanings with which scientifically sophisticated people use them when they are off their guard, and yet it might not be a correct account of the status of colours.

180

Error could well result, then, from a failure to distinguish factual from conceptual analysis with regard to colours, from taking an account of the meanings of statements as a full account of what there is. There is a similar and in practice even greater risk of error in moral philosophy. There is another reason, too, why it would be a mistake to concentrate second order ethical discussions on questions of meaning. The more work philosophers have done on meaning, both in ethics and elsewhere, the more complications have come to light. It is by now pretty plain that no simple account of the meanings of first order moral statements will be correct, will cover adequately even the standard, conventional, senses of the main moral terms; I think, none the less, that there is a relatively clear-cut issue about the objectivity of moral values which is in danger of being lost among the complications of meaning.

4. Is Objectivity a Real Issue?

It has, however, been doubted whether there is a real issue here. I must concede that it is a rather old-fashioned one. I do not mean merely that it was raised by Hume, who argued that 'The vice entirely escapes you ... till you turn your reflexion into your own breast,' and before him by Hobbes, and long before that by some of the Greek sophists. I mean rather that it was discussed vigorously in the nineteen thirties and forties, but since then has received much less attention. This is not because it has been solved or because agreement has been reached: instead it seems to have been politely shelved.

But was there ever a genuine problem? R. M. Hare has said that he does not understand what is meant by 'the objectivity of values', and that he has not met anyone who does. We all know how to recognize the activity called 'saying, thinking it to be so, that some act is wrong', and he thinks that it is to this activity that the subjectivist and the objectivist are both alluding, though one calls it 'an attitude of disapproval' and the other 'a moral intuition': these are only different names for the same thing. It is true that if one person says that a certain act is wrong and another that it is not wrong the objectivist will say that they are contradicting one another; but this yields no significant discrimination between objectivism and subjectivism, because the subjectivist too will concede that the second person is negating what the first has said, and Hare sees no difference betwen contradicting and negating. Again, the objectivist will say that one of the two must be wrong; but Hare argues that to say that the judgement that a certain act is wrong is itself wrong is merely to negate that judgement, and the subjectivist too must negate one or other of the two judgements, so that still no clear difference between objectivism and subjectivism has emerged. He sums up his case thus: 'Think of one world into whose fabric values are objectively built; and think of another in which those values have been annihilated. And remember that in both worlds the people in them go on being concerned about the same things—there is no difference in the "subjective" concern which people have for things, only in their "objective" value. Now I ask, "What is the difference between the states of affairs in these two worlds?" Can any answer be given except "None whatever"?'

Now it is quite true that it is logically possible that the subjective concern, the activity of valuing or of thinking things wrong, should go on in just the same way whether there are objective values or not. But to say this is only to reiterate that there is a logical distinction between first and second order ethics: first order judgements are not necessarily affected by the truth or falsity of a second order view. But it does not follow, and it is not true, that there is no difference whatever between these two worlds. In the one there is something that backs up and validates some of the subjective concern which people have for things, in the other there is not. Hare's argument is similar to the positivist claim that there is no difference between a phenomenalist or Berkeleian world in which there are only minds and their ideas and the commonsense realist one in which there are also material things, because it is logically possible that people should have the same experiences in both. If we reject the positivism that would make the dispute between realists and phenomenalists a pseudo-question, we can reject Hare's similarly supported dismissal of the issue of the objectivity of values.

In any case, Hare has minimized the difference between his two worlds by considering only the situation where people already have just such subjective concern; further differences came to light if we consider how subjective concern is acquired or changed. If there were something in the fabric of the world that validated certain kinds of concern, then it would be possible to acquire these merely by finding something out, by letting one's thinking be controlled by how things were. But in the world in which objective values have been annihilated the acquiring of some new subjective concern means the development of something new on the emotive side by the person who acquires it, something that eighteenth-century writers would put under the head of passion or sentiment.

The issue of the objectivity of values needs, however, to be distinguished from others with which it might be confused. To say that there are objective values would not be to say merely that there are some things which are valued by everyone, nor does it entail this. There could be agreement in valuing even if valuing is just something that people do, even if this activity is not further validated. Subjective agreement would give intersubjective values, but intersubjectivity is not objectivity. Nor is objectivity simply universalizability: someone might well be prepared to universalize his prescriptive judgements or approvals—that is, to prescribe and approve in just the same ways in all relevantly similar cases, even ones in which he was involved differently or not at all—and yet he could recognize that such prescribing and approving were his activities, nothing more. Of course if there were objective values they would presumably belong to *kinds* of things or actions or states of affairs, so that the judgements that reported them would be universalizable; but the converse does not hold.

A more subtle distinction needs to be made between objectivism and descriptivism. Descriptivism is again a doctrine about the meanings of ethical terms and statements, namely that their meanings are purely descriptive rather than even partly prescriptive or emotive or evaluative, or that it is not an essential feature of the conventional meaning of moral statements that they have some special illocutionary force, say of commending rather than asserting. It contrasts with the view that commendation is in principle distinguishable from description (however difficult they may be to separate in practice) and that moral statements have it as at least part of their meaning that they are commendatory and hence in some uses intrinsically action-guiding. But descriptive meaning neither entails nor is entailed by objectivity. Berkeley's subjective idealism about material objects would be quite compatible with the admission that material object statements have purely descriptive meaning. Conversely, the main tradition of European moral philosophy from Plato onwards has combined the view that moral values are objective with the recognition that moral judgements are partly prescriptive or directive or action-guiding. Values themselves have been seen as at once prescriptive and objective. In Plato's theory the Forms, and in particular the Form of the Good, are eternal, extra-mental, realities. They are a very central structural element in the fabric of the world. But it is held also that just knowing them or 'seeing' them will not merely tell men what to do but will ensure that they do it, overruling any contrary inclinations. The philosopher-kings in the *Republic* can, Plato thinks, be trusted with unchecked power because their education will have given them knowledge of the Forms. Being acquainted with the Forms of the Good and Justice and Beauty and the rest they will, by this knowledge alone, without any further motivation, be impelled to pursue and promote these ideals. Similarly, Kant believes that pure reason can by itself be practical, though he does not pretend to be able to explain how it can be so. Again, Sidgwick argues that if there is to be a science of ethics—and he assumes that there can be, indeed he defines ethics as 'the science of conduct'—what ought to be 'must in another sense have objective existence: it must be an object of knowledge and as such the same for all minds'; but he says that the affirmations of this science 'are also precepts', and he speaks of happiness as 'an end *absolutely* prescribed by reason'. Since many philosophers have thus held that values are objectively prescriptive, it is clear that the ontological doctrine of objectivism must be distinguished from descriptivism, a theory about meaning.

But perhaps when Hare says that he does not understand what is meant by 'the objectivity of values' he means that he cannot understand how values could be objective, he cannot frame for himself any clear, detailed, picture of what it would be like for values to be part of the fabric of the world. This would be a much more plausible claim; as we have seen, even Kant hints at a similar difficulty. Indeed, even Plato warns us that it is only through difficult studies spread over many years that one can approach the knowledge of the Forms. The difficulty of seeing how values could be objective is a fairly strong reason for thinking that they are not so; ... but it is not a good reason for saying that this is not a real issue.

I believe that as well as being a real issue it is an important one. It clearly matters for general philosophy. It would make a radical difference to our metaphysics if we had to find room for objective values—perhaps something like Plato's Forms—somewhere in our picture of the world. It would similarly make a difference to our epistemology if it had to explain how such objective values are or can be known, and to our philosophical psychology if we had to allow such knowledge, or Kant's pure practical reason, to direct choices and actions. Less obviously, how this issue is settled will affect the possibility of certain kinds of moral argument. For example, Sidgwick considers a discussion between an egoist and a utilitarian, and points out that if the egoist claims that his happiness or pleasure is objectively desirable or good, the utilitarian can argue that the egoist's happiness 'cannot be more objectively desirable or more a good than the similar happiness of any other person: the mere fact . . . that *he is he* can have nothing to do with its objective desirability or goodness'. In other words, if ethics is built on the concept of objective goodness, then egoism as a first order system or method of ethics can be refuted, whereas if it is assumed that goodness is only subjective it cannot. But Sidgwick correctly stresses what a number of other philosophers have missed, that this argument against egoism would require the objectivity specifically of goodness: the objectivity of what ought to be or of what it is rational to do would not be enough. If the egoist claimed that it was objectively rational, or obligatory upon him, to seek his own happiness, a similar argument about the irrelevance of the fact that he is he would lead only to the conclusion that it was objectively rational or obligatory for each other person to seek *his* own happiness, that is, to a universalized form of egoism, not to the refutation of egoism. And of course insisting on the universalizability of moral judgements, as opposed to the objectivity of goodness, would yield only the same result.

5. Standards of Evaluation

One way of stating the thesis that there are no objective values is to say that value statements cannot be either true or false. But this formulation, too, lends itself to misinterpretation. For there are certain kinds of value statements which undoubtedly can be true or false, even if, in the sense I intend, there are no objective values. Evaluations of many sorts are commonly made in relation to agreed and assumed standards. The classing of wool, the grading of apples, the awarding of prizes at sheepdog trials, flower shows, skating and diving championships, and even the marking of examination papers are carried out in relation to standards of quality or merit which are peculiar to each particular subject-matter or type of contest, which may be explicitly laid down but which, even if they are nowhere explicitly stated, are fairly well understood and agreed by those who are recognized as judges or experts in each particular field. Given any sufficiently determinate standards, it will be an objective issue, a matter of truth and falsehood, how well any particular specimen measures up to those standards. Comparative judgements in particular will be capable of truth and falsehood: it will be a factual question whether this sheepdog has performed better than that one.

The subjectivist about values, then, is not denying that there can be objective evaluations relative to standards, and these are as possible in the aesthetic and moral fields as in any of those just mentioned. More than this, there is an objective distinction which applies in many such fields, and yet would itself be regarded as a peculiarly moral one: the distinction between justice and injustice. In one important sense of the word it is a paradigm case of injustice if a court declares someone to be guilty of an offence of which it knows him to be innocent. More generally, a finding is unjust if it is at variance with what the relevant law and the facts together require, and particularly if it is known by the court to be so. More generally still, any award of marks, prizes, or the like is unjust if it is at variance with the agreed standards for the contest in question: if one diver's performance in fact measures up better to the accepted standards for diving than another's, it will be injust if the latter is awarded higher marks or the prize. In this way the justice or injustice of decisions relative to standards can be a thoroughly objective matter, though there may still be a subjective element in the interpretation or application of standards. But the statement that a certain decision is thus just or unjust will not be objectively prescriptive: in so far as it can be simply true it leaves open the question whether there is any objective requirement to do what is just and to refrain from what is unjust, and equally leaves open the practical decision to act in either way.

Recognizing the objectivity of justice in relation to standards, and of evaluative judgements relative to standards, then, merely shifts the question of the objectivity of values back to the standards themselves. The subjectivist may try to make his point by insisting that there is no objective validity about the choice of standards. Yet he would clearly be wrong if he said that the choice of even the most basic standards in any field was completely arbitrary. The standards used in sheepdog trials clearly bear some relation to the work that sheepdogs are kept to do, the standards for grading apples bear some relation to what people generally want in or like about apples, and so on. On the other hand, standards are not as a rule strictly validated by such purposes. The appropriateness of standards is neither fully determinate nor totally indeterminate in relation to independently specifiable aims or desires. But however determinate it is, the objective appropriateness of standards in relation to aims or desires is no more of a threat to the denial of objective values than is the objectivity of evaluation relative to standards. In fact it is logically no different from the objectivity of goodness relative to desires. Something may be called good simply in so far as it satisfies or is such as to satisfy a certain desire; but the objectivity of such relations of satisfaction does not constitute in our sense an objective value.

6. Hypothetical and Categorical Imperatives

We may make this issue clearer by referring to Kant's distinction between hypothetical and categorical imperatives, though what he called imperatives are more naturally expressed as 'ought'-statements than in the imperative mood. 'If you want X, do Y' (or 'You ought to do Y') will be a hypothetical imperative if it is based on the supposed fact that Y is, in the circumstances, the only (or the best) available means to X, that is, on a causal relation between Y and X. The reason for doing Y lies in its causal connection with the desired end, X;

the oughtness is contingent upon the desire. But 'You ought to do Y' will be a categorical imperative if you ought to do Y irrespective of any such desire for any end to which Y would contribute, if the oughtness is not thus contingent upon any desire. But this distinction needs to be handled with some care. An 'ought'-statement is not in this sense hypothetical merely because it incorporates a conditional clause. 'If you promised to do Y, you ought to do Y' is not a hypothetical imperative merely on account of the stated if-clause; what is meant may be either a hypothetical or a categorical imperative, depending upon the implied reason for keeping the supposed promise. If this rests upon some such further unstated conditional as 'If you want to be trusted another time', then it is a hypothetical imperative; if not, it is categorical. Even a desire of the agent's can figure in the antecedent of what, though conditional in grammatical form, is still in Kant's sense of a categorical imperative. 'If you are strongly attracted sexually to young children you ought not to go in for school teaching' is not, in virtue of what it explicitly says, a hypothetical imperative: the avoidance of school teaching is not being offered as a means to the satisfaction of the desires in question. Of course, it could still be a hypothetical imperative, if the implied reason were a prudential one; but it could also be a categorical imperative, a moral requirement where the reason for the recommended action (strictly, avoidance) does not rest upon that action's being a means to the satisfaction of any desire that the agent is supposed to have. Not every conditional ought-statement or command, then, is a hypothetical imperative; equally, not every non-conditional one is a categorical imperative. An appropriate if-clause may be left unstated. Indeed, a simple command in the imperative mood, say a parade-ground order, which might seem most literally to qualify for the title of a categorical imperative, will hardly ever be one in the sense we need here. The implied reason for complying with such an order will almost always be some desire of the person addressed, perhaps simply the desire to keep out of trouble. If so, such an apparently categorical order will be in our sense a hypothetical imperative. Again, an imperative remains hypothetical even if we change the 'if' to 'since': the fact that the desire for X is actually present does not alter the fact that the reason for doing Y is contingent upon the desire for X by way of Y's being a means to X. In Kant's own treatment, while imperatives of skill relate to desires which an agent may or may not have, imperatives of prudence relate to the desire for happiness which, Kant assumes, everyone has. So construed, imperatives of prudence are no less hypothetical than imperatives of skill, no less contingent upon desires that the agent has at the time the imperatives are addressed to him. But if we think rather of a counsel of prudence as being related to the agent's future welfare, to the satisfaction of desires that he does not yet have— not even to a present desire that his future desires should be satisfied—then a counsel of prudence is a categorical imperative, different indeed from a moral one, but analogous to it.

A categorical imperative, then, would express a reason for acting which was unconditional in the sense of not being contingent upon any present desire of the agent to whose satisfaction the recommended action would contribute as a means—or more directly: 'You ought to dance', if the implied reason is just that you want to dance or like dancing, is still a hypothetical imperative. Now Kant himself held that moral judgements are categorical imperatives, or perhaps are all applications of one categorical imperative, and it can plausibly be maintained at least that many moral judgements contain a categorically imperative element. So far as ethics is concerned, my thesis that there are no objective values is specifically the denial that any such categorically imperative element is objectively valid. The objective values which I am denying would be action-directing absolutely, not contingently (in the way indicated) upon the agent's desires and inclinations.

Another way of trying to clarify this issue is to refer to moral reasoning or moral arguments. In practice, of course, such reasoning is seldom fully explicit: but let us suppose that we could make explicit the reasoning that supports some evaluative conclusion, where this conclusion has some action-guiding force that is not contingent upon desires or purposes or chosen ends. Then what I am saying is that somewhere in the input to this argument—perhaps in one or more of the premisses, perhaps in some part of the form of the argument—there will be something which cannot be objectively validated—some premiss which is not capable of being simply true, or some form of argument which is not valid as a matter of general logic, whose authority or cogency is not objective, but is constituted by our choosing or deciding to think in a certain way.

7. The Claim to Objectivity

If I have succeeded in specifying precisely enough the moral values whose objectivity I am denying, my thesis may now seem to be trivially true. Of course, some will say, valuing, preferring, choosing, recommending, rejecting, condemning, and so on, are human activities, and there is no need to look for values that are prior to and logically independent of all such activities. There may be widespread agreement in valuing, and particular value-judgements are not in general arbitrary or isolated: they typically cohere with others, or can be criticized if they do not, reasons can be given for them, and so on: but if all that the subjectivist is maintaining is that desires, ends, purposes, and the like figure somewhere in the system of reasons, and that no ends or purposes are objective as opposed to being merely intersubjective, then this may be conceded without much fuss.

But I do not think that this should be conceded so easily. As I have said, the main tradition of European moral philosophy includes the contrary claim, that there are objective values of just the sort I have denied. I have referred already to Plato, Kant, and Sidgwick. Kant in particular holds that the categorical imperative is not only categorical and imperative but objectively so: though a rational being gives the moral law to himself, the law that he thus makes is determinate and necessary. Aristotle begins the *Nicomachean Ethics* by saying that the good is that at which all things aim, and that ethics is part of a science which he calls 'politics', whose goal is not knowledge but practice; yet he does not doubt that there can be *knowledge* of what is the good for man, nor, once he has identified this as well-being or happiness, *eudaimonia,* that it can be known, rationally determined, in what happiness consists; and it is plain that he thinks that this happiness is intrinsically desirable, not good simply because it is desired. The rationalist Samuel Clarke holds that

> these eternal and necessary differences of things make it *fit and reasonable* for creatures so to act . . . even separate from the consideration of these rules being the *positive will* or *command of God;* and also antecedent to any respect or regard, expectation or apprehension, of any *particular private and personal advantage or disadvantage, reward or punishment,* either present or future . . .

Even the sentimentalist Hutcheson defines moral goodness as 'some quality apprehended in actions, which procures approbation . . .', while saying that the moral sense by which we perceive virtue and vice has been given to us (by the Author of nature) to direct our actions. Hume indeed was on the other side, but he is still a witness to the dominance of the objectivist tradition, since he claims that when we 'see that the distinction of vice and virtue is not founded merely on the relations of objects, nor is perceiv'd by reason', this 'wou'd subvert all the vulgar systems of morality'. And Richard Price insists that right and wrong are 'real characters of actions', not 'qualities of our minds', and are perceived by the understanding; he criticizes the notion of moral sense on the ground that it would make virtue an affair of taste, and moral right and wrong 'nothing in the objects themselves'; he rejects Hutcheson's view because (perhaps mistakenly) he sees it as collapsing into Hume's.

But this objectivism about values is not only a feature of the philosophical tradition. It has also a firm basis in ordinary thought, and even in the meanings of moral terms. No doubt it was an extravagance for Moore to say that 'good' is the name of a non-natural quality, but it would not be so far wrong to say that in moral contexts it is used as if it were the name of a supposed non-natural quality, where the description 'non-natural' leaves room for the peculiar evaluative, prescriptive, intrinsically action-guiding aspects of this supposed quality. This point can be illustrated by reflection on the conflicts and swings of opinion in recent years between non-cognitivist and naturalist views about the central, basic, meanings of ethical terms. If we reject the view that it is the function of such terms to introduce objective values into discourse about conduct and choices of action, there seem to be two main alternative types of account. One (which has importantly different subdivisions) is that they conventionally express either attitudes which the speaker purports to adopt towards whatever it is that he characterizes morally, or prescriptions or recommendations, subject perhaps to the logical constraint of universalizability. Different views of this type share the central thesis that ethical terms have, at least partly and primarily, some sort of non-cognitive, non-descriptive, meaning. Views of the other type hold that they are descriptive in meaning, but descriptive of natural features, partly of such features as everyone, even the non-cognitivist, would recognize as distinguishing kind actions from cruel ones, courage from cowardice, politeness from rudeness, and so on, and partly (though these two overlap) of relations between the actions and some human wants, satisfactions, and the like, I believe that views of both these types capture part of the truth. Each approach can account for the fact that moral judgements are action-guiding or practical. Yet each gains much of its plausibility from the felt inadequacy of the other. It is a very natural reaction to any non-cognitive analysis of ethical terms to protest that there is more to ethics than this, something more external to the maker of moral judgements, more authoritative over both him and those of or to whom he speaks, and this reaction is likely to persist even when full allowance has been made for the logical, formal, constraints of full-blooded prescriptivity and universalizability. Ethics, we are inclined to believe, is more a matter of knowledge and less a matter of decision than any non-cognitive analysis allows. And of course naturalism satisfies this demand. It will not be a matter of choice or decision whether an action is cruel or unjust or imprudent or whether it is likely to produce more distress than pleasure. But in satisfying this demand, it introduces a converse deficiency. On a naturalist analysis, moral judgements can be practical, but their practicality is wholly relative to desires or possible satisfactions of the person or persons whose actions are to be guided; but moral judgements seem to say more than this. This view leaves out the categorical quality of moral requirements. In fact both naturalist and non-cognitive analyses leave out the apparent authority of ethics, the one by excluding the categorically imperative aspect, the other the claim to objective validity or truth. The ordinary user of moral language means to say something about whatever it is that he characterizes morally, for example a possible action, as it is in itself, or would be if it were realized, and not about, or even simply expressive of, his, or anyone else's, attitude or relation to it. But the something he wants to say is not purely descriptive, certainly not inert, but something that involves a call for action or for the refraining from action, and one that is absolute, not contingent upon any desire or preference or policy or choice, his own or anyone else's. Someone in a state of moral perplexity, wondering whether it would be wrong for him to engage, say, in research related to bacteriological warfare, wants to arrive at some judgement about this concrete case, his doing this work at this time in these actual circumstances; his relevant characteristics will be part of the subject of the judgement, but no relation between him and the proposed action will be part of the predicate. The question is not, for example, whether he really wants to do this work, whether it will satisfy or dissatisfy him, whether he will in the long run have a pro-attitude towards it, or even whether this is an action of a sort that he can happily and sincerely recommend in all relevantly similar cases. Nor is he even wondering just whether to recommend such action in all relevantly similar cases. He wants to know whether this course of action would be wrong in itself. Something like this is the everyday objectivist concept of which talk about non-natural qualities is a philosopher's reconstruction.

The prevalence of this tendency to objectify values—and not only moral ones—is confirmed by a pattern of thinking that we find in existentialists and those influenced by them. The denial of objective values can carry with it an extreme emotional reaction, a feeling that nothing matters at all, that life has lost its purpose. Of course this does not follow; the lack of objective values is not a good reason for abandoning subjective concern or for ceasing to want anything. But the abandonment of a belief in objective values can cause, at least temporarily, a decay of subjective concern and sense of purpose. That it does so is evidence that the people in whom this reaction occurs have been tending to objectify their concerns and purposes, have been giving them a fictitious external authority. A claim to objectivity has been so strongly associated with their subjective concerns and purposes that the collapse of the former seems to undermine the latter as well.

This view, that conceptual analysis would reveal a claim to objectivity, is sometimes dramatically confirmed by philosophers who are officially on the other side. Bertrand Russell, for example, says that 'ethical propositions should be expressed in the optative mood, not in the indicative'; he defends himself effectively against the charge of inconsistency in both holding ultimate ethical valuations to be subjective and expressing emphatic opinions on ethical questions. Yet at the end he admits:

> Certainly there *seems* to be something more. Suppose, for example, that some one were to advocate the introduction of bull-fighting in this country. In opposing the proposal, I should *feel,* not only that I was expressing my desires, but that my desires in the matter are *right,* whatever that may mean. As a matter of argument, I can, I think, show that I am not guilty of any logical inconsistency in holding to the above interpretation of ethics and at the same time expressing strong ethical preferences. But in feeling I am not satisfied.

But he concludes, reasonably enough, with the remark: 'I can only say that, while my own opinions as to ethics do not satisfy me, other people's satisfy me still less.'

I conclude, then, that ordinary moral judgements include a claim to objectivity, an assumption that there are objective values in just the sense in which I am concerned to deny this. And I do not think it is going too far to say that this assumption has been incorporated in the basic, conventional, meanings of moral terms. Any analysis of the meanings of moral terms which omits this claim to objective, intrinsic, prescriptivity is to that extent incomplete; and this is true of any non-cognitive analysis, any naturalist one, and any combination of the two.

If second order ethics were confined, then, to linguistic and conceptual analysis, it ought to conclude that moral values at least are objective: that they are so is part of what our ordinary moral statements mean: the traditional moral concepts of the ordinary man as well as of the main line of western philosophers are concepts of objective value. But it is precisely for this reason that linguistic and conceptual analysis is not enough. The claim to objectivity, however ingrained in our language and thought, is not self-validating. It can and should be questioned. But the denial of objective values will have to be put forward not as the result of an analytic approach, but as an 'error theory', a theory that although most people in making moral judgements implicitly claim, among other things, to be pointing to something objectively prescriptive, these claims are all false. It is this that makes the name 'moral scepticism' appropriate.

But since this is an error theory, since it goes against assumptions ingrained in our thought and built into some of the ways in which language is used, since it conflicts with what is sometimes called common sense, it needs very solid support. It is not something we can accept lightly or casually and then quietly pass on. If we are to adopt this view, we must argue explicitly for it. Traditionally it has been supported by arguments of two main kinds, which I shall call the argument from relativity and the argument from queerness, but these can, as I shall show, be supplemented in several ways.

8. The Argument From Relativity

The argument from relativity has as its premiss the well-known variation in moral codes from one society to another and from one period to another, and also the differences in moral beliefs between different groups and classes within a complex community. Such variation is in itself merely a truth of descriptive morality, a fact of anthropology which entails neither first order nor second order ethical views. Yet it may indirectly support second order subjectivism: radical differences between first order moral judgements make it difficult to treat those judgements as apprehensions of objective truths. But it is not the mere occurrence of disagreements that tells against the objectivity of values. Disagreement on questions in history or biology or cosmology does not show that there are no objective issues in these fields for investigators to disagree about. But such scientific disagreement results from speculative inferences or explanatory hypotheses based on inadequate evidence, and it is hardly plausible to interpret moral disagreement in the same way. Disagreement about moral codes seems to reflect people's adherence to and participation in different ways of life. The causal connection seems to be mainly that way round: it is that people approve of monogamy because they participate in a monogamous way of life rather than that they participate in a monogamous way of life because they approve of monogamy. Of course, the standards may be an idealization of the way of life from which they arise: the monogamy in which people participate may be less complete, less rigid, than that of which it leads them to approve. This is not to say that moral judgements are purely conventional. Of course there have been and are moral heretics and moral reformers, people who have turned against the established rules and practices of their own communities for moral reasons, and often for moral reasons that we would endorse. But this can usually be understood as the extension, in ways which, though new and unconventional, seemed to them to be required for consistency, of rules to which they already adhered as arising out of an existing way of life. In short, the argument from relativity has some force simply because the actual variations in the moral codes are more readily explained by the hypothesis that they reflect ways of life than by the hypothesis that they express perceptions, most of them seriously inadequate and badly distorted, of objective values.

But there is a well-known counter to this argument from relativity, namely to say that the items for which objective validity is in the first place to be claimed are not specific moral rules or codes but very general basic principles which are recognized at least implicitly to some extent in all society—such principles as provide the foundations of what Sidgwick has called different methods of ethics: the principle of universalizability, perhaps, or the rule that one ought to conform to the specific rules of any way of life in which one takes part, from which one profits, and on which one relies, or some utilitarian principle of doing what tends, or seems likely, to promote the general happiness. It is easy to show that such general principles, married with differing concrete circumstances, different existing social patterns or different preferences, will beget different specific moral rules; and there is some plausibility in the claim that the specific rules thus generated will vary from community to community or from group to group in close agreement with the actual variations in accepted codes.

The argument from relativity can be only partly countered in this way. To take this line the moral objectivist has to say that it is only in these principles that the objective moral character attaches immediately to its descriptively specified ground or subject: other moral judgements are objectively valid or true, but only derivatively and contingently—if things had been otherwise, quite different sorts of actions would have been right. And despite the prominence in recent philosophical ethics of universalization, utilitarian principles, and the like, these are very far from constituting the whole of what is actually affirmed as basic in ordinary moral thought. Much of this is concerned rather with what Hare calls 'ideals' or, less kindly, 'fanaticism'. That is, people judge that some things are good or right, and others are bad or wrong, not because— or at any rate not only because—they exemplify some general principle for which widespread implicit acceptance could be claimed, but because something about those things arouses certain responses immediately in them, though they would arouse radically and irresolvably different responses in others. 'Moral sense' or 'intuition' is an initially more plausible description of what supplies many of our basic moral judgements than 'reason'. With regard to all these starting points of moral thinking the argument from relativity remains in full force.

9. The Argument From Queerness

Even more important, however, and certainly more generally applicable, is the argument from queerness. This has two parts, one metaphysical, the other epistemological. If there were objective values, then they would be entities or qualities or relations of a very strange sort, utterly different from anything else in the universe. Correspondingly, if we were aware of them, it would have to be by some special faculty of moral perception or intuition, utterly different from our ordinary ways of knowing everything else. These points were recognized by Moore when he spoke of non-natural qualities, and by the intuitionists in their talk about a 'faculty of moral intuition'. Intuitionism has long been out of favour, and it is indeed easy to point out its implausibilities. What is not so often stressed, but is more important, is that the central thesis of intuitionism is one to which any objectivist view of values is in the end committed: intuitionism merely makes unpalatably plain what other forms of objectivism wrap up. Of course the suggestion that moral judgements are made or moral problems solved by just sitting down and having an ethical intuition is a travesty of actual moral thinking. But, however complex the real process, it will require (if it is to yield authoritatively prescriptive conclusions) some input of this distinctive sort, either premisses or forms of argument or both. When we ask the awkward question, how we can be aware of this authoritative prescriptivity, of the truth of these distinctively ethical premisses or of the cogency of this distinctively ethical pattern of reasoning, none of our ordinary accounts of sensory perception or introspection or the framing and confirming of explanatory hypotheses or inference or logical construction or conceptual analysis, or any combination of these, will provide a satisfactory answer; 'a special sort of intuition' is a lame answer, but it is the one to which the clear-headed objectivist is compelled to resort.

Indeed, the best move for the moral objectivist is not to evade this issue, but to look for companions in guilt. For example, Richard Price argues that it is not moral knowledge alone that such an empiricism as those of Locke and Hume is unable to account for, but also our knowledge and even our ideas of essence, number, identity, diversity, solidity, inertia, substance, the necessary existence and infinite extension of time and space, necessity and possibility in general, power, and causation. If the understanding, which Price defines as the faculty within us that discerns truth, is also a source of new simple ideas of so many other sorts, may it not also be a power of immediately perceiving right and wrong, which yet are real characters of action?

This is an important counter to the argument from queerness. The only adequate reply to it would be to show how, on empiricist foundations, we can construct an account of the ideas and beliefs and knowledge that we have of all these matters. I cannot even begin to do that here, though I have undertaken some parts of the task elsewhere. I can only state my belief that satisfactory accounts of most of these can be given in empirical terms. If some supposed metaphysical necessities or essences resist such treatment, then they too should be included, along with objective values, among the targets of the argument from queerness.

This queerness does not consist simply in the fact that ethical statements are 'unverifiable'. Although logical positivism with its verifiability theory of descriptive meaning gave an impetus to non-cognitive accounts of ethics, it is not only logical positivists but also empiricists of a much more liberal sort who should find objective values hard to accommodate. Indeed, I would not only reject the verifiability principle but also deny the conclusion commonly drawn from it, that moral judgements lack descriptive meaning. The assertion that there are objective values or intrinsically prescriptive entities or features of some kind, which ordinary moral judgements presuppose, is, I hold, not meaningless but false.

Plato's Forms give a dramatic picture of what objective values would have to be. The Form of the Good is such that knowledge of it provides the knower with both a direction and an overriding motive; something's being good both tells the person who knows this to pursue it and makes him pursue it. An objective good would be sought by anyone who was acquainted with it, not because of any contingent fact that this person, or every person, is so constituted that he desires this end, but just because the end has to-be-pursuedness somehow built into it. Similarly, if there were objective principles of right and wrong, any wrong (possible) course of action would have not-to-be-doneness somehow built into it. Or we should have something like Clarke's necessary relations of fitness between situations and actions, so that a situation would have a demand for such-and-such and action somehow built into it.

The need for an argument of this sort can be brought out by reflection on Hume's argument that 'reason'—in which at this stage he includes all sorts of knowing as well as reasoning—can never be an 'influencing motive of the will'. Someone might object that Hume has argued unfairly from the lack of influencing power (not contingent upon desires) in ordinary objects of knowledge and ordinary reasoning, and might maintain that values differ from natural objects precisely in their power, when known, automatically to influence the will. To this Hume could, and would need to, reply that this objection involves the postulating of value-entities or value-features of quite a different order from anything else with which we are acquainted, and of a corresponding faculty with which to detect them. That is, he would have to supplement his explicit argument with what I have called the argument from queerness.

Another way of bringing out this queerness is to ask, about anything that is supposed to have some objective moral quality, how this is linked with its natural features. What is the connection between the natural fact that an action is a piece of deliberate cruelty—say, causing pain just for fun—and the moral fact that it is wrong? It cannot be an entailment, a logical or semantic necessity. Yet it is not merely that the two features occur together. The wrongness must somehow be 'consequential' or 'supervenient'; it is wrong because it is a piece of deliberate cruelty. But just what *in the world* is signified by this 'because'? And how do we know the relation that it signifies, if this is something more than such actions being socially condemned, and condemned by us too, perhaps through our having absorbed attitudes from our social environment? It is not even sufficient to postulate a faculty which 'sees' the wrongness: something must be postulated which can see at once the natural features that constitute the cruelty, and the wrongness, and the mysterious consequential link between the two. Alternatively, the intuition required might be the perception that wrongness is a higher order property belonging to certain natural properties; but what is this belonging of properties to other properties, and how can we discern it? How much simpler and more comprehensible the situation would be if we could replace the moral quality with some sort of subjective response which could be causally related to the detection of the natural features on which the supposed quality is said to be consequential.

It may be thought that the argument from queerness is given an unfair start if we thus relate it to what are admittedly among the wilder products of philosophical fancy—Platonic Forms, non-natural qualities, self-evident relations of fitness, faculties of intuition, and the like. Is it equally forceful if applied to the terms in which everyday moral judgements are more likely to be expressed—though still, as has been argued in Section 7, with a claim to objectivity—'you must do this', 'you can't do that', 'obligation', 'unjust', 'rotten', 'disgraceful', 'mean', or talk about good reasons for or against possible actions? Admittedly not; but that is because the objective prescriptivity, the element a claim for whose authoritativeness is embedded in ordinary moral thought and language, is not yet isolated in these forms of speech, but is presented along with relations to desires and feelings, reasoning about the means to desired ends, interpersonal demands, the injustice which consists in the violation of what are in the context the accepted standards of merit, the psychological constituents of meanness, and so on. There is nothing queer about any of these, and under cover of them the claim for moral authority may pass unnoticed. But if I am right in arguing that it is ordinarily there, and is therefore very likely to be incorporated almost automatically in philosophical accounts of ethics which systematize our ordinary thought even in such apparently innocent terms as these, it needs to be examined, and for this purpose it needs to be isolated and exposed as it is by the less cautious philosophical reconstructions.

10. Patterns of Objectification

Considerations of these kinds suggest that it is in the end less paradoxical to reject than to retain the common-sense belief in the objectivity of moral values, provided that we can explain how this belief, if it is false, has become established and is so resistant to criticisms. This proviso is not difficult to satisfy.

On a subjectivist view, the supposedly objective values will be based in fact upon attitudes which the person has who takes himself to be recognizing and responding to those values. If we admit what Hume calls the mind's 'propensity to spread itself on external objects', we can understand the supposed objectivity of moral qualities as arising from what we can call the projection or objectification of moral attitudes. This would be analogous to what is called the 'pathetic fallacy', the tendency to read our feelings into their objects. If a fungus, say, fills us with disgust, we may be inclined to ascribe to the fungus itself a non-natural quality of foulness. But in moral contexts there is more than this propensity at work. Moral attitudes themselves are at least partly social in origin: socially established—and socially necessary—patterns of behaviour put pressure on individuals, and each individual tends to internalize these pressures and to join in requiring these patterns of behaviour of himself and of others. The attitudes that are objectified into moral values have indeed an external source, though not the one assigned to them by the belief in their absolute authority. Moreover, there are motives that would support objectification. We need morality to regulate interpersonal relations, to control some of the ways in which people behave towards one another, often in opposition to contrary inclinations. We therefore want our moral judgements to be authoritative for other agents as well as for ourselves: objective validity would give them the authority required. Aesthetic values are logically in the same position as moral ones; much the same metaphysical and epistemological considerations apply to them. But aesthetic values are less strongly objectified than moral ones; their subjective status, and an 'error theory' with regard to such claims to objectivity as are incorporated in aesthetic judgements, will be more readily accepted, just because the motives for their objectification are less compelling.

But it would be misleading to think of the objectification of moral values as primarily the projection of feelings, as in the pathetic fallacy. More important are wants and demands. As Hobbes says, 'whatsoever is the object of any man's Appetite or Desire, that is it, which he for his part called *Good*'; and certainly both the adjective 'good' and the noun 'goods' are used in non-moral contexts of things because they are such as to satisfy desires. We get the notion of something's being objectively good, or having intrinsic value, by reversing the direction of dependence here, by making the desire depend upon the goodness, instead of the goodness on the desire. And this is aided by the fact that the desired thing will indeed have features that make it desired, that enable it to arouse a desire or that make it such as to satisfy some desire that is already there. It is fairly easy to confuse the way in which a thing's desirability is indeed objective with its having in our sense objective value. The fact that the word 'good' serves as one of our main moral terms is a trace of this pattern of objectification.

Similarly related uses of words are covered by the distinction between hypothetical and categorical imperatives. The statement that someone 'ought to' or, more strongly, 'must' do such-and-such may be backed up explicitly or implicitly by reference to what he wants or to what his purposes and objects are. Again, there may be a reference to the purposes of someone else, perhaps the speaker: 'You must do this'—'Why?'—'Because I want such-and-such'. The moral categorical imperative which could be expressed in the same words can be seen as resulting from the suppression of the conditional clause in a hypothetical imperative without its being replaced by any such reference to the speaker's wants. The action in question is still required in something like the way in which it would be if it were appropriately related to a want, but it is no longer admitted that there is any contingent want upon which is being required depends. Again this move can be understood when we remember that at least our central and basic moral judgements represent social demands, where the source of the demand is indeterminate and diffuse. Whose demands or wants are in question, the agent's, or the speaker's, or those of an indefinite multitude of other people? All of these in a way, but there are advantages in not specifying them precisely. The speaker is expressing demands which he makes as a member of a community, which he has developed in and by participation in a joint way of life; also, what is required of this particular agent would be required of any other in a relevantly similar situation; but the agent too is expected to have internalized the relevant demands, to act as if the ends for which the action is required were his own. By suppressing any explicit reference to demands and making the imperatives categorical we facilitate conceptual moves from one such demand relation to another. The moral uses of such words as 'must' and 'ought' and 'should', all of which are used also to express hypothetical imperatives, are traces of this pattern of objectification.

It may be objected that this explanation links normative ethics too closely with descriptive morality, with the mores or socially enforced patterns of behaviour that anthropologists record. But it can hardly be denied that moral thinking starts from the enforcement of social codes. Of course it is not confined to that. But even when moral judgements are detached from the mores of any actual society they are liable to be framed with reference to an ideal community of moral agents, such as Kant's kingdom of ends, which but for the need to give God a special place in it would have been better called a commonwealth of ends.

Another way of explaining the objectification of moral values is to say that ethics is a system of law from which the legislator has been removed. This might have been derived either from the positive law of a state or from a supposed system of divine law. There can be no doubt that some features of modern European moral concepts are traceable to the theological ethics of Christianity. The stress on quasi-imperative notions, on what ought to be done or on what is wrong in a sense that is close to that of 'forbidden', are surely relics of divine commands. Admittedly, the central ethical concepts for Plato and Aristotle also are in a broad sense prescriptive or intrinsically action-guiding, but in concentrating rather on 'good' than on 'ought' they show that their moral thought is an objectification of the desired and the satisfying rather than of the commanded. Elizabeth Anscombe has argued that modern, non-Aristotelian, concepts of *moral* obligation, *moral* duty, of what is *morally* right and wrong, and of the *moral* sense of 'ought' are survivals outside the framework of thought that made them really intelligible, namely the belief in divine law. She infers that 'ought' has 'become a word of mere mesmeric force', with only a 'delusive appearance of content', and that we would do better to discard such terms and concepts altogether, and go back to Aristotelian ones.

There is much to be said for this view. But while we can explain some distinctive features of modern moral philosophy in this way, it would be a mistake to see the whole problem of the claim to objective prescriptivity as merely local and unnecessary, as a post-operative complication of a society from which a dominant system of theistic belief has recently been rather hastily excised. As Cudworth and Clarke and Price, for example, show, even those who still admit divine commands, or the positive law of God, may believe moral values to have an independent objective but still action-guiding authority. Responding to Plato's *Euthyphro* dilemma, they believe that God commands what he commands because it is in itself good or right, not that it is good or right merely because and in that he commands it. Otherwise God himself could not be called good. Price asks, 'What can be more preposterous, than to make the Deity nothing but will; and to exalt this on the ruins of all his attributes?' The apparent objectivity of moral value is a widespread phenomenon which has more than one source: the persistence of a belief in something like divine law when the belief in the divine legislator has faded out is only one factor among others. There are several different patterns of objectification, all of which have left characteristic traces in our actual moral concepts and moral language.

11. The General Goal of Human Life

The argument of the preceding sections is meant to apply quite generally to moral thought, but the terms in which it has been stated are largely those of the Kantian and post-Kantian tradition of English moral philosophy. To those who are more familiar with another tradition, which runs through Aristotle and Aquinas, it may seem wide of the mark. For them, the fundamental notion is that of the good for man, or the general end or goal of human life, or perhaps of a set of basic goods or primary human purposes. Moral reasoning consists partly in achieving a more adequate understanding of this basic goal (or set of goals), partly in working out the best way of pursuing and realizing it. But this approach is open to two radically different interpretations. According to one, to say that something is the good for man or the general goal of human life is just to say that this is what men in fact pursue or will find ultimately satisfying, or perhaps that it is something which, if postulated as an implicit goal, enables us to make sense of actual human strivings and to detect a coherent pattern in what would otherwise seem to be a chaotic jumble of conflicting purposes. According to the other interpretation, to say that something is the good for man or the general goal of human life is to say that this is man's proper end, that this is what he ought to be striving after, whether he in fact is or not. On the first interpretation we have a descriptive statement, on the second a normative or evaluative or prescriptive one. But this approach tends to combine the two interpretations, or to slide from one to the other, and to borrow support for what are in effect claims of the second sort from the plausibility of statements of the first sort.

I have no quarrel with this notion interpreted in the first way. I would only insert a warning that there may well be more diversity even of fundamental purposes, more variation in what different human beings will find ultimately satisfying, than the terminology of '*the* good for man' would suggest. Nor indeed, have I any quarrel with the second, prescriptive, interpretation, provided that it is recognized as subjectively prescriptive, that the speaker is here putting forward his own demands or proposals, or those of some movement that he represents, though no doubt linking these demands or proposals with what he takes to be already in the first, descriptive, sense fundamental human goals. In fact, I shall myself make use of the notion of the good for man, interpreted in both these ways, when I try in Chapter 8 to sketch a positive

moral system. But if it is claimed that something is objectively the right or proper goal of human life, then this is tantamount to the assertion of something that is objectively categorically imperative, and comes fairly within the scope of our previous arguments. Indeed, the running together of what I have here called the two interpretations is yet another pattern of objectification: a claim to objective prescriptivity is constructed by combining the normative element in the second interpretation with the objectivity allowed by the first, by the statement that such and such are fundamentally pursued or ultimately satisfying human goals. The argument from relativity still applies: the radical diversity of the goals that men actually pursue and find satisfying makes it implausible to construe such pursuits as resulting from an imperfect grasp of a unitary true good. So too does the argument from queerness; we can still ask what this objectively prescriptive rightness of the true goal can be, and how this is linked on the one hand with the descriptive features of this goal and on the other with the fact that it is *to some extent* an actual goal of human striving.

To meet these difficulties, the objectivist may have recourse to the purpose of God: the true purpose of human life is fixed by what God intended (or, intends) men to do and to be. Actual human strivings and satisfactions have some relation to this true end because God made men for this end and made them such as to pursue it—but only *some* relation, because of the inevitable imperfection of created beings.

I concede that if the requisite theological doctrine could be defended, a kind of objective ethical prescriptivity could be thus introduced. Since I think that theism cannot be defended, I do not regard this as any threat to my argument. But I shall take up the question of relations between morality and religion again in Chapter 10. Those who wish to keep theism as a live option can read the arguments of the intervening chapters hypothetically, as a discussion of what we can make of morality without recourse to God, and hence of what we can say about morality if, in the end, we dispense with religious belief.

12. Conclusion

I have maintained that there is a real issue about the status of values, including moral values. Moral scepticism, the denial of objective moral values, is not to be confused with any one of several first order normative views, or with any linguistic or conceptual analysis. Indeed, ordinary moral judgements involve a claim to objectivity which both non-cognitive and naturalist analyses fail to capture. Moral scepticism must, therefore, take the form of an error theory, admitting that a belief in objective values is built into ordinary moral thought and language, but holding that this ingrained belief is false. As such, it needs arguments to support it against 'common sense'. But solid arguments can be found. The considerations that favour moral scepticism are: first, the relativity or variability of some important starting points of moral thinking and their apparent dependence on actual ways of life; secondly, the metaphysical peculiarity of the supposed objective values, in that they would have to be intrinsically action-guiding and motivating; thirdly, the problem of how such values could be consequential or supervenient upon natural features; fourthly, the corresponding epistemological difficulty of accounting for our knowledge of value entities or features and of their links with the features on which they would be consequential; fifthly, the possibility of explaining, in terms of several different patterns of objectification, traces of which remain in moral language and moral concepts, how even if there were no such objective values people not only might have come to suppose that there are but also might persist firmly in that belief. These five points sum up the case for moral scepticism; but of almost equal importance are the preliminary removal of misunderstandings that often prevent this thesis from being considered fairly and explicitly, and the isolation of those items about which the moral sceptic is sceptical from many associated qualities and relations whose objective status is not in dispute.

. . .

15

Moral Explanations

NICHOLAS STURGEON

Nicholas Sturgeon (b. 1942) is Associate Professor of Philosophy at Cornell University. He has published a number of articles on moral philosophy.

Sturgeon's topic is a problem raised by Gilbert Harman. In reading 13, Harman notes that morality seems importantly different from science. Unlike scientific facts, moral facts appear to play no role in explaining our observations (or anything else). But Sturgeon argues that this has not been established. In his view, a plausible explanation of behavior such as that of Adolf Hitler makes reference to the (moral) fact that Hitler was depraved. Of course, anyone with exactly Hitler's psychology would have acted just as Hitler did. But in Sturgeon's view, to have Hitler's psychology is to be depraved. It is thus impossible to explain Hitler's behavior without appealing to moral facts.

We might, of course, be wrong in holding that persons with that psychology are depraved. Despite the evidence, the moral theory in which this belief is embedded might be mistaken. But, just so, we might, despite all the evidence, be mistaken in holding our theories of subatomic physics or of the external world. Thus construed, Harman's argument is a special case of a much wider skepticism. For this reason, Sturgeon argues, it poses no special threat to ethics.

THERE IS ONE ARGUMENT for moral skepticism that I respect even though I remain unconvinced. It has sometimes been called the argument from moral diversity or relativity, but that is somewhat misleading, for the problem arises not from the diversity of moral views, but from the apparent difficulty of *settling* moral disagreements, or even of knowing what would be required to settle them, a difficulty thought to be noticeably greater than any found in settling disagreements that arise in, for example, the sciences. This provides an argument for moral skepticism because one obviously possible explanation of our difficulty in settling moral disagreements is that they are really unsettleable, that there is no way of justifying one rather than another competing view on these issues; and a possible further explanation for the unsettleability of moral disagreements, in turn, is moral nihilism, the view that on these issues there just is no fact of the matter, that the impossibility of discovering and establishing moral truths is due to there not being any.

I am, as I say, unconvinced: partly because I think this argument exaggerates the difficulty we actually find in settling moral disagreements, partly because there are alternative explanations to be considered for the difficulty we do find.

Under the latter heading, for example, it certainly matters to what extent moral disagreements depend on disagreements about other questions which, however, disputed they may be, are nevertheless regarded as having objective answers: questions such as which, if any, religion is true, which account of human psychology, which theory of human society. And it also matters to what extent consideration of moral questions is in practice skewed by distorting factors such as personal interest and social ideology. These are large issues. Although it is possible to say some useful things to put them in perspective,[1] it appears impossible to settle them quickly or in any a priori way. Consideration of them is likely to have to be piecemeal and, in the short run at least, frustratingly indecisive.

These large issues are not my topic here. But I mention them, and the difficulty of settling them, to show why it is natural that moral skeptics have hoped to find some quicker way of establishing their thesis. I doubt that any exist, but some have of course been proposed. Verificationist attacks on ethics should no doubt be seen in this light, and J. L. Mackie's recent "argument from queerness" is a clear instance.[2] The quicker response on which I shall concentrate, however, is neither of these, but instead an argument by Gilbert Harman designed to bring out the "basic problem" about morality, which in his view is "its apparent immunity from observational testing" and "the seeming irrelevance of observational evidence."[3] The argument is that reference to moral facts appears unnecessary for the *explanation* of our moral observations and beliefs.

Harman's view, I should say at once, is not in the end a skeptical one, and he does not view the argument I shall discuss as a decisive defense of moral skepticism or moral nihilism. Someone else might easily so regard it, however. For Harman himself regards it as creating a strong *prima facie* case for skepticism and nihilism, strong enough to justify calling it "the problem with ethics."[4] And he believes it shows that the only recourse for someone who wishes to avoid moral skepticism is to find defensible reductive definitions for ethical terms; so skepticism would be the obvious conclusion to draw for anyone who doubted the possibility of such definitions. I believe, however, that Harman is mistaken on both counts. I shall show that his argument for skepticism either rests on claims that most people would find quite implausible (and so cannot be what constitutes, for *them,* the problem with ethics); or else becomes just the application to ethics of a familiar *general* skeptical strategy, one which, if it works for ethics, will work equally well for unobservable

[1] As, for example, in Alan Gewirth, "Positive 'Ethics' and Normative 'Science' ", *The Philosophical Review* 69 (1960), pp. 311–30, in which there are some useful remarks about the first of them.

[2] J. L. Mackie, *Ethics: Inventing Right and Wrong* (Harmondsworth, England: Penguin, 1977), pp. 38–42.

[3] Gilbert Harman, *The Nature of Morality: An Introduction to Ethics* (New York: Oxford University Press, 1977), pp. vii, viii. Parenthetical page references are to this work.

[4] Harman's title for the entire first section of his book.

theoretical entities, or for other minds, or for an external world (and so, again, can hardly be what constitutes the distinctive problem with *ethics*). I have argued elsewhere,[5] moreover, that one can in any case be a moral realist, and indeed an ethical naturalist, without believing that we are now or ever will be in possession of reductive naturalistic definitions for ethical terms.

I. The Problem With Ethics

Moral theories are often tested in thought experiments, against imagined examples; and, as Harman notes, trained researchers often test scientific theories in the same way. The problem, though, is that scientific theories can also be tested against the world, by observations or real experiments; and, Harman asks, "can moral principles be tested in the same way, out in the world?"

This would not be a very interesting or impressive challenge, of course, if it were merely a resurrection of standard verificationist worries about whether moral assertions and theories have any testable empirical implications, implications statable in some relatively austere "observational" vocabulary. One problem with that form of the challenge, as Harman points out, is that there are no "pure" observations, and in consequence no purely observational vocabulary either. But there is also a deeper problem that Harman does not mention, one that remains even if we shelve worries about "pure" observations and, at least for the sake of argument, grant the verificationist his observational language, pretty much as it was usually conceived: that is, as lacking at the very least any obviously theoretical terminology from any recognized science, and of course as lacking any moral terminology. For then the difficulty is that moral principles fare just as well (or just as badly) against the verificationist challenge as do typical scientific principles. For it is by now a familiar point about scientific principles—principles such as Newton's law of universal gravitation or Darwin's theory of evolution—that they are entirely devoid of empirical implications when considered in isolation.[6] We do of course base observational predictions on such theories and so test them against experience, but that is because we do *not* consider them in isolation. For we can derive these predictions only by relying at the same time on a large background of additional assumptions, many of which are equally theoretical and equally incapable of being tested in isolation.

A less familiar point, because less often spelled out, is that the relation of moral principles to observation is similar in *both* these respects. Candidate moral principles—for example, that an action is wrong just in case there is

---

[5] In the longer article of which this is an abridgement.

[6] This point is generally credited to Pierre Duhem; see *The Aim and Structure of Physical Theory*, trans. Philip P. Wiener (Princeton, N.J.: Princeton University Press, 1954). It is a prominent theme in the influential writings of W. V. O. Quine. For an especially clear application of it, see Hilary Putnam, "The 'Corroboration' of Theories," in *Mathematics, Matter and Method: Philosophical Papers, Volume I,* second ed. (Cambridge: Cambridge University Press, 1977), pp. 250–69.

something else the agent could have done that would have produced a greater balance of pleasure over pain—lack empirical implications when considered in isolation. But it is easy to derive empirical consequences from them, and thus to test them against experience, if we allow ourselves, as we do in the scientific case, to rely on a background of other assumptions of comparable status. Thus, if we conjoin the act-utilitarian principle I just cited with the further view, also untestable in isolation, that it is always wrong deliberately to kill a human being, we can deduce from these two premises together the consequence that deliberately killing a human being always produces a lesser balance of pleasure over pain than some available alternative act; and this claim is one any positivist would have conceded we know, in principle at least, how to test. If we found it to be false, moreover, then we would be forced by this empirical test to abandon at least one of the moral claims from which we derived it.

It might be thought a worrisome feature of this example, however, and a further opening for skepticism, that there could be controversy about which moral premise to abandon, and that we have not explained how our empirical test can provide an answer to *this* question. And this may be a problem. It should be a familiar problem, however, because the Duhemian commentary includes a precisely corresponding point about the scientific case: that if we are at all cautious in characterizing what we observe, then the requirement that our theories merely be *consistent* with observation is a very weak one. There are always many, perhaps indefinitely many, different mutually inconsistent ways to adjust our views to meet this constraint. Of course, in practice we are often confident of how to do it: if you are a freshman chemistry student, you do not conclude from your failure to obtain the predicted value in an experiment that it is all over for the atomic theory of gases. And the decision can be equally easy, one should note, in a moral case. Consider two examples. From the surprising moral thesis that Adolf Hitler was a morally admirable person, together with a modest piece of moral theory to the effect that no morally admirable person would, for example, instigate and oversee the degradation and death of millions of persons, one can derive the testable consequence that Hitler did not do this. But he did, so we must give up one of our premises; and the choice of which to abandon is neither difficult nor controversial.

Or, to take a less monumental example, contrived around one of Harman's own, suppose you have been thinking yourself lucky enough to live in a neighborhood in which no one would do anything wrong, at least not in public; and that the modest piece of theory you accept, this time, is that malicious cruelty, just for the hell of it, is wrong. Then, as in Harman's example, "you round a corner and see a group of young hoodlums pour gasoline on a cat and ignite it." At this point, either your confidence in the neighborhood or your principle about cruelty has got to give way. But the choice is easy, if dispiriting, so easy as hardly to require thought. As Harman says, "You do not need to *conclude* that what they are doing is wrong; you do not need to figure anything out; you can *see* that it is wrong" (p. 4). But a skeptic can still wonder whether this practical confidence, or this "seeing," rests in either sort of case on anything more than deeply ingrained conventions of thought—respect for scientific experts, say, and for certain moral traditions—as opposed to anything answerable to the facts of the matter, any reliable strategy for getting it right about the world.

Now, Harman's challenge is interesting partly because it does not rest on these verificationist doubts about whether moral beliefs have observational implications, but even more because what it does rest on is a partial answer to the kind of general skepticism to which, as we have seen, reflection on the verificationist picture can lead. Many of our beliefs are justified, in Harman's view, by their providing or helping to provide a reasonable *explanation* of our observing what we do. It would be consistent with your failure, as a beginning student, to obtain the experimental result predicted by the gas laws, that the laws are mistaken. But a better explanation, in light of your inexperience and the general success experts have had in confirming and applying these laws, is that you made some mistake in running the experiment. So our scientific beliefs can be justified by their explanatory role; and so too, in Harman's view, can mathematical beliefs and many commonsense beliefs about the world.

Not so, however, moral beliefs: they appear to have no such explanatory role. That is "the problem with ethics." Harman spells out his version of this contrast:

> You need to make assumptions about certain physical facts to explain the occurrence of the observations that support a scientific theory, but you do not seem to need to make assumptions about any moral facts to explain the occurrence of the so-called moral observations I have been talking about. In the moral case, it would seem that you need only make assumptions about the psychology or moral sensibility of the person making the moral observation. (p. 6)

More precisely, and applied to his own example, it might be reasonable, in order to explain your judging that the hoodlums are wrong to set the cat on fire, to assume "that the children really are pouring gasoline on a cat and you are seeing them do it." But there is no

> obvious reason to assume anything about "moral facts," such as that it is really wrong to set the cat on fire. . . . Indeed, an assumption about moral facts would seem to be totally irrelevant to the explanation of your making the judgment you make. It would seem that all we need assume is that you have certain more or less well articulated moral principles that are reflected in the judgments you make, based on your moral sensibility. (p. 7)

And Harman thinks that if we accept this conclusion, suitably generalized, then, subject to one possible qualification concerning reduction that I have discussed elsewhere,[7] we must conclude that moral theories cannot be tested against the world as scientific theories can, and that we have no reason to

---

[7] See note 5.

believe that moral facts are part of the order of nature or that there is any moral knowledge (pp. 23, 35).

My own view is that Harman is quite wrong, not in thinking that the explanatory role of our beliefs is important to their justification, but in thinking that moral beliefs play no such role.[8] I shall have to say something about the initial plausibility of Harman's thesis as applied to his own example, but part of my reason for dissenting should be apparent from the other example I just gave. We find it easy (and so does Harman [p. 108]) to conclude from the evidence not just that Hitler was not morally admirable, but that he was morally depraved. But isn't it plausible that Hitler's moral depravity—the fact of his really having been morally depraved—forms part of a reasonable explanation of why we believe he was depraved? I think so, and I shall argue concerning this and other examples that moral beliefs very commonly play the explanatory role Harman denies them. Before I can press my case, however, I need to clear up several preliminary points about just what Harman is claiming and just how his argument is intended to work.

II. Observation and Explanation

(1) For there are several ways in which Harman's argument invites misunderstanding. One results from his focusing at the start on the question of whether there can be moral *observations*.[9] But this question turns out to be a side issue, in no way central to his argument that moral principles cannot be tested against the world. There are a couple of reasons for this, of which the more important[10] by far is that Harman does not really require of moral facts, if belief in them is to be justified, that they figure in the explanation of moral observations. It would be enough, on the one hand, if they were needed for the explanation of moral beliefs that are not in any interesting sense obser-

---

[8] Harman is careful always to say only that moral beliefs *appear* to play no such role, and since he eventually concludes that there *are* moral facts (p. 132), this caution may be more than stylistic. I shall argue that this more cautious claim, too, is mistaken (indeed, that is my central thesis). But to avoid issues about Harman's intent, I shall simply mean by "Harman's argument" the skeptical argument of his first two chapters, whether or not he means to endorse all of it. This argument surely deserves discussion in its own right in either case, especially since Harman never explains what is wrong with it.

[9] He asks: "Can moral principles be tested in the same way [as scientific hypotheses can], out in the world? You can observe someone do something, but can you ever perceive the rightness or wrongness of what he does?" (p. 4).

[10] The other is that Harman appears to use "observe" (and "perceive" and "see") in a surprising way. One would normally take observing (or perceiving, or seeing) something to involve *knowing* it was the case. But Harman apparently takes an observation to be *any* opinion arrived at as "a direct result of perception" (p. 5) or, at any rate (see next footnote), "immediately and without conscious reasoning" (p. 7). This means that observations need not even be true, much less known to be true. A consequence is that the existence of moral observations, in Harman's sense, would not be sufficient to show that there is moral knowledge, although this *would* be sufficient if "observe" were being used in a more standard sense. What I argue in the text is that the existence of moral observations (in either Harman's or the standard sense) is not *necessary* for showing that there is moral knowledge, either.

vations. For example, Harman thinks belief in moral facts would be vindicated if they were needed to explain our drawing the moral conclusions we do when we reflect on hypothetical cases, but I think there is no illumination in calling these conclusions observations.[11] It would also be enough, on the other hand, if moral facts were needed for the explanation of what were clearly observations, but not moral observations. Harman thinks mathematical beliefs are justified, but he does not suggest that there are mathematical observations; it is rather that appeal to mathematical truths helps to explain why we make the physical observations we do (p. 10). Moral beliefs would surely be justified, too, if they played such a role, whether or not there are any moral observations.

So the claim is that moral facts are not needed to explain our having any of the moral beliefs we do, whether or not those beliefs are observations, and are equally unneeded to explain any of the observations we make, whether or not those observations are moral. In fact, Harman's view appears to be that moral facts aren't needed to explain anything at all: though it would perhaps be question-begging for him to begin with this strong a claim, since he grants that if there were any moral facts, then appeal to other moral facts—more general ones, for example—might be needed to explain *them* (p. 8). But he is certainly claiming, at the very least, that moral facts aren't needed to explain any nonmoral facts we have any reason to believe in.

(2) Other possible misunderstandings concern what is meant in asking whether reference to moral facts is *needed* to explain moral beliefs. One warning about this question I have dealt with in my discussion of reduction elsewhere;[12] but another, about what Harman is clearly *not* asking, and about what sort of answer I can attempt to defend to the question he is asking, I can spell out

---

[11] This sort of case does not meet Harman's characterization of an observation as an opinion that is "a direct result of perception" (p. 5), but he is surely right that moral facts would be as well vindicated if they were needed to explain our drawing conclusions about hypothetical cases as they would be if they were needed to explain observations in the narrower sense. To be sure, Harman is still confining his attention to cases in which we draw the moral conclusion from our thought experiment "immediately and without conscious reasoning" (p. 7), and it is no doubt the existence of such cases that gives purchase to talk of a "moral sense." But this feature, again, can hardly matter to the argument: would belief in moral facts be less justified if they were needed only to explain the instances in which we draw the moral conclusion *slowly?* Nor can it make any difference for that matter whether the case we are reflecting on is hypothetical: so my example in which we, quickly or slowly, draw a moral conclusion about Hitler from what we know of him, is surely relevant.

[12] In the longer paper from which this one is abridged. The salient point is that there are two very *different* reasons one might have for thinking that no reference to moral facts is needed in the explanation of moral beliefs. One—Harman's reason, and my target in this essay—is that no moral explanations even *seem* plausible, that reference to moral facts always strikes us as "completely irrelevant" to the explanation of moral beliefs. This claim, if true, would tend to support moral skepticism. The other, which might appeal to a "reductive" naturalist in ethics, is that any moral explanations that *do* seem plausible can be paraphrased without explanatory loss in entirely nonmoral terms. I doubt this view, too, and I argue in the longer version of this paper that no ethical naturalist need hold it. But anyone tempted by it should note that it is anyway no version of moral skepticism: for what it says is that we know *so much* about ethics that we are always able to say, in entirely nonmoral terms, exactly which natural properties the moral terms in any plausible moral explanations refer to—that's why the moral expressions are dispensable. These two reasons should not be confused with one another.

here. For Harman's question is clearly not just whether there is *an* explanation of our moral beliefs that does not mention moral facts. Almost surely there is. Equally surely, however, there is *an* explanation of our commonsense non-moral beliefs that does not mention an external world: one which cites only our sensory experience, for example, together with whatever needs to be said about our psychology to explain why with that history of experience we would form just the beliefs we do. Harman means to be asking a question that will lead to skepticism about moral facts, but not to skepticism about the existence of material bodies or about well-established scientific theories of the world.

Harman illustrates the kind of question he is asking, and the kind of answer he is seeking, with an example from physics that it will be useful to keep in mind. A physicist sees a vapor trail in a cloud chamber and thinks, "There goes a proton." What explains his thinking this? Partly, of course, his psychological set, which largely depends on his beliefs about the apparatus and all the theory he has learned; but partly also, perhaps, the hypothesis that "there really was a proton going through the cloud chamber, causing the vapor trail, which he saw as a proton." We will *not* need this latter assumption, however, "if his having made that observation could have been equally well explained by his psychological set alone, without the need for any assumption about a proton" (p. 6).[13] So for reference to moral facts to be *needed* in the explanation of our beliefs and observations, is for this reference to be required for an explanation that is somehow *better* than competing explanations. Correspondingly, reference to moral facts will be unnecessary to an explanation, in Harman's view, not just because we can find some explanation that does not appeal to them, but because *no* explanation that appeals to them is any better than some competing explanation that does not.

Now, fine discriminations among competing explanations of almost anything are likely to be difficult, controversial, and provisional. Fortunately, however, my discussion of Harman's argument will not require any fine discriminations. This is because Harman's thesis, as we have seen, is *not* that moral explanations lose out by a small margin; nor is it that moral explanations, though sometimes initially promising, always turn out on further examination to be inferior to nonmoral ones. It is, rather, that reference to moral facts always looks, right from the start, to be "completely irrelevant" to the explanation of any of our observations and beliefs. And my argument will be that this is mistaken: that many moral explanations appear to be good explanations, or components in good explanations, that are not obviously undermined by anything else that we know. My suspicion, in fact, is that moral facts are needed in the sense explained, that they will turn out to belong in our best

---

[13] It is surprising that Harman does not mention the obvious intermediate possibility, which would occur to any instrumentalist: to cite the physicist's psychological set *and* the vapor trail, but say nothing about protons or other unobservables. It is *this* explanation, as I emphasize below, that is most closely parallel to an explanation of beliefs about an external world in terms of sensory experience and psychological makeup, or of moral beliefs in terms of nonmoral facts together with our "moral sensibility."

overall explanatory picture of the world, even in the long run, but I shall not attempt to establish that here. Indeed, it should be clear why I could not pretend to do so. For I have explicitly put to one side the issue (which I regard as incapable in any case of quick resolution) of whether and to what extent actual moral disagreements can be settled satisfactorily; but I assume it would count as a defect in any sort of explanation to rely on claims about which rational agreement proved unattainable. So I concede that it *could* turn out, for anything I say here, that moral explanations are all defective and should be discarded. What I shall try to show is merely that many moral explanations look reasonable enough to be in the running; and, more specifically, that nothing Harman says provides any reason for thinking they are not. This claim is surely strong enough (and controversial enough) to be worth defending.

(3) It is implicit in this statement of my project, but worth noting separately, that I take Harman to be proposing an *independent* skeptical argument—independent not merely of the argument from the difficulty of settling disputed moral questions, but also of other standard arguments for moral skepticism. Otherwise his argument is not worth separate discussion. For *any* of these more familiar skeptical arguments will of course imply that moral explanations are defective, on the reasonable assumption that it would be a defect in any explanation to rely on claims as doubtful as these arguments attempt to show all moral claims to be. But if *that* is why there is a problem with moral explanations, one should surely just cite the relevant skeptical argument, rather than this derivative difficulty about moral explanations, as the basic "problem with ethics," and it is that argument we should discuss. So I take Harman's interesting suggestion to be that there is a *different* difficulty that remains even if we put other arguments for moral skepticism aside and *assume,* for the sake of argument, that there are moral facts (for example, that what the children in his example are doing is really wrong): namely, that these assumed facts *still* seem to play no explanatory role.

This understanding of Harman's thesis crucially affects my argumentative strategy in a way to which I should alert the reader in advance. For it should be clear that assessment of this thesis not merely permits, but *requires,* that we provisionally assume the existence of moral facts. I can see no way of evaluating the claim that *even if* we assumed the existence of moral facts they would still appear explanatorily irrelevant, without assuming the existence of some, to see how they would look. So I do freely assume this in each of the examples I discuss in the next section. (I have tried to choose plausible examples, moreover, moral facts most of us would be inclined to believe in if we did believe in moral facts, since those are the easiest to think about; but the precise examples don't matter, and anyone who would prefer others should feel free to substitute her own.) I grant, furthermore, that if Harman were right about the outcome of this thought experiment—that even after we assumed these facts they still looked irrelevant to the explanation of our moral beliefs and other nonmoral facts—then we might conclude with him that there were, after all, no such facts. But I claim he is wrong: that once we have provisionally assumed the existence of moral facts they *do* appear relevant, by perfectly ordinary standards, to the explanation of moral beliefs and of a good deal else besides. Does this prove that there *are* such facts? Well of course it helps support that view, but here I carefully make no claim to have shown so much. What I *show* is that any remaining reservations about the existence of moral facts must be based on those *other* skeptical arguments, of which Harman's argument is independent. In short, there may still be a "problem with ethics," but it has *nothing* special to do with moral explanations.

III. Moral Explanations

Now that I have explained how I understand Harman's thesis, I turn to my arguments against it. I shall first add to my example of Hitler's moral character several more in which it seems plausible to cite moral facts as part of an explanation of nonmoral facts, and in particular of people's forming the moral opinions they do. I shall then argue that Harman gives us no plausible reason to reject or ignore these explanations; I shall claim, in fact, that the same is true for his own example of the children igniting the cat. I shall conclude, finally, by attempting to diagnose the source of the disagreement between Harman and me on these issues.

My Hitler example suggests a whole range of extremely common cases that appear not to have occurred to Harman, cases in which we cite someone's moral character as part of an explanation of his or her deeds, and in which that whole story is then available as a plausible further explanation of someone's arriving at a correct assessment of that moral character. Take just one other example. Bernard DeVoto, in *The Year of Decision: 1846,* describes the efforts of American emigrants already in California to rescue another party of emigrants, the Donner Party, trapped by snows in the High Sierras, once their plight became known. At a meeting in Yerba Buena (now San Francisco), the relief efforts were put under the direction of a recent arrival, Passed Midshipman Selim Woodworth, described by a previous acquaintance as "a great busybody and ambitious of taking a command among the emigrants."[14] But Woodworth not only failed to lead rescue parties into the mountains himself, where other rescuers were counting on him (leaving children to be picked up by him, for example), but had to be "shamed, threatened and bullied" even into organizing the efforts of others willing to take the risk; he spent time arranging comforts for himself in camp, preening himself on the importance of his position; and as a predictable result of his cowardice and his exercises in vainglory, many died who might have been saved, including four known still to be alive when he turned back for the last time in mid-March.

DeVoto concludes: "Passed Midshipman Woodworth was just no damned good" (1942, p. 442). I cite this case partly because it has so clearly the structure of an inference to a reasonable explanation. One can think of competing

---

[14] Bernard DeVoto, *The Year of Decision: 1846* (Boston: Houghton Mifflin, 1942), p. 426; a quotation from the notebooks of Francis Parkman. The account of the entire rescue effort is on pp. 424–444.

explanations, but the evidence points against them. It isn't, for example, that Woodworth was a basically decent person who simply proved too weak when thrust into a situation that placed heroic demands on him. He volunteered, he put no serious effort even into tasks that required no heroism, and it seems clear that concern for his own position and reputation played a much larger role in his motivation that did any concern for the people he was expected to save. If DeVoto is right about this evidence, moreover, it seems reasonable that part of the explanation of his believing that Woodworth was no damned good is just that Woodworth *was* no damned good.

DeVoto writes of course with more moral intensity (and with more of a flourish) than academic historians usually permit themselves, but it would be difficult to find a serious work of biography, for example, in which actions are not explained by appeal to moral character: sometimes by appeal to specific virtues and vices, but often enough also by appeal to a more general assessment. A different question, and perhaps a more difficult one, concerns the sort of example on which Harman concentrates, the explanation of judgments of right and wrong. Here again he appears just to have overlooked explanations in terms of moral character: a judge's thinking that it would be wrong to sentence a particular offender to the maximum prison term the law allows, for example, may be due in part to her decency and fairmindedness, which I take to be moral properties if any are. But do moral features of the action or institution being judged ever play an explanatory role? Here is an example in which they appear to. An interesting historical question is why vigorous and reasonably widespread moral opposition to slavery arose for the first time in the eighteenth and nineteenth centuries, even though slavery was a very old institution; and why this opposition arose primarily in Britain, France, and in French- and English-speaking North America, even though slavery existed throughout the New World.[15] There is a standard answer to this question. It is that chattel slavery in British and French America, and then in the United States, was much *worse* than previous forms of slavery, and much worse than slavery in Latin America. This is, I should add, a controversial explanation. But as is often the case with historical explanations, its proponents do not claim it is the whole story, and many of its opponents grant that there may be some truth in these comparisons, and that they may after all form a small part of a larger explanation.[16] This latter concession is all I require for my example. Equally good for my purpose would be the more limited thesis which explains the growth

[15] What is being explained, of course, is not just why people came to think slavery wrong, but why people who were not themselves slaves or in danger of being enslaved came to think it so seriously wrong as to be intolerable. There is a much larger and longer history of people who thought it wrong but tolerable and an even longer one of people who appear not to have gotten past the thought that the world would be a better place without it. See David Brion Davis, *The Problem of Slavery in Western Culture* (Ithaca, N.Y.: Cornell University Press, 1966).

[16] For a version of what I am calling the standard view of slavery in the Americas, see Frank Tannenbaum, *Slave and Citizen* (New York: Alfred A. Knopf, 1947). For an argument against both halves of the standard view, see Davis, *The Problem of Slavery,* esp. pp. 60–61, 223–25, 262–63.

of antislavery sentiment in the United States, between the Revolution and the Civil War, in part by saying that slavery in the United States became a more oppressive institution during that time. The appeal in these standard explanations is straightforwardly to moral facts.

What is supposed to be wrong with all these explanations? Harman says that assumptions about moral facts seem "completely irrelevant" in explaining moral observations and moral beliefs (p. 7), but on its more natural reading that claim seems pretty obviously mistaken about these examples. For it is natural to think that if a particular assumption is completely irrelevant to the explanation of a certain fact, then that fact would have obtained, and we could have explained it just as well, even if the assumption had been false.[17] But I do not believe that Hitler would have done all he did if he had not been morally depraved, nor, on the assumption that he was not depraved, can I think of any plausible explanation for his doing those things. Nor is it plausible that we would all have believed he was morally depraved even if he hadn't been. Granted, there is a tendency for writers who do not attach much weight to fascism as a social movement to want to blame its evils on a single maniacal leader, so perhaps some of them would have painted Hitler as a moral monster even if he had not been one. But this is only a tendency, and one for which many people know how to discount, so I doubt that our moral belief really is overdetermined in this way. Nor, similarly, do I believe that Woodworth's actions were overdetermined, so that he would have done just as he did even if he had been a more admirable person. I suppose one could have doubts about DeVoto's objectivity and reliability; it is obvious he dislikes Woodworth, so perhaps he would have thought him a moral loss and convinced his readers of this no matter what the man was really like. But it is more plausible that the dislike is mostly based on the same evidence that supports DeVoto's moral view of him, and that very different evidence, at any rate, would have produced a different verdict. If so, then Woodworth's moral character is part of the explanation of DeVoto's belief about his moral character.

It is more plausible of course that serious moral opposition to slavery would have emerged in Britain, France, and the United States even if slavery hadn't been worse in the modern period than before, and worse in the United States than in Latin America, and that the American antislavery movement would have grown even if slavery had not become more oppressive as the nineteenth century progressed. But that is because these moral facts are offered as at best a partial explanation of these developments in moral opinion. And if they really *are* part of the explanation, as seems plausible, then it is also plausible that whatever effect they produced was not entirely overdetermined; that, for example, the growth of the antislavery movement in the United States would at least have been somewhat slower if slavery had been and remained less bad an institution. Here again it hardly seems "completely irrelevant" to the explanation whether or not these moral facts obtained.

[17] This counterfactual test requires qualification to be exactly right, but none of the plausible qualifications matters to my examples. See the longer version of this paper.

212

It is more puzzling, I grant, to consider Harman's own example in which you see the children igniting a cat and react immediately with the thought that this is wrong. Is it true, as Harman claims, that the assumption that the children are really doing something wrong is "totally irrelevant" to any reasonable explanation of your making that judgment? Would you, for example, have reacted in just the same way, with the thought that the action is wrong, even if what they were doing *hadn't* been wrong, and could we explain your reaction equally well on this assumption? Now, there is more than one way to understand this counterfactual question, and I shall return below to a reading of it that might appear favorable to Harman's view. What I wish to point out for now is merely that there is a natural way of taking it, parallel to the way in which I have been understanding similar counterfactual questions about my own examples, on which the answer to it has to be simply: it depends. For to answer the question, I take it,[18] we must consider a situation in which what the children are doing is not wrong, but which is otherwise as much like the actual situation as possible, and then decide what your reaction would be in that situation. But since what makes their action wrong, what its wrongness *consists* in, is presumably something like its being an act of gratuitous cruelty (or, perhaps we should add, of intense cruelty, and to a helpless victim), to imagine them not doing something wrong we are going to have to imagine their action different in this respect. More cautiously and more generally, if what they are actually doing is wrong, and if moral properties are, as many writers have held, supervenient on natural ones,[19] then in order to imagine them not doing something wrong we are going to have to suppose their action different from the actual one in some of its natural features as well. So our question becomes: Even if the children had been doing something else, something just different enough not to be wrong, would you have taken them even so to be doing something wrong?

Surely there is no one answer to this question. It depends on a lot about you, including your moral views and how good you are at seeing at a glance what some children are doing. It probably depends also on a debatable moral issue;

---

[18] Following, informally, Stalnaker and Lewis on counterfactuals. See Robert Stalnaker, "A Theory of Conditionals," in Nicholas Rescher, ed., *Studies in Logical Theory,* APQ Monograph No. 2 (Oxford: Basil Blackwell, 1968); and David Lewis, *Counterfactuals* (Cambridge, MA: Harvard University Press, 1973).

[19] What would be generally granted is just that *if* there are moral properties they supervene on natural properties. But, remember, we are assuming for the sake of argument that there are.

I think moral properties *are* natural properties; and from this view it of course follows trivially that they supervene on natural properties: that, necessarily, nothing could differ in its moral properties without differing in some natural respect. But I also accept the more interesting thesis usually intended by the claim about supervenience—that there are more basic natural features such that, necessarily, once they are fixed, so are the moral properties. (In supervening on more basic natural facts of some sort, moral facts are like *most* natural facts. Social facts like unemployment, for example, supervene on complex histories of many individuals and their relations; and facts about the existence and properties of macroscopic physical objects—colliding billiard balls, say—clearly supervene on the microphysical constitution of the situations that include them.)

namely, just *how* different the children's action would have to be in order not to be wrong. (Is unkindness to animals, for example, also wrong?) I believe we can see how, in a case in which the answer was clearly affirmative, we might be tempted to agree with Harman that the wrongness of the action was no part of the explanation of your reaction. For suppose you are like this. You hate children. What you especially hate, moreover, is the sight of children enjoying themselves; so much so that whenever you see children having fun, you immediately assume they are up to no good. The more they seem to be enjoying themselves, furthermore, the readier you are to fasten on any pretext for thinking them engaged in real wickedness. Then it is true that even if the children had been engaged in some robust but innocent fun, you would have thought they were doing something wrong; and Harman is perhaps right[20] about you that the actual wrongness of the action you see is irrelevant to your thinking it wrong. This is because your reaction is due to a feature of the action that coincides only very accidentally with the ones that make it wrong.[21] But, of course, and fortunately, many people aren't like this (nor does Harman argue that they are). It isn't true of them, in general, that if the children had been doing something similar, although different enough not to be wrong, they would still have thought the children were doing something wrong. And it isn't true either, therefore, that the wrongness of the action is irrelevant to the explanation of why they think it wrong.

Now, one might have the sense from my discussion of all these examples, but perhaps especially from my discussion of this last one, Harman's own, that I have perversely been refusing to understand his claim about the explanatory irrelevance of moral facts in the way he intends. And perhaps I have not been understanding it as he wishes. In any case, I agree, I have certainly not been understanding the crucial counterfactual question, of whether we would have drawn the same moral conclusion even if the moral facts had been different, in the way he must intend. But I am not being perverse. I believe, as I have said, that my way of taking the question is the more natural one. And, more

---

[20] Not *certainly* right, because there is still the possibility that your reaction is to some extent overdetermined, and is to be explained partly by your sympathy for the cat and your dislike of cruelty, as well as by your hatred for children (although this last alone would have been sufficient to produce it).

We could of course rule out this possibility by making you an even less attractive character, indifferent to the suffering of animals and not offended by cruelty. But it may then be hard to imagine that such a person (whom I shall cease calling "you") could retain enough of a grip on moral thought for us to be willing to say he thought the action *wrong*, as opposed to saying that he merely pretended to do so. This difficulty is perhaps not insuperable, but it is revealing. Harman says that the actual wrongness of the action is "completely irrelevant" to the explanation of the observer's reaction. Notice that what is in fact true, however, is that it is *very hard* to imagine someone who reacts in the way Harman describes, but whose reaction is *not* due, at least in part, to the actual wrongness of the action.

[21] Perhaps deliberate cruelty is worse the more one enjoys it (a standard counterexample to hedonism). If so, the fact that the children are enjoying themselves makes their action worse, but presumably isn't what makes it wrong to begin with.

importantly: although there is, I grant, a reading of that question on which it will always yield the answer Harman wants—namely, that a difference in the moral facts would *not* have made a difference in our judgment—I do not believe this reading can support his argument. I must now explain why.

It will help if I contrast my general approach with his. I am approaching questions about the justification of belief in the spirit of what Quine has called "epistemology naturalized."[22] I take this to mean that we have in general no a priori way of knowing which strategies for forming and refining our beliefs are likely to take us closer to the truth. The only way we have of proceeding is to assume the approximate truth of what seems to us the best overall theory we already have of what we are like and what the world is like, and to decide in the light of *that* what strategies of research and reasoning are likely to be reliable in producing a more nearly true overall theory. One result of applying these procedures, in turn, is likely to be the refinement or perhaps even the abandonment of parts of the tentative theory with which we began.

I take Harman's approach, too, to be an instance of this one. He says we are justified in believing in those facts that we need to assume to explain why we observe what we do. But he does not think that our knowledge of this principle about justification is a priori. Furthermore, as he knows, we cannot decide whether one explanation is better than another without relying on beliefs we already have about the world. Is it really a better explanation of the vapor trail the physicist sees in the cloud chamber to suppose that a proton caused it, as Harman suggests in his example, rather than some other charged particle? Would there, for example, have been no vapor trail in the absence of that proton? There is obviously no hope of answering such questions without assuming at least the approximate truth of some quite far-reaching microphysical theory, and our knowledge of such theories is not a priori.

But my approach differs from Harman's in one crucial way. For among the beliefs in which I have enough confidence to rely on in evaluating explanations, at least at the outset, are some moral beliefs. And I have been relying on them in the following way.[23] Harman's thesis implies that the supposed moral fact of Hitler's being morally depraved is irrelevant to the explanation of Hitler's doing what he did. (For we may suppose that if it explains his doing what he did, it also helps explain, at greater remove, Harman's belief and mine in his moral depravity.) To assess this claim, we need to conceive a situation in which

[22] W. V. O. Quine, "Epistemology Naturalized," in *Ontological Relativity and Other Essays* (New York: Columbia University Press, 1969), pp. 69–90. In the same volume, see also "Natural Kinds," pp. 114–38.

[23] Harman of course allows us to assume the moral facts whose explanatory relevance is being assessed: that Hitler was depraved, or that what the children in his example are doing is wrong. But I have been assuming something more—something about what depravity *is*, and about what *makes* the children's action wrong. (At a minimum, in the more cautious version of my argument, I have been assuming that *something* about its more basic features makes it wrong, so that it could not have differed in its moral quality without differing in those other features as well.)

Hitler was *not* morally depraved and consider the question whether in that situation he would still have done what he did. My answer is that he would not, and this answer relies on a (not very controversial) moral view: that in any world at all like the actual one, only a morally depraved person could have initiated a world war, ordered the "final solution," and done any number of other things Hitler did. That is why I believe that, if Hitler hadn't been morally depraved, he wouldn't have done those things, and hence that the fact of his moral depravity is relevant to an explanation of what he did.

Harman, however, cannot want us to rely on any such moral views in answering this counterfactual question. This comes out most clearly if we return to his example of the children igniting the cat. He claims that the wrongness of this act is irrelevant to an explanation of your thinking it wrong, that you would have *thought* it wrong even if it wasn't. My reply was that in order for the action not to be wrong it would have had to lack the feature of deliberate, intense, pointless cruelty, and that if it had differed in this way you might very well *not* have thought it wrong. I also suggested a more cautious version of this reply: that since the action is in fact wrong, and since moral properties supervene on more basic natural ones, it would have had to be different in *some* further natural respect in order not to be wrong; and that we do not know whether if it had so differed you would still have thought it wrong. Both of these replies, again, rely on moral views, the latter merely on the view that there is *something* about the natural features of the action in Harman's example that makes it wrong, the former on a more specific view as to which of these features do this.

But Harman, it is fairly clear, intends for us *not* to rely on any such moral views in evaluating his counterfactual claim. His claim is not that if the action had not been one of deliberate cruelty (or had otherwise differed in whatever way would be required to remove its wrongness), you would still have thought it wrong. It is, instead, that if the action were one of deliberate, pointless cruelty, but this *did not make it wrong,* you would still have thought it was wrong. And to return to the example of Hitler's moral character, the counterfactual claim that Harman will need in order to defend a comparable conclusion about that case is not that if Hitler had been, for example, humane and fairminded, free of nationalistic pride and racial hatred, he would still have done exactly as he did. It is, rather, that if Hitler's psychology, and anything else about his situation that could strike us as morally relevant, had been exactly as it in fact was, but this had *not constituted moral depravity,* he would still have done exactly what he did.

Now the antecedents of these two conditionals are puzzling. For one thing, both are, I believe, necessarily false. I am fairly confident, for example, that Hitler really was morally depraved;[24] and since I also accept the view that

---

[24] And anyway, remember, this is the sort of fact Harman allows us to assume in order to see whether, if we assume it, it will look explanatory.

moral features supervene on more basic natural properties,[25] I take this to imply that there is no possible world in which Hitler has just the personality he in fact did, in just the situation he was in, but is not morally depraved. Any attempt to describe such a situation, moreover, will surely run up against the limits of our moral concepts—what Harman calls our "moral sensibility"— and this is no accident. For what Harman is asking us to do, in general, is to consider cases in which absolutely *everything* about the nonmoral facts that could seem morally relevant to us, in light of whatever moral theory we accept and of the concepts required for understanding that theory, is held fixed, but in which the moral judgment that our theory yields about the case is nevertheless mistaken. So it is hardly surprising that, using that theory and those concepts, we should find it difficult to conceive in any detail what such a situation would be like. It is especially not surprising when the cases in question are as paradigmatic in light of the moral outlook we in fact have as is Harman's example or is, even more so, mine of Hitler's moral character. The only way we could be wrong about this latter case (assuming we have the nonmoral facts right) would be for our whole theory to be hopelessly wrong, so radically mistaken that there could be no hope of straightening it out through adjustments from within.

But I do not believe we should conclude, as we might be tempted to,[26] that we therefore know a priori that this is not so, or that we cannot understand these conditionals that are crucial to Harman's argument. Rather, now that we have seen how we have to understand them, we should grant that they are

---

[25] It is about here that I have several times encountered the objection: but surely *supervenient* properties aren't needed to explain anything. It is a little hard, however, to see just what this objection is supposed to come to. If it includes endorsement of the conditional I here attribute to Harman, then I believe the remainder of my discussion is an adequate reply to it. If it is the claim that, because moral properties are supervenient, we can always exploit the insights in any moral explanations, however plausible, without resort to moral *language,* then I have already dealt with it in my discussion of reductionism (see note 10, above): the claim is probably false, but even if it is true it is no support for Harman's view, which is not that moral explanations are plausible but reducible, but that they are totally implausible. And doubts about the causal efficacy of supervenient facts seem misplaced in any case, as attention to my earlier examples (note 17) illustrates. High unemployment causes widespread hardship, and can also bring down the rate of inflation. The masses and velocities and two colliding billiard balls causally influence the subsequent trajectories of the two balls. There is no doubt some sense in which these facts are causally efficacious *in virtue of* the way they supervene on—that is, are constituted out of, or causally realized by—more basic facts, but this hardly shows them *inefficacious.* (Nor does Harman appear to think it does: for his *favored* explanation of your moral belief about the burning cat, recall, appeals to psychological facts [about your moral sensibility], a biological fact (that it's a cat), and macrophysical facts [that it's on fire]—supervenient facts all, on his physicalist view and mine.) If anyone does hold to a general suspicion of causation by supervenient facts and properties, however, as Jaegwon Kim appears to (see "Causality, Identity, and Supervenience in the Mind-Body Problem," *Midwest Studies in Philosophy* 4 (1979), pp. 31–49), it is enough to note that this suspicion cannot diagnose any special difficulty with *moral* explanations, any distinctive "problem with ethics." The "problem," arguably, will be with every discipline but fundamental physics.

[26] And as I take it Philippa Foot, for example, is still prepared to do, at least about paradigmatic cases. See her *Moral Relativism* (Lawrence, Kansas: The University of Kansas, 1978).

true: that if our moral theory were somehow hopelessly mistaken, but all the nonmoral facts remained exactly as they in fact are, then, since we do *accept* that moral theory, we would still draw exactly the moral conclusions we in fact do. But we should deny that any skeptical conclusion follows from this. In particular, we should deny that it follows that moral facts play no role in explaining our moral judgments.

For consider what follows from the parallel claim about microphysics, in particular about Harman's example in which a physicist concludes from his observation of a vapor trail in a cloud chamber, and from the microphysical theory he accepts, that a free proton has passed through the chamber. The parallel claim, notice, is *not* just that if the proton had not been there the physicist would still have thought it was. This claim is implausible, for we may assume that the physicist's theory is generally correct, and it follows from that theory that if there hadn't been a proton there, then there wouldn't have been a vapor trail. But in a perfectly similar way it is implausible that if Hitler hadn't been morally depraved we would still have thought he was: for we may assume that our moral theory also is at least roughly correct, and it follows from the most central features of that theory that if Hitler hadn't been morally depraved, he wouldn't have done what he did. The *parallel* claim about the microphysical example is, instead, that if there hadn't been a proton there, but there *had* been a vapor trail, the physicist would still have concluded that a proton was present. More precisely, to maintain a perfect parallel with Harman's claims about the moral cases, the antecedent must specify that although no proton is present, absolutely *all* the non-microphysical facts that the physicist, in light of his theory, might take to be relevant to the question of whether or not a proton is present, are exactly as in the actual case. (These macrophysical facts, as we may for convenience call them, surely include everything one would normally think of as an observable fact.) Of course, we shall be unable to imagine this without imagining that the physicist's theory is pretty badly mistaken;[27] but I believe we should grant that, *if* the physicist's theory were somehow this badly mistaken, but all the macrophysical facts (including all the observable facts) were held fixed, then the physicist, since he does accept that theory, would still draw all the same conclusions that he actually does. That is, this conditional claim, like Harman's parallel claim about the moral cases, is true.

---

[27] If we imagine the physicist *regularly* mistaken in this way, moreover, we will have to imagine his theory not just mistaken but hopelessly so. And we can easily reproduce the other notable feature of Harman's claims about the moral cases, that what we are imagining is *necessarily* false, if we suppose that one of the physicist's (or better, chemist's) conclusions is about the microstructure of some common substance, such as water. For I agree with Saul Kripke that whatever microstructure water has is essential to it, that it has this structure in every possible world in which it exists. (Saul Kripke, *Naming and Necessity* [Cambridge, MA: Harvard University Press, 1980].) If we are right (as we have every reason to suppose) in thinking that water is actually H_2O, therefore, the conditional, "If water were not H_2O, but all the observable, macrophysical facts were just as they actually are, chemists would still have come to *think* it was H_2O," has a necessarily false antecedent; just as, if we are right (as we also have good reason to suppose) in thinking that Hitler was actually morally depraved, the conditional, "If

But no skeptical conclusions follow; nor can Harman, since he does not intend to be a skeptic about physics, think that they do. It does not follow, in the first place, that we have any reason to think the physicist's theory *is* generally mistaken. Nor does it follow, furthermore, that the hypothesis that a proton really did pass through the cloud chamber is not part of a good explanation of the vapor trail, and hence of the physicist's thinking this has happened. This looks like a reasonable explanation, of course, only on the assumption that the physicist's theory is at least roughly true, for it is this theory that tells us, for example, what happens when charged particles pass through a supersaturated atmosphere, what other causes (if any) there might be for a similar phenomenon, and so on. But, as I say, we have not been provided with any reason for not trusting the theory to this extent.

Similarly, I conclude, we should draw no skeptical conclusions from Harman's claims about the moral cases. It is true that if our moral theory were seriously mistaken, but we still believed it, and the nonmoral facts were held fixed, we would still make just the moral judgments we do. But *this* fact by itself provides us with no reason for thinking that our moral theory *is* generally mistaken. Nor, again, does it imply that the fact of Hitler's really having been morally depraved forms no part of a good explanation of his doing what he did and hence, at greater remove, of our thinking him depraved. This explanation will appear reasonable, of course, only on the assumption that our accepted moral theory is at least roughly correct, for it is this theory that assures us that only a depraved person could have thought, felt, and acted as Hitler did. But, as I say, Harman's argument has provided us with no reason for not trusting our moral views to this extent, and hence with no reason for doubting that it is sometimes moral facts that explain our moral judgments.

I conclude with three comments about my argument.

(1) I have tried to show that Harman's claim—that we would have held the particular moral beliefs we do even if those beliefs were untrue—admits of two readings, one of which makes it implausible, and the other of which reduces it to an application of a general skeptical strategy, a strategy which could as easily be used to produce doubt about microphysical as about moral facts. The general strategy is this. Consider any conclusion C we arrive at by relying both on some distinguishable "theory" T and on some body of evidence not being

---

Hitler were just as he was in all natural respects, but not morally depraved, we would still have *thought* he was depraved," has a necessarily false antecedent. Of course, I am not suggesting that in either case our knowledge that the antecedent is false is a priori.

These counterfactuals, because of their impossible antecedents, will have to be interpreted over worlds that are (at best) only "epistemically" possible; and, as Richard Boyd has pointed out to me, this helps to explain why anyone who accepts a causal theory of knowledge (or any theory according to which the justification of our belief depends on what explains our holding them) will find their truth irrelevant to the question of how much we know, either in chemistry or in morals. For although there certainly are counterfactuals that are relevant to questions about what causes what (and, hence, about what explains what), these have to be counterfactuals about real possibilities, not merely epistemic ones.

challenged, and ask whether we would have believed C even if it had been false. The plausible answer, *if* we are allowed to rely on T, will often be no: for if C had been false, then (according to T) the evidence would have had to be different, and in that case we wouldn't have believed C. (I have illustrated the plausibility of this sort of reply for all my moral examples, as well as for the microphysical one.) But the skeptic of course intends us *not* to rely on T in this way, and so rephrases the question: Would we have believed C even if it were false *but* all the evidence had been exactly as it in fact was? Now the answer has to be yes; and the skeptic concludes that C is doubtful. (It should be obvious how to extend this strategy to belief in other minds, or in an external world.) I am of course not convinced: I do not think answers to the rephrased question show anything interesting about what we know or justifiably believe. But it is enough for my purposes here that no such *general* skeptical strategy could pretend to reveal any problems peculiar to belief in *moral* facts.

(2) My conclusion about Harman's argument, although it is not exactly the same as, is nevertheless similar to and very much in the spirit of the Duhemian point I invoked earlier against verificationism. There the question was whether typical moral assertions have testable implications, and the answer was that they do, so long as you include additional moral assumptions of the right sort among the background theories on which you rely in evaluating these asser- tions. Harman's more important question is whether we should ever regard moral facts as relevant to the explanation of nonmoral facts, and in particular of our having the moral beliefs we do. But the answer, again, is that we should, so long as we are willing to hold the right sorts of *other* moral assumptions fixed in answering counterfactual questions. Neither answer shows morality to be on any shakier ground than, say, physics, for typical microphysical hypotheses, too, have testable implications, and appear relevant to explana- tions, only if we are willing to assume at least the approximate truth of an elaborate microphysical theory and to hold this assumption fixed in answering counterfactual questions.

(3) Of course, this picture of how explanations depend on background the- ories, and moral explanations in particular on moral background theories, does show why someone already tempted toward moral skepticism on other grounds (such as those I mentioned at the beginning of this essay) might find Harman's claim about moral explanations plausible. To the extent that you already have pervasive doubts about moral theories, you will also find moral facts nonexplanatory. So I grant that Harman has located a natural symptom of moral skepticism; but I am sure he has neither traced this skepticism to its roots nor provided any independent argument for it. His claim (p. 22) that we do not *in fact* cite moral facts in explanation of moral beliefs and observations cannot provide such an argument, for that claim is false. So, too, is the claim that assumptions about moral facts seem irrelevant to such explanations, for many do not. The claim that we *should* not rely on such assumptions because they *are* irrelevant, on the other hand, unless it is supported by some indepen- dent argument for moral skepticism, will just be question-begging: for the principal test of whether they are relevant, in any situation in which it appears

they might be, is a counterfactual question about what would have happened if the moral fact had not obtained, and how we answer that question depends precisely upon whether we *do* rely on moral assumptions in answering it.

My own view I stated at the outset: that the only argument for moral skepticism with any independent weight is the argument from the difficulty of settling disputed moral questions. I have shown that anyone who finds Harman's claim about moral explanations plausible must already have been tempted toward skepticism by some other considerations, and I suspect that the other considerations will typically be the ones I sketched. So that is where discussion should focus. I also suggested that those considerations may provide less support for moral skepticism than is sometimes supposed, but I must reserve a thorough defense of that thesis for another occasion.[28]

[28] This essay has benefited from helpful discussion of earlier versions read at the University of Virginia, Cornell University, Franklin and Marshall College, Wayne State University, and the University of Michigan. I have been aided by a useful correspondence with Gilbert Harman; and I am grateful also for specific comments from Richard Boyd, David Brink, David Copp, Stephen Darwall, Terence Irwin, Norman Kretzmann, Ronald Nash, Peter Railton, Bruce Russell, Sydney Shoemaker, and Judith Slein.

16

Outline of a Decision
Procedure for Ethics

JOHN RAWLS

John Rawls (b. 1921) is Professor of Philosophy at Harvard University. He is among the leading moral and political theorists of the twentieth century. His book, A Theory of Justice, is already a contemporary classic.

In this early paper, Rawls presents an alternative to the view that objectivity in ethics requires that moral judgments be capable of corresponding to moral facts. This assumption is shared by many who question the objectivity of morality (see Harman and Mackie, readings 13 and 14) and by many who defend it (see Sturgeon, reading 15). But according to Rawls, the assumption is inappropriate. In its place, he argues that we should require only that correct moral principles be reasonable or justifiable. Moreover, justifiability should be understood as derivability through a rationally defensible procedure.

When moral objectivity is conceived in this way, the obvious challenge is to describe the procedure that confers justification upon moral principles. Rawls does this in a series of stages. First, he specifies certain features (a degree of intelligence, rationality, and so on) that make someone a competent judge. Next, he specifies certain features of the judgments of such judges (the fact that the judge is not influenced by fear or by the promise of gain, feels certain of his judgment, and so on) that make these judgments worthy of acceptance. Finally, he suggests that there may well be moral principles that imply precisely the judgments that share these features. Such principles provide what he calls an "explication" of the considered judgments of competent judges. If any moral principles are worthy of acceptance, and so are objectively justified, these are.

1.1 THE QUESTION WITH which we shall be concerned can be stated as follows: Does there exist a reasonable decision procedure which is sufficiently strong, at least in some cases, to determine the manner in which competing interests should be adjudicated, and, in instances of conflict, one interest given preference over another; and, further, can the existence of this procedure, as well as its reasonableness, be established by rational methods of inquiry? In order to answer both parts of this question in the affirmative, it is necessary to describe a reasonable procedure and then to evidence that it satisfies certain criteria. This I attempt to do beginning at 2.1 below.

1.2 It should be noted that we are concerned here only with the existence of a reasonable method, and not with the problem of how to make it psychologically effective in the settling of disputes. How much allegiance the method is able to gain is irrelevant for our present purposes.

1.3 The original question has been framed the way it is because the objectivity or the subjectivity of moral knowledge turns, not on the question whether ideal value entities exist or whether moral judgments are caused by emotions or whether there is a variety of moral codes the world over, but simply on the question: does there exist a reasonable method for validating and invalidating given or proposed moral rules and those decisions made on the basis of them? For to say of scientific knowledge that it is objective is to say that the propositions expressed therein may be evidenced to be true by a reasonable and reliable method, that is, by the rules and procedures of what we may call "inductive logic";* and, similarly, to establish the objectivity of moral rules, and the decisions based upon them, we must exhibit the decision procedure, which can be shown to be both reasonable and reliable, at least in some cases, for deciding between moral rules and lines of conduct consequent to them.

2.1 For the present, we may think of ethics as being more analogous to the study of inductive logic than to any other established inquiry. Just as in inductive logic we are concerned with discovering reasonable criteria which, when we are given a proposition, or theory, together with the empirical evidence for it, will enable us to decide the extent to which we ought to consider it to be true so in ethics we are attempting to find reasonable principles which, when we are given a proposed line of conduct and the situation in which it is to be carried out and the relevant interests which it affects, will enable us to determine whether or not we ought to carry it out and hold it to be just and right.

2.2 There is no way of knowing ahead of time how to find and formulate these reasonable principles. Indeed, we cannot even be certain that they exist, and it is well known that there are no mechanical methods of discovery. In what follows, however, a method will be described, and it remains for the reader to judge for himself to what extent it is, or can be, successful.

2.3 First it is necessary to define a class of competent moral judges as follows: All those persons having to a certain requisite degree each of the following characteristics, which can, if desired, be made more determinate:

(i) A competent moral judge is expected to have a certain requisite degree of intelligence, which may be thought of as that ability which intelligence tests are designed to measure. The degree of this ability required should not be set too high, on the assumption that what we call "moral insight" is the possession of the normally intelligent man as well as of the more brilliant. Therefore I am inclined to say that a competent moral judge need not be more than normally intelligent.

(ii) A competent judge is required to know those things concerning the world about him and those consequences of frequently performed actions, which it

---

* What Rawls calls "inductive logic" is what we have referred to as "non-deductive logic" in our introduction.

is reasonable to expect the average intelligent man to know. Further, a competent judge is expected to know, in all cases whereupon he is called to express his opinion, the peculiar facts of those cases. It should be noted that the kind of knowledge here referred to is to be distinguished from sympathetic knowledge discussed below.

(iii) A competent judge is required to be a reasonable man as this characteristic is evidenced by his satisfying the following tests: First, a reasonable man shows a willingness, if not a desire, to use the criteria of inductive logic in order to determine what is proper for him to believe. Second, a reasonable man, whenever he is confronted with a moral question, shows a disposition to find reasons for and against the possible lines of conduct which are open to him. Third, a reasonable man exhibits a desire to consider questions with an open mind, and consequently, while he may already have an opinion on some issue, he is always willing to reconsider it in the light of further evidence and reasons which may be presented to him in discussion. Fourth, a reasonable man knows, or tries to know, his own emotional, intellectual, and moral predilections and makes a conscientious effort to take them into account in weighing the merits of any question. He is not unaware of the influences of prejudice and bias even in his most sincere efforts to annul them; nor is he fatalistic about their effect so that he succumbs to them as being those factors which he thinks must sooner or later determine his decision.

(iv) Finally, a competent judge is required to have a sympathetic knowledge of those human interests which, by conflicting in particular cases, give rise to the need to make a moral decision. The presence of this characteristic is evidenced by the following: First, by the person's direct knowledge of those interests gained by experiencing, in his own life, the goods they represent. The more interests which a person can appreciate in terms of his own direct experience, the greater the extent to which he satisfies this first test. Yet it is obvious that no man can know all interests directly, and therefore the second test is that, should a person not be directly acquainted with an interest, his competency as a judge is seen, in part, by his capacity to give that interest an appraisal by means of an imaginative experience of it. This test also requires of a competent judge that he must not consider his own *de facto* preferences as the necessarily valid measure of the actual worth of those interests which come before him, but that he be both able and anxious to determine, by imaginative appreciation, what those interests mean to persons who share them, and to consider them accordingly. Third, a competent judge is required to have the capacity and the desire to lay before himself in imagination all the interests in conflict, together with the relevant facts of the case, and to bestow upon the appraisal of each the same care which he would give to it if that interest were his own. He is required to determine what he would think to be just and unjust if each of the interests were as thoroughly his own as they are in fact those of other persons, and to render his judgment on the case as he feels his sense of justice requires after he has carefully framed in his mind the issues which are to be decided.

. . .

2.5 The next step in the development of our procedure is to define the class of considered moral judgments, the determining characteristics of which are as follows:

(i) It is required first that the judgment on a case be given under such conditions that the judge is immune from all of the reasonably foreseeable consequences of the judgment. For example, he will not be punished for deciding the case one way rather than another.

(ii) It is required that the conditions be such that the integrity of the judge can be maintained. So far as possible, the judge must not stand to gain in any immediate and personal way by his decision. These two tests are designed to exclude judgments wherein a person must weigh the merit of one of his own interests. The imposition of these conditions is justified on the grounds that fear and partiality are recognized obstructions in the determination of justice.

(iii) It is required that the case, on which the judgment is given, be one in which there is an actual conflict of interests. Thus, all judgments on hypothetical cases are excluded. In addition, it is preferable that the case be not especially difficult and be one that is likely to arise in ordinary life. These restrictions are desirable in order that the judgments in question be made in the effort to settle problems with which men are familiar and whereupon they have had an opportunity to reflect.

(iv) It is required that the judgment be one which has been preceded by a careful inquiry into the facts of the question at issue, and by a fair opportunity for all concerned to state their side of the case. This requirement is justified on the ground that it is only by chance that a just decision can be made without a knowledge of the relevant facts.

(v) It is required that the judgment be felt to be certain by the person making it. This characteristic may be called "certitude" and it is to be sharply distinguished from certainty, which is a logical relation between a proposition, or theory, and its evidence. This test is justified on the ground that it seems more profitable to study those judgments which are felt to be correct than those which seem to be wrong or confused even to those who make them.

(vi) It is required that the judgment be stable, that is, that there be evidence that at other times and at other places competent judges have rendered the same judgment on similar cases, understanding similar cases to be those in which the relevant facts and the competing interests are similar. The stability must hold, by and large, over the class of competent judges and over their judgments at different times. Thus, if on similar cases of a certain type, competent judges decided one way one day, and another the next, or if a third of them decided one way, a third the opposite way, while the remaining third said they did not know how to decide the cases, then none of these judgments would be stable judgments, and therefore none would be considered judgments. These restrictions are justified on the grounds that it seems unreasonable to have any confidence that a judgment is correct if competent persons disagree about it.

(vii) Finally, it is required that the judgment be intuitive with respect to ethical principles, that is, that it should not be determined by a conscious application of principles so far as this may be evidenced by introspection. By the term "intuitive" I do not mean the same as that expressed by the terms "impulsive" and "instinctive." An intuitive judgment may be consequent to a thorough inquiry into the facts of the case, and it may follow a series of reflections on the possible effects of different decisions, and even the application of a common sense rule, e.g., promises ought to be kept. What is required is that the judgment not be determined by a systematic and conscious use of ethical principles. The reason for this restriction will be evident if one keeps in mind the aim of the present inquiry, namely, to describe a decision procedure whereby principles, by means of which we may justify specific moral decisions, may themselves be shown to be justifiable. Now part of this procedure will consist in showing that these principles are implicit in the considered judgments of competent judges. It is clear that if we allowed these judgments to be determined by a conscious and systematic application of these principles, then the method is threatened with circularity. We cannot test a principle honestly by means of judgments wherein it has been consciously and systematically used to determine the decision.

2.6 Up to this point I have defined, first, a class of competent judges and, second, a class of considered judgments. If competent judges are those persons most likely to make correct decisions, then we should take care to abstract those judgments of theirs which, from the conditions and circumstances under which they are made, are most likely to be correct. With the exception of certain requirements, which are needed to prevent circularity, the defining characteristics of considered judgments are such that they select those judgments most likely to be decided by the habits of thought and imagination deemed essential for a competent judge. One can say, then, that those judgments which are relevant for our present purposes are the considered judgments of competent judges as these are made from day to day on the moral issues which continually arise. No other judgments, for reasons previously stated, are of any concern.

· · ·

3.1 The next step in the present method is as follows: once the class of considered judgments of competent judges has been selected, there remains to discover and formulate a satisfactory explication of the total range of these judgments. This process is understood as being a heuristic device which is likely to yield reasonable and justifiable principles.

3.2 The term "explication" is given meaning somewhat graphically as follows: Consider a group of competent judges making considered judgments in review of a set of cases which would be likely to arise in ordinary life. Then an explication of these judgments is defined to be a set of principles, such that, if any competent man were to apply them intelligently and consistently to the same cases under review, his judgments, made systematically nonintuitive by the explicit and conscious use of the principles, would be, nevertheless, identical, case by case, with the considered judgments of the group of competent judges. . . .

4.3 In what follows we shall assume that a satisfactory and comprehensive explication of the considered judgments of competent judges is already known (note proviso under fourth test below). Now consider the question as to what reasons we can have for accepting these principles as justifiable.

The first reason for accepting them has already been touched upon: namely, since the principles explicate the considered judgments of competent judges, and since these judgments are more likely than any other judgments to represent the mature convictions of competent men as they have been worked out under the most favorable existing conditions, the invariant in what we call "moral insight," if it exists, is more likely to be approximated by the principles of a successful explication than by principles which a man might fashion out of his own head. Individual predilections will tend to be canceled out once the explication has included judgments of many persons made on a wide variety of cases. Thus the fact that the principles constitute a comprehensive explication of the considered judgments of competent judges is reason for accepting them. That this should be so is understandable if we reflect, to take the contrary case, how little confidence we would have in principles which should happen to explicate the judgments of men under strong emotional or physical duress, or of those mentally ill. Hence the type of judgments which make up the range of the explication is the first ground for accepting the principles thereof.

Secondly, the reasonableness of a principle is tested by seeing whether it shows a capacity to become accepted by competent moral judges after they have freely weighed its merits by criticism and open discussion, and after each has thought it over and compared it with his own considered judgments. It is hoped that some principles will exhibit a capacity to win free and willing allegiance and be able to implement a gradual convergence of uncoerced opinion.

Thirdly, the reasonableness of a principle is tested by seeing whether it can function in existing instances of conflicting opinion, and in new cases causing difficulty, to yield a result which, after criticism and discussion, seems to be acceptable to all, or nearly all, competent judges, and to conform to their intuitive notion of a reasonable decision. For example, the problem of punishment has been a troublesome moral issue for some time, and if a principle or set of principles should be formulated which evidenced a capacity to settle this problem to the satisfaction of all, or nearly all, competent judges, then this principle, or set of principles, would meet this test in one possible instance of its application. In general, a principle evidences its reasonableness by being able to resolve moral perplexities which existed at the time of its formulation and which will exist in the future. This test is somewhat analogous to a test which we impose upon an empirical theory: namely, its ability to foresee laws and facts hitherto unknown, and to explain facts and laws hitherto unexplainable.

Finally, the reasonableness of a principle is tested by seeing whether it shows a capacity to hold its own (that is, to continue to be felt reasonable), against a subclass of the considered judgments of competent judges, as this fact may be evidenced by our intuitive conviction that the considered judgments are incorrect rather than the principle, when we confront them with the principle. A principle satisfies this test when a subclass of considered judgments, rather than the principle, is felt to be mistaken when the principle fails to explicate it. For example, it often happens that competent persons, in judging the moral worth of character, blame others in conflict with the rule that a man shall not be morally condemned for the possession of characteristics which would not have been otherwise even if he had so chosen. Frequently, however, when we point out that their judgments conflict with this rule, these persons, upon reflection, will decide that their judgments are incorrect, and acknowledge the principle. To the extent that principles exhibit this capacity to alter what we think to be our considered judgments in cases of conflict, they satisfy the fourth test. It is, of course, desirable, although not essential, that whenever a principle does successfully militate against what is taken to be a considered judgment, some convincing reason can be found to account for the anomaly. We should like to find that the once accepted intuitive conviction is actually caused by a mistaken belief as to a matter fact of which we were unaware or fostered by what is admittedly a narrow bias of some kind. The rationale behind this fourth test is that while the considered judgments of competent judges are the most likely repository of the working out of men's sense of right and wrong, a more likely one, for example, than that of any particular individual's judgments alone, they may, nevertheless, contain certain deviations, or confusions, which are best discovered by comparing the considered judgments with principles which pass the first three tests and seeing which of the two tends to be felt incorrect in the light of reflection. . . .

4.4 A principle is evidenced to be reasonable to the extent that it satisfies jointly all of the foregoing tests. In practice, however, we are wise if we expect less than this. We are not likely to find easily a comprehensive explication which convinces all competent judges, which resolves all existing difficulties, and which, should there be anomalies in the considered judgments themselves, always tends to overcome them. We should expect satisfactory explications of but delimited areas of the considered judgments. Ethics must, like any other discipline, work its way piece by piece.

. . .

6.4 The manner of describing the decision procedure here advocated may have led the reader to believe that it claims to be a way of discovering justifiable ethical principles. There are, however, no precisely describable methods of discovery, and certainly the finding of a successful explication satisfying the tests of 4.3 will require at least some ingenuity. Therefore it is best to view the exposition as a description of the procedure of justification stated in reverse. Thus if a man were asked to justify his decision on a case, he should proceed as follows: first, he should show that, given the circumstances and the interests in conflict, his decision is capable of being explicated by the principles of justice. Second, he should evidence that these principles satisfy the tests in 4.3. If asked to proceed further, he should remark on the nature of considered judgments and competent judges and urge that one could hardly be expected to prefer judgments made under emotional duress, or in ignorance of the facts by unintelligent or mentally sick persons, and so on. Finally, he should stress that such considerations arise, if the demands for justification are pushed far enough, in validating inductive criteria as well as in justifying ethical principles. Provided an explication exists satisfying the tests in 4.3, moral actions can be justified in a manner analogous to the way in which decisions to believe a proposition, or theory, are justified.

6.5 Two possible objections remain to be considered. First, it may be said that, even if the foregoing decision procedure could be carried out in a particular case, the decision in question still would not be justified. To this I should say that we ought to inquire whether the person making the objection is not expecting too much. Perhaps he expects a justification procedure to show him how the decision is deducible from a synthetic a priori proposition. The answer to a person with such hopes is that they are logically impossible to satisfy and that all we should expect is that moral decisions and ethical principles are capable of the same sort of justification as decisions to believe and inductive criteria. Secondly, it may be said that a set of principles satisfying the tests of 4.3 does not exist. To this I should say that while it is obvious that moral codes and customs have varied in time, and change from place to place, yet when we think of a successful explication as representing the invariant in the considered judgments of competent judges, then the variation of codes and customs is not decisive against the existence of such an explication. Such a question cannot be decided by analysis or by talking about possibilities, but only by exhibiting explications which are capable of satisfying the tests which are properly applied to them.

III

THE JUSTIFICATION
FOR BEING MORAL

To ACT MORALLY, a person must consider the interests of others. He must keep his promises, act fairly, and not cause harm. But acting in these ways is often not the best way of achieving our own goals. Whether we want to win an election, succeed in business, or move quickly through a grocery line, we may fare better by doing what is wrong. Why, then, should we do what is right?

One possible answer is that being moral serves our overall interest. Despite his temporary sacrifices, the upright person may be better off, all things considered, than the immoral one. Thus, Plato notes in reading 17 that virtue can bring honor and rewards. And Thomas Hobbes argues forcefully in reading 18 that conformity to moral rules is necessary for self-preservation. Although Hobbes believes that in the absence of government, "every man has a right to every thing," he insists that where there is civil order, we best protect our interests by keeping agreements, displaying gratitude, and, generally, treating others as we wish to be treated. By not mistreating others, we avoid mistreatment by them. At first glance, this seems to invite the reply that we sometimes *can* benefit by acting wrongly. But Hobbes's position may be that it is difficult to know in advance which immoral acts will benefit us, and that the costs of finding out are often prohibitive. For these reasons, the cautiously self-interested person may do best by consistently following morality.

Quite clearly, these suggestions contain much truth. Yet because they appeal to such facts as our inability to know when our wrongdoing will be discovered, they do not rule out wrongdoing under all conceivable circumstances. In reading 17, Plato tells the story of the ancestor of Gyges, who found a ring that made him invisible. If someone had such a ring, he *would* know that he could get away with doing what is wrong. Thus, if self-interest is to prevent him from acting wrongly, it must do so on some further grounds. The prospects for finding such grounds are explored in reading 19 by Peter Singer. Singer considers, but is skeptical of, the suggestion that furtive immorality always brings guilt and unhappiness. He is more impressed with the suggestion that purely self-interested persons lead empty and unfulfilled lives. At least for some, the ethical point of view, which considers the interests of all, may be the key to a rich and meaningful existence.

These arguments defend morality as being in each person's interest. But is establishing that something will benefit a person the only way of justifying it to him? In reading 20, David Hume defends a very different conception of justification. According to Hume, what is reasonable for someone depends entirely on the desires, or "passions," he actually has. These desires may or may not include a dominant desire to further his own self-interest. As Hume writes, "[i]t is not contrary to reason to prefer the destruction of the whole world to the scratching of my finger. It is not contrary to reason for me to choose my total ruin to prevent the least uneasiness of an Indian, or person wholly unknown to me. It is as little contrary to reason to prefer even my own acknowledged lesser good to my greater, and have a more ardent affection for the former than the latter."

Hume's view, if correct, opens up new possibilities. It suggests that, at least to some people, we can justify being moral without showing that it will bring personal benefits. Rather, we can argue that being moral coincides with, or is the best way of fulfilling, the totality of one's desires. Because Hume believed that we all identify sympathetically with the pleasures and pains of others, he believed that everyone has desires that are directed at others' well-being. Thus, his theory points to a justification both of observing the conventions of justice, which serve the common good, and of acts of beneficence, charity, and the like. Similarly, but more straightforwardly, Philippa Foot argues in reading 21 that the moral life can be defended only to those who want to be kind, fair, and just. Many people do have such desires, and find such lives inspiring. But one who lacks a commitment to charity, justice, and honesty does not frustrate his own purposes by acting immorally. For that person, being immoral is not irrational.

As Foot recognizes, justifications that appeal to either self-interest or desire may seem unsatisfying. Thus, Kant notes in reading 29 that when a shopkeeper's reason for dealing honestly with a child is only to preserve his reputation, his actions seem to lack moral worth. Though not immoral, his actions are not motivated by duty—by respect for the moral law. But if respect for moral law is different from mere desire, then the justification for following the moral law must also be independent of any agent's desires. The justification must appeal to considerations accessible to all rational beings. It must, in Kant's view, be supplied by reason itself.

The Kantian idea that it is somehow inconsistent or irrational to ignore the interests of others has been developed in various ways. According to R. M. Hare (reading 22), to say that we ought to do something is both to commit ourselves to doing it and to prescribe a similar action for anyone else who is similarly situated. Hence, when we say that we ought to harm or cheat another, we prescribe that we be harmed or cheated when the roles are reversed. Because few are willing to prescribe this, most who say that they ought to harm or cheat others, or who act on that conviction, are being inconsistent. As Hare recognizes, one might attempt to avoid the inconsistency by harming or cheating another without saying that one ought to do it. However, in Hare's view, this stance is much harder to maintain consistently than it first appears.

Because Hare ties the obligation not to harm others to the unwillingness not to be harmed, his theory assigns a role to desire as well as reason. Thus, Hare must allow that the obligation does not apply to one who is willing to be harmed in order to further some ideal or political cause. In this respect, Hare's justification of morality falls short of Kant's ideal of inescapability and necessity. In reading 23, Alan Gewirth ties morality to reason in a way that may avoid this problem. Gewirth's strategy is to appeal not to the logic of moral discourse, but to the requirements of purposive action. In his view, anyone who acts is committed to believing that he has a right to act, and thus also that he has a right to the freedom and well-being that make action possible. These rights are violated when others act immorally toward him. Because each person's reason for believing that he has rights is simply that he acts, and because each person knows that all others are agents as well, each person must be committed to believing that all others have similar rights. And because our status as agents is unavoidable, the resulting commitment to morality must be unavoidable too.

Thus far, we have encountered justifications of morality that appeal to different combinations of self-interest, desire, and reason. In our final selection, we encounter still a further way of combining these elements. In reading 24, Kurt Baier argues that little is accomplished when only a few people follow moral rules, but that everyone's life is greatly improved when everyone follows such rules. Thus, Baier contends that we have no reason to follow such rules if others do not also follow them, but every reason to do so if others do. In the latter case, our reason consists of the many benefits made possible by morality, when these are considered from an impersonal perspective. Because we would receive these benefits even if we did *not* follow the rules, this may not seem to be an adequate justification for our following the rules. But because Baier contends that the proper perspective is "the point of view of *anyone*," he can reply that if I were justified in making an exception of myself, then anyone else would be also. This would mean that the case for having the rules would collapse. Clearly Baier's "point of view of *anyone*," is similar to the perspective that Kantians believe to be forced on us by reason. Thus, Baier's theory combines appeals to reason and self-interest in a novel way.

17

The Ring of Gyges

PLATO

Plato (427–347 B.C.) wrote a series of dialogues that immortalized his teacher Socrates. In these dialogues, Plato poses in striking form many of the issues and competing answers that have been at the center of philosophical study for more than two thousand years.

In this selection from his dialogue The Republic, *Plato articulates a central challenge to morality: Why should anyone do what is just (or, more generally, what is right)? If, like Gyges, we had a ring that could render us invisible, why should we not do whatever foul deeds we pleased? If what matters is worldly reward and honor, then it is not important to act justly, but only to appear just. In that case, we should feign justice, but secretly practice injustice whenever possible. If we are to avoid this conclusion, our justification of morality must go deeper. We must ask, "in what way does its very possession benefit a man?"*

WHEN I HAD SAID THIS I thought I had done with the discussion, but evidently this was only a prelude. Glaucon on this occasion too showed that boldness which is characteristic of him, and refused to accept Thrasymachus' abandoning the argument. He said: Do you, Socrates, want to appear to have persuaded us, or do you want truly to convince us that it is better in every way to be just than unjust?

I would certainly wish to convince you truly, I said, if I could.

Well, he said, you are certainly not attaining your wish. Tell me, do you think there is a kind of good which we welcome not because we desire its consequences but for its own sake: joy, for example, and all the harmless pleasures which have no further consequences beyond the joy which one finds in them?

Certainly, said I, I think there is such a good.

Further, there is the good which we welcome for its own sake and also for its consequences, knowledge for example and sight and health. Such things we somehow welcome on both counts.

Yes, said I.

Are you also aware of a third kind, he asked, such as physical training, being treated when ill, the practice of medicine, and other ways of making money? We should say that these are wearisome but beneficial to us; we should not want them for their own sake, but because of the rewards and other benefits which result from them.

There is certainly such a third kind, I said, but why do you ask?

Under which of these headings do you put justice? he asked.

I would myself put it in the finest class, I said, that which is to be welcomed both for itself and for its consequences by any man who is to be blessed with happiness.

That is not the opinion of the many, he said; they would put it in the wearisome class, to be pursued for the rewards and popularity which come from a good reputation, but to be avoided in itself as being difficult.

I know that is the general opinion, I said. Justice has now for some time been objected to by Thrasymachus on this score while injustice was extolled, but it seems I am a slow learner.

Come then, he said, listen to me also to see whether you are still of the same opinion, for I think that Thrasymachus gave up before he had to, charmed by you as by a snake charmer. I am not yet satisfied by the demonstration on either side. I am eager to hear the nature of each, of justice and injustice, and what effect its presence has upon the soul. I want to leave out of account the rewards and consequences of each. So, if you agree, I will do the following: I will renew the argument of Thrasymachus; I will first state what people consider the nature and origin of justice; secondly, that all who practise it do so unwillingly as being something necessary but not good; thirdly, that they have good reason to do so, for, according to what people say, the life of the unjust man is much better than that of the just.

It is not that I think so, Socrates, but I am perplexed and my ears are deafened listening to Thrasymachus and innumerable other speakers; I have never heard from anyone the sort of defence of justice that I want to hear, proving that it is better than injustice. I want to hear it praised for itself, and I think I am most likely to hear this from you. Therefore I am going to speak at length in praise of the unjust life and in doing so I will show you the way I want to hear you denouncing injustice and praising justice. See whether you want to hear what I suggest.

I want it more than anything else, I said. Indeed, what subject would a man of sense talk and hear about more often with enjoyment?

Splendid, he said, then listen while I deal with the first subject I mentioned: the nature and origin of justice.

They say that to do wrong is naturally good, to be wronged is bad, but the suffering of injury so far exceeds in badness the good of inflicting it that when men have done wrong to each other and suffered it, and have had a taste of both, those who are unable to avoid the latter and practise the former decide that it is profitable to come to an agreement with each other neither to inflict injury nor to suffer it. As a result they begin to make laws and covenants, and the law's command they call lawful and just. This, they say, is the origin and essence of justice; it stands between the best and the worst, the best being to do wrong without paying the penalty and the worst to be wronged without the power of revenge. The just then is a mean between two extremes; it is welcomed and honoured because of men's lack of the power to do wrong. The man who has that power, the real man, would not make a compact with anyone not to inflict injury or suffer it. For him that would be madness. This then, Socrates, is, according to their argument, the nature and origin of justice.

Even those who practise justice do so against their will because they lack the power to do wrong. This we could realize very clearly if we imagined ourselves granting to both the just and the unjust the freedom to do whatever they liked. We could then follow both of them and observe where their desires led them, and we would catch the just man redhanded travelling the same road as the unjust. The reason is the desire for undue gain which every organism by nature pursues as a good, but the law forcibly sidetracks him to honour equality. The freedom I just mentioned would most easily occur if these men had the power which they say the ancestor of the Lydian Gyges possessed. The story is that he was a shepherd in the service of the ruler of Lydia. There was a violent rainstorm and an earthquake which broke open the ground and created a chasm at the place where he was tending sheep. Seeing this and marvelling, he went down into it. He saw, besides many other wonders of which we are told, a hollow bronze horse. There were window-like openings in it; he climbed through them and caught sight of a corpse which seemed of more than human stature, wearing nothing but a ring of gold on its finger. This ring the shepherd put on and came out. He arrived at the usual monthly meeting which reported to the king on the state of the flocks, wearing the ring. As he was sitting among the others he happened to twist the hoop of the ring towards himself, to the inside of his hand, and as he did this he became invisible to those sitting near him and they went on talking as if he had gone. He marvelled at this and, fingering the ring, he turned the hoop outward again and became visible. Perceiving this he tested whether the ring had this power and so it happened: if he turned the hoop inwards he became invisible, but was visible when he turned it outwards. When he realized this, he at once arranged to become one of the messengers to the king. He went, committed adultery with the king's wife, attacked the king with her help, killed him, and took over the kingdom.

Now if there were two such rings, one worn by the just man, the other by the unjust, no one, as these people think, would be so incorruptible that he would stay on the path of justice or bring himself to keep away from other people's property and not touch it, when he could with impunity take whatever he wanted from the market, go into houses and have sexual relations with anyone he wanted, kill anyone, free all those he wished from prison, and do the other things which would make him like a god among men. His actions would be in no way different from those of the other and they would both follow the same path. This, some would say, is a great proof that no one is just willingly[1] but under compulsion, so that justice is not one's private good, since wherever either thought he could do wrong with impunity he would do so. Every man believes that injustice is much more profitable to himself than

---

[1] This of course directly contradicts the famous Socratic paradox that no one is willingly bad and that people do wrong because they have not the knowledge to do right, which is virtue.—TRANS.

justice, and any exponent of this argument will say that he is right. The man who did not wish to do wrong with that opportunity, and did not touch other people's property, would be thought by those who knew it to be very foolish and miserable. They would praise him in public, thus deceiving one another, for fear of being wronged. So much for my second topic.

As for the choice between the lives we are discussing, we shall be able to make a correct judgment about it only if we put the most just man and the most unjust man face to face; otherwise we cannot do so. By face to face I mean this: let us grant to the unjust the fullest degree of injustice and to the just the fullest justice, each being perfect in his own pursuit. First, the unjust man will act as clever craftsmen do—a top navigator for example or physician distinguishes what his craft can do and what it cannot; the former he will undertake, the latter he will pass by, and when he slips he can put things right. So the unjust man's correct attempts at wrongdoing must remain secret; the one who is caught must be considered a poor performer, for the extreme of injustice is to have a reputation for justice, and our perfectly unjust man must be granted perfection in injustice. We must not take this from him, but we must allow that, while committing the greatest crimes, he has provided himself with the greatest reputation for justice; if he makes a slip he must be able to put it right; he must be a sufficiently persuasive speaker if some wrongdoing of his is made public; he must be able to use force, where force is needed, with the help of his courage, his strength, and the friends and wealth with which he has provided himself.

Having described such a man, let us now in our argument put beside him the just man, simple as he is and noble, who, as Aeschylus put it,[2] does not wish to appear just but to be so. We must take away his reputation, for a reputation for justice would bring him honour and rewards, and it would then not be clear whether he is what he is for justice's sake or for the sake of rewards and honour. We must strip him of everything except justice and make him the complete opposite of the other. Though he does no wrong, he must have the greatest reputation for wrongdoing so that he may be tested for justice by not weakening under ill repute and its consequences. Let him go his incorruptible way until death with a reputation for injustice throughout his life, just though he is, so that our two men may reach the extremes, one of justice, the other of injustice, and let them be judged as to which of the two is the happier.

Whew! My dear Glaucon, I said, what a mighty scouring you have given those two characters, as if they were statues in a competition.

I do the best I can, he replied. The two being such as I have described, there should be no difficulty in following the argument through as to what kind of life awaits each of them, but it must be said. And if what I say sounds rather boorish, Socrates, realize that it is not I who speak, but those who praise

[2] In *Seven Against Thebes*, 592–4, it is said of Amphiaraus that "he did not wish to appear but to be the best," and it continues with the words quoted below: "He harbours in his heart a deep furrow, from which good counsels grow."—TRANS.

injustice as preferable to justice. They will say that the just man in these circumstances will be whipped, stretched on the rack, imprisoned, have his eyes burnt out, and, after suffering every kind of evil, he will be impaled and realize that one should not want to be just but to appear so. Indeed, Aeschylus' words are far more correctly applied to the unjust than to the just, for we shall be told that the unjust man pursues a course which is based on truth and not on appearances; he does not want to appear but to be unjust:

> He harvests in his heart a deep furrow
> from which good counsels grow.

He rules his city because of his reputation for justice, he marries into any family he wants to, he gives his children in marriage to anyone he wishes, he has contractual and other associations with anyone he may desire, and, beside all these advantages, he benefits in the pursuit of gain because he does not scruple to practise injustice. In any contest, public or private, he is the winner, getting the better of his enemies and accumulating wealth; he benefits his friends and does harm to his enemies. To the gods he offers grand sacrifices and gifts which will satisfy them, he can serve the gods much better than the just man, and also such men as he wants to, with the result that he is likely to be dearer to the gods. This is what they say, Socrates, that both from gods and men the unjust man secures a better life than the just.

After Glaucon has thus spoken I again had it in mind to say something in reply, but his brother Adeimantus intervened: You surely do not think that enough has been said from this point of view, Socrates?

Why not? said I.

The most important thing, that should have been said, has not been said, he replied.

Well then, I said, let brother stand by brother. If Glaucon has omitted something, you come to his help. Yet what he has said is sufficient to throw me and to make me incapable of coming to the help of justice.

Nonsense, he said. Hear what more I have to say, for we should also go fully into the arguments opposite to those he mentioned, those which praise justice and censure injustice, so that what I take to be Glaucon's intention may be clearer. When fathers speak to their sons, they say one must be just—and so do all who care for them, but they do not praise justice itself, only the high reputations it leads to, in order that the son, thought to be just, shall enjoy those public offices, marriages, and the rest which Glaucon mentioned, as they belong to the just man because of his high repute; they lay even greater emphasis on the results of reputation. They add popularity granted by the gods, and mention abundant blessings which, they say, the gods grant to the pious. So too the noble Hesiod and Homer declare,[3] the one that for the just the gods make "the oak trees bear acorns at the top and bees in the middle and their

---

[3] The two quotations which immediately follow are from Hesiod's *Works and Days*, 232-3, and Homer, *Odyssey*, 19, 109.—TRANS.

fleecy sheep are heavy with their burden of wool" and many other blessings of like nature. The other says similar things:

> (like the fame) of a goodly king who, in his piety,
> upholds justice; for him the black earth bears wheat
> and barley and the trees are heavy with fruit; his
> sheep bear lambs continually and the sea provides its fish.

Musaeus[4] and his son grant from the gods more robust pleasures to the just. Their words lead the just to the underworld, and, seating them at table, provide them with a banquet of the saints, crown them with wreaths, and make them spend all their time drinking, as if they thought that the finest reward of virtue was perpetual drunkenness. Others stretch the rewards of virtue from the gods even further, for they say that the children and the children's children and the posterity of the pious man who keeps his oaths will survive into the future. Thus, and in other such ways, do they praise justice. The impious and unjust they bury in mud in the underworld, they force them to carry water in a sieve, they bring them into disrepute while still living, and they attribute to them all the punishments which Glaucon enumerated in the case of the just with a reputation for injustice, but they have nothing else to say. This then is the way people praise and blame justice and injustice.

Besides this, Socrates, look at another kind of argument which is spoken in private, and also by the poets, concerning justice and injustice. All go on repeating with one voice that justice and moderation are beautiful, but certainly difficult and burdensome, while incontinence and injustice are sweet and easy, and shameful only by repute and by law. They add that unjust deeds are for the most part more profitable than just ones. They freely declare, both in private and in public, that the wicked who have wealth and other forms of power are happy. They honour them but pay neither honour nor attention to the weak and the poor, though they agree that these are better men than the others.

What men say about the gods and virtue is the most amazing of all, namely that the gods too inflict misfortunes and a miserable life upon many good men, and the opposite fate upon their opposites. Begging priests and prophets frequent the doors of the rich and persuade them that they possess a god-given power to remedy by sacrifices and incantations at pleasant festivals any crime that the rich man or one of his ancestors may have committed. Moreover, if one wishes to harass some enemy, then at little expense he will be able to harm the just and the unjust alike, for by means of spells and enchantments they can persuade the gods to serve them. They bring the poets as witnesses to all this, some harping on the easiness of vice, that

> Vice is easy to choose in abundance, the path is
> smooth and it dwells very near, but sweat is placed by
> the gods on the way to virtue,

---

[4] Musaeus was a legendary poet closely connected with the mystery religion of Orphism.—TRANS.

and a path which is long, rough, and steep;[5] others quote Homer as a witness that the gods can be influenced by men, for he too said:[6]

> the gods themselves can be swayed by prayer, for
> suppliant men can turn them from their purpose by
> sacrifices and gentle prayers, by libations and burnt offerings
> whenever anyone has transgressed and sinned.

They offer in proof a mass of writings by Musaeus and Orpheus, offspring, as they say, of Selene and the Muses. In accordance with these they perform their ritual and persuade not only individuals but whole cities that, both for the living and for the dead, there are absolutions and purifications for sin by means of sacrifices and pleasurable, playful rituals. These they call initiations which free from punishment yonder, where a dreadful fate awaits the uninitiated.

When all such sayings about the attitudes of men and gods toward virtue and vice are so often repeated, what effect, my dear Socrates, do we think they have upon the minds of our youth? One who is naturally talented and able, like a bee flitting from flower to flower gathering honey, to flit over these sayings and to gather from them an impression of what kind of man he should be and of how best to travel along the road of life, would surely repeat to himself the saying of Pindar: should I by justice or by crooked deceit scale this high wall and thus live my life fenced off from other men? The advantages said to be mine if I am just are of no use, I am told, unless I also appear so; while the troubles and penalties are obvious. The unjust man, on the other hand, who has secured for himself a reputation for justice, lives, they tell me, the life of a god. Therefore, since appearance, as the wise men tell me, forcibly overwhelms truth and controls happiness, this is altogether the way I should live. I should build around me a façade that gives the illusion of justice to those who approach me and keep behind this the greedy and crafty fox of the wise Archilochus.[7]

"But surely" someone objects, "it is not easy for vice to remain hidden always." We shall reply that nothing is easy which is of great import. Nevertheless, this is the way we must go if we are to be happy, and follow along the lines of all we have been told. To protect our secret we shall form sworn conspiratorial societies and political clubs. Besides, there are teachers of persuasion who make one clever in dealing with assemblies and with the courts. This will enable us to use persuasion here and force there, so that we can secure our own advantage without penalty.

"But one cannot force the gods nor have secrets from them." Well, if either they do not exist or do not concern themselves with human affairs, why should we worry about secrecy? If they do exist and do concern themselves, we have heard about them and know them from no other source than our laws and

---

[5] Hesiod, *Work and Days*, 287-89.—TRANS.

[6] Homer, *Iliad*, 9, 497-501.—TRANS.

[7] I.e. the fox mentioned by Archilochus. The fable in question is not extant.—TRANS.

our genealogising poets, and these are the very men who tell us that the gods can be persuaded and influenced by gentle prayers and by offerings. We should believe both or neither. If we believe them, we should do wrong and then offer sacrifices from the proceeds. If we are just, we shall not be punished by the gods but we shall lose the profits of injustice. If we are unjust we shall get the benefit of sins and transgressions, and afterwards persuade the gods by prayer and escape without punishment. "But in Hades we will pay the penalty for the crimes committed here, either ourselves or our children's children." "My friend," the young man will reply as he does his reckoning, "mystery rites have great potency, and so have the gods of absolution, as the greatest cities tell us, and the children of the gods who have become poets and prophets tell us that this is so."

For what reason then should we still choose justice rather than the greatest injustice? If we practise the latter with specious decorum we shall do well at the hands of gods and of men; we shall live and die as we intend, for so both the many and the eminent tell us. From all that has been said, Socrates, what possibility is there that any man of power, be it the power of mind or of wealth, of body or of birth, will be willing to honour justice and not laugh aloud when he hears it praised? And surely any man who can show that what we have said is untrue and has full knowledge that justice is best, will be full of forgiveness, and not of anger, for the unjust. He knows that only a man of godlike character whom injustice disgusts, or one who has superior knowledge, avoids injustice, and that no other man is willingly just, but through cowardice or old age or some other weakness objects to injustice, because he cannot practise it. That this is so is obvious, for the first of these men to acquire power is the first to do wrong as much as he is able.

The only reason for all this talk, Socrates, which led to Glaucon's speech and mine, is to say to you: Socrates, you strange man, not one of all of you who profess to praise justice, beginning with the heroes of old, whose words are left to us, to the present day—not one has ever blamed injustice or praised justice in any other way than by mentioning the reputations, honours, and rewards which follow justice. No one has ever adequately described, either in poetry or in private conversation, what the very presence of justice or injustice in his soul does to a man even if it remains hidden from gods and men; one is the greatest evil the soul can contain, while the other, justice, is the greatest good. If you had treated the subject in this way and had persuaded us from youth, we should then not be watching one another to see we do no wrong, but every man would be his own best guardian and he would be afraid lest, by doing wrong, he live with the greatest evil.

Thrasymachus or anyone else might say what we have said, and perhaps more in discussing justice and injustice. I believe they would be vulgarly distorting the effect of each. To be quite frank with you, it is because I am eager to hear the opposite from you that I speak with all the emphasis I can muster. So do not merely give us a theoretical proof that justice is better than injustice, but tell us how each, in and by itself, affects a man, the one for good, the other for evil. Follow Glaucon's advice and do not take reputations into account, for if you do not deprive them of true reputation and attach false reputations to them, we shall say that you are not praising justice but the reputation for it, or blaming injustice but the appearance of it, that you are encouraging one to be unjust in secret, and that you agree with Thrasymachus that the just is another's good, the advantage of the stronger, while the unjust is one's own advantage and profit, though not the advantage of the weaker.

Since you have agreed that justice is one of the greatest goods, those which are worthy of attainment for their consequences, but much more for their own sake—sight, hearing, knowledge, health, and all other goods which are creative by what they are and not by what they seem—do praise justice in this regard: in what way does its very possession benefit a man and injustice harm him? Leave rewards and reputations for others to praise.

For others would satisfy me if they praised justice and blamed injustice in this way, extolling the rewards of the one and denigrating those of the other, but from you, unless you tell me to, I will not accept it, because you have spent your whole life investigating this and nothing else. Do not, therefore, give us a merely theoretical proof that justice is better than injustice, but tell us what effect each has in and by itself, the one for good, the other for evil, whether or not it be hidden from gods and men.

I had always admired the character of Glaucon and Adeimantus, and on this occasion I was quite delighted with them as I listened and I said: You are the sons of a great man, and Glaucon's lover began his elegy well when he wrote, celebrating the repute you gained at the battle of Megara:

Sons of Ariston, godlike offspring of a famous man.

That seems well deserved, my friends; you must be divinely inspired if you are not convinced that injustice is better than justice, and yet can speak on its behalf as you have done. And I do believe that you are really unconvinced by your own words. I base this belief on my knowledge of the way you live, for, if I had only your words to go by, I would not trust you. The more I trust you, however, the more I am at a loss what to do. I do not see how I can be of help; I feel myself incapable. I see a proof of this in the fact that I thought what I said to Thrasymachus showed that justice is better than injustice, but you refuse to accept this as adequate. On the other hand I do not see how I can refuse my help, for I fear it is even impious to be present when justice is being charged and to fail to come to her help as long as there is breath in one's body and one is still able to speak. So the best course is to give her any assistance I can.

· · ·

18

Morality and Self-Interest

THOMAS HOBBES

> *Thomas Hobbes (1588–1679) made important contributions in metaphysics and psychology as well as political theory and ethics. The following selection is from his masterpiece* Leviathan.
>
> *According to Hobbes, morality is ultimately grounded in self-interest. In his view, people act solely to achieve gratification and to avoid being harmed. If this view is correct (it is criticized by Joel Feinberg in reading 1), the only effective reason for being moral is that morality serves each person's interest. And this is, in fact, Hobbes's position. He argues that justice, gratitude, and other elements of morality serve to ward off strife and disorder. For this reason, conformity to them is dictated by various "laws of nature."*
>
> *Do such laws always apply? According to Hobbes, they do not. When we keep an agreement without assurance that others will do likewise, we needlessly jeopardize ourselves. Since this is not reasonable, moral requirements apply only when backed by force. As Hobbes himself puts it, "covenants without the sword are but words." To provide the required force, we need a government, or "sovereign," that is stonger than any citizen or group of citizens. By imposing severe penalties for disobedience, the government removes incentives to attack or betray others for gain or through fear. It thus makes possible both morality and peace.*

Of the Natural Condition of Mankind as Concerning Their Felicity and Misery

NATURE HATH MADE men so equal, in the faculties of the body, and mind; as that though there be found one man sometimes manifestly stronger in body, or of quicker mind than another; yet when all is reckoned together, the difference between man, and man, is not so considerable, as that one man can thereupon claim to himself any benefit, to which another may not pretend, as well as he. For as to the strength of body, the weakest has strength enough to kill the strongest, either by secret machination, or by confederacy with others, that are in the same danger with himself.

And as to the faculties of the mind, setting aside the arts grounded upon words, and especially that skill of proceeding upon general, and infallible rules, called science; which very few have, and but in few things; as being not a native faculty, born with us; nor attained, as prudence, while we look after somewhat else, I find yet a greater equality amongst men, than that of strength. For prudence, is but experience; which equal time, equally bestows on all men, in those things they equally apply themselves unto. That which may perhaps make such equality incredible, is but a vain conceit of one's own wisdom, which almost all men think they have in a greater degree, than the vulgar; that is, than all men but themselves, and a few others, whom by fame, or for concurring with themselves, they approve. For such is the nature of men, that howsoever they may acknowledge many others to be more witty, or more eloquent, or more learned; yet they will hardly believe there be many so wise as themselves; for they see their own wit at hand, and other men's at a distance. But this proveth rather that men are in that point equal, than unequal. For there is not ordinarily a greater sign of the equal distribution of any thing, than that every man is contented with his share.

From this equality of ability, ariseth equality of hope in the attaining of our ends. And therefore if any two men desire the same thing, which nevertheless they cannot both enjoy, they become enemies; and in the way to their end, which is principally their own conservation, and sometimes their delectation only, endeavour to destroy, or subdue one another. And from hence it comes to pass, that where an invader hath no more to fear, than another man's single power; if one plant, sow, build, or possess a convenient seat, others may probably be expected to come prepared with forces united, to dispossess, and deprive him, not only of the fruit of his labour, but also of his life, or liberty. And the invader again is in the like danger of another.

And from this diffidence of one another, there is no way for any man to secure himself, so reasonable, as anticipation; that is, by force, or wiles, to master the persons of all men he can, so long, till he see no other power great enough to endanger him: and this is no more than his own conservation requireth, and is generally allowed. Also because there be some, that taking pleasure in contemplating their own power in the acts of conquest, which they pursue farther than their security requires; if others, that otherwise would be glad to be at ease within modest bounds, should not by invasion increase their power, they would not be able, long time, by standing only on their defence, to subsist. And by consequence, such augmentation of dominion over men being necessary to a man's conservation, it ought to be allowed him.

Again, men have no pleasure, but on the contrary a great deal of grief, in keeping company, where there is no power able to over-awe them all. For every man looketh that his companion should value him, at the same rate he sets upon himself: and upon all signs of contempt, or undervaluing, naturally endeavours, as far as he dares, (which amongst them that have no common power to keep them in quiet, is far enough to make them destroy each other), to extort a greater value from his contemners, by damage; and from others, by the example.

So that in the nature of man, we find three principal causes of quarrel. First, competition; secondly, diffidence; thirdly, glory.

The first, maketh men invade for gain; the second, for safety; and the third, for reputation. The first use violence, to make themselves masters of other men's persons, wives, children, and cattle; the second, to defend them; the third, for trifles, as a word, a smile, a different opinion, and any other sign of undervalue, either direct in their persons, or by reflection in their kindred, their friends, their nation, their profession, or their name.

Hereby it is manifest, that during the time men live without a common power to keep them all in awe, they are in that condition which is called war; and such a war, as is of every man, against every man. For WAR, consisteth not in battle only, or the act of fighting; but in a tract of time, wherein the will to contend by battle is sufficiently known: and therefore the notion of *time,* is to be considered in the nature of war; as it is in the nature of weather. For as the nature of foul weather, lieth not in a shower or two of rain; but in an inclination thereto of many days together: so the nature of war, consisteth not in actual fighting; but in the known disposition thereto, during all the time there is no assurance to the contrary. All other time is PEACE.

Whatsoever therefore is consequent to a time of war, where every man is enemy to every man; the same is consequent to the time, wherein men live without other security, than what their own strength, and their own invention shall furnish them withal. In such condition, there is no place for industry; because the fruit thereof is uncertain: and consequently no culture of the earth; no navigation, nor use of the commodities that may be imported by sea; no commodious building; no instruments of moving, and removing, such things as require much force; no knowledge of the face of the earth; no account of time; no arts; no letters; no society; and which is worst of all, continual fear, and danger of violent death; and the life of man, solitary, poor, nasty, brutish, and short.

It may seem strange to some man, that has not well weighed these things; that nature should thus dissociate, and render men apt to invade, and destroy one another: and he may therefore, not trusting to this inference, made from the passions, desire perhaps to have the same confirmed by experience. Let him therefore consider with himself, when taking a journey, he arms himself, and seeks to go well accompanied; when going to sleep, he locks his doors; when even in his house he locks his chests; and this when he knows there be laws, and public officers, armed, to revenge all injuries shall be done him; what opinion he has of his fellow-subjects, when he rides armed; of his fellow citizens, when he locks his doors; and of his children, and servants, when he locks his chests. Does he not there as much accuse mankind by his actions, as I do by my words? But neither of us accuse man's nature in it. The desires, and other passions of man, are in themselves no sin. No more are the actions, that proceed from those passions, till they know a law that forbids them: which till laws be made they cannot know: nor can any law be made, till they have agreed upon the person that shall make it.

It may peradventure be thought, there was never such a time, nor condition of war as this; and I believe it was never generally so, over all the world: but there are many places, where they live so now. For the savage people in many places of America, except the government of small families, the concord whereof dependeth on natural lust, have no government at all; and live at this day in that brutish manner, as I said before. Howsoever, it may be perceived what manner of life there would be, where there were no common power to fear, by the manner of life, which men that have formerly lived under a peaceful government, use to degenerate into, in a civil war.

But though there had never been any time, wherein particular men were in a condition of war one against another; yet in all times, kings, and persons of sovereign authority, because of their independency, are in continual jealousies, and in the state and posture of gladiators; having their weapons pointing, and their eyes fixed on one another; that is, their forts, garrisons, and guns upon the frontiers of their kingdoms; and continual spies upon their neighbours; which is a posture of war. But because they uphold thereby, the industry of their subjects; there does not follow from it, that misery, which accompanies the liberty of particular men.

To this war of every man, against every man, this also is consequent; that nothing can be unjust. The notions of right and wrong, justice and injustice have there no place. Where there is no common power, there is no law: where no law, no injustice. Force, and fraud, are in war the two cardinal virtues. Justice, and injustice are none of the faculties neither of the body, nor mind. If they were, they might be in a man that were alone in the world, as well as his senses, and passions. They are qualities, that relate to men in society, not in solitude. It is consequent also to the same condition, that there be no propriety, no dominion, no *mine* and *thine* distinct; but only that to be every man's, that he can get: and for so long, as he can keep it. And thus much for the ill condition, which man by mere nature is actually placed in; though with a possibility to come out of it, consisting partly in the passions, partly in his reason.

The passions that incline men to peace, are fear of death; desire of such things as are necessary to commodious living; and a hope by their industry to obtain them. And reason suggesteth convenient articles of peace, upon which men may be drawn to agreement. These articles, are they, which otherwise are called the Laws of Nature: whereof I shall speak more particularly, in the two following chapters.

Of the First and Second Natural Laws, and of Contracts

THE RIGHT OF NATURE, which writers commonly call *jus naturale,* is the liberty each man hath, to use his own power, as he will himself, for the preservation of his own nature; that is to say, of his own life; and consequently, of doing any thing, which in his own judgment, and reason, he shall conceive to be the aptest means thereunto.

By LIBERTY, is understood, according to the proper signification of the word, the absence of external impediments: which impediments, may oft take away part of a man's power to do what he would; but cannot hinder him from using the power left him, according as his judgment, and reason shall dictate to him.

A LAW OF NATURE, *lex naturalis,* is a precept or general rule, found out by reason, by which a man is forbidden to do that, which is destructive of his life, or taketh away the means of preserving the same; and to omit that, by which he thinketh it may be best preserved. For though they that speak of this subject, use to confound *jus,* and *lex, right* and *law:* yet they ought to be distinguished; because RIGHT, consisteth in liberty to do, or to forbear: whereas LAW, determineth, and bindeth to one of them: so that law, and right, differ as much, as obligation, and liberty; which in one and the same matter are inconsistent.

And because the condition of man, as hath been declared in the precedent chapter, is a condition of war of every one against every one; in which case every one is governed by his own reason; and there is nothing he can make use of, that may not be a help unto him, in preserving his life against his enemies; it followeth, that in such a condition, every man has a right to every thing; even to one another's body. And therefore, as long as this natural right of every man to every thing endureth, there can be no security to any man, how strong or wise soever he be, of living out the time, which nature ordinarily alloweth men to live. And consequently it is a precept, or general rule of reason, *that every man, ought to endeavour peace, as far as he has hope of obtaining it; and when he cannot obtain it, that he may seek, and use, all helps, and advantages of war.* The first branch of which rule, containeth the first, and fundamental law of nature; which is, *to seek peace, and follow it.* The second, the sum of the right of nature; which is, *by all means we can, to defend ourselves.*

From this fundamental law of nature, by which men are commanded to endeavour peace, is derived this second law; *that a man be willing, when others are so too, as far-forth, as for peace, and defence of himself he shall think it necessary, to lay down this right to all things; and be contented with so much liberty against other men, as he would allow other men against himself.* For as long as every man holdeth this right, of doing any thing he liketh; so long are all men in the condition of war. But if other men will not lay down their right, as well as he; then there is no reason for any one, to divest himself of his: for that were to expose himself to prey, which no man is bound to, rather than to dispose himself to peace. This is that law of the Gospel; *whatsoever you require that others should do to you, that do ye to them.* And that law of all men, *quod tibi fieri non vis, alteri ne feceris.*

To *lay down* a man's *right* to any thing, is to *divest* himself of the *liberty,* of hindering another of the benefit of his own right to the same. For he that renounceth, or passeth away his right, giveth not to any other man a right which he had not before; because there is nothing to which every man had not right by nature: but only standeth out of his way, that he may enjoy his own original right, without hindrance from him; not without hindrance from another. So that the effect which redoundeth to one man, by another man's defect of right, is but so much diminution of impediments to the use of his own right original.

Right is laid aside, either by simply renouncing it; or by transferring it to another. By *simply* RENOUNCING; when he cares not to whom the benefit thereof redoundeth. By TRANSFERRING; when he intendeth the benefit thereof to some certain person, or persons. And when a man hath in either manner abandoned, or granted away his right; then he is said to be OBLIGED, or BOUND, not to hinder those, to whom such right is granted, or abandoned, from the benefit of it: and that he *ought,* and it is his DUTY, not to make void that voluntary act of his own: and that such hindrance is INJUSTICE, and INJURY, as being *sine jure;* the right being before renounced, or transferred. So that *injury,* or *injustice,* in the controversies of the world, is somewhat like to that, which in the disputations of scholars is called *absurdity.* For as it is there called an absurdity, to contradict what one maintained in the beginning: so in the world, it is called injustice, and injury, voluntarily to undo that, which from the beginning he had voluntarily done. The way by which a man either simply renounceth, or transferreth his right, is a declaration, or signification, by some voluntary and sufficient sign, or signs, that he doth so renounce, or transfer; or hath so renounced, or transferred the same, to him that accepteth it. And these signs are either words only, or actions only; or, as it happeneth most often, both words, and actions. And the same are the BONDS, by which men are bound, and obliged: bonds, that have their strength, not from their own nature, for nothing is more easily broken than a man's word, but from fear of some evil consequence upon the rupture.

Whensoever a man transferreth his right, or renounceth it; it is either in consideration of some right reciprocally transferred to himself; or for some other good he hopeth for thereby. For it is a voluntary act: and of the voluntary acts of every man, the object is some *good to himself.* And therefore there be some rights, which no man can be understood by any words, or other signs, to have abandoned, or transferred. As first a man cannot lay down the right of resisting them, that assault him by force, to take away his life; because he cannot be understood to aim thereby, at any good to himself. The same may be said of wounds, and chains, and imprisonment; both because there is no benefit consequent to such patience; as there is to the patience of suffering another to be wounded, or imprisoned: as also because a man cannot tell, when he seeth men proceed against him by violence, whether they intend his death or not. And lastly the motive, and end for which this renouncing, and transferring of right is introduced, is nothing else but the security of a man's person, in his life, and in the means of so preserving life, as not to be weary of it. And therefore if a man by words, or other signs, seem to despoil himself of the end, for which those signs were intended; he is not to be understood as if he meant it, or that it was his will; but that he was ignorant of how such words and actions were to be interpreted.

The mutual transferring of right, is that which men call CONTRACT.

There is difference between transferring of right to the thing; and transferring, or tradition, that is delivery of the thing itself. For the thing may be delivered together with the translation of the right; as in buying and selling with ready-money; or exchange of goods, or lands: and it may be delivered some time after.

Again, one of the contractors, may deliver the thing contracted for on his part, and leave the other to perform his part at some determinate time after, and in the mean time be trusted; and then the contract on his part, is called PACT, or COVENANT: or both parts may contract now, to perform hereafter: in which cases, he that is to perform in time to come, being trusted, his performance is called *keeping of promise,* or faith; and the failing of performance, if it be voluntary, *violation of faith.*

. . .

If a covenant be made, wherein neither of the parties perform presently, but trust one another; in the condition of mere nature, which is a condition of war of every man against every man, upon any reasonable suspicion, it is void: but if there be a common power set over them both, with right and force sufficient to compel performance, it is not void. For he that performeth first, has no assurance the other will perform after; because the bonds of words are too weak to bridle men's ambition, avarice, anger, and other passions, without the fear of some coercive power; which in the condition of mere nature, where all men are equal, and judges of the justness of their own fears, cannot possibly be supposed. And therefore he which performeth first, does but betray himself to his enemy; contrary to the right, he can never abandon, of defending his life, and means of living.

But in a civil estate, where there is a power set up to constrain those that would otherwise violate their faith, that fear is no more reasonable; and for that cause, he which by the covenant is to perform first, is obliged so to do.

The cause of fear, which maketh such a covenant invalid, must be always something arising after the covenant made; as some new fact, or other sign of the will not to perform: else it cannot make the covenant void. For that which could not hinder a man from promising, ought not to be admitted as a hindrance of performing.

. . .

A covenant not to defend myself from force, by force, is always void. For, as I have showed before, no man can transfer, or lay down his right to save himself from death, wounds, and imprisonment, the avoiding whereof is the only end of laying down any right; and therefore the promise of not resisting force, in no covenant transferreth any right; nor is obliging. For though a man may covenant thus, *unless I do so, or so, kill me;* he cannot covenant thus, *unless I do so, or so, I will not resist you, when you come to kill me.* For man by nature chooseth the lesser evil, which is danger of death in resisting; rather than the greater, which is certain and present death in not resisting. And this is granted to be true by all men, in that they lead criminals to execution, and prison, with armed men, notwithstanding that such criminals have consented to the law, by which they are condemned.

. . .

Of Other Laws of Nature

From that law of nature, by which we are obliged to transfer to another, such rights, as being retained, hinder the peace of mankind, there followeth a third; which is this, *that men perform their covenants made:* without which,

250

covenants are in vain, and but empty words; and the right of all men to all things remaining, we are still in the condition of war.

And in this law of nature, consisteth the fountain and original of JUSTICE. For where no covenant hath preceded, there hath no right been transferred, and every man has right to every thing; and consequently, no action can be unjust. But when a covenant is made, then to break it is *unjust:* and the definition of INJUSTICE, is no other than *the not performance of covenant.* And whatsoever is not unjust, is *just.*

But because covenants of mutual trust, where there is a fear of not performance on either part, as hath been said in the former chapter, are invalid; though the original of justice be the making of covenants; yet injustice actually there can be none, till the cause of such fear be taken away; which while men are in the natural condition of war, cannot be done. Therefore before the names of just, and unjust can have place, there must be some coercive power, to compel men equally to the performance of their covenants, by the terror of some punishment, greater than the benefit they expect by the breach of their covenant; and to make good that propriety, which by mutual contract men acquire, in recompense of the universal right they abandon: and such power there is none before the erection of a commonwealth. And this is also to be gathered out of the ordinary definition of justice in the Schools: for they say, that *justice is the constant will of giving to every man his own.* And therefore where there is no *own,* that is no propriety, there is no injustice; and where there is no coercive power erected, that is, where there is no commonwealth, there is no propriety; all men having right to all things: therefore where there is no commonwealth, there nothing is unjust. So that the nature of justice, consisteth in keeping of valid covenants: but the validity of covenants begins not but with the constitution of a civil power, sufficient to compel men to keep them: and then it is also that propriety begins.

. . .

Whatsoever is done to a man, conformable to his own will signified to the doer, is no injury to him. For if he that doeth it, hath not passed away his original right to do what he please, by some antecedent covenant, there is no breach of covenant; and therefore no injury done him. And if he have; then his will to have it done being signified, is a release of that covenant: and so again there is no injury done him.

Justice of actions, is by writers divided into *commutative,* and *distributive:* and the former they say consisteth in proportion arithmetical; the latter in proportion geometrical. Commutative therefore, they place in the equality of value of the things contracted for; and distributive, in the distribution of equal benefit, to men of equal merit. As if it were injustice to sell dearer than we buy; or to give more to a man than he merits. The value of all things contracted for, is measured by the appetite of the contractors: and therefore the just value, is that which they be contented to give. And merit (besides that which is by covenant, where the performance on one part, meriteth the performance on the other part, and falls under justice commutative, not distributive) is not due to justice; but is rewarded of grace only. And therefore this distinction, in the sense wherein it useth to be expounded, is not right. To speak properly, commutative justice, is the justice, of a contractor; that is, a performance of covenant, in buying, and selling; hiring, and letting to hire; lending, and borrowing; exchanging, bartering, and other acts of contract.

And distributive justice, the justice of an arbitrator; that is to say, the act of defining what is just. Wherein, being trusted by them that make him arbitrator, if he perform his trust, he is said to distribute to every man his own: and this is indeed just distribution, and may be called, though improperly, distributive justice; but more properly equity; which also is a law of nature, as shall be shown in due place.

As justice dependeth on antecedent covenant; so does GRATITUDE depend on antecedent grace; that is to say, antecedent free gift: and is the fourth law of nature; which may be conceived in this form, *that a man which receiveth benefit from another of mere grace, endeavour that he which giveth it, have no reasonable cause to repent him of his good will.* For no man giveth, but with intention of good to himself; because gift is voluntary; and of all voluntary acts, the object is to every man his own good; of which if men see they shall be frustrated, there will be no beginning of benevolence, or trust; nor consequently of mutual help; nor of reconciliation of one man to another; of *war;* which is contrary to the first and fundamental law of nature, which commandeth men to *seek peace.* The breach of this law, is called *ingratitude;* and hath the same relation to grace, that injustice hath to obligation by covenant.

A fifth law of nature, is COMPLAISANCE; that is to say, *that every man strive to accommodate himself to the rest.* For the understanding whereof, we may consider, that there is in men's aptness to society, a diversity of nature, rising from their diversity of affections; not unlike to that we see in stones brought together for building of an edifice. For as that stone which by the asperity, and irregularity of figure, takes more room from others, than itself fills; and for the hardness, cannot be easily made plain, and thereby hindereth the building, is by the builders cast away as unprofitable, and troublesome: so also, a man that by asperity of nature, will strive to retain those things which to himself are superfluous, and to others necessary; and for the stubbornness of his passions, cannot be corrected, is to be left, or cast out of society, as cumbersome thereunto. For seeing every man, not only by right, but also by necessity of nature, is supposed to endeavour all he can, to obtain that which is necessary for his conservation; he that shall oppose himself against it, for things superfluous, is guilty of the war that thereupon is to follow; and therefore doth that, which is contrary to the fundamental law of nature, which commandeth *to seek peace.* The observers of this law, may be called SOCIABLE, the Latins call them *commodi;* the contrary, *stubborn, insociable, forward, intractable.*

A sixth law of nature, is this, *that upon caution of the future time, a man ought to pardon the offences past of them that repenting, desire it.* For PARDON, is nothing but granting of peace; which though granted to them that persevere in their hostility, be not peace, but fear; yet not granted to them that give caution of the future time, is sign of an aversion to peace; and therefore contrary to the law of nature.

A seventh is, *that in revenges,* that is, retribution of evil for evil, *men look not at the greatness of the evil past, but the greatness of the good to follow.* Whereby we are forbidden to inflict punishment with any other design, than for correction of the offender, or direction of others. For this law is consequent to the next before it, that commandeth pardon, upon security of the future time. Besides, revenge without respect to the example, and profit to come, is a triumph, or glorying in the hurt of another, tending to no end; for the end is always somewhat to come; and glorying to no end, is vain-glory, and contrary to reason, and to hurt without reason, tendeth to the introduction of war; which is against the law of nature; and is commonly styled by the name of *cruelty.*

. . .

And because, though men be never so willing to observe these laws, there may nevertheless arise questions concerning a man's action; first, whether it were done, or not done; secondly, if done, whether against the law, or not against the law; the former whereof, is called a question *of fact;* the latter a question *of right,* therefore unless the parties to the question, covenant mutually to stand to the sentence of another, they are as far from peace as ever. This other to whose sentence they submit is called an ARBITRATOR. And therefore it is of the law of nature, *that they that are at controversy, submit their right to the judgment of an arbitrator.*

And seeing every man is presumed to do all things in order to his own benefit, no man is a fit arbitrator in his own cause; and if he were never so fit; yet equity allowing to each party equal benefit, if one be admitted to be judge, the other is to be admitted also; and so the controversy, that is, the cause of war, remains, against the law of nature.

For the same reason no man in any cause ought to be received for arbitrator, to whom greater profit, or honour, or pleasure apparently ariseth out of the victory of one party, than of the other: for he hath taken, though an unavoidable bribe, yet a bribe; and no man can be obliged to trust him. And thus also the controversy, and the condition of war remaineth, contrary to the law of nature.

And in a controversy of *fact,* the judge being to give no more credit to one, than to the other, if there be no other arguments, must give credit to a third; or to a third and fourth; or more: for else the question is undecided, and left to force, contrary to the law of nature.

These are the laws of nature, dictating peace, for a means of the conservation of men in multitudes; and which only concern the doctrine of civil society. There be other things tending to the destruction of particular men; as drunkenness, and all other parts of intemperance; which may therefore also be reckoned amongst those things which the law of nature hath forbidden; but are not necessary to be mentioned, nor are pertinent enough to this place.

And though this may seem too subtle a deduction of the laws of nature, to be taken notice of by all men; whereof the most part are too busy in getting food, and the rest too negligent to understand; yet to leave all men inexcusable, they have been contracted into one easy sum, intelligible even to the meanest capacity; and that is, *Do not that to another, which thou wouldest not have done to thyself;* which sheweth him, that he had no more to do in learning the laws of nature, but, when weighing the actions of other men with his own, they seem too heavy, to put them into the other part of the balance, and his own into their place, that his own passions, and self-love, may add nothing to the weight; and then there is none of these laws of nature that will not appear unto him very reasonable.

The laws of nature oblige *in foro interno;* that is to say, they bind to a desire they should take place: but *in foro externo;* this is, to the putting them in act, not always. For he that should be modest, and tractable, and perform all he promises, in such time, and place, where no man else should do so, should but make himself a prey to others, and procure his own certain ruin, contrary to the ground of all laws of nature, which tend to nature's preservation. And again, he that having sufficient security, that others shall observe the same laws towards him, observes them not himself, seeketh not peace, but war; and consequently the destruction of his nature by violence.

And whatsoever laws bind *in foro interno,* may be broken, not only by a fact contrary to the law, but also by a fact according to it, in case a man think it contrary. For though his action in this case, be according to the law; yet his purpose was against the law; which, where the obligation is *in foro interno,* is a breach.

The laws of nature are immutable and eternal; for injustice, ingratitude, arrogance, pride, iniquity, acception of persons, and the rest, can never be made lawful. For it can never be that war shall preserve life, and peace destroy it.

The same laws, because they oblige only to a desire, and endeavour, I mean an unfeigned and constant endeavour, are easy to be observed. For in that they require nothing but endeavor, he that endeavoureth their performance, fulfilleth them; and he that fulfilleth the law, is just.

And the science of them, is the true and only moral philosophy. For moral philosophy is nothing else but the science of what is *good,* and *evil,* in the conversation, and society of mankind. *Good,* and *evil,* are names that signify our appetites, and aversions; which in different tempers, customs, and doctrines of men, are different: and divers men, differ not only in their judgment, on the senses of what is pleasant, and unpleasant to the taste, smell, hearing, touch, and sight; but also of what is conformable, or disagreeable to reason, in the actions of common life. Nay, the same man, in divers times, differs from himself; and one time praiseth, that is, calleth good, what another time he dispraiseth, and calleth evil: from whence arise disputes, controversies, and at last war. And therefore so long a man is in the condition of mere nature, which is a condition of war, as private appetite is the measure of good, and evil: and consequently all men agree on this, that peace is good, and therefore also the way, or means of peace, which, as I have shewed before, are *justice, gratitude, modesty, equity, mercy,* and the rest of the laws of nature, are good; that is to say; *moral virtues;* and their contrary *vices,* evil. Now the science of virtue and vice, is moral philosophy; and therefore the true doctrine of the laws of nature, is the true moral philosophy. But the writers of moral philosophy, though they acknowledge the same virtues and vices; yet not seeing wherein consisted their goodness; nor that they come to be praised, as the means of peaceable, sociable, and comfortable living, place them in a mediocrity of passions: as if not the cause, but the degree of daring, made fortitude; or not the cause, but the quantity of a gift, made liberality.

These dictates of reason, men used to call by the names of laws, but improperly: for they are but conclusions, or theorems concerning what conduceth to the conservation and defence of themselves; whereas law, properly, is the word of him, that by right hath command over others. But yet if we consider the same theorems, as delivered in the word of God, that by right commandeth all things; then are they properly called laws.

Of the Causes, Generation, and Definition of a Commonwealth

The final cause, end, or design of men, who naturally love liberty, and dominion over others, in the introduction of that restraint upon themselves, in which we see them live in commonwealths, is the foresight of their own preservation, and of a more contented life thereby; that is to say, of getting themselves out from that miserable condition of war, which is necessarily consequent, as hath been shown (chapter 13), to the natural passions of men, when there is no visible power to keep them in awe, and tie them by fear of punishment to the performance of their covenants, and observation of those laws of nature set down in the fourteenth and fifteenth chapters.

For the laws of nature, as *justice, equity, modesty, mercy,* and, in sum, *doing to others, as we would be done to,* of themselves, without the terror of some power, to cause them to be observed, are contrary to our natural passions, that carry us to partiality, pride, revenge, and the like. And covenants, without the sword, are but words, and of no strength to secure a man at all. Therefore notwithstanding the laws of nature (which every one hath then kept, when he has the will to keep them, when he can do it safely) if there be no power erected, or not great enough for our security; every man will, and may lawfully rely on his own strength and art, for caution against all other men. And in all places, where men have lived by small families, to rob and spoil one another, has been a trade, and so far from being reputed against the law of nature, that the greater spoils they gained, the greater was their honour; and men observed no other laws therein, but the laws of honour; that is, to abstain from cruelty, leaving to men their lives, and instruments of husbandry. And as small families did then; so now do cities and kingdoms which are but greater families, for their own security, enlarge their dominions, upon all pretences of danger, and fear of invasion, or assistance that may be given to invaders, and endeavour as much as they can, to subdue, or weaken their neighbours, by open force, and secret arts, for want of other caution, justly; and are remembered for it in after ages with honour.

. . .

It is true, that certain living creatures, as bees, and ants, live sociably one with another, which are therefore by Aristotle numbered amongst political creatures; and yet have no other direction, than their particular judgments and appetites; nor speech, whereby one of them can signify to another, what he thinks expedient for the common benefit: and therefore some man may perhaps desire to know, why mankind cannot do the same. To which I answer,

First, that men are continually in competition for honour and dignity, which these creatures are not; and consequently amongst men there ariseth on that ground, envy and hatred, and finally war; but amongst these not so.

Secondly, that amongst these creatures, the common good differeth not from the private; and being by nature inclined to their private, they procure thereby the common benefit. But man, whose joy consisteth in comparing himself with other men, can relish nothing but what is eminent.

Thirdly, that these creatures, having not, as man, the use of reason, do not see, nor think they see any fault, in the administration of their common business; whereas amongst men, there are very many, that think themselves wiser, and abler to govern the public, better than the rest; and these strive to reform and innovate, one this way, another that way; and thereby bring it into distraction and civil war.

Fourthly, that these creatures, though they have some use of voice, in making known to one another their desires, and other affections; yet they want that art of words, by which some men can represent to others, that which is good, in the likeness of evil; and evil, in the likeness of good; and augment, or diminish the apparent greatness of good and evil; discontenting men, and troubling their peace at their pleasure.

Fifthly, irrational creatures cannot distinguish between *injury*, and *damage;* and therefore as long as they be at ease, they are not offended with their fellows: whereas man is then most troublesome, when he is most at ease: for then it is that he loves to shew his wisdom, and control the actions of them that govern the commonwealth.

Lastly, the agreement of these creatures is natural; that of men, is by covenant only, which is artificial: and therefore it is no wonder if there be somewhat else required, besides covenant, to make their agreement constant and lasting; which is a common power, to keep them in awe, and to direct their actions to the common benefit.

The only way to erect such a common power, as may be able to defend them from the invasion of foreigners, and the injuries of one another, and thereby to secure them in such sort, as that by their own industry, and by the fruits of the earth, they may nourish themselves and live contentedly; is, to confer all their power and strength upon one man, or upon one assembly of men, that may reduce all their wills, by plurality of voices, unto one will: which is as much as to say, to appoint one man, or assembly of men, to bear their person; and every one to own, and acknowledge himself to be author of whatsoever he that so beareth their person, shall act, or cause to be acted, in those things which concern the common peace and safety; and therein to submit their wills, every one to his will, and their judgments, to his judgment. This is more than consent, or concord; it is a real unity of them all, in one and the same person, made by covenant of every man with every man, in such manner, as if every man should say to every man, *I authorize and give up my right of governing myself, to this man, or to this assembly of men, on this condition, that thou give up thy right to him, and authorize all his actions in like manner.* This done, the multitude so united in one person, is called a COMMONWEALTH, in Latin CIVITAS. This is the generation of that great LEVIATHAN, or rather, to speak more reverently, of that *mortal god,* to which we owe under the *immortal God,* our peace and defence. For by this authority, given him by every particular man in the commonwealth, he hath the use of so much power and strength conferred on him, that by terror thereof, he is enabled to form the wills of them all, to peace at home, and mutual aid against their enemies abroad. And in him consisteth the essence of the commonwealth; which, to define it, is *one person, of whose acts a great multitude, by mutual covenants one with another, have made themselves every one the author, to the end he may use the strength and means of them all, as he shall think expedient, for their peace and common defence.*

And he that carrieth this person is called SOVEREIGN, and said to have *sovereign power;* and every one besides, his SUBJECT.

. . .

19
Why Act Morally?

PETER SINGER

Peter Singer (b. 1946) teaches philosophy at Monash University in Australia. He has written several books and many philosophical essays on social and political problems. His book, Animal Liberation, *was influential in bringing many people to reflect on the way we treat animals.*

In this selection from his book Practical Ethics, *Singer asks why anyone should adopt the moral point of view. Why give equal consideration to the interests of all those whom our actions will affect, rather than thinking only of ourselves? In answer, many have argued that equal consideration of interests is a requirement of reason. For variants of this view, see the selections by Kant, Hare, and Gewirth (readings 29, 22, and 23). But Singer contends that there is nothing irrational about egoism. Like Hume (reading 20), he maintains that reason provides no ends, but only the means to achieve what people want.*

Might being moral itself be a means to something we want? In particular, might it be a means to true happiness? Against this, Singer cites examples of psychopaths who profess to be happy despite their unconcern for others. But he also notes that psychopaths seem bored and aimless. He therefore speculates that a meaningful life may require purposes beyond one's momentary pleasures. More speculatively yet, it may require concern for others. If so, then the quest for meaning in life may itself lead us to the moral standpoint.

PREVIOUS CHAPTERS of this book have discussed what we ought, morally, to do about several practical issues and what means we are justified in adopting to achieve our ethical goals. The nature of our conclusions about these issues—the demands they make upon us—raises a further, more fundamental question: why should we act morally?

Take our conclusions about the use of animals for food, or the aid the rich should give the poor. Some readers may accept these conclusions, become vegetarians, and do what they can to reduce absolute poverty. Others may disagree with our conclusions, maintaining that there is nothing wrong with eating animals and that they are under no moral obligation to do anything about reducing absolute poverty. There is also, however, likely to be a third group, consisting of readers who find no fault with the ethical arguments of these chapters, yet do not change their diets or their contributions to overseas aid. Of this third group, some will just be weak-willed, but others may want an answer to a further practical question. If the conclusions of ethics require so much of us, they may ask, should we bother about ethics at all?

Understanding the Question

'Why should I act morally?' is a different type of question from those that we have been discussing up to now. Questions like 'Why should I treat blacks and whites equally?' or 'Why is abortion justifiable?' seek ethical reasons for acting in a certain way. These are questions within ethics. They presuppose the ethical point of view. 'Why should I act morally?' is on another level. It is not a question within ethics, but a question about ethics.

'Why should I act morally?' is therefore a question about something normally presupposed. Such questions are perplexing. Some philosophers have found this particular question so perplexing that they have rejected it as logically improper, as an attempt to ask something which cannot properly be asked.

One ground for this rejection is the claim that our ethical principles are, by definition, the principles we take as overridingly important. This means that whatever principles are overriding for a particular person are necessarily that person's ethical principles, and a person who accepts as an ethical principle that she ought to give her wealth to help the poor must, by definition, have actually decided to give away her wealth. On this definition of ethics once a person has made an ethical decision no further practical question can arise. Hence it is impossible to make sense of the question: 'Why should I act morally?'

It might be thought a good reason for accepting the definition of ethics as overriding that it allows us to dismiss as meaningless an otherwise troublesome question. Adopting this definition cannot solve real problems, however, for it leads to correspondingly greater difficulties in establishing any ethical conclusion. Take, for example, the conclusion that the rich ought to aid the poor. We were able to argue for this in Chapter 8 only because we assumed that, as suggested in the first two chapters of this book, the universalizability of ethical judgments requires us to go beyond thinking only about our own interests, and leads us to take a point of view from which we must give equal consideration to the interests of all affected by our actions. We cannot hold that ethical judgments must be universalizable and *at the same time* define a person's ethical principles as whatever principles that person takes as overridingly important—for what if I take as overridingly important some non-universalizable principle, like 'I ought to do whatever benefits me'? If we define ethical principles as whatever principles one takes as overriding, then anything whatever may count as an ethical principle, for one may take any principle whatever as overridingly important. Thus what we gain by being able to dismiss the question: 'Why should I act morally?' we lose by being unable to use the universalizability of ethical judgments—or any other feature of ethics—to argue for particular conclusions about what is morally right. Taking ethics as in some sense necessarily involving a universal point of view seems to me a more natural and less confusing way of discussing these issues.

Other philosophers have rejected 'Why should I act morally?' for a different reason. They think it must be rejected for the same reason that we must reject another question, 'Why should I be rational?' which, like 'Why should I act morally?' also questions something—in this case rationality—normally presupposed. 'Why should I be rational?' really is logically improper because in answering it we would be giving reasons for being rational. Thus we would presuppose rationality in our attempt to justify rationality. The resulting justification of rationality would be circular—which shows, not that rationality lacks a necessary justification, but that it needs no justification, because it cannot intelligibly be questioned unless it is already presupposed.

Is 'Why should I act morally?' like 'Why should I be rational?' in that it presupposes the very point of view it questions? It would be, if we interpreted the 'should' as a moral 'should'. Then the question would ask for moral reasons for being moral. This would be absurd. Once we have decided that an action is morally obligatory, there is no further *moral* question to ask. It is redundant to ask why I should, morally, do the action that I morally should do.

There is, however, no need to interpret the question as a request for an ethical justification of ethics. 'Should' need not mean 'should, morally'. It could simply be a way of asking for reasons for action, without any specification about the kind of reasons wanted. We sometimes want to ask a very general practical question, from no particular point of view. Faced with a difficult choice, we ask a close friend for advice. Morally he says, we ought to do A, but B would be more in our interests, while etiquette demands C and D would contribute most to art and culture. This answer may not satisfy us. We want advice on which of these standpoints to adopt. If it is possible to ask such a question we must ask it from a position of neutrality between all these points of view, not of commitment to any one of them.

'Why should I act morally?' is this sort of question. If it is not possible to ask practical questions without presupposing a point of view, we are unable to say anything intelligible about the most ultimate practical choices. Whether to act according to considerations of ethics, self-interest, etiquette, or aesthetics would be a choice 'beyond reason'—in a sense, an arbitrary choice. Before we resign ourselves to this conclusion we should at least attempt to interpret the question so that the mere asking of it does not commit us to any particular point of view.

We can now formulate the question more precisely. It is a question about the ethical point of view, asked from a position outside it. But what is 'the ethical point of view'? I have suggested that a distinguishing feature of ethics is that ethical judgments are universalizable. Ethics requires us to go beyond our own personal point of view to a standpoint like that of the impartial spectator who takes a universal point of view.

Given this conception of ethics, 'Why should I act morally?' is a question which may properly be asked by anyone wondering whether to act only on grounds that would be acceptable from this universal point of view. It is, after all, possible to act—and some people do act—without thinking of anything except one's own interests. The question asks for reasons for going beyond this personal basis of action and acting only on judgments one is prepared to prescribe universally.

Reason and Ethics

There is an ancient line of philosophical thought which attempts to demonstrate that to act rationally is to act ethically. The argument is today associated with Kant and is mainly found in the writings of modern Kantians, though it goes back at least as far as the Stoics. The form in which the argument is presented varies, but the common structure is as follows:

1. Some requirement of universalizability or impartiality is essential to ethics.
2. Reason is universally or objectively valid. If, for example, it follows from the premises 'All humans are mortal' and 'Socrates is human' that Socrates is mortal, then this inference must follow universally. It cannot be valid for me and invalid for you. This is a general point about reason, whether theoretical or practical.

Therefore:

3. Only a judgment which satisfies the requirement described in (1) as a necessary condition of an ethical judgment will be an objectively rational judgment in accordance with (2). For I cannot expect any other rational agents to accept as valid for them a judgment which I would not accept if I were in their place; and if two rational agents could not accept each other's judgments, they could not be rational judgments, for the reason given in (2). To say that I would accept the judgment I make, even if I were in someone else's position and they in mine is, however, simply to say that my judgment is one I can prescribe from a universal point of view. Ethics and reason both require us to rise above our own particular point of view and take a perspective from which our own personal identity—the role we happen to occupy—is unimportant. Thus reason requires us to act on universalizable judgments and, to that extent, to act ethically.

Is this argument valid? I have already indicated that I accept the first point, that ethics involves universalizability. The second point also seems undeniable. Reason must be universal. Does the conclusion therefore follow? Here is the flaw in the argument. The conclusion appears to follow directly from the premises; but this move involves a slide from the limited sense in which it is true that a rational judgment must be universally valid, to a stronger sense of 'universally valid' which is equivalent to universalizability.

The difference between these two senses can be seen by considering a non-universalizable imperative, like the purely egoistic: 'Let everyone do what is in *my* interests.' This differs from the imperative of universalizable egoism—

'Let everyone do what is in *her own* interests'—because it contains an inelim-
inable reference to a particular person. It therefore cannot be an ethical imperative. Does it also lack the universality required if it is to be a rational basis
for action? Surely not. Every rational agent could accept that the purely egoistic
activity of other rational agents is rationally justifiable. Pure egoism could be
rationally adopted by everyone.

Let us look at this more closely. It must be conceded that there is a sense in
which one purely egoistic rational agent—call him Jack—could not accept the
practical judgments of another purely egoistic rational agent—call her Jill.
Assuming Jill's interests differ from Jack's, Jill may be acting rationally in
urging Jack to do *A*, while Jack is also acting rationally in deciding against
doing *A*.

This disagreement is, however, compatible with all rational agents accepting
pure egoism. Though they accept pure egoism, it points them in different directions because they start from different places. When Jack adopts pure egoism,
it leads him to further his interests and when Jill adopts pure egoism it leads
her to further her interests. Hence the disagreement over what to do. On the
other hand—and this is the sense in which pure egoism could be accepted as
valid by all rational agents—if we were to ask Jill (off the record and promising
not to tell Jack) what she thinks it would be rational for Jack to do, she would,
if truthful, have to reply that it would be rational for Jack to do what is in his
own interests, rather than what is in her interests.

So when purely egoistic rational agents oppose each other's acts, it does not
indicate disagreement over the rationality of pure egoism. Pure egoism, though
not a universalizable principle, could be accepted as a rational basis of action
by all rational agents. This sense in which rational judgments must be universally acceptable is weaker than the sense in which ethical judgments must be.
That an action will benefit *me* rather than anyone else could be a valid reason
for doing it, though it could not be an ethical reason for doing it.

A consequence of this conclusion is that rational agents may rationally try
to prevent each other doing what they admit the other is rationally justified in
doing. There is, unfortunately, nothing paradoxical about this. Two businessmen competing for an important sale will accept each other's conduct as rational,
though each aims to thwart the other. The same holds of two soldiers meeting
in battle, or two footballers vying for the ball.

Accordingly this attempted demonstration of a link between reason and
ethics fails. There may be other ways of forging this link, but it is difficult to
see any that hold greater promise of success. The chief obstacle to be overcome
is the nature of practical reason. Long ago David Hume argued that reason in
action applies only to means, not to ends. The ends must be given by our wants
and desires. Hume unflinchingly drew out the implications of this view:

> 'Tis not contrary to reason to prefer the destruction of the whole world to the
> scratching of my finger. 'This not contrary to reason for me to choose my total
> ruin, to prevent the least uneasiness of an Indian or person wholly unknown to

me.' Tis as little contrary to reason to prefer even my own acknowledged lesser good to my greater, and have a more ardent affection for the former than the latter.[1]

Extreme as it is, Hume's view of practical reason has stood up to criticism remarkably well. His central claim —that in practical reasoning we start from something wanted—is difficult to refute; yet it must be refuted if any argument is to succeed in showing that it is rational for all of us to act ethically irrespective of what we want.

Nor is the refutation of Hume all that is needed for a demonstration of the rational necessity of acting ethically. In *The Possibility of Altruism*, Thomas Nagel has argued forcefully that not to take one's own future desires into account in one's practical deliberations—irrespective of whether one *now* happens to desire the satisfaction of those future desires—would indicate a failure to see oneself as a person existing over time, the present being merely one time among others in one's life. So it is my conception of myself as a person that makes it rational for me to consider my long-term interests. This holds true even if I have 'a more ardent affection' for something that I acknowledge is not really, all things considered, in my own interest.

Whether Nagel's argument succeeds in vindicating the rationality of prudence is one question: whether a similar argument can also be used in favour of a form of altruism based on taking the desires of *others* into account is another question altogether. Nagel attempts this analogous argument. The role occupied by 'seeing the present as merely one time among others' is, in the argument for altruism, taken by 'seeing oneself as merely one person among others'. But whereas it would be extremely difficult for most of us to cease conceiving of ourselves existing over time, with the present merely one time among others that we will live through, the way we see ourselves as a person among others is quite different. Henry Sidgwick's observation on this point seems to me exactly right:

> It would be contrary to Common Sense to deny that the distinction between any one individual and any other is real and fundamental, and that consequently 'I' am concerned with the quality of my existence as an individual in a sense, fundamentally important, in which I am not concerned with the quality of the existence of other individuals: and this being so, I do not see how it can be proved that this distinction is not to be taken as fundamental in determining the ultimate end of rational action for an individual.[2]

So it is not only Hume's view of practical reason that stands in the way of attempts to show that to act rationally is to act ethically; we might succeed in

---

[1] David Hume, *Treatise of Human Nature*, Bk. II, Pt. iii, sec. 3.

[2] Henry Sidgwick, *The Methods of Ethics* (7th ed. London, 1907), p.498.

overthrowing that barrier, only to find our way blocked by the commonsense distinction between self and others. Taken together, these are formidable obstacles and I know of no way of overcoming them.

Ethics and Self-Interest

If practical reasoning begins with something wanted, to show that it is rational to act morally would involve showing that in acting morally we achieve something we want. If, agreeing with Sidgwick rather than Hume, we hold that it is rational to act in our long-term interests irrespective of what we happen to want at the present moment, we could show that it is rational to act morally by showing that it is in our long-term interests to do so. There have been many attempts to argue along one or other of these lines, ever since Plato, in *The Republic,* portrayed Socrates as arguing that to be virtuous is to have the different elements of one's personality ordered in a harmonious manner, and this is necessary for happiness. We shall look at these arguments shortly; but first it is necessary to assess an objection to this whole approach to 'Why should I act morally?'

People often say that to defend morality by appealing to self-interest is to misunderstand what ethics is all about. F. H. Bradley stated this eloquently:

> What answer can we give when the question Why should I be Moral?, in the sense of What will it advantage Me?, is put to us? Here we shall do well, I think, to avoid all praises of the pleasantness of virtue. We may believe that it transcends all possible delights of vice, but it would be well to remember that we desert a moral point of view, that we degrade and prostitute virtue, when to those who do not love her for herself we bring ourselves to recommend her for the sake of her pleasures.[3]

In other words, we can never get people to act morally by providing reasons of self-interest, because if they accept what we say and act on the reasons given, they will only be acting self-interestedly, not morally.

One reply to this objection would be that the substance of the action, what is actually done, is more important than the motive. People might give money to famine relief because their friends will think better of them, or they might give the same amount because they think it their duty. Those saved from starvation by the gift will benefit to the same extent either way.

This is true but crude. It can be made more sophisticated if it is combined with an appropriate account of the nature and function of ethics. Ethics, though not consciously created, is a product of social life which has the function of promoting values common to the members of the society. Ethical judgments do this by praising and encouraging actions in accordance with these values. Ethical judgments are concerned with motives because this is a good indication of the tendency of an action to promote good or evil, but also because it is here

---

[3] F. H. Bradley, *Ethical Studies* (Oxford, 1876, reprinted 1962), p. 63.

that praise and blame may be effective in altering the tendency of a person's actions. Conscientiousness (that is, acting for the sake of doing what is right) is a particularly useful motive, from the community's point of view. People who are conscientious will, if they accept the values of their society (and if most people did not accept these values they would not be the values of the society) always tend to promote what the society values. They may have no generous or sympathetic inclinations, but if they think it their duty to give famine relief, they will do so. Moreover, those motivated by the desire to do what is right can be relied upon to act as they think right in all circumstances, whereas those who act from some other motive, like self-interest, will only do what they think right when the believe it will also be in their interest. Conscientiousness is thus a kind of multi-purpose gap-filler that can be used to motivate people towards whatever is valued, even if the natural virtues normally associated with action in accordance with those values (generosity, sympathy, honesty, tolerance, humility, etc.) are lacking. (This needs some qualification: a conscientious mother may provide as well for her children as a mother who loves them, but she cannot love them because it is the right thing to do. Sometimes conscientiousness is a poor substitute for the real thing.)

On this view of ethics it is still results, not motives, that really matter. Conscientiousness is of value because of its consequences. Yet, unlike, say, benevolence, conscientiousness can be praised and encouraged only for its own sake. To praise a conscientious act for its consequences would be to praise not conscientiousness, but something else altogether. If we appeal to sympathy or self-interest as a reason for doing one's duty, then we are not encouraging people to do their duty for its own sake. If conscientiousness is to be encouraged, it must be thought of as good for its own sake.

It is different in the case of an act done from a motive that people act upon irrespective of praise and encouragement. The use of ethical language is then inappropriate. We do not normally say that people ought to do, or that it is their duty to do, whatever gives them the greatest pleasure, for most people are sufficiently motivated to do this anyway. So, whereas we praise good acts done for the sake of doing what is right, we withhold our praise when we believe the act was done from some motive like self-interest.

This emphasis on motives and on the moral worth of doing right for its own sake is now embedded in our notion of ethics. To the extent that it is so embedded, we will feel that to provide considerations of self-interest for doing what is right is to empty the action of its moral worth.

My suggestion is that our notion of ethics has become misleading to the extent that moral worth is attributed only to action done because it is right, without any ulterior motive. It is understandable, and from the point of view of society desirable, that this attitude should prevail; nevertheless, those who accept this view of ethics, and are led by it to do what is right because it is right, without asking for any further reason, are falling victim to a kind of confidence trick — though not, of course, a consciously perpetrated one.

That this view of ethics is unjustifiable has already been indicated by the failure of the argument discussed earlier in this chapter for a rational justification of ethics. In the history of Western philosophy, no one has urged more strongly than Kant that our ordinary moral consciousness finds moral worth only when duty is done for duty's sake. Yet Kant himself saw that without a rational justification this common conception of ethics would be 'a mere phantom of the brain'. And this is indeed the case. If we reject—as in general terms we have done—the Kantian justification of the rationality of ethics, but try to retain the Kantian conception of ethics, ethics is left hanging without support. It becomes a closed system, a system that cannot be questioned because its first premise—that only action done because it is right has any moral worth—rules out any possible justification for accepting this very premise. Morality is, on this view, no more rational an end than any other allegedly self-justifying practice, like etiquette or the kind of religious faith that comes only to those who first set aside all skeptical doubts.

Taken as a view of ethics as a whole, we should abandon this Kantian notion of ethics. This does not mean, however, that we should never do what we see to be right simply because we see it to be right without further reasons. Here we need to appeal to the distinction Hare has made between intuitive and critical thinking. When we stand back from our day-to-day ethical decisions and ask why we should act morally, we should not allow ourselves to be put off seeking reasons, even self-interested ones. If our search is successful, however, it may provide us with reasons for taking up the ethical point of view as a settled policy, a way of living. We would not then ask, in our day-to-day ethical decision making, whether each particular right action was in our interest. In all but the most extraordinary situations, we would assume that it was, and once we had decided what was right we would go ahead and do it, without thinking about further reasons for doing what is right. To deliberate over the ultimate reasons for doing what is right in each case would impossibly complicate our lives; it would also be inadvisable because in particular situations we might be too greatly influenced by strong but temporary desires and inclinations, and so make decisions we would later regret.

So a justification of ethics in terms of self-interest would not defeat its own aim, and we can now ask if such a justification exists. There is a daunting list of those who, following Plato's lead, have offered one: Aristotle, Aquinas, Spinoza, Butler, Hegel, even—for all his strictures against prostituting virtue—Bradley. Like Plato, these philosophers made broad claims about human nature and the conditions under which human beings can be happy. Some were also able to fall back on a belief that virtue will be rewarded and wickedness punished in a life after our bodily death. Philosophers cannot use this argument if they want to carry conviction nowadays; nor can they adopt sweeping psychological theories on the basis of their own general experience of their fellows, as philosophers used to do when psychology was a branch of philosophy.

It might be said that since philosophers are not empirical scientists, discussion of the connection between acting ethically and living a fulfilled and happy life should be left to psychologists, sociologists and other appropriate experts. The question is not, however, dealt with by any other single discipline and its relevance to practical ethics is reason enough for our looking into it.

266

What facts about human nature could show that ethics and self-interest coincide? One theory is that we all have benevolent or sympathetic inclinations which make us concerned about the welfare of others. Another relies on a natural conscience which gives rise to guilt feelings when we do what we know to be wrong. But how strong are these benevolent desires or feelings of guilt? Is it possible to suppress them? If so, isn't it possible that in a world in which humans and other animals are suffering in great numbers, suppressing one's conscience and sympathy for others is the surest way to happiness?

To meet this objection those who would link ethics and happiness must assert that we cannot be happy if these elements of our nature are suppressed. Benevolence and sympathy, they might argue, are tied up with the capacity to take part in friendly or loving relations with others, and there can be no real happiness without such relationships. For the same reason it is necessary to take at least some ethical standards seriously, and to be open and honest in living by them—for a life of deception and dishonesty is a furtive life, in which the possibility of discovery always clouds the horizon. Genuine acceptance of ethical standards is likely to mean that we feel some guilt—or at least that we are less pleased with ourselves than we otherwise would be—when we do not live up to them.

These claims about the connection between our character and our prospects of happiness are no more than hypotheses. Attempts to confirm them by detailed research are sparse and inadequate. A. H. Maslow, an American psychologist, asserts that human beings have a need for self-actualization, which involves growing towards courage, kindness, knowledge, love, honesty, and unselfishness. When we fulfil this need we feel serene, joyful, filled with zest, sometimes euphoric, and generally happy. When we act contrary to our need for self-actualization we experience anxiety, despair, boredom, shame, emptiness and are generally unable to enjoy ourselves. It would be nice if Maslow should turn out to be right; unfortunately the data Maslow produces in support of his theory consists of very limited studies of selected people. The theory must await confirmation or falsification from larger, more rigorous and more representative studies.

Human nature is so diverse that one may doubt if any generalization about the kind of character that leads to happiness could hold for all human beings. What, for instance, of those we call 'psychopaths'? Psychiatrists use this term as a label for a person who is asocial, impulsive, egocentric, unemotional, lacking in feelings of remorse, shame or guilt, and apparently unable to form deep and enduring personal relationships. Psychopaths are certainly abnormal, but whether it is proper to say that they are mentally ill is another matter. At least on the surface, they do not *suffer* from their condition, and it is not obvious that it is in their interest to be 'cured'. Hervey Cleckley, the author of a classic study of psychopathy entitled *The Mask of Sanity,* notes that since his book was first published he has received countless letters from people desperate for help—but they are from the parents, spouses and other relatives of psychopaths, almost never from the psychopaths themselves. This is not surprising, for while psychopaths are asocial and indifferent to the welfare of others, they seem to enjoy life. Psychopaths often appear to be charming, intelligent people, with no delusions or other signs of irrational thinking. When interviewed they say things like:

> A lot has happened to me, a lot more will happen. But I enjoy living and I am always looking forward to each day. I like laughing and I've done a lot. I am essentially a clown at heart—but a happy one. I always take the bad with the good.

There is no effective therapy for psychopathy, which may be explained by the fact that psychopaths see nothing wrong with their behaviour and often find it extremely rewarding, at least in the short term. Of course their impulsive nature and lack of sense of shame or guilt means that some psychopaths end up in prison, though it is hard to tell how many do not, since those who avoid prison are also more likely to avoid contact with psychiatrists. Studies have shown that a surprisingly large number of psychopaths are able to avoid prison despite grossly antisocial behaviour, probably because of their well-known ability to convince others that they are truly repentant, that it will never happen again, that they deserve another chance, etc., etc.

The existence of psychopathic people counts against the contention that benevolence, sympathy and feelings of guilt are present in everyone. It also appears to count against attempts to link happiness with the possession of these inclinations. But let us pause before we accept this latter conclusion. Must we accept psychopaths' own evaluations of their happiness? They are, after all, notoriously persuasive liars. Moreover even if they are telling the truth as they see it, are they qualified to say that they are really happy, when they seem unable to experience the emotional states that play such a large part in the happiness and fulfilment of more normal people? Admittedly, a psychopath could use the same argument against us: how can we say that we are truly happy when we have not experienced the excitement and freedom that comes from complete irresponsibility? Since we cannot enter into the subjective states of psychopathic people, nor they into ours, the dispute is not easy to resolve.

Cleckley suggests that the psychopaths' behaviour can be explained as a response to the meaninglessness of their lives. It is characteristic of psychopaths to work for a while at a job and then just when their ability and charm have taken them to the crest of success, commit some petty and easily detectable crime. A similar pattern occurs in their personal relationships. (There is support to be found here for Thomas Nagel's account of imprudence as rational only if one fails to see oneself as a person existing over time, with the present merely one among other times one will live through. Certainly psychopathic people live largely in the present and lack any coherent life plan.)

Cleckley explains this erratic and to us inadequately motivated behaviour by likening the psychopath's life to that of children forced to sit through a performance of *King Lear*. Children are restless and misbehave under these conditions because they cannot enjoy the play as adults do. They act to relieve boredom. Similarly, Cleckley says, psychopaths are bored because their emotional poverty means that they cannot take interest in, or gain satisfaction from, what for others are the most important things in life: love, family, success in business or professional life, etc. These things simply do not matter to them. Their unpredictable and anti-social behaviour is an attempt to relieve what would otherwise be a tedious existence.

These claims are speculative and Cleckley admits that they may not be possible to establish scientifically. They do suggest, however, an aspect of the psychopath's life that undermines the otherwise attractive nature of the psychopath's free-wheeling life. Most reflective people, at some time or other, want their life to have some kind of meaning. Few of us could deliberately choose a way of life which we regarded as utterly meaningless. For this reason most of us would not choose to live a psychopathic life, however enjoyable it might be.

Yet there is something paradoxical about criticizing the psychopath's life for its meaninglessness. Don't we have to accept, in the absence of religious belief, that life really is meaningless, not just for the psychopath but for all of us? And if this is so, why should we not choose—if it were in our power to choose our personality—the life of a psychopath? But is it true that, religion aside, life is meaningless? Now our pursuit of reasons for acting morally has led us to what is often regarded as the ultimate philosophical question.

Has Life a Meaning?

In what sense does rejection of belief in a god imply rejection of the view that life has any meaning? If this world had been created by some divine being with a particular goal in mind, it could be said to have a meaning, at least for that divine being. If we could know what the divine being's purpose in creating us was, we could then know what the meaning of our life was for our creator. If we accepted our creator's purpose (though why we should do that would need to be explained) we could claim to know the meaning of life.

When we reject belief in a god we must give up the idea that life on this planet has some preordained meaning. Life as a whole has no meaning. Life began, as the best available theories tell us, in a chance combination of gases; it then evolved through random mutations and natural selection. All this just happened; it did not happen for any overall purpose. Now that it has resulted in the existence of beings who prefer some states of affairs to others, however, it may be possible for particular lives to be meaningful. In this sense atheists can find meaning in life.

Let us return to the comparison between the life of a psychopath and that of a more normal person. Why should the psychopath's life not be meaningful? We have seen that psychopaths are egocentric to an extreme: neither other people, nor worldly success, nor anything else really matters to them. But why is their own enjoyment of life not sufficient to give meaning to their lives?

Most of us would not be able to find happiness by deliberately setting out to enjoy ourselves without caring about anyone or anything else. The pleasures we obtained in that way would seem empty, and soon pall. We seek a meaning for our lives beyond our own pleasures, and find fulfilment and happiness in doing what we see to be meaningful. If our life has no meaning other than our own happiness, we are likely to find that when we have obtained what we think we need to be happy, happiness itself still eludes us.

That those who aim at happiness for happiness's sake often fail to find it, while others find happiness in pursuing altogether different goals, has been called 'the paradox of hedonism'. It is not, of course, a logical paradox but a claim about the way in which we come to be happy. Like other generalizations on this subject it lacks empirical confirmation. Yet it matches our everyday observations, and is consistent with our nature as evolved, purposive beings. Human beings survive and reproduce themselves through purposive action. We obtain happiness and fulfilment by working towards and achieving our goals. In evolutionary terms we could say that happiness functions as an internal reward for our achievements. Subjectively, we regard achieving the goal (or progressing towards it) as a reason for happiness. Our own happiness, therefore, is a by-product of aiming at something else, and not to be obtained by setting our sights on happiness alone.

The psychopath's life can now be seen to be meaningless in a way that a normal life is not. It is meaningless because it looks inward to the pleasures of the present moment and not outward to anything more long-term or far-reaching. More normal lives have meaning because they are lived to some larger purpose.

All this is speculative. You may accept or reject it to the extent that it agrees with your own observation and introspection. My next—and final—suggestion is more speculative still. It is that to find an enduring meaning in our lives it is not enough to go beyond psychopaths who have no long-term commitments or life plans; we must also go beyond more prudent egoists who have long-term plans concerned only with their own interests. The prudent egoists may find meaning in their lives for a time, for they have the purpose of furthering their own interests; but what, in the end, does that amount to? When everything in our interests has been achieved, do we just sit back and be happy? Could we be happy in this way? Or would we decide that we had still not quite reached our target, that there was something else we needed before we could sit back and enjoy it all? Most materially successful egoists take the latter route, thus escaping the necessity of admitting that they cannot find happiness in permanent holidaying. People who slaved to establish small businesses, telling themselves they would do it only until they had made enough to live comfortably, keep working long after they have passed their original target. Their material 'needs' expand just fast enough to keep ahead of their income. Retirement is a problem for many because they cannot enjoy themselves without a purpose in life. The recommended solution is, of course, to find a new purpose, whether it be stamp collecting or voluntary work for a charity.

Now we begin to see where ethics comes into the problem of living a meaningful life. If we are looking for a purpose broader than our own interests, something which will allow us to see our lives as possessing significance beyond the narrow confines of our own conscious states, one obvious solution is to take up the ethical point of view. The ethical point of view does, as we have seen, require us to go beyond a personal point of view to the standpoint of an impartial spectator. Thus looking at things ethically is a way of transcending our inward-looking concerns and identifying ourselves with the most objective point of view possible—with, as Sidgwick put it, 'the point of view of the universe'.

The point of view of the universe is a lofty standpoint. In the rarefied air that surrounds it we may get carried away into talking, as Kant does, of the moral point of view 'inevitably' humbling all who compare their own limited nature with it. I do not want to suggest anything as sweeping as this. Earlier in this chapter, in rejecting Thomas Nagel's argument for the rationality of altruism, I said that there is nothing irrational about being concerned with the quality of one's own existence in a way that one is not concerned with the quality of existence of other individuals. Without going back on this, I am now suggesting that rationality, in the broad sense which includes self-awareness and reflection on the nature and point of our own existence, may push us towards concerns broader than the quality of our own existence; but the process is not a necessary one and those who do not take part in it—or, in taking part, do not follow it all the way to the ethical point of view—are not irrational or in error. Psychopaths, for all I know, may simply be unable to obtain as much happiness through caring about others as they obtain by antisocial acts. Other people find collecting stamps an entirely adequate way of giving purpose to their lives. There is nothing irrational about that; but others again grow out of stamp collecting as they become more aware of their situation in the world and more reflective about their purposes. To this third group the ethical point of view offers a meaning and purpose in life that one does not grow out of.

(At least, one cannot grow out of the ethical point of view until all ethical tasks have been accomplished. If that utopia were ever achieved, our purposive nature might well leave us dissatisfied, much as the egoist is dissatisfied when he has everything he needs to be happy. There is nothing paradoxical about this, for we should not expect evolution to have equipped us, in advance, with the ability to enjoy a situation that has never previously occurred. Nor is this going to be a practical problem in the near future.)

'Why act morally?' cannot be given an answer that will provide everyone with overwhelming reasons for acting morally. Ethically indefensible behaviour is not always irrational. We will probably always need the sanctions of the law and social pressure to provide additional reasons against serious violations of ethical standards. On the other hand, those reflective enough to ask the question we have been discussing in this chapter are also those most likely to appreciate the reasons that can be offered for taking the ethical point of view.

20

Morality and Natural Sentiment

DAVID HUME

David Hume (1711–76), made enduring contributions to ethics, social philosophy, the theory of knowledge, and the philosophy of religion. His masterpiece, A Treatise of Human Nature, *was published when he was twenty-eight.*

Hume's theory of ethics is elaborate and subtle. This selection, excerpted from the Treatise, *presents some of its main elements. To begin, Hume examines the view that morality is grounded in reason. Since morality sometimes moves us to act, this view implies that reason can motivate actions. But Hume argues that reason supplies no motives. At best, it tells us how to achieve what we independently desire. Since reason "is, and ought only to be, the slave of the passions," it is not the source of moral judgments.*

What, then, is? According to Hume, the crucial role is played by the passions themselves. When we judge a character to be virtuous or vicious, or an act to be good or bad, we are projecting our own feelings upon it. These feelings are not merely reactions to the fact that we are benefited or harmed. Rather, they reflect pleasures and pains we feel through sympathetic identification with other affected parties. In stressing the connection between moral judgments and the judge's own feelings, Hume anticipates Ayer's emotive theory (reading 12). In stressing the role of sympathetic identification with others, he anticipates theories like Hare's (reading 22).

Although Hume's general theory applies to all moral judgments, he makes an important distinction between natural and artificial virtues. Such traits as beneficence and generosity are always beneficial, and thus are natural virtues. But other virtues, such as justice, are different. If goods were plentiful or not easily transferred, or if people were less covetous than they are, there would be no need for justice. But given the world as it is, rules of ownership are in everyone's interest. For this reason, we develop conventions that each person observes in expectation that others will do likewise. Since justice is the observation of such conventions, it is an artificial virtue.

Of the Influencing Motives of the Will

NOTHING IS MORE usual in philosophy, and even in common life, than to talk of the combat of passion and reason, to give the preference to reason, and assert that men are only so far virtuous as they conform themselves to its dictates. Every rational creature, it is said, is obliged to regulate his actions by reason; and if any other motive or principle challenge the direction of his conduct, he ought to oppose it till it be entirely subdued or at least brought to a conformity with that superior principle. On this method of thinking the greatest part of moral philosophy, ancient and modern, seems to be founded; nor is there an ampler field as well for metaphysical arguments as popular declamations than this supposed pre-eminence of reason above passion. The eternity, invariableness, and divine origin of the former have been displayed to the best advantage; the blindness, inconstancy, and deceitfulness of the latter have been as strongly insisted on. In order to show the fallacy of all this philosophy, I shall endeavour to prove, *first*, that reason alone can never be a motive to any action of the will; and, *secondly*, that it can never oppose passion in the direction of the will.

The understanding exerts itself after two different ways, as it judges from demonstration or probability; as it regards the abstract relations of our ideas, or those relations of objects of which experience only gives us information. I believe it scarce will be asserted that the first species of reasoning alone is ever the cause of any action. As its proper province is the world of ideas, and as the will always places us in that of realities, demonstration and volition seem upon that account to be totally removed from each other. Mathematics, indeed, are useful in all mechanical operations, and arithmetic in almost every art and profession: but it is not of themselves they have any influence. Mechanics are the art of regulating the motions of bodies *to some designed end* or *purpose*; and the reason why we employ arithmetic in fixing the proportions of numbers is only that we may discover the proportions of their influence and operation. A merchant is desirous of knowing the sum total of his accounts with any person: why? but that he may learn what sum will have the same *effects* in paying his debt, and going to market, as all the particular articles taken together. Abstract or demonstrative reasoning, therefore, never influences any of our actions, but only as it directs our judgment concerning causes and effects; which leads us to the second operation of the understanding.

It is obvious that when we have the prospect of pain or pleasure from any object, we feel a consequent emotion of aversion or propensity, and are carried to avoid or embrace what will give us this uneasiness or satisfaction. It is also obvious that this emotion rests not here, but, making us cast our view on every side, comprehends whatever objects are connected with its original one by the relation of cause and effect. Here then reasoning takes place to discover this relation; and according as our reasoning varies, our actions receive a subsequent variation. But it is evident in this case that the impulse arises not from reason, but is only directed by it. It is from the prospect of pain or pleasure that the aversion or propensity arises towards any object: and these emotions extend themselves to the causes and effects of that object, as they are pointed out to us by reason and experience. It can never in the least concern us to know that such objects are causes, and such others effects, if both the causes and effects be indifferent to us. Where the objects themselves do not affect us, their connection can never give them any influence; and it is plain that, as reason is nothing but the discovery of this connection, it cannot be by its means that the objects are able to affect us.

Since reason alone can never produce any action or give rise to volition, I infer that the same faculty is as incapable of preventing volition or of disputing the preference with any passion or emotion. This consequence is necessary. It is impossible reason could have the latter effect of preventing volition, but by giving an impulse in a contrary direction to our passions; and that impulse, had it operated alone, would have been ample to produce volition. Nothing can oppose or retard the impulse of passion but a contrary impulse; and if this contrary impulse ever arises from reason, that latter faculty must have an original influence on the will and must be able to cause as well as hinder any act of volition. But if reason has no original influence, it is impossible it can withstand any principle which has such an efficacy, or ever keep the mind in suspense a moment. Thus it appears that the principle which opposes our passion cannot be the same with reason, and is only called so in an improper sense. We speak not strictly and philosophically when we talk of the combat of passion and of reason. Reason is, and ought only to be, the slave of the passions, and can never pretend to any other office than to serve and obey them. As this opinion may appear somewhat extraordinary, it may not be improper to confirm it by some other considerations.

A passion is an original existence or, if you will, modification of existence, and contains not any representative quality which renders it a copy of any other existence or modification. When I am angry, I am actually possessed with the passion, and in that emotion have no more a reference to any other object than when I am thirsty, or sick, or more that five feet high. It is impossible, therefore, that this passion can be opposed by, or be contradictory to, truth and reason; since this contradiction consists in the disagreement of ideas, considered as copies, with those objects which they represent.

What may at first occur on this head is that as nothing can be contrary to truth or reason, except what has a reference to it, and as the judgments of our understanding only have this reference, it must follow that passions can be contrary to reason only so far as they are *accompanied* with some judgment or opinion. According to this principle, which is so obvious and natural, it is only in two senses that any affection can be called unreasonable. First, when a passion, such as hope or fear, grief or joy, despair or security, is founded on the supposition of the existence of objects which really do not exist. Secondly, when, in exerting any passion in action, we choose means sufficient for the designed end, and deceive ourselves in our judgment of causes and effects. Where a passion is neither founded on false suppositions, nor chooses means insufficient for the end, the understanding can neither justify nor condemn it. It is not contrary to reason to prefer the destruction of the whole world to the scratching of my finger. It is not contrary to reason for me to choose my total ruin to prevent the least uneasiness of an Indian, or person wholly unknown to me. It is as little contrary to reason to prefer even my own acknowledged lesser good to my greater, and have a more ardent affection for the former than the latter. A trivial good may, from certain circumstances, produce a desire superior to what arises from the greatest and most valuable enjoyment; nor is there anything more extraordinary in this than in mechanics to see one pound weight raise up a hundred by the advantage of its situation. In short, a passion must be accompanied with some false judgment in order to its being unreasonable; and even then it is not the passion, properly speaking, which is unreasonable, but the judgment.

. . .

Moral Distinctions Not Derived from Reason

. . .

Those who affirm that virtue is nothing but a conformity to reason; that there are eternal fitnesses and unfitnesses of things which are the same to every rational being that considers them; that the immutable measure of right and wrong impose an obligation, not only on human creatures, but also on the Deity himself: all these systems concur in the opinion that morality, like truth, is discerned merely by ideas, and by their juxtaposition and comparison. In order, therefore, to judge of these systems, we need only consider whether it be possible from reason alone to distinguish betwixt moral good and evil, or whether there must concur some other principles to enable us to make that distinction.

If morality had naturally no influence on human passions and actions, it were in vain to take such pains to inculcate it; and nothing would be more fruitless than that multitude of rules and precepts with which all moralists abound. Philosophy is commonly divided into *speculative* and *practical;* and as morality is always comprehended under the latter division, it is supposed to influence our passions and actions, and to go beyond the calm and indolent judgments of the understanding. And this is confirmed by common experience, which informs us that men are often governed by their duties, and are deterred from some actions by the opinion of injustice, and impelled to others by that of obligation.

Since morals, therefore, have an influence on the actions and affections, it follows that they cannot be derived from reason, and that because reason alone, as we have already proved, can never have any such influence. Morals excite passions, and produce or prevent actions. Reason of itself is utterly impotent in this particular. The rules of morality, therefore, are not conclusions of our reason.

No one, I believe, will deny the justness of this inference; nor is there any other means of evading it than by denying that principle on which it is founded. As long as it is allowed that reason has no influence on our passions and actions, it is in vain to pretend that morality is discovered only by a deduction of reason. An active principle can never be founded on an inactive; and if reason be inactive in itself, it must remain so in all its shapes and appearances, whether it exerts itself in natural or moral subjects, whether it considers the powers of external bodies or the actions of rational beings.

It would be tedious to repeat all the arguments by which I have proved that reason is perfectly inert and can never either prevent or produce any action or affection. It will be easy to recollect what has been said upon that subject. I shall only recall on this occasion one of these arguments, which I shall endeavour to render still more conclusive and more applicable to the present subject.

Reason is the discovery of truth or falsehood. Truth or falsehood consists in an agreement or disagreement either to the *real* relations of ideas, or to *real* existence and matter of fact. Whatever, therefore, is not susceptible of this agreement or disagreement is incapable of being true or false, and can never be an object of our reason. Now, it is evident our passions, volitions, and actions, are not susceptible of any such agreement or disagreement; being original facts and realities, complete in themselves, and implying no reference to other passions, volitions, and actions. It is impossible, therefore, they can be pronounced either true or false, and be either contrary or conformable to reason.

This argument is of double advantage to our present purpose. For it proves *directly* that actions do not derive their merit from a conformity to reason, nor their blame from a contrariety to it; and it proves the same truth more *indirectly,* by showing us that as reason can never immediately prevent or produce any action by contradicting or approving of it, it cannot be the source of moral good and evil, which are found to have that influence. Actions may be laudable or blamable, but they cannot be reasonable or unreasonable: laudable or blamable, therefore, are not the same with reasonable or unreasonable. The merit and demerit of actions frequently contradict, and sometimes control our natural propensities. But reason has no such influence. Moral distinctions, therefore, are not the offspring of reason. Reason is wholly inactive, and can never be the source of so active a principle as conscience, or a sense of morals.

. . .

But, to be more particular, and to show that those eternal immutable fitnesses and unfitnesses of things cannot be defended by sound philosophy, we may weigh the following considerations.

If the thought and understanding were alone capable of fixing the boundaries of right and wrong, the character of virtuous and vicious either must lie in some relations of objects, or must be a matter of fact which is discovered by our reasoning. This consequence is evident. As the operations of human understanding divide themselves into two kinds—the comparing of ideas and the inferring of matter of fact—were virtue discovered by the understanding, it must be an object of one of these operations; nor is there any third operation of the understanding which can discover it. There has been an opinion very industriously propagated by certain philosophers that morality is susceptible of demonstration; and though no one has ever been able to advance a single step in those demonstrations, yet it is taken for granted that this science may be brought to an equal certainty with geometry or algebra. Upon this supposition vice and virtue must consist in some relations, since it is allowed on all hands that no matter of fact is capable of being demonstrated. Let us therefore begin with examining this hypothesis and endeavour, if possible, to fix those moral qualities which have been so long the objects of our fruitless researches, point out distinctly the relations which constitute morality or obligation, that we may know wherein they consist, and after what manner we must judge of them.

If you assert that vice and virtue consist in relations susceptible of certainty and demonstration, you must confine yourself to those *four* relations which alone admit of that degree of evidence; and in that case you run into absurdities from which you will never be able to extricate yourself. For as you make the very essence of morality to lie in the relations and as there is no one of these relations but what is applicable not only to an irrational but also to an inanimate object, it follows that even such objects must be susceptible of merit or demerit. *Resemblance, contrariety, degrees in quality,* and *proportions in quantity and number;* all these relations belong as properly to matter as to our actions, passions, and volitions. It is unquestionable, therefore, that morality lies not in any of these relations, nor in the sense of it in their discovery.[1]

Should it be asserted that the sense of morality consists in the discovery of some relation distinct from these, and that our enumeration was not complete when we comprehended all demonstrable relations under four general heads; to this I know not what to reply, till some one be so good as to point out to me this new relation. It is impossible to refute a system which has never yet been explained. In such a manner of fighting in the dark, a man loses his blows in the air and often places them where the enemy is not present.

. . .

Nor does this reasoning only prove that morality consists not in any relations that are the objects of science; but, if examined, will prove with equal certainty that it consists not in any *matter of fact* which can be discovered by the understanding. This is the *second* part of our argument; and if it can be made evident, we may conclude that morality is not an object of reason. But can there be any difficulty in proving that vice and virtue are not matters of fact whose existence we can infer by reason? Take any action allowed to be vicious—wilful murder, for instance. Examine it in all lights, and see if you can find that matter of fact or real existence which you call *vice*. In whichever way you take it, you find only certain passions, motives, volitions, and thoughts. There is no other matter of fact in the case. The vice entirely escapes you, as long as you consider the object. You never can find it till you turn your reflection into your own

---

[1] As a proof how confused our way of thinking on this subject commonly is, we may observe that those who assert that morality is demonstrable do not say that morality lies in the relations, and that the relations are distinguishable by reason. They only say that reason can discover such an action in such relations to be virtuous, and such another vicious. It seems they thought it sufficient if they could bring the word "relation" into the proposition, without troubling themselves whether it was to the purpose or not. But here, I think, is plain argument. Demonstrative reason discovers only relations. But that reason, according to this hypothesis, discovers also vice and virtue. These moral qualities, therefore, must be relations. When we blame any action, in any situation, the whole complicated object of action and situation must form certain relations, wherein the essence of vice consists. This hypothesis is not otherwise intelligible. For what does reason discover, when it pronounces any action vicious? Does it discover a relation or a matter of fact? These questions are decisive, and must not be eluded.

breast and find a sentiment of disapprobation which arises in you towards this action. Here is a matter of fact; but it is the object of feeling, not of reason. It lies in yourself, not in the object. So that when you pronounce any action or character to be vicious, you mean nothing, but that from the constitution of your nature you have a feeling or sentiment of blame from the contemplation of it. Vice and virtue, therefore, may be compared to sounds, colours, heat, and cold, which, according to modern philosophy, are not qualities in objects but perceptions in the mind: and this discovery in morals, like that other in physics, is to be regarded as a considerable advancement of the speculative sciences; though, like that too, it has little or no influence on practice. Nothing can be more real, or concern us more, than our own sentiments of pleasure and uneasiness; and if these be favourable to virtue, and unfavourable to vice, no more can be requisite to the regulation of our conduct and behaviour.

I cannot forbear adding to these reasonings an observation which may, perhaps, be found of some importance. In every system of morality which I have hitherto met with, I have always remarked that the author proceeds for some time in the ordinary way of reasoning, and establishes the being of a god, or makes observations concerning human affairs; when of a sudden I am surprised to find that instead of the usual copulations of propositions *is* and *is not*, I meet with no proposition that is not connected with an *ought* or an *ought not*. This change is imperceptible, but is, however, of the last consequence. For as this *ought* or *ought not* expresses some new relation or affirmation, it is necessary that it should be observed and explained; and at the same time that a reason should be given for what seems altogether inconceivable, how this new relation can be a deduction from others which are entirely different from it. But as authors do not commonly use this precaution, I shall presume to recommend it to the readers; and am persuaded that this small attention would subvert all the vulgar systems of morality and let us see that the distinction of vice and virtue is not founded merely on the relations of objects, nor is perceived by reason.

Moral Distinctions Derived from a Moral Sense

Thus the course of the argument leads us to conclude that since vice and virtue are not discoverable merely by reason, or the comparison of ideas, it must be by means of some impression or sentiment they occasion, that we are able to mark the difference betwixt them. Our decisions concerning moral rectitude and depravity are evidently perceptions; and as all perceptions are either impressions or ideas, the exclusion of the one is a convincing argument for the other. Morality, therefore, is more properly felt than judged of; though this feeling or sentiment is commonly so soft and gentle that we are apt to confound it with an idea, according to our common custom of taking all things for the same which have any near resemblance to each other.

The next question is of what nature are these impressions, and after what manner do they operate upon us? Here we cannot remain long in suspense, but must pronounce the impression arising from virtue to be agreeable, and that proceeding from vice to be uneasy. Every moment's experience must convince us of this. There is no spectacle so fair and beautiful as a noble and generous action; nor any which gives us more abhorrence than one that is cruel and treacherous. No enjoyment equals the satisfaction we receive from the company of those we love and esteem; as the greatest of all punishments is to be obliged to pass our lives with those we hate or contemn. A very play or romance may afford us instances of this pleasure which virtue conveys to us; and pain which arises from vice.

Now, since the distinguishing impressions by which moral good or evil is known are nothing but *particular* pains or pleasures, it follows that in all inquiries concerning these moral distinctions it will be sufficient to show the principles which make us feel a satisfaction or uneasiness from the survey of any character, in order to satisfy us why the character is laudable or blamable. An action, or sentiment, or character, is virtuous or vicious; why? because its view causes a pleasure or uneasiness of a particular kind. In giving a reason, therefore, for the pleasure or uneasiness, we sufficiently explain the vice or virtue. To have the sense of virtue is nothing but to *feel* a satisfaction of a particular kind from the contemplation of a character. The very *feeling* constitutes or praise or admiration. We go no further; nor do we inquire into the cause of the satisfaction. We do not infer a character to be virtuous because it pleases; but in feeling that it pleases after such a particular manner we in effect feel that it is virtuous. The case is the same as in our judgments concerning all kinds of beauty, and tastes, and sensations. Our approbation is implied in the immediate pleasure they convey to us.

I have objected to the system which establishes eternal rational measures of right and wrong, that it is impossible to show in the actions of reasonable creatures any relations which are not found in external objects; and therefore, if morality always attended these relations, it were possible for inanimate matter to become virtuous or vicious. Now it may, in like manner, be objected to the present system, that if virtue and vice be determined by pleasure and pain, these qualities must in every case arise from the sensations; and consequently any object, whether animate or inanimate, rational or irrational, might become morally good or evil, provided it can excite a satisfaction or uneasiness. But though this objection seems to be the very same, it has by no means the same force in the one case as in the other. For, *first,* it is evident that under the term *pleasure* we comprehend sensations which are very different from each other, and which have only such a distant resemblance as is requisite to make them be expressed by the same abstract term. A good composition of music and a bottle of good wine equally produce pleasure; and, what is more, their goodness is determined merely by the pleasure. But shall we say, upon that account, that the wine is harmonious, or the music of a good flavour? In like manner, an inanimate object and the character or sentiments of any person may, both of them, give satisfaction; but, as the satisfaction is different, this keeps our sentiments concerning them from being confounded, and makes us ascribe virtue to the one and not to the other. Nor is every sentiment of pleasure or pain, which arises from characters and actions, of that *peculiar* kind which makes us praise or condemn. The good qualities of an enemy are hurtful to us, but may still command our esteem and respect. It is only when a character is considered in general, without reference to our particular interest, that it causes such a feeling or sentiment as denominates it morally good or evil. It is true, those sentiments from interest and morals are apt to be confounded, and naturally run into one another. It seldom happens that we do not think an enemy vicious, and can distinguish betwixt his opposition to our interest and real villainy or baseness. But this hinders not but that the sentiments are in themselves distinct, and a man of temper and judgment may preserve himself from these illusions. In like manner, though it is certain a musical voice is nothing but one that naturally gives a *particular* kind of pleasure, yet it is difficult for a man to be sensible that the voice of an enemy is agreeable, or to allow it to be musical. But a person of a fine ear, who has the command of himself, can separate these feelings and give praise to what deserves it.

Secondly, we may call to remembrance the preceding system of the passions, in order to remark a still more considerable difference among our pains and pleasures. Pride and humility, love and hatred, are excited when there is anything presented to us that both bears a relation to the object of the passion and produces a separate sensation related to the sensation of the passion. Now, virtue and vice are attended with these circumstances. They must necessarily be placed either in ourselves or others, and excite either pleasure or uneasiness; and therefore must give rise to one of these four passions, which clearly distinguishes them from the pleasure and pain arising from inanimate objects that often bear no relation to us; and this is, perhaps, the most considerable effect that virtue and vice have upon the human mind.

It may now be asked *in general* concerning this pain or pleasure that distinguishes moral good and evil, *from what principle is it derived, and whence does it arise in the human mind?* To this I reply, *first,* that it is absurd to imagine that, in every particular instance, these sentiments are produced by an *original* quality and *primary* constitution. For as the number of our duties is in a manner infinite, it is impossible that our original instincts should extend to each of them, and from our very first infancy impress on the human mind all that multitude of precepts which are contained in the completest system of ethics. Such a method of proceeding is not conformable to the usual maxims by which nature is conducted, where a few principles produce all that variety we observe in the universe, and everything is carried on in the easiest and most simple manner. It is necessary, therefore, to abridge these primary impulses and find some more general principles upon which all our notions of morals are founded.

But, in the *second* place, should it be asked, whether we ought to search for these principles in *nature,* or whether we must look for them in some other origin? I would reply that our answer to this question depends upon the definition of the word *nature,* than which there is none more ambiguous and equivocal. If *nature* be opposed to miracles, not only the distinction betwixt vice and virtue is natural, but also every event which has ever happened in the world, *excepting those miracles on which our religion is founded.* In saying, then, that the sentiments of vice and virtue are natural in this sense, we make no very extraordinary discovery.

But *nature* may also be opposed to rare and unusual; and in this sense of the word, which is the common one, there may often arise disputes concerning what is natural or unnatural; and one may in general affirm that we are not possessed of any very precise standard by which these disputes can be decided. Frequent and rare depend upon the number of examples we have observed; and as this number may gradually increase or diminish, it will be impossible to fix any exact boundaries betwixt them. We may only affirm on this head that if ever there was anything which could be called natural in this sense, the sentiments of morality certainly may; since there never was any nation of the world, nor any single person in any nation, who was utterly deprived of them, and who never, in any instance, showed the least approbation or dislike of manners. These sentiments are so rooted in our constitution and temper that, without entirely confounding the human mind by disease or madness, it is impossible to extirpate and destroy them.

But *nature* may also be opposed to artifice as well as to what is rare and unusual; and in this sense it may be disputed whether the notions of virtue be natural or not. We readily forget that the designs, and projects, and views of men are principles as necessary in their operation as heat and cold, moist and dry; but, taking them to be free and entirely our own, it is usual for us to set them in opposition to the other principles of nature. Should it therefore be demanded whether the sense of virtue be natural or artificial, I am of opinion that it is impossible for me at present to give any precise answer to this question. Perhaps it will appear afterwards that our sense of some virtues is artificial, and that of others natural. The discussion of this question will be more proper, when we enter upon an exact detail of each particular vice and virtue.[2]

Meanwhile, it may not be amiss to observe from these definitions of *natural* and *unnatural* that nothing can be more unphilosophical than those systems which assert that virtue is the same with what is natural, and vice with what is unnatural. For in the first sense of the word "nature," as opposed to miracles, both vice and virtue are equally natural; and in the second sense, as opposed to what is unusual, perhaps virtue will be found to be the most unnatural. At least it must be owned that heroic virtue, being as unusual, is as little natural as the most brutal barbarity. As to the third sense of the word, it is certain that both vice and virtue are equally artificial and out of nature. For, however it may be disputed whether the notion of a merit or demerit in certain actions be natural or artificial, it is evident that the actions themselves are artificial, and performed with a certain design and intention; otherwise they could never be ranked under any of these denominations. It is impossible, therefore, that the character of natural and unnatural can ever, in any sense, mark the boundaries of vice and virtue.

Thus we are still brought back to our first position that virtue is distinguished

---

[2] In the following discourse, *natural* is also opposed sometimes to *civil*, sometimes to *moral*. The opposition will always discover the sense in which it is taken.

by the pleasure, and vice by the pain, that any action, sentiment, or character, gives us by the mere view and contemplation. This decision is very commodious; because it reduces us to this simple question, *why any action or sentiment, upon the general view or survey, gives a certain satisfaction or uneasiness,* in order to show the origin of its moral rectitude or depravity, without looking for any incomprehensible relations and qualities which never did exist in nature, nor even in our imagination, by any clear and distinct conception? I flatter myself I have executed a great part of my present design by a state of the question which appears to me so free from ambiguity and obscurity.

Of the Origin of Justice and Property

We now proceed to examine two questions, viz., *concerning the manner in which the rules of justice are established by the artifice of men;* and *concerning the reasons which determine us to attribute to the observance or neglect of these rules a moral beauty and deformity.* These questions will appear afterwards to be distinct. We shall begin with the former.

. . .

There are three different species of goods which we are possessed of: the internal satisfaction of our minds, the external advantages of our body, and the enjoyment of such possessions as we have acquired by our industry and good fortune. We are perfectly secure in the enjoyment of the first. The second may be ravished from us, but can be of no advantage to him who deprives us of them. The last only are both exposed to the violence of others, and may be transferred without suffering any loss or alteration; while at the same time there is not a sufficient quantity of them to supply every one's desires and necessities. As the improvement, therefore, of these goods is the chief advantage of society, so the *instability* of their possession, along with their *scarcity,* is the chief impediment.

In vain should we expect to find in *uncultivated nature* a remedy to this inconvenience; or hope for any inartificial principle of the human mind which might control those partial affections, and make us overcome the temptations arising from our circumstances. The idea of justice can never serve to this purpose, or be taken for a natural principle capable of inspiring men with an equitable conduct towards each other. That virtue, as it is now understood, would never have been dreamed of among rude and savage men. For the notion of injury or injustice implies an immorality or vice committed against some other person. And as every immorality is derived from some defect or unsoundness of the passions, and as this defect must be judged of, in a great measure, from the ordinary course of nature in the constitution of the mind, it will be easy to know whether we be guilty of any immorality with regard to others, by considering the natural and usual force of those several affections which are directed towards them. Now, it appears that in the original frame of our mind our strongest attention is confined to ourselves; our next is extended to our relations and acquaintance; and it is only the weakest which reaches to strangers and indifferent persons. This partiality, then, and unequal affection must not only have an influence on our behaviour and conduct in society, but even on our ideas of vice and virtue; so as to make us regard any remarkable transgression of such a degree of partiality, either by too great an enlargement or contraction of the affections, as vicious and immoral. This we may observe in our common judgments concerning actions, where we blame a person who either centers all his affections in his family, or is so regardless of them as, in any opposition of interest, to give the preference to a stranger or mere chance acquaintance. From all which it follows that our natural uncultivated ideas of morality, instead of providing a remedy for the partiality of our affections, do rather conform themselves to that partiality and give it an additional force and influence.

The remedy, then, is not derived from nature but from *artifice;* or, more properly speaking, nature provides a remedy in the judgment and understanding for what is irregular and incommodious in the affections. For when men, from their early education in society, have become sensible of the infinite advantages that result from it, and have besides acquired a new affection to company and conversation, and when they have observed that the principal disturbance in society arises from those goods which we call external, and from their looseness and easy transition from one person to another, they must seek for a remedy by putting these goods as far as possible on the same footing with the fixed and constant advantages of the mind and body. This can be done after no other manner than by a convention entered into by all the members of the society to bestow stability on the possession of those external goods, and leave every one in the peaceable enjoyment of what he may acquire by his fortune and industry. By this means every one knows what he may safely possess; and the passions are restrained in their partial and contradictory motions. Nor is such a restraint contrary to these passions; for if so, it could never be entered into nor maintained; but it is only contrary to their heedless and impetuous movement. Instead of departing from our own interest, or from that of our nearest friends, by abstaining from the possessions of others, we cannot better consult both these interests than by such a convention; because it is by that means we maintain society, which is so necessary to their well-being and subsistence as well as to our own.

This convention is not of the nature of a *promise;* for even promises themselves, as we shall see afterwards, arise from human conventions. It is only a general sense of common interest; which sense all the members of the society express to one another, and which induces them to regulate their conduct by certain rules. I observe that it will be for my interest to leave another in the possession of his goods, *provided* he will act in the same manner with regard to me. He is sensible of a like interest in the regulation of his conduct. When this common sense of interest is mutually expressed and is known to both, it produces a suitable resolution and behaviour. And this may properly enough be called a convention or agreement betwixt us, though without the interposition of a promise; since the actions of each of us have a reference to those of the other, and are performed upon the supposition that something is to be performed on the other part. Two men who pull the oars of a boat do it by an agreement or convention, though they have never given promises to each other. Nor is the rule concerning the stability of possessions the less derived from human conventions, that it arises gradually, and acquires force by a slow progression and by our repeated experience of the inconveniences of transgressing it. On the contrary, this experience assures us still more that the sense of interest has become common to all our fellows, and gives us a confidence of the future regularity of their conduct; and it is only on the expectation of this that our moderation and abstinence are founded. In like manner are languages gradually established by human conventions, without any promise. In like manner do gold and silver become the common measures of exchange, and are esteemed sufficient payment for what is of a hundred times their value.

After this convention concerning abstinence from the possessions of others is entered into, and every one has acquired a stability in his possessions, there immediately arise the ideas of justice and injustice; as also those of *property, right,* and *obligation.* The latter are altogether unintelligible without first understanding the former. Our property is nothing but those goods whose constant possession is established by the laws of society—that is, by the laws of justice. Those, therefore, who make use of the words *property,* or *right,* or *obligation,* before they have explained the origin of justice, or even make use of them in that explication, are guilty of a very gross fallacy, and can never reason upon any solid foundation. A man's property is some object related to him. This relation is not natural but moral, and founded on justice. It is very preposterous, therefore, to imagine that we can have any idea of property without fully comprehending the nature of justice, and showing its origin in the artifice and contrivance of men. The origin of justice explains that of property. The same artifice gives rise to both. As our first and most natural sentiment of morals is founded on the nature of our passions, and gives the preference to ourselves and friends above strangers, it is impossible there can be naturally any such thing as fixed right or property, while the opposite passions of men impel them in contrary directions, and are not restrained by any convention or agreement.

. . .

. . . I have already observed that justice takes its rise from human conventions, and that these are intended as a remedy to some inconveniences which proceed from the concurrence of certain *qualities* of the human mind with the *situation* of external objects. The qualities of the mind are *selfishness* and *limited generosity;* and the situation of external objects is their *easy change,* joined to their *scarcity* in comparison of the wants and desires of men. But however philosophers may have been bewildered in those speculations, poets have been guided more infallibly by a certain taste or common instinct which, in most kinds of reasoning, goes further than any of that art and philosophy with which we have been yet acquainted. They easily perceived, if every man had a tender regard for another, or if nature supplied abundantly all our wants and desires, that the jealousy of interest, which justice supposes, could no longer have place; nor would there be any occasion for those distinctions and limits of property and possession which at present are in use among mankind. Increase to a sufficient degree the benevolence of men, or the bounty of nature, and you render justice useless by supplying its place with much nobler virtues and more valuable blessings. The selfishness of men is animated by the few possessions we have in proportion to our wants; and it is to restrain this selfishness that men have been obliged to separate themselves from the community, and to distinguish betwixt their own goods and those of others.

Nor need we have recourse to the fictions of poets to learn this, but, beside the reason of the thing, may discover the same truth by common experience and observation. It is easy to remark that a cordial affection renders all things common among friends, and that married people in particular mutually lose their property and are unacquainted with the *mine* and *thine*, which are so necessary and yet cause such disturbance in human society. The same effect arises from any alteration in the circumstances of mankind; as when there is such a plenty of anything as satisfies all the desires of men; in which case the distinction of property is entirely lost, and everything remains in common. This we may observe with regard to air and water, though the most valuable of all external objects; and may easily conclude that if men were supplied with everything in the same abundance, or if *every one* had the same affection and tender regard for *every one* as for himself, justice and injustice would be equally unknown among mankind.

. . .

. . . Though the rules of justice are established merely by interest, their connection with interest is somewhat singular, and is different from what may be observed on other occasions. A single act of justice is frequently contrary to *public interest;* and were it to stand alone, without being followed by other acts, may in itself be very prejudicial to society. When a man of merit, of a beneficent disposition, restores a great fortune to a miser or a seditious bigot, he has acted justly and laudably; but the public is a real sufferer. Nor is every single act of justice, considered apart, more conducive to private interest than to public; and it is easily conceived how a man may impoverish himself by a single instance of integrity, and have reason to wish that, with regard to that single act, the laws of justice were for a moment suspended in the universe. But however single acts of justice may be contrary either to public or private interest, it is certain that the whole plan or scheme is highly conducive, or indeed absolutely requisite, both to the support of society and the well-being of every individual. It is impossible to separate the good from the ill. Property must be stable, and must be fixed by general rules. Though in one instance the public be a sufferer, this momentary ill is amply compensated by the steady prosecution of the rule and by the peace and order which it establishes in society. And even every individual person must find himself a gainer on balancing the account; since without justice society must immediately dissolve, and every one must fall into that savage and solitary condition which is infinitely worse than the worst situation that can possibly be supposed in society. When, therefore, men have had experience enough to observe that, whatever may be the consequence of any single act of justice performed by a single person, yet the whole system of actions concurred in by the whole society is infinitely advantageous to the whole and to every part, it is not long before justice and property take place. Every member of society is sensible of this interest; every one expresses this sense to his fellows along with the resolution he has taken of squaring his actions by it, on condition that others will do the same. No more is requisite to induce any one of them to perform an act of justice, who has the first opportunity. This becomes an example to others; and thus justice establishes itself by a kind of convention or agreement, that is, by a sense of interest, supposed to be common to all, and where every single act is performed in expectation that others are to perform the like. Without such a convention no one would ever have dreamed that there was such a virtue as justice, or have been induced to conform his actions to it. Taking any single act, my justice may be pernicious in every respect; and it is only upon the supposition that others are to imitate my example that I can be induced to embrace that virtue; since nothing but this combination can render justice advantageous, or afford me any motives to conform myself to its rules.

We come now to the *second* question we proposed, viz., *Why we annex the idea of virtue to justice, and of vice to injustice.* This question will not detain us long after the principles which we have already established. All we can say of it at present will be dispatched in a few words; and for further satisfaction the reader must wait till we come to the third part of this book. The *natural* obligation to justice, viz., interest, has been fully explained; but as to the *moral* obligation, or the sentiment of right and wrong, it will first be requisite to examine the natural virtues before we can give a full and satisfactory account of it.

After men have found by experience that their selfishness and confined generosity, acting at their liberty, totally incapacitate them for society, and at the same time have observed that society is necessary to the satisfaction of those very passions, they are naturally induced to lay themselves under the restraint of such rules as may render their commerce more safe and commodious. To the imposition, then, and observance of these rules, both in general and in every particular instance, they are at first induced only by a regard to interest; and this motive, on the first formation of society, is sufficiently strong and forcible. But when society has become numerous and has increased to a tribe or nation, this interest is more remote; nor do men so readily perceive that disorder and confusion follow upon every breach of these rules, as in a more narrow and contracted society. But though in our own actions we may frequently lose sight of that interest which we have in maintaining order, and may follow a lesser and more present interest, we never fail to observe the prejudice we receive either mediately or immediately from the injustice of others, as not being in that case either blinded by passion or biassed by any contrary temptation. Nay, when the injustice is so distant from us as no way to affect our interest, it still displeases us, because we consider it as prejudicial to human society and pernicious to every one that approaches the person guilty of it. We partake of their uneasiness by *sympathy;* and as everything which gives uneasiness in human actions, upon the general survey, is called *vice*, and whatever produces satisfaction, in the same manner, is denominated *virtue*, this is the reason why the sense of moral good and evil follows upon justice and injustice. And though this sense in the present case be derived only from contemplating the actions of others, yet we fail not to extend it even to our own actions. The *general rule* reaches beyond those instances from which it arose; while at the same time we naturally *sympathize* with others in the sentiments they entertain of us.

. . .

Of the Origin of the Natural Virtues and Vices

We come now to the examination of such virtues and vices as are entirely natural, and have no dependence on the artifice and contrivance of men. The examination of these will conclude this system of morals.

. . .

We have already observed that moral distinctions depend entirely on certain peculiar sentiments of pain and pleasure, and that whatever mental quality in ourselves or others gives us a satisfaction by the survey or reflection is of course virtuous; as everything of this nature that gives uneasiness is vicious. Now, since every quality in ourselves or others which gives pleasure always causes pride or love, as every one that produces uneasiness excites humility or hatred, it follows that these two particulars are to be considered as equivalent with regard to our mental qualities; *virtue* and the power of producing love or pride; *vice* and the power of producing humility or hatred. In every case, therefore, we must judge of the one by the other, and may pronounce any *quality* of the mind virtuous which causes love or pride, and any one vicious which causes hatred or humility.

If any *action* be either virtuous or vicious, it is only as a sign of some quality or character. It must depend upon durable principles of the mind which extend over the whole conduct and enter into the personal character. Actions themselves, not proceeding from any constant principle, have no influence on love or hatred, pride or humility; and consequently are never considered in morality.

This reflection is self-evident and deserves to be attended to as being of the utmost importance in the present subject. We are never to consider any single action in our inquiries concerning the origin of morals, but only the quality or character from which the action proceeded. These alone are *durable* enough to affect our sentiments concerning the person. Actions are indeed better indications of a character than words, or even wishes and sentiments; but it is only so far as they are such indications that they are attended with love or hatred, praise or blame.

To discover the true origin of morals, and of that love or hatred which arises from mental qualities, we must take the matter pretty deep and compare some principles which have been already examined and explained.

We may begin with considering anew the nature and force of *sympathy*. The minds of all men are similar in their feelings and operations; nor can any one be actuated by any affection of which all others are not in some degree susceptible. As in strings equally wound up the motion of one communicates itself to the rest, so all the affections readily pass from one person to another, and beget correspondent movements in every human creature. When I see the *effects* of passion in the voice and gesture of any person, my mind immediately passes from these effects to their causes, and forms such a lively idea of the passion as is presently converted into the passion itself. In like manner, when I perceive the *causes* of any emotion, my mind is conveyed to the effects, and is actuated with a like emotion. Were I present at any of the more terrible operations of surgery, it is certain that, even before it begun, the preparation of the instruments, the laying of the bandages in order, the heating of the irons, with all the signs of anxiety and concern in the patient and assistants, would have a great effect upon my mind, and excite the strongest sentiments of pity and terror. No passion of another discovers itself immediately to the mind. We are only sensible of its causes or effects. From *these* we infer the passion; and consequently, *these* give rise to our sympathy.

. . .

No virtue is more esteemed than justice, and no vice more detested than injustice; nor are there any qualities which go further to the fixing the character, either as amiable or odious. Now, justice is a moral virtue, merely because it has that tendency to the good of mankind, and indeed is nothing but an artificial invention to that purpose. The same may be said of allegiance, of the laws of nations, of modesty, and of good manners. All these are mere human contrivances for the interest of society. And since there is a very strong sentiment of morals, which in all nations and all ages has attended them, we must allow that the reflecting on the tendency of characters and mental qualities is sufficient to give us the sentiments of approbation and blame. Now, as the means to an end can only be agreeable where the end is agreeable, and as the good of society, where our own interest is not concerned or that of our friends, pleases only by sympathy, it follows that sympathy is the source of the esteem which we pay to all the artificial virtues.

Thus it appears that *sympathy* is a very powerful principle in human nature, that it has a great influence on our taste of beauty, and that it produces our sentiment of morals in all the artificial virtues. From thence we may presume that it also gives rise to many of the other virtues, and that qualities acquire our approbation because of their tendency to the good of mankind. This presumption must become a certainty, when we find that most of those qualities which we *naturally* approve of have actually that tendency and render a man a proper member of society; while the qualities which we *naturally* disapprove of have a contrary tendency and render any intercourse with the person dangerous or disagreeable. For having found that such tendencies have force enough to produce the strongest sentiment of morals, we can never reasonably, in these cases, look for any other cause of approbation or blame; it being an inviolable maxim in philosophy that where any particular cause is sufficient for an effect, we ought to rest satisfied with it, and ought not to multiply causes without necessity. We have happily attained experiments in the artificial virtues, where the tendency of qualities to the good of society is the *sole* cause of our approbation, without any suspicion of the concurrence of another principle. From thence we learn the force of that principle. And where that principle may take place, and the quality approved of is really beneficial to society, a true philosopher will never require any other principle to account for the strongest approbation and esteem.

That many of the natural virtues have this tendency to the good of society, no one can doubt of. Meekness, beneficence, charity, generosity, clemency, moderation, equity, bear the greatest figure among the moral qualities, and are commonly denominated the *social* virtues, to mark their tendency to the good of society.

. . .

The only difference betwixt the natural virtues and justice lies in this, that the good which results from the former rises from every single act, and is the object of some natural passion; whereas a single act of justice, considered in itself, may often be contrary to the public good; and it is only the concurrence of mankind in a general scheme or system of action which is advantageous. When I relieve persons in distress, my natural humanity is my motive; and so far as my succour extends, so far have I promoted the happiness of my fellow creatures. But if we examine all the questions that come before any tribunal of justice, we shall find that, considering each case apart, it would as often be an instance of humanity to decide contrary to the laws of justice as comformable to them. Judges take from a poor man to give to a rich; they bestow on the dissolute the labour of the industrious; and put into the hands of the vicious the means of harming both themselves and others. The whole scheme, however, of law and justice is advantageous to the society; and it was with a view to this advantage that men, by their voluntary conventions, established it. After it is once established by these conventions, it is *naturally* attended with a strong sentiment of morals which can proceed from nothing but our sympathy with the interests of society. We need no other explication of that esteem which attends such of the natural virtues as have a tendency to the public good.

. . .

Before I proceed further, I must observe two remarkable circumstances in this affair which may seem objections to the present system. The first may be thus explained. When any quality or character has a tendency to the good of mankind, we are pleased with it and approve of it because it presents the lively idea of pleasure; which idea affects us by sympathy, and is itself a kind of pleasure. But as this sympathy is very variable, it may be thought that our sentiments of morals must admit of all the same variations. We sympathize more with persons contiguous to us than with persons remote from us; with our acquaintance, than with strangers; with our countrymen, than with foreigners. But notwithstanding this variation of our sympathy, we give the same approbation to the same moral qualities in China as in England. They appear equally virtuous and recommend themselves equally to the esteem of a judicious spectator. The sympathy varies without a variation in our esteem. Our esteem, therefore, proceeds not from sympathy.

To this I answer, the approbation of moral qualities most certainly is not derived from reason or any comparison of ideas; but proceeds entirely from a moral taste and from certain sentiments of pleasure or disgust which arise upon the contemplation and view of particular qualities or characters. Now, it is evident that those sentiments, whencever they are derived, must vary according to the distance or contiguity of the objects; nor can I feel the same lively pleasure from the virtues of a person who lived in Greece two thousand years ago that I feel from the virtues of a familiar friend and acquaintance. Yet I do not say that I esteem the one more than the other; and therefore, if the variation of the sentiment without a variation of the esteem be an objection, it must have equal force against every other system, as against that of sympathy. But to consider the matter aright, it has no force at all; and it is the easiest matter in the world to account for it. Our situation with regard both to persons and things is in continual fluctuation; and a man that lies at a distance from us may in a little time become a familiar acquaintance. Besides, every particular man has a peculiar position with regard to others; and it is impossible we could ever converse together on any reasonable terms, were each of us to consider characters and persons only as they appear from his peculiar point of view. In order, therefore, to prevent those continual *contradictions* and arrive at a more *stable* judgment of things, we fix on some *steady* and *general* points of view, and always in our thoughts, place ourselves in them, whatever may be our present situation. In like manner, external beauty is determined merely by pleasure; and it is evident a beautiful countenance cannot give so much pleasure when seen at a distance of twenty paces as when it is brought nearer us. We say not, however, that it appears to us less beautiful; because we know what effect it will have in such a position, and by that reflection we correct its momentary appearance.

In general, all sentiments of blame or praise are variable, according to our situation of nearness or remoteness with regard to the person blamed or praised, and according to the present disposition of our mind. But these variations we regard not in our general decisions, but still apply the terms expressive of our liking or dislike in the same manner as if we remained in one point of view. Experience soon teaches us this method of correcting our sentiments, or at least of correcting our language, where the sentiments are more stubborn and unalterable. Our servant, if diligent and faithful, may excite stronger sentiments of love and kindness than Marcus Brutus, as represented in history; but we say not upon that account that the former character is more laudable than the latter. We know that, were we to approach equally near to that renowned patriarch, he would command a much higher degree of affection and admiration. Such corrections are common with regard to all the senses; and, indeed, it were impossible we could ever make use of language or communicate our sentiments to one another, did we not correct the momentary appearances of things and overlook our present situation.

. . .

. . . When we form our judgments of persons merely from the tendency of their characters to our own benefit, or to that of our friends, we find so many contradictions to our sentiments in society and conversation, and such an uncertainty from the incessant changes of our situation, that we seek some other standard of merit and demerit which may not admit of so great variation. Being thus loosened from our first station, we cannot afterwards fix ourselves so commodiously by any means as by a sympathy with those who have any commerce with the person we consider. This is far from being as lively as when our own interest is concerned, or that of our particular friends; nor has it such an influence on our love and hatred; but being equally conformable to our calm and general principles, it is said to have an equal authority over our reason, and to command our judgment and opinion. We blame equally a bad action which we read of in history, with one performed in our neighbourhood the other day; the meaning of which is that we know from reflection that the former action would excite as strong sentiments of disapprobation as the latter, were it placed in the same position.

I now proceed to the *second* remarkable circumstance which I propose to take notice of. Where a person is possessed of a character that in its natural tendency is beneficial to society, we esteem him virtuous, and are delighted with the view of his character, even though particular accidents prevent its operation and incapacitate him from being serviceable to his friends and country. Virtue in rags is still virtue; and the love which it procures attends a man into a dungeon or desert, where the virtue can no longer be exerted in action and is lost to all the world. Now, this may be esteemed an objection to the present system. Sympathy interests us in the good of mankind; and if sympathy were the source of our esteem for virtue, that sentiment of approbation could only take place where the virtue actually attained its end and was beneficial to mankind. Where it fails of its end, it is only an imperfect means and, therefore, can never acquire any merit from that end. The goodness of an end can bestow a merit on such means alone as are complete and actually produce the end.

To this we may reply that, where any object, in all its parts, is fitted to attain any agreeable end, it naturally gives us pleasure and is esteemed beautiful, even though some external circumstances be wanting to render it altogether effectual. It is sufficient if everything be complete in the object itself. A house that is contrived with great judgment for all the commodities of life pleases us upon that account, though perhaps we are sensible that no one will ever dwell in it. A fertile soil and a happy climate delight us by a reflection on the happiness which they would afford the inhabitants, though at present the country be desert and uninhabited. A man whose limbs and shape promise strength and activity is esteemed handsome, though condemned to perpetual imprisonment. The imagination has a set of passions belonging to it upon which our sentiments of beauty much depend. These passions are moved by degrees of liveliness and strength, which are inferior to *belief,* and independent of the real existence of their objects. Where a character is in every respect fitted to be beneficial to society, the imagination passes easily from the cause to the effect, without considering that there are still some circumstances wanting to render the cause a complete one. *General rules* create a species of probability which sometimes influences the judgment, and always the imagination.

It is true, when the cause is complete and a good disposition is attended with good fortune which renders it really beneficial to society, it gives a stronger pleasure to the spectator, and is attended with a more lively sympathy. We are more affected by it; and yet we do not say that it is more virtuous, or that we esteem it more. We know that an alteration of fortune may render the benevolent disposition entirely impotent; and therefore we separate as much as possible the fortune from the disposition. The case is the same as when we correct the different sentiments of virtue which proceed from its different distances from ourselves. The passions do not always follow our corrections; but these corrections serve sufficiently to regulate our abstract notions, and are alone regarded when we pronounce in general concerning the degrees of vice and virtue.

. . .

21

Morality as a System of Hypothetical Imperatives

PHILIPPA FOOT

Philippa Foot (b. 1920) is Professor of Philosophy at the University of California at Los Angeles, and Senior Research Fellow at Somerville College, Oxford. She has published influential articles on free will, the problem of abortion, and other topics in moral philosophy. Some of her essays are collected under the title Virtues and Vices.

In this essay, Foot takes issue with the central Kantian claim that morality must be grounded in categorical rather than in hypothetical imperatives. Kant's position (see reading 29) is that any genuinely moral reason for acting must operate independently of any desires or inclinations that an agent merely happens to have. Foot disagrees. She acknowledges that it may make sense to say that a person should do something that will not further his desires, as when we say that even a person who cares nothing about etiquette should, according to the rules, not eat peas with a knife. However, Foot insists that the rules of etiquette provide no reason for acting unless one wants to obey them, and that the rules of morality are precisely similar in this regard. Contrary to what Kantians say, an amoral person can rationally and consistently disregard moral rules.

If moral rules do not compel rational assent, then do they not lose all their force and special status? According to Foot, they do not. Even if moral considerations only provide reasons for acting when someone wants to act morally, it hardly follows that the desire to act morally must be shallow or transient. To the contrary, among those who have it, that desire is often extremely deep and stable. If we reject psychological hedonism and other forms of psychological egoism (see reading 1), we will have to agree that such a desire can lead people to make great sacrifices to achieve moral ends. This, Foot argues, is all that any moralist needs or should ask.

THERE ARE MANY difficulties and obscurities in Kant's moral philosophy, and few contemporary moralists will try to defend it all. Many, for instance, agree in rejecting Kant's derivation of duties from the mere form of the law expressed in terms of a universally legislative will. Nevertheless, it is generally supposed, even by those who would not dream of calling themselves his followers, that Kant established one thing beyond doubt—namely, the necessity of distinguishing moral judgements from hypothetical imperatives. That moral judgements cannot be hypothetical imperatives has come to seem an unquestionable truth. It will be argued here that it is not.

In discussing so thoroughly Kantian a notion as that of the hypothetical imperative, one naturally begins by asking what Kant himself meant by a hypothetical imperative, and it may be useful to say a little about the idea of an imperative as this appears in Kant's works. In writing about imperatives Kant seems to be thinking at least as much of statements about what ought to be or should be done, as of injunctions expressed in the imperative mood. He even describes as an imperative the assertion that it would be 'good to do or refrain from doing something'[1] and explains that for a will that 'does not always do something simply because it is presented to it as a good thing to do' this has the force of a command of reason. We may therefore think of Kant's imperatives as statements to the effect that something ought to be done or that it would be good to do it.

The distinction between hypothetical imperatives and categorical imperatives, which plays so important a part in Kant's ethics, appears in characteristic form in the following passages from the *Foundations of the Metaphysics of Morals:*

> All imperatives command either hypothetically or categorically. The former present the practical necessity of a possible action as a means to achieving something else which one desires (or which one may possibly desire). The categorical imperative would be one which presented an action as of itself objectively necessary, without regard to any other end.[2]

> If the action is good only as a means to something else, the imperative is hypothetical; but if it is thought of as good in itself, and hence as necessary in a will which of itself conforms to reason as the principle of this will, the imperative is categorical.[3]

The hypothetical imperative, as Kant defines it, 'says only that the action is good to some purpose' and the purpose, he explains, may be possible or actual. Among imperatives related to actual purposes Kant mentions rules of prudence, since he believes that all men necessarily desire their own happiness. Without committing ourselves to this view it will be useful to follow Kant in classing together as 'hypothetical imperatives' those telling a man what he ought to do because (or if) he wants something and those telling him what he ought to do on grounds of self-interest. Common opinion agrees with Kant in insisting that a moral man must accept a rule of duty whatever his interests or desires.

Having given a rough description of the class of Kantian hypothetical imperatives it may be useful to point to the heterogeneity within it. Sometimes what a man should do depends on his passing inclination, as when he wants his

---

[1] *Foundations of the Metaphysics of Morals,* Sec. II, trans. by L. W. Beck.

[2] Ibid.

[3] Ibid.

294

coffee hot and should warm the jug. Sometimes it depends on some long-term project, when the feelings and inclinations of the moment are irrelevant. If one wants to be a respectable philosopher one should get up in the mornings and do some work, though just at that moment when one should do it the thought of being a respectable philosopher leaves one cold. It is true nevertheless to say of one, at that moment, that one wants to be a respectable philosopher, and this can be the foundation of a desire-dependent hypothetical imperative. The term 'desire' as used in the original account of the hypothetical imperative was meant as a grammatically convenient substitute for 'want', and was not meant to carry any implication of inclination rather than long-term aim or project. Even the word 'project', taken strictly, introduces undesirable restrictions. If someone is devoted to his family or his country or to any cause, there are certain things he wants, which may then be the basis of hypothetical imperatives, without either inclinations or projects being quite what is in question. Hypothetical imperatives should already be appearing as extremely diverse; a further important distinction is between those that concern an individual and those that concern a group. The desires on which a hypothetical imperative is dependent may be those of one man, or may be taken for granted as belonging to a number of people engaged in some common project or sharing common aims.

Is Kant right to say that moral judgements are categorical, not hypothetical, imperatives? It may seem that he is, for we find in our language two different uses of words such as 'should' and 'ought', apparently corresponding to Kant's hypothetical and categorical imperatives, and we find moral judgements on the 'categorical' side. Suppose, for instance, we have advised a traveller that he should take a certain train, believing him to be journeying to his home. If we find that he has decided to go elsewhere, we will most likely have to take back what we said: the 'should' will now be unsupported and in need of support. Similarly, we must be prepared to withdraw our statement about what he should do if we find that the right relation does not hold between the action and the end—that it is either no way of getting what he wants (or doing what he wants to do) or not the most eligible among possible means. The use of 'should' and 'ought' in moral contexts is, however, quite different. When we say that a man should do something and intend a moral judgement we do not have to back up what we say by considerations about his interests or his desires; if no such connexion can be found the 'should' need not be withdrawn. It follows that the agent cannot rebut an assertion about what, morally speaking, he should do by showing that the action is not ancillary to his interests or desires. Without such a connexion the 'should' does not stand unsupported and in need of support; the support that *it* requires is of another kind.

There is, then, one clear difference between moral judgements and the class of 'hypothetical imperatives' so far discussed. In the latter 'should' is 'used hypothetically', in the sense defined, and if Kant were merely drawing attention to this piece of linguistic usage his point would easily be proved. But obviously Kant meant more than this; in describing moral judgements as non-hypothetical—that is, categorical imperatives—he is ascribing to them a special dignity and necessity which this usage cannot give. Modern philosophers follow Kant in talking, for example, about the 'unconditional requirement' expressed in moral judgements. These, they say, tell us what we have to do whatever our interests or desires, and by their inescapability they are distinguished from hypothetical imperatives.

The problem is to find proof for this further feature of moral judgements. If anyone fails to see the gap that has to be filled it will be useful to point out to him that we find 'should' used non-hypothetically in some non-moral statements to which no one attributes the special dignity and necessity conveyed by the description 'categorical imperative'. For instance, we find this non-hypothetical use of 'should' in sentences enunciating rules of etiquette, as, for example, that an invitation in the third person should be answered in the third person, where the rule does not *fail to apply* to someone who has his own good reasons for ignoring this piece of nonsense, or who simply does not care about what, from the point of view of etiquette, he should do. Similarly, there is a non-hypothetical use of 'should' in contexts where something like a club rule is in question. The club secretary who has told a member that he should not bring ladies into the smoking-room does not say, 'Sorry, I was mistaken' when informed that this member is resigning tomorrow and cares nothing about his reputation in the club. Lacking a connexion with the agent's desires or interests, this 'should' does not stand 'unsupported and in need of support'; it requires only the backing of the rule. This use of 'should' is therefore 'non-hypothetical' in the sense defined.

It follows that if a hypothetical use of 'should' gave a hypothetical imperative, and a non-hypothetical use of 'should' a categorical imperative, then 'should' statements based on rules of etiquette, or rules of a club would be categorical imperatives. Since this would not be accepted by defenders of the categorical imperative in ethics, who would insist that these other 'should' statements give hypothetical imperatives, they must be using this expression in some other sense. We must therefore ask what they mean when they say that 'You should answer . . . in the third person' is a hypothetical imperative. Very roughly the idea seems to be that one may reasonably ask why anyone should bother about what should (from the point of view of etiquette) be done, and that such considerations deserve no notice unless reason is shown. So although people give as their reason for doing something the fact that it is required by etiquette, we do not take this consideration as *in itself giving us reason to act*. Considerations of etiquette do not have any automatic reason-giving force, and a man might be right if he denied that he had reason to do 'what's done'.

This seems to take us to the heart of the matter, for, by contrast, it is supposed that moral considerations necessarily give reasons for acting to any man. The difficulty is, of course, to defend this proposition which is more often repeated than explained. Unless it is said, implausibly, that all 'should' or 'ought' statements give reasons for acting, which leaves the old problem of assigning a special categorical status to moral judgement, we must be told what it is that makes the moral 'should' relevantly different from the 'shoulds' appearing in normative statements of other kinds.[4] Attempts have sometimes been made to show that some kind of irrationality is involved in ignoring the 'should' of morality: in saying "Immoral—so what?" as one says "Not *comme il faut*—so what?' But as far as I can see these have all rested on some illegitimate assumption, as, for instance, of thinking that the amoral man, who agrees that some piece of conduct is immoral but takes no notice of that, is inconsistently disregarding a rule of conduct that he has accepted; or again of thinking it inconsistent to desire that others will not do to one what one proposes to do to them. The fact is that the man who rejects morality because he sees no reason to obey its rules can be convicted of villainy but not of inconsistency. Nor will his action necessarily be irrational. Irrational actions are those in which a man in some way defeats his own purposes, doing what is calculated to be disadvantageous or to frustrate his ends. Immorality does not *necessarily* involve any such thing.

It is obvious that the normative character of moral judgement does not guarantee its reason-giving force. Moral judgements are normative, but so are judgements of manners, statements of club rules, and many others. Why should the first provide reasons for acting as the others do not? In every case it is because there is a background of teaching that the non-hypothetical 'should' can be used. The behaviour is required, not simply recommended, but the question remains as to why we should do what we are required to do. It is true that moral rules are often enforced much more strictly than the rules of etiquette, and our reluctance to press the non-hypothetical 'should' of etiquette may be one reason why we think of the rules of etiquette as hypothetical imperatives. But are we then to say that there is nothing behind the idea that moral judgements are categorical imperatives but the relative stringency of our moral teaching? I believe that this may have more to do with the matter than the defenders of the categorical imperative would like to admit. For if we look at the kind of thing that is said in its defence we may find ourselves puzzled about what the words can even mean unless we connect them with the feelings that this stringent teaching implants. People talk, for instance, about the 'binding force' of morality, but it is not clear what this means if not that we *feel*

---

[4] To say that moral considerations are *called* reasons is blatantly to ignore the problem.

In the case of etiquette or club rules it is obvious that the non-hypothetical use of 'should' has resulted in the loss of the usual connexion between what one should do and what one has reason to do. Someone who objects that in the moral case a man cannot be justified in restricting his practical reasoning in this way, since every moral 'should' gives reasons for acting, must face the following dilemma. Either it is possible to create reasons for acting simply by putting together any silly rules and introducing a non-hypothetical 'should', or else the non-hypothetical 'should' does not necessarily imply reasons for acting. If it does not necessarily imply reasons for acting we may ask why it is supposed to do so in the case of morality. Why cannot the indifferent amoral man say that for him 'should$_m$' gives no reason for acting, treating 'should$_m$' as most of us treat 'should$_e$'? Those who insist that 'should$_m$' is categorical in this second 'reason-giving' sense do not seem to realise that they never prove this to be so. They sometimes say that moral considerations 'just do' give reasons for acting, without explaining why some devotee of etiquette could not say the same about the rules of etiquette.

ourselves unable to escape. Indeed the 'inescapability' of moral requirements is often cited when they are being contrasted with hypothetical imperatives. No one, it is said, escapes the requirements of ethics by having or not having particular interests or desires. Taken in one way this only reiterates the contrast between the 'should' of morality and the hypothetical 'should', and once more places morality alongside of etiquette. Both are inescapable in that behaviour does not cease to offend against either morality or etiquette because the agent is indifferent to their purposes and to the disapproval he will incur by flouting them. But morality is supposed to be inescapable in some special way and this may turn out to be merely the reflection of the way morality is taught. Of course, we must try other ways of expressing the fugitive thought. It may be said, for instance, that moral judgements have a kind of necessity since they tell us what we 'must do' or 'have to do' whatever our interests and desires. The sense of this is, again, obscure. Sometimes when we use such expressions we are referring to physical or mental compulsion. (A man has to go along if he is pulled by strong men and he has to give in if tortured beyond endurance.) But it is only in the absence of such conditions that moral judgements apply. Another and more common sense of the words is found in sentences such as 'I caught a bad cold and had to stay in bed' where a penalty for acting otherwise is in the offing. The necessity of acting morally is not, however, supposed to depend on such penalties. Another range of examples, not necessarily having to do with penalties, if found where there is an unquestioned acceptance of some project or rôle, as when a nurse tells us that she has to make her rounds at a certain time, or we say that we have to run for a certain train. But these too are irrelevant in the present context, since the acceptance condition can always be revoked.

No doubt it will be suggested that it is in some other sense of the words 'have to' or 'must' that one has to or must do what morality demands. But why should one insist that there must be such a sense when it proves so difficult to say what it is? Suppose that what we take for a puzzling thought were really no thought at all but only the reflection of our *feelings* about morality? Perhaps it makes no sense to say that we 'have to' submit to the moral law, or that morality is 'inescapable' in some special way. For just as one may feel as if one is falling without believing that one is moving downward, so one may feel as if one has to do what is morally required without believing oneself to be under physical or psychological compulsion, or about to incur a penalty if one does not comply. No one thinks that if the word 'falling' is used in a statement reporting one's sensations it must be used in a special sense. But this kind of mistake may be involved in looking for the special sense in which one 'has to' do what morality demands. There is no difficulty about the idea that we feel we *have to* behave morally, and given the psychological conditions of the learning of moral behaviour it is natural that we should have such feelings. What we cannot do is quote them in support of the doctrine of the categorical imperative. It seems, then, that in so far as it is backed up by statements to the effect that the moral law *is* inescapable, or that we *do* have to do what is morally required of us, it is uncertain whether the doctrine of the categorical imperative even makes sense.

The conclusion we should draw is that moral judgements have no better claim to be categorical imperatives than do statements about matters of etiquette. People may indeed follow either morality or etiquette without asking why they should do so, but equally well they may not. They may ask for reasons and may reasonably refuse to follow either if reasons are not to be found.

It will be said that this way of viewing moral considerations must be totally destructive of morality, because no one could ever act morally unless he accepted such considerations as in themselves sufficient reason for action. Actions that are truly moral must be done 'for their own sake', 'because they are right', and not for some ulterior purpose. This argument we must examine with care, for the doctrine of the categorical imperative has owed much to its persuasion.

Is there anything to be said for the thesis that a truly moral man acts 'out of respect for the moral law' or that he does what is morally right because it is morally right? That such propositions are not prima facie absurd depends on the fact that moral judgement concerns itself with a man's reasons for acting as well as with what he does. Law and etiquette require only that certain things are done or left undone, but no one is counted as charitable if he gives alms 'for the praise of men', and one who is honest only because it pays him to be honest does not have the virtue of honesty. This kind of consideration was crucial in shaping Kant's moral philosophy. He many times contrasts acting out of respect for the moral law with acting from an ulterior motive, and what is more from one that is self-interested. In the early *Lectures on Ethics* he gave the principle of truth-telling under a system of hypothetical imperatives as that of not lying *if it harms one to lie*. In the *Metaphysics of Morals* he says that ethics cannot start from the ends which a man may propose to himself, since these are all 'selfish'.[5] In the *Critique of Practical Reason* he argues explicitly that when acting not out of respect for moral law but 'on a material maxim' men do what they do for the sake of pleasure or happiness.

> All material practical principles are, as such, of one and the same kind and belong under the general principle of self love or one's own happiness.[6]

Kant, in fact, was a psychological hedonist* in respect of all actions except those done for the sake of the moral law, and this faulty theory of human nature was one of the things preventing him from seeing that moral virtue might be compatible with the rejection of the categorical imperative.

If we put this theory of human action aside, and allow as ends the things that seem to be ends, the picture changes. It will surely be allowed that quite

---

[5] Pt. II, Introduction, sec. II.

[6] Immanuel Kant, *Critique of Practical Reason*, trans. L. W. Beck, p. 133.

* One who believes that actions are performed to gain pleasure or avoid pain. For discussion, see Joel Feinberg, "Psychological Egoism," reading 1.

apart from thoughts of duty a man may care about the suffering of others, having a sense of identification with them, and wanting to help if he can. Of course he must want not the reputation of charity, nor even a gratifying rôle helping others, but, quite simply, their good. If this is what he does care about, then he will be attached to the end proper to the virtue of charity and a comparison with someone acting from an ulterior motive (even a respectable ulterior motive) is out of place. Nor will the conformity of his action to the rule of charity be merely contingent. Honest action may happen to further a man's career; charitable actions do not *happen* to further the good of others.[7]

Can a man accepting only hypothetical imperatives possess other virtues besides that of charity? Could he be just or honest? This problem is more complex because there is no end related to such virtues as the good of others is related to charity. But what reason could there be for refusing to call a man a just man if he acted justly because he loved truth and liberty, and wanted every man to be treated with a certain respect? And why should the truly honest man not follow honesty for the sake of the good that honest dealing brings to men? Of course, the usual difficulties can be raised about the rare case in which no good is foreseen from an individual act of honesty. But it is not evident that a man's desires could not give him reason to act honestly even here. He wants to live openly and in good faith with his neighbours; it is not all the same to him to lie and conceal.

If one wants to know whether there could be a truly moral man who accepted moral principles as hypothetical rules of conduct, as many people accept rules of etiquette as hypothetical rules of conduct, one must consider the right kind of example. A man who demanded that morality should be brought under the heading of self-interest would not be a good candidate, nor would anyone who was ready to be charitable or honest only so long as he felt inclined. A cause such as justice makes strenuous demands, but this is not peculiar to morality, and men are prepared to toil to achieve many ends not endorsed by morality. That they are prepared to fight so hard for moral ends—for example, for liberty and justice—depends on the fact that these are the kinds of ends that arouse devotion. To sacrifice a great deal for the sake of etiquette one would need to be under the spell of the emphatic 'ought'. One could hardly be devoted to behaving *comme il faut*.

In spite of all that has been urged in favour of the hypothetical imperative in ethics, I am sure that many people will be unconvinced and will argue that one element essential to moral virtue is still missing. This missing feature is the recognition of a *duty* to adopt those ends which we have attributed to the moral man. We have said that he *does* care about others, and about causes such as liberty and justice; that it is on this account that he will accept a system of morality. But what if he never cared about such things, or what if he ceased to care? Is it not the case that he *ought* to care? This is exactly what Kant

---

[7] It is not, of course, necessary that charitable actions should *succeed* in helping others; but when they do so they do not *happen* to do so, since that is necessarily their aim. (Footnote added, 1977.)

would say, for though at times he sounds as if he thought that morality is not concerned with ends, at others he insists that the adoption of ends such as the happiness of others is itself dictated by morality.[8] How is this proposition to be regarded by one who rejects all talk about the binding force of the moral law? He will agree that a moral man has moral ends and cannot be indifferent to matters such as suffering and injustice. Further, he will recognise in the statement that one *ought* to care about these things a correct application of the non-hypothetical moral 'ought' by which society is apt to voice its demands. He will not, however, take the fact that he ought to have certain ends as in itself reason to adopt them. If he himself is a moral man then he cares about such things, but not 'because he ought'. If he is an amoral man he may deny that he has any reason to trouble his head over this or any other moral demand. Of course he may be mistaken, and his life as well as others' lives may be most sadly spoiled by his selfishness. But this is not what is urged by those who think they can close the matter by an emphatic use of 'ought'. My argument is that they are relying on an illusion, as if trying to give the moral 'ought' a magic force.[9]

This conclusion may, as I said, appear dangerous and subversive of morality. We are apt to panic at the thought that we ourselves, or other people, might stop caring about the things we do care about, and we feel that the categorical imperative gives us some control over the situation. But it is interesting that the people of Leningrad were not struck by the thought that only the *contingent* fact that other citizens shared their loyalty and devotion to the city stood between them and the Germans during the terrible years of the siege. Perhaps we should be less troubled than we are by fear of defection from the moral cause; perhaps we should even have less reason to fear it if peopled thought of themselves as volunteers banded together to fight for liberty and justice and against inhumanity and oppression. It is often felt, even if obscurely, that there is an element of deception in the official line about morality. And while some have been persuaded by talk about the authority of the moral law, others have turned away with a sense of distrust.

[8] See e.g., *The Metaphysics of Morals*, pt. II, sec. 30.

[9] See G. E. M. Anscombe, 'Modern Moral Philosophy', *Philosophy* (1958). My view is different from Miss Anscombe's, but I have learned from her.

22

Freedom and Reason

R. M. HARE

R. M. Hare (b. 1919) is White's Professor of Moral Philosophy at Corpus Christi College, Oxford University. He has done important work both in moral theory and in the application of moral theory to practical problems. His major works include The Language of Morals, Freedom and Reason, *and* Moral Thinking.

In Hare's view, every moral judgment involves two elements. When someone judges that he morally ought to do something, he commits himself to doing it and also extends his principle of action to anyone else in a similar position. As Hare puts it, all moral judgments are both prescriptive and universalizable.

In this selection, Hare argues that these rules place important constraints on our moral thought. To show this, he proposes a simple example. Suppose that A owes B money, and B owes C money. Suppose further that B is considering imprisoning A for nonpayment. Given the universalizability requirement, accepting this judgment would force B to judge that C ought to imprison him for not paying. But B does not want to go to jail, and so cannot prescribe that C imprison him. Thus, B must withdraw his judgment that he ought to imprison A. Moreover, he must withdraw this judgment even if his creditor C is not real, but only imagined.

Could B escape this conclusion? As Hare recognizes, he might try. For one thing B might either reject Hare's definition of morality or refuse to think in moral terms. Failing that, he might look for differences between himself and A. Or he might simply accept the prescription that he too be sent to jail. In the later part of the selection, Hare considers such maneuvers. His conclusion is that few if any are effective.

THE RULES OF MORAL REASONING ARE, basically, two, corresponding to the two features of moral judgements which I argued for in the first half of this book, prescriptivity and universalizability. When we are trying, in a concrete case, to decide what we ought to do, what we are looking for (as I have already said) is an action to which we can commit ourselves (prescriptivity) but which we are at the same time prepared to accept as exemplifying a principle of action to be prescribed for others in like circumstances (universalizability). If, when we consider some proposed action, we find that, when universalized, it yields prescriptions which we cannot accept, we reject this action as a solution to our moral problem—if we cannot universalize the prescription, it cannot become an 'ought'.

. . .

I will now try to exhibit the bare bones of the theory of moral reasoning that I wish to advocate by considering a very simple (indeed over-simplified) example. As we shall see, even this very simple case generates the most baffling complexities; and so we may be pardoned for not attempting anything more difficult to start with.

This example is adapted from a well-known parable.[1] *A* owes money to *B*, and *B* owes money to *C*, and it is the law that creditors may exact their debts by putting their debtors into prison. *B* asks himself, 'Can I say that I ought to take this measure against *A* in order to make him pay? He is no doubt *inclined* to do this, or *wants* to do it. Therefore, if there were no question of universalizing his prescriptions, he would assent readily to the *singular* prescription 'Let me put *A* into prison' (4.3). But when he seeks to turn this prescription into a moral judgement, and say, 'I *ought* to put *A* into prison because he will not pay me what he owes', he reflects that this would involve accepting the principle 'Anyone who is in my position ought to put his debtor into prison if he does not pay'. But then he reflects that *C* is in the same position of unpaid creditor with regard to himself (*B*), and that the cases are otherwise identical; and that if anyone in this position ought to put his debtors into prison, then so ought *C* to put him (*B*) into prison. And to accept the moral prescription '*C* ought to put me into prison' would commit him (since, as we have seen, he must be using the word 'ought' prescriptively) to accepting the singular prescription 'Let *C* put me into prison'; and this he is not ready to accept. But if he is not, then neither can he accept the original judgement that he (*B*) ought to put *A* into prison for debt. Notice that the whole of this argument would break down if 'ought' were not being used both universalizably *and prescriptively*; for if it were not being used prescriptively, the step from '*C* ought to put me into prison' to 'Let *C* put me into prison' would not be valid.

The structure and ingredients of this argument must now be examined. We must first notice an analogy between it and the Popperian theory of scientific method. What has happened is that a provisional or suggested moral principle has been rejected because one of its particular consequences proved unacceptable. But an important difference between the two kinds of reasoning must also be noted; it is what we should expect, given that the data of scientific observation are recorded in descriptive statements, whereas we are here dealing with prescriptions. What knocks out a suggested hypothesis, on Popper's theory, is a singular statement of fact: the hypothesis has the consequence that p; but not-p. Here the logic is just the same, except that in place of the observation-statements 'p' and 'not-p' we have the singular *prescriptions* 'Let *C* put *B* into prison for debt' and its contradictory. Nevertheless, given that *B* is disposed to reject the first of these prescriptions, the argument against him is just as cogent as in the scientific case.

We may carry the parallel further. Just as science, seriously pursued, is the search for hypotheses and the testing of them by the attempt to falsify their

---

[1] Matthew xviii. 23.

particular consequences, so morals, as a serious endeavour, consists in the search for principles and the testing of them against particular cases. Any rational activity has its discipline, and this is the discipline of moral thought: to test the moral principles that suggest themselves to us by following out their consequences and seeing whether we can accept *them*.

No argument, however, starts from nothing. We must therefore ask what we have to have before moral arguments of the sort of which I have given a simple example can proceed. The first requisite is that the facts of the case should be given; for all moral discussion is about some particular set of facts, whether actual or supposed. Secondly we have the logical framework provided by the meaning of the word 'ought' (i.e. prescriptivity and universalizability, both of which we saw to be necessary). Because moral judgements have to be universalizable, *B* cannot say that he ought to put *A* into prison for debt without committing himself to the view that *C*, who is *ex hypothesi* in the same position *vis-à-vis* himself, ought to put *him* into prison; and because moral judgements are prescriptive, this would be, in effect, prescribing to *C* to put him into prison; and this he is unwilling to do, since he has a strong inclination not to go to prison. This inclination gives us the third necessary ingredient in the argument: if *B* were a completely apathetic person, who literally did not mind what happened to himself or to anybody else, the argument would not touch him. The three necessary ingredients which we have noticed, then, are (1) facts; (2) logic; (3) inclinations. These ingredients enable us, not indeed to arrive at an evaluative conclusion, but to *reject* an evaluative proposition. We shall see later that these are not, in all cases, the only necessary ingredients.

In the example which we have been using, the position was deliberately made simpler by supposing that *B* actually stood to some other person in exactly the same relation as *A* does to him. Such cases are unlikely to arise in practice. But it is not necessary for the force of the argument that *B* should *in fact* stand in this relation to anyone; it is sufficient that he should consider hypothetically such a case, and see what would be the consequences in it of those moral principles between whose acceptance and rejection he has to decide. Here we have an important point of difference from the parallel scientific argument, in that the crucial case which leads to rejection of the principle can itself be a supposed, not an observed, one. That hypothetical cases will do as well as actual ones is important, since it enables us to guard against a possible misinterpretation of the argument which I have outlined. It might be thought that what moves *B* is the *fear* that *C* will actually do to him as he does to *A*—as happens in the gospel parable. But this fear is not only irrelevant to the moral argument; it does not even provide a particularly strong non-moral motive unless the circumstances are somewhat exceptional. *C* may, after all, not find out what *B* has done to *A*; or *C*'s moral principles may be different from *B*'s, and independent of them, so that what moral principle *B* accepts makes no difference to the moral principles on which *C* acts.

Even, therefore, if *C* did not exist, it would be no answer to the argument for *B* to say 'But in my case there is no fear that anybody will ever be in a position to do to me what I am proposing to do to *A*'. For the argument does not rest on any such fear. All that is essential to it is that *B* should disregard the fact that he plays the particular role in the situation which he does, without disregarding the inclinations which people have in situations of this sort. In other words, he must be prepared to give weight to *A*'s inclinations and interests as if they were his own. This is what turns selfish prudential reasoning into moral reasoning. It is much easier, psychologically, for *B* to do this if he is actually placed in a situation like *A*'s *vis-à-vis* somebody else; but this is not necessary, provided that he has sufficient imagination to envisage what it is like to be *A*. For our first example, a case was deliberately chosen in which little imagination was necessary; but in most normal cases a certain power of imagination and readiness to use it is a fourth necessary ingredient in moral arguments, alongside those already mentioned, viz. logic (in the shape of universalizability and prescriptivity), the facts, and the inclinations or interests of the people concerned.

It must be pointed out that the absence of even one of these ingredients may render the rest ineffective. For example, impartiality by itself is not enough. If, in becoming impartial, *B* became also completely dispassionate and apathetic, and moved as little by other people's interests as by his own, then, as we have seen, there would be nothing to make him accept or reject one moral principle rather than another. That is why those who, like Adam Smith and Professor Kneale, advocate what have been called 'Ideal Observer Theories' of ethics, sometimes postulate as their imaginary ideal observer not merely an impartial spectator, but an impartially *sympathetic* spectator.[2] To take another example, if the person who faces the moral decision has no imagination, then even the fact that someone can do the very same thing to him may pass him by. If, again, he lacks the readiness to universalize, then the vivid imagination of the sufferings which he is inflicting on others may only spur him on to intensify them, to increase his own vindictive enjoyment. And if he is ignorant of the material facts (for example about what is likely to happen to a person if one takes out a writ against him), then there is nothing to tie the moral argument to particular choices.

The best way of testing the argument which we have outlined will be to consider various ways in which somebody in *B*'s position might seek to escape from it. There are indeed a number of ways; and all of them may be successful, at a price. It is important to understand what the price is in each case. We may classify these manœuvres which are open to *B* into two kinds. There are first of all the moves which depend on his using the moral words in a different way from that on which the argument relied. We saw that for the success of the

---

[2] It will be plain that there are affinities, though there are also differences, between this type of theory and my own. For such theories see W. C. Kneale, *Philosophy*, xxv (1950), 162; R. Firth and R. B Brandt, *Philosophy and Phenomenological Research*, xii (1951/2), 317, and xv (1954/5), 407, 414, 422; and J. Harrison, *Aristotelian Society*, supp. vol. xxviii (1954), 132. Firth, unlike Kneale, says that the observer must be 'dispassionate', but see Brandt, op. cit., p. 411 n. For a shorter discussion see Brandt, *Ethical Theory*, p. 173. Since for many Christians God occupies the role of 'ideal observer', the moral judgements which they make may be expected to coincide with those arrived at by the method of reasoning which I am advocating.

argument it was necessary that 'ought' should be used universalizably and prescriptively. If *B* uses it in a way that is either not prescriptive or not universalizable, then he can escape the force of the argument, at the cost of resigning from the kind of discussion that we thought we were having with him. We shall discuss these two possibilities separately. Secondly, there are moves which can still be made by *B*, even though he is using the moral words in the same way as we are. We shall examine three different sub-classes of these.

Before dealing with what I shall call the *verbal* manœuvres in detail, it may be helpful to make a general remark. Suppose that we are having a simple mathematical argument with somebody, and he admits, for example, that there are five eggs in this basket, and six in the other, but maintains that there are a dozen eggs in the two baskets taken together; and suppose that this is because he is using the expression 'a dozen' to mean 'eleven'. It is obvious that we cannot compel him logically to admit that there are not a dozen eggs, in *his* sense of 'dozen'. But it is equally obvious that this should not disturb us. For such a man only appears to be dissenting from us. His dissent is only apparent, because the proposition which his words express is actually consistent with the conclusion which we wish to draw; he *says* 'There are a dozen eggs'; but he *means* what we should express by saying 'There are eleven eggs'; and this we are not disputing. It is important to remember that in the moral case also the dissent may be only apparent, if the words are being used in different ways, and that it is no defect in a method of argument if it does not make it possible to prove a conclusion to a person when he is using words in such a way that the conclusion does not follow.

It must be pointed out, further (since this is a common source of confusion), that in this argument nothing whatever hangs upon our *actual* use of words in common speech, any more than it does in the arithmetical case. That we use the sound 'dozen' to express the meaning that we customarily do use it to express is of no consequence for the argument about the eggs; and the same may be said of the sound 'ought'. There is, however, something which I, at any rate, customarily express by the sound 'ought', whose character is correctly described by saying that it is a universal or universalizable prescription. I hope that what I customarily express by the sound 'ought' is the same as what most people customarily express by it; but if I am mistaken in this assumption, I shall still have given a correct account, so far as I am able, of that which I express by this sound.[3] Nevertheless, this account will interest other people mainly in so far as my hope that they understand the same thing as I do by 'ought' is fulfilled; and since I am moderately sure that this is indeed the case with many people, I hope that I may be of use to them in elucidating the logical properties of the concept which they thus express.

At this point, however, it is of the utmost importance to stress that the fact that two people express the same thing by 'ought' does not entail that they share the same moral opinions. For the formal, logical properties of the word

---

[3] Cf. Moore, *Principia Ethica*, p. 6.

'ought' (those which are determined by its *meaning*) are only one of the four factors (listed earlier) whose combination governs a man's moral opinion on a given matter. Thus ethics, the study of the logical properties of the moral words, remains morally neutral (its conclusions neither are substantial moral judgements, nor entail them, even in conjunction with factual premises); its bearing upon moral questions lies in this, that it makes logically impossible certain combinations of moral and other prescriptions. Two people who are using the word 'ought' in the same way may yet disagree about what ought to be done in a certain situation, either because they differ about the facts, or because one or other of them lacks imagination, or because their different inclinations make one reject some singular prescription which the other can accept. For all that, ethics (i.e. the logic of moral language) is an immensely powerful engine for producing moral agreement; for if two people are willing to use the moral word 'ought', and to use it in the same way (viz. the way that I have been describing), the other possible sources of moral disagreement are all eliminable. People's inclinations about most of the important matters in life tend to be the same (very few people, for example, like being starved or run over by motor-cars); and, even when they are not, there is a way of generalizing the argument, to be described in the next chapter, which enables us to make allowance for differences in inclinations. The facts are often, given sufficient patience, ascertainable. Imagination can be cultivated. If these three factors are looked after, as they can be, agreement on the use of 'ought' is the only other necessary condition for producing moral agreement, at any rate in typical cases. And, if I am not mistaken, this agreement in use is already there in the discourse of anybody with whom we are at all likely to find ourselves arguing; all that is needed is to think clearly, and so make it evident.

After this methodological digression, let us consider what is to be done with the man who professes to be using 'ought' in some different way from that which I have described—because he is not using it prescriptively, or not universalizably. For the reasons that I have given, if he takes either of these courses, he is no longer in substantial moral disagreement with us. Our apparent moral disagreement is really only verbal; for although, as we shall see shortly, there may be a residuum of substantial disagreement, this cannot be moral. It cannot even be an evaluative disagreement, in the sense of 'evaluative' above defined.

Let us take first the man who is using the word 'ought' prescriptively, but not universalizably. He can say that he ought to put his debtor into prison, although he is not prepared to agree that his creditor ought to put *him* into prison. We, on the other hand, since we are not prepared to admit that our creditors in these circumstances ought to put us into prison, cannot say that we ought to put our debtors into prison. So there is an appearance of substantial moral disagreement, which is intensified by the fact that, since we are both using the word 'ought' prescriptively, our respective views will lead to different particular actions. Different *singular* prescriptions about what to do are (since both our judgements are prescriptive) derivable from what we are respectively saying. But this is not enough to constitute a moral disagreement. For there to be a moral disagreement, or even an evaluative one of any kind, we must differ, not only about what *is* to be done is some particular case, but about some universal principle concerning what *ought* to be done in cases of a certain sort; and since *B* is (on the hypothesis considered) advocating no such universal principle, he is saying nothing with which we can be in moral or evaluative disagreement. Considered purely as prescriptions, indeed, our two views are in substantial disagreement; but the moral, evaluative (i.e. the *universal* prescriptive) disagreement is only verbal, because, when the expression of *B*'s view is understood as he means it, the view turns out not to be a view about the morality of the action at all. So *B*, by this manœuvre, can go on prescribing to himself to put *A* into prison, but has to abandon the claim that he is justifying the action morally, as we understand the word 'morally'. One may, of course, use any word as one pleases, at a price. But he can no longer claim to be giving that sort of justification of his action for which, as I think, the common expression is 'moral justification'.

I need not deal at length with the second way in which *B* might be differing from us in his use of 'ought', viz. by not using it prescriptively. If he were not using it prescriptively, it will be remembered, he could assent to the singular prescription 'Let not *C* put me into prison for debt', and yet assent also to the non-prescriptive moral judgement '*C* ought to put me into prison for debt'. And so his disinclination to be put into prison for debt by *C* would furnish no obstacle to his saying that he (*B*) ought to put *A* into prison for debt. And thus he could carry out his own inclination to put *A* into prison with apparent moral justification. The justification would be, however, only apparent. For if *B* is using the word 'ought' non-prescriptively, then 'I ought to put *A* into prison for debt' does not entail the singular prescription 'Let me put *A* into prison for debt'; the 'moral' judgement becomes quite irrelevant to the choice of what to do. There would also be the same lack of substantial moral disagreement as we noticed in the preceding case. *B* would not be disagreeing with us other than verbally, so far as the moral question is concerned (though there might be points of *factual* disagreement between us, arising from the *descriptive* meaning of our judgements). The 'moral' disagreement could be only verbal, because whereas we should be dissenting from the universalizable prescription '*B* ought to put *A* into prison for debt', *this* would not be what *B* was expressing, though the words he would be using would be the same. For *B* would not, by these words, be expressing a prescription at all.

So much for the ways (of which my list may well be incomplete) in which *B* can escape from our argument by using the word 'ought' in a different way from us. The remaining ways of escape are open to him even if he is using 'ought' in the same way as we are, viz. to express a universalizable prescription.

We must first consider that class of escape-routes whose distinguishing feature is that *B*, while using the moral words in the same way as we are, refuses to make positive moral judgements at all in certain cases. There are two main variations of this manœuvre. *B* may either say that it is indifferent, morally, whether he imprisons *A* or not; or he may refuse to make any moral judgement at all, even one of indifference, about the case. It will be obvious that if he adopts either of these moves, he can evade the argument as so far set out. For

that argument only forced him to *reject* the moral judgement 'I ought to imprison
A for debt'. It did not force him to assent to any moral judgement; in particular,
he remained free to assent, either to the judgement that he ought not to imprison
A for debt (which is the one that we want him to accept) or to the judgement
that it is neither the case that he ought, nor the case that he ought not (that
it is, in short, indifferent); and he remained free, also, to say 'I am just not
making any moral judgements at all about this case'.

We have not yet, however, exhausted the arguments generated by the demand
for universalizability, provided that the moral words are being used in a way
which allows this demand. For it is evident that these manœuvres could, in
principle, be practised in any case whatever in which the morality of an act is
in question. And this enables us to place *B* in a dilemma. Either he practises
this manœuvre in *every* situation in which he is faced with a moral decision;
or else he practises it only *sometimes*. The first alternative, however, has to be
sub-divided; for 'every situation' might mean 'every situation in which he himself has to face a moral decision regarding one of his own actions', or it might
mean 'every situation in which a moral question arises for him, whether about
his own actions or about somebody else's'. So there are three courses that he
can adopt: (1) He either refrains altogether from making moral judgements,
or makes none except judgements of indifference (that is to say, he either
observes a complete moral silence, or says 'Nothing matters morally'; either
of these two positions might be called a sort of amoralism); (2) He makes
moral judgements in the normal way about other people's actions, but adopts
one or other of the kinds of amoralism, just mentioned, with regard to his
own; (3) He expresses moral indifference, or will make no moral judgement
at all, with regard to *some* of his own actions and those of other people, but
makes moral judgements in the normal way about others.

Now it will be obvious that in the first case there is nothing that we can do,
and that this should not disturb us. Just as one cannot win a game of chess
against an opponent who will not make any moves—and just as one cannot
argue mathematically with a person who will not commit himself to any mathematical statements—so moral argument is impossible with a man who will
make no moral judgements at all, or—which for practical purposes comes to
the same thing—makes only judgements of indifference. Such a person is not
entering the arena of moral dispute, and therefore it is impossible to contest
with him. He is compelled also—and this is important—to abjure the protection of morality for his own interests.

In the other two cases, however, we have an argument left. If a man is
prepared to make positive moral judgements about other people's actions, but
not about his own, or if he is prepared to make them about some of his own
decisions, but not about others, then we can ask him on what principle he
makes the distinction between these various cases. This is a particular application of the demand for universalizability. He will still have left to him the
ways of escape from this demand which are available in all its applications,
and which we shall consider later. But there is no way of escape which is
available in this application, but not in others. He must either produce (or at

least admit the existence of) some principle which makes him hold different moral opinions about apparently similar cases, or else admit that the judgements he is making are not moral ones. But in the latter case, he is in the same position, in the present dispute, as the man who will not make any moral judgements at all; he has resigned from the contest.

In the particular example which we have been considering, we supposed that the cases of *B* and of *C*, his own creditor, were identical. The demand for universalization therefore compels *B* to make the same moral judgement, whatever it is, about both cases. He had therefore, unless he is going to give up the claim to be arguing morally, either to say that neither he nor *C* ought to exercise their legal rights to imprison their debtors; or that both ought (a possibility to which we shall recur in the next section); or that it is indifferent whether they do. But the last alternative leaves it open to *B* and *C* to do what they like in the matter; and we may suppose that, though *B* himself would like to have this freedom, he will be unwilling to allow it to *C*. It is as unlikely that he will *permit* *C* to put him (*B*) into prison as that he will *prescribe* it. We may say, therefore, that while move (1), described above, constitutes an abandonment of the dispute, moves (2) and (3) really add nothing new to it.

We must next consider a way of escape which may seem much more respectable than those which I have so far mentioned. Let us suppose that *B* is a firm believer in the rights of property and the sanctity of contracts. In this case he may say roundly that debtors ought to be imprisoned by their creditors whoever they are, and that, specifically, *C* ought to imprison him (*B*), and he (*B*) ought to imprison *A*. And he may, unlike the superficially similar person described earlier, be meaning by 'ought' just what we usually mean by it—i.e. he may be using the word prescriptively, realizing that in saying that *C* ought to put him into prison, he is prescribing that *C* put him in prison. *B*, in this case, is perfectly ready to go to prison for his principles, in order that the sanctity of contracts may be enforced. In real life, *B* would be much more likely to take this line if the situation in which he himself played the role of debtor were not actual but only hypothetical; but this, as we saw earlier, ought not to make any difference to the argument.

We are not yet, however, in a position to deal with this escape-route. All we can do is to say why we cannot now deal with it, and leave this loose end to be picked up later. *B*, if he is sincere in holding the principle about the sanctity of contracts (or any other universal moral principle which has the same effect in this particular case), may have two sorts of grounds for it. He may hold it on utilitarian grounds, thinking that, unless contracts are rigorously enforced, the results will be so disastrous as to outweigh any benefits that *A*, or *B* himself, may get from being let off. This could, in certain circumstances, be a good argument. But we cannot tell whether it is, until we have generalized the type of moral argument which has been set out in this chapter, to cover cases in which the interests of more than two parties are involved. As we saw, it is only the interests of *A* and *B* that come into the argument as so far considered (the interests of the third party, *C*, do not need separate consideration, since *C* was introduced only in order to show *B*, if necessary fictionally, a situation in which the roles were reversed; therefore C's interests, being a mere replica of B's, will vanish, as a separate factor, once the A/B situation, and the moral judgements made on it, are universalized). But if utilitarian grounds of the sort suggested are to be adduced, they will bring with them a reference to all the other people whose interests would be harmed by laxity in the enforcement of contracts. This escape-route, therefore, if this is its basis, introduces considerations which cannot be assessed until we have generalized our form of argument to cover 'multilateral' moral situations. At present, it can only be said that if B can show that leniency in the enforcement of contracts would really have the results he claims for the community at large, he might be justified in taking the severer course. This will be apparent after we have considered in some detail an example (that of the judge and the criminal) which brings out these considerations even more clearly.

On the other hand, B might have a quite different, non-utilitarian kind of reason for adhering to his principle. He might be moved, not by any weight which he might attach to the interests of other people, but by the thought that to enforce contracts of this sort is necessary in order to conform to some moral or other *ideal* that he has espoused. Such ideals might be of various sorts. He might be moved, for example, by an ideal of abstract justice, of the *fiat justitia, ruat caelum* variety. We have to distinguish such an ideal of justice, which pays no regard to people's interests, from that which is concerned merely to do justice *between* people's interests. It is very important, if considerations of justice are introduced into a moral argument, to know of which sort they are. Justice of the second kind can perhaps be accommodated within a moral view which it is not misleading to call utilitarian. But this is not true of an ideal of the first kind. It is characteristic of this sort of non-utilitarian ideals that, when they are introduced into moral arguments, they render ineffective the appeal to universalized self-interest which is the foundation of the argument that we have been considering. This is because the person who has whole-heartedly espoused such an ideal (we shall call him the 'fanatic') does not mind if people's interests—even his own—are harmed in the pursuit of it.

It need not be justice which provides the basis of such an escape-route as we are considering. Any moral ideal would do, provided that it were pursued regardless of other people's interests. For example, B might be a believer in the survival of the fittest, and think that, in order to promote this, he (and everyone else) ought to pursue their own interests by all means in their power and regardless of everyone else's interests. This ideal might lead him, in this particular case, to put A in prison, and he might agree that C ought to do the same to him, if he were not clever enough to avoid this fate. He might think that universal obedience to such a principle would maximize the production of supermen and so make the world a better place. If these were his grounds, it is possible that we might argue with him factually, showing that the universal observance of the principle would not have the results he claimed. But we might be defeated in this factual argument if he had an ideal which made him call the world 'a better place' when the jungle law prevailed; he could then agree to our factual statements, but still maintain that the condition of the world described by us as resulting from the observance of his principle would be better than its present condition. In this case, the argument might take two courses. If we could get him to imagine himself in the position of the weak, who went to the wall in such a state of the world, we might bring him to realize that to hold his principle involved prescribing that things should be done to him, in hypothetical situations, which he could not sincerely prescribe. If so, then the argument would be on the rails again, and could proceed on lines which we have already sketched. But he might stick to his principle and say "If I were weak, then I ought to go to the wall'. If he did this, he would be putting himself beyond the reach of what we shall call 'golden rule' or 'utili-tarian' arguments by becoming what we shall call a 'fanatic'. Since a great part of the rest of this book will be concerned with people who take this sort of line, it is unnecessary to pursue their case further at this point.

The remaining manœuvre that *B* might seek to practise is probably the commonest. It is certainly the one which is most frequently brought up in philosophical controversies on this topic. This consists in a fresh appeal to the facts—i.e. in asserting that there are in fact morally relevant differences between his case and that of others. In the example which we have been considering, we have artificially ruled out this way of escape by assuming that the case of *B* and *C* is exactly similar to that of *A* and *B*; from this it follows *a fortiori* that there are no morally relevant differences. Since the *B/C* case may be a hypothetical one, this condition of exact similarity can always be fulfilled, and therefore this manœuvre is based on a misconception of the type of argument against which it is directed. Nevertheless it may be useful, since this objection is so commonly raised, to deal with it at this point, although nothing further will be added thereby to what has been said already.

It may be claimed that no two actual cases would ever be exactly similar; there would always be some differences, and B might allege that some of these were morally relevant. He might allege, for example, that, whereas his family would starve if C put him into prison, this would not be the case if he put *A* into prison, because *A*'s family would be looked after by *A*'s relatives. If such a difference existed, there might be nothing logically disreputable in calling it morally relevant, and such arguments are in fact often put forward and accepted.

The difficulty, however, lies in drawing the line between those arguments of this sort which are legitimate, and those which are not. Suppose that *B* alleges that the fact that *A* has a hooked nose or a black skin entitles him, *B*, to put him in prison, but that *C* ought not to do the same thing to him, *B*, because his nose is straight and his skin white. Is this an argument of equal logical respectability? Can I say that the fact that I have a mole in a particular place on my chin entitles me to further my own interests at others' expense, but that they are forbidden to do this by the fact that they lack this mark of natural pre-eminence?

The answer to this manœuvre is implicit in what has been said already about the relevance, in moral arguments, of hypothetical as well as actual cases. The fact that no two actual cases are ever identical has no bearing on the problem. For all we have to do is to imagine an identical case in which the roles are reversed. Suppose that my mole disappears, and that my neighbor grows one in the very same spot on his chin. Or, to use our other example, what does B say about a hypothetical case in which he has a black skin or a hooked nose, and A and C are both straight-nosed and white-skinned? Since this is the same argument, in essentials, as we used at the very beginning, it need not be repeated here. B is in fact faced with a dilemma. Either the property of his own case, which he claims to be morally relevant, is a properly universal property (i.e. one describable without reference to individuals), or it is not. If it is a universal property, then, because of the meaning of the word 'universal', it is a property which might be possessed by another case in which he played a different role (though in fact it may not be); and we can therefore ask him to ignore the fact that it is he himself who plays the role which he does in this case. This will force him to count as morally relevant only those properties which he is prepared to allow to be relevant even when other people have them. And this rules out all the attractive kinds of special pleading. On the other hand, if the property in question is not a properly universal one, then he has not met the demand for universalizability, and cannot claim to be putting forward a moral argument at all.

It is necessary, in order to avoid misunderstanding, to add two notes to the foregoing discussion. The misunderstanding arises through a too literal interpretation of the common forms of expression—which constantly recur in arguments of this type—'How would you like it if . . . ?' and 'Do as you would be done by'. Though I shall later, for convenience, refer to the type of arguments here discussed as 'golden-rule' arguments, we must not be misled by these forms of expression.

First of all, we shall make the nature of the argument clearer if, when we are asking B to imagine himself in the position of his victim, we phrase our question, never in the form 'What *would* you say, or feel, or think, or how *would* you like it, if you were he?', but always in the form 'What *do* you say (*in propria persona*) about a hypothetical case in which you are in your victim's position?' The importance of this way of phrasing the question is that, if the question were put in the first way, B might reply 'Well, of course, if anybody did this to me I should resent it very much and make all sorts of adverse moral judgements about the act; but this has absolutely no bearing on the validity of the moral opinion which I am *now* expressing'. To involve him in contradiction, we have to show that he *now* holds an opinion about the hypothetical case which is inconsistent with his opinion about the actual case.

The second thing which has to be noticed is that the argument, as set out, does not involve any sort of deduction of a moral judgement, or even of the negation of a moral judgement, from a factual statement about people's inclinations, interests, &c. We are not saying to B 'You are as a matter of fact averse to this being done to you in a hypothetical case; and from this it follows logically that you ought not to do it to another'. Such a deduction would be a breach of Hume's Law ('No "ought" from an "is"'), to which I have repeatedly declared my adherence. The point is, rather, that because of his aversion to its being done to him in the hypothetical case, he cannot accept the singular *prescription* that in the hypothetical case it should be done to him; and this, because of the logic of 'ought', precludes him from accepting the moral judgement that he ought to do likewise to another in the actual case. It is not a question of a factual statement about a person's inclinations being inconsistent with a moral judgement; rather, his inclinations being what they are, he cannot assent sincerely to a certain singular prescription, and if he cannot do this, he cannot assent to a certain universal prescription which entails it, when conjoined with factual statements about the circumstances whose truth he admits. Because of this entailment, if he assented to the factual statements and to the universal prescription, but refused (as he must, his inclinations being what they are) to assent to the singular prescription, he would be guilty of a logical inconsistency.

If it be asked what the relation is between his aversion to being put in prison in the hypothetical case, and his inability to accept the hypothetical singular prescription that if he were in such a situation he should be put into prison, it would seem that the relation is not unlike that between a belief that the cat is on the mat, and an inability to accept the proposition that the cat is not on the mat. Further attention to this parallel will perhaps make the position clearer. Suppose that somebody advances the hypothesis that cats never sit on mats, and that we refute him by pointing to a cat on a mat. The logic of our refutation proceeds in two stages. Of these, the second is: 'Here is a cat sitting on a mat, so it is not the case that cats never sit on mats'. This is a piece of logical deduction; and to it, in the moral case, corresponds the step from 'Let this not be done to me' to 'It is not the case that I ought to do it to another in similar circumstances'. But in both cases there is a first stage whose nature is more obscure, and different in the two cases, though there is an analogy between them.

In the 'cat' case, it is logically possible for a man to look straight at the cat on the mat, and yet believe that there is no cat on the mat. But if a person with normal eyesight and no psychological aberrations does this, we say that he does not understand the meaning of the words, 'The cat is on the mat'. And even if he does not have normal eyesight, or suffers from some psychological aberration (such as a phobia of cats, say, that he just *cannot* admit to himself that he is face to face with one), yet, if we can convince him that everyone else can see a cat there, he will have to admit that there *is* a cat there, or be accused of misusing the language.

If, on the other hand, a man says 'But I *want* to be put in prison, if ever I am in that situation', we can, indeed, get as far as accusing him of having eccentric desires; but we cannot, when we have proved to him that nobody else has such a desire, face him with the choice of either saying, with the rest, 'Let this not be done to me', or else being open to the accusation of not understanding what he is saying. For it is not an incorrect use of words to want eccentric things. Logic does not prevent me wanting to be put in a gas chamber if a Jew. It is perhaps true that I logically cannot want for its own sake an experience which I think of as *unpleasant*; for to say that I think of it as unpleasant may be logically inconsistent with saying that I want it for its own sake. If this is so, it is because 'unpleasant' is a prescriptive expression. But 'to be put in prison' and 'to be put in a gas chamber if a Jew', are not prescriptive expressions; and therefore these things can be wanted without offence to logic. It is, indeed, in the logical possibility of wanting *anything* (neutrally described) that the 'freedom' which is alluded to in my title essentially consists. And it is this, as we shall see, that lets by the person whom I shall call the 'fanatic'.

There is not, then, a complete analogy between the man who says 'There is no cat on the mat' when there is, and the man who wants things which others do not. But there is a partial analogy, which, having noticed this difference, we may be able to isolate. The analogy is between two relations: the relations between, in both cases, the 'mental state' of these men and what they say. If I believe that there is a cat on the mat I cannot sincerely say that there is not; and, if I want not to be put into prison more than I want anything else, I cannot sincerely say 'Let me be put into prison'. When, therefore, I said above 'His inclinations being what they are, he cannot assent sincerely to a certain singular prescription', I was making an analytic statement (although the 'cannot' is not a logical 'cannot'); for if he were to assent sincerely to the prescription, that would entail *ex vi terminorum* that his inclinations had changed—in the very same way that it is analytically true that, if the other man were to say sincerely that there was a cat on the mat, when before he had sincerely denied this, he must have changed his belief.

If, however, instead of writing 'His inclinations being what they are, he cannot . . .', we leave out the first clause and write simply 'He cannot . . .', the statement is no longer analytic; we are making a statement about his psychology which might be false. For it is logically possible for inclinations to change; hence it is possible for a man to come sincerely to hold an ideal which requires that he himself should be sent to a gas chamber if a Jew. That is the price we have to pay for our freedom. But, as we shall see, in order for reason to have a place in morals it is not necessary for us to close this way of escape by means of a logical barrier; it is sufficient that, men and the world being what they are, we can be very sure that hardly anybody is going to take it with his eyes open. And when we are arguing with one of the vast majority who are not going to take it, the reply that somebody else *might* take it does not help his case against us. In this respect, all moral arguments are *ad hominem*.

23

The 'Is-Ought' Problem Resolved

ALAN GEWIRTH

Alan Gewirth (b. 1912) taught philosophy for many years at the University of Chicago. He is the author of Reason and Morality *and many essays on ethical theory, and is a past president of the American Philosophical Association's Western Division. This selection was originally his presidential address to that body. Its middle section is omitted here.*

The "is-ought problem" to which Gewirth's title refers was first posed by David Hume (see reading 20). Hume asked how it can ever be legitimate to draw conclusions about what we ought to do, or what ought to happen, from premises about what is the case. In other words, how can we derive normative conclusions from factual premises?

In this essay, Gewirth first refines this problem and then proposes a solution to it. To reach that solution, Gewirth employs what he calls the "dialectically necessary method." His method is dialectical because, like Plato in the Socratic dialogues, he starts from the claims of others. But unlike Plato, Gewirth does not begin with claims that people just happen to make. Instead, he proceeds from assumptions to which we commit ourselves merely by acting. Since we cannot avoid acting, these assumptions are, for practical purposes, necessary.

What, then, are the assumptions? Since all action is purposive, all agents must regard their purposes as valuable. And since freedom and well-being are needed to achieve any purposes, all agents must also regard their freedom and well-being as valuable. Because of this, all agents must see themselves as having rights to freedom and well-being. And because these rights are seen to follow from agency alone, each agent must ascribe them to all other agents. But if all other agents have these rights, then we ought not to harm or interfere with them. Thus, the transition from "is" to "ought" is made.

WHEN I TOLD one of my philosophical friends the title of this paper, he suggested that I make a slight addition, so that the title would read: "The 'Is-Ought' Problem Resolved—Again?!" Indeed, I agree with his implied conviction that on certain interpretations of it the 'Is-Ought' Problem has already been resolved several times; and I wish to emphasize that these resolutions and the polemical exchanges generated by them have done much to sharpen the issues. Nevertheless, I also maintain that the real 'Is-Ought' Problem has not yet been resolved. I therefore want to do three main things in this paper. First,

I shall present what I take to be the real 'Is-Ought' Problem and shall indicate why it is the real one. Second, I shall review the main recent attempts to resolve the Problem and shall show that none of these has succeeded so far as the real 'Is-Ought' Problem is concerned. Third, I shall give my resolution of this real Problem.

I

First, then, what is the real 'Is-Ought' Problem? It will come as no surprise that the Problem is concerned with moral 'oughts'. After all, it was in the context of a discussion of the basis of "moral distinctions" that Hume wrote his famous passage about the need for explaining and justifying the transition from 'is' to 'ought' as copulas of propositions.[1] And in the introduction to a recent anthology devoted to the subject, the editor writes that the 'Is-Ought' Problem is "the central problem in moral philosophy."[2]

Now the word 'moral' is used in several different senses. While taking account of these differences, I shall focus on certain paradigm cases of what are undeniably moral 'ought'-judgments which persons have sought to derive from 'is'-statements. These judgments are of two main kinds. One kind sets forth negative moral duties to refrain from inflicting serious harm on other persons. Their paradigm uses have been of this form: "A intends to do X to B in order to gratify A's inclinations although he knows this will bring only great suffering to B; therefore, A ought not to do X to B." The other kind sets forth positive duties to perform certain actions for the benefit of other persons, especially where the latter would otherwise suffer serious harm. Their paradigm uses have been of this sort: "B is drowning and A by throwing him a rope can rescue him; therefore A ought to throw the rope to B;" or "B is starving while A has plenty of food; therefore A ought to give some food to B;" and so forth. In addition to such individual moral duties, persons have also sought to derive more specifically sociopolitical moral 'oughts' from 'is'-statements; for example, "That society is characterized by great inequalities of wealth and power; therefore it ought to be changed;" or "This state respects civil liberties; therefore we ought to that extent to support it;" and so forth.

The 'oughts' presented in these judgments have five important formal and material characteristics, which will constitute five interrelated conditions or tests that must be satisfied by any solution of the real 'Is-Ought' Problem. First, the 'oughts' are moral ones in the sense that they take positive account of the interests of other persons as well as the agent or speaker, especially as regards the distribution of what is considered to be basic well-being. It is this well-being, indicated in the antecedent 'is'-statements, that provides the reasons for the actions urged in the 'ought'-judgments.

---

[1] *Treatise of Human Nature*, III. i. 1 (ed. Selby-Bigge, pp. 469–470).

[2] W.D. Hudson, ed., *The Is-Ought Question* (London: Macmillan and Co., 1969), p. 11.

Second, these 'oughts' are prescriptive in that their users advocate or seek to guide or influence actions, which they set forth as required by the facts presented in the antecedents. Although not all uses of 'ought' are prescriptive, such advocacy marks the unconditional use of 'ought' as in the above cases, where the antecedent empirical statements serve not to qualify or restrict the 'oughts' but rather to indicate the facts or reasons which make them mandatory.

Third, the 'oughts' are egalitarian in that they require that at least basic well-being be distributed equally as between the agent addressed and his potential recipients, or as among the members of a society. Although such egalitarianism is sometimes made part of the definition of 'moral', and I shall myself sometimes use 'moral' to include both this and the prescriptiveness just mentioned, it seems best to distinguish these considerations, since there may, after all, be non-egalitarian moralities.

A fourth important characteristic of these 'oughts' is that they are determinate. By this I mean that the actions they prescribe have definite contents such that the opposite contents cannot be obtained by the same mode of derivation. Thus, in my above examples, the 'oughts' require, respectively, rescuing, feeding, not harming; at the same time they are opposite-excluding in that one cannot, by the mode of derivation in question, obtain as conclusions 'oughts' which permit or require not rescuing, not feeding, or harming.

A fifth characteristic of these 'oughts', which to some extent encompasses some of the other characteristics, is that they are categorical, not merely hypothetical. By this characteristic, which applies more directly to the individual 'ought'-judgments, I mean that the requirements set forth therein are normatively overriding and ineluctable or necessary, in that their bindingness cannot be removed by, and hence is not contingent on or determined by, variable, escapable features either of the persons addressed or of their social relations. These escapable, non-determining features include the self-interested desires of the persons addressed, their variable choices, opinions, and attitudes, and institutional rules whose obligatoriness may itself be doubtful or variable.

Now it is with 'ought'-judgments having these five characteristics of being moral, prescriptive, egalitarian, determinate, and categorical that the real 'Is-Ought' Problem is concerned. The Problem is this: how can 'ought'-judgments having these five characteristics be logically derived from, or be justified on the basis of, premisses which state empirical facts? As this question suggests, a sixth condition which must be satisfied by any solution of the real 'Is-Ought' Problem is that of non-circularity, especially in the respect that the premisses from which the 'ought'-conclusions are derived must not themselves be moral or prescriptive. The resolution of the Problem calls not only for presenting a derivation which satisfies these six conditions but also for a theory which adequately explains why this derivation is successful and why previous attempts at derivation have been unsuccessful. There may indeed be problems about deriving from empirical statements 'ought'-judgments which lack one or more of these five characteristics; but they are not the real 'Is-Ought' Problem, not only because, having fewer conditions to satisfy, they are easier to resolve, but also because they necessarily fail to cope with the issue of justifying categorical moral 'ought'-judgments, judgments which bear on the most basic requirements of how persons ought to live in relation to one another.

It is the decisive importance of this issue of justification that makes the real 'Is-Ought' Problem at once so central and so difficult for moral philosophy. There is a familiar sequence of considerations at this point. The moral 'ought'-judgments of the sort I mentioned above are not self-evident; hence if they are to be justified at all they must be derived in some way from other statements. These other, justifying statements must themselves be either moral or non-moral (where 'moral' here includes also the characteristics of prescriptiveness and categoricalness). If the justifying statements are moral ones, then there recurs the question of how *they* are to be justified, since they too are not self-evident, and the question continues to recur as we mount through more general moral rules and principles. If, on the other hand, the statements from which the moral 'ought'-judgments are to be derived are non-moral ones, such as the empirical statements that figured in my paradigm cases, then there is the difficulty that the 'ought'-judgments are not derivable from those statements either inductively or deductively, unless we define 'ought' in empirical terms; and such a definition raises many questions of adequacy, including how the 'ought'-judgments can pass the tests of prescriptiveness and categoricalness. But it seems clear that if the moral 'ought'-judgments cannot in any way be justified on the basis of empirical and logical considerations, i.e. by logical derivation from 'is'-statements, then they cannot be definitively justified at all. Hence the crucial importance of the real 'Is-Ought' Problem.

I shall use the expression *external model* and *internal model* to distinguish the two chief positions on this issue. The external model holds that 'ought' is external to 'is' in that there is a basic logical gap between them: 'ought' cannot be correctly defined in terms of empirical and logical considerations alone, nor can these considerations constitute determinate criteria of 'ought' because any facts adduced as such criteria must ultimately reflect personal and hence variable decisions; consequently, 'ought' cannot be logically derived from 'is.' The internal model upholds the opposite position. The external model asserts also that 'ought'-judgments are not self-evident, so it concludes that they are not capable of any definitive justification at all; they reflect decisions or attitudes to which, at least at an ultimate level, questions of justification are inapplicable. Although logical gaps of some sort have also been held to underlie various other philosophical Problems—for example, in the Problem of Induction there is the logical gap between particular observation-statements and general laws, and in the Mind-Body Problem there is the logical gap between statements about bodily movements and statements about intentional human actions— the 'is-ought' gap is declared by the external model to be much wider than any of these others, for while both sides of the other gaps fall within the 'is', the 'is-ought' gap involves a difference between 'is' and something belonging to an entirely separate category.

. . .

III

In this final section I want to show how 'ought'-judgments which are categorical, determinate, prescriptive, egalitarian, and moral can be logically and non-circularly derived from 'is'-statements which describe empirical facts about the world. I shall do this by presenting a certain version of what I have called the internal model. But my version differs in important respects from those considered above. The main bases of these differences comprise two interrelated points, one about the context, the other about method.

The factual context within which my argument will proceed is that of the generic features of action. This context is both logically prior to and more invariable and inescapable than the other contexts appealed to in the attempted material 'is-ought' derivations considered above. In those derivations, as we have seen, there were two sorts of variabilities, each of which made the 'ought'-conclusions hypothetical rather than categorical. The arguments went as follows: Given a certain structured context, certain actions are necessary or required by that context. The necessities here were hence hypothetical in that, while one had first to accept the respective contexts as normatively binding, as justifiably setting forth requirements for action, this acceptance was not itself necessary, but was rather a matter of one's choice. I shall call this the acceptance-variability of the respective contexts. In addition, the specific contents of each context could vary; that is, even if one accepted the context in general, one might adopt different ends, participate in different institutions, have different conceptions of well-being, and these diversities generated quite different and even opposed 'ought'-conclusions. I shall call this the content-variability of the respective contexts. So there was a double hypotheticalness in these arguments, and this accounted for their failure to satisfy the conditions of categoricalness and determinacy.

In the context of the generic features of action, on the other hand, neither of these variabilities is found. There is no acceptance-variability, for it is not open to any person intentionally to evade or reject the context of action. To be sure, one might try to carry out such rejection by intentionally committing suicide, ingesting sleep-inducing drugs, selling oneself into slavery, and so forth. But not only would this intentional removal of oneself from the context of action obviously carry a crushing price, but moreover the very acts of taking these evading steps would themselves be actions, and hence the necessary conditions of actions, their generic features, would be fulfilled in the very process of removing oneself from further involvement in the context of action. Similarly, if one views actions in terms of their generic features there is no content-variability in the context of actions; for although actions may, of course, be of many different sorts, they all have certain generic features in common, features which are necessarily exhibited by any instance of action, and these necessary features logically generate certain requirements or 'oughts' regardless of the specific differences of kinds of action. Because of this lack of acceptance-variability and content-variability, the 'oughts' derived from the context of the generic features of action have a necessity which enables them to satisfy the conditions of categoricalness and determinacy. I shall, in fact, try to show that the relation of the theory of action to moral philosophy is much closer and more substantive than has hitherto been thought.

It is to be noted that I am here using the word 'action' in a quite strict sense. In this sense, human movements or behaviors are not actions if they occur from one or more of the following kinds of cause: (a) direct compulsion by someone or something external to the person; (b) causes internal to the person, such as reflexes, ignorance, or disease, which decisively contribute, in ways beyond his control, to the occurrence of the behavior; (c) indirect compulsion whereby the person's choice to emit some behavior is forced by someone else's coercion. In contrast to such behaviors, actions in the strict sense have the generic features of being voluntary and purposive. By 'voluntary' I mean that the agent occurrently or dispositionally controls his behavior by his unforced choice, knowing the various proximate circumstances of his action. By 'purposive' I mean that the agent intends to do what he does, envisaging some purpose or goal which may consist either in the performance of the action itself or in some outcome of that performance; in either case, insofar as it is the purpose of his action the agent regards it as some sort of good. These generic features also mean that actions are characterized by freedom and relative well-being on the part of the agent: by freedom in virtue of their uncoerced character and the agent's control over them; by well-being in the relative sense that the agent's purpose is to do or obtain something he regards as good, although not necessarily good in terms either of morality or even of his own self-interest.

The direct relevance of action in the strict sense to the 'Is-Ought' Problem can be seen from the fact that 'ought'-judgments are primarily concerned with action in this sense. When it is said, not only in moral or political precepts but also in prudential, technical, institutional, and other practical precepts, that some person ought to do something, the assumption of the speaker, at least prospectively, is that the person addressed is an actual or potential agent who can control his behavior with a view to achieving the objective set forth in the precept, and that the agent will set some sort of preferred priority either on this objective or on the ones for which he would otherwise act. As this last point indicates, actions in the strict sense include behaviors whereby agents may violate as well as fulfill moral, political, and other practical precepts, and they also include behaviors which are indifferent in relation to such precepts.

In addition to this consideration, the direct rational justification for focusing on the generic features of action is that, being invariable, they impose themselves on every agent, as against the particular contents of his actions which vary with his different and possibly arbitrary inclinations, and also that, being necessary to all action, they take priority for the agent over the particular purposes for which he may contingently act.

Before proceeding to the derivation, I must say something about the method I shall follow. Philosophers have, of course, dealt with and disagreed over the nature of their operations and results; in this regard they have used such phrases as 'rational reconstruction', 'conceptual analysis', 'criteriological connection', 'phenomenological description', 'inductive generalization', and so forth. I cannot, of course, deal with this issue here. But in order to facilitate understanding of what I shall try to do, I should point out that I shall use what I call a dialectically necessary method. My method is dialectical in a sense closely related to that referred to in the Socratic dialogues and in Aristotle: that is, it begins from assumptions, statements, or claims made by protagonists—in this case, the agent—and it examines what these logically imply. The method is dialectically necessary, however, in that the assumptions or claims in question are necessarily made by agents; they reflect not some protagonist's variable opinions, interests, or ideals but rather the necessary structure of purposive action as viewed by the agent. One aspect of this necessity has already been suggested in my statements about the invariability of the context of the generic features of action. On the basis of these necessary contents, I shall show that every agent is logically committed to making or at least accepting certain determinate, categorical moral 'ought'-judgments. Although I shall characterize the steps leading to this logical commitment as entailments, my argument will not be materially affected if the connections in question are interpreted in some less stringent way, so long as their necessary connection with the context of the generic features of action is kept in view.

It will constitute no objection to my use of this method that agents do not necessarily perform speech acts or make linguistic utterances. For on the basis of their actions certain thought-contents can be attributed to them in either direct or indirect discourse. If we see someone running very hard in order to catch a bus, we can safely infer, without stopping him and asking him, that he thinks it is worth his effort to try to catch that bus, just as if we see someone reading a book with avid interest we don't have to see whether he is moving his lips in order to attribute to him such a judgment as, "It is worth my attention reading this book," according to whatever criterion of worth is involved in his purpose of reading. Moreover, although there is in general a difference between entailment-relations among propositions and relations of belief of those propositions—if p entails q, this does not entail that someone's believing that p entails his believing that q—nevertheless I shall here attribute to the agent belief in or acceptance of certain propositions on the basis of their being entailed by other propositions he accepts. The justification for this is that the entailments in question are so direct that awareness of them can safely be attributed to any person who is sufficiently rational to be able to control his behavior by his unforced choice with a view to achieving his purposes.

Enough of preliminaries. I shall now undertake to show how 'ought'-judgments having the five required characteristics are logically derivable from 'is'-statements which describe the occurrence of actions in the strict sense defined above. Although the argument will involve various complexities, some of which I have treated in detail elsewhere, I can indicate enough of the main lines in what follows.

To begin with, that purposive actions occur or that some person performs an action is an empirical fact which can be stated in descriptive, empirical propositions regardless of whether the statements are made by the agent himself or by other persons. As made by the agent himself, the statement may be put formally as, "I do X for purpose E." Although there has been an abortive attempt to argue that assertions of the performance or occurrence of actions are ascriptive rather than descriptive in that they make moral or legal judgments about the agent's responsibility, this attempt has, by general agreement, been definitively refuted.[3] And although some utterances of this form are performatory in Austin's sense, most are not. In a somewhat different direction we can also disregard here Cartesian doubts about the possibility of empirically ascertaining that the choices and purposes involved in action are in fact occurrently or dispositionally present. This disregard is especially warranted because, in accordance with my dialectical method, I shall be considering actions as they are viewed and referred to by the agent himself.

From this empirical premiss, the agent's statement that he performs an action, the derivation will now proceed in four main steps. The first step involves the point that the action as viewed by the agent has, in virtue of its purposiveness, a certain evaluative element. To see this, we must note that action is not a mere physical occurrence in which the entities concerned make no choices and guide themselves for the sake of no purposes. Nor is the agent's attitude toward his action merely a passive or contemplative one; the action is not something that happens to him from causes beyond his control. On the contrary, the agent's relation to the action he brings about is conative and evaluative, for he acts for some purpose which seems to him to be good. In acting, the agent envisages more or less clearly some preferred outcome, some objective or goal which he wants to achieve, where such wanting may be either intentional or inclinational. This goal is regarded by the agent as worth aiming at or pursuing; for if he did not so regard it he would not unforcedly choose to move from quiescence or non-action to action with a view to achieving the goal. This conception of worth constitutes a valuing on the part of the agent; he regards the object of his action as having at least sufficient value to merit his acting to attain it, according to whatever criteria are involved in his action. These criteria of value need not be moral nor even hedonic; they run the full range of the purposes for which the agent acts. Now 'value' in this broad sense is synonymous with 'good' in a similarly broad sense encompassing a wide range of nonmoral as well as moral criteria. Hence, since the agent values, at least instrumentally, the purposes or objects for which he acts, it can also be said that he regards these objects as at least instrumentally good according to whatever criteria lead him to try to achieve his purpose. He may, of course, also regard his purpose as bad on other criteria, and he may regret the narrow range of alternatives open to him among which he chooses. Still, so long as his choice is not forced, by the very fact that he chooses to act he shows that he regards his action as worth performing and hence as good at least relatively to his not acting at all or to his acting for other purposes which are open to him. The

---

[3] See H. I. A. Hart, "The Ascription of Rights and Responsibilities," *Proceedings of the Aristotelian Society*, vol. 49 (1948–49); P. T. Geach, "Ascriptivism," *Philosophical Review*, vol. 69 (1960), pp. 221 ff.; Hart, *Punishment and Responsibility* (Oxford: Clarendon Press, 1968), Preface.

presence of choice and purpose in action thus gives it a structure such that, from the standpoint of the agent, "I do X for purpose E" entails "X and E are good." Since the latter statement is a value-judgment, or at least the function of such a judgment, to this extent from the standpoint of the agent the 'fact-value' gap, even if not the 'is-ought' gap, is already bridged in action.

The agent's positive evaluative judgment extends not only to his particular action and purpose but also to the generic features which characterize all his actions. Since his action is a means to attaining something he regards as good, even if this is only the performance of the action itself, he regards as good the voluntariness or freedom which is an essential feature of his action, for without this he would not be able to act for any purpose at all. He also regards as good those basic aspects of his well-being which are the necessary conditions both of the existence and of the success of all his actions, and which hence are not relative to his particular purposes and not subject to the disagreements that we saw earlier attach to different interpretations of well-being as a whole. This basic well-being comprises certain physical and psychological dispositions ranging from life and physical integrity to a feeling of confidence as to the general possibility of attaining one's goals.

In connection with this point, it should be noted that whereas the eudae-monist derivation considered above, like other naturalistic doctrines, left itself open to the objection that what it regards as well-being is not really good or is not considered good by some persons, my present argument does not incur this objection. For, being dialectical, the argument proceeds from within the standpoint of the agent himself and his own purposes and conceptions of well-being, whatever they may be. But as against the means-end derivation considered above, my argument, being dialectically *necessary*, does not depend for its direct content upon the contingent and variable purposes which different persons may have and the means required for these; it depends rather upon the necessary means which are required for any purposive actions, and which any agent must therefore regard as good. Thus, because freedom and basic well-being are at least instrumentally necessary to all the agent's actions for purposes, from the agent's standpoint his statement, "I do X for purpose E" entails not only "X and E are good" but also "My freedom and basic well-being are good as the necessary conditions of all my actions."

From this first main step there follows a second, bearing on justifications and right-claims. In virtue of his positive evaluations the agent regards himself as justified in performing his actions and in having the freedom and basic well-being which generically figure in all his actions, and he implicitly makes a corresponding right-claim. To regard something as justified on some criterion is to hold that its rightness is or can be established according to that criterion, and to have toward it a corresponding attitude of endorsement. Now an important, even if not the only, basis of an action's being right from the standpoint of its agent is that he regards it as having a good purpose. The agent therefore regards his action as justified by this goodness. But, *a fortiori*, he especially regards himself as justified in having freedom and basic well-being, since these are the necessary conditions of all his actions and hence of any purposes or goals he may attain or pursue through action.

This justificatory attitude takes the logical form of a claim on the part of the agent that he has a right to perform his actions and to have freedom and basic well-being. Even if there is not in every case a correct inference from an agent's regarding X as good to his claiming a right to X, the inference does hold from within the agent's standpoint insofar as X consists in freedom and basic well-being, because of the strategic relation of these goods to all his purposive actions. In the case of every claim to have a right to X, a necessary condition is that X seem directly or indirectly good to the claimant, and a sufficient condition is that he regard X as a basic good such as is required for his pursuit of any other goods. For it is central to the concept of a right, at least where it is advanced as a claim by individuals, that its primary, even if not its only, application is to the proximate prerequisites of any purposive actions, since without the direct capacity for such action the claimant, beyond making the claim itself, would not be able to move toward anything he regards as good. It is this elemental aspect of right-claims that seems to me to underlie Jefferson's asserting as self-evident that all men have inalienable rights to life, liberty, and the pursuit of happiness. Put in the dialectically necessary terms I am using here, this says that since every agent regards as basic goods the freedom and basic well-being which are the proximate necessary conditions of his acting for the achievement of any of his purposes, and since the criterion of claiming justifications and rights, so far as the agent is concerned, consists in the first instance in such proximate necessary conditions, it follows that any agent must claim, at least implicitly, that he has a right to freedom and basic well-being. And this right-claim is prescriptive: it carries the agent's advocacy or endorsement.

According to this second main step, then, action as viewed by the agent has a normative as well as an evaluative structure, in that it involves right-claims as well as judgments of good. From the agent's standpoint, his judgment "My freedom and basic well-being are good as the necessary conditions of all my actions" entails "I have a right to freedom and basic well-being"[4] This second step is, of course, crucial for the 'is-ought' derivation, since the normative concept of having a right either already is, or is directly translatable into, a deontic concept. Nevertheless, in order to show how all five conditions of the real 'Is-Ought' Problem are to be satisfied, I must go through two further steps.

The third main step involves the consideration that, given the agent's claim that he has a right to freedom and basic well-being, he is logically committed to a generalization of this right-claim to all prospective agents and hence to all persons. To see this, we must note that every right-claim is made on behalf of some person or group with an at least implicit recognition of the description

---

[4] For more detailed arguments for the above two steps, see my "The Normative Structure of Action," *Review of Metaphysics*, vol. 25 (1971), pp. 238 ff.

or sufficient reason which is held to ground the right. This description or sufficient reason may be quite general or quite particular, but in any case the person who claims some right must admit, on pain of contradiction, that this right also belongs to any other persons to whom that description or reason applies. This necessity is an exemplification of the logical principle of universalizability: if some predicate P belongs to some subject S because S has the property Q (where the 'because' is that of sufficient reason or condition), then P must also belong to all other subjects S_1, S_2, . . . S_n which have Q. If one denies this implication in the case of some individual, such as S_1, which has Q, then one contradicts oneself, for in saying that P belongs to S because S has Q one implies that all Q is P, but in denying this in the case of S_1, which has Q, one says that some Q is not P.

The crucial question in the present context concerns the description or sufficient reason which the agent adduces as decisively relevant in claiming that he has a right to freedom and basic well-being. Many philosophers have held that there is no logical limit in this respect, that any agent can choose whatever description or sufficient reason he likes without committing any logical error. He may claim that he has the rights in question because and only because, for example, he is white or male or American or a philosopher or an atheist, or for that matter because he is named Wordsworth Donisthorpe or because he was born on such and such a date at such and such a place, and so forth. And, of course, depending on the property he adduces as a sufficient reason for his right-claim, he will be logically required to grant only that these rights belong to all other persons who have this property, including, at the extreme, the class consisting only of one member, himself.

In opposition to this view, I hold that the agent logically must adduce only a certain description or sufficient reason as the ground of his claim that he has a right to freedom and basic well-being. This description or sufficient reason is that he is a prospective agent who has purposes he wants to fulfill. If the agent adduces anything less general than this as his exclusive justifying description, then, by the preceding argument, he can be shown to contradict himself. Let us designate by the letter R such a more restrictive description. Examples of R would include, "My name is Wordsworth Donisthorpe" and the other descriptions just mentioned. Now let us ask the agent whether, while being an agent, he would still claim to have the rights of freedom and basic well-being even if he were not R. If he answers yes, then he contradicts his assertion that he has these rights only insofar as he is R. He would hence have to admit that he is mistaken in restricting his justificatory description to R. But if he answers no, i.e. if he says that while being an agent he would not claim these rights if he were not R, then he can be shown to contradict himself with regard to the generic features of action. For, as we have seen, it is necessarily true of every agent both that he requires freedom and basic well-being in order to act and that he hence implicitly claims the right to have freedom and basic well-being. For an agent not to claim these rights would mean that he does not act for purposes he regards as good at all and that he does not regard his actions, with their necessary conditions of freedom and basic well-being, as justified by the goodness of his purpose. But this in turn would mean that he is not an agent, which contradicts the initial assumption. Thus, to avoid contradicting himself, the agent must admit that he would claim to have the rights of freedom and basic well-being even if he were not R, and hence that the description or sufficient reason for which he claims these rights is not anything less general than that he is a prospective agent who has purposes he wants to fulfill.[5]

It is also this generality that explains why, in the necessary description or sufficient reason of his having these rights, I have referred to a '*prospective* agent who has purposes he wants to fulfill.' For the agent claims these rights not only in his present action with its particular purpose but in all his actions. To restrict to his present purpose his reason for claiming the rights of freedom and basic well-being would be to overlook the fact that he regards these as goods in respect of all his actions and purposes, not only his present one.

Since, then, the agent, in order to avoid contradicting himself, must claim that he has the rights of freedom and basic well-being for the sufficient reason that he is a prospective agent who has purposes he wants to fulfill, he logically must accept the generalization that all prospective agents who have purposes they want to fulfill, and hence all persons, have the rights of freedom and basic well-being. This generalization is a direct application of the principle of universalizability; and if the agent denies the generalization, then, as we have seen, he contradicts himself. For on the one hand in holding, as he logically must, that he has the rights of freedom and basic well-being because he is a prospective purposive agent, he implies that all prospective purposive agents have these rights; but on the other hand he holds that some prospective purposive agent does not have these rights.

I shall henceforth refer to the agent who avoids such contradictions, and who hence accepts the opposed logically necessary statements, as a 'rational agent.' It will be noted that this is the minimal and most basic sense of 'rational' as applied to persons and that its criterion is a purely logical one, involving consistency or the avoidance of self-contradiction. Thus we have seen that, by virtue of accepting the statement "I have a right to freedom and basic well-being," the rational agent must also accept "I have these rights for the sufficient reason that I am a prospective purposive agent," and hence that "All prospective purposive agents have a right to freedom and basic well-being." The rational agent must therefore advocate or endorse these rights for all other persons on the same ground as he advocates them for himself.

The fourth and final main step moves directly from this generalized right-claim to a correlative 'ought'-judgment. For all rights are logically correlative with at least negative duties or 'oughts', in that for any person A to have a right to have or do something X entails that all other persons ought to refrain from interfering either with A's having or doing X or at least with A's trying to have or do X. Hence, since the agent logically had to admit that "All pro-

---

[5] I have presented this and related arguments more fully in "The Justification of Egalitarian Justice," *American Philosophical Quarterly*, vol. 8 (1971), pp. 331 ff., and in *Moral Rationality*, The Lindley Lecture for 1972 (University of Kansas, 1972).

spective purposive agents have a right to freedom and basic well-being," he must also logically accept the 'ought'-judgment, "I ought to refrain from interfering with the freedom and basic well-being of all prospective purposive agents," and hence of all persons. Interference with their freedom would constitute coercion; interference with their basic well-being would constitute basic harm. Thus we have seen that from the initial empirical premiss, "I do X for purpose E," there logically follows the 'ought'-judgment, "I ought to refrain from coercing other persons or inflicting basic harm on them." The agent is logically compelled to admit these 'oughts', on pain of contradiction.

The general principle of these 'oughts' or duties may be expressed as the following precept addressed to every agent: *Apply to your recipient the same generic features of action that you apply to yourself.* I shall call this the *Principle of Generic Consistency (PGC)*, since it combines the formal consideration of consistency, as found in the above universalization argument, with the material consideration of the generic features of action, including the right-claims which the agent necessarily makes. The *PGC* is an egalitarian universalist moral principle since it requires an equal distribution of the most basic rights of action. It says to every agent that just as, in acting, he necessarily applies to himself and claims as rights for himself the generic features of action, voluntariness or freedom and purposiveness at least in the sense of basic well-being, so he ought to apply these same generic features to all the recipients of his actions by allowing them also to have freedom and basic well-being and hence by refraining from coercing them or inflicting basic harm on them. This means that the agent ought to be impartial as between himself and other persons when the latter's freedom and basic well-being are at stake, so that he ought to respect other persons' freedom and basic well-being as well as his own. And as we have seen, if the agent denies or violates this principle, then he contradicts himself.

The *PGC* has as direct or indirect logical consequences egalitarian moral 'ought'-judgments of the paradigmatic sort that I presented at the outset. Given the *PGC*, there directly follows the negative duty not to inflict serious gratuitous harm on other persons. There also directly follows the positive duty to perform such actions as rescuing drowning persons or feeding starving persons, especially when this can be done at relatively little cost to oneself. For the *PGC* prohibits inflicting basic harms on other persons; but to refrain from performing such actions as rescuing and feeding in the circumstances described would be to inflict basic harms on the persons in need and would hence violate the impartiality required by the *PGC*. It would mean that while the agent participates in the situation voluntarily and with basic well-being, not to mention his other purposes, he prevents his recipients from doing so. Although there is indeed a distinction between causing a basic harm to occur and merely permitting it to occur by one's inaction, such intentional inaction in the described circumstances is itself an action that interferes with the basic well-being of the persons in need. For it prevents, by means under the agent's control and with his knowledge, the occurrence of transactions which would remove the basic harms in question.

The *PGC* also has as its indirect consequences sociopolitical moral 'ought'-judgments requiring actions in support of civil liberties and in opposition to great inequalities of wealth and power. While I do not have the time now to go into such institutional applications, the general point is that since the *PGC* requires an equal distribution of the most basic rights of action, freedom and basic well-being, it also requires legal, political, and economic institutions which foster such libertarian and egalitarian rights, and it hence requires actions which support such institutions. Unlike the direct institutional derivations considered earlier, if the obligations grounded in various institutions are to be justified, then the institutions themselves must first be justifiable through the *PGC*.[6] And it is by rules based on such justified institutions that conflicts arising from agents' use of their freedom are to be resolved.

This, then, concludes my argument. So far as concerns the particular paradigmatic moral 'ought'-judgments which I presented at the outset, I have not derived them directly from their antecedent 'is'-statements about B's starving and so forth; rather I have treated these combinations as enthymemes having such specific 'ought'-premisses as: "Whenever some person is starving and someone else can relieve him at no comparable cost to himself, he ought to do so." These 'ought'-premisses, however, follow from the *PGC*, and the *PGC* in turn follows, through the steps I have indicated, from the 'is'-statement made by the agent that he performs actions for purposes. Hence, the particular moral 'ought'-judgments have been derived, through several intermediate steps, from an empirical 'is'-statement.

I have here presented, then, a complex version of what I have called the internal model of the relation between 'ought' and 'is'. I have not directly defined 'ought' in terms of 'is'; rather, I have held that the application of 'ought' is entailed by the correlative concept of having a right. The agent's application of this concept, in turn, has been derived from the concept of goods which are the necessary conditions of all his actions, since he necessarily claims that he has a right to at least these goods. And the agent's application of the concept of good, finally, has been derived from his acting for purposes. Since the agent's assertion that he acts for purposes is an empirical, descriptive statement, I have in this indirect way derived 'ought' from 'is'. Whether the derivation is at each point definitional or is rather of some other non-arbitrary sort does not materially affect my argument, so long as its necessary relation to the context of action is recognized.

If this derivation has been successful, if it constitutes a resolution of the real 'Is-Ought' Problem, then the 'ought'-judgments which I have derived have the five characteristics indicated in my first section. Let us examine whether this is so. We have already seen that the *PGC* and the more specific 'ought'-judgments that follow from it are moral and egalitarian. They are also prescriptive, since they follow logically from the agent's prescriptive claim that he has a

---

[6] For fuller discussion of how institutional obligations are derived from the *PGC*, see my "Obligation: Political, Legal, Moral," *op. cit.*, (above, n. 10). See also my "Categorial Consistency in Ethics," *Philosophical Quarterly*, vol. 17 (1967), pp. 289 ff.

right to freedom and basic well-being. And they are determinate, for they rule out the coercion and basic harm which we saw were permitted by other 'is-ought' derivations.

It may be questioned, however, whether the condition of categoricalness has been satisfied. The objection would be that there is a conflict between the categorical and the dialectical. Since my argument has been dialectical in that it proceeds from within the standpoint of the agent, including the evaluations and right-claims he makes, the *PGC* and the ensuing ought-judgments I have derived are valid, so holds the objection, only relatively to the agent's stand-point, but not absolutely. Even if the agent is logically compelled to uphold certain 'ought'-judgments, given his initial statement that he performs actions for purposes, this does not establish that those judgments are really correct or binding. Hence, their 'oughts' are not categorical.

My reply to this objection is that the dialectically *necessary* aspect of my method gives the 'ought'-conclusions a more than contingent or hypothetical status. Since moral 'oughts' apply only or primarily to the context of action and hence to agents, to have shown that certain 'ought'-judgments logically must be granted by all agents, on pain of contradiction, is to give the judgments an absolute status since their validity is logically ineluctable within the whole context of their possible application. It will be recalled that in my original specification I said that for 'ought'-judgments to be categorical the normative bindingness of the requirements they set forth cannot be removed or evaded by variable, escapable features of the persons addressed, including their self-interested desires or their contingent choices, opinions, and attitudes. This condition of categoricalness is fulfilled by the *PGC*'s 'ought'-judgment.

This necessity also explicates the respect in which moral judgments have truth-value. The *PGC* and the moral judgments that follow from it are true in that they correspond to the concept of a rational agent, for they indicate what logically must be admitted by such an agent. As I noted above, the criterion of 'rational' here is a purely logical one.

Finally, what of the condition of non-circularity? Although my argument began from the agent's empirical statements that he performs actions, I then pointed out that actions as viewed by him have certain ineluctable evaluative and normative elements. Doesn't this mean that I have reached a normative or at least a prescriptive 'ought'-conclusion only by putting normativeness or prescriptiveness into my premiss about action? It was this question that figured in the 'dilemma of commitment' that I presented above. Now an assumption of this dilemma was that for any person who undertakes to derive 'ought' from 'is' within some context, it is open to him to choose or to refrain from choosing to commit himself to that context with its requirements. As we have seen, however, it is impossible intentionally to refrain from committing oneself to the context of the generic features of action, for any such refraining would itself exhibit those features. Hence, the 'ought' which is derived within that context is prescriptive; but nevertheless the derivation is not circular, because the derived 'ought' reflects not a dispensable choice or commitment but rather a necessity which is not subject to any choice or decision on the part of the agent. The objector hence cannot say, "You've reached a commitment or pre-scription in the conclusion only because you've already chosen to put the com-mitment or prescription into your premiss;" for the latter commitment in the premiss is not one that the deriver has *chosen* or has *put into* the premiss. Rather, the commitment is there in the nature of the case, and all he is doing is recognize it; but he cannot evade it. In any event, as already noted, the initial premiss of the derivation is the agent's empirical statement that he performs actions for purposes; and the prescriptiveness of the moral 'ought'-conclusion is accounted for more specifically by the advocacy embodied in his right-claim together with its logical generalization.

What I have tried to show here, then, is that the 'is' of the performance of actions having the generic features logically generates the 'ought' of categorical moral judgments; or, in other words, that the fact of being a purposive agent logically requires, on pain of self-contradiction, an acknowledgment that one ought to act in certain basic moral ways. To summarize: Because actions are conative and value-pursuing, they commit the agent to advocate or endorse for himself the rights of freedom and basic well-being which are the proximate necessary prerequisites of all his acting; hence, he makes judgments which fulfill the condition of prescriptiveness. Because the agent must advocate these rights for general reasons stemming from his simply being a prospective purposive agent, his advocacy must logically be extended to all other persons; hence, his judgments fulfill the conditions of being moral and egalitarian. And because this extension is based on the generic and hence inescapable features of action, it logically cannot be evaded or reversed regardless of any variable desires, choices, or attitudes on the part of the agent; hence, his judgments fulfill the conditions of determinacy and categoricalness. In this way, then, by an analysis of the generic features of action and their normative implications, I have argued that the real 'Is-Ought' Problem is resolved.

24

The Moral Point of View

KURT BAIER

Kurt Baier (b. 1917) is Professor of Philosophy at the University of Pittsburgh. This selection is taken from Baier's major work, The Moral Point of View.

In the selection, Baier attempts to provide a test of truth for moral convictions. In Baier's view, such convictions are true if they are acceptable from the moral point of view. That point of view is the "highest court of appeal" for adjudicating conflicts of interest. As such, it cannot be the same as the perspective of self-interest. Rather, it requires a commitment to principles that apply to all, and that are for the good of everyone alike. According to Baier, our behavior fails to be for the good of everyone alike if we treat others as we do not want them to treat us, and also (roughly) if we violate societal rules whose violation by everyone would be undesirable.

Why should we take the moral point of view? Since self-interested reasons may not apply, and since moral reasons would be circular, this question may seem unanswerable. But Baier argues that there is an answer. Though subject to interpretation, his argument appears to be that because we and all others benefit from the general existence of morality, we have reason to conform to the moral rules acknowledged by others even when doing so will not benefit us. For a related discussion to which Baier acknowledges a substantial debt, see reading 18 by Thomas Hobbes.

WHAT, THEN, IS the test (if any) which a moral conviction must pass in order to be called true? Many philosophers have held that there is not and cannot be such a test. They would perhaps admit that we may reduce our moral convictions to a few basic moral principles, or perhaps even only one, from which all others can be derived, but they would hold that at least one such principle must simply be selected as we please. Such basic principles are matters for deciding, not for finding out.

I shall argue, on the contrary, that our moral convictions are true if they can be seen to be required or acceptable *from the moral point of view*. It is indeed true that a person must adopt the moral point of view if he is to be moral. But it is not true that this is an arbitrary decision. On the contrary, I shall show, in Chapter Twelve, that there are the very best reasons for adopting this point of view.

Answers to practical questions can be arrived at by reference to a point of view, which may be defined by a principle. When we adopt a certain point of view, we adopt its defining principle. To look at practical problems from that point of view is to be prepared to answer practical questions of the form 'What shall I do?' 'What should be done?' by reference to its defining principle.

Suppose the problem under discussion is whether or not a certain traffic roundabout should be erected at a certain intersection. I can look at this from various points of view, that of a pedestrian or a motorist, a local politician or a manufacturer of roundabouts, and so on. In cases such as these, we have in mind the point of view of self-interest as applied to certain special positions or jobs or functions in a society. To look at our problem from the point of view of a motorist is to ask whether the erection of a roundabout at this intersection is in the interest of a motorist. For different points of view there may, of course, be different, even opposing, answers to the same practical questions. The roundabout may be in the interest of a motorist but not of a pedestrian, in the interest of a manufacturer of roundabouts but not of a local politician who depends for his votes on the poorer section (the pedestrians) of the population.

However, a point of view is not necessarily defined by the principle of self-interest or its more specific application to a particular position in society. We can, for instance, look at this problem from the point of view of town planners or traffic experts, who may favor the roundabout because their special task is to solve traffic problems. Their point of view is defined by the principle 'Favor anything that keeps the traffic flowing; oppose anything that is likely to cause traffic holdups.' But the erection of the roundabout can hardly be said to be *in their interest.* They do not derive any personal advantage or benefit from the scheme. There are many such disinterested points of view, for example, the point of view of a social worker, a social reformer, an advocate of public health schemes, a missionary.

A person is of good will if he adopts the moral point of view as supreme, that is, as overriding all other points of view. When asking the question 'What shall I do?' or 'What is to be done?' such a person will always engage in moral deliberation, survey and weigh the moral considerations, and give them greater weight than any others. A person has adopted the moral point of view when he reviews the facts in the light of *his* moral convictions. We do not require him to test his moral convictions every time, but only because we presume that he already has true moral convictions. This presumption may be false. He may simply have accepted without much questioning the moral convictions of his group, or he may have departed from them without getting any nearer the truth. In such a case, he merely *means* to adopt the moral point of view, but has not succeeded. He has adopted something which he wrongly believes to be the moral point of view. He must still be called a person of good will because of his intentions, but he cannot arrive at true answers to his question.

Clearly, our central problem is to define the moral point of view.

. . .

Throughout the history of philosophy, by far the most popular candidate for the position of the moral point of view has been self-interest. There are obvious parallels between these two standpoints. Both aim at the good. Both are rational. Both involve deliberation, the surveying and weighing of reasons. The adoption of either yields statements containing the word 'ought.' Both involve the notion of self-mastery and control over the desires. It is, moreover, plausible to hold that a person could not have a reason for doing anything whatsoever unless his behavior was designed to promote his own good. Hence, if morality is to have the support of reason, moral reasons must be self-interested, hence the point of view of morality and self-interest must be the same. On the other hand, it seems equally obvious that morality and self-interest are very frequently opposed. Morality often requires us to refrain from doing what self-interest recommends or to do what self-interest forbids. Hence morality and self-interest cannot be the same points of view.

Self-Interest and Morality

Can we save the doctrine that the moral point of view is that of self-interest? One way of circumventing the difficulty just mentioned is to draw a distinction between two senses of 'self-interest,' shortsighted and enlightened. The shortsighted egoist always follows his short-range interest without taking into consideration how this will affect others and how their reactions will affect him. The enlightened egoist, on the other hand, knows that he cannot get the most out of life unless he pays attention to the needs of others on whose good will he depends. On this view, the standpoint of (immoral) egoism differs from that of morality in that it fails to consider the interests of others even when this costs little or nothing or when the long-range benefits to oneself are likely to be greater than the short-range sacrifices.

This view can be made more plausible still if we distinguish between those egoists who consider each course of action on its own merits and those who, for convenience, adopt certain rules of thumb which they have found will promote their long-range interest. Slogans such as 'Honesty is the best policy,' 'Give to charity rather than to the Department of Internal Revenue,' 'Always give a penny to a beggar when you are likely to be watched by your acquaintances,' 'Treat your servants kindly and they will work for you like slaves,' 'Never be arrogant to anyone—you may need his services one day,' are maxims of this sort. They embody the "wisdom" of a given society. The enlightened long-range egoist may adopt these as rules of thumb, that is, as *prima-facie* maxims, as rules which he will observe unless he has good evidence that departing from them will pay him better than abiding by them. It is obvious that the rules of behavior adopted by the enlightened egoist will be very similar to those of a man who rigidly follows our own moral code.

Sidgwick appears to believe that egoism is one of the legitimate "methods of ethics," although he himself rejects it on the basis of an "intuition" that it is false. He supports the legitimacy of egoism by the argument that everyone could consistently adopt the egoistic point of view. "I quite admit that when the painful necessity comes for another man to choose between his own happiness and the general happiness, he must as a reasonable being prefer his own, i.e. it is right for him to do this on my principle."[1] The consistent enlightened egoist satisfies the categorical imperative, or at least one version of it, 'Act only on that maxim whereby thou canst at the same time will that it should become a universal law.'

However, no "intuition" is required to see that this is not the point of view of morality, even though it can be universally adopted without self-contradiction. In the first place, a consistent egoist adopts for all occasions the principle 'everyone for himself' which we allow (at most) only in conditions of chaos, when the normal moral order breaks down. Its adoption marks the return to the law of the jungle, the state of nature, in which the "softer," "more chivalrous" ways of morality have no place.[2]

This point can be made more strictly. It can be shown that those who adopt consistent egoism cannot make moral judgments. Moral talk is impossible for consistent egoists. But this amounts to a *reductio ad absurdum* of consistent egoism.

Let B and K be candidates for the presidency of a certain country and let it be granted that it is in the interest of either to be elected, but that only one can succeed. It would then be in the interest of B but against the interest of K if B were elected, and vice versa, and therefore in the interest of B but against the interst of K if K were liquidated, and vice versa. But from this it would follow that B ought to liquidate K, that it is wrong for B not to do so, that B has not "done his duty" until he has liquidated K; and vice versa. Similarly K, knowing that his own liquidation is in the interest of B and therefore anticipating B's attempts to secure it, ought to take steps to foil B's endeavors. It would be wrong for him not to do so. He would "not have done his duty" until he had made sure of stopping B. It follows that if K prevents B from liquidating him, his act must be said to be both wrong and not wrong—wrong because it is the prevention of what B ought to do, his duty, and wrong for B not to do it; not wrong because it is what K ought to do, his duty, and wrong for K not to do it. But one and the same act (logically) cannot be both morally wrong and not morally wrong. Hence in cases like these morality does not apply.

This is obviously absurd. For morality is designed to apply in just such cases, namely, those where interests conflict. But if the point of view of morality were that of self-interest, then there could *never* be moral solutions of conflicts of interest. However, when there are conflicts of interest, we always look for a "higher" point of view, one from which such conflicts can be settled. Consistent egoism makes everyone's private interest the "highest court of appeal." But by 'the moral point of view' we *mean* a point of view which is a court of appeal for conflicts of interest. Hence it cannot (logically) be identical with the point of view of self-interest. Sidgwick is, therefore, wrong in thinking that consistent

---

[1] Henry Sidgwick, *The Methods of Ethics*, 7th ed. (London: Macmillan and Co., 1907), pref. to the 6th ed., p. xvii.

[2] See below, Chapter Twelve, section 3.

egoism is one of the "legitimate methods of ethics." He is wrong in thinking that an "intuition" is required to see that it is not the correct moral point of view. That it is not can be seen in the same way in which we can "see" that the Court of Petty Sessions is not the Supreme Court.

Morality Involves Doing Things on Principle

Another feature of consistent egoism is that the rules by which a consistent egoist abides are merely rules of thumb. A consistent egoist has only one supreme principle, to do whatever is necessary for the realization of his one aim, the promotion of his interest. He does not have *principles*, he has only an aim. If one has adopted the moral point of view, then one acts on principle and not merely on rules of thumb designed to promote one's aim. This involves conforming to the rules whether or not doing so favors one's own or anyone else's aim.

Kant grasped this point even if only obscurely. He saw that adopting the moral point of view involves acting on principle. It involves conforming to rules even when doing so is unpleasant, painful, costly, or ruinous to oneself. Kant, furthermore, argued rightly that, since moral action is action on principle (and not merely in accordance with rules of thumb), a moral agent ought not to make exceptions in his own favor, and he interpreted this to mean that moral rules are absolutely inflexible and without exceptions. Accordingly he concluded that if 'Thou shalt not kill' states a moral rule, then any and every act correctly describable as an act of killing someone must be said to be morally wrong.

Kant also saw that this view required him to reject some of our deepest moral convictions; we certainly think that the killing of a man in self-defense or by the hangman is not morally wrong. Kant was prepared to say that our moral convictions are wrong on this point. Can we salvage these moral convictions? The only alternative, to say that acting on principle does not require us not to make exceptions in our own favor, seems to be equally untenable.

It is therefore not surprising that many philosophers have abandoned Kant's (and the commonsense) view that the moral rightness of an act is its property of being in accordance with a moral rule or principle. Thus, the deontologists claim that rightness is a simple property which we can "see" or "intuit" in an act, and the utilitarians, that rightness is a complex property, namely, the tendency of an act to promote the greatest happiness of the greatest number. But, as is well known, these accounts are not plausible and lead to considerable difficulties.

However, this whole problem arises only because of a confusion, the confusion of the expression 'making an exception to a rule' with the expression 'a rule has an exception.' As soon as this muddle is cleared away it can be seen that Kant is right in saying that acting on principle implies making no exception in anyone's favor, but wrong in thinking that therefore all moral rules must be absolutely without exception.

'No parking in the city' has a number of recognized exceptions which are part of the rule itself, for example, 'except in the official parking areas,' 'except in front of a parking meter,' 'except on Saturday mornings and after 8 P.M. every day.' A person who does not know the recognized exceptions does not completely know the rule, for these exceptions more precisely define its range of application. A policeman who is not booking a motorist parking in front of a parking meter is not granting exemption to (making an exception in favor of) this motorist. On the contrary, he is administering the rule correctly. If he did apply the no-parking rule to the motorist, *he* would be applying it where *it* does not apply, because this is one of the recognized exceptions which are *part of* the rule. On the other hand, a policeman who does not book a motorist parking his vehicle in a prohibited area at peak hour on a busy day is making an exception in the motorist's favor. If he does so because the man is his friend, he illegitimately grants an exemption. If he does so because the motorist is a doctor who has been called to attend to a man lying unconscious on the pavement, this is a "deserving case" and he grants the exemption legitimately.

Apply this distinction to the rules of a given morality. Notice first that moral rules differ from laws and regulations in that they are not administered by special administrative organs such as policemen and magistrates. Everyone "administers" them himself. Nevertheless, it makes sense to speak of making exceptions in one's own favor. For one may refuse to apply the rule to oneself when one knows that it does apply, that is to say, one may refuse to observe it even when one knows one should. And what is true of making exceptions in one's own favor is true also of making them in favor of someone else. It is almost as immoral to make exceptions in favor of one's wife, son, or nephew as in favor of oneself.

When we say, therefore, that a person who has killed a burglar in self-defense has not done anything wrong, we are not making an exception in the house-owner's favor. It is much nearer the truth to say that, in our morality, the rule 'Thou shalt not kill' *has several recognized exceptions*, among them 'in self-defense.' We can say that a man does not know fully our moral rule 'Thou shalt not kill' if he does not know that it has, among others, this exception.

Like other rules of reason, our moral convictons are so only *presumptively*. Killing is wrong *unless* it is killing in self-defense, killing by the hangman, killing of an enemy in wartime, accidental killing, and possibly mercy killing. If it is one of these types of killing, then it is *not* wrong.

Even if it is one of the wrongful acts of killing, it is so only *prima facie*, other things being equal. For there may have been an overriding moral reason in favor of killing the man, for example, that he is about to blow up a train and that this is the only way of stopping him.

One further point should be made to avoid misunderstanding. Unlike laws and regulations, moral rules have not been laid down by anyone. Knowing moral rules cannot, therefore, involve knowing exactly what a certain person has enjoined and forbidden and what exceptions he has allowed, because there is no such person. In the case of regulations and laws, it was precisely this

knowledge which enabled us to draw the distinction between saying that someone was granting an exception and saying that he was merely applying the
rule which, for cases of this sort, provided for an exception. Our distinction
seems to collapse for moral rules.

However, the answer to this is simple. When a magistrate is empowered to
make exceptions or grant exemptions in "deserving cases," the question of
what is a "deserving case" is not of course answered in the regulation itself. If
it were, the magistrate would not be exercising his power to grant exemption,
but would simply apply the regulation as provided in it. How, then, does the
magistrate or policeman know what is a deserving case? The doctor who parks
his car in a prohibited spot in order to attend to an injured man is such a case,
namely, a *morally deserving* case. The principles in accordance with which
policemen or magistrates grant exemptions to existing regulations are moral
principles. In the case of moral rules, there cannot be any distinction between
exceptions which are part of the rule and deserving cases. *Only* deserving cases
can be part of the moral rule, and *every* deserving case is properly part of it.
Hence while in the case of laws and regulations there is a reason for going
beyond the exceptions allowed in the regulation itself (when there is a morally
deserving instance), in the case of moral rules there is no such reason. For all
deserving cases are, from the nature of the case, part of the moral rule itself.
Hence it is never right to make an exception to a moral rule in anyone's favor.
Kant is therefore quite right in saying that it is always wrong to make exceptions
to moral rules in one's own favor (and for that matter in anyone else's), but
he is wrong in thinking that this makes moral rules inflexible.

All this follows from the very nature of moral principles. They are binding
on everyone alike quite irrespective of what are the goals or purposes of the
person in question. Hence self-interest cannot be the moral point of view, for
it sets every individual one supreme goal, his own interest, which overrules all
his other maxims.

Moral Rules Are Meant for Everybody

The point of view of morality is inadequately characterized by saying that
I have adopted it if *I* act on principles, that is, on rules to which I do not make
exceptions whenever acting on them would frustrate one or the other of my
purposes or desires. It is characterized by greater universality than that. It must
be thought of as a standpoint from which principles are considered as being
acted on *by everyone.* Moral principles are not merely principles on which a
person must always act without making exceptions, but they are principles
meant for everybody.

It follows from this that the teaching of morality must be completely universal and open. Morality is meant to be taught to all members of the group
in such a way that everyone can and ought always to act in accordance with
these rules. It is not the preserve of an oppressed or privileged class or individual. People are neglecting their duties if they do not teach the moral rules to

their children. Chidlren are removed from the homes of criminals because they are not likely to be taught the moral rules there. Furthermore, moral rules must be taught quite openly and to everybody without discrimination. An esoteric code, a set of precepts known only to the initiated and perhaps jealously concealed from outsiders, can at best be a religion, not a morality. 'Thou shalt not eat beans and this is a secret' or 'Always leave the third button of your waistcoat undone, but don't tell anyone except the initiated members' may be part of an esoteric religion, but not of a morality. 'Thou shalt not kill, but it is a strict secret' is absurd. 'Esoteric morality' is a contradiction in terms. It is no accident that the so-called higher religions were imbued with the missionary spirit, for they combine the beliefs of daemons and gods and spirits characteristic of primitive religions with *a system of morality*. Primitive religions are not usually concerned to proselytize. On the contrary, they are imbued with the spirit of the exclusive trade secret. If one thinks of one's religion as concentrated wisdom of life revealed solely to the *chosen* people, one will regard it as the exclusive property of the club, to be confined to the elect. If, on the other hand, the rules are thought to be for everyone, one must in consistency want to spread the message.

The condition of universal teachability yields . . . other criteria of moral rules. They must not, in the first place, be "self-frustrating." They are so if their purpose is frustrated as soon as everybody acts on them, if they have a point only when a good many people act on the opposite principle. Someone might, for instance, act on the maxim 'When you are in need, ask for help, but never help another man when he is in need.' If everybody adopted this principle, then their adoption of the second half would frustrate what obviously is the point of the adoption of the first half, namely, to get help when one is in need. Although such a principle is not self-contradictory—for anybody could consistently adopt it—it is nevertheless objectionable from the moral point of view, for it could not be taught openly to everyone. It would then lose its point. It is a parasitic principle, useful to anyone only if many people act on its opposite.

The same is true of "self-defeating" and "morally impossible" rules. A principle is self-defeating if its point is defeated as soon as a person lets it be known that he has adopted it, for example, the principle 'Give a promise even when you know or think that you can never keep it, or when you don't intend to keep it.' The very point of giving promises is to reassure and furnish a guarantee to the promisee. Hence any remark that throws doubt on the sincerity of the promiser will defeat the purpose of making a promise. And clearly to *let it be known* that one gives promises even when one knows or thinks one cannot, or when one does not intend to keep them, is to raise such doubts. And to say that one acts on the above principle is to imply that one may well give promises in these cases. Hence to reveal that one acts on this principle will tend to defeat one's own purpose.

It has already been said that moral rules must be capable of being taught openly, but this rule is self-defeating when taught openly, for then everyone would be known to act on it. Hence it cannot belong to the morality of any group.

339

Moral Rules Must Be for the Good of Everyone Alike

The conditions so far mentioned are merely formal. They exclude certain sorts of rule as not coming up to the formal requirements. But moral rules should also have a certain sort of content. Observation of these rules should be *for the good of everyone alike*. Thrasymachus' view that justice is the advantage of the stronger, if true of the societies of his day, is an indictment of their legal systems from the moral point of view. It shows that what goes by the name of morality in these societies is no more than a set of rules and laws which enrich the ruling class at the expense of the masses. But this is wrong because unjust, however much the rules satisfy the formal criteria. For given certain initial social conditions, formal equality before the law may favor certain groups and exploit others.

There is one obvious way in which a rule may be for the good of everyone alike, namely, if it furthers the common good. When I am promoted and my salary is raised, this is to my advantage. It will also be to the advantage of my wife and my family and possibly of a few other people—it will not be to the advantage of my colleague who had hoped for promotion but is now excluded. It may even be to his detriment if his reputation suffers as a result. If the coal miners obtain an increase in their wages, then this is to the advantage of coal miners. It is for their common good. But it may not be to the advantage of anyone else. On the other hand, if production is raised and with it everyone's living standard, that is literally to everyone's advantage. The rule 'Work harder,' if it has these consequences, is for the common good of all.

Very few rules, if any, will be for the common good of everyone. But a rule may be in the interest of everyone alike, even though the results of the observation of the rule are not for the common good in the sense explained. Rules such as 'Thou shalt not kill,' 'Thou shalt not be cruel,' 'Thou shalt not lie' are obviously, in some other sense, for the good of everyone alike. What is this sense? It becomes clear if we look at these rules from the moral point of view, that is, that of an independent, unbiased, impartial, objective, dispassionate, disinterested observer. Taking such a God's-eye point of view, we can see that it is in the interest of everyone alike that everyone should abide by the rule 'Thou shalt not kill.' From the moral point of view, it is clear that it is in the interest of everyone alike if everyone alike should be allowed to pursue his own interest provided this does not adversely affect someone else's interests. Killing someone in the pursuit of my interests would interfere with his.

There can be no doubt that such a God's-eye point of view is involved in the moral standpoint. The most elementary teaching is based on it. The negative version of the so-called Golden Rule sums it up: 'Don't do unto others as you would not have them do unto you.' When we teach children the moral point of view, we try to explain it to them by getting them to put themselves in another person's place: 'How would you like to have that done to you!' 'Don't do evil,' the most readily accepted moral rule of all, is simply the most general form of stating this prohibition. For doing evil is the opposite of doing good. Doing good is doing for another person what, if he were following (self-interested) reason, he would do for himself. Doing evil is doing to another person what it would be contrary to reason for him to do to himself. Harming another, hurting another, doing to another what he dislikes having done to him are the specific forms this takes. Killing, cruelty, inflicting pain, maiming, torturing, deceiving, cheating, rape, adultery are instances of this sort of behavior. They all violate the condition of "reversibility," that is, that the behavior in question must be acceptable to a person whether he is at the "giving" or "receiving" end of it.

It is important to see just what is established by this condition of being for the good of everyone alike. In the first place, anyone is doing wrong who engages in nonreversible behavior. It is irrelevant whether he knows that it is wrong or not, whether the morality of his group recognizes it or not. Such behavior is "wrong in itself," irrespective of individual or social recognition, irrespective of the consequences it has. Moreover, every single act of such behavior is wrong. We need not consider the whole group or the whole of humanity engaging in this sort of behavior, but only a single case. Hence we can say that all nonreversible behavior is morally wrong; hence that anyone engaging in it is doing what, prima facie, he ought not to do. We need not consider whether this sort of behavior has harmful consequences, whether it is forbidden by the morality of the man's group, or whether he himself thinks it wrong.

The principle of reversibility does not merely impose certain prohibitions on a moral agent, but also certain positive injunctions. It is, for instance, wrong—an omission—not to help another person when he is in need and when we are in a position to help him. The story of the Good Samaritan makes this point. The positive version of the Golden Rule makes the same point more generally: 'Do unto others as you would have them do unto you.' Note that it is wrong—not merely not meritorious—to omit to help others when they are in need and when you are in a position to help them. It does not follow from this, however, that it is wrong not to promote the greatest good of the greatest number, or not to promote the greatest amount of good in the world. Deontologists and utilitarians alike make the mistake of thinking that it is one, or the only one, of our moral duties to "do the optimific act." Nothing could be further from the truth. We do not have a duty to do good to others or to ourselves, or to others and/or to ourselves in a judicious mixture such that it produces the greatest possible amount of good in the world. We are morally required to do good only to those who are actually in need of our assistance. The view that we always ought to do the optimific act, or whenever we have no more stringent duty to perform, would have the absurd result that we are doing wrong whenever we are relaxing, since on those occasions there will always be opportunities to produce greater good than we can by relaxing. For the relief of suffering is always a greater good than mere enjoyment. Yet it is quite plain that the worker who, after a tiring day, puts on his slippers and listens to the wireless is not doing anything he ought not to, is not neglecting any of his duties, even though it may be perfectly true that there are things he might do which produce more good in the world, even for himself, than merely relaxing by the fireside.

Social Morality

We have so far considered absolute morality only. As we have noted, the moral point of view is characterized by a formal and a material condition. The formal condition is this: a man cannot be said to have adopted the moral point of view unless he is prepared to treat the moral rules as principles rather than mere rules of thumb, that is, to do things *on principle* rather than merely to act purposively, merely to aim at a certain end. And, furthermore, he must act on rules which are meant for everybody, and not merely for himself or some favored group. The material condition is this: the rules must be for the good of everyone alike. This does not mean that they must be for the common good of all human beings, past, present, and future, for such a condition would be impossible to satisfy. Its meaning can be elucidated by setting forth the criteria of saying that a rule is for the good of everyone alike. As far as absolute morality is concerned, only one condition must be satisfied, namely, that these rules should be "reversible," that is, not merely for the good of the agent, but at least not detrimental to the persons who are affected by the agent's behavior.

An examination of social conditions will yield some further criteria of 'being for the good of everyone alike.' A society is more than just a number of individuals living in a certain area and behaving in ways directly affecting others, such as killing, maiming, and robbing. Life in society involves a social framework which multiplies the points of contact between individuals and which can transform the effects of a man's behavior on his fellow men. Within a given social framework, behavior may be harmful which is not, from its nature, the infliction of harm on another. It may be harmful only if and because a great many people in that society engage in it. No harm is done if one person walks across the lawn. But the lawn is ruined if everyone does. No harm is done if one person uses the gas. But if everyone uses it during peak hours, then the gas supply may break down, and everyone will be adversely affected.

That such behavior is morally objectionable is widely recognized. We acknowledge that it is, by the well-known formula 'You can't do that; what if everyone did the same!" Kant thought of it as the core of his categorical imperative, 'Act only on that maxim whereby thou canst at the same time will that it should become a universal law.' This is precisely what we "cannot will" in the cases in question. Although it is not true that, as Kant put it, a will willing such a maxim to become a universal law would, literally, contradict itself, nevertheless, in making such a maxim *a universal law*, one would enjoin people to do evil, and such a law would obviously be wrong.

It is, however, important to distinguish behavior which is "nonuniversalizable" from behavior that is "nonreversible." The latter can be seen to be *wrong in itself*, irrespective of the consequences and of how many people engage in it. This is not so in the case of nonuniversalizable behavior. There we have to consider the consequences, and not merely of a single act but of a great many of them. There is nothing wrong in itself with putting one straw on the camel's back, but one of them will be the last.

What exactly does this prove? That no one is allowed to lay even one straw on the camel's back? That every act of this kind is wrong? Surely not. Before we can say that any act of this sort is wrong, a number of conditions must be satisfied.

In the first place, all concerned must be *equally entitled* to behave in the nonuniversalizable way. It would, for instance, be most undesirable if everyone had dinner at 6:30 P.M., for all the nation's service would then come to a standstill at that time. But it cannot follow from this that eating at 6:30 P.M. is wrong for everyone. It cannot follow because the argument applies equally for any time, and it must be all right to eat at *some* time. Of course, there is no serious problem here. Not everyone is equally entitled to have his dinner at 6:30 P.M. Those who are on duty at that time must have it before or after or while they are attending to their duties.

There are further conditions. If everyone were celibate all his life, mankind would die out, or, at any rate, the number would soon be so seriously reduced as to make life unbearable. Those who do not find the prospect of the end of the human race upsetting will have to admit that the return to primitive conditions is undesirable. Again, if everyone suddenly stopped smoking, drinking, gambling, and going to the pictures, some states might go bankrupt and this would be undesirable. All the same, it can hardly be true that abstinence in matters of sex, smoking, drinking, gambling, and visits to the cinema can be wrong in any and every case, even though we are surely all equally entitled to refrain from these ways of spending our time.

There must, therefore, be a further condition. Everyone must not only be equally entitled to engage in these forms of activity, but people must also be inclined to do so. There would have to be a real danger that, unless they are stopped somehow, many will engage in this sort of behavior. People are lazy, so they will not go to the polling booth or make the detour round the newly planted lawn. People like picking flowers, so they will destroy the rare wild flowers. People want to heat their rooms, so they will want to use their radiators during peak hours. But there is no great danger that they will all go celibate, or give up smoking and drinking.

This point, by the way, shows that nonuniversalizability cannot be adduced to show that suicide is wrong. Suicide is no more wrong than celibacy and for the same reason. People are less keen on suicide even than on celibacy. There is no danger of the race dying out. In fact, all over the world people are so keen on procreation that the suicide rate could go up a long way before anyone need be alarmed. Of course if, one day, life and sex were to become burdens to all of us and if, nevertheless, it really is desirable that the race should go on, then reckless suicide or slothful celibacy might become morally wrongful types of conduct. Until then, those weary of life and sex need not have a bad conscience about their uncommon indulgences.

There is one further point in this. To say that it is wrong to walk across the lawn or switch on the gas during peak hours provided (a) it would have undesirable consequences *if* everyone did it, (b) we are all equally entitled to do it, and (c) doing it is an indulgence, not a sacrifice, amounts to saying that since refraining from doing these things is a sacrifice such a sacrifice for the common good should not be demanded of one or a few only, but equally of all, even if a universal sacrifice is not needed. Since no one is more entitled than anyone else to indulge himself and since *all* cannot do so without the undesirable consequences which no one wants, *no one* should be allowed to indulge himself.

Now the conditions are complete. If the behavior in question is such that (i) the consequences would be undesirable if everyone did it, (ii) all are equally entitled to engage in it, and (iii) engaging in this sort of behavior is an indulgence, not a sacrifice, then such behavior *should be prohibited by the morality of the group.*

But now suppose that it is not prohibited. Is it wrong all the same? Kant certainly thought so. I think he is mistaken. For since, by indulging in the behavior in question, I am not actually doing any harm, my behavior is not wrong in itself, but only when taken in conjunction with that of others. I cannot prevent the evil by refraining. Others must refrain too. In the case of nonreversible behavior, *my action alone* is the cause of the evil. I can avoid the evil if I refrain. In the case under discussion, however, if I have reason to suppose that the others will not refrain, I surely have reason not to refrain either, as my only reason for refraining is my desire to avoid causing the evil consequences. If these cannot be avoided, I have no reason not to indulge myself. If the grass is not going to grow anyway, why should I make the detour?

It is no good arguing that I am not entitled to do wrong just because other people might or probably would. For I am not doing wrong. I have no moral reason for the sacrifice. I need no justification or excuse, for my behavior is wrong only *if I have no reason to think* that others will refuse to make the sacrifice. If I have reason to think they will refuse to make it, then I have reason to think that my own sacrifice will be in vain; hence I have reason against making it.

Of course, if the results are *very* undesirable and my sacrifice is *very* small and I am not very certain what the others will do, I should take the risk of making the sacrifice even if it turns out to have been in vain. But, otherwise, reason will support the opposite course.

The situation is different if the morality or the custom or the law of the group does not already contain a rule forbidding such behavior. If there is such a rule, then the behavior is wrong, for such a rule has the backing of morality. As we have said, a group ought to have rules forbidding nonuniversalizable behavior. And when there is such a rule, then the community has regulated behavior of this sort and I ought to do my share toward the success of the regulation.

I should like to add one word about the morality of individual initiative in these matters. Some people think that individuals should go ahead with a good example and not wait until the rule-making powers of the group are used. Others argue that this is putting too great a burden on the public-spirited. Thus, compulsory military service with exemptions granted to those engaged in important national industries is said by some to be fairer, volunteering for national service is said by others to be morally preferable. I can see no reason for the latter view. It may indeed seem preferable from the military point of view, for it may be argued that volunteers are better soldiers. But there is no reason why if keenness is wanted volunteers should not have preferential rights to serve in the army rather than in industry. On the other hand, there is no reason why the sacrifices involved in the defense of their country should be borne only by those who are taking their moral responsibilities seriously, and no reason why those who are not should benefit gratuitously. In the absence of argument showing that the method of individual initiative yields a more efficient army, the other seems to me preferable and, in any case, obviously fairer. Hesitation to use the lawmaking force of the community is understandable, for such use may endanger individual freedom, but often this hesitation is supported on the grounds of the moral preferability of individual sacrifice and initiative. Such arguments seem to me unsound.

The Supremacy of Moral Reasons

Are moral reasons really superior to reasons of self-interest as we all believe? Do we really have reason on our side when we follow moral reasons against self-interest? What reasons could there be for being moral? Can we really give an answer to 'Why should we be moral?' It is obvious that all these questions come to the same thing. When we ask, 'Should we be moral?' or 'Why should we be moral?' or 'Are moral reasons superior to all others?' we ask to be shown the reason for being moral. What is this reason?

Let us begin with a state of affairs in which reasons of self-interest are supreme. In such a state everyone keeps his impulses and inclinations in check when and only when they would lead him into behavior detrimental to his own interest. Everyone who follows reason will discipline himself to rise early, to do his exercises, to refrain from excessive drinking and smoking, to keep good company, to marry the right sort of girl, to work and study hard in order to get on, and so on. However, it will often happen that people's interests conflict. In such a case, they will have to resort to ruses or force to get their own way. As this becomes known, men will become suspicious, for they will regard one another as scheming competitors for the good things in life. The universal supremacy of the rules of self-interest must lead to what Hobbes called the state of nature. At the same time, it will be clear to everyone that universal obedience to certain rules overriding self-interest would produce a state of affairs which serves everyone's interest much better than his unaided pursuit of it in a state where everyone does the same. Moral rules are universal rules designed to override those of self-interest when following the latter is harmful to others. 'Thou shalt not kill,' 'Thou shalt not lie,' 'Thou shalt not steal' are rules which forbid the inflicting of harm on someone else even when this might be in one's interest.

The very *raison d'être* of a morality is to yield reasons which overrule the reasons of self-interest in those cases when everyone's following self-interest would be harmful to everyone. Hence moral reasons are superior to all others.

"But what does this mean?" it might be objected. "If it merely means that we do so regard them, then you are of course right, but your contention is useless, a mere point of usage. And how could it mean any more? If it means that we not only do so regard them, but *ought* to regard them, then there must be *reasons* for saying this. But there could not be any reasons for it. If you offer reasons of self-interest, you are arguing in a circle. Moreover, it cannot be true that it is always in my interest to treat moral reasons as superior to reasons of self-interest. If it were, self-interest and morality could never conflict, but they notoriously do. It is equally circular to argue that there are moral reasons for saying that one ought to treat moral reasons as superior to reasons of self-interest. And what other reasons are there?"

The answer is that we are now looking at the world from the point of view of *anyone*. We are not examining particular alternative courses of action before this or that person; we are examining two alternative worlds, one in which moral reasons are always treated by everyone as superior to reasons of self-interest and one in which the reverse is the practice. And we can see that the first world is the better world, because we can see that the second world would be the sort which Hobbes describes as the state of nature.

This shows that I ought to be moral, for when I ask the question 'What ought I to do?' I am asking, 'Which is the course of action supported by the best reasons?' But since it has just been shown that moral reasons are superior to reasons of self-interest, I have been given a reason for being moral, for following moral reasons rather than any other, namely, they are better reasons than any other.

But is this always so? Do we have a reason for being moral whatever the conditions we find ourselves in? Could there not be situations in which it is not true that we have reasons for being moral, that, on the contrary, we have reasons for ignoring the demands of morality? Is not Hobbes right in saying that in a state of nature the laws of nature, that is, the rules of morality, bind only *in foro interno*?

Hobbes argues as follows.

(i) To live in a state of nature is to live outside society. It is to live in conditions in which there are no common ways of life and, therefore, no reliable expectations about other people's behavior other than that they will follow their inclination or their interest.

(ii) In such a state reason will be the enemy of co-operation and mutual trust. For it is too risky to hope that other people will refrain from protecting their own interests by the preventive elimination of probable or even possible dangers to them. Hence reason will counsel everyone to avoid these risks by preventive action. But this leads to war.

(iii) It is obvious that everyone's following self-interest leads to a state of affairs which is desirable from no one's point of view. It is, on the contrary, desirable that everybody should follow rules overriding self-interest whenever that is to the detriment of others. In other words, it is desirable to bring about a state of affairs in which all obey the rules of morality.

(iv) However, Hobbes claims that in the state of nature it helps nobody if a single person or a small group of persons begins to follow the rules of morality, for this could only lead to the extinction of such individuals or groups. In such a state, it is therefore contrary to reason to be moral.

(v) The situation can change, reason can support morality, only when the presumption about other people's behavior is reversed. Hobbes thought that this could be achieved only by the creation of an absolute ruler with absolute power to enforce his laws. We have already seen that this is not true and that it is quite different if people live in a society, that is, if they have common ways of life, which are taught to all members and somehow enforced by the group. Its members have reason to expect their fellows generally to obey its rules, that is, its religion, morality, customs, and law, even when doing so is not, on certain occasions, in their interest. Hence they too have reason to follow these rules.

Is this argument sound? One might, of course, object to step (i) on the grounds that this is an empirical proposition for which there is little or no evidence. For how can we know whether it is true that people in a state of nature would follow only their inclinations or, at best, reasons of self-interest, when nobody now lives in that state or has ever lived in it?

However, there is some empirical evidence to support this claim. For in the family of nations, individual states are placed very much like individual persons in a state of nature. The doctrine of the sovereignty of nations and the absence of an effective international law and police force are a guarantee that nations live in a state of nature, without commonly accepted rules that are somehow enforced. Hence it must be granted that living in a state of nature leads to living in a state in which individuals act either on impulse or as they think their interest dictates. For states pay only lip service to morality. They attack their hated neighbors when the opportunity arises. They start preventive wars in order to destroy the enemy before he can deliver his knockout blow. Where interests conflict, the stronger party usually has his way, whether his claims are justified or not. And where the relative strength of the parties is not obvious, they usually resort to arms in order to determine "whose side God is on." Treaties are frequently concluded but, morally speaking, they are not worth the paper they are written on. Nor do the partners regard them as contracts binding in the ordinary way, but rather as public expressions of the belief of the governments concerned that for the time being their alliance is in the interest of the allies. It is well understood that such treaties may be canceled before they reach their predetermined end or simply broken when it suits one partner. In international affairs, there are very few examples of *Nibelungen-treue*, although statesmen whose countries have profited from keeping their treaties usually make such high moral claims.

It is, moreover, difficult to justify morality in international affairs. For suppose a highly moral statesman were to demand that his country adhere to a treaty obligation even though this meant its ruin or possibly its extinction. Suppose he were to say that treaty obligations are sacred and must be kept whatever the consequences. How could he defend such a policy? Perhaps one might argue that someone has to make a start in order to create mutual confidence in international affairs. Or one might say that setting a good example is the best way of inducing others to follow suit. But such a defense would hardly be sound. The less skeptical one is about the genuineness of the cases in which nations have adhered to their treaties from a sense of moral obligation, the more skeptical one must be about the effectiveness of such examples of virtue in effecting a change of international practice. Power politics still govern in international affairs.

We must, therefore, grant Hobbes the first step in his argument and admit that in a state of nature people, as a matter of psychological fact, would not follow the dictates of morality. But we might object to the next step that knowing this psychological fact about other people's behavior constitutes a reason for behaving in the same way. Would it not still be immoral for anyone to ignore the demands of morality even though he knows that others are likely or certain to do so, too? Can we offer as a justification for morality the fact that no one is entitled to do wrong just because someone else is doing wrong? This argument begs the question whether it *is* wrong for anyone in this state to disregard the demands of morality. It cannot be wrong to break a treaty or make preventive war if we have no reason to obey the moral rules. For to say that it is wrong to do so is to say that we ought not to do so. But if we have no reason for obeying the moral rule, then we have no reason overruling self-interest, hence no reason for keeping the treaty when keeping it is not in our interest, hence it is not true that we have a reason for keeping it, hence not true that we ought to keep it, hence not true that it is wrong not to keep it.

I conclude that Hobbes's argument is sound. Moralities are systems of principles whose acceptance by everyone as overruling the dictates of self-interest is in the interest of everyone alike, though following the rules of a morality is not of course identical with following self-interest. If it were, there could be no conflict between a morality and self-interest and no point in having moral rules overriding self-interest. Hobbes is also right in saying that the application of this system of rules is in accordance with reason only in social conditions, that is, when there are well-established ways of behavior.

The answer to our question 'Why should we be moral?' is therefore as follows. We should be moral because being moral is following rules designed to overrule self-interest whenever it is in the interest of everyone alike that everyone should set aside his interest. It is not self-contradictory to say this, because it may be in one's interest *not* to follow one's interest at times. We have already seen that enlightened self-interest acknowledges this point. But while enlightened self-interest does not require any genuine sacrifice from anyone, morality does. In the interest of the possibility of the good life for everyone, voluntary sacrifices are sometimes required from everybody. Thus, a person might do better for himself by following enlightened self-interest rather than morality. It is not possible, however, that *everyone* should do better for himself by following enlightened self-interest rather than morality. The best possible life *for everyone* is possible only by everyone's following the rules of morality, that is, rules which quite frequently may require individuals to make genuine sacrifices.

It must be added to this, however, that such a system of rules has the support of reason only where people live in societies, that is, in conditions in which there are established common ways of behavior. Outside society, people have no reason for following such rules, that is, for being moral. In other words, outside society, the very distinction between right and wrong vanishes.

IV

NORMATIVE
ETHICS

OUR MORAL JUDGMENTS are extremely varied. We praise many actions as admirable and upright, and condemn many others as despicable. Moreover, in planning our own activities, we reject many possible acts because they are wrong, and decide on others because they are morally required. On what underlying principles are these judgments and decisions based? And, whatever our actual principles, why accept these and not others? In posing such questions, we are asking which moral norms should govern our lives. We are thus seeking a theory of *normative ethics*.

One historically influential theory says that what persons ought to do depends on what God approves of their doing or commands them to do. This theory—the *Divine Command Theory* of ethics—may be viewed either as setting forth the basic normative principle, "Do what God commands," or as holding that God's commands are the *source* of whatever normative principles we ought to accept. Either way, the theory invests morality with God's authority and majesty. Yet just because of this, the theory cannot convince those who doubt God's existence. Moreover, before accepting it, even believers must respond to a dilemma first noticed by Plato. In reading 25, Plato asks, in effect, whether actions are made right by the fact that God commands them, or whether God commands acts because they are independently right. If we accept the first alternative, God's commands will appear arbitrary. If we accept the second, what is right will not depend on God's commands.

By itself, the Divine Command Theory singles out no substantive principles. Even those who accept it may disagree about *what* God commands. Thus, whether or not we accept it, we must go on to ask which sorts of acts are right. In general, substantive normative principles can take two forms. A principle may tell us to perform acts either because they produce good consequences or for some other reason. A principle of the first type is called *consequentialist*; one of the second type is called *deontological*. Because there are different views about what is good—these are explored in the readings in part V—there are also different consequentialist principles. But by far the most popular is the *principle of utility*, which tells us to do what produces the greatest amount of pleasure, happiness, or satisfaction of desire. Versions of this principle are set forth by Jeremy Bentham in reading 34 and John Stuart Mill in reading 26. Those who accept it are called *utilitarians*.

Utilitarianism offers many advantages. Because it considers each person's happiness equally, it displays the impartiality that many take to characterize morality. And because every act produces some determinate amount of happiness, utilitarianism allows us to compare the rightness of any two acts. With enough information, utilitarians can always tell us which acts to perform. Of course, in the actual world, we rarely can foresee all the effects of any possible act. Yet just because of this, the utilitarian can plausibly explain our commitment to such apparently nonutilitarian principles as, "Do not harm others," "Treat people fairly," and "Do not kill." As Mill argues, these common-sense principles may serve as guides to the maximization of happiness when we must act under conditions of incomplete information. Given the circumstances of ordinary life, we may produce the best results by not considering happiness every time we act.

The ability to account for our common-sense moral beliefs is a point in favor of utilitarianism. But in another way, these beliefs may work *against* utilitarianism. For if the only reason not to steal or kill is that such acts generally fail to maximize happiness, then we will lack a reason not to steal or kill when such acts clearly *would* maximize happiness. For example, if we can best promote utility by killing a rich miser and redistributing his money, the utility principle must endorse this act. According to critics, this shows that utilitarianism is unacceptable. As Thomas Nagel argues in reading 49 while discussing the rules of war, utilitarianism seems incapable of limiting the means we may use to promote worthwhile ends. But some versions of utilitarianism may escape this charge. In reading 27, Richard Brandt distinguishes between *act-utilitarianism*, which judges individual acts by the amount of happiness they bring, and *rule-utilitarianism*, which judges acts by their conformity to rules whose *general acceptance* would maximize utility. Because the latter rules would presumably forbid killing the miser and redistributing his money, the rule-utilitarian may be able to explain why this act is wrong even though it *would* maximize utility.

Other difficulties, however, remain. In reading 28, John Rawls suggests that utilitarianism rests on a false analogy between individuals and society. It is rational for individuals to try to maximize the sum of their satisfactions, because their sacrifices are offset by their own larger gains. For example, a person may rationally endure pain at the dentist's office to avoid worse pain later. But

Rawls argues that it is not similarly rational for society to try to maximize the sum of its members' satisfactions; for those whose interests are sacrificed are not compensated by the larger gains of others. Given this and related problems, consequentialism may not properly capture the insight that morality is impersonal. We may, instead, need a deontological theory.

In reading 29, Immanuel Kant proposes such a theory. He defends several versions of a basic principle—a "Categorical Imperative"—that he thinks should regulate all behavior. One way of putting this principle is "Act only according to that maxim [i.e., that rule of conduct] by which you can at the same time will that it should become a universal law." Another is "Act so that you treat humanity, whether in your own person or in that of another, always as an end and never as a means only." In either formulation, Kant's basic principle rules out such acts as making promises that cannot be kept. If everyone made such promises, then no promises would be credible and the institution of promising itself would disappear. Thus, the maxim cannot be a universal law. Moreover, when we make a promise we know we cannot keep, we treat the person to whom we make it as a mere means to the accomplishment of our own ends. Since the prohibition against such promises applies even when making them would have better consequences than not making them, Kant's theory is clearly deontological. In fact, Kant argues that consequences are irrelevant in two senses. An act's anticipated consequences cannot determine whether one ought to perform it, and its actual consequences cannot affect its moral worth when it *is* performed. Even an unsuccessful attempt to do the right thing "would sparkle like a jewel in its own right." In saying this, Kant articulates the common belief that we are only responsible for what we can control. But, as Thomas Nagel notes in reading 30, Kant thereby rejects the equally common belief that results sometimes *do* matter. We believe that reckless driving that causes death is worse than reckless driving that does not, yet "whether a reckless driver hits a pedestrian depends on the presence of the pedestrian at the point where he recklessly passes a red light."

There are also other questions. Because the Categorical Imperative generates many duties, we may wonder how to resolve conflicts among these. If we have duties both to keep our promises and to help others, then what should we do when helping requires that we break a promise? And are there really acts that we should perform whatever the consequences? Should we keep a promise when breaking it might save hundreds of lives? Thousands? Millions? Impressed by such questions, some, such as W. D. Ross, have advanced theories that combine deontological and consequentialist elements. In reading 31, Ross argues that there is no single principle of morality. Rather, we have basic duties both to promote good consequences and to avoid dishonesty, ingratitude, and injustice. Because these duties may conflict, none is absolute. To resolve conflicts, we must use our judgment to determine which duties take priority in our particular situation.

As a description of our actual practice, Ross's account seems accurate enough. But what are we doing when we make judgments about priorities, if not seeking further principles? If no such principles exist, what makes one judgment better than another? Although Ross believes that there are no priority rules, a theory that explicitly incorporates such a rule is defended by John Rawls in reading 32. Because Rawls's main concern is not the rightness of individual acts, but rather the justice of social institutions such as the legal and economic system, his priority rule applies to principles governing such institutions. In Rawls's view, just social institutions must allow all citizens the greatest possible amount of equal liberty and also maximize the economic position of society's worst-off group. Of these requirements, the first takes precedence: no increase in economic well-being—even for the worst-off—may be achieved at the cost of any sacrifice of basic liberties. In proposing these principles, and in suggesting that his approach may also yield principles of individual action, Rawls aligns himself with the deontological tradition in general, and with Kant's ethical theory in particular.

Proposing priority rules is one way of responding to the apparent plurality of duties. But a very different response is also possible. In reading 33, Jean-Paul Sartre denies that there is any single answer to the question of which principle takes precedence in a given situation. According to Sartre, how much weight we attach to any duty is entirely up to us. In the absence of a divine lawgiver, both our priority rules and the first-level principles they govern are entirely self-imposed. If we are honest, we will acknowledge that we create our own morality. When we seek advice, we make our decisions through our choice of adviser; when we are given a code, we ourselves decide how to interpret it and whether to follow it. According to Sartre, we can never transfer our responsibility to the code itself. In the end, our priorities are what we make them.

25

Euthyphro

PLATO

For biographical information about Plato, see reading 17.

In this selection, Plato discusses the relation between morality and the gods. The topic is important because many believe that God is the source of moral principles. As Hare observes in reading 22, moral principles are prescriptive, and thus resemble laws or commands. Hence it is tempting to trace them to some commander or lawgiver. But no ordinary person has the authority to issue binding moral commands. Thus it is natural to suppose that the moral lawgiver is divine.

But Plato's argument implies that this cannot be correct. Through his spokesman Socrates, Plato examines the beliefs of Euthyphro, who intends to prosecute his own father for killing a servant. In defense of this, Euthyphro insists that prosecuting murderers is pious because such actions are loved by the gods. But Socrates goes further, and asks why the gods love the actions that they do. If they have no reasons, then their love is arbitrary. Yet if they do have reasons, then the actions are not pious because they are loved by the gods. Instead, the acts are loved by the gods because they are pious. If this argument is successful, a similar argument will show that acts are not made right simply by God's commands.

EUTHYPHRO: What's new, Socrates, to make you leave your usual haunts in the Lyceum and spend your time here by the king-archon's court. Surely you are not prosecuting any one before the king archon as I am?

SOCRATES: The Athenians do not call this a prosecution but an indictment, Euthyphro.

E: What is this you say? Someone must have indicted you, for you are not going to tell me that you have indicted someone else.

S: No indeed.

E: But someone else has indicted you?

S: Quite so.

E: Who is he?

S: I do not really know myself, Euthyphro. He is apparently young and unknown. They call him Meletus, I believe. He belongs to the Pitthean deme, if you know anyone from that deme called Meletus, with long hair, not much of a beard, and a rather acquiline nose.

E: I don't know him, Socrates. What charge does he bring against you?

S: What charge? A not ignoble one I think, for it is no small thing for a young man to have knowledge of such an important subject. He says he knows how our young men are corrupted and who corrupts them. He is likely to be wise, and when he sees my ignorance corrupting his contemporaries, he proceeds to accuse me to the city as to their mother. I think he is the only one of our public men to start out the right way, for it is right to care first that the young should be as good as possible, just as a good farmer is likely to take care of the young plants first, and of the others later. So, too, Meletus first gets rid of us who corrupt the growth of the young, as he says, and then afterwards he will obviously take care of the older and become a source of great blessings for the city, as seems likely to happen to one who started out this way.

E: I could wish this were true, Socrates, but I fear the opposite may happen. He seems to me to start out by harming the very heart of the city by attempting to wrong you. Tell me, what does he say you do to corrupt the young?

S: Strange things, to hear him tell it, for he says that I am a maker of gods, that I create new gods while not believing in the old gods, and he has indicted me for this very reason, as he puts it.

E: I understand, Socrates. This is because you say that the divine sign keeps coming to you. So he has written this indictment against you as one who makes innovations in religious matters, and he comes to court to slander you, knowing that such things are easily misrepresented to the crowd. The same is true in my case. Whenever I speak of divine matters in the assembly and foretell the future, they laugh me down as if I were crazy; and yet I have foretold nothing that did not happen. Nevertheless, they envy all of us who do this. One need not give them any thought, but carry on just the same.

S: My dear Euthyphro, to be laughed at does not matter perhaps, for the Athenians do not mind anyone they think clever, as long as he does not teach his own wisdom, but if they think that he makes others to be like himself they get angry, whether through envy, as you say, or for some other reason.

E: I have certainly no desire to test their feelings toward me in this matter.

S: Perhaps you seem to make yourself but rarely available, and not to be willing to teach your own wisdom, but my liking for people makes them think that I pour out to anybody anything I have to say, not only without charging a fee but appearing glad to reward anyone who is willing to listen. If then they were intending to laugh at me, as you say they laugh at you, there would be nothing unpleasant in their spending their time in court laughing and jesting, but if they are going to be serious, the outcome is not clear except to you prophets.

E: Perhaps it will come to nothing, Socrates, and you will fight your case as you think best, as I think I will mine.

S: What is your case, Euthyphro? Are you the defendant or the prosecutor?

E: The prosecutor.

S: Whom do you prosecute?

E: One whom I am thought crazy to prosecute.

S: Are you pursuing someone who will easily escape you?

E: Far from it, for he is quite old.

S: Who is it?

E: My father.

S: My dear sir! Your own father?

E: Certainly.

S: What is the charge? What is the case about?

E: Murder, Socrates.

S: Good heavens! Certainly, Euthyphro, most men would not know how they could do this and be right. It is not the part of anyone to do this, but of one who is far advanced in wisdom.

E: Yes by Zeus, Socrates, that is so.

S: Is then the man your father killed one of your relatives? Or is that obvious, for you would not prosecute your father for the murder of a stranger.

E: It is ridiculous, Socrates, for you to think that it makes any difference whether the victim is a stranger or a relative. One should only watch whether the killer acted justly or not; if he acted justly, let him go, but if not, one should prosecute, even if the killer shares your hearth and table. The pollution is the same if you knowingly keep company with such a man and do not cleanse yourself and him by bringing him to justice. The victim was a dependent of mine, and when we were farming in Naxos he was a servant of ours. He killed one of our household slaves in drunken anger, so my father bound him hand and foot and threw him in a ditch, then sent a man here to enquire from the priest what should be done. During that time he gave no thought or care to the bound man, as being a killer, and it was no matter if he died, which he did. Hunger and cold and his bonds caused his death before the messenger came back from the seer. Both my father and my other relatives are angry that I am prosecuting my father for murder on behalf of a murderer, as he did not even kill him. They say that such a victim does not deserve a thought and that it is impious for a son to prosecute his father for murder. But their ideas of the divine attitude to piety and impiety are wrong, Socrates.

S: Whereas, by Zeus, Euthyphro, you think that your knowledge of the divine, and of piety and impiety, is so accurate that, when those things happened as you say, you have no fear of having acted impiously in bringing your father to trial?

E: I should be of no use, Socrates, and Euthyphro would not be superior to the majority of men, if I did not have accurate knowledge of all such things.

S: It is indeed most important, my admirable Euthyphro, that I should become your pupil, and as regards this indictment challenge Meletus about these very things and say to him: that in the past too I considered knowledge about the divine to be most important, and that now that he says that I improvise and innovate about the gods I have become your pupil. I would say to him: "If, Meletus, you agree that Euthyphro is wise in these matters, consider me, too, to have the right beliefs and do not bring me to trial. If you do not think so, then prosecute that teacher of mine for corrupting the older men, me and his own father, by teaching me and by exhorting and punishing him.

If he is not convinced, does not discharge me, or indicts you instead of me, I shall repeat the same challenge in court.

E: Yes by Zeus, Socrates, and, if he should try to indict me, I think I would find his weak spots and the talk in court would be about him rather than about me.

S: It is because I realize this that I am eager to become your pupil, my dear friend. I know that other people as well as this Meletus do not even seem to notice you, whereas he sees me so sharply and clearly that he indicts me for ungodliness. So tell me now, by Zeus, what you just now maintained you clearly knew: what kind of thing do you say that godliness and ungodliness are, both as regards murder and other things; or is the pious not the same and alike in every action, and the impious the opposite of all that is pious and like itself, and everything is to be impious presents us with one form or appearance in so far as it is impious.

E: Most certainly, Socrates.

S: Tell me then, what is the pious, and what the impious, do you say?

E: I say that the pious is to do what I am doing now, to prosecute the wrong-doer, be it about murder or temple robbery or anything else, whether the wrongdoer is your father or your mother or anyone else; not to prosecute is impious. And observe, Socrates, that I can quote the law as a great proof that this is so. I have already said to others that such actions are right, not to favour the ungodly, whoever they are. These people themselves believe that Zeus is the best and most just of the gods, yet they agree that he bound his father because he unjustly swallowed his sons, and that he in turn castrated his father for similar reasons. But they are angry with me because I am prosecuting my father for his wrongdoing. They contradict themselves in what they say about the gods and about me.

S: Indeed, Euthyphro, this is the reason why I am a defendant in the case, because I find it hard to accept things like that being said about the gods, and it is likely to be the reason why I shall be told I do wrong. Now, however, if you, who have full knowledge of such things, share their opinions, then we must agree with them, too, it would seem. For what are we to say, we who agree that we ourselves have no knowledge? Tell me, by the god of friendship, do you really believe these things are true?

E: Yes, Socrates, and so are even more surprising things, of which the majority has no knowledge.

S: And do you believe that there really is war among the gods, and terrible enmities and battles, and other such things as are told by the poets, and other sacred stories such as are embroidered by good writers and by representations of which the robe of the goddess is adorned when it is carried up to the Acropolis? Are we to say these things are true, Euthyphro?

E: Not only these, Socrates, but, as I was saying just now, I will, if you wish, relate many other things about the gods which I know will amaze you.

S: I should not be surprised, but you will tell me these at leisure some other time. For now, try to tell me more clearly what I was asking just now, for, my friend, you did not teach me adequately when I asked you what the pious was, but you told me that what you are doing now, to prosecute your father for murder, is pious.

E: And I told the truth, Socrates.

S: Perhaps. You agree, however, that there are many other pious actions.

E: There are.

S: Bear in mind then that I did not bid you tell me one or two of the many pious actions but that form itself that makes all pious actions pious, for you agreed that all impious actions are impious and all pious actions pious through one form, or don't you remember?

E: I do.

S: Tell me then what form itself is, so that I may look upon it, and using it as a model, say that any action of yours or another's that is of that kind is pious, and if it is not that it is not.

E: If that is how you want it, Socrates, that is how I will tell you.

S: That is what I want.

E: Well then, what is dear to the gods is pious, what is not is impious.

S: Splendid, Euthyphro! You have now answered in the way I wanted. Whether your answer is true I do not know yet, but you will obviously show me that what you say is true.

E: Certainly.

S: Come then, let us examine what we mean. An action or a man dear to the gods is pious, but an action or a man hated by the gods is impious. They are not the same, but opposites, the pious and the impious. Is that not so?

E: It is indeed.

S: And that seems to be a good statement?

E: I think so, Socrates.

S: We have also stated that the gods are in a state of discord, that they are at odds with each other, Euthyphro, and that they are at enmity with each other. That too has been said.

E: It has.

S: What are the subjects of difference that cause hatred and anger? Let us look at it this way. If you and I were to differ about numbers as to which is the greater, would this difference make us enemies and angry with each other, or would we proceed to count and soon resolve our difference about this?

E: We would certainly do so.

S: Again, if we differed about the larger and the smaller, we would turn to measurement and soon cease to differ.

E: That is so.

S: And about the heavier and the lighter, we would resort to weighing and be reconciled.

E: Of course.

S: What subject of difference would make us angry and hostile to each other if we were unable to come to a decision? Perhaps you do not have an answer ready, but examine as I tell you whether these subjects are the just and the unjust, the beautiful and the ugly, the good and the bad. Are these not the subjects of difference about which, when we are unable to come to a satisfactory decision, you and I and other men become hostile to each other whenever we do.

E: That is the difference, Socrates, about those subjects.

S: What about the gods, Euthyphro? If indeed they have differences, will it not be about these same subjects?

E: It certainly must be so.

S: Then according to your argument, my good Euthyphro, different gods consider different things to be just, beautiful, ugly, good and bad, for they would not be at odds with one another unless they differed about these subjects, would they?

E: You are right.

S: And they like what each of them considers beautiful, good, and just, and hate the opposites of these?

E: Certainly.

S: But you say that the same things are considered just by some gods and unjust by others, and as they dispute about these things they are at odds and at war with each other. Is that not so?

E: It is.

S: The same things then are loved by the gods and hated by the gods, both god-loved and god-hated.

E: It seems likely.

S: And the same things would be both pious and impious, according to this argument?

E: I'm afraid so.

S: So you did not answer my question, you surprising man. I did not ask you what same thing is both pious and impious, and it appears that what is loved by the gods is also hated by them. So it is in no way surprising if your present action, namely punishing your father, may be pleasing to Zeus but displeasing to Kronos and Ouranos, pleasing to Hephaestus but displeasing to Hera, and so with any other gods who differ from each other on this subject.

E: I think, Socrates, that on this subject no gods would differ from one another, that whoever has killed anyone unjustly should pay the penalty.

S: Well now, Euthyphro, have you ever heard any man maintaining that one who has killed or done anything else unjustly should not pay the penalty?

E: They never cease to dispute on this subject, both elsewhere and in the courts, for when they have committed many wrongs they do and say anything to avoid the penalty.

S: Do they agree they have done wrong, Euthyphro, and in spite of so agreeing do they nevertheless say they should not be punished?

E: No, they do not agree on that point.

S: So they do not say or do anything. For they do not venture to say this, or dispute that they must not pay the penalty if they have done wrong, but I think they deny doing wrong. Is that not so?

E: That is true.

S: Then they do not dispute that the wrongdoer must be punished, but they may disagree as to who the wrongdoer is, what he did and when.

E: You are right.

S: Do not the gods have the same experience, if indeed they are at odds with each other about the just and the unjust, as your argument maintains? Some assert that they wrong one another, while others deny it, but no one among gods or men ventures to say that the wrongdoer must not be punished.

E: Yes, that is true, Socrates, as to the main point.

S: And those who disagree, whether men or gods, dispute about each action, if indeed the gods disagree. Some say it is done justly, others unjustly. Is that not so?

E: Yes indeed.

S: Come now, my dear Euthyphro, tell me, too, that I may become wiser, what proof you have that all the gods consider that man to have been killed unjustly who became a murderer while in your service, was bound by the master of his victim, and died in his bonds before the one who bound him found out from the seers what was to be done with him, and that it is right for a son to denounce and to prosecute his father on behalf of such a man. Come, try to show me a clear sign that all the gods definitely believe this action to be right. If you can give me adequate proof of this, I shall never cease to extol your wisdom.

E: This is perhaps no light task, Socrates, though I could show you very clearly.

S: I understand that you think me more dull-witted than the jury, as you will obviously show them that these actions were unjust and that all the gods hate such actions.

E: I will show it to them clearly, Socrates, if only they will listen to me.

S: They will listen if they think you show them well. But this thought came to me as I was speaking, and I am examining it, saying to myself: "If Euthyphro shows me conclusively that all the gods consider such a death unjust, to what greater extent have I learned from him the nature of piety and impiety? This action would then, it seems, be hated by the gods, but the pious and the impious were not thereby now defined, for what is hated by the gods has also been shown to be loved by them." So I will not insist on this point; let us assume, if you wish, that all the gods consider this unjust and that they all hate it. However, is this the correction we are making in our discussion, that what all the gods hate is impious, and what they all love is pious, and that what some gods love and others hate is neither or both? Is that how you now wish us to define piety and impiety?

E: What prevents us from doing so, Socrates?

S: For my part nothing, Euthyphro, but you look whether on your part this proposal will enable you to teach me most easily what you promised.

E: I would certainly say that the pious is what all the gods love, and the opposite, which all the gods hate, is the impious.

S: Then let us again examine whether that is a sound statement, or do we let it pass, and if one of us, or someone else, merely says that this is so, do we accept that it is so? Or should we examine what the speaker means?

E: We must examine it, but I certainly think that this is now a fine statement.

S: We shall soon know better whether it is. Consider this: Is the pious loved by the gods because it is pious, or is it pious because it is loved by the gods?

E: I don't know what you mean, Socrates.

S: I shall try to explain more clearly; we speak of something being carried and something carrying, of something being led and something leading, of something being seen and something seeing, and you understand that these things are all different from one another and how they differ?

E: I think I do.

S: So there is something being loved and something loving, and the loving is a different thing.

E: Of course.

S: Tell me then whether that which is (said to be) being carried is being carried because someone carries it or for some other reason.

E: No, that is the reason.

S: And that which is being led is so because someone leads it, and that which is being seen because someone sees it?

E: Certainly.

S: It is not seen by someone because it is being seen but on the contrary it is being seen because someone sees it, nor is it because it is being led that someone leads it but because someone leads it that it is being led; nor does someone carry an object because it is being carried, but it is being carried because someone carries it. Is what I want to say clear, Euthyphro? I want to say this, namely, that if anything comes to be, or is affected, it does not come to be because it is coming to be, but it is coming to be because it comes to be; nor is it affected because it is being affected but because something affects it. Or do you not agree?

E: I do.

S: What is being loved is either something that comes to be or something that is affected by something?

E: Certainly.

S: So it is in the same case as the things just mentioned; it is not loved by those who love it because it is being loved, but it is being loved because they love it?

E: Necessarily.

S: What then do we say about the pious, Euthyphro? Surely that is loved by all the gods, according to what you say?

E: Yes.

S: Is it loved because it is pious, or for some other reason?

E: For no other reason.

S: It is loved then because it is pious, but it is not pious because it is loved.

E: Apparently.

S: And because it is loved by the gods it is being loved and is dear to the gods?

E: Of course.

s: The god-beloved is then not the same as the pious, Euthyphro, nor the pious the same as the god-beloved, as you say it is, but one differs from the other.

E: How so, Socrates?

s: Because we agree that the pious is beloved for the reason that it is pious, but it is not pious because it is loved. Is that not so?

E: Yes.

s: And that the god-beloved, on the other hand, is so because it is loved by the gods, by the very fact of being loved, but it is not loved because it is god-beloved.

E: True.

s: But if the god-beloved and the pious were the same, my dear Euthyphro, and the pious were loved because it was pious, then the god-beloved would be loved because it was god-beloved, and if the god-beloved was god-beloved because it was loved by the gods, then the pious would also be pious because it was loved by the gods; but now you see that they are in opposite cases as being altogether different from each other: the one is of a nature to be loved because it is loved, the other is loved because it is of a nature to be loved. I'm afraid, Euthyphro, that when you were asked what piety is, you did not wish to make its nature clear to me, but you told me an affect or quality of it, that the pious has the quality of being loved by all the gods, but you have not yet told me what the pious is. Now, if you will, do not hide things from me but tell me again from the beginning what piety is, whether loved by the gods or having some other quality—we shall not quarrel about that—but be keen to tell me what the pious and the impious are.

E: But Socrates, I have no way of telling you what I have in mind, for whatever proposition we put forward goes around and refuses to stay put where we establish it.

s: Your statements, Euthyphro, seem to belong to my ancestor, Daedalus. If I were stating them and putting them forward, you would perhaps be making fun of me and say that because of my kinship with him my conclusions in discussion run away and will not stay where one puts them. As these propositions are yours, however, we need some other jest, for they will not stay put for you, as you say yourself.

E: I think the same jest will do for our discussion, Socrates, for I am not the one who makes them go round and not remain in the same place; it is you who are the Daedalus; for as far as I am concerned they would remain as they were.

s: It looks as if I was cleverer than Daedalus in using my skill, my friend, in so far as he could only cause to move the things he made himself, but I can make other people's move as well as my own. And the smartest part of my skill is that I am clever without wanting to be, for I would rather have my arguments remain unmoved than possess the wealth of Tantalus as well as the cleverness of Daedalus. But enough of this. Since I think you are making unnecessary difficulties, I am as eager as you are to find a way to teach me about piety, and do not give up before you do. See whether you think all that is pious is of necessity just.

E: I think so.

S: And is then all that is just pious? Or is all that is pious just, but not all that is just pious, but some of it is and some is not?

E: I do not follow what you are saying, Socrates.

S: Yet you are younger than I by as much as you are wiser. As I say, you are making difficulties because of your wealth of wisdom. Pull yourself together, my dear sir, what I am saying is not difficult to grasp. I am saying the opposite of what the poet said who wrote:

> You do not wish to name Zeus, who had done it, and who made all things grow, for where there is fear there is also shame.

I disagree with the poet. Shall I tell you why?

E: Please do.

S: I do not think that "where there is fear there is also shame," for I think that many people who fear disease and poverty and many other such things feel fear, but are not ashamed of the things they fear. Do you not think so?

E: I do indeed.

S: But where there is shame there is also fear. Does anyone feel shame at something who is not also afraid at the same time of a reputation for wickedness?

E: He is certainly afraid.

S: It is then not right to say "where there is fear there is also shame," but that where there is shame there is also fear, for fear covers a larger area than shame. Shame is a part of fear just as odd is a part of number, with the result that it is not true that where there is number there is also oddness, but that where there is oddness there is also number. Do you follow me?

E: Surely.

S: This is the kind of thing I was asking before, whether where there is piety there is also justice, but where there is justice there is not always piety, for the pious is a part of justice. Shall we say that, or do you think otherwise?

E: No, but like that, for what you say appears to be right.

S: See what comes next; if the pious is a part of the just, we must, it seems, find out what part of the just it is. Now if you asked me something of what we mentioned just now, such as what part of number is the even, and what number that is, I would say it is the number that is divisible into two equal, not unequal, parts. Or do you not think so?

E: I do.

S: Try in this way to tell me what part of the just the pious is, in order to tell Meletus not to wrong us any more and not to indict me for ungodliness, since I have learned from you sufficiently what is godly and pious and what is not.

E: I think, Socrates, that the godly and pious is the part of the just that is concerned with the care of the gods, while that concerned with the care of men is the remaining part of justice.

s: You seem to me to put that very well, but I still need a bit of information. I do not know yet what you mean by care, for you do not mean it in the sense as the care of other things, as, for example, not everyone knows how to care for horses, but the horse breeder does.

E: Yes, I do mean it that way.

s: So horse breeding is care of horses.

E: Yes.

s: Nor does everyone know how to care for dogs, but the hunter does.

E: That is so.

s: So hunting is the care of dogs.

E: Yes.

s: And cattle raising is the care of cattle.

E: Quite so.

s: While piety and godliness is the care of the gods, Euthyphro. Is that what you mean?

E: It is.

s: Now care in each case has the same effect; it aims at the good and the benefit of the object cared for, as you can see that horses cared for by horse breeders are benefited and become better. Or do you not think so?

E: I do.

s: So dogs are benefited by dog breeding, cattle by cattle raising, and so with all the others. Or do you think that care aims to harm the object of its care?

E: By Zeus, no.

s: It aims to benefit the object of its care.

E: Of course.

s: Is piety then, which is the care of the gods, also to benefit the gods and make them better? Would you agree that when you do something pious you make some one of the gods better?

E: By Zeus, no.

s: Nor do I think that this is what you mean—far from it—but that is why I asked you what you meant by the care of gods, because I did not believe you meant this kind of care.

E: Quite right, Socrates, that is not the kind of care I mean.

s: Very well, but what kind of care of the gods would piety be?

E: The kind of care, Socrates, that slaves take of their masters.

s: I understand. It is likely to be the service of the gods.

E: Quite so.

s: Could you tell me to the achievement of what goal service to doctors tends? Is it not, do you think to achieving health?

E: I think so.

s: What about service to shipbuilders? To what achievement is it directed?

E: Clearly, Socrates, to the building of a ship.

s: And service to housebuilders to the building of a house?

E: Yes.

S: Tell me then, my good sir, to the achievement of what aim does service to the gods tend? You obviously know since you say that you, of all men, have the best knowledge of the divine.

E: And I am telling the truth, Socrates.

S: Tell me then, by Zeus, what is that excellent aim that the gods achieve, using us as their servants?

E: Many fine things, Socrates.

S: So do generals, my friend. Nevertheless you could tell me their main concern, which is to achieve victory in war, is it not?

E: Of course.

S: The farmers too, I think, achieve many fine things, but the main point of their efforts is to produce food from the earth.

E: Quite so.

S: Well then, how would you sum up the many fine things that the gods achieve?

E: I told you a short while ago, Socrates, that it is a considerable task to acquire any precise knowledge of these things, but, to put it simply, I say that if a man knows how to say and do what is pleasing to the gods at prayer and sacrifice, those are pious actions such as preserve both private houses and public affairs of state. The opposite of these pleasing actions are impious and overturn and destroy everything.

S: You could tell me in far fewer words, if you were willing, the sum of what I asked, Euthyphro, but you are not keen to teach me, that is clear. You were on the point of doing so, but you turned away. If you had given that answer, I should now have acquired from you sufficient knowledge of the nature of piety. As it is, the lover of inquiry must follow it wherever it may lead him. Once more then, what do you say that piety and the pious are, and also impiety? Are they a knowledge of how to sacrifice and pray?

E: They are.

S: To sacrifice is to make a gift to the gods, whereas to pray is to beg from the gods?

E: Definitely, Socrates.

S: It would follow from this statement that piety would be a knowledge of how to give to, and beg from, the gods.

E: You understood what I said very well, Socrates.

S: That is because I am so desirous of your wisdom, and I concentrate my mind on it, so that no word of yours may fall to the ground. But tell me, what is this service to the gods? You say it is to beg from them and to give to them?

E: I do.

S: And to beg correctly would be to ask from them things that we need?

E: What else?

S: And to give correctly is to give them what they need from us, for it would not be skillful to bring gifts to anyone that are in no way needed.

E: True, Socrates.

S: Piety would then be a sort of trading skill between gods and men?

E: Trading yes, if you prefer to call it that.

S: I prefer nothing, unless it is true. But tell me, what benefit do the gods derive from the gifts they receive from us? What they give us is obvious to all. There is for us no good that we do not receive from them, but how are they benefited by what they receive from us? Or do we have such an advantage over them in the trade that we receive all our blessings from them and they receive nothing from us?

E: Do you suppose, Socrates, that the gods are benefited by what they receive from us?

S: What could those gifts from us to the gods be, Euthyphro?

E: What else, you think, than honour, reverence, and what I mentioned before, gratitude.

S: The pious is then, Euthyphro, pleasing to the gods, but not beneficial or dear to them?

E: I think it is of all things most dear to them.

S: So the pious is once again what is dear to the gods.

E: Most certainly.

S: When you say this, will you be surprised if your arguments seem to move about instead of staying put? And will you accuse me of being Daedalus who makes them move, though you are yourself much more skillful than Daedalus and make them go round in a circle? Or do you not realize that our argument has moved around and come again to the same place? You surely remember that earlier the pious and the god-beloved were shown not to be the same but different from each other. Or do you not remember?

E: I do.

S: Do you then not realize that when you say now that that what is dear to the gods is the pious? Is this not the same as the god-beloved? Or is it not?

E: It certainly is.

S: Either we were wrong when we agreed before, or, if we were right then, we are wrong now.

E: That seems to be so.

S: So we must investigate again from the beginning what piety is, as I shall not willingly give up before I learn this. Do not think me unworthy, but concentrate your attention and tell the truth. For you know it, if any man does, and I must not let you go, like Proteus, before you tell me. If you had no clear knowledge of piety and impiety you would never have ventured to prosecute your old father for murder on behalf of a servant. For fear of the gods you would have been afraid to take the risk lest you should not be acting rightly, and would have been ashamed before men, but now I know well that you believe you have clear knowledge of piety and impiety. So tell me, my good Euthyphro, and do not hide what you believe.

E: Some other time, Socrates, for I am in a hurry now, and it is time for me to go.

s: What a thing to do, my friend! By going you have cast me down from a great hope I had, that I would learn from you the nature of the pious and the impious and so escape Meletus' indictment by showing that I had acquired wisdom in divine matters from Euthyphro, and my ignorance would no longer cause me to be careless and inventive about such things, and that I would be better for the rest of my life.

26

Utilitarianism

JOHN STUART MILL

John Stuart Mill (1806–1873) was among the most important British thinkers of the nineteenth century. A philosopher in the Empiricist tradition, he published works on logic, scientific method, and epistemology, as well as on ethics and social and political philosophy. His books include A System of Logic, Utilitarianism, On Liberty, *and* The Subjection of Women.

In this selection, Mill presents an extended defense of utilitarianism. Utilitarianism is the view that the ultimate principle of morality is to "Strive to produce as much overall happiness as possible." Mill was taught this approach by his father, James Mill, who in turn learned it from the philosopher and social reformer Jeremy Bentham. However, whereas Bentham makes no distinctions among types of pleasures (see reading 34), Mill believes that some forms of happiness are more worthwhile than others. He argues that the pleasures of a Socrates are more valuable than those we share with animals because anyone who was "competently acquainted" with both would choose the former.

In whatever form we favor, utilitarianism offers many advantages. As Mill notes, it provides a ready-made answer to the question of what to do when obligations conflict. For example, suppose you have promised to meet a friend for lunch. On the way there, you encounter someone drowning in a lake. If no single moral principle dominates, you will have no principled way of deciding between your conflicting obligations to provide aid and to keep your promise. However, if you are a utilitarian, you will perform whichever act brings more happiness—in this case, rescuing the drowning person. Moreover, besides adjudicating moral conflicts, utilitarianism explains why we accept the conflicting principles, and why we ought to accept them. In Mill's view, we generally ought to help others and keep our promises, because doing these things brings great social benefits. Our familiar principles are like signposts that reflect collective past experience about what maximizes happiness.

One further aspect of Mill's account deserves brief mention. Toward the end of this selection, Mill offers a famous argument for the principle of utility. He argues that whatever is desired is desirable, and that in the last analysis people desire happiness and nothing else. Therefore, happiness is the only truly desirable thing, and it should be maximized. This argument offers a number of opportunities for careful reflection and analysis. You may find it helpful to refer to Feinberg's discussion of psychological egoism (reading 1) as you weigh Mill's argument.

WHAT UTILITARIANISM IS

. . .

THE CREED WHICH accepts as the foundation of morals "utility" or the "greatest happiness principle" holds that actions are right in proportion as they tend to promote happiness; wrong as they tend to produce the reverse of happiness. By happiness is intended pleasure and the absence of pain; by unhappiness, pain and the privation of pleasure. To give a clear view of the moral standard set up by the theory, much more requires to be said; in particular, what things it includes in the ideas of pain and pleasure, and to what extent this is left an open question. But these supplementary explanations do not affect the theory of life on which this theory of morality is grounded—namely, that pleasure and freedom from pain are the only things desirable as ends; and that all desirable things (which are as numerous in the utilitarian as in any other scheme) are desirable either for pleasure inherent in themselves or as means to the promotion of pleasure and the prevention of pain.

Now such a theory of life excites in many minds, and among them in some of the most estimable in feeling and purpose, inveterate dislike. To suppose that life has (as they express it) no higher end than pleasure—no better and nobler object of desire and pursuit—they designate as utterly mean and groveling, as a doctrine worthy only of swine, to whom the followers of Epicurus were, at a very early period, contempuously likened; and modern holders of the doctrine are occasionally made the subject of equally polite comparisons by its German, French, and English assailants.

When thus attacked, the Epicureans have always answered that it is not they, but their accusers, who represent human nature in a degrading light, since the accusation supposes human beings to be capable of no pleasures except those of which swine are capable. If this supposition were true, the charge could not be gainsaid, but would then be no longer an imputation; for if the sources of pleasure were precisely the same to human beings and to swine, the rule of life which is good enough for the one would be good enough for the other. The comparison of the Epicurean life to that of beasts is felt as degrading, precisely because a beast's pleasures do not satisfy a human being's conceptions of happiness. Human beings have faculties more elevated than the animal appetites and, when once made conscious of them, do not regard anything as happiness which does not include their gratification. I do not indeed, consider the Epicureans to have been by any means faultless in drawing out their scheme of consequences from the utilitarian principle. To do this in any sufficient manner, many Stoic, as well as Christian, elements require to be included. But there is no known Epicurean theory of life which does not assign to the pleasures of the intellect, of the feelings and imagination, and of the moral sentiments a much higher value as pleasures than to those of mere sensation. It must be admitted, however, that utilitarian writers in general have placed the superiority of mental over bodily pleasures chiefly in the greater permanency, safety, uncostliness, etc., of the former—that is, in their circumstantial advantages rather than in their intrinsic nature. And on all these points utilitarians have fully proved their case; but they might have taken the other and, as it may be called, higher ground with entire consistency. It is quite compatible with the principle of utility to recognize the fact that some kinds of pleasure are more desirable and more valuable than others. It would be absurd that, while in estimating all other things quality is considered as well as quantity, the estimation of pleasure should be supposed to depend on quantity alone.

If I am asked what I mean by difference of quality in pleasures, or what makes one pleasure more valuable than another, merely as a pleasure, except its being greater in amount, there is but one possible answer. Of two pleasures, if there be one to which all or almost all who have experience of both give a decided preference, irrespective of any feeling of moral obligation to prefer it, that is the more desirable pleasure. If one of the two is, by those who are competently acquainted with both, placed so far above the other that they prefer it, even though knowing it to be attended with a greater amount of discontent, and would not resign it for any quantity of the other pleasure which their nature is capable of, we are justified in ascribing to the preferred enjoyment a superiority in quality so far outweighing quantity as to render it, in comparison, of small account.

Now it is an unquestionable fact that those who are equally acquainted with and equally capable of appreciating and enjoying both do give a most marked preference to the manner of existence which employs their higher faculties. Few human creatures would consent to be changed into any of the lower animals for a promise of the fullest allowance of a beast's pleasures; no intelligent human being would consent to be a fool, no instructed person would be an ignoramus, no person of feeling and conscience would be selfish and base, even though they should be persuaded that the fool, the dunce, or the rascal is better satisfied with his lot than they are with theirs. They would not resign what they possess more than he for the most complete satisfaction of all the desires which they have in common with him. If they ever fancy they would, it is only in cases of unhappiness so extreme that to escape from it they would exchange their lot for almost any other, however undesirable in their own eyes. A being of higher faculties requires more to make him happy, is capable probably of more acute suffering, and certainly accessible to it at more points, than one of an inferior type; but in spite of these liabilities, he can never really wish to sink into what he feels to be a lower grade of existence. We may give what explanation we please of this unwillingness; we may attribute it to pride, a name which is given indiscriminately to some of the most and to some of the least estimable feelings of which mankind are capable; we may refer it to the love of liberty and personal independence, an appeal to which was with the Stoics one of the most effective means for the inculcation of it; to the love of power or to the love of excitement, both of which do really enter into and contribute to it; but its most appropriate appellation is a sense of dignity, which all human beings possess in one form or other, and in some, though by no means in exact, proportion to their higher faculties, and which is so essential a part of the happiness of those in whom it is strong that nothing which conflicts with it could be otherwise than momentarily an object of desire to them. Whoever supposes that this preference takes place at a sacrifice of happiness—that the superior being, in anything like equal circumstances, is not happier than the inferior—confounds the two very different ideas of happiness and content. It is indisputable that the being whose capacities of enjoyment are low has the greatest chance of having them fully satisfied; and a highly endowed being will always feel that any happiness which he can look for, as the world is constituted, is imperfect. But he can learn to bear its imperfections, if they are at all bearable; and they will not make him envy the being who is indeed unconscious of the imperfections, but only because he feels not at all the good which those imperfections qualify. It is better to be a human being dissatisfied than a pig satisfied; better to be Socrates dissatisfied than a fool satisfied. And if the fool, or the pig, are of a different opinion, it is because they only know their own side of the question. The other party to the comparison knows both sides.

It may be objected than many who are capable of the higher pleasures occasionally, under the influence of temptation, postpone them to the lower. But this is quite compatible with a full appreciation of the intrinsic superiority of the higher. Men often, from infirmity of character, make their election for the nearer good, though they know it to be the less valuable; and this no less when the choice is between two bodily pleasures than when it is between bodily and mental. They pursue sensual indulgences to the injury of health, though perfectly aware that health is the greater good. It may be further objected that many who begin with youthful enthusiasm for everything noble, as they advance in years, sink into indolence and selfishness. But I do not believe that those who undergo this very common change voluntarily choose the lower description of pleasures in preference to the higher. I believe that, before they devote themselves exclusively to the one, they have already become incapable of the other. Capacity for the nobler feelings is in most natures a very tender plant, easily killed, not only by hostile influences, but by mere want of sustenance; and in the majority of young persons it speedily dies away if the occupations to which their position in life has devoted them, and the society into which it has thrown them, are not favorable to keeping that higher capacity in exercise. Men lose their high aspirations as they lose their intellectual tastes, because they have not time or opportunity for indulging them; and they addict themselves to inferior pleasures, not because they deliberately prefer them, but because they are either the only ones to which they have access or the only ones which they are any longer capable of enjoying. It may be questioned whether anyone who has remained equally susceptible to both classes of pleasures ever knowingly and calmly preferred the lower, though many, in all ages, have broken down in an ineffectual attempt to combine both.

From this verdict of the only competent judges, I apprehend there can be no appeal. On a question which is the best worth having of two pleasures, or which of two modes of existence is the most grateful to the feelings, apart from its moral attributes and from its consequences, the judgment of these who are qualified by knowledge of both, or, if they differ, that of the majority among them, must be admitted as final. And there needs be the less hesitation to accept this judgment respecting the quality of pleasures, since there is no other tribunal to be referred to even on the question of quantity. What means are there of determining which is the acutest of two pains, or the intensest of two pleasurable sensations, except the general suffrage of those who are familiar with both? Neither pains nor pleasures are homogeneous, and pain is always heterogeneous with pleasure. What is there to decide whether a particular pleasure is worth purchasing at the cost of a particular pain, except the feelings and judgment of the experienced? When, therefore, those feelings and judgment declare the pleasures derived from the higher faculties to be preferable *in kind,* apart from the question of intensity, to those of which the animal nature, disjoined from the higher faculties, is susceptible, they are entitled on this subject to the same regard.

. . .

I must again repeat what the assailants of utilitarianism seldom have the justice to acknowledge, that the happiness which forms the utilitarian standard of what is right in conduct is not the agent's own happiness but that of all concerned. As between his own happiness and that of others, utilitarianism requires him to be as strictly impartial as a disinterested and benevolent spectator. In the golden rule of Jesus of Nazareth, we read the complete spirit of the ethics of utility. "To do as you would be done by," and " to love your neighbor as yourself," constitute the ideal perfection of utilitarian morality. As the means of making the nearest approach to this ideal, utility would enjoin, first, that laws and social arrangements should place the happiness or (as, speaking practically, it may be called) the interest of every individual as nearly as possible in harmony with the interest of the whole; and, secondly, that education and opinion, which have so vast a power over human character, should so use that power as to establish in the mind of every individual an indissoluble association between his own happiness and the good of the whole, especially between his own happiness and the practice of such modes of conduct, negative and positive, as regard for the universal happiness prescribes; so that not only he may be unable to conceive the possibility of happiness to himself, consistently with conduct opposed to the general good, but also that a direct impulse to promote the general good may be in every individual one of the habitual motives of action, and the sentiments connected therewith may fill a large and prominent place in every human being's sentient existence. If the impugners of the utilitarian morality represented it to their own minds in this its true character, I know not what recommendation possessed by any other morality they could possibly affirm to be wanting to it; what more beautiful or more exalted developments of human nature any other ethical system can be supposed to foster, or what springs of action, not accessible to the utilitarian, such systems rely on for giving effect to their mandates.

The objectors to utilitarianism cannot always be charged with representing it in a discreditable light. On the contrary, those among them who entertain anything like a just idea of its disinterested character sometimes find fault with its standard as being too high for humanity. They say it is exacting too much to require that people shall always act from the inducement of promoting the general interest of society. But this is to mistake the very meaning of a standard of morals and confound the rule of action with the motive of it. It is the business of ethics to tell us what are our duties, or by what test we may know them; but no system of ethics requires that the sole motive of all we do shall be a feeling of duty; on the contrary, ninety-nine hundredths of all our actions are done from other motives, and rightly so done if the rule of duty does not condemn them. It is the more unjust to utilitarianism that this particular mis-apprehension should be made a ground of objection to it, inasmuch as utili-tarian moralists have gone beyond almost all others in affirming that the motive has nothing to do with the morality of the action, though much with the worth of the agent. He who saves a fellow creature from drowning does what is morally right, whether his motive be duty or the hope of being paid for his trouble; he who betrays the friend that trusts him is guilty of a crime, even if his object be to serve another friend to whom he is under greater obligations.[1] But to speak only of actions done from the motive or duty, and in direct obedience to principle: it is a misapprehension of the utilitarian mode of thought to conceive it as implying that people should fix their minds upon so wide a generality as the world, or society at large. The great majority of good actions are intended not for the benefit of the world, but for that of indivduals, of which the good of the world is made up; and the thoughts of the most virtuous man need not on these occasions travel beyond the particular persons con-cerned, except so far as is necessary to assure himself that in benefiting them he is not violating the rights, that is, the legitimate and authorized expectations, of anyone else. The multiplication of happiness is, according to the utilitarian

[1] An opponent, whose intellectual and moral fairness it is a pleasure to acknowledge (the Rev. J. Llewellyn Davies), has objected to this passage, saying, "Surely the rightness or wrongness of saving a man from drowning does depend very much upon the motive with which it is done. Suppose that a tyrant, when his enemy jumped into the sea to escape from him, saved him from drowning simply in order that he might inflict upon him more exquisite tortures, would it tend to clearness to speak of that rescue as 'a morally right action'? Or suppose again, according to one of the stock illustrations of ethical inquiries, that a man betrayed a trust received from a friend, because the discharge of it would fatally injure that friend himself or someone belonging to him, would utilitarianism compel one to call the betrayal 'a crime' as much as if it had been done from the meanest motive?"

I submit that he who saves another from drowning in order to kill him by torture afterwards does not differ only in motive from him who does the same thing from duty or benevolence; the act itself is different. The rescue of the man is, in the case supposed, only the necessary first step of an act far more atrocious than leaving him to drown would have been. Had Mr. Davies said, "The rightness or wrongness of saving a man from drowning does depend very much"—not upon the motive, but—"upon the *intention*," no utilitarian would have differed from him. Mr. Davies, by an oversight too common not to be quite venial, has in this case confounded the very different ideas of Motive and Intention. There is no point which utilitarian thinkers (and Bentham pre-eminently) have taken more pains to illustrate than this. The morality of the action depends entirely upon the intention—that is, upon what the agent *wills to do*. But the motive, that is, the feeling which makes him will so to do, if it makes no difference in the act, makes none in the morality: though it makes a great difference in our moral estimation of the agent, especially if it indicates a good or a bad habitual *disposition*—a bent of character from which useful, or from which hurtful actions are likely to arise.

ethics, the object of virtue: the occasions on which any person (except one in a thousand) has it in his power to do this on an extended scale—in other words, to be a public benefactor—are but exceptional; and on these occasions alone is he called on to consider public utility; in every other case, private utility, the interest or happiness of some few persons, is all he has to attend to. Those alone the influence of whose actions extends to society in general need concern themselves habitually about so large an object. In the case of abstinences indeed—of things which people forbear to do from moral considerations, though the consequences in the particular case might be beneficial— it would be unworthy of an intelligent agent not to be consciously aware that the action is of a class which, if practiced generally, would be generally injurious, and that this is the ground of the obligation to abstain from it. The amount of regard for the public interest implied in this recognition is no greater than is demanded by every system of morals, for they all enjoin to abstain from whatever is manifestly pernicious to society.

The same considerations dispose of another reproach against the doctrine of utility, founded on a still grosser misconception of the purpose of a standard of morality and of the very meaning of the words "right" and "wrong." It is often affirmed that utilitarianism renders men cold and unsympathizing; that it chills their moral feelings toward individuals; that it makes them regard only the dry and hard consideration of the consequences of actions, not taking into their moral estimate the qualities from which those actions emanate. If the assertion means that they do not allow their judgment respecting the rightness or wrongness of an action to be influenced by their opinion of the qualities of the person who does it, this is a complaint not against utilitarianism, but against any standard or morality at all; for certainly no known ethical standard decides an action to be good or bad because it is done by a good or bad man, still less because done by an amiable, a brave, or a benevolent man, or the contrary. These considerations are relevant, not to the estimation of actions, but of persons; and there is nothing in the utilitarian theory inconsistent with the fact that there are other things which interest us in persons besides the rightness and wrongness of their actions. The Stoics, indeed, with the paradoxical misuse of language which was part of their system, and by which they strove to raise themselves above all concern about anything but virtue, were fond of saying that he who has that has everything; that he, and only he, is rich, is beautiful, is a king. But no claim of this description is made for the virtuous man by the utilitarian doctrine. Utilitarians are quite aware that there are other desirable possessions and qualities besides virtue, and are perfectly willing to allow to all of them their full worth. They are also aware that a right action does not necessarily indicate a virtuous character, and that actions which are blamable often proceed from qualities entitled to praise. When this is apparent in any particular case, it modifies their estimation, not certainly of the act, but of the agent. I grant that they are, notwithstanding, of opinion that in the long run the best proof of a good character is good actions; and resolutely refuse to consider any mental disposition as good of which the predominant tendency is to produce bad conduct. This makes them unpopular with many people, but it is an unpopularity which they must share with everyone who regards the distinction between right and wrong in a serious light; and the reproach is not one which a conscientious utilitarian need be anxious to repel.

. . .

Again, utility is often summarily stigmatized as an immoral doctrine by giving it the name of "expediency," and taking advantage of the popular use of that term to contrast it with principle. But the expedient, in the sense in which it is opposed to the right, generally means that which is expedient for the particular interest of the agent himself; as when a minister sacrifices the interests of his country to keep himself in place. When it means anything better than this, it means that which is expedient for some immediate object, some temporary purpose, but which violates a rule whose observance is expedient in a much higher degree. The expedient, in this sense, instead of being the same thing with the useful, is a branch of the hurtful. Thus it would often be expedient, for the purpose of getting over some momentary embarrassment, or attaining some object immediately useful to ourselves or others, to tell a lie. But inasmuch as the cultivation in ourselves of a sensitive feeling on the subject of veracity is one of the most useful, and the enfeeblement of that feeling one of the most hurtful, things to which our conduct can be instrumental; and inasmuch as any, even unintentional, deviation from truth does that much toward weakening the trustworthiness of human assertion, which is not only the principal support of all present social well-being, but the insufficiency of which does more than any one thing that can be named to keep back civilization, virtue, everything on which human happiness on the largest scale depends—we feel that the violation, for a present advantage, of a rule of such transcendent expediency is not expedient, and that he who, for the sake of convenience to himself or to some other individual, does what depends on him to deprive mankind of the good, and inflict upon them the evil, involved in the greater or less reliance which they can place in each other's words, acts the part of one of their worst enemies. Yet that even this rule, sacred as it is, admits of possible exceptions is acknowledged by all moralists; the chief of which is when the withholding of some fact (as of information from a malefactor, or of bad news from a person dangerously ill) would save an individual (especially an individual other than oneself) from great and unmerited evil, and when the withholding can only be effected by denial. But in order that the exception many not extend itself beyond the need, and may have the least possible effect in weakening reliance on veracity, it ought to be recognized and, if possible, its limits defined; and, if the principle of utility is good for anything, it must be good for weighing these conflicting utilities against one another and marking out the region within which one or the other preponderates.

Again, defenders of utility often find themselves called upon to reply to such objections as this—that there is not time, previous to action, for calculating and weighing the effects of any line of conduct on the general happiness. This is exactly as if anyone were to say that it is impossible to guide our conduct by Christianity because there is not time, on every occasion on which anything has to be done, to read through the Old and New Testaments. The answer to the objection is that there has been ample time, namely, the whole past duration of the human species. During all that time mankind have been learning by experience the tendencies of actions; on which experience all the prudence as well as all the morality of life are dependent. People talk as if the commencement of this course of experience had hitherto been put off, and as if, at the moment when some man feels tempted to meddle with the property or life of another, he had to begin considering for the first time whether murder and theft are injurious to human happiness. Even then I do not think that he would find the question very puzzling; but, at all events, the matter is now done to his hand. It is truly a whimsical supposition that, if mankind were agreed in considering utility to be the test of morality, they would remain without any agreement as to what *is* useful, and would take no measures for having their notions on the subject taught to the young and enforced by law and opinion. There is no difficulty in proving any ethical standard whatever to work ill if we suppose universal idiocy to be conjoined with it; but on any hypothesis short of that, mankind must by this time have acquired positive beliefs as to the effects of some actions on their happiness; and the beliefs which have thus come down are the rules of morality for the multitude, and for the philosopher until he has succeeded in finding better. That philosophers might easily do this, even now, on many subjects; that the received code of ethics is by no means of divine right; and that mankind have still much to learn as to the effects of actions on the general happiness, I admit or rather earnestly maintain. The corollaries from the principle of utility, like the precepts of every practical art, admit of indefinite improvement, and, in a progressive state of the human mind, their improvement is perpetually going on. But to consider the rules of morality as improvable is one thing; to pass over the intermediate generalization entirely and endeavor to test each individual action directly by the first principle is another. It is a strange notion that the acknowledgment of a first principle is inconsistent with the admission of secondary ones. To inform a traveler respecting the place of his ultimate destination is not to forbid the use of landmarks and direction-posts on the way. The proposition that happiness is the end and aim of morality does not mean that no road ought to be laid down to that goal, or that persons going thither should not be advised to take one direction rather than another. Men really ought to leave off talking a kind of nonsense on this subject, which they would neither talk nor listen to on other matters of practical concernment. Nobody argues that the art of navigation is not founded on astronomy because sailors cannot wait to calculate the Nautical Almanac. Being rational creatures, they go to sea with it ready calculated; and all rational creatures go out upon the sea of life with their minds made up on the common questions of right and wrong, as well as on many of the far more difficult questions of wise and foolish. And this, as long as foresight is a human quality, it is to be presumed they will continue to do. Whatever we adopt as the fundamental principle of morality, we require subordinate principles to apply it by; the impossibility of doing without them, being common to all systems, can afford no argument against any one in particular; but gravely to argue as if no such secondary principles could be had, and as if mankind had remained till now, and always must remain, without drawing any general conclusions from the experience of human life is as high a pitch, I think, as absurdity has ever reached in philosophical controversy.

The remainder of the stock arguments against utilitarianism mostly consist in laying to its charge the common infirmities of human nature, and the general difficulties which embarrass conscientious persons in shaping their course through life. We are told that a utilitarian will be apt to make his own particular case an exception to moral rules, and, when under temptation, will see a utility in the breach of a rule, greater than he will see in its observance. But is utility the only creed which is able to furnish us with excuses for evil-doing and means of cheating our own conscience? They are afforded in abundance by all doctrines which recognize as a fact in morals the existence of conflicting considerations, which all doctrines do that have been believed by sane persons. It is not the fault of any creed, but of the complicated nature of human affairs, that rules of conduct cannot be so framed as to require no exceptions, and that hardly any kind of action can safely be laid down as either always obligatory or always condemnable. There is no ethical creed which does not temper the rigidity of its laws by giving a certain latitude, under the moral responsibility of the agent, for accomodation to peculiarities of circumstances; and under every creed, at the opening thus made, self-deception and dishonest casuistry get in. There exists no moral system under which there do not arise unequivocal cases of conflicting obligation. These are the real difficulties, the knotty points both in the theory of ethics and in the conscientious guidance of personal conduct. They are overcome practically, with greater or with less success, according to the intellect and virtue of the individual; but it can hardly be pretended that anyone will be the less qualified for dealing with them, from possessing an ultimate standard to which conflicting rights and duties can be referred. If utility is the ultimate source of moral obligations, utility may be invoked to decide between them when their demands are incompatible. Though the application of the standard may be difficult, it is better than none at all; while in other systems, the moral laws all claiming independent authority, there is no common umpire entitled to interfere between them; their claims to precedence one over another rest on little better than sophistry, and, unless determined, as they generally are, by the unacknowledged influence of consideration of utility, afford a free scope for the action of personal desires and partialities. We must remember that only in these cases of conflict between secondary principles is it requisite that first principles should be appealed to. There is no case of moral obligation in which some secondary principle is not involved; and if only one, there can seldom be any real doubt which one it is, in the mind of any person by whom the principle itself is recognized.

OF WHAT SORT OF PROOF
THE PRINCIPLE OF UTILITY IS SUSCEPTIBLE

It has already been remarked that questions of ultimate ends do not admit of proof, in the ordinary acceptation of the term. To be incapable of proof by reasoning is common to all first principles, to the first premises of our knowledge, as well as to those of our conduct. But the former, being matters of fact, may be the subject of a direct appeal to the faculties which judge of fact—namely, our senses and our internal consciousness. Can an appeal be made to the same faculties on questions of practical ends? Or by what other faculty is cognizance taken of them?

Questions about ends are, in other words, questions what things are desirable. The utilitarian doctrine is that happiness is desirable, and the only thing desirable, as an end; all other things being only desirable as means to that end. What ought to be required of this doctrine, what conditions is it requisite that the doctrine should fulfill—to make good its claim to be believed?

The only proof capable of being given that an object is visible is that people actually see it. The only proof that a sound is audible is that people hear it; and so of the other sources of our experience. In like manner, I apprehend, the sole evidence it is possible to produce that anything is desirable is that people do actually desire it. If the end which the utilitarian doctrine proposes to itself were not, in theory and in practice, acknowledged to be an end, nothing could ever convince any person that it was so. No reason can be given why the general happiness is desirable, except that each person, so far as he believes it to be attainable, desires his own happiness. This, however, being a fact, we have not only all the proof which the case admits of, but all which it is possible to require, that happiness is a good, that each person's happiness is a good to that person, and the general happiness, therefore, a good to the aggregate of all persons. Happiness has made out its title as *one* of the ends of conduct and, consequently, one of the criteria of morality.

But it has not, by this alone, proved itself to be the sole criterion. To do that, it would seem, by the same rule, necessary to show, not only that people desire happiness, but that they never desire anything else. Now it is palpable that they do desire things which, in common language, are decidedly distinguished from happiness. They desire, for example, virtue and the absence of vice no less really than pleasure and the absence of pain. The desire of virtue is not as universal, but it is as authentic a fact as the desire of happiness. And hence the opponents of the utilitarian standard deem that they have a right to infer that there are other ends of human action besides happiness, and that happiness is not the standard of approbation and disapprobation.

But does the utilitarian doctrine deny that people desire virtue, or maintain that virtue is not a thing to be desired? The very reverse. It maintains not only that virtue is to be desired, but that it is to be desired disinterestedly, for itself. Whatever may be the opinion of utilitarian moralists as to the original conditions by which virtue is made virtue, however they may believe (as they do) that actions and dispositions are only virtuous because they promote another end than virtue, yet this being granted, and it having been decided, from considerations of this description, what *is* virtuous, they not only place virtue at the very head of the things which are good as means to the ultimate end, but they also recognize as a psychological fact the possibility of its being, to the individual, a good in itself, without looking to any end beyond it; and hold that the mind is not in a right state, not in a state conformable to utility, not in the state most conducive to the general happiness, unless it does love virtue in this manner—as a thing desirable in itself, even although, in the individual instance, it should not produce those other desirable consequences which it tends to produce, and on account of which it is held to be virtue. This opinion is not, in the smallest degree, a departure from the happiness principle. The ingredients of happiness are very various, and each of them is desirable in itself, and not merely when considered as swelling an aggregate. The principle of utility does not mean that any given pleasure, as music, for instance, or any given exemption from pain, as for example health, is to be looked upon as means to a collective something termed happiness, and to be desired on that account. They are desired and desirable in and for themselves; besides being means, they are a part of the end. Virtue, according to the utilitarian doctrine, is not naturally and originally part of the end, but it is capable of becoming so; and in those who live it disinterestedly it has become so, and is desired and cherished, not as a means to happiness, but as part of their happiness.

To illustrate this further, we may remember that virtue is not the only thing originally a means, and which if it were not a means to anything else would be and remain indifferent, but which by association with what it is a means to comes to be desired for itself, and that too with the utmost intensity. What, for example, shall we say of the love of money? There is nothing originally more desirable about money than about any heap of glittering pebbles. Its worth is solely that of the things which it will buy; the desires for other things than itself, which it is a means of gratifying. Yet the love of money is not only one of the strongest moving forces of human life, but money is, in many cases, desired in and for itself; the desire to possess it is often stronger than the desire to use it, and goes on increasing when all the desires which point to ends beyond it, to be compassed by it, are falling off. It may, then, be said truly that money is desired not for the sake of an end, but as part of the end. From being a means to happiness, it it has come to be itself a principal ingredient of the individual's conception of happiness. The same may be said of the majority of the great objects of human life: power, for example, or fame, except that to each of these there is a certain amount of immediate pleasure annexed, which has at least the semblance of being naturally inherent in them—a thing which cannot be said of money. Still, however, the strongest natural attraction, both of power and of fame, is the immense aid they give to the attainment of our other wishes; and it is the strong association thus generated between them and all our objects of desire which gives to the direct desire of them the intensity it often assumes, so as in some characters to surpass in strength all other desires. In these cases the means have become a part of the end, and a more important part of it than any of the things which they are means to. What was once desired as an instrument for the attainment of happiness has come to be desired for its own sake. In being desired for its own sake it is, however, desired as *part* of happiness. The person is made, or thinks he would be made, happy by its mere possession; and is made unhappy by failure to obtain it. The desire of it is not a different thing from the desire of happiness any more than the love of music or the desire of health. They are included in happiness. They are some of the elements of which the desire of happiness is made up. Happiness is not an abstract idea but a concrete whole; and these are some of its parts. And the utilitarian standard sanctions and approves their being so. Life would be a poor thing, very ill provided with sources of happiness, if there were not this provision of nature by which things originally indifferent, but conducive to, or otherwise associated with, the satisfaction of our primitive desires, become in themselves sources of pleasure more valuable than the primitive pleasures, both in permanency, in the space of human existence that they are capable of covering, and even in intensity.

Virtue, according to the utilitarian conception is a good of this description. There was no original desire of it, or motive to it, save its conduciveness to pleasure, and especially to protection from pain. But through the association thus formed it may be felt a good in itself, and desired as such with as great intensity as any other good; and with this difference between it and the love of money, of power, or of fame—that all of these may, and often do, render the individual noxious to the other members of the society to which he belongs, whereas there is nothing which makes him so much a blessing to them as the cultivation of the disinterested love of virtue. And consequently, the utilitarian standard, while it tolerates and approves those other acquired desires, up to the point beyond which they would be more injurious to the general happiness than promotive of it, enjoins and requires the cultivation of the love of virtue up to the greatest strength possible, as being above all things important to the general happiness.

It results from the preceding considerations that there is in reality nothing desired except happiness. Whatever is desired otherwise than as a means to some end beyond itself, and ultimately to happiness, is desired as itself a part of happiness, and is not desired for itself until it has become so. Those who desire virtue for its own sake desire it either because the consciousness of it is a pleasure, or because the consciousness of being without it is a pain, or for both reasons united; as in truth the pleasure and pain seldom exist separately, but almost always together—the same person feeling pleasure in the degree of virtue attained, and pain in not having attained more. If one of these gave him no pleasure, and the other no pain, he would not love or desire virtue, or would desire it only for the other benefits which it might produce to himself or to persons whom he cared for.

We have now, then, an answer to the question, of what sort of proof the principle of utility is susceptible. If the opinion which I have now stated is psychologically true—if human nature is so constituted as to desire nothing which is not either a part of happiness or a means of happiness—we can have no other proof, and we require no other, that these are the only things desirable. If so, happiness is the sole end of human action, and the promotion of it the test by which to judge of all human conduct; from whence it necessarily follows that it must be the criterion of morality, since a part is included in the whole.

And now to decide whether this is really so, whether mankind do desire nothing for itself but that which is a pleasure to them, or of which the absence is a pain, we have evidently arrived at a question of fact and experience, dependent, like all similar questions, upon evidence. It can only be determined by practiced self-consciousness and self-observation, assisted by observation of others. I believe that these sources of evidence, impartially consulted, will declare that desiring a thing and finding it pleasant, aversion to it and thinking of it as painful, are phenomena entirely inseparable or, rather, two parts of the same phenomenon—in strictness of language, two different modes of naming the same psychological fact; that to think of an object as desirable (unless for the sake of its consequences) and to think of it as pleasant are one and the same thing; and that to desire anything except in proportion as the idea of it is pleasant is a physical and metaphysical impossibility.

So obvious does this appear to me that I expect it will hardly be disputed; and the objection made will be, not that desire can possibly be directed to anything ultimately except pleasure and exemption from pain, but that the will is a different thing from desire; that a person of confirmed virtue or any other person whose purposes are fixed carries out his purposes without any thought of the pleasure he has in contemplating them or expects to derive from their fulfillment, and persists in acting on them, even though these pleasures are much diminished by changes in his character or decay of his passive sensibilities, or are outweighed by the pains which the pursuit of the purposes may bring upon him. All this I fully admit and have stated it elsewhere as positively and emphatically as anyone. Will, the active phenomenon, is a different thing from desire, the state of passive sensibility, and, though originally an offshoot from it, may in time take root and detach itself from the parent stock, so much so that in the case of a habitual purpose, instead of willing the thing because we desire it, we often desire it only because we will it. This, however, is but an instance of that familiar fact, the power of habit, and is nowise confined to the case of virtuous actions. Many indifferent things which men originally did from a motive of some sort they continue to do from habit. Sometimes this is done unconsciously, the consciousness coming only after the action; at other times with conscious volition, but volition which has become habitual and is put in operation by the force of habit, in opposition perhaps to the deliberate preference, as often happens with those who have contracted habits of vicious or hurtful indulgence. Third and last comes the case in which the habitual act of will in the individual instance is not in contradiction to the general intention prevailing at other times, but in fulfillment of it, as in the case of the person of confirmed virtue and of all who pursue deliberately and consistently any determinate end. The distinction between will and desire thus understood is an authentic and highly important psychological fact; but the fact consists solely in this—that will, like all other parts of our constitution, is amenable to habit, and that we may will from habit what we no longer desire for itself, or desire only because we will it. It is not the less true that will, in the beginning, is entirely produced by desire, including in that term the repelling influence of pain as well as the attractive one of pleasure. Let us take into consideration no longer the person who has a confirmed will to do right, but him in whom that virtuous will is still feeble, conquerable by temptation, and not to be fully relied on; by what means can it be strengthened? How can the will to be virtuous, where it does not exist in sufficient force, be implanted or awakened? Only by making the person *desire* virtue—by making him think of it in a pleasurable light, or of its absence in a painful one. It is by associating the doing right with pleasure, or the wrong with pain, or by eliciting and impressing and bringing home to the person's experience the pleasure naturally involved in the one or the pain in the other, that it is possible to call forth that will to be virtuous which, when confirmed, acts without any thought of either pleasure or pain. Will is the child of desire, and passes out of the dominion of its parent only to come under that of habit. That which is the result of habit affords no presumption of being intrinsically good; and there would be no reason for wishing that the purpose of virtue should become independent of pleasure and pain were it not that the influence of the pleasurable and painful associations which prompt to virtue is not sufficiently to be depended on for unerring constancy of action until it has acquired the support of habit. Both in feeling and in conduct, habit is the only thing which imparts certainty; and it is because of the importance to others of being able to rely absolutely on one's feelings and conduct, and to oneself of being able to rely on one's own, that the will to do right ought to be cultivated into this habitual independence. In other words, this state of the will is a means to good, not intrinsically a good; and does not contradict the doctrine that nothing is a good to human beings but in so far as it is either itself pleasurable or a means of attaining pleasure or averting pain.

But if this doctrine be true, the principle of utility is proved. Whether it is so or not must now be left to the consideration of the thoughtful reader.

27

Toward a Credible
Form of Utilitarianism

RICHARD BRANDT

*Richard Brandt (b. 1910) has taught philosophy at Swarthmore College and,
more recently, at the University of Michigan. He has published many articles
on ethics and the philosophy of mind. His books include* Hopi Ethics,
Ethical Theory, *and* A Theory of the Good and the Right.

  *In this selection, Brandt tries to formulate a version of rule-utilitarianism
that is not open to decisive objections. Rule-utilitarianism says that we
should apply the principle of utility ("do what will produce the best results")
to choices among rules or systems of rules rather than to individual acts. But
how, exactly, should we do this? Should we ask what would happen if
everyone followed a given set of rules? What would happen if the rules were
learned and accepted by a society of people of average conscientiousness?
What would happen if the rules were learned and accepted by all actual
members of the agent's society? In posing the question, should we consider
members of other societies? And how, in any case, can we formulate systems
of rules to resolve potential conflicts within those systems? As Brandt
proceeds, he offers detailed and careful answers to these questions. By
working through these answers, we learn much about the resources of rule-
utilitarianism.*

Introduction

THIS PAPER IS an attempt to formulate, in a tolerably precise way, a type of
utilitarian ethical theory which is not open to obvious and catastrophic objections. It is not my aim especially to advocate the kind of view finally stated,
although I do believe it is more acceptable than any other type of utilitarianism.

. . .

The view to be discussed is a form of "rule-utilitarianism." This terminology
must be explained. I call a utilitarianism "act-utilitarianism" if it holds that
the rightness of an act is fixed by the utility of *its* consequences, as compared
with those of other acts the agent might perform instead. Act-utilitarianism is
hence an atomistic theory: the value of the effects of a single act on the world
is decisive for its rightness. "Rule-utilitarianism," in contrast, applies to views
according to which the rightness of an act is not fixed by *its* relative utility,
but by conformity with general rules or principles; the utilitarian feature of
these theories consists in the fact that the correctness of these rules or principles
is fixed in some way by the utility of their general acceptance. In contrast with

the atomism of act-utilitarianism, rule-utilitarianism is in a sense an organic theory: the rightness of individual acts can be ascertained only by assessing a whole social policy.

Neither form of utilitarianism is necessarily committed on the subject of what counts as "utility": not on the meaning or function of such phrases as "maximize intrinsic good," and not on the identity of intrinsic goods—whether enjoyments, or states of persons, or states of affairs, such as equality of distribution.

In recent years, types of rule-utilitarianism have been the object of much interest. And for good reason. Act-utilitarianism, at least given the assumptions about what is valuable which utilitarians commonly make, has implications which it is difficult to accept. It implies that if you have employed a boy to mow your lawn and he has finished the job and asks for his pay, you should pay him what you promised only if you cannot find a better use for your money. It implies that when you bring home your monthly pay-check you should use it to support your family and yourself only if it cannot be used more effectively to supply the needs of others. It implies that if your father is ill and has no prospect of good in his life, and maintaining him is a drain on the energy and enjoyments of others, then, if you can end his life without provoking any public scandal or setting a bad example, it is your positive duty to take matters into your own hands and bring his life to a close. A virtue of rule-utilitarianism, in at least some of its forms, is that it avoids at least some of such objectionable implications.

In the present paper I wish to arrive at a more precise formulation of a rule-utilitarian type of theory which is different from act-utilitarianism and which is not subject to obvious and catastrophic difficulties. To this end I shall, after an important preliminary discussion, begin by considering two formulations, both supported by distinguished philosophers, which, as I shall show, lead us in the wrong direction. This discussion will lead to a new formulation devised to avoid the consequences of the first theories. I shall then describe three problems which the new theory seems to face, and consider how—by amendments or otherwise—these difficulties may be met.

1
Utilitarianism as a Theory About the Objectively Right

Before we can proceed there is a preliminary issue to be settled. It is generally agreed that utilitarianism is a proposal about which acts are *right* or *wrong*. Unfortunately it is also widely held—although this is a matter of dispute— that these terms are used in several senses. Hence, in order to state the utilitarian thesis clearly, we must identify which sense of these words (if there is more than one) we have in mind. Utilitarianism may be clearly false in all of its forms if it is construed as a universal statement about which acts are right or wrong, in some of the senses in which these words are, or at least are supposed to be, used.

It is plausible to say that "wrong" is sometimes used in a sense equivalent to "morally blameworthy" or "reprehensible," in a sense which implies the propriety of disapproval of the agent for his deed. Now, if utilitarianism is understood as a theory about right and wrong actions in this sense, I believe it is an indefensible theory in all its forms. For we have good reason to think that whether an act is wrong in this sense depends in part on such things as whether the agent sincerely believed he was doing his duty, whether the temptation to do what he did was so strong that only a person of very unusual firmness of will would have succeeded in withstanding it, and whether the agent's action was impulsive and provoked, or deliberate and unprovoked. If whether an act is wrong depends in part on any one of these factors, then it is difficult to see how the utilitarian thesis that rightness or wrongness is in some sense a function of utility can be correct.

We can, however, construe utilitarianism as a thesis about which acts are right or wrong in some other sense. It may, for instance, be taken as a theory about which acts are right or wrong in a forward-looking sense, which I shall call the "objective" sense. But what is this sense?

. . .

If we . . . say that "duty" is sometimes used in a sense such that whether something is one's duty depends on what the facts really are, then we are conceding that the word (and, presumably, "right" and "wrong" *and* "moral obligation") is sometimes used in an "objective" sense—the sense in which G. E. Moore thought it was sometimes used when he wrote *Ethics and Principia Ethica*. And if so, it is not entirely stupid to propose, as Moore did, that furthermore, an act is right, in that objective sense of "right," if and only if its *actual* consequences, whether foreseeable at the time or not, are such that the performance of the act produces at least as much intrinsic good as could be produced by any other act the agent could perform instead. It is this sense of these terms—the sense in which duty (etc.) depends on what the facts really are and not on what the agent thinks about them—which I am terming the "objective" sense. I shall construe utilitarianism as a proposal about which acts are right or wrong in this objective sense.

It would be foolish, however, . . . to affirm without doubt that there is a sense of "duty" in which duty depends on what the facts are and not on what the agent thinks they are—and much more foolish to affirm without doubt that there is *no* sense of "duty" in which duty depends, not on the facts, but on what the agent thinks the facts are, at least after properly careful investigation.

Philosophers who think these words have no "objective" sense at all, or who at least think there is still a third sense of these terms, over and above the two I have sketched, probably can mostly be said to think that these words are used in what we may call the "subjective" sense—and either that this is their only sense or that it is one ordinary sense. They do not agree among themselves about what this sense is. Some of them hold that "right" (etc.) is sometimes so used that—if I may identify their conception by my own terminology, which, of course, some of them would not accept—an act is right in that sense if and only if it would have been right in my objective sense, if the facts had really been what the agent thought they were, or at least would have thought they were if he had investigated properly. What is one's duty, on this view, depends on what the agent thinks about the facts—or would think if he investigated properly—not on what the facts really are. Naturally, if one has this (alleged) sense of "duty" or "right" in mind when formulating the principle of utilitarianism, one will say the principle is that an act is right if and only if the agent *thinks*—or would think, if he investigated properly—it will maximize utility (or have some such relation to utility). Or, perhaps, the principle will say that an act is right if and only if it will maximize expectable utility, or something of the sort.

The question whether there is an objective sense, or a subjective sense, or perhaps both such senses, is a difficult one. Although I think it plausible to suppose there is an "objective" sense, I do feel doubt about the matter. I propose, nevertheless, to discuss utilitarianism as a theory about right and wrong in this sense. I do so for several reasons. First, there are many philosophers who think there is such a sense, and an examination of utilitarianism construed in this way "speaks to their condition."[1] Second, even if there were no such ordinary sense of "right," we could define such a sense by reference to the "subjective" sense of "right" (assuming there is one); and it so happens that we could say all the things that we have occasion to say in ethics by using this defined "objective" sense of "right" and also terms like "blameworthy" and "reprehensible." We could say "all we have occasion to say" in the sense that any statement we make, and think important, could be put in terms of this vocabulary. Third, it is important to see how types of rule-utilitarian theory fare if they are construed as theories about which acts are right or wrong in this sense. Doubtless sometimes writers on this topic have not kept clearly in mind just which sense of "right" they were talking about; it is useful to see what difficulties arise *if* they are to be taken as talking of what is right or wrong in the objective sense. Finally, an assessment of utilitarianisms as theories about which acts are objectively right will enable us to make at least some assessments of utilitarianisms as theories about which acts are subjectively right, in view of the logical connection indicated above between "right" in the objective sense and "right" in the subjective sense.

2
Accepted Rules vs. Justifiable Rules as the Test of Rightness

It is convenient to begin by taking as our text some statements drawn from an interesting article by J. O. Urmson. In this paper, Urmson suggested that John Stuart Mill should be interpreted as a rule-utilitarian; and Urmson's

---

[1] Notice that such philosophers are not refuted by the mere consideration that sometimes we say "is right" and not "is probably right" even when we know we lack evidence about some facts that might be relevant to what is right in the objective sense. It would be a mistake to infer from such usage that we are not employing "right" in the objective sense. For, in general, we are entitled to make any assertion roundly without the qualifying word "probable" if we know of no definite grounds for questioning the truth of the assertion.

opinion was that Mill's view would be more plausible if he were so interpreted. Urmson summarized the possible rule-utilitarian interpretation of Mill in four propositions, of which I quote the first two:

A. A particular action is justified as being right [in the sense of being morally obligatory] by showing that it is in accord with [is required by] some moral rule. It is shown to be wrong by showing that it transgresses some moral rule.
B. A moral rule is shown to be correct by showing that the recognition of that rule promotes the ultimate end.[2]

Urmson's first proposition could be taken in either of two ways. When it speaks of a "moral rule," it may refer to an *accepted* moral rule, presumably one accepted in the society of the agent. Alternatively, it may refer to a *correct* moral rule, presumably one the recognition of which promotes the ultimate end. If we ask in which way the proposed theory should be taken, in order to arrive at a defensible theory, part of the answer is that qualifications are going to be required, whichever way we take it. I think it more worthwhile and promising, however, to try to develop it in the second interpretation.

. . .

For a start, we might summarize the gist of Urmson's proposal, construed in the second way, as follows: "An act is right if and only if it conforms with that set of moral rules, the recognition of which would have significantly desirable consequences." A somewhat modified version of this is what I shall be urging.

One minor amendment I wish to make immediately. I think we should replace the second clause by the expression, "the recognition of which would have the *best* consequences." This amendment may be criticized on the ground that the business of moral rules is with commanding or prohibiting actions whose performance or omission would be quite harmful if practiced widely, but not to require actions which just maximize benefits, especially if the benefit concerns only the agent. It may be said, then, that the amendment I propose is possibly a clue to *perfect* behavior but not to right behavior. But this objection overlooks an important point. We must remember that it is a serious matter to have a moral rule at all, for moral rules take conduct out of the realm of preference and free decision. So, for the recognition of a certain moral rule to have good consequences, the benefits of recognition must outweigh the costliness of restricting freedom. Therefore, to recognize a moral rule restricting self-regarding behavior will rarely have the best consequences; rules of prudence should normally not be moral rules. Again, my proposal implies that moral rules will require services for other people only when it is better to have such services performed from a sense of obligation than not performed at all;

---

[2] J. O. Urmson, "The Interpretation of the Moral Philosophy of J. S. Mill," *Philosophical Quarterly*, Vol. III (1953), 33–39.

so the amendment does not commit us to saying that it is morally obligatory to perform minor altruistic services for others.

But why insist on the amendment? The reason is that the original, as I stated it (but not necessarily as Urmson intended it), is insufficiently comparative in form. The implication is that a rule is acceptable so long as it is significantly better than no regulation at all. But the effect of this is tolerantly to accept a great many rules which we should hardly regard as morally acceptable. Consider promises. There are various possible rules about when promises must be kept. One such possible rule is to require keeping *all* promises, absolutely irrespective of unforseeable and uncontemplated hardships on the promisee. Recognition of this rule might have good consequences as compared with no rule at all. Therefore it seems to satisfy the unamended formula. Many similar rules would satisfy it. But we know of another rule—the one we recognize—with specifications about allowable exceptions, which would have much better consequences. If we are utilitarian in spirit, we shall want to endorse such a rule but not both of these rules; and the second one is much closer to our view about what our obligations are. The amendment in general endorses as correct many rules which command our support for parallel reasons, and refuses to endorse many others which we reject for parallel reasons.

3

A Specious Rule-Utilitarianism

I shall now digress briefly, in order to bring out the importance of avoiding a form of rule-utilitarianism which seems to differ only insignificantly from our above initial suggestion, and which at first seems most attractive. It is worthwhile doing so, partly because two very interesting and important papers developing a rule-utilitarian theory may be construed as falling into the trap I shall describe.[3] I say only that they "may be" so construed because their authors are possibly using somewhat different concepts and, in particular, may not be thinking of utilitarianism as a thesis about right and wrong in the objective sense.

Suppose that we wrote, instead of the above suggested formulation, the following: "An act is right if and only if it conforms with that set of moral rules, general conformity with which would have best consequences." This phrasing is a bit vague, however, so let us expand it to this: "An act is right if and only if it conforms with that set of general prescriptions for action such that, if everyone always did, from among all the things which he could do on a given occasion, what conformed with these prescriptions, then at least as much intrinsic good would be produced as by conformity with any other set of general prescriptions." This sounds very like our above formulation. It is,

---

[3] These articles are: J. Harrison, "Utilitarianism, Universalisation, and Our Duty to Be Just," *Proceedings of the Aristotelian Society*, Vol. LIII (1952–53), pp. 105–134; and R. F. Harrod, "Utilitarianism Revised," *Mind*, n.s. XLV (1936), 137–156.

however, different in a very important way: for its test of whether an act is right, or a general rule correct, is what would happen if people *really all did act* in a certain way. The test is not the consequences of recognizing a rule, or of acting with such a rule in mind; the test as stated does not require that people do, or even can, think of or formulate, much less apply the rule of a moral code. What is being said is simply that a rule is correct, and corresponding conduct right, if it would have best consequences for everyone actually to act, for whatever reason, in accordance with the rule. Of course, one of the consequences to be taken into account may be the fact that expectations of conduct according to the rule might be built up, and that people could count on conforming behavior.

This theory is initially attractive. We seem to be appealing to it in our moral reasoning when we say, "You oughtn't to do so-and-so, because if everybody in your circumstances did this, the consequences would be bad."

Nevertheless, the fact is that this theory—however hard it may be to see that it does—has identically the same consequences for behavior as does act-utilitarianism. And since it does, it is a mistake to advocate it as a theory preferable to act-utilitarianism, as some philosophers may have done. Let us see how this is.

Let us ask ourselves: What would a set of moral prescriptions be like, such that general conformity with it, in the sense intended, would have the best consequences? The answer is that the set would contain just one rule, the prescription of the *act-utilitarians:* "Perform an act, among those open to you, which will have at least as good consequences as any other." There cannot be a moral rule, conformity with which could have better consequences than this one. If it really is true that doing a certain thing will have the very best consequences in the long run, everything considered, of all the things I can do, then there is nothing better I can do than this. If everyone always did the very best thing it was possible for him to do, the total intrinsic value produced would be at a maximum. Any act which deviated from this principle would produce less good than some other act which might have been performed. It is clear, then, that the moral rule general conformity with which would produce most good is a rule corresponding to the principle of act-utilitarianism. The two theories, then, have identical consequences for behavior. I am, of course, not at all suggesting that everyone *trying* to produce the best consequences will have the same consequences as everyone *trying* to follow some different set of rules—or that everyone trying to follow some different set of rules may not have better consequences than everyone trying just to produce the best consequences. Far from it. What I am saying is that *succeeding* in producing the best consequences is a kind of success which cannot be improved upon. And it is this which is in question, when we are examining the formula we are now looking at.

To say that succeeding in producing the best consequences cannot be improved upon is consistent with admitting that what will in fact have the best consequences, in view of what other people in fact have done or will do, may be different from what would have had the best consequences if other people were to behave differently from the way in which they did or will do. The behavior of others is part of the context relevant for determining the effects of a given act of any agent.

It may be thought that this reasoning is unfair to this rule-utilitarian view. For what this theory has in mind, it may be said, is rules forbidding classes of actions described in ways other than by reference to their utility—rules forbidding actions like lies, adultery, theft, etc. So, it may be said, the principle of act-utilitarianism is not even a competitor for the position of one of the rules admitted by this theory.

My reply to this objection is twofold. In the first place, it would be rather foolish to suppose that any system of moral rules could omit rules about doing good, rules about doing what will maximize utility. Surely we do wish to include among our rules one roughly to the effect that, if we have the opportunity to do a great deal of good for others at little cost, we should do it. And also a rule to the effect that we should avoid harming others. It is no accident that W. D. Ross's list of seven prima facie obligations contains four which refer to doing good, in one way or another. But the point would still stand even if we ignore this fact. For suppose we set about to describe a set of rules, none of which is explicitly to prescribe *doing good,* but general conformity with which will maximize utility. Now obviously, the set of rules in question will be that set which prescribes, by descriptions which make no reference to having good consequences, exactly that very class of actions which would also be prescribed by the act-utilitarian principle. And one can find a set of rules which will prescribe exactly this class of acts without referring to utility. We can find such a set, because every member of the class of acts prescribed by the act-utilitarian principle will have some other property *on account of which* it will maximize utility in the circumstances. Every act, that is to say, which maximizes utility does so because of some doubtless very complex property that it has. As a result, we can set up a system of prescriptions for action which refer to these complex properties, such that our system of rules will prescribe exactly the set of acts prescribed by the act-utilitarian principle. The set of rules may be enormously long and enormously complex. But this set of rules will have the property of being that set, general conformity with which will maximize utility. And the acts prescribed will be identical with the acts prescribed by the act-utilitarian principle. So, again, the prescriptions for conduct of this form of rule-utilitarianism are identical with those of the act-utilitarian theory.

4
Rule-Utilitarianism: A Second Approximation

The whole point of the preceding remarks has been to focus attention on the point that a rule-utilitarianism like Urmson's is different from act-utilitarianism only when it speaks of something like "*recognition* of a rule having the best consequences" instead of something like "*conformity* with a certain rule having the best consequences." With this in mind, we can see clearly one of the virtues of Urmson's proposal, which we interpreted as being: "An act is right if and only if it conforms with that set of moral rules, *the recognition of which* would have the best consequences."

But, having viewed the difficulties of a view verbally very similar to the above, we are now alert to the fact that the formulation we have suggested is itself open to interpretations that may lead to problems. How may we construe Urmson's proposal, so that it is both unambiguous and credible? Of course we do not wish to go to the opposite extreme and take "recognition of" to mean merely "doffing the hat to" without attempt to practice. But how shall we take it?

I suggest the following as a second approximation.

First, let us speak of a set of moral rules as being "learnable" if people of ordinary intelligence are able to learn or absorb its provisions, so as to believe the moral propositions in question in the ordinary sense of "believe" for such contexts.[4] Next, let us speak of "the adoption" of a moral code by a person as meaning "the learning and belief of its provisions (in the above sense) and conformity of behavior to these to the extent we may expect people of ordinary conscientiousness to conform their behavior to rules they believe are principles about right or obligatory behavior." Finally, let us, purely arbitrarily and for the sake of brevity, use the phrase "maximizes intrinsic value" to mean "would produce at least as much intrinsic good as would be produced by any relevant alternative action." With these stipulations, we can now propose, as a somewhat more precise formulation of Urmson's proposal, the following rule-utilitarian thesis: "An act is right if and only if it conforms with that learnable set of rules, the adoption of which by everyone would maximize intrinsic value."

This principle does not at all imply that the rightness or wrongness of an act is contingent upon the agent's having *thought about* all the complex business of the identity of a set of ideal moral rules; it asserts, rather, that an act is right if and only if it *conforms* to such a set of rules, regardless of what the agent may think. Therefore the principle is not disqualified from being a correct principle about what is objectively right or wrong, in Moore's sense; for it makes rightness and wrongness a matter of the facts, and totally independent of what the agent thinks is right, or of what the agent thinks about the facts, or of the evidence the agent may have, or of what is probably the case on the basis of this evidence.

An obvious merit of this principle is that it gives expression to at least part of our practice or procedure in trying to find out what is right or wrong. For when we are in doubt about such matters, we often try to think out how it would work in practice to have a moral code which prohibited or permitted various actions we are considering. We do not, of course, ordinarily do any-

---

[4] To say that a moral code can be learned by a person is not to say he can learn to *recite* it. It is enough if he learns it well enough to recall the relevant rule when stimulated by being in a context to which it is relevant. Learning a moral code is thus like learning a complex route into a large city: we may not be able to draw it or explain to others what it is, but when we drive it and have the landmarks before us, we remember each turn we are to make.

thing as complicated as try to think out the *complete* ideal moral code; we are content with considering whether certain specific injunctions relevant to the problem we are considering might be included in a good and workable code. Nevertheless, we are prepared to admit that the whole ideal code is relevant. For if someone shows us that a specific injunction which we think would be an acceptable part of a moral code clearly would not work out in view of other provisions necessary to an ideal code, we should agree that a telling point had been made and revise our thinking accordingly.

In order to get a clearer idea of the kind of "set of rules" (with which right actions must conform) which could satisfy the conditions this rule-utilitarian principle lays down, let us note some general features such a set presumably would have. First, it would contain rules giving directions for recurrent situations which involve conflicts of human interests. Presumably, then, it would contain rules rather similar to W. D. Ross's list of prima facie obligations: rules about the keeping of promises and contracts, rules about debts of gratitude such as we may owe to our parents, and, of course, rules about not injuring other persons and about promoting the welfare of others where this does not work a comparable hardship on us. Second, such a set of rules would not include petty restrictions; nor, at least for the most part, would it contain purely prudential rules. Third, the rules would not be very numerous; an upper limit on quantity is set by the ability of ordinary people to learn them. Fourth, such a set of rules would not include unbearable demands; for their inclusion would only serve to bring moral obligation into discredit. Fifth, the set of rules adoption of which would have the best consequences could not leave too much to discretion. It would make concessions to the fact that ordinary people are not capable of perfectly fine discriminations, and to the fact that, not being morally perfect, people of ordinary conscientiousness will have a tendency to abuse a moral rule where it suits their interest. We must remember that a college dormitory rule like "Don't play music at such times or in such a way as to disturb the study or sleep of others" would be ideally flexible if people were perfect; since they aren't, we have to settle for a rule like "No music after 10 P.M." The same thing is true for a moral code. The best moral code has to allow for the fact that people are what they are; it has to be less flexible and less efficient than a moral code that was to be adopted by perfectly wise and perfectly conscientious people could be.

Should we think of such a moral code as containing only prescriptions for situations likely to arise in *everyone's* life—rules like "If you have made a promise, then . . ." or "If you have a parent living, then treat him thus-and-so"? Or should we think of it as containing distinct sets of prescriptions for *different roles or statuses,* such as "If you are a policeman, then . . ." or "If you are a physician, then . . ."? And if the ideal code is to contain different prescriptions for different roles and statuses, would it not be so complex that it could not be learned by people of ordinary intelligence? The answer to these questions is that the rule-utilitarian is not committed, by his theory, to the necessity of such special codes, although I believe he may well admit their desirability—admit, for instance, that it is a good thing for a physician to carry a rule in his mental kit, specially designed to answer the question, "Shall I treat a patient who does not pay his bill?" In any case, our rule-utilitarian theory can *allow* for such special rules. Nor is there a difficulty in the fact that people of normal intelligence could hardly learn all these special sets of rules. For we can mean, by saying that a code can be "learned" by people of ordinary intelligence, that any person can learn all the rules relevant to the problems *he* will face. A rule-utilitarian will not, of course, have in mind a moral code which in some part is secret—for instance, lawyers having a moral code known only to themselves, a code which it would be harmful for others to know about. For surely in the long run it could not have best consequences for a society to have a moral code, perhaps granting special privileges to some groups, which could not stand the light of public knowledge.

5
First Problem: Moral Codes for an Imperfect Society

Our "second approximation" to a rule-utilitarian principle has proposed that an act is right if and only if it conforms with the requirements of a learnable moral code, the adoption of which by *everyone* would maximize utility—and meaning by "adoption of a code" the learning and belief that the code lays down the requirements for moral behavior, and conformity to it to the extent we may expect from people of *ordinary conscientiousness*.

The italicized words in the preceding paragraph indicate two respects in which the proposed test of rightness in a sense departs from reality. In actuality moral codes are not subscribed to by everybody in all particulars: there is virtual unanimity on some items of what we call "the code of the community" (such as the prohibition of murder and incest), but on other matters there is less unanimity (in the United States, the "code" permits artificial birth-control measure despite disapproval by many Catholics), and it is a somewhat arbitrary matter to decide when the disagreement has become so general that we ought not to speak of something as part of the code of the community at all. There is probably some measure of disagreement on many or most moral matters in most modern communities (and, surely, in at least many primitive communities). Furthermore, our proposal, in an effort to be definite about the degree of commitment involved in the "adoption" of a code, spoke of an "ordinary conscientiousness." This again departs from reality. Ordinary conscientiousness may be the exception: many people are extremely, perhaps even overly conscientious; at the other extreme, some people act as if they have developed no such thing as a conscience at all. It is characteristic of actual communities that there is a wide range in degrees of conscientiousness.

As a result of these departures from reality, our test for rightness savors a bit of the utopian. We are invited to think of different worlds, each populated by people of "ordinary conscientiousness," all of whom are inoculated with a standard moral code. We are to decide whether given types of action are right or wrong by considering which of these hypothetical communities would realize a maximum of value.

There is force in the proposal. In fact, if we are thinking of sponsoring some ideal, this conception is a useful one for appraising whatever ideal we are considering. Just as we might ask whether large military establishments or a capitalist economy would be suitable for the ideal community of the future, so we can ask whether certain features of our present moral code would be suitable in such a community. It may be that such a conception should play a large role in deciding what ultimate ideals we should espouse.

Nevertheless, this conception may, from its very framework, necessarily be unsuitable for deciding the rightness of actions in the real world. It appears that, in fact, this is the case with both of the features mentioned above.

First, the proposal is to test rightness by the desirability of a rule in a moral code among people of ordinary conscientiousness. Now, in a community composed of people of ordinary conscientiousness we do not have to provide for the contingency of either saints or great sinners. In particular, we do not have to provide for the occurrence of people like Adolf Hitler. In such a community, presumably, we could get along with a minimal police force, perhaps an unarmed police force. Similarly, it would seem there would be no value in a moral prescription like "Resist evil men." In the community envisaged, problems of a certain sort would presumably not arise, and therefore the moral code need not have features designed to meet those problems. Very likely, for instance, a moral code near to that of extreme pacifism would work at least as well as a code differing in its nonpacifism.

More serious is the flaw in the other feature: that the test of rightness is to be compatibility with the requirements of the moral code, adoption of which *by everyone* would maximize utility. The trouble with this is that it permits behavior which really would be desirable if everyone agreed, but which might be objectionable and undesirable if not everyone agreed. For instance, it may well be that it would have the best consequences if the children are regarded as responsible for an elderly parent who is ill or needy; but it would be most unfortunate if the members of a Hopi man's native household—primarily his sisters and their families—decided that their presently recognized obligation had no standing on this account, since the result would be that as things now stand, no one at all would take the responsibility. Again, if everyone recognized an obligation to share in duties pertaining to national defense, it would be morally acceptable to require this legally; but it would hardly be morally acceptable to do so if there are pacifists who on moral grounds are ready to die rather than bear arms. And similarly for other matters about which there are existing and pronounced moral convictions.

It seems clear that some modification must be made if our rule-utilitarian proposal is to have implications consistent with the moral convictions of thoughtful people. Unfortunately it is not clear just what the modification should be. The one I am inclined to adopt is as follows. First, we must drop that part of our conception which assumes that people in our hypothetical societies are of ordinary conscientiousness. We want to allow for the existence of both saints and sinners and to have a moral code to cope with them. In order to do this, we had better move closer to Urmson's original suggestion.

We had better drop the notion of "adoption" and replace it by his term "recognition," meaning by "recognition by all" simply "belief by all that the rules formulate moral requirements." Second, we must avoid the conception of the acceptance of all the rules of a given moral code by *everybody* and replace it by something short of this, something which does not rule out the problems created by actual convictions about morals. Doing so means a rather uneasy compromise, because we cannot sacrifice the central feature of the rule-utilitarian view, which is that the rightness of an act is to be tested by whether it conforms with rules the (somehow) general acceptance of which would maximize utility. The compromise I propose is this: that the test whether an act is right is whether it is compatible with that set of rules which, were it to replace the moral commitments of members of the *actual society* at the time, *except where there are already fairly decided moral convictions,* would maximize utility.

The modified theory, then, is this: "An act is right if and only if it conforms with that learnable set of rules, the recognition of which as morally binding, roughly at the time of the act, by all actual people insofar as these rules are not incompatible with existing fairly decided moral commitments, would maximize intrinsic value."[5]

The modification has the effect that whether an act is right depends to some extent on such things as (1) how large a proportion of the actual population is conscientious and (2) what are the existing fairly decided moral beliefs at the time. This result is not obviously a mistake.

6

Second Problem: Conflicts of Rules

The objection is sure to be raised against any rule-utilitarian theory of the general sort we are considering that the whole conception is radically misconceived. For the theory proposes that what makes an act right is its conformity to the set of rules, recognition of which would maximize utility; and it is proposed that if we are in serious doubt whether an action would be right, we should ask ourselves whether it would conform with a utility-maximizing set of rules. Now, the objection will run, the very conception of such a set of rules evaporates, or else appears to involve contradictions, when we try to get it in sharp focus. The very idea of a set of rules simple enough to be learned and different from act-utilitarianism, and at the same time sufficiently comprehen-

---

[5] This formulation is rather similar in effect to one suggested to me by Wilfrid Sellars. (I have no idea whether he now inclines toward it, or whether he ever did lean toward it strongly.) This is: "An act is right if and only if it conforms with that set of rules the *teaching of which* to the society of the agent, at the time of the action, would maximize welfare." This formulation is simpler, but it has its own problems. Teaching to which and how many individuals? By whom? With what skill and means? We should remember that it may be unwise to teach children the rules that are best for adults and that it may sometimes be desirable to teach ideals which are more extreme than we want people actually to live by, e.g., those of the Sermon on the Mount.

sive and precise to yield directions for conduct in every situation which may arise, is an impossible dream.

The reason is that moral problems are often quite complex. There are pros and cons—obligations and counter-obligations—which have to be weighed delicately. For instance, a promise that has been made to do something is normally a point in favor of saying that doing it is obligatory; but just how much force the promise will have depends on various circumstances, such as when it was made, how solemnly it was made, whether it was fully understood by both parties, etc. The force of these circumstances cannot be stated and weighed by any set of rules. There is a moral to be drawn, it may be said, from W. D. Ross's theory of prima facie obligations: Ross could provide no general direction for what to do when prima facie obligations conflict; he had to leave the resolution of such conflicts to conscience or intuition. So, in general, no code simple enough to be written down and learned (and different from act-utilitarianism) can prescribe what is right in complex cases.

The difficulty is obviously a serious one. If the very concept of a complete code, the recognition of which would maximize utility, cannot be explained in detail, then the proposal that the rightness of every action is fixed by its conformity with the provisions of such a code must be abandoned.

What must be done to meet this charge? Of course, it cannot be demanded that we actually produce the ideal moral code for our society, or even a complete code of which the correct code might be supposed to be a variation. What can be fairly demanded is that we describe classes of rules or elements which may be expected in the ideal code, and that we make clear, in the course of this description, that the rules constituting the classes are simple enough to be learned, and that a person who had learned the rules of the several classes would be in a position to give an answer to all moral questions—or at least as definite an answer as can reasonably be expected. We may suppose that, if the theory is to be plausible, these classes of rules will be familiar—that they will be rules which thoughtful people do use in deciding moral issues. Let us see what can be said.

It is clear that a complete moral code must contain rules or principles of more than one level. The lowest level will consist of rules devised to cover familiar recurrent situations, presumably rather like those proposed by Ross in his formulation of prima facie obligations. Thus, it will contain rules like "Do not injure conscious beings," "Do what you have promised to do," etc. On reflection, we can see that such rules must be qualified in two ways. First, each of them must conclude with an exceptive clause something like "except as otherwise provided in this code." But second, they must be more complex than our samples; as Ross well knew, such simple rules do not state accurately what we think are our prima facie obligations—and presumably such rules are not the rules it would maximize welfare to have recognized as first-order rules. Consider, for instance the rule I have suggested about promises. It is too simple, for we do not seriously believe that *all* promises have even a prima facie claim to be fulfilled; nor would it be a good thing for people to think they ought. For instance, we think there is no obligation at all to keep a promise made on the basis of deliberate misrepresentation by the promisee; and it is to the public interest that we should think as we do. Just as the law of contracts lists various types of contracts which it is against the public interest for the courts to enforce, so there are types of promises the fulfillment of which we do not think obligatory, and a moral requirement to fulfill them would be contrary to the public interest. The lowest-level group of rules, then, will include one about promise-keeping which will state explicitly which types of promises must be kept except when some more stringent obligation intervenes. And the same for the other basic moral rules.

I do not know if anyone would contend that it would be impossible to write down an exact statement formulating our total prima facie obligations—the kinds of considerations which to some extent make a moral claim on agents. I do not know if anyone would say that in principle we cannot state exactly the list of prima facie obligations it would maximize utility for everyone to feel. Whether or not anyone does say that a list of exact prima facie obligations cannot be stated, I know of no solid argument which can be put forward to show that this is the case. I do not believe a satisfactory list *has* been provided (Ross's statement being quite abbreviated), but I know of no sound reason for thinking that it cannot be. It would not, I think, be an impossible inquiry to determine what is the total set of distinct fundamental prima facie obligations people in fact do recognize in their moral thinking.

A set of first-level rules, however, is not enough. For moral perplexities arise most often where there are conflicts of prima facie obligations, where there would be conflicts of the first-level moral rules. If the rule-utilitarian theory is to work, it must provide for the resolution of such perplexities. How can this be done?

The problem can be partially met by supposing that a complete moral code will contain second-level rules specifically prescribing for conflicts of the basic rules. One second-level rule might be: "Do not injure anyone solely in order to produce something good, unless the good achieved be substantially greater than the injury." In fact we already learn and believe rules roughly of this kind. For instance, Ross suggested in *The Right and the Good* that we think there is normally a stronger obligation to avoid injury to others than to do good or to keep one's promises. A moral code can contain some such second-order rules without intolerable complexity.

But such rules will hardly be numerous enough to solve all the problems. And the rule we stated was not precise: it used the vague phrase "substantially greater," which is clear enough, in context, to decide for many situations, but it is by no means precise enough to legislate for all. I think, therefore, that if the very conception of a set of rules simple enough to be learned and adequate to adjudicate all possible cases is to be intelligible, it must be possible to formulate a consistent and plausible "remainder-rule," that is, a top-level rule giving adequate directions for all cases for which the lower-level rules do not prescribe definitely enough or for which their prescriptions are conflicting. We are not here called upon to identify the correct remainder-rule—although we know that the rule-utilitarian theory is that the correct one is the one the recognition of which (etc.) would do most good. What we are called upon to do is to sketch out what such a rule might well be like.

It is worthwhile to mention two possibilities for a remainder-rule.[6] First, such a rule might specify that all cases not legislated for by other clauses in the code be decided simply on the basis of comparative utility of consequences. For such cases, then, the remainder-rule would prescribe exactly what the act-utilitarian principle prescribes. Second (and I think this possibility the more interesting), the remainder-rule might be: "One is obligated to perform an action if and only if a person who knew the relevant facts and had them vividly in mind, had been carefully taught the other rules of this code, and was uninfluenced by interests beyond those arising from learning the code, would feel obligated to perform that action." Such a rule could decide cases not legislated for by the remainder of the code only if the explicit rules were taught so as to be connected with different degrees of *felt obligation*. In some cases such an association could be established by the very content of the rule, for instance, in the case of a rule stating that there is an obligation not to injure others, and that the obligation increases in strength with the amount of injury involved. Another example is that of second-level rules about the priorities of first-level rules. In other cases the association might be fixed simply by the relative insistence or firmness of the teachers, with respect to the rule in question. As a result of the rules being taught in this way, conscientious people would have established in them hesitations, of different degrees of strength, to do certain sorts of things—in other words, a sense of obligation to do or avoid certain things, the sense having different force for different things. Therefore, when persons so trained were faced with a situation in which lower-order rules gave conflicting directions (and where no higher-order rule assigned an explicit priority), they would hesitate to resolve the problem in various ways because of the built-in sense of obligation. Now, the proposed remainder-rule would in effect be a somewhat qualified prescription to take whatever course of action would leave morally well-trained people least dissatisfied. (I imagine that something like this is what Ross had in mind when he said that in complex situations one must rely on one's intuition.) The rule-utilitarian proposal is, of course, that the correct degree of felt obligation to be associated with a rule is, like the order of priorities expressed in the second-level rules, fixed by the relative utilities of the various possible arrangements—partly the utilities of the adjudications of complex cases by the remainder-rule.

It is after all possible, then, for a moral code different from act-utilitarianism to be simple enough to be learned and still able to decide for all problems which may arise.

---

[6] It will probably be clear why the remainder-rule cannot simply be the rule-utilitarian principle itself. For the rule-utilitarian principle states that an act is right if and only if it conforms with the rules of a certain kind of code. If one of the rules of the code were the rule-utilitarian principle, it would contain reference to a code which presumably would itself contain again the rule-utilitarian principle, and so on ad infinitum.

7
Third Problem: Relativity to the Agent's Society

One final complication may be needed in the rule-utilitarian proposal. In place of saying that the rightness of an act is fixed by conformity with the prescriptions of the moral code, the recognition of which as morally binding by people (etc.) *everywhere* would maximize intrinsic good, we might say that the rightness of an act is fixed by conformity with the prescriptions of that moral code, the recognition of which as morally binding by people *in the agent's society* would maximize intrinsic good. This kind of complication should be avoided if possible, because it is difficult to assign a definite meaning to the phrase "in the agent's society." We should notice, incidentally, that it is *not* suggested that the test be the maximizing of intrinsic good only in the agent's society; such a thesis would promise quite dubious consequences.

A modification of this sort would admit a kind of relativism into ethics. For, while it is consistent with the rule-utilitarian principle itself being correct for everyone, it has the consequence that an act might be right in one society which would be wrong in another society. For instance, it might be a moral obligation for a man to support his elderly father in one society, but not his obligation in another society. Most philosophers, however, would probably view this kind of relativism as innocuous, since such differences in obligation could occur only when conditions in the two societies were different in such a way that recognition of one rule by one society would have best consequences, and recognition of a different rule by another society would also have best consequences.

But is there any reason for adopting this complicating feature? Why not say that, if a moral code is valid for anybody it is valid for everybody? Surely, it will be said, *some* moral rules are universally valid—perhaps, for instance, a rule forbidding a person from causing another pain merely in order to give himself pleasure. And if so, perhaps we can go on, with Ross, to say that the fundamental principles of obligation are universally true, although their application in special circumstances may give rise to an *appearance* of society-bound rules. For instance, Ross would say that "Keep your promises" is universally a true and important first-level rule. But in some places a thing is promised with certain mutually-understood but not explicitly stated conditions, while in other places the implicit conditions are different. As a result, the conduct required, in view of the explicit promise, by the universally valid principle is different in different societies. Or again, "Thou shalt not steal" or "Thou shalt not commit adultery" might be construed as universally valid injunctions, the first being not to take property which, according to the institutions of the society, is recognized as belonging to another, and the second, not to have sexual relations with any person if either party is, according to the custom of the society, the marriage partner of another. All fundamental moral principles, then, may be thought to have intersocietal validity; only the specific conduct enjoined or prohibited may vary from one society to another because of local conditions.

This view, however, faces serious difficulties. In order to bring these into focus, let us consider an example: the obligations of a father to his children. In the United States, I believe, it is thought that a father should see to it—within the limits of his financial capacities—that his children receive a good education, enjoy physical and mental health, and have some security against unforeseeable catastrophes. Contrast this with a society, like that of the Hopi, in which responsibility for children falls primarily on a household, "household" being defined primarily by blood-ties with the mother. In this situation, responsibility for children is primarily a problem for the mother and her blood relatives. (The factual accuracy of these assertions is not, I believe, a material consideration.) In the United States, the father is generally charged with responsibility for bringing the welfare, or prospects of welfare, of his children up to a certain rough minimum; in the Hopi society this responsibility falls roughly on other persons, although the father may share in it as far as affection dictates. Correspondingly, in the United States grown children have responsibility for their father, whereas among the Hopi the responsibility for the father belongs elsewhere—not on a man's own children but on the household of the father, the one to which he belongs through blood-ties with his mother and siblings.

I take it nobody is going to argue that fathers in the United States do not have the obligations they are generally thought to have, or that Hopi fathers do have obligations which are generally thought to fall elsewhere. (There may be some exceptions to this.) Therefore, if there is to be a *universal* moral rule locating obligations for the welfare of children, it will be one which roughly places it, at least for the present, where it is recognized to be in these societies. What kind of rule might this be? It is hard to say. Very possibly there is uniformity of assignment of such responsibilities in societies with a certain kind of social structure, and hence one could conceivably state a general rule prescribing that fathers do certain things in societies of a specified sociological description. It is doubtful, however, whether such a rule is simple enough to be learned. Moreover, social structures may be too much organic wholes to permit even such generalizations; if so, in respect of some kinds of conduct there can be no general, intersocietally valid moral rule at all.

There is another way of putting much the same point. Instead of asking whether we can frame a general rule which will have implications for particular societies coincident with what we should want to say are the actual locations of responsibilities in these societies, we might ask whether any universal rules can be framed, recognition of which as morally binding would have consequences comparably as good as local rules, devised on the basis of examination of individual institutional structures as a whole. Is the universality of moral rules to be so sacrosanct that we shall not recognize a moral rule as binding on a given society unless it can be viewed as a special case of some universally valid rule? A person who wishes to make utility the test of moral rules will, I think, wish to make the utility of local rules his test.

It may be supposed that the example of family obligations is untypically complex. But to do so would be a mistake. The responsibilities of physicians and teachers—or professional men in general—to the individuals whom they serve pose similar difficulties. So do the ethics of borrowing and the charging of interest. It is possible that the broad outlines of prohibited and required behavior will be rather similar in all societies. But when we come to the fine points—the exceptions, the qualifications, the priorities—we are in for difficulties if we must defend the view that statable universal rules are the best ones for everybody to feel bound by, or that they conform to serious opinions about the location of obligations in various types of society. This, I think, has been the conclusion of various "self-realizationist" philosophers like A. MacBeath and C. A. Campbell.

Let us then consider (without necessarily insisting that it be adopted) the view that the rightness of an act is fixed by conformity with the prescriptions of that moral code, the recognition of which as morally binding by people (etc.) *in the agent's society* would maximize intrinsic good. Can we propose a meaning of "in the agent's society" sufficiently definite that we can say the proposal is at least a clear one?

How shall we identify "the society" of the agent? This question could have been answered fairly simply in much earlier times when all societies were rather clearly demarcated atomic units, although when we remember the relationships of the *kula* reported by Malinowski, we can see that matters were not always so simple even among primitive peoples. The question is difficult in a modern civilization. What is a Columbia University professor who lives in the suburbs to count as his "society"? The faculty club? His suburb? New York City? The state of New York? Any choice seems a bit arbitrary. Or suppose Khrushchev makes a promise to Eisenhower. What society should we bear in mind as the one the utility of a set of rules in which sets the standard of right and wrong?

Very tentatively, I am inclined to suggest that we understand the "society of an agent" in the following way. An individual, I suggest, may live in several "moral worlds," and the rules for these several moral worlds may be different. For one thing, he is a member of a succession of local groups, each one more inclusive than the last: the local community, the metropolitan area, etc. Now a good part of one's life is lived as a resident, a neighbor, a citizen. Insofar as moral problems arise as part of one's life in this capacity, the problem is to be settled by reference to the rules best for the geographical community. How wide a geographical community should we pick? The best answer seems to be: the largest area over which common rules can be adopted without loss of utility. If it were costly in utility to apply to a borough the rules which were the best for the metropolitan area, then we had better consider our case in the light of rules useful for the smaller group. But a person has other roles besides that of citizen and neighbor. One may be a member of groups which transcend the local community—perhaps nation-wide associations, class, or caste. Most important, perhaps, are transactions resulting from the institutional involvement of the participants; for example, business transactions involving corporations or unions, or the affairs of the church, or educational affairs, or the activities of the press or radio. In these cases a segment of the life-relations of the individuals involved consists in their interactions with others who have the same role or who participate in the same institution. In such cases, I suggest that the moral rules governing behavior should be the rules adoption of which by the relevant group (for example, the group participating in a given institution) would be best, as governing the transactions of that group. It may be, of course, that we do not need some of these complications, that there is no need to distinguish the rules for businessmen in dealing with each other or with a union from the ones properly followed in one's relations with wife and neighbor.[7]

8
Concluding Remarks

The principle with which we end is this: "An act is right if and only if it conforms with that learnable set of rules the recognition of which as morally binding—roughly at the time of the act—by everyone in the society of the agent, except for the retention by individuals of already formed and decided moral convictions, would maximize intrinsic value."[8]

I wish to make three final comments on this principle.

First, one may ask whether a set of moral roles which would maximize intrinsic value in the way described would necessarily be a *just* set of rules. Surely, if the rules are not just, conformity with them will by no means guarantee that an action is right. A further inquiry must be made about whether additional requirements are needed to assure that moral rules are just. It may be that, as I have suggested elsewhere, none is called for if equality of some sort is an intrinsic good.

Second, if the proposed principle is correct, we can give at least a partial answer to a person who asks *why* he ought to perform actions he is obligated to perform, if they conflict with his self-interest. Perhaps a person who asks such a question is merely confused, and his query not worth our attention. But we can say to him that one reason for meeting his obligation is that by doing so he plays the game of living according to the rules which will maximize welfare. And this will be, at least partially, a satisfying answer to a man who is activated by love or sympathy or respect directed at other sentient beings generally.

Finally, some reflections on the employment of the principle. It is, perhaps, obvious that it is not necessary to advocate that everyone always bear the rule-utilitarian principle in mind in deciding what he ought to do. Not that it would be harmful—beyond the waste of time—to do so; for it is obvious that the clear moral obligations are prescribed by the principle. For example, only an instant's thought is required to see that it is socially useful to recognize the

---

[7] The above discussion shows that the theory that what is right is behavior conforming with the *accepted* rules of the agent's society has complications which have not been adequately discussed.

[8] As the principle now stands, a given individual might have to learn several codes, corresponding to his several roles in society.

rule that solemn promises should be kept—doubtless with some qualifications. The rule's employment is important, however, in analyzing more difficult cases, in making clear whether a given moral rule should be qualified in a certain way. Of course, it would be foolish to suggest that application of the principle is an easy road to the resolution of moral problems. It may very often be that after most careful reflection along the lines suggested, the most that can be said is that a given action is probably the one which the principle requires. If so, if we accept the principle, we can go on to say that this action is probably the right one.

28
Classical Utilitarianism

JOHN RAWLS

For biographical information about John Rawls, see reading 16.

In this selection, taken from A Theory of Justice, *Rawls elaborates and criticizes what he views as the intuitive basis of utilitarianism. He argues that utilitarianism draws its plausibility from an analogy between the individual and society. Just as a rational individual tries to maximize his satisfactions over time, so too will a rational society try to maximize the satisfactions of all its members. Thus understood, the principle of utility has a basis that is plausible and elegant.*

Yet that basis also raises problems. When individuals sacrifice for their own future welfare, they themselves are the ultimate beneficiaries. But when a society burdens some for the greater benefit of others, the losers and gainers are different persons. This leads Rawls to end by remarking that "utilitarianism does not take seriously the distinction between persons."

THERE ARE MANY forms of utilitarianism, and the development of the theory has continued in recent years. I shall not survey these forms here, nor take account of the numerous refinements found in contemporary discussions. My aim is to work out a theory of justice that represents an alternative to utilitarian thought generally and so to all of these different versions of it. I believe that the contrast betwen the contract view and utilitarianism remains essentially the same in all these cases. Therefore I shall compare justice as fairness with familiar variants of intuitionism, perfectionism, and utilitarianism in order to bring out the underlying differences in the simplest way. With this end in mind, the kind of utilitarianism I shall describe here is the strict classical doctrine which receives perhaps its clearest and most accessible formulation in Sidgwick. The main idea is that society is rightly ordered, and therefore just, when its major institutions are arranged so as to achieve the greatest net balance of satisfaction summed over all the individuals belonging to it.[1]

We may note first that there is, indeed, a way of thinking of society which makes it easy to suppose that the most rational conception of justice is utilitarian. For consider: each man in realizing his own interests is certainly free

---

[1] I shall take Henry Sidgwick's *The Methods of Ethics,* 7th ed. (London, 1907), as summarizing the development of utilitarian moral theory. Book III of his *Principles of Political Economy* (London, 1883) applies this doctrine to questions of economic and social justice, and is a precursor of A. C. Pigou, *The Economics of Welfare* (London, Macmillan, 1920). Sidgwick's *Outlines of the History of Ethics,* 5th ed. (London, 1902), contains a brief history of the utilitarian tradition. We may follow him in assuming, somewhat arbitrarily, that it begins with Shaftesbury's *An Inquiry Concerning Virtue and Merit* (1711) and Hutcheson's *An Inquiry Concerning Moral Good and Evil* (1725). Hutcheson seems to have been the first to state clearly the principle of

to balance his own losses against his own gains. We may impose a sacrifice on ourselves now for the sake of a greater advantage later. A person quite properly acts, at least when others are not affected, to achieve his own greatest good, to advance his rational ends as far as possible. Now why should not a society act on precisely the same principle applied to the group and therefore regard that which is rational for one man as right for an association of men? Just as the well-being of a person is constructed from the series of satisfactions that are experienced at different moments in the course of his life, so in very much the same way the well-being of society is to be constructed from the fulfillment of the systems of desires of the many individuals who belong to it. Since the principle for an individual is to advance as far as possible his own welfare, his own system of desires, the principle for society is to advance as far as possible the welfare of the group, to realize to the greatest extent the comprehensive system of desire arrived at from the desires of its members. Just as an individual balances present and future gains against present and future losses, so a society may balance satisfactions and dissatisfactions between different individuals. And so by these reflections one reaches the principle of utility in a natural way: a society is properly arranged when its institutions maximize the net balance of satisfaction. The principle of choice for an association of men is interpreted as an extension of the principle of choice for one man. Social justice is the principle of rational prudence applied to an aggregative conception of the welfare of the group (§30).[2]

---

utility. He says in *Inquiry,* sec. III, §8, that "that action is best, which procures the greatest happiness for the greatest numbers; and that, worst, which, in like manner, occasions misery." Other major eighteenth century works are Hume's *A Treatise of Human Nature* (1739), and *An Enquiry Concerning the Principles of Morals* (1751); Adam Smith's *A Theory of the Moral Sentiments* (1759); and Bentham's *The Principles of Morals and Legislation* (1789). To these we must add the writings of J. S. Mill represented by *Utilitarianism* (1863) and F. Y. Edgeworth's *Mathematical Psychics* (London, 1888).

The discussion of utilitarianism has taken a different turn in recent years by focusing on what we may call the coordination problem and related questions of publicity. This development stems from the essays of R. F. Harrod, "Utilitarianism Revised," *Mind,* vol. 45 (1936); J. D. Mabbott, "Punishment," *Mind,* vol. 48 (1939); Jonathan Harrison, "Utilitarianism, Universalisation, and Our Duty to Be Just," *Proceedings of the Aristotelian Society,* vol. 53 (1952–53); and J. O. Urmson, "The Interpretation of the Philosophy of J. S. Mill," *Philosophical Quarterly,* vol. 3 (1953). See also J. J. C. Smart, "Extreme and Restricted Utilitarianism," *Philosophical Quarterly,* vol. 6 (1956), and his *An Outline of a System of Utilitarian Ethics* (Cambridge, The University Press, 1961). For an account of these matters, see David Lyons, *Forms and Limits of Utilitarianism* (Oxford, The Clarendon Press, 1965); and Allan Gibbard, "Utilitarianisms and Coordination" (dissertation, Harvard University, 1971). The problems raised by these works, as important as they are, I shall leave aside as not bearing directly on the more elementary question of distribution which I wish to discuss.

Finally, we should note here the essays of J. C. Harsanyi, in particular, "Cardinal Utility in Welfare Economics and in the Theory of Risk-Taking," *Journal of Political Economy,* 1953, and "Cardinal Welfare, Individualistic Ethics, and Interpersonal Comparisons of Utility," *Journal of Political Economy,* 1955; and R. B. Brandt, "Some Merits of One Form of Rule-Utilitarianism," *University of Colorado Studies* (Boulder, Colorado, 1967).

[2] On this point see also D. P. Gauthier, *Practical Reasoning* (Oxford, Clarendon Press, 1963), pp. 126f. The text elaborates the suggestion found in "Constitutional Liberty and the Concept of

This idea is made all the more attractive by a further consideration. The two main concepts of ethics are those of the right and the good; the concept of a morally worthy person is, I believe, derived from them. The structure of an ethical theory is, then, largely determined by how it defines and connects these two basic notions. Now it seems that the simplest way of relating them is taken by teleological theories: the good is defined independently from the right, and then the right is defined as that which maximizes the good.[3] More precisely, those institutions and acts are right which of the available alternatives produce the most good, or at least as much good as any of the other institutions and acts open as real possibilities (a rider needed when the maximal class is not a singleton). Teleological theories have a deep intuitive appeal since they seem to embody the idea of rationality. It is natural to think that rationality is maximizing something and that in morals it must be maximizing the good. Indeed, it is tempting to suppose that it is self-evident that things should be arranged so as to lead to the most good.

It is essential to keep in mind that in a teleological theory the good is defined independently from the right. This means two things. First, the theory accounts for our considered judgments as to which things are good (our judgments of value) as a separate class of judgments intuitively distinguishable by common sense, and then proposes the hypothesis that the right is maximizing the good as already specified. Second, the theory enables one to judge the goodness of things without referring to what is right. For example, if pleasure is said to be the sole good, then presumably pleasures can be recognized and ranked in value by criteria that do not presuppose any standards of right, or what we would normally think of as such. Whereas if the distribution of goods is also counted as a good, perhaps a higher order one, and the theory directs us to produce the most good (including the good of distribution among others), we no longer have a teleological view in the classical sense. The problem of distribution falls under the concept of right as one intuitively understands it, and so the theory lacks an independent definition of the good. The clarity and simplicity of classical teleological theories derives largely from the fact that they factor our moral judgments into two classes, the one being characterized separately while the other is then connected with it by a maximizing principle.

Teleological doctrines differ, pretty clearly, according to how the conception of the good is specified. If it is taken as the realization of human excellence in

---

Justice," *Nomos VI: Justice,* ed. C. J. Friedrich and J. W. Chapman (New York, Atherton Press, 1963), pp. 124f, which in turn is related to the idea of justice as a higher-order administrative decision. See "Justice as Fairness," *Philosophical Review,* 1958, pp. 185–187. . . . That the principle of social integration is distinct from the principle of personal integration is stated by R. B. Perry *General Theory of Value* (New York, Longmans, Green, and Company, 1926), pp. 674–677. He attributes the error of overlooking this fact to Emile Durkheim and others with similar views. His conception of social integration is that brought about by a shared and dominant benevolent purpose.

[3] Here I adopt W. K. Frankena's definition of teleological theories in *Ethics* (Englewood Cliffs, N.J., Prentice Hall, Inc., 1963), p. 13.

the various forms of culture, we have what may be called perfectionism. This notion is found in Aristotle and Nietzsche, among others. If the good is defined as pleasure, we have hedonism; if as happiness, eudaimonism, and so on. I shall understand the principle of utility in its classical form as defining the good as the satisfaction of desire, or perhaps better, as the satisfaction of rational desire. This accords with the view in all essentials and provides, I believe, a fair interpretation of it. The appropriate terms of social cooperation are settled by whatever in the circumstances will achieve the greatest sum of satisfaction of the rational desires of individuals. It is impossible to deny the initial plausibility and attractiveness of this conception.

The striking feature of the utilitarian view of justice is that it does not matter, except indirectly, how this sum of satisfactions is distributed among individuals any more than it matters, except indirectly, how one man distributes his satisfactions over time. The correct distribution in either case is that which yields the maximum fulfillment. Society must allocate its means of satisfaction whatever these are, rights and duties, opportunities and privileges, and various forms of wealth, so as to achieve this maximum if it can. But in itself no distribution of satisfaction is better than another except that the more equal distribution is to be preferred to break ties.[4] It is true that certain common sense precepts of justice, particularly those which concern the protection of liberties and rights, or which express the claims of desert, seem to contradict this contention. But from a utilitarian standpoint the explanation of these precepts and of their seemingly stringent character is that they are those precepts which experience shows should be strictly respected and departed from only under exceptional circumstances if the sum of advantages is to be maximized.[5] Yet, as with all other precepts, those of justice are derivative from the one end of attaining the greatest balance of satisfaction. Thus there is no reason in principle why the greater gains of some should not compensate for the lesser losses of others; or more importantly, why the violation of the liberty of a few might not be made right by the greater good shared by many. It simply happens that under most conditions, at least in a reasonably advanced stage of civilization, the greatest sum of advantages is not attained in this way. No doubt the strictness of common sense precepts of justice has a certain usefulness in limiting men's propensities to injustice and to socially injurious actions, but the utilitarian believes that to affirm this strictness as a first principle of morals is a mistake. For just as it is rational for one man to maximize the fulfillment of his system of desires, it is right for a society to maximize the net balance of satisfaction taken over all of its members.

The most natural way, then, of arriving at utilitarianism (although not, of course, the only way of doing so) is to adopt for society as a whole the principle of rational choice for one man. Once this is recognized, the place of the impartial spectator and the emphasis on sympathy in the history of utilitarian thought

---

[4] On this point see Sidgwick, *The Methods of Ethics*, pp. 416f.

[5] See J. S. Mill, *Utilitarianism*, ch. V, last two pars.

is readily understood. For it is by the conception of the impartial spectator and the use of sympathetic identification in guiding our imagination that the principle for one man is applied to society. It is this spectator who is conceived as carrying out the required organization of the desires of all persons into one coherent system of desire; it is by this construction that many persons are fused into one. Endowed with ideal powers of sympathy and imagination, the impartial spectator is the perfectly rational individual who identifies with and experiences the desires of others as if these desires were his own. In this way he ascertains the intensity of these desires and assigns them their appropriate weight in the one system of desire the satisfaction of which the ideal legislator then tries to maximize by adjusting the rules of the social system. On this conception of society separate individuals are thought of as so many different lines along which rights and duties are to be assigned and scarce means of satisfaction allocated in accordance with rules so as to give the greatest fulfillment of wants. The nature of the decision made by the ideal legislator is not, therefore, materially different from that of an entrepreneur deciding how to maximize his profit by producing this or that commodity, or that of a consumer deciding how to maximize his satisfaction by the purchase of this or that collection of goods. In each case there is a single person whose system of desires determines the best allocation of limited means. The correct decision is essentially a question of efficient administration. This view of social cooperation is the consequence of extending to society the principle of choice for one man, and then, to make this extension work, conflating all persons into one through the imaginative acts of the impartial sympathetic spectator. Utilitarianism does not take seriously the distinction between persons.

29

Morality and
Rationality

IMMANUEL KANT

*Any short list of the greatest philosophers in Western thought will include
Immanuel Kant (1724–1804). Kant made major contributions to most of
the central areas of philosophy: ethics, political philosophy, epistemology,
metaphysics, philosophy of art, philosophy of mind, and philosophy of
religion. His two most important works are* The Critique of Pure Reason
(1781) and The Foundations of the Metaphysics of Morals *(1785).*

   The Foundations of the Metaphysics of Morals, *excerpted here, has had a
profound influence on the development of ethical thought. Kant's theory is
extremely difficult to understand, and the reader must be prepared to exert
considerable intellectual effort to come to grips with this very important
perspective on ethics. Because Kant's approach is superficially rather
puzzling, this introduction provides a roadmap that points out some of the
major landmarks in Kant's theory. The text has also been divided into
sections, and descriptive titles have been provided for different parts of
Kant's long argument.*

   *In a sense, the true starting places for Kant's essays are his reflections on
the need for philosophy in ethical thinking (see section D in the reading).
Kant believes that the ordinary person knows perfectly well which actions
are right and which actions are wrong. (As we read, we will see why Kant
has such faith in the average person.) Therefore, the role of philosophy is not
to tell people what is right or wrong, but to enable them to defend their
ordinary moral views when attacked by a skeptic. Kant's work in this
reading falls into two halves. First, he will try to provide an illuminating
description of our ordinary moral views; second, he will try to show how
those common moral views may be defended.*

   *Kant describes our common moral views in the two passages we have
called "The Good Will" and "Acting From the Motive of Duty." His point
in "The Good Will" is that we usually do not consider the consequences
when evaluating the moral worth of an action, but rather the intention with
which the act was done. If the intention was good—if the agent had a good
will—then the action is good. Kant expands upon this theme in the section
on duty. He claims that we believe that an agent deserves moral praise for
an action, not simply because he or she has in fact done the right thing, but
because the agent was motivated by the intention to do the right thing. The
agent was motivated by a sense of duty.*

   *How do we decide what our duties are? Kant believes that persons, unlike
animals, are capable of formulating laws of conduct for themselves and of
acting on those laws (section E). The fundamental law of conduct—the
"moral law"—is that one should perform an act only if one would will that*

anyone in similar circumstances do the same thing. That is, one should will to perform an act only if one would will that behavior of that type be a law of human conduct. Kant believes that it is a fundamental fact about human reason that whenever we think about performing a particular act, we always think about that act from a more general standpoint. We always ask: should that be a universal law governing human action? This is why Kant believes that the ordinary person can always tell right from wrong. When considering an action, the ordinary person, possessed of reason, will always ask: should it be a universal law of conduct that people do this action? Immorality arises when we flout the moral law. Even though we would not want a particular type of behavior to be the law, we selfishly make an exception in our own case and allow ourselves to engage in the beahvior anyway.

In section G, Kant draws out a startling consequence of his theory of morality. According to that theory, persons themselves are the ultimate source of morality. Hence, Kant claims that all persons have ultimate and intrinsic worth. No "market value" can be placed on any individual person. This leads Kant to restate the moral law in a different way: we must always treat persons with respect and never as a mere means to some goal. Finally, in section H, Kant tries to illuminate the moral law from yet another standpoint. He suggests that when acting we must always think of ourselves as belonging to a community of persons, each of whom creates the laws governing this realm by his or her own actions.

[A. The Good Will]

NOTHING IN THE world—indeed nothing even beyond the world—can possibly be conceived which could be called good without qualification except a *good will*. Intelligence, wit, judgment, and the other talents of the mind, however they may be named, or courage, resoluteness, and perseverance as qualities of temperament, are doubtless in many respects good and desirable. But they can become extremely bad and harmful if the will, which is to make use of these gifts of nature and which in its special constitution is called character, is not good. It is the same with the gifts of fortune, power, riches, honor, even health, general well-being, and the contentment with one's condition which is called happiness, make for pride and even arrogance if there is not a good will to correct their influence on the mind and on its principles of action so as to make it universally conformable to its end. It need hardly be mentioned that the sight of a being adorned with no feature of a pure and good will, yet enjoying uninterrupted prosperity, can never give pleasure to a rational impartial observer. Thus the good will seems to constitute the indispensable condition even of worthiness to be happy.

Some qualities seem to be conducive to this good will and can facilitate its action, but, in spite of that, they have no intrinsic unconditional worth. They rather presuppose a good will, which limits the high esteem which one otherwise rightly has for them and prevents their being held to be absolutely good. Moderation in emotions and passions, self-control, and calm deliberation not only are good in many respects but even seem to constitute a part of the inner worth of the person. But however unconditionally they were esteemed by the ancients, they are far from being good without qualification. For without the principle of a good will they can become extremely bad, and the coolness of a villain makes him not only far more dangerous but also more directly abominable in our eyes than he would have seemed without it.

The good will is not good because of what it effects or accomplishes or because of its adequacy to achieve some proposed end; it is good only because of its willing, i.e., it is good of itself. And, regarded for itself, it is to be esteemed incomparably higher than anything which could be brought about by it in favor of any inclination or even of the sum total of all inclinations. Even if it should happen that, by a particularly unfortunate fate or by the niggardly provision of a stepmotherly nature, this will should be wholly lacking in power to accomplish its purpose, and if even the greatest effort should not avail it to achieve anything of its end, and if there remained only the good will (not as a mere wish but as the summoning of all the means in our power), it would sparkle like a jewel in its own right, as something that had its full worth in itself. Usefulness or fruitlessness can neither diminish nor augment this worth. Its usefulness would be only its setting, as it were, so as to enable us to handle it more conveniently in commerce or to attract the attention of those who are not yet connoisseurs, but not to recommend it to those who are experts or to determine its worth.

But there is something so strange in this idea of the absolute worth of the will alone, in which no account is taken of any use, that, notwithstanding the agreement even of common sense, the suspicion must arise that perhaps only high-flown fancy is its hidden basis, and that we may have misunderstood the purpose of nature in its appointment of reason as the ruler of our will. We shall therefore examine this idea from this point of view.

In the natural constitution of an organized being, i.e., one suitably adapted to life, we assume as an axiom that no organ will be found for any purpose which is not the fittest and best adapted to that purpose. Now if its preservation, its welfare—in a word, its happiness—were the real end of nature in a being having reason and will, then nature would have hit upon a very poor arrangement in appointing the reason of the creature to be the executor of this purpose. For all the actions which the creature has to perform with this intention, and the entire rule of its conduct, would be dictated much more exactly by instinct, and that end would be far more certainly attained by instinct than it ever could be by reason. And if, over and above this, reason should have been granted to the favored creature, it would have served only to let it contemplate the happy constitution of its nature, to admire it, to rejoice in it, and to be grateful for it to its beneficent cause. But reason would not have been given in order that the being should subject its faculty of desire to that weak and delusive guidance and to meddle with the purpose of nature. In a word, nature would have taken care that reason did not break forth into practical use nor have the presumption, with its weak insight, to think out for itself the plan of happiness and the means of attaining it. Nature would have taken over not only the choice of ends but also that of the means, and with wise foresight she would have entrusted both to instinct alone.

And, in fact, we find that the more a cultivated reason deliberately devotes itself to the enjoyment of life and happiness, the more the man falls short of true contentment. From this fact there arises in many persons, if only they are candid enough to admit it, a certain degree of misology, hatred of reason. This is particularly the case with those who are most experienced in its use. After counting all the advantages which they draw—I will not say from the invention of the arts of common luxury—from the sciences (which in the end seem to them to be also a luxury of the understanding), they nevertheless find that they have actually brought more trouble on their shoulders instead of gaining in happiness; they finally envy, rather than despise, the common run of men who are better guided by mere natural instinct and who do not permit their reason much influence on their conduct. And we must at least admit that a morose attitude or ingratitude to the goodness with which the world is governed is by no means found always among those who temper or refute the boasting eulogies which are given of the advantages of happiness and contentment with which reason is supposed to supply us. Rather their judgment is based on the idea of another and far more worthy purpose of their existence for which, instead of happiness, their reason is properly intended, this purpose, therefore, being the supreme condition to which the private purposes of men must for the most part defer.

Reason is not, however, competent to guide the will safely with regard to its objects and the satisfaction of all our needs (which it in part multiplies), and to this end an innate instinct would have led with far more certainty. But reason is given to us as a practical faculty, i.e., one which is meant to have an influence on the will. As nature has elsewhere distributed capacities suitable to the functions they are to perform, reason's proper function must be to produce a will good in itself and not one good merely as a means, for to the former reason is absolutely essential. This will must indeed not be the sole and complete good but the highest good and the condition of all others, even of the desire for happiness. In this case it is entirely compatible with the wisdom of nature that the cultivation of reason, which is required for the former unconditional purpose, at least in this life restricts in many ways—indeed can reduce to less than nothing—the achievement of the latter conditional purpose, happiness. For one perceives that nature here does not proceed unsuitably to its purpose, because reason, which recognizes its highest practical vocation in the establishment of a good will, is capable only of a contentment of its own kind, i.e., one that springs from the attainment of a purpose which is determined by reason, even though this injures the ends of inclination.

We have, then, to develop the concept of a will which is to be esteemed as good of itself without regard to anything else. It dwells already in the natural sound understanding and does not need so much to be taught as only to be brought to light. In the estimation of the total worth of our actions it always takes first place and is the condition of everything else. In order to show this, we shall take the concept of duty. It contains that of a good will, though with certain subjective restrictions and hindrances; but these are far from concealing it and making it unrecognizable, for they rather bring it out by contrast and make it shine forth all the brighter.

[B. Acting from the Motive of Duty]

I here omit all actions which are recognized as opposed to duty, even though they may be useful in one respect or another, for with these the question does not arise at all as to whether they may be carried out *from* duty, since they conflict with it. I also pass over the actions which are really in accordance with duty and to which one has no direct inclination, rather executing them because impelled to do so by another inclination. For it is easily decided whether an action in accord with duty is performed from duty or for some selfish purpose. It is far more difficult to note this difference when the action is in accordance with duty and, in addition, the subject has a direct inclination to do it. For example, it is in fact in accordance with duty that a dealer should not over-charge an inexperienced customer, and wherever there is much business the prudent merchant does not do so, having a fixed price for everyone, so that a child may buy of him as cheaply as any other. Thus the customer is honestly served. But this is far from sufficient to justify the belief that the merchant has behaved in this way from duty and principles of honesty. His own advantage required this behavior; but it cannot be assumed that over and above that he had a direct inclination to the purchaser and that, out of love, as it were, he gave none an advantage in price over another. Therefore the action was done neither from duty nor from direct inclination but only for a selfish purpose.

On the other hand, it is a duty to preserve one's life, and moreover everyone has a direct inclination to do so. But for that reason the often anxious care which most men take of it has no intrinsic worth, and the maxim of doing so has no moral import. They preserve their lives according to duty, but not from duty. But if adversities and hopeless sorrow completely take away the relish for life, if an unfortunate man, strong in soul, is indignant rather than despond-ent or dejected over his fate and wishes for death, and yet preserves his life without loving it and from neither inclination nor fear but from duty—then his maxim has a moral import.

To be kind where one can is duty, and there are, moreover, many persons so sympathetically constituted that without any motive of vanity or selfishness they find an inner satisfaction in spreading joy, and rejoice in the contentment of others which they have made possible. But I say that, however dutiful and amiable it may be, that kind of action has no true moral worth. It is on a level with [actions arising from] other inclinations, such as the inclination to honor, which, if fortunately directed to what in fact accords with duty and is generally useful and thus honorable, deserve praise and encouragement but no esteem. For the maxim lacks the moral import of an action done not from inclination but from duty. But assume that the mind of that friend to mankind was clouded by a sorrow of his own which extinguished all sympathy with the lot of others and that he still had the power to benefit others in distress, but that their need

414

left him untouched because he was preoccupied with his own need. And now supposed him to tear himself, unsolicited by inclination, out of this dead insensibility and to perform this action only from duty and without any inclination—then for the first time his action has genuine moral worth. Furthermore, if nature has put little sympathy in the heart of a man, and if he, though an honest man, is by temperament cold and indifferent to the sufferings of others, perhaps because he is provided with special gifts of patience and fortitude and expects or even requires that others should have the same—and such a man would certainly not be the meanest product of nature—would not he find in himself a source from which to give himself a far higher worth than he could have got by having a good-natured temperament? This is unquestionably true even though nature did not make him philanthropic, for it is just here that the worth of the character is brought out, which is morally and incomparably the highest of all: he is beneficent not from inclination but from duty.

To secure one's own happiness is at least indirectly a duty, for discontent with one's condition under pressure from many cares and amid unsatisfied wants could easily become a great temptation to transgress duties. But without any view to duty all men have the strongest and deepest inclination to happiness, because in this idea all inclinations are summed up. But the precept of happiness is often so formulated that it definitely thwarts some inclinations, and men can make no definite and certain concept of the sum of satisfaction of all inclinations which goes under the name of happiness. It is not to be wondered at, therefore, that a single inclination, definite as to what it promises and as to the time at which it can be satisfied, can outweigh a fluctuating idea, and that, for example, a man with the gout can choose to enjoy what he likes and to suffer what he may, because according to his calculations at least on this occasion he has not sacrificed the enjoyment of the present moment to a perhaps groundless expectation of a happiness supposed to lie in health. But even in this case, if the universal inclination to happiness did not determine his will, and if health were not at least for him a necessary factor in these calculations, there yet would remain, as in all other cases, a law that he ought to promote his happiness, not from inclination but from duty. Only from this law would his conduct have true moral worth.

It is in this way, undoubtedly, that we should understand those passages of Scripture which command us to love our neighbor and even our enemy, for love as an inclination cannot be commanded. But beneficence from duty, when no inclination impels it and even when it is opposed by a natural and unconquerable aversion, is practical love, not pathological love; it resides in the will and not in the propensities of feeling, in principles of action and not in tender sympathy; and it alone can be commanded.

[Thus the first proposition of morality is that to have moral worth an action must be done from duty.] The second proposition is: An action performed from duty does not have its moral worth in the purpose which is to be achieved through it but in the maxim by which it is determined. Its moral value, therefore, does not depend on the realization of the object of the action but merely on the principle of volition by which the action is done, without any regard to the objects of the faculty of desire. From the preceding discussion it is clear that the purposes we may have for our actions and their effects as ends and incentives of the will cannot give the actions any unconditional and moral worth. Wherein, then, can this worth lie, if it is not in the will in relation to its hoped-for effect? It can lie nowhere else than in the principle of the will, irrespective of the ends which can be realized by such action. For the will stands, as it were, at the crossroads halfway between its a priori principle which is formal and its a posteriori incentive which is material. Since it must be determined by something, if it is done from duty it must be determined by the formal principle of volition as such since every material principle has been withdrawn from it.

The third principle, as a consequence of the two preceding, I would express as follows: Duty is the necessity of an action executed from respect for law. I can certainly have an inclination to the object as an effect of the proposed action, but I can never have respect for it precisely because it is a mere effect and not an activity of a will. Similarly, I can have no respect for any inclination whatsoever, whether my own or that of another; in the former case I can at most approve of it and in the latter I can even love it, i.e., see it as favorable to my own advantage. But that which is connected with my will merely as ground and not as consequence, that which does not serve my inclination but overpowers it or at least excludes it from being considered in making a choice— in a word, law itself—can be an object of respect and thus a command. Now as an act from duty wholly excludes the influence of inclination and therewith every object of the will, nothing remains which can determine the will objectively except the law, and nothing subjectively except pure respect for this practical law. This subjective element is the maxim[1] that I ought to follow such a law even if it thwarts all my inclinations.

Thus the moral worth of an action does not lie in the effect which is expected from it or in any principle of action which has to borrow its motive from this expected effect. For all these effects (agreeableness of my own condition, indeed even the promotion of the happiness of others) could be brought about through other causes and would not require the will of a rational being, while the highest and unconditional good can be found only in such a will. Therefore, the preeminent good can consist only in the conception of the law in itself (which can be present only in a rational being) so far as this conception and not the hoped-for effect is the determining ground of the will. This pre-eminent good, which we call moral, is already present in the person who acts according to this conception, and we do not have to look for it first in the result.[2]

---

[1] A maxim is the subjective principle of volition. The objective principle (i.e., that which would serve all rational beings also subjectively as a practical principle if reason had full power over the faculty of desire) is the practical law.

[2] It might be objected that I seek to take refuge in an obscure feeling behind the word "respect," instead of clearly resolving the question with a concept of reason. But though respect is a feeling, it is not one received through any [outer] influence but is self-wrought by a rational concept; thus it differs specifically from all feelings of the former kind which may be referred to inclination

[C. The Moral Law]

But what kind of a law can that be, the conception of which must determine the will without reference to the expected result? Under this condition alone the will can be called absolutely good without qualification. Since I have robbed the will of all impulses which could come to it from obedience to any law, nothing remains to serve as a principle of the will except universal conformity of its action to law as such. That is, I should never act in such a way that I could not also will that my maxim should be a universal law. Mere conformity to law as such (without assuming any particular law applicable to certain actions) serves as the principle of the will, and it must serve as such a principle if duty is not to be a vain delusion and chimerical concept. The common reason of mankind in its practical judgments is in perfect agreement with this and has this principle constantly in view.

Let the question, for example, be: May I, when in distress, make a promise with the intention not to keep it? I easily distinguish the two meanings which the question can have, viz., whether it is prudent to make a false promise, or whether it conforms to my duty. Undoubtedly the former can often be the case, though I do see clearly that it is not sufficient merely to escape from the present difficulty by this expedient, but that I must consider whether inconveniences much greater than the present one may not later spring from this lie. Even with all my supposed cunning, the consequences cannot be so easily foreseen. Loss of credit might be far more disadvantageous than the misfortune I now seek to avoid, and it is hard to tell whether it might not be more prudent to act according to a universal maxim and to make it a habit not to promise anything without intending to fulfill it. But it is soon clear to me that such a maxim is based only on an apprehensive concern with consequences.

To be truthful from duty, however, is an entirely different thing from being truthful out of fear of disadvantageous consequences, for in the former case the concept of the action itself contains a law for me, while in the latter I must first look about to see what results for me may be connected with it. For to deviate from the principle of duty is certainly bad, but to be unfaithful to my

---

or fear. What I recognize directly as a law for myself I recognize with respect, which means merely the consciousness of the submission of my will to a law without the intervention of other influences on my mind. The direct determination of the will by the law and the consciousness of this determination is respect; thus respect can be regarded as the effect of the law on the subject and not as the cause of the law. Respect is properly the conception of a worth which thwarts my self-love. Thus it is regarded as an object neither of inclination nor of fear, though it has something analogous to both. The only object of respect is the law, and indeed only the law which we impose on ourselves and yet recognize as necessary in itself. As a law, we are subject to it without consulting self-love; as imposed on us by ourselves, it is a consequence of our will. In the former respect it is analogous to fear and in the latter to inclination. All respect for a person is only respect for the law (of rightousness, etc.) of which the person provides an example. Because we see the improvement of our talents as a duty, we think of a person of talents as the example of a law, as it were (the law that we should by practice become like him in his talents), and that constitutes our respect. All so-called moral interest consists solely in respect for the law.

maxim of prudence can sometimes be very advantageous to me, though it is certainly safe to abide by it. The shortest but most infallible way to find the answer to the question as to whether a deceitful promise is consistent with duty is to ask myself: Would I be content that my maxim (of extricating myself from difficulty by a false promise) should hold as a universal law for myself as well as for others? And could I say to myself that everyone may make a false promise when he is in a difficulty from which he otherwise cannot escape? I immediately see that I could will the lie but not a universal law to lie. For with such a law there would be no promises at all, inasmuch as it would be futile to make a pretense of my intention in regard to future actions to those who would not believe this pretense or—if they overhastily did so—who would pay me back in my own coin. Thus my maxim would necessarily destroy itself as soon as it was made a universal law.

[D. Common Morality and the Need for Philosophy]

I do not, therefore, need any penetrating acuteness in order to discern what I have to do in order that my volition may be morally good. Inexperienced in the course of the world, incapable of being prepared for all its contingencies, I ask myself only: Can I will that my maxim become a universal law? If not, it must be rejected, not because of any disadvantage accruing to myself or even to others, but because it cannot enter as a principle into a possible universal legislation, and reason extorts from me an immediate respect for such legislation. I do not as yet discern on what it is grounded (a question the philosopher may investigate), but I at least understand that it is an estimation of the worth which far outweighs all the worth of whatever is recommended by the inclinations, and that the necessity of my actions from pure respect for the practical law constitutes duty. To duty every other motive must give place, because duty is the condition of a will good in itself, whose worth transcends everything.

Thus within the moral knowledge of common human reason we have attained its principle. To be sure, common human reason does not think of it abstractly in such a universal form, but it always has it in view and uses it as the standard of its judgments. It would be easy to show how common human reason, with this compass, knows well how to distinguish what is good, what is bad, and what is consistent or inconsistent with duty. Without in the least teaching common reason anything new, we need only to draw its attention to its own principle, in the manner of Socrates, thus showing that neither science nor philosophy is needed in order to know what one has to do in order to be honest and good, and even wise and virtuous. We might have conjectured beforehand that the knowledge of what everyone is obliged to do and thus also to know would be within the reach of everyone, even the most ordinary man. Here we cannot but admire the great advantages which the practical faculty of judgment has over the theoretical in ordinary human understanding. In the theoretical, if ordinary reason ventures to go beyond the laws of experience and perceptions of the senses, it falls into sheer inconceivabilities and self-contradictions, or at least into a chaos of uncertainty, obscurity, and instability. In the practical, on the other hand, the power of judgment first shows itself to advantage when common understanding excludes all sensuous incentives from practical laws. It then becomes even subtle, quibbling with its own conscience or with other claims to what should be called right, or wishing to determine correctly for its own instruction the worth of certain actions. But the most remarkable thing about ordinary reason in its practical concern is that it may have as much hope as any philosopher of hitting the mark. In fact, it is almost more certain to do so than the philosopher, because he has no principle which the common understanding lacks, while his judgment is easily confused by a mass of irrelevant considerations, so that it easily turns aside from the correct way. Would it not, therefore, be wiser in moral matters to acquiesce in the common rational judgment, or at most to call in philosophy in order to make the system of morals more complete and comprehensible and its rules more convenient for use (especially in disputation) than to steer the common understanding from its happy simplicity in practical matters and to lead it through philosophy into a new path of inquiry and instruction?

Innocence is indeed a glorious thing, but, on the other hand, it is very sad that it cannot well maintain itself, being easily led astray. For this reason, even wisdom—which consists more in acting than in knowing—needs science, not to learn from it but to secure admission and permanence to its precepts. Man feels in himself a powerful counterpoise against all commands of duty which reason presents to him as so deserving of respect; this counterpoise is his needs and inclinations, the complete satisfaction of which he sums up under the name of happiness. Now reason issues inexorable commands without promising anything to the inclinations. It disregards, as it were, and holds in contempt those claims which are so impetuous and yet so plausible, and which will not allow themselves to be abolished by any command. From this a natural dialectic arises, i.e., a propensity to argue against the stern laws of duty and their validity, or at least to place their purity and strictness in doubt and, where possible, to make them more accordant with our wishes and inclinations. This is equivalent to corrupting them in their very foundations and destroying their dignity—a thing which even common practical reason cannot ultimately call good.

In this way common human reason is impelled to go outside its sphere and to take a step into the field of practical philosophy. But it is forced to do so not by any speculative need, which never occurs to it so long as it is satisfied to remain merely healthy reason; rather, it is so impelled on practical grounds in order to obtain information and clear instruction respecting the source of its principle and the correct determination of this principle in its opposition to the maxims which are based on need and inclination. It seeks this information in order to escape from the perplexity of opposing claims and to avoid the danger of losing all genuine moral principles through the equivocation in which it is easily involved. Thus, when practical common reason cultivates itself, a dialectic surreptitiously ensues which forces it to seek aid in philosophy, just as the same thing happens in the theoretical use of reason. In this case, as in the theoretical, it will find rest only in a thorough critical examination of our reason.

. . .

[E. Acting According to the Concept of Law]

In this study we do not advance merely from the common moral judgment (which here is very worthy of respect) to the philosophical, as this has already been done, but we advance by natural stages from a popular philosophy (which goes no further than it can grope by means of examples) to metaphysics (which is not held back by anything empirical and which, as it must measure out the entire scope of rational knowledge of this kind, reaches even Ideas, where examples fail us). In order to make this advance, we must follow and clearly present the practical faculty of reason from its universal rules of determination to the point where the concept of duty arises from it.

Everything in nature works according to laws. Only a rational being has the capacity of acting according to the conception of laws, i.e., according to principles. This capacity is will. Since reason is required for the derivation of actions from laws, will is nothing else than practical reason. If reason infallibly determines the will, the actions which such a being recognizes as objectively necessary are also subjectively necessary. That is, the will is a faculty of choosing only that which reason, independently of inclination, recognizes as practically necessary, i.e., as good. But if reason of itself does not sufficiently determine the will, and if the will is subjugated to subjective conditions (certain incentives) which do not always agree with objective conditions; in a word, if the will is not of itself in complete accord with reason (the actual case of men), then the actions which are recognized as objectively necessary are subjectively contingent, and the determination of such a will according to objective laws is constraint. That is, the relation of objective laws to a will which is not completely good is conceived as the determination of the will of a rational being by principles of reason to which this will is not by nature necessarily obedient.

The conception of an objective principle, so far as it constrains a will, is a command (of reason), and the formula of this command is called an *imperative*.

All imperatives are expressed by an "ought" and thereby indicate the relation of an objective law of reason to a will which is not in its subjective constitution necessarily determined by this law. This relation is that of constraint. Imperatives say that it would be good to do or to refrain from doing something, but they say it to a will which does not always do something simply because it is presented as a good thing to do. Practical good is what determines the will by means of the conception of reason and hence not by subjective causes but, rather, objectively, i.e., on grounds which are valid for every rational being as such. It is distinguished from the pleasant as that which has an influence on the will only by means of a sensation from merely subjective causes, which hold only for the senses of this or that person and not as a principle of reason which holds for everyone.

A perfectly good will, therefore, would be equally subject to objective laws (of the good), but it could not be conceived as constrained by them to act in accord with them, because, according to its own subjective constitution, it can be determined to act only through the conception of the good. Thus no imperatives hold for the divine will or, more generally, for a holy will. The "ought" is here out of place, for the volition of itself is necessarily in unison with the law. Therefore imperatives are only formulas expressing the relation of objective laws of volition in general to the subjective imperfection of the will of this or that rational being, e.g., the human will.

All imperatives command either hypothetically or categorically. The former present the practical necessity of a possible action as a means to achieving something else which one desires (or which one may possibly desire). The categorical imperative would be one which presented an action as of itself objectively necessary, without regard to any other end.

Since every practical law presents a possible action as good and thus as necessary for a subject practically determinable by reason, all imperatives are formulas of the determination of action which is necessary by the principle of a will which is in any way good. If the action is good only as a means to something else, the imperative is hypothetical; but if it is thought of as good in itself, and hence as necessary in a will which of itself conforms to reason as the principle of this will, the imperative is categorical.

The imperative thus says what action possible to me would be good, and it presents the practical rule in relation to a will which does not forthwith perform an action simply because it is good, in part because the subject does not always know that the action is good and in part (when he does know it) because his maxims can still be opposed to the objective principles of practical reason.

The hypothetical imperative, therefore, says only that the action is good to some purpose, possible or actual. In the former case it is a problematical, in the latter an assertorical, practical principle. The categorical imperative, which declares the action to be of itself objectively necessary without making any reference to a purpose, i.e., without having any other end, holds as an apodictical (practical) principle.

. . .

[F. How Is the Categorical Imperative Possible?]

In attacking this problem, we will first inquire whether the mere concept of a categorical imperative does not also furnish the formula containing the proposition which alone can be a categorical imperative. For even when we know the formula of the imperative, to learn how such an absolute law is possible will require difficult and special labors which we shall postpone to the last section.

If I think of a hypothetical imperative as such, I do not know what it will contain until the condition is stated [under which it is an imperative]. But if I think of a categorical imperative, I know immediately what it contains. For since the imperative contains besides the law only the necessity that the maxim should accord with this law, while the law contains no condition to which it is restricted, there is nothing remaining in it except the universality of law as such to which the maxim of the action should conform; and in effect this conformity alone is represented as necessary by the imperative.

There is, therefore, only one categorical imperative. It is: Act only according to that maxim by which you can at the same time will that it should become a universal law.

Now if all imperatives of duty can be derived from this one imperative as a principle, we can at least show what we understand by the concept of duty and what it means, even though it remain undecided whether that which is called duty is an empty concept or not.

The universality of law according to which effects are produced constitutes what is properly called nature in the most general sense (as to form), i.e., the existence of things so far as it is determined by universal laws. [By analogy], then, the universal imperative of duty can be expressed as follows: Act as though the maxim of your action were by your will to become a universal law of nature.

We shall now enumerate some duties, adopting the usual division of them into duties to ourselves and to others and into perfect and imperfect duties.

1. A man who is reduced to despair by a series of evils feels a weariness with life but is still in possession of his reason sufficiently to ask whether it would not be contrary to his duty to himself to take his own life. Now he asks whether the maxim of his action could become a universal law of nature. His maxim, however, is: For love of myself, I make it my principle to shorten my life when by a longer duration it threatens more evil than satisfaction. But it is questionable whether this principle of self-love could become a universal law of nature. One immediately sees a contradiction in a system of nature whose law would be to destory life by the feeling whose special office is to impel the improvement of life. In this case it would not exist as nature; hence that maxim cannot obtain as a law of nature, and thus it wholly contradicts the supreme principle of all duty.

2. Another man finds himself forced by need to borrow money. He well knows that he will not be able to repay it, but he also sees that nothing will be loaned him if he does not firmly promise to repay it at a certain time. He desires to make such a promise, but he has enough conscience to ask himself whether it is not improper and opposed to duty to relieve his distress in such a way. Now, assuming he does decide to do so, the maxim of his action would be as follows: When I believe myself to be in need of money, I will borrow money and promise to repay it, although I know I shall never do so. Now this principle of self-love or of his own benefit may very well be compatible with his whole future welfare, but the question is whether it is right. He changes the pretension of self-love into a universal law and then puts the question:

How would it be if my maxim became a universal law? He immediately sees that it could never hold as a universal law of nature and be consistent with itself; rather it must necessarily contradict itself. For the universality of a law which says that anyone who believes himself to be in need could promise what he pleased with the intention of not fulfilling it would make the promise itself and the end to be accomplished by it impossible; no one would believe what was promised to him but would only laugh at any such assertion as vain pretense.

3. A third finds in himself a talent which could, by means of some cultivation, make him in many respects a useful man. But he finds himself in comfortable circumstances and prefers indulgence in pleasure to troubling himself with broadening and improving his fortunate natural gifts. Now, however, let him ask whether his maxim of neglecting his gifts, besides agreeing with his propensity to idle amusement, agrees also with what is called duty. He sees that a system of nature could indeed exist in accordance with such a law, even though man (like the inhabitants of the South Sea Islands) should let his talents rust and resolve to devote his life merely to idleness, indulgence, and propagation—in a word, to pleasure. But he cannot possibly will that this should become a universal law of nature or that it should be implanted in us by a natural instinct. For, as a rational being, he necessarily wills that all his faculties should be developed, inasmuch as they are given to him for all sorts of possible purposes.

4. A fourth man, for whom things are going well, sees that others (whom he could help) have to struggle with great hardships, and he asks, "What concern of mine is it? Let each one be as happy as heaven wills, or as he can make himself; I will not take anything from him or even envy him; but to his welfare or to his assistance in time of need I have no desire to contribute." If such a way of thinking were a universal law of nature, certainly the human race could exist, and without doubt even better than in a state where everyone talks of sympathy and good will, or even exerts himself occasionally to practice them while, on the other hand, he cheats when he can and betrays or otherwise violates the rights of man. Now although it is possible that a universal law of nature according to that maxim could exist, it is nevertheless impossible to will that such a principle should hold everywhere as a law of nature. For a will which resolved this would conflict with itself, since instances can often arise in which he would need the love and sympathy of others, and in which he would have robbed himself, by such a law of nature springing from his own will, of all hope of the aid he desires.

The foregoing are a few of the many actual duties, or at least of duties we hold to be actual, whose derivation from the one stated principle is clear. We must be able to will that a maxim of our action become a universal law; this is the canon of the moral estimation of our action generally. Some actions are of such a nature that their maxim cannot even be *thought* as a universal law of nature without contradiction, far from it being possible that one could will that it should be such. In others this internal impossibility is not found, though it is still impossible to *will* that their maxim should be raised to the universality of a law of nature, because such a will would contradict itself. We easily see that the former maxim conflicts with the stricter or narrower (imprescriptible) duty, the latter with broader (meritorious) duty. Thus all duties, so far as the kind of obligation (not the object of their action) is concerned, have been completely exhibited by these examples in their dependence on the one principle.

When we observe ourselves in any transgression of a duty, we find that we do not actually will that our maxim should become a universal law. That is impossible for us; rather, the contrary of this maxim should remain as a law generally, and we only take the liberty of making an exception to it for ourselves or for the sake of our inclination, and for this one occasion. Consequently, if we weighed everything from one and the same standpoint, namely, reason, we would come upon a contradiction in our own will, viz., that a certain principle is objectively necessary as a universal law and yet subjectively does not hold universally but rather admits exceptions. However, since we regard our action at one time from the point of view of a will wholly conformable to reason and then from that of a will affected by inclinations, there is actually no contradiction, but rather an opposition of inclination to the precept of reason (*antagonismus*). In this the universality of the principle (*universalitas*) is changed into mere generality (*generalitas*), whereby the practical principle of reason meets the maxim halfway. Although this cannot be justified in our own impartial judgment, it does show that we actually acknowledge the validity of the categorical imperative and allow ourselves (with all respect to it) only a few exceptions which seem to us to be unimportant and forced upon us.

We have thus at least established that if duty is a concept which is to have significance and actual legislation for our actions, it can be expressed only in categorical imperatives and not at all in hypothetical ones. For every application of it we have also clearly exhibited the content of the categorical imperative which must contain the principle of all duty (if there is such). This is itself very much. But we are not yet advanced far enough to prove a priori that that kind of imperative really exists, that there is a practical law which of itself commands absolutely and without any incentives, and that obedience to this law is duty.

[G. The Ultimate Worth of Persons]

[*We must now inquire how such a categorical imperative is possible.*]
With a view to attaining this, it is extremely important to remember that we must not let ourselves think that the reality of this principle can be derived from the particular constitution of human nature. For duty is practical unconditional necessity of action; it must, therefore, hold for all rational beings (to which alone an imperative can apply), and only for that reason can it be a law for all human wills. Whatever is derived from the particular natural situation of man as such, or from certain feelings and propensities, or even from a particular tendency of the human reason which might not hold necessarily for the will of every rational being (if such a tendency is possible), can give a

maxim valid for us but not a law; that is, it can give a subjective principle by which we might act only if we have the propensity and inclination, but not an objective principle by which we would be directed to act even if all our propensity, inclination, and natural tendency were opposed to it. This is so far the case that the sublimity and intrinsic worth of the command is the better shown in a duty the fewer subjective causes there are for it and the more there are against it; the latter do not weaken the constraint of the law or diminish its validity.

Here we see philosophy brought to what is, in fact, a precarious position, which should be made fast even though it is supported by nothing in either heaven or earth. Here philosophy must show its purity as the absolute sustainer of its laws, and not as the herald of those which an implanted sense or who knows what tutelary nature whispers to it. Those may be better than no laws at all, but they can never afford fundamental principles, which reason alone dictates. These fundamental principles must originate entirely a priori and thereby obtain their commanding authority; they can expect nothing from the inclination of men but everything from the supremacy of the law and due respect for it. Otherwise they condemn man to self-contempt and inner abhorrence.

Thus everything empirical is not only wholly unworthy to be an ingredient in the principle of morality but is even highly prejudicial to the purity of moral practices themselves. For, in morals, the proper and inestimable worth of an absolutely good will consists precisely in the freedom of the principle of action from all influences from contingent grounds which only experience can furnish. We cannot too much or too often warn against the lax or even base manner of thought which seeks principles among empirical motives and laws, for human reason in its weariness is glad to rest on this pillow. In a dream of sweet illusions (in which it embraces not Juno but a cloud), it substitutes for morality a bastard patched up from limbs of very different parentage, which looks like anything one wishes to see in it, but not like virtue to anyone who has ever beheld her in her true form.

The question then is: Is it a necessary law for all rational beings that they should always judge their actions by such maxims as they themselves could will to serve as universal laws? If it is such a law, it must be connected (wholly a priori) with the concept of the will of a rational being as such. But in order to discover this connection we must, however reluctantly, take a step into metaphysics, although into a region of it different from speculative philosophy, i.e., into metaphysics of morals. In a practical philosophy it is not a question of assuming grounds for what happens but of assuming laws of what ought to happen even though it may never happen—that is to say, objective, practical laws. Hence in practical philosophy we need not inquire into the reasons why something pleases or displeases, how the pleasure of mere feeling differs from taste, and whether this is distinct from a general satisfaction of reason. Nor need we ask on what the feeling of pleasure or displeasure rests, how desires and inclinations arise, and how, finally, maxims arise from desires and inclination under the co-operation of reason. For all these matters belong to an empirical psychology, which would be the second part of physics if we consider it as philosophy of nature so far as it rests on empirical laws. But here it is a question of objectively practical laws and thus of the relation of a will to itself so far as it determines itself only by reason; for everything which has a relation to the empirical automatically falls away, because if reason of itself alone determines conduct it must necessarily do so a priori. The possibility of reason thus determining conduct must now be investigated.

The will is thought of as a faculty of determining itself to action in accordance with the conception of certain laws. Such a faculty can be found only in rational beings. That which serves the will as the objective ground of its self-determination is an end, and, if it is given by reason alone, it must hold alike for all rational beings. On the other hand, that which contains the ground of the possibility of the action, whose result is an end, is called the means. The subjective ground of desire is the incentive, while the objective ground of volition is the motive. Thus arises the distinction between subjective ends, which rest on incentives, and objective ends, which depend on motives valid for every rational being. Practical principles are formal when they disregard all subjective ends; they are material when they have subjective ends, and thus certain incentives, as their basis. The ends which a rational being arbitrarily proposes to himself as consequences of his action are material ends and are without exception only relative, for only their relation to a particularly constituted faculty of desire in the subject gives them their worth. And this worth cannot, therefore, afford any universal principles for all rational beings or valid and necessary principles for every volition. That is, they cannot give rise to any practical laws. All these relative ends, therefore, are grounds for hypothetical imperatives only.

But suppose that there were something the existence of which in itself had absolute worth, something which, as an end in itself, could be a ground of definite laws. In it and only in it could lie the ground of a possible categorical imperative, i.e., of a practical law.

Now, I say, man and, in general, every rational being exists as an end in himself and not merely as a means to be arbitrarily used by this or that will. In all his actions, whether they are directed to himself or to other rational beings, he must always be regarded at the same time as an end. All objects of inclinations have only a conditional worth, for if the inclinations and the needs founded on them did not exist, their object would be without worth. The inclinations themselves as the sources of needs, however, are so lacking in absolute worth that the universal wish of every rational being must be indeed to free himself completely from them. Therefore, the worth of any objects to be obtained by our actions is at all times conditional. Beings whose existence does not depend on our will but on nature, if they are not rational beings, have only a relative worth as means and are therefore called "things"; on the other hand, rational beings are designated "persons" because their nature indicates that they are ends in themselves, i.e., things which may not be used merely as means. Such a being is thus an object of respect and, so far, restricts all [arbitrary] choice. Such beings are not merely subjective ends whose existence as a result of our action has a worth for us, but are objective ends, i.e., beings whose existence in itself is an end. Such an end is one for which no other end can be substituted, to which these beings should serve merely as means. For, without them, nothing of absolute worth could be found, and if all worth is conditional and thus contingent, no supreme practical principle for reason could be found anywhere.

Thus if there is to be a supreme practical principle and a categorical imperative for the human will, it must be one that forms an objective principle of the will from the conception of that which is necessarily an end for everyone because it is an end in itself. Hence this objective principle can serve as a universal practical law. The ground of this principle is: rational nature exists as an end in itself. Man necessarily thinks of his own existence in this way; thus far it is a subjective principle of human actions. Also every other rational being thinks of his existence by means of the same rational ground which holds also for myself; thus it is at the same time an objective principle from which, as a supreme practical ground, it must be possible to derive all laws of the will. The practical imperative, therefore, is the following: Act so that you treat humanity, whether in your own person or in that of another, always as an end and never as a means only.

. . .

[H. Moral Agents as Law—Givers to Themselves]

If we now look back upon all previous attempts which have ever been undertaken to discover the principle of morality, it is not to be wondered at that they all had to fail. Man was seen to be bound to laws by his duty, but it was not seen that he is subject only to his own, yet universal, legislation, and that he is only bound to act in accordance with his own will, which is, however, designed by nature to be a will giving universal laws. For if one thought of him as subject only to a law (whatever it may be), this necessarily implied some interest as a stimulus or compulsion to obedience because the law did not arise from his will. Rather, his will was constrained by something else according to a law to act in a certain way. By this strictly necessary consequence, however, all the labor of finding a supreme ground for duty was irrevocably lost, and one never arrived at duty but only at the necessity of action from a certain interest. This might be his own interest or that of another, but in either case the imperative always had to be conditional and could not at all serve as a moral command. This principle I will call the principle of *autonomy* of the will in contrast to all other principles which I accordingly count under heteronomy.

The concept of each rational being as a being that must regard itself as giving universal law through all the maxims of its will, so that it may judge itself and its actions from this standpoint, leads to a very fruitful concept, namely, that of a *realm of ends*.

By "realm" I understand the systematic union of different rational beings through common laws. Because laws determine ends with regard to their universal validity, if we abstract from the personal difference of rational beings and thus from all content of their private ends, we can think of a whole of all ends in systematic connection, a whole of rational beings as ends in themselves as well as of the particular ends which each may set for himself. This is a realm of ends, which is possible on the aforesaid principles. For all rational beings stand under the law that each of them should treat himself and all others never merely as means but in every case also as an end in himself. Thus there arises a systematic union of rational beings through common objective laws. This is a realm which may be called a realm of ends (certainly only an ideal), because what these laws have in view is just the relation of these beings to each other as ends and means.

A rational being belongs to the realm of ends as a member when he gives universal laws in it while also himself subject to these laws. He belongs to it as sovereign when he, as legislating, is subject to the will of no other. The rational being must regard himself always as legislative in a realm of ends possible through the freedom of the will, whether he belongs to it as member or as sovereign. He cannot maintain the latter position merely through the maxims of his will but only when he is a completely independent being without need and with power adequate to his will.

Morality, therefore, consists in the relation of every action to that legislation through which alone a realm of ends is possible. This legislation, however, must be found in every rational being. It must be able to arise from his will, whose principle then is to take no action according to any maxim which would be inconsistent with its being a universal law and thus to act only so that the will through its maxims could regard itself at the same time as universally lawgiving. If now the maxims do not by their nature already necessarily conform to this objective principle of rational beings as universally lawgiving, the necessity of acting according to that principle is called practical constraint, i.e., duty. Duty pertains not to the sovereign in the realm of ends, but rather to each member, and to each in the same degree.

The practical necessity of acting according to this principle, i.e., duty, does not rest at all on feelings, impulses, and inclinations; it rests merely on the relation of rational beings to one another, in which the will of a rational being must always be regarded as legislative, for otherwise it could not be thought of as an end in itself. Reason, therefore, relates every maxim of the will as giving universal laws to every other will and also to every action toward itself; it does so not for the sake of any other practical motive or future advantage but rather from the idea of the dignity of a rational being who obeys no law except that which he himself also gives.

In the realm of ends everything has either a *price* or a *dignity*. Whatever has a price can be replaced by something else as its equivalent; on the other hand, whatever is above all price, and therefore admits of no equivalent, has a dignity.

That which is related to general human inclinations and needs has a *market price*. That which, without presupposing any need, accords with a certain taste, i.e., with pleasure in the mere purposeless play of our faculties, has an *affective price*. But that which constituted the condition under which alone something can be an end in itself does not have mere relative worth, i.e., a price, but an intrinsic worth, i.e., *dignity*.

Now morality is the condition under which alone a rational being can be an end in itself, because only through it is it possible to be a legislative member in the realm of ends. Thus morality and humanity, so far as it is capable of morality, alone have dignity. Skill and diligence in work have a market value; wit, lively imagination, and humor have an affective price; but fidelity in promises and benevolence on principle (not from instinct) have intrinsic worth. Nature and likewise art contain nothing which could replace their lack, for their worth consists not in effects which flow from them, nor in advantage and utility which they procure; it consists only in intentions, i.e., maxims of the will which are ready to reveal themselves in this manner through actions even though success does not favor them. These actions need no recommendation from any subjective disposition or taste in order that they may be looked upon with immediate favor and satisfaction, nor do they have need of any immediate propensity or feeling directed to them. They exhibit the will which performs them as the object of an immediate respect, since nothing but reason is required in order to impose them on the will. The will is not to be cajoled into them, for this, in the case of duties, would be a contradiction. This esteem lets the worth of such a turn of mind be recognized as dignity and puts it infinitely beyond any price, with which it cannot in the least be brought into competition or comparison without, as it were, violating its holiness.

And what is it that justifies the morally good disposition or virtue in making such lofty claims? It is nothing less than the participation it affords the rational being in giving universal laws. He is thus fitted to be a member in a possible realm of ends to which his own nature already destined him. For, as an end in himself, he is destined to be legislative in the realm of ends, free from all laws of nature and obedient only to those which he himself gives. Accordingly, his maxims can belong to a universal legislation to which he is at the same time also subject. A thing has no worth other than that determined for it by the law. The legislation which determines all worth must therefore have a dignity, i.e., unconditional and incomparable worth. For the esteem which a rational being must have for it, only the word "respect" is a suitable expression. Autonomy is thus the basis of the dignity of both human nature and every rational nature.

The three aforementioned ways of presenting the principle of morality are fundamentally only so many formulas of the very same law, and each of them unites the others in itself.

. . .

30

Moral Luck

THOMAS NAGEL

Thomas Nagel (b. 1937) taught philosophy at Princeton University and is now chairman of the philosophy department at New York University. He is the author of The Possibility of Altruism, *an important work of moral theory, and, more recently, of* The View from Nowhere. *This selection is from his collection of essays,* Mortal Questions.

Nagel's topic here is a tension within our attitudes toward moral responsibility. On the one hand, it seems that persons are not responsible for what they cannot control. As Kant asserts in reading 29, a good will appears to retain its moral worth even when it achieves nothing or actually brings bad results. Yet as Nagel notes, this is not the way we actually think. We consider it worse to run a red light and kill a pedestrian than to run a red light and not harm anyone. But a pedestrian's unforeseen presence is not within the driver's control. Hence, how wrongly the driver turns out to have acted depends on his "moral luck."

Other factors have similar effects. A person has no control over his basic character traits, nor does he have control over the opportunities and temptations he encounters, yet these also influence our evaluation of him. In fact, when we strip away everything a person cannot control, very little, if anything, remains. This leads some to say that persons can be blamed and held responsible even for things they could not control.

But Nagel argues that this response is inadequate. To come to grips with the problem, we must understand its source. According to Nagel, this is the need to view ourselves as both components of an objective world and subjective initiators of action. For contrasting attempts to draw moral conclusions from facts about agency, see reading 23 by Alan Gewirth, and reading 46 by Charles Fried.

KANT BELIEVED THAT good or bad luck should influence neither our moral judgment of a person and his actions, nor his moral assessment of himself.

> The good will is not good because of what it effects or accomplishes or because of its adequacy to achieve some proposed end; it is good only because of its willing, i.e., it is good of itself. And, regarded for itself, it is to be esteemed incomparably higher than anything which could be brought about by it in favor of any inclination or even of the sum total of all inclinations. Even if it should happen that,

by a particularly unfortunate fate or by the niggardly provision of a stepmotherly nature, this will should be wholly lacking in power to accomplish its purpose, and if even the greatest effort should not avail it to achieve anything of its end, and if there remained only the good will (not as a mere wish but as the summoning of all the means in our power), it would sparkle like a jewel in its own right, as something that had its full worth in itself. Usefulness or fruitlessness can neither diminish nor augment this worth.[1]

He would presumably have said the same about a bad will: whether it accomplishes its evil purposes is morally irrelevant. And a course of action that would be condemned if it had a bad outcome cannot be vindicated if by luck it turns out well. There cannot be moral risk. This view seems to be wrong, but it arises in response to a fundamental problem about moral responsibility to which we possess no satisfactory solution.

The problem develops out of the ordinary conditions of moral judgment. Prior to reflection it is intuitively plausible that people cannot be morally assessed for what is not their fault, or for what is due to factors beyond their control. Such judgment is different from the evaluation of something as a good or bad thing, or state of affairs. The latter may be present in addition to moral judgment, but when we blame someone for his actions we are not merely saying it is bad that they happened, or bad that he exists: we are judging *him,* saying he is bad, which is different from his being a bad thing. This kind of judgment takes only a certain kind of object. Without being able to explain exactly why, we feel that the appropriateness of moral assessment is easily undermined by the discovery that the act or attribute, no matter how good or bad, is not under the person's control. While other evaluations remain, this one seems to lose its footing. So a clear absence of control, produced by involuntary movement, physical force, or ignorance of the circumstances, excuses what is done from moral judgment. But what we do depends in many more ways than these on what is not under our control—what is not produced by a good or a bad will, in Kant's phrase. And external influences in this broader range are not usually thought to excuse what is done from moral judgment, positive or negative.

Let me give a few examples, beginning with the type of case Kant has in mind. Whether we succeed or fail in what we try to do nearly always depends to some extent on factors beyond our control. This is true of murder, altruism, revolution, the sacrifice of certain interests for the sake of others—almost any morally important act. What has been done, and what is morally judged, is partly determined by external factors. However jewel-like the good will may be in its own right, there is a morally significant difference between rescuing someone from a burning building and dropping him from a twelfth-story window while trying to rescue him. Similarly, there is a morally significant difference between reckless driving and manslaughter. But whether a reckless

---

[1] *Foundations of the Metaphysics of Morals,* first section, third paragraph.

driver hits a pedestrian depends on the presence of the pedestrian at the point where he recklessly passes a red light. What we do is also limited by the opportunities and choices with which we are faced, and these are largely determined by factors beyond our control. Someone who was an officer in a concentration camp might have led a quiet and harmless life if the Nazis had never come to power in Germany. And someone who led a quiet and harmless life in Argentina might have become an officer in a concentration camp if he had not left Germany for business reasons in 1930.

I shall say more later about these and other examples. I introduce them here to illustrate a general point. Where a significant aspect of what someone does depends on factors beyond his control, yet we continue to treat him in that respect as an object of moral judgment, it can be called moral luck. Such luck can be good or bad. And the problem posed by this phenomenon, which led Kant to deny its possibility, is that the broad range of external influences here identified seems on close examination to undermine moral assessment as surely as does the narrower range of familiar excusing conditions. If the condition of control is consistently applied, it threatens to erode most of the moral assessments we find it natural to make. The things for which people are morally judged are determined in more ways than we at first realize by what is beyond their control. And when the seemingly natural requirement of fault or responsibility is applied in light of these facts, it leaves few pre-reflective moral judgments intact. Ultimately, nothing or almost nothing about what a person does seems to be under his control.

Why not conclude, then, that the condition of control is false—that it is an initially plausible hypothesis refuted by clear counter-examples? One could in that case look instead for a more refined condition which picked out the *kinds* of lack of control that really undermine certain moral judgments, without yielding the unacceptable conclusion derived from the broader condition, that most or all ordinary moral judgments are illegitimate.

What rules out this escape is that we are dealing not with a theoretical conjecture but with a philosophical problem. The condition of control does not suggest itself merely as a generalization from certain clear cases. It seems *correct* in the further cases to which it is extended beyond the original set. When we undermine moral assessment by considering new ways in which control is absent, we are not just discovering what *would* follow given the general hypothesis, but are actually being persuaded that in itself the absence of control is relevant in these cases too. The erosion of moral judgment emerges not as the absurd consequence of an over-simple theory, but as a natural consequence of the ordinary idea of moral assessment, when it is applied in view of a more complete and precise account of the facts. It would therefore be a mistake to argue from the unacceptability of the conclusions to the need for a different account of the conditions of moral responsibility. The view that moral luck is paradoxical is not a *mistake,* ethical or logical, but a perception of one of the ways in which the intuitively acceptable conditions of moral judgment threaten to undermine it all.

It resembles the situation in another area of philosophy, the theory of knowledge. There too conditions which seem perfectly natural, and which grow out of the ordinary procedures for challenging and defending claims to knowledge, threaten to undermine all such claims if consistently applied. Most skeptical arguments have this quality: they do not depend on the imposition of arbitrarily stringent standards of knowledge, arrived at by misunderstanding, but appear to grow inevitably from the consistent application of ordinary standards.[2] There is a substantive parallel as well, for epistemological skepticism arises from consideration of the respects in which our beliefs and their relation to reality depend on factors beyond our control. External and internal causes produce our beliefs. We may subject these processes to scrutiny in an effort to avoid error, but our conclusions at this next level also result, in part, from influences which we do not control directly. The same will be true no matter how far we carry the investigation. Our beliefs are always, ultimately, due to factors outside our control, and the impossibility of encompassing those factors without being at the mercy of others leads us to doubt whether we know anything. It looks as though, if any of our beliefs are true, it is pure biological luck rather than knowledge.

Moral luck is like this because while there are various respects in which the natural objects of moral assessment are out of our control or influenced by what is out of our control, we cannot reflect on these facts without losing our grip on the judgments.

There are roughly four ways in which the natural objects of moral assessment are disturbingly subject to luck. One is the phenomenon of constitutive luck—the kind of person you are, where this is not just a question of what you deliberately do, but of your inclinations, capacities, and temperament. Another category is luck in one's circumstances—the kind of problems and situations one faces. The other two have to do with the causes and effects of action: luck in how one is determined by antecedent circumstances, and luck in the way one's actions and projects turn out. All of them present a common problem. They are all opposed by the idea that one cannot be more culpable or estimable for anything than one is for that fraction of it which is under one's control. It seems irrational to take or dispense credit or blame for matters over which a person has no control, or for their influence on results over which he has partial control. Such things may create the conditions for action, but action can be judged only to the extent that it goes beyond these conditions and does not just result from them.

Let us first consider luck, good and bad, in the way things turn out. Kant, in the above-quoted passage, has one example of this in mind, but the category covers a wide range. It includes the truck driver who accidentally runs over a child, the artist who abandons his wife and five children to devote himself to

---

[2] See Thompson Clark, 'The Legacy of Skepticism', *Journal of Philosophy*, LXIX, no. 20 (November 9, 1972), 754–69.

painting,[3] and other cases in which the possibilities of success and failure are even greater. The driver, if he is entirely without fault, will feel terrible about his role in the event, but will not have to reproach himself. Therefore this example of agent-regret[4] is not yet a case of *moral* bad luck. However, if the driver was guilty of even a minor degree of negligence—failing to have his brakes checked recently, for example—then if that negligence contributes to the death of the child, he will not merely feel terrible. He will blame himself for the death. And what makes this an example of moral luck is that he would have to blame himself only slightly for the negligence itself if no situation arose which required him to brake suddenly and violently to avoid hitting a child. Yet the *negligence* is the same in both cases, and the driver has no control over whether a child will run into his path.

The same is true at higher levels of negligence. If someone has had too much to drink and his car swerves on to the sidewalk, he can count himself morally lucky if there are no pedestrians in its path. If there were, he would be to blame for their deaths, and would probably be prosecuted for manslaughter. But if he hurts no one, although his recklessness is exactly the same, he is guilty of a far less serious legal offense and will certainly reproach himself and be reproached by others much less severely. To take another legal example, the penalty for attempted murder is less than that for successful murder—however similar the intentions and motives of the assailant may be in the two cases. His degree of culpability can depend, it would seem, on whether the victim happened to be wearing a bullet-proof vest, or whether a bird flew into the path of the bullet—matters beyond his control.

Finally, there are cases of decision under uncertainty—common in public and in private life. Anna Karenina goes off with Vronsky, Gauguin leaves his family, Chamberlain signs the Munich agreement, the Decembrists persuade the troops under their command to revolt against the czar, the American colonies declare their independence from Britain, you introduce two people in an attempt at match-making. It is tempting in all such cases to feel that some decision must be possible, in the light of what is known at the time, which will make reproach unsuitable no matter how things turn out. But this is not true; when someone acts in such ways he takes his life, or his moral position, into his hands, because how things turn out determines what he has done. It is possible *also* to assess the decision from the point of view of what could be

---

[3] Such a case, modelled on the life of Gauguin, is discussed by Bernard Williams in 'Moral Luck,' *Proceedings of the Aristotelian Society,* supplementary vol. L (1976), 115–35 (to which the original version of this essay was a reply). He points out that though success or failure cannot be predicted in advance, Gauguin's most basic retrospective feelings about the decision will be determined by the development of his talent. My disagreement with Williams is that his account fails to explain why such retrospective attitudes can be called moral. If success does not permit Gauguin to justify himself to others, but still determines his most basic feelings, that shows only that his most basic feelings need not be moral. It does not show that morality is subject to luck. If the restrospective judgment were moral, it would imply the truth of a hypothetical judgment made in advance, of the form 'If I leave my family and become a great painter, I will be justified by success; if I don't become a great painter, the act will be unforgivable.'

[4] Williams' term (*ibid.*).

known at the time, but this is not the end of the story. If the Decembrists had succeeded in overthrowing Nicholas I in 1825 and establishing a constitutional regime, they would be heroes. As it is, not only did they fail and pay for it, but they bore some responsibility for the terrible punishments meted out to the troops who had been persuaded to follow them. If the American Revolution had been a bloody failure resulting in greater repression, then Jefferson, Franklin and Washington would still have made a noble attempt, and might not even have regretted it on their way to the scaffold, but they would also have had to blame themselves for what they had helped to bring on their compatriots. (Perhaps peaceful efforts at reform would eventually have succeeded.) If Hitler had not overrun Europe and exterminated millions, but instead had died of a heart attack after occupying the Sudetenland, Chamberlain's action at Munich would still have utterly betrayed the Czechs, but it would not be the great moral disaster that has made his name a household word.[5]

In many cases of difficult choice the outcome cannot be foreseen with certainty. One kind of assessment of the choice is possible in advance, but another kind must await the outcome, because the outcome determines what has been done. The same degree of culpability or estimability in intention, motive, or concern is compatible with a wide range of judgments, positive or negative, depending on what happened beyond the point of decision. The *mens rea* which could have existed in the absence of any consequences does not exhaust the grounds of moral judgment. Actual results influence culpability or esteem in a large class of unquestionably ethical cases ranging from negligence through political choice.

That these are genuine moral judgments rather than expressions of temporary attitude is evident from the fact that one can say *in advance* how the moral verdict will depend on the results. If one negligently leaves the bath running with the baby in it, one will realize, as one bounds up the stairs toward the bathroom, that if the baby has drowned one has done something awful, whereas if it has not one has merely been careless. Someone who launches a violent revolution against an authoritarian regime knows that if he fails he will be responsible for much suffering that is in vain, but if he succeeds he will be justified by the outcome. I do not mean that *any* action can be retroactively justified by history. Certain things are so bad in themselves, or so risky, that no results can make them all right. Nevertheless, when moral judgment does depend on the outcome, it is objective and timeless and not dependent on a change of standpoint produced by success or failure. The judgment after the fact follows from an hypothetical judgment that can be made beforehand, and it can be made as easily by someone else as by the agent.

From the point of view which makes responsibility dependent on control, all this seems absurd. How is it possible to be more or less culpable depending

---

[5] For a fascinating but morally repellent discussion of the topic of justification by history, see Maurice Merleau-Ponty, *Humanisme et Terreur* (Paris: Gallimard, 1947), translated as *Humanism and Terror* (Boston: Beacon Press, 1969).

on whether a child gets into the path of one's car, or a bird into the path of one's bullet? Perhaps it is true that what is done depends on more than the agent's state of mind or intention. The problem then is, why is it not irrational to base moral assessment on what people do, in this broad sense? It amounts to holding them responsible for the contributions of fate as well as for their own—provided they have made some contribution to begin with. If we look at cases of negligence or attempt, the pattern seems to be that overall culpability corresponds to the product of mental or intentional fault and the seriousness of the outcome. Cases of decision under uncertainty are less easily explained in this way, for it seems that the overall judgment can even shift from positive to negative depending on the outcome. But here too it seems rational to subtract the effects of occurrences subsequent to the choice, that were merely possible at the time, and concentrate moral assessment on the actual decision in light of the probabilities. If the object of moral judgment is the *person,* then to hold him accountable for what he has done in the broader sense is akin to strict liability, which may have its legal uses but seems irrational as a moral position.

The result of such a line of thought is to pare down each act to its morally essential core, an inner act of pure will assessed by motive and intention. Adam Smith advocates such a position in *The Theory of Moral Sentiments,* but notes that it runs contrary to our actual judgments.

> But how well soever we may seem to be persuaded of the truth of this equitable maxim, when we consider it after this manner, in abstract, yet when we come to particular cases, the actual consequences which happen to proceed from any action, have a very great effect upon our sentiments concerning its merit or demerit, and almost always either enhance or diminish our sense of both. Scarce, in any one instance, perhaps, will our sentiments be found, after examination, to be entirely regulated by this rule, which we all acknowledge ought entirely to regulate them.[6]

Joel Feinberg points out further that restricting the domain of moral responsibility to the inner world will not immunize it to luck. Factors beyond the agent's control, like a coughing fit, can interfere with his decisions as surely as they can with the path of a bullet from his gun.[7] Nevertheless the tendency to cut down the scope of moral assessment is pervasive, and does not limit itself to the influence of effects. It attempts to isolate the will from the other direction, so to speak, by separating out constitutive luck. Let us consider that next.

Kant was particularly insistent on the moral irrelevance of qualities of temperament and personality that are not under the control of the will. Such

[6] Pt II, sect. 3, Introduction, para. 5.

[7] 'Problematic Responsibility in Law and Morals', in Joel Feinberg, *Doing and Deserving* (Princeton: Princeton University Press, 1970).

qualities as sympathy or coldness might provide the background against which obedience to moral requirements is more or less difficult, but they could not be objects of moral assessment themselves, and might well interfere with confident assessment of its proper object—the determination of the will by the motive of duty. This rules out moral judgment of many of the virtues and vices, which are states of character that influence choice but are certainly not exhausted by dispositions to act deliberately in certain ways. A person may be greedy, envious, cowardly, cold, ungenerous, unkind, vain, or conceited, but *behave* perfectly by a monumental effort of will. To possess these vices is to be unable to help having certain feelings under certain circumstances, and to have strong spontaneous impulses to act badly. Even if one controls the impulses, one still has the vice. An envious person hates the greater success of others. He can be morally condemned as envious even if he congratulates them cordially and does nothing to denigrate or spoil their success. Conceit, likewise, need not be displayed. It is fully present in someone who cannot help dwelling with secret satisfaction on the superiority of his own achievements, talents, beauty, intelligence, or virtue. To some extent such a quality may be the product of earlier choices; to some extent it may be amenable to change by current actions. But it is largely a matter of constitutive bad fortune. Yet people are morally condemned for such qualities, and esteemed for others equally beyond control of the will: they are assessed for what they are *like*.

To Kant this seems incoherent because virtue is enjoined on everyone and therefore must in principle be possible for everyone. It may be easier for some than for others, but it must be possible to achieve it by making the right choices, against whatever temperamental background.[8] One may want to have a generous spirit, or regret not having one, but it makes no sense to condemn oneself or anyone else for a quality which is not within the control of the will. Condemnation implies that you should not be like that, not that it is unfortunate that you are.

Nevertheless, Kant's conclusion remains intuitively unacceptable. We may be persuaded that these moral judgments are irrational, but they reappear involuntarily as soon as the argument is over. This is the pattern throughout the subject.

The third category to consider is luck in one's circumstances, and I shall mention it briefly. The things we are called upon to do, the moral tests we face, are importantly determined by factors beyond our control. It may be true of someone that in a dangerous situation he would behave in a cowardly or

[8] 'if nature has put little sympathy in the heart of a man, and if he, though an honest man, is by temperament cold and indifferent to the sufferings of others, perhaps because he is provided with special gifts of patience and fortitude and expects or even requires that others should have the same—and such a man would certainly not be the meanest product of nature—would not he find in himself a source from which to give himself a far higher worth than he could have got by having a good-natured temperament?' (*Foundations of the Metaphysics of Morals*, first section, eleventh paragraph).

heroic fashion, but if the situation never arises, he will never have the chance to distinguish or disgrace himself in this way, and his moral record will be different.[9]

A conspicuous example of this is political. Ordinary citizens of Nazi Germany had an opportunity to behave heroically by opposing the regime. They also had an opportunity to behave badly, and most of them are culpable for having failed this test. But it is a test to which the citizens of other countries were not subjected, with the result that even if they, or some of them, would have behaved as badly as the Germans in like circumstances, they simply did not and therefore are not similarly culpable. Here again one is morally at the mercy of fate, and it may seem irrational upon reflection, but our ordinary moral attitudes would be unrecognizable without it. We judge people for what they actually do or fail to do, not just for what they would have done if circumstances had been different.[10]

This form of moral determination by the actual is also paradoxical, but we can begin to see how deep in the concept of responsibility the paradox is embedded. A person can be morally responsible only for what he does; but what he does results from a great deal that he does not do; therefore he is not morally responsible for what he is and is not responsible for. (This is not a contradiction, but it is a paradox.)

It should be obvious that there is a connection between these problems about responsibility and control and an even more familiar problem, that of freedom of the will. That is the last type of moral luck I want to take up, though I can do no more within the scope of this essay than indicate its connection with the other types.

If one cannot be responsible for consequences of one's acts due to factors beyond one's control, or for antecedents of one's acts that are properties of temperament not subject to one's will, or for the circumstances that pose one's moral choices, then how can one be responsible even for the stripped-down

---

[9] Cf. Thomas Gray, 'Elegy Written in a Country Churchyard':
    Some mute inglorious Milton here may rest,
    Some Cromwell, guiltless of his country's blood.
An unusual example of circumstantial moral luck is provided by the kind of moral dilemma with which someone can be faced through no fault of his own, but which leaves him with nothing to do which is not wrong. See chapter 5; and Bernard Williams, 'Ethical Consistency', *Proceedings of the Aristotelian Society*, supplementary vol. XXXIX (1965), reprinted in *Problems of the Self* (Cambridge: Cambridge University Press, 1973), pp. 166–86.

[10] Circumstantial luck can extend to aspects of the situation other than individual behavior. For example, during the Vietnam War even U.S. citizens who had opposed their country's actions vigorously from the start often felt compromised by its crimes. Here they were not even responsible; there was probably nothing they could do to stop what was happening, so the feeling of being implicated may seem unintelligible. But it is nearly impossible to view the crimes of one's own country in the same way that one views the crimes of another country, no matter how equal one's lack of power to stop them in the two cases. One *is* a citizen of one of them, and has a connection with its actions (even if only through taxes that cannot be withheld)—that one does not have with the other's. This makes it possible to be ashamed of one's country, and to feel a victim of moral bad luck that one was an American in the 1960s.

acts of the will itself, if *they* are the product of antecedent circumstances outside of the will's control?

The area of genuine agency, and therefore of legitimate moral judgment, seems to shrink under this scrutiny to an extensionless point. Everything seems to result from the combined influence of factors, antecedent and posterior to action, that are not within the agent's control. Since he cannot be responsible for them, he cannot be responsible for their results—though it may remain possible to take up the aesthetic or other evaluative analogues of the moral attitudes that are thus displaced.

It is also possible, of course, to brazen it out and refuse to accept the results, which indeed seem unacceptable as soon as we stop thinking about the arguments. Admittedly, if certain surrounding circumstances had been different, then no unfortunate consequences would have followed from a wicked intention, and no seriously culpable act would have been performed; but since the circumstances were *not* different, and the agent *in fact* succeeded in perpetrating a particularly cruel murder, *that* is what he did, and that is what he is responsible for. Similarly, we may admit that if certain antecedent circumstances had been different, the agent would never have developed into the sort of person who would do such a thing; but since he *did* develop (as the inevitable result of those antecedent circumstances) into the sort of swine he is, and into the person who committed such a murder, *that* is what he is blameable for. In both cases one is responsible for what one actually does—even if what one actually does depends in important ways on what is not within one's control. This compatibilist account of our moral judgments would leave room for the ordinary conditions of responsibility—the absence of coercion, ignorance, or involuntary movement—as part of the determination of what someone has done—but it is understood not to exclude the influence of a great deal that he has not done.[11]

The only thing wrong with this solution is its failure to explain how skeptical problems arise. For they arise not from the imposition of an arbitrary external requirement, but from the nature of moral judgment itself. Something in the ordinary idea of what someone does must explain how it can seem necessary to subtract from it anything that merely happens—even though the ultimate consequence of such subtraction is that nothing remains. And something in the ordinary idea of knowledge must explain why it seems to be undermined by any influences on belief not within the control of the subject—so that knowledge seems impossible without an impossible foundation in autonomous reason. But let us leave epistemology aside and concentrate on action, character, and moral assessment.

---

[11] The corresponding position in epistemology would be that knowledge consists of true beliefs formed in certain ways, and that it does not require all aspects of the process to be under the knower's control, actually or potentially. Both the correctness of these beliefs and the process by which they are arrived at would therefore be importantly subject to luck. The Nobel Prize is not awarded to people who turn out to be wrong, no matter how brilliant their reasoning.

The problem arises, I believe, because the self which acts and is the object of moral judgment is threatened with dissolution by the absorption of its acts and impulses into the class of events. Moral judgment of a person is judgment not of what happens to him, but of him. It does not say merely that a certain event or state of affairs is fortunate or unfortunate or even terrible. It is not an evaluation of a state of the world, or of an individual as part of the world. We are not thinking just that it would be better if he were different, or did not exist, or had not done some of the things he has done. We are judging *him*, rather than his existence or characteristics. The effect of concentrating on the influence of what is not under his control is to make this responsible self seem to disappear, swallowed up by the order of mere events.

What, however, do we have in mind that a person must *be* to be the object of these moral attitudes? While the concept of agency is easily undermined, it is very difficult to give it a positive characterization. That is familiar from the literature on Free Will.

I believe that in a sense the problem has no solution, because something in the idea of agency is incompatible with actions being events, or people being things. But as the external determinants of what someone has done are gradually exposed, in their effect on consequences, character, and choice itself, it becomes gradually clear that actions are events and people things. Eventually nothing remains which can be ascribed to the responsible self, and we are left with nothing but a portion of the larger sequence of events, which can be deplored or celebrated, but not blamed or praised.

Though I cannot define the idea of the active self that is thus undermined, it is possible to say something about its sources. There is a close connection between our feelings about ourselves and our feelings about others. Guilt and indignation, shame and contempt, pride and admiration are internal and external sides of the same moral attitudes. We are unable to view ourselves simply as portions of the world, and from inside we have a rough idea of the boundary between what is us and what is not, what we do and what happens to us, what is our personality and what is an accidental handicap. We apply the same essentially internal conception of the self to others. About ourselves we feel pride, shame, guilt, remorse—and agent-regret. We do not regard our actions and our characters merely as fortunate or unfortunate episodes—though they may also be that. We cannot *simply* take an external evaluative view of ourselves—of what we most essentially are and what we do. And this remains true even when we have seen that we are not responsible for our own existence, or our nature, or the choices we have to make, or the circumstances that give our acts the consequences they have. Those acts remain ours and we remain ourselves, despite the persuasiveness of the reasons that seem to argue us out of existence.

It is this internal view that we extend to others in moral judgment—when we judge *them* rather than their desirability or utility. We extend to others the refusal to limit ourselves to external evaluation, and we accord to them selves like our own. But in both cases this comes up against the brutal inclusion of humans and everything about them in a world from which they cannot be separated and of which they are nothing but contents. The external view forces itself on us at the same time that we resist it. One way this occurs is through the gradual erosion of what we do by the subtraction of what happens.[12]

The inclusion of consequences in the conception of what we have done is an acknowledgment that we are parts of the world, but the paradoxical character of moral luck which emerges from this acknowledgment shows that we are unable to operate with such a view, for it leaves us with no one to be. The same thing is revealed in the appearance that determinism obliterates responsibility. Once we see an aspect of what we or someone else does as something that happens, we lose our grip on the idea that it has been done and that we can judge the doer and not just the happening. This explains why the absence of determinism is no more hospitable to the concept of agency than is its presence—a point that has been noticed often. Either way the act is viewed externally, as part of the course of events.

The problem of moral luck cannot be understood without an account of the internal conception of agency and its special connection with the moral attitudes as opposed to other types of value. I do not have such an account. The degree to which the problem has a solution can be determined only by seeing whether in some degree the incompatibility between this conception and the various ways in which we do not control what we do is only apparent. I have nothing to offer on that topic either. But it is not enough to say merely that our basic moral attitudes toward ourselves and others are determined by what is actual; for they are also threatened by the sources of that actuality, and by the external view of action which forces itself on us when we see how everything we do belongs to a world that we have not created.

---

[12] See P. F. Strawson's discussion of the conflict between the objective attitude and personal reactive attitudes in 'Freedom and Resentment', *Proceedings of the British Academy*, 1962, reprinted in *Studies in the Philosophy of Thought and Action*, ed. P. F. Strawson (London: Oxford University Press, 1968), and in P. F. Strawson, *Freedom and Resentment and Other Essays* (London: Methuen, 1974).

31

What Makes Right Acts Right?

W. D. ROSS

For biographical information about W. D. Ross, see reading 10.

Ross's view about what makes acts right incorporates elements of both utilitarianism and Kantianism. He rejects the utilitarian assumptions that happiness is the only good thing, and that our only duty is to maximize what is good. However, he agrees that our duties include the promotion of happiness (and other goods) as well as keeping promises, promoting justice, and developing our talents. Because an act that satisfies one of these duties will often not satisfy another, Ross calls all such duties prima facie. We have a prima facie duty to perform an act when the act "would be a duty proper if it were not at the same time of another kind which is morally significant." By contrast, our duty proper in a particular situation is what we should do, all things considered.

How do we know our prima facie and all-things-considered duties? According to Ross, we know that the keeping of promises, gratitude, and the production of happiness are among our prima facie duties through a kind of direct apprehension. It is simply self-evident that these features always count in favor of acts. But what we should do in any particular situation is not self-evident. To ascertain this, we must carefully weigh all the relevant factors. For example, if telling someone the truth would pain him, we must balance our prima facie duty of fidelity against our prima facie duty not to do harm. This requires the conscientious exercise of judgment. For further consideration of these issues, see Ross's discussion in reading 10.

As many critics have noted, Ross's account gives little guidance about how to exercise judgment in particular cases. Yet even if we are dissatisfied with this, we may remain attracted to his views about which considerations are relevant. In claiming that there is a variety of irreducibly different moral duties, Ross captures the considered belief of many thoughtful people.

THE REAL POINT at issue between hedonism and utilitarianism on the one hand and their opponents on the other is not whether 'right' means 'productive of so and so'; for it cannot with any plausibility be maintained that it does. The point at issue is that to which we now pass, viz. whether there is any general character which makes right acts right, and if so, what it is. Among the main historical attempts to state a single characteristic of all right actions which is the foundation of their rightness are those made by egoism and utilitarianism. But I do not propose to discuss these, not because the subject is unimportant, but because it has been dealt with so often and so well already, and because there has come to be so much agreement among moral philosophers that neither of these theories is satisfactory. A much more attractive theory has been put forward by Professor Moore: that what makes actions right is that they are productive of more *good* than could have been produced by any other action open to the agent.

This theory is in fact the culmination of all the attempts to base rightness on productivity of some sort of result. The first form this attempt takes is the attempt to base rightness on conduciveness to the advantage or pleasure of the agent. This theory comes to grief over the fact, which stares us in the face, that a great part of duty consists in an observance of the rights and a furtherance of the interests of others, whatever the cost to ourselves may be. Plato and others may be right in holding that a regard for the rights of others never in the long run involves a loss of happiness for the agent, that 'the just life profits a man'. But this, even if true, is irrelevant to the rightness of the act. As soon as a man does an action *because* he thinks he will promote his own interests thereby, he is acting not from a sense of its rightness but from self-interest.

To the egoistic theory hedonistic utilitarianism supplies a much-needed amendment. It points out correctly that the fact that a certain pleasure will be enjoyed by the agent is no reason why he *ought* to bring it into being rather than an equal or greater pleasure to be enjoyed by another, though, human nature being what it is, it makes it not unlikely that he *will* try to bring it into being. But hedonistic utilitarianism in its turn needs a correction. On reflection it seems clear that pleasure is not the only thing in life that we think good in itself, that for instance we think the possession of a good character, or an intelligent understanding of the world, as good or better. A great advance is made by the substitution of 'productive of the greatest good' for 'productive of the greatest pleasure'.

Not only is this theory more attractive than hedonistic utilitarianism, but its logical relation to that theory is such that the latter could not be true unless *it* were true, while it might be true though hedonistic utilitarianism were not. It is in fact one of the logical bases of hedonistic utilitarianism. For the view that what produces the maximum pleasure is right has for its bases the views (1) that what produces the maximum good is right, and (2) that pleasure is the only thing good in itself. If they were not assuming that what produces the maximum *good* is right, the utilitarians' attempt to show that pleasure is the only thing good in itself, which is in fact the point they take most pains to establish, would have been quite irrelevant to their attempt to prove that only what produces the maximum *pleasure* is right. If, therefore, it can be shown that productivity of the maximum good is not what makes all right actions right, we shall *a fortiori* have refuted hedonistic utilitarianism.

When a plain man fulfills a promise because he thinks he ought to do so, it seems clear that he does so with no thought of its total consequences, still less with any opinion that these are likely to be the best possible. He thinks in fact much more of the past than of the future. What makes him think it right to act in a certain way is the fact that he has promised to do so—that and, usually, nothing more. That his act will produce the best possible consequences is not his reason for calling it right. What lends colour to the theory we are examining, then, is not the actions (which form probably a great majority of our actions) in which some such reflection as 'I have promised' is the only reason we give ourselves for thinking a certain action right, but the exceptional cases in which the consequences of fulfilling a promise (for instance) would be so disastrous to others that we judge it right not to do so. It must of course be admitted that such cases exist. If I have promised to meet a friend at a particular time for some trivial purpose, I should certainly think myself justified in breaking my engagement if by doing so I could prevent a serious accident or bring relief to the victims of one. And the supporters of the view we are examining hold that my thinking so is due to my thinking that I shall bring more good into existence by the one action than by the other. A different account may, however, be given of the matter, an account which will, I believe, show itself to be the true one. It may be said that besides the duty of fulfilling promises I have and recognize a duty of relieving distress, and that when I think it right to do the latter at the cost of not doing the former, it is not because I think I shall produce more good thereby but because I think it the duty which is in the circumstances more of a duty. This account surely corresponds much more closely with what we really think in such a situation. If, so far as I can see, I could bring equal amounts of good into being by fulfilling my promise and by helping some one to whom I had made no promise, I should not hesitate to regard the former as my duty. Yet on the view that what is right is right because it is productive of the most good I should not so regard it.

There are two theories, each in its way simple, that offer a solution of such cases of conscience. One is the view of Kant, that there are certain duties of perfect obligation, such as those of fulfilling promises, of paying debts, of telling the truth, which admit of no exception whatever in favour of duties of imperfect obligation, such as that of relieving distress. The other is the view of, for instance, Professor Moore and Dr. Rashdall, that there is only the duty of producing good, and that all 'conflicts of duties' should be resolved by asking 'by which action will most good be produced?' But it is more important that our theory fit the facts than that it be simple, and the account we have given above corresponds (it seems to me) better than either of the simpler theories with what we really think, viz. that normally promise-keeping, for example, should come before benevolence, but that when and only when the good to be produced by the benevolent act is very great and the promise comparatively trivial, the act of benevolence becomes our duty.

In fact the theory of 'ideal utilitarianism', if I may for brevity refer so to the theory of Professor Moore, seems to simplify unduly our relations to our fellows. It says, in effect, that the only morally significant relation in which my neighbours stand to me is that of being possible beneficiaries by my action. They do stand in this relation to me, and this relation is morally significant. But they may also stand to me in the relation of promisee to promiser, of creditor to debtor, of wife to husband, of child to parent, of friend to friend, of fellow countryman to fellow countryman, and the like; and each of these relations is the foundation of a *prima facie* duty, which is more or less incumbent on me according to the circumstances of the case. When I am in a situation, as perhaps I always am, in which more than one of these *prima facie* duties is incumbent on me, what I have to do is to study the situation as fully as I can until I form the considered opinion (it is never more) that in the circumstances one of them is more incumbent than any other; then I am bound to think that to do this *prima facie* duty is my duty *sans phrase* in the situation.

I suggest '*prima facie* duty' or 'conditional duty' as a brief way of referring to the characteristic (quite distinct from that of being a duty proper) which an act has, in virtue of being of a certain kind (e.g. the keeping of a promise), of being an act which would be a duty proper if it were not at the same time of another kind which is morally significant. Whether an act is a duty proper or actual duty depends on *all* the morally significant kinds it is an instance of. The phrase '*prima facie* duty' must be apologized for, since (1) it suggests that what we are speaking of is a certain kind of duty, whereas it is in fact not a duty, but something related in a special way to duty. Strictly speaking, we want not a phrase in which duty is qualified by an adjective, but a separate noun. (2) '*Prima*' facie suggests that one is speaking only of an appearance which a moral situation presents at first sight, and which may turn out to be illusory; whereas what I am speaking of is an objective fact involved in the nature of the situation, or more strictly in an element of its nature, though not, as duty proper does, arising from its *whole* nature. . . .

There is nothing arbitrary about these *prima facie* duties. Each rests on a definite circumstance which cannot seriously be held to be without moral significance. Of *prima facie* duties I suggest, without claiming completeness or finality for it, the following division.

(1) Some duties rest on previous acts of my own. These duties seem to include two kinds, (*a*) those resting on a promise or what may fairly be called an implicit promise, such as the implicit undertaking not to tell lies which seems to be implied in the act of entering into conversation (at any rate by civilized men), or of writing books that purport to be history and not fiction. These may be called the duties of fidelity. (*b*) Those resting on a previous wrongful act. These may be called the duties of reparation. (2) Some rest on previous acts of other men, i.e. services done by them to me. These may be loosely described as the duties of gratitude. (3) Some rest on the fact or possibility of a distribution of pleasure or happiness (or of the means thereto) which is not in accordance with the merit of the persons concerned; in such cases there arises a duty to upset or prevent such a distribution. These are the duties of justice. (4) Some rest on the mere fact that there are other beings in the world whose condition we can make better in respect of virtue, or of intelligence, or of pleasure. These are the duties of benificence. (5) Some rest on the fact that we can improve our own condition in respect of virtue or of intelligence. These are the duties of self-improvement. (6) I think that we should distinguish from (4) the duties that may be summed up under the title of 'not injuring others'. No doubt to injure others is incidentally to fail to do them good; but it seems to me clear that nonmaleficence is apprehended as a duty distinct from that of

benificence, and as a duty of a more stringent character. . . . We should not in general consider it justifiable to kill one person in order to keep another alive, or to steal from one in order to give alms to another.

The essential defect of the 'ideal utilitarian' theory is that it ignores, or at least does not do full justice to, the highly personal character of duty. If the only duty is to produce the maximum of good, the question who is to have the good—whether it is myself, or my benefactor, or a person to whom I have made a promise to confer that good on him, or a mere fellow man to whom I stand in no such special relation—should make no difference to my having a duty to produce that good. But we are all in fact sure that it makes a vast difference.

. . .

If the objection be made, that this catalogue of the main types of duty is an unsystematic one resting on no logical principle, it may be replied, first, that it makes no claim to being ultimate. It is a *prima facie* classification of the duties which reflection on our moral convictions seems actually to reveal. And if these convictions are, as I would claim that they are, of the nature of knowledge, and if I have not misstated them, the list will be a list of authentic conditional duties, correct as far as it goes though not necessarily complete. The list of *goods* put forward by the rival theory is reached by exactly the same method—the only sound one in the circumstances—viz. that of direct reflection on what we really think. Loyalty to the facts is worth more than a symmetrical architectonic or a hastily reached simplicity. If further reflection discovers a perfect logical basis for this or for a better classification, so much the better.

It may, again, be objected that our theory that there are these various and often conflicting types of *prima facie* duty leaves us with no principle upon which to discern what is our actual duty in particular circumstances. But this objection is not one which the rival theory is in a position to bring forward. For when we have to choose between the production of two heterogeneous goods, say knowledge and pleasure, the 'ideal utilitarian' theory can only fall back on an opinion, for which no logical basis can be offered, that one of the goods is the greater; and this is no better than a similar opinion that one of two duties is the more urgent. And again, when we consider the infinite variety of the effects of our actions in the way of pleasure, it must surely be admitted that the claim which *hedonism* sometimes makes, that it offers a readily applicable criterion of right conduct, is quite illusory.

I am unwilling, however, to content myself with an *argumentum ad hominem,* and I would contend that in principle there is no reason to anticipate that every act that is our duty is so for one and the same reason. Why should two sets of circumstances, or one set of circumstances, *not* possess different characteristics, any one of which makes a certain act our *prima facie* duty? When I ask what it is that makes me in certain cases sure that I have a *prima facie* duty to do so and so, I find that it lies in the fact that I have made a promise; when I ask the same question in another case, I find the answer lies in the fact that I have done a wrong. And if on reflection I find (as I think I do) that neither of these reasons is reducible to the other, I must not on any *a priori* ground assume that such a reduction is possible.

. . .

The duty of justice is particularly complicated, and the word is used to cover things which are really very different—things such as the payment of debts, the reparation of injuries done by oneself to another, and the bringing about of a distribution of happiness between other people in proportion to merit. I use the word to denote only the last of these three. In the fifth chapter I shall try to show that besides the three (comparatively) simple goods, virtue, knowledge, and pleasure, there is a more complex good, not reducible to these, consisting in the proportionment of happiness to virtue. The bringing of this about is a duty which we owe to all men alike, though it may be reinforced by special responsibilities that we have undertaken to particular men. This, therefore, with benificence and self-improvement, comes under the general principle that we should produce as much good as possible, though the good here involved is different in kind from any other.

But besides this general obligation, there are special obligations. These may arise, in the first place, incidentally, from acts which were not essentially meant to create such an obligation, but which nevertheless create it. From the nature of the case such acts may be of two kinds—the infliction of injuries on others, and the acceptance of benefits from them. It seems clear that these put us under a special obligation to other men, and that only these acts can do so incidentally. From these arise the twin duties of reparation and gratitude.

And finally there are special obligations arising from acts the very intention of which, when they were done, was to put us under such an obligation. The name for such acts is 'promises'; the name is wide enough if we are willing to include under it implicit promises, i.e. modes of behaviour in which without explicit verbal promise we intentionally create an expectation that we can be counted on to behave in a certain way in the interest of another person.

These seem to be, in principle, all the ways in which *prime facie* duties arise. In actual experience they are compounded together in highly complex ways. Thus, for example, the duty of obeying the laws of one's country arises partly (as Socrates contends in the *Crito*) from the duty of gratitude for the benefits one has received from it; partly from the implicit promise to obey which seems to be involved in permanent residence in a country whose laws we know we are *expected* to obey, and still more clearly involved when we ourselves invoke the protection of its laws (this is the truth underlying the doctrine of the social contract); and partly (if we are fortunate in our country) from the fact that its laws are potent instruments for the general good.

Or again, the sense of a general obligation to bring about (so far as we can) a just apportionment of happiness to merit is often greatly reinforced by the fact that many of the existing injustices are due to a social and economic system which we have, not indeed created, but taken part in and assented to; the duty of justice is then reinforced by the duty of reparation.

It is necessary to say something by way of clearing up the relation between *prima facie* duties and the actual or absolute duty to do one particular act in particular circumstances. If, as almost all moralists except Kant are agreed, and as most plain men think, it is sometimes right to tell a lie or to break a promise, it must be maintained that there is a difference between *prima facie* duty and actual or absolute duty. When we think ourselves justified in breaking, and indeed morally obliged to break, a promise in order to relieve some one's distress, we do not for a moment cease to recognize a *prima facie* duty to keep our promise, and this leads us to feel, not indeed shame or repentance, but certainly compunction, for behaving as we do; we recognize, further, that it is our duty to make up somehow to the promisee for the breaking of the promise. We have to distinguish from the characteristic of being our duty that of tending to our duty. Any act that we do contains various elements in virtue of which it falls under various categories. In virtue of being the breaking of a promise, for instance, it tends to be wrong; in virtue of being an instance of relieving distress it tends to be right. . . .

Another instance of the same distinction may be found in the operation of natural laws. *Qua* subject to the force of gravitation towards some other body, each body tends to move in a particular direction with a particular velocity; but its actual movement depends on *all* the forces to which it is subject. It is only by recognizing this distinction that we can preserve the absoluteness of laws of nature, and only by recognizing a corresponding distinction that we can preserve the absoluteness of the general principles of morality. But an important difference between the two cases must be pointed out. When we say that in virtue of gravitation a body tends to move in a certain way, we are referring to a causal influence actually exercised on it by another body or other bodies. When we say that in virtue of being deliberately untrue a certain remark tends to be wrong, we are referring to no causal relation, to no relation that involves succession in time, but to such a relation as connects the various attributes of a mathematical figure. And if the word 'tendency' is thought to suggest too much a causal relation, it is better to talk of certain types of act as being *prima facie* right or wrong (or of different persons as having different and possibly conflicting claims upon us), than of their tending to be right or wrong.

Something should be said of the relation between our apprehension of the *prima facie* rightness of certain types of act and our mental attitude towards particular acts. It is proper to use the word 'apprehension' in the former case and not in the latter. That an act, *qua* fulfilling a promise, or *qua* effecting a just distribution of good, or *qua* returning services rendered, or *qua* promoting the good of others, or *qua* promoting the virtue or insight of the agent, is *prima facie* right, is self-evident; not in the sense that it is evident from the beginning of our lives, or as soon as we attend to the proposition for the first time, but in the sense that when we have reached sufficient mental maturity and have given sufficient attention to the proposition it is evident without any need of proof, or of evidence beyond itself. It is self-evident just as a mathematical axiom, or the validity of a form of inference, is evident. The moral order expressed in these propositions is just as much part of the fundamental nature of the universe (and, we may add, of any possible universe in which there were moral agents at all) as is the spatial or numerical structure expressed in the axioms of geometry or arithmetic. In our confidence that these propositions are true there is involved the same trust in our reason that is involved in our confidence in mathematics; and we should have no justification for trusting it in the latter sphere and distrusting it in the former. In both cases we are dealing with propositions that cannot be proved, but that just as certainly need no proof.

. . .

Our judgements about our actual duty in concrete situations have none of the certainty that attaches to our recognition of the general principles of duty. A statement is certain, i.e. is an expression of knowledge, only in one or other of two cases: when it is either self-evident, or a valid conclusion from self-evident premises. And our judgements about our particular duties have neither of these characters. (1) They are not self-evident. Where a possible act is seen to have two characteristics, in virtue of one of which it is *prima facie* right, and in virtue of the other *prima facie* wrong, we are (I think) well aware that we are not certain whether we ought or ought not to do it; that whether we do it or not, we are taking a moral risk. We come in the long run, after consideration, to think one duty more pressing than the other, but we do not feel certain that it is so. And though we do not always recognize that a possible act has two such characteristics, and though there *may* be cases in which it has not, we are never certain that any particular possible act has not, and therefore never certain that it is right, nor certain that it is wrong. For, to go no further in the analysis, it is enough to point out that any particular act will in all probability in the course of time contribute to the bringing about of good or of evil for many human beings, and thus have a *prima facie* rightness or wrongness of which we know nothing. (2) Again, our judgements about our particular duties are not logical conclusions from self-evident premises. The only possible premises would be the general principles stating their *prima facie* rightness or wrongness *qua* having the different characteristics they do have; and even if we could (as we cannot) apprehend the extent to which an act will tend on the one hand, for example, to bring out advantages for our benefactors, and on the other hand to bring about disadvantages for fellow men who are not our benefactors, there is no principle by which we can draw the conclusion that it is on the whole right or on the whole wrong. In this respect the judgement as to the rightness of a particular act is just like the judgement as to the beauty of a particular natural object or work of art. A poem is, for instance, in respect of certain qualities beautiful and in respect of certain others not beautiful; and our judgement as to the degree of beauty it possesses on the whole is never reached by logical reasoning from the apprehension of its particular beauties or particular defects. Both in this and in the moral case we have more or less probable opinions which are not logically justified conclusions from the general principles that are recognized as self-evident.

There is therefore much truth in the description of the right act as a fortunate act. If we cannot be certain that it is right, it is our good fortune if the act we do is the right act. This consideration does not, however, make the doing of our duty a mere matter of chance. There is a parallel here between the doing of duty and the doing of what will be to our personal advantage. We never *know* what act will in the long run be to our advantage. Yet it is certain that we are more likely in general to secure our advantage if we estimate to the best of our ability the probable tendencies of our actions in this respect, than if we act on caprice. And similarly we are more likely to do our duty if we reflect to the best of our ability on the *prima facie* rightness or wrongness of various possible acts in virtue of the characteristics we perceive them to have, than if we act without reflection. With this greater likelihood we must be content.

Many people would be inclined to say that the right act for me is not that whose general nature I have been describing, viz. that which if I were omniscient I should see to be my duty, but that which on all the evidence available to me I should think to be my duty. But suppose that from the state of partial knowledge in which I think act A to be my duty, I could pass to a state of perfect knowledge in which I saw act B to be my duty, should I not say 'act B was the right act for me to do'? I should no doubt add 'though I am not to be blamed for doing act A'. . . .

It might seem absurd to suggest that it could be right for any one to do an act which would produce consequences less good than those which would be produced by some other act in his power. Yet a little thought will convince us that this is not absurd. The type of case in which it is easiest to see that this is so is, perhaps, that in which one has made a promise. In such a case we all think that *prima facie* it is our duty to fulfill the promise irrespective of the precise goodness of the total consequences. And though we do not think it is necessarily our actual or absolute duty to do so, we are far from thinking that any, even the slightest, gain in the value of the total consequences will necessarily justify us in doing something else instead. Suppose, to simplify the case by abstraction, that the fulfillment of a promise to A would produce 1,000 units of good for him, but that by doing some other act I would produce 1,001 units of good for B, to whom I have made no promise, the other consequences of the two acts being of equal value; should we really think it self-evident that it was our duty to do the second act and not the first? I think not. We should, I fancy, hold that only a much greater disparity of value between the total consequences would justify us in failing to discharge our *prima facie* duty to A. After all, a promise is a promise, and is not to be treated so lightly as the theory we are examining would imply. What, exactly, a promise is, is not so easy to determine, but we are surely agreed that it constitutes a serious moral limitation to our freedom of action. To produce the 1,001 units of goods for B rather than fulfill our promise to A would be to take, not perhaps our duty as philanthropists too seriously, but certainly our duty as makers of promises too lightly.

. . .

I conclude that the attributes 'right' and 'optimific'* are not identical, and that we do not know either by intuition, by deduction, or by induction that they coincide in their application, still less that the latter is the foundation of the former. It must be added, however, that if we are ever under no special obligation such as that of fidelity to a promisee or of gratitude to a benefactor, we ought to do what will produce most good; and that even when we are under a special obligation the tendency of acts to promote general good is one of the main factors in determining whether they are right.

In what has preceded, a good deal of use has been made of 'what we really think' about moral questions; a certain theory has been rejected because it does not agree with what we really think. It might be said that this is in principle wrong; that we should not be content to expound what our present moral consciousness tells us but should aim at a criticism of our existing moral consciousness in the light of theory. Now I do not doubt that the moral consciousness of men has in detail undergone a good deal of modification as regards the things we think right, at the hands of moral theory. But if we are told, for instance, that we should give up our view that there is a special obligatoriness attaching to the keeping of promises because it is self-evident that the only duty is to produce as much good as possible, we have to ask ourselves whether we really, when we reflect, *are* convinced that this is self-evident, and whether we really *can* get rid of our view that promise-keeping has a bindingness independent of productiveness of maximum good. In my own experience I find that I cannot, in spite of a very genuine attempt to do so; and I venture to think that most people will find the same, and that just because they cannot lose the sense of special obligation, they cannot accept as self-evident, or even as true, the theory which would require them to do so. In fact it seems, on reflection, self-evident that a promise, simply as such, is something that *prima facie* ought to be kept, and it does *not,* on reflection, seem self-evident that production of maximum good is the only thing that makes an act obligatory. And to ask us to give up at the bidding of a theory our actual apprehension of what is right and what is wrong seems like asking people to repudiate their actual experience of beauty, at the bidding of a theory which says 'only that which satisfies such and such conditions can be beautiful'. If what I have called our actual apprehension is (as I would maintain that it is) truly an apprehension, i.e. an instance of knowledge, the request is nothing less than absurd.

I would maintain, in fact, that what we are apt to describe as 'what we think' about moral questions contains a considerable amount that we do not think but know, and that this forms the standard by reference to which the truth of any moral theory has to be tested, instead of having itself to be tested by reference to any theory. I hope that I have in what precedes indicated what in

---

* Productive of the most possible good.

my view these elements of knowledge are that are involved in our ordinary moral consciousness.

It would be a mistake to found a natural science on 'what we really think', i.e. on what reasonably thoughtful and well-educated people think about the subjects of the science before they have studied them scientifically. For such opinions are interpretations, and often misinterpretations, of sense-experience; and the man of science must appeal from these to sense-experience itself, which furnishes his real data. In ethics no such appeal is possible. We have no more direct way of access to the facts about rightness and goodness and about what things are right or good, than by thinking about them; the moral convictions of thoughtful and well-educated people are the data of ethics just as sense-perceptions are the data of a natural science. Just as some of the latter have to be rejected as illusory, so have some of the former; but as the latter are rejected only when they are in conflict with other more accurate sense-perceptions, the former are rejected only when they are in conflict with convictions which stand better the test of reflection. The existing body of moral convictions of the best people is the cumulative product of the moral reflection of many generations, which has developed an extremely delicate power of appreciation of moral distinctions; and this the theorist cannot afford to treat with anything other than the greatest respect. The verdicts of the moral consciousness of the best people are the foundation on which we must build; though he must first compare them with one another and eliminate any contradictions they may contain.

32

A Theory of Justice

JOHN RAWLS

For biographical information about John Rawls, see reading 16.

In this selection, taken from his book A Theory of Justice, *Rawls argues that social arrangements are just, and actions are right, when they conform to principles arising out of certain choices. These choices are not actual, but rather are choices that would be made by ideally situated persons. Such persons would know only the most general facts about the world. They would not know their own race, sex, degree of wealth, or natural abilities. Being ignorant of these things, they could not tailor principles to their own advantage. Because they would not even know their actual preferences and psychological tendencies, they would want only "primary goods"—goods that it is rational to want whatever else one wants. According to Rawls, such goods include rights and liberties, powers and opportunities, wealth and income, and the social bases of self-respect.*

What principles would persons who are behind this "veil of ignorance" choose? To structure basic social institutions, such as the political constitution and economic system, they would choose that "each person have a right to the most extensive basic liberty compatible with a similar liberty for others." However, they would tolerate some social and economic inequalities provided that (a) they did not restrict equality of opportunity, and (b) they raised the position of even the worst-off (for example, by providing the better-off with incentives that raised productivity). Because such inequalities help both the worse-off and the better-off, it would be irrational not to accept them. Because Rawls is more concerned with social justice than individual action, he says far less about the choice of principles regulating personal behavior. However, he believes that persons in his "original position" would choose principles imposing such familiar duties and obligations as fidelity, mutual aid, mutual respect, and noninfliction of harm.

Because Rawls does not equate justice or rightness with the maximization of benefit, his theory is a deep and systematic alternative to utilitarianism (readings 26 and 27). In this and other respects, the theory resembles Kant's (reading 29). For illuminating discussion of the parallels, see Rawls' own "Kantian interpretation" of his theory at the selection's end.

The Main Idea of the Theory of Justice

MY AIM IS to present a conception of justice which generalizes and carries to a higher level of abstraction the familiar theory of the social contract as found, say, in Locke, Rousseau, and Kant.[1] In order to do this we are not to think of the original contract as one to enter a particular society or to set up a particular form of government. Rather, the guiding idea is that the principles of justice for the basic structure of society are the object of the original agreement. They are the principles that free and rational persons concerned to further their own interests would accept in an initial position of equality as defining the fundamental terms of their association. These principles are to regulate all further agreements; they specify the kinds of social cooperation that can be entered into and the forms of government that can be established. This way of regarding the principles of justice I shall call justice as fairness.

Thus we are to imagine that those who engage in social cooperation choose together, in one joint act, the principles which are to assign basic rights and duties and to determine the division of social benefits. Men are to decide in advance how they are to regulate their claims against one another and what is to be the foundation charter of their society. Just as each person must decide by rational reflection what constitutes his good, that is, the system of ends which it is rational for him to pursue, so a group of persons must decide once and for all what is to count among them as just and unjust. The choice which rational men would make in this hypothetical situation of equal liberty, assuming for the present that this choice problem has a solution, determines the principles of justice.

In justice as fairness the original position of equality corresponds to the state of nature in the traditional theory of the social contract. This original position is not, of course, thought of as an actual historical state of affairs, much less as a primitive condition of culture. It is understood as a purely hypothetical situation characterized so as to lead to a certain conception of justice.[2] Among the essential features of this situation is that no one knows his place in society, his class position or social status, nor does any one know his fortune in the distribution of natural assets and abilities, his intelligence, strength, and the like. I shall even assume that the parties do not know their conceptions of the good or their special psychological propensities. The principles of justice are chosen behind a veil of ignorance. This ensures that no one is advantaged

[1] As the text suggests, I shall regard Locke's *Second Treatise of Government,* Rousseau's *The Social Contract,* and Kant's ethical works beginning with *The Foundations of the Metaphysics of Morals* as definitive of the contract tradition. For all of its greatness, Hobbes's *Leviathan* raises special problems. A general historical survey is provided by J. W. Gough, *The Social Contract,* 2nd ed. (Oxford, The Clarendon Press, 1957), and Otto Gierke, *Natural Law and the Theory of Society,* trans. with an introduction by Ernest Barker (Cambridge, The University Press, 1934). A presentation of the contract view as primarily an ethical theory is to be found in G. R. Grice, *The Grounds of Moral Judgment* (Cambridge, The University Press, 1967). See also §19, note 30.

[2] Kant is clear that the original agreement is hypothetical. See *The Metaphysics of Morals,* pt. I (*Rechtslehre*), especially §§47, 52; and pt. II of the essay "Concerning the Common Saying: This May Be True in Theory but It Does Not Apply in Practice," in *Kant's Political Writings,* ed. Hans Reiss and trans. by H. B. Nisbet (Cambridge, The University Press, 1970), pp. 73–87. See Georges Vlachos, *La Pensée politique de Kant* (Paris, Presses Universitaires de France, 1962), pp. 326–335; and J. G. Murphy, *Kant: The Philosophy of Right* (London, Macmillan, 1970), pp. 109–112, 133–136, for a further discussion.

or disadvantaged in the choice of principles by the outcome of natural chance or the contingency of social circumstances. Since all are similarly situated and no one is able to design principles to favor his particular condition, the principles of justice are the result of a fair agreement or bargain. For given the circumstances of the original position, the symmetry of everyone's relations to each other, this initial situation is fair between individuals as moral persons, that is, as rational beings with their own ends and capable, I shall assume, of a sense of justice. The original position is, one might say, the appropriate initial status quo, and thus the fundamental agreements reached in it are fair. This explains the propriety of the name "justice as fairness": it conveys the idea that the principles of justice are agreed to in an initial situation that is fair. The name does not mean that the concepts of justice and fairness are the same, any more than the phrase "poetry as metaphor" means that the concepts of poetry and metaphor are the same.

Justice as fairness begins, as I have said, with one of the most general of all choices which persons might make together, namely, with the choice of the first principles of a conception of justice which is to regulate all subsequent criticism and reform of institutions. Then, having chosen a conception of justice, we can suppose that they are to choose a constitution and a legislature to enact laws, and so on, all in accordance with the principles of justice initially agreed upon. Our social situation is just if it is such that by this sequence of hypothetical agreements we would have contracted into the general system of rules which defines it. Moreover, assuming that the original position does determine a set of principles (that is, that a particular conception of justice would be chosen), it will then be true that whenever social institutions satisfy these principles those engaged in them can say to one another that they are cooperating on terms to which they would agree if they were free and equal persons whose relations with respect to one another were fair. They could all view their arrangements as meeting the stipulations which they would acknowledge in an initial situation that embodies widely accepted and reasonable constraints on the choice of principles. The general recognition of this fact would provide the basis for a public acceptance of the corresponding principles of justice. No society can, of course, be a scheme of cooperation which men enter voluntarily in a literal sense; each person finds himself placed at birth in some particular position in some particular society, and the nature of this position materially affects his life prospects. Yet a society satisfying the principles of justice as fairness comes as close as a society can to being a voluntary scheme, for it meets the principles which free and equal persons would assent to under circumstances that are fair. In this sense its members are autonomous and the obligations they recognize self-imposed.

One feature of justice as fairness is to think of the parties in the initial situation as rational and mutually disinterested. This does not mean that the parties are egoists, that is, individuals with only certain kinds of interests, say in wealth, prestige, and domination. But they are conceived as not taking an interest in one another's interests. They are to presume that even their spiritual aims may be opposed, in the way that the aims of those of different religions may be opposed. Moreover, the concept of rationality must be interpreted as far as possible in the narrow sense, standard in economic theory, of taking the most effective means to given ends. I shall modify this concept to some extent, as explained later, but one must try to avoid introducing into it any controversial ethical elements. The initial situation must be characterized by stipulations that are widely accepted.

In working out the conception of justice as fairness one main task clearly is to determine which principles of justice would be chosen in the original position. To do this we must describe this situation in some detail and formulate with care the problem of choice which it presents. These matters I shall take up in the immediately succeeding chapters. It may be observed, however, that once the principles of justice are thought of as arising from an original agreement in a situation of equality, it is an open question whether the principle of utility would be acknowledged. Offhand it hardly seems likely that persons who view themselves as equals, entitled to press their claims upon one another, would agree to a principle which may require lesser life prospects for some simply for the sake of a greater sum of advantages enjoyed by others. Since each desires to protect his interests, his capacity to advance his conception of the good, no one has a reason to acquiesce in an enduring loss for himself in order to bring about a greater net balance of satisfaction. In the absence of strong and lasting benevolent impulses, a rational man would not accept a basic structure merely because it maximized the algebraic sum of advantages irrespective of its permanent effects on his own basic rights and interests. Thus it seems that the principle of utility is incompatible with the conception of social cooperation among equals for mutual advantage. It appears to be inconsistent with the idea of reciprocity implicit in the notion of a well-ordered society. Or, at any rate, so I shall argue.

I shall maintain instead that the persons in the initial situation would choose two rather different principles: the first requires equality in the assignment of basic rights and duties, while the second holds that social and economic inequalities, for example, inequalities of wealth and authority, are just only if they result in compensating benefits for everyone, and in particular for the least advantaged members of society. These principles rule out justifying institutions on the grounds that the hardships of some are offset by a greater good in the aggregate. It may be expedient but it is not just that some should have less in order that others may prosper. But there is no injustice in the greater benefits earned by a few provided that the situation of persons not so fortunate is thereby improved. The intuitive idea is that since everyone's well-being depends upon a scheme of cooperation without which no one could have a satisfactory life, the division of advantages should be such as to draw forth the willing cooperation of everyone taking part in it, including those less well situated. Yet this can be expected only if reasonable terms are proposed. The two principles mentioned seem to be a fair agreement on the basis of which those better endowed, or more fortunate in their social position, neither of which we can be said to deserve, could expect the willing cooperation of others when some workable scheme is a necessary condition of the welfare of all.[3] Once we decide to look for a conception of justice that nullifies the accidents of natural endowment and the contingencies of social circumstance as counters in quest for political and economic advantage, we are led to these principles. They express the result of leaving aside those aspects of the social world that seem arbitrary from a moral point of view.

The problem of the choice of principles, however, is extremely difficult. I do not expect the answer I shall suggest to be convincing to everyone. It is, therefore, worth noting from the outset that justice as fairness, like other contract views, consists of two parts: (1) an interpretation of the initial situation and of the problem of choice posed there, and (2) a set of principles which, it is argued, would be agreed to. One may accept the first part of the theory (or some variant thereof), but not the other, and conversely. The concept of the initial contractual situation may seem reasonable although the particular principles proposed are rejected. To be sure, I want to maintain that the most appropriate conception of this situation does lead to principles of justice contrary to utilitarianism and perfectionism, and therefore that the contract doctrine provides an alternative to these views. Still, one may dispute this contention even though one grants that the contractarian method is a useful way of studying ethical theories and of setting forth their underlying assumptions.

. . .

A final remark. Justice as fairness is not a complete contract theory. For it is clear that the contractarian idea can be extended to the choice of more or less an entire ethical system, that is, to a system including principles for all the virtues and not only for justice. Now for the most part I shall consider only principles of justice and others closely related to them; I make no attempt to discuss the virtues in a systematic way. Obviously if justice as fairness succeeds reasonably well, a next step would be to study the more general view suggested by the name "rightness as fairness." But even this wider theory fails to embrace all moral relationships, since it would seem to include only our relations with other persons and to leave out of account how we are to conduct ourselves toward animals and the rest of nature. I do not contend that the contract notion offers a way to approach these questions which are certainly of the first importance; and I shall have to put them aside. We must recognize the limited scope of justice as fairness and of the general type of view that it exemplifies. How far its conclusions must be revised once these other matters are understood cannot be decided in advance.

The Original Position and Justification

I have said that the original position is the appropriate initial status quo which ensures that the fundamental agreements reached in it are fair. This fact

---

[3] For the formulation of this intuitive idea I am indebted to Allan Gibbard.

yields the name "justice as fairness." It is clear, then, that I want to say that one conception of justice is more reasonable than another, or justifiable with respect to it, if rational persons in the initial situation would choose its principles over those of the other for the role of justice. Conceptions of justice are to be ranked by their acceptability to persons so circumstanced. Understood in this way the question of justification is settled by working out a problem of deliberation: we have to ascertain which principles it would be rational to adopt given the contractual situation. This connects the theory of justice with the theory of rational choice.

If this view of the problem of justification is to succeed, we must, of course, describe in some detail the nature of this choice problem. A problem of rational decision has a definite answer only if we know the beliefs and interests of the parties, their relations with respect to one another, the alternatives between which they are to choose, the procedure whereby they make up their minds, and so on. As the circumstances are presented in different ways, correspondingly different principles are accepted. The concept of the original position, as I shall refer to it, is that of the most philosophically favored interpretation of this initial choice situation for the purposes of a theory of justice.

But how are we to decide what is the most favored interpretation? I assume, for one thing, that there is a broad measure of agreement that principles of justice should be chosen under certain conditions. To justify a particular description of the initial situation one shows that it incorporates these commonly shared presumptions. One argues from widely accepted but weak premises to more specific conclusions. Each of the presumptions should by itself be natural and plausible; some of them may seem innocuous or even trivial. The aim of the contract approach is to establish that taken together they impose significant bounds on acceptable principles of justice. The ideal outcome would be that these conditions determine a unique set of principles; but I shall be satisfied if they suffice to rank the main traditional conceptions of social justice.

One should not be misled, then, by the somewhat unusual conditions which characterize the original position. The idea here is simply to make vivid to ourselves the restrictions that it seems reasonable to impose on arguments for principles of justice, and therefore on these principles themselves. Thus is seems reasonable and generally acceptable that no one should be advantaged or disadvantaged by natural fortune or social circumstances in the choice of principles. It also seems widely agreed that it should be impossible to tailor principles to the circumstances of one's own case. We should ensure further that particular inclinations and aspirations, and persons' conceptions of their good do not affect the principles adopted. The aim is to rule out those principles that it would be rational to propose for acceptance, however little the chance of success, only if one knew certain things that are irrelevant from the standpoint of justice. For example, if a man knew that he was wealthy, he might find it rational to advance the principle that various taxes for welfare measures be counted unjust; if he knew that he was poor, he would most likely propose the contrary principle. To represent the desired restrictions one imagines a situation in which everyone is deprived of this sort of information. One excludes the knowledge of those contingencies which sets men at odds and allows them to be guided by their prejudices. In this manner the veil of ignorance is arrived at in a natural way. This concept should cause no difficulty if we keep in mind the constraints on arguments that it is meant to express. At any time we can enter the original position, so to speak, simply by following a certain procedure, namely, by arguing for principles of justice in accordance with these restrictions.

It seems reasonable to suppose that the parties in the original position are equal. That is, all have the same rights in the procedure for choosing principles; each can make proposals, submit reasons for their acceptance, and so on. Obviously the purpose of these conditions is to represent equality between human beings as moral persons, as creatures having a conception of their good and capable of a sense of justice. The basis of equality is taken to be similarity in these two respects. Systems of ends are not ranked in value; and each man is presumed to have the requisite ability to understand and to act upon whatever principles are adopted. Together with the veil of ignorance, these conditions define the principles of justice as those which rational persons concerned to advance their interests would consent to as equals when none are known to be advantaged or disadvantaged by social and natural contingencies.

There is, however, another side to justifying a particular description of the original position. This is to see if the principles which would be chosen match our considered convictions of justice or extend them in an acceptable way. We can note whether applying these principles would lead us to make the same judgments about the basic structure of society which we now make intuitively and in which we have the greatest confidence; or whether, in cases where our present judgments are in doubt and given with hesitation, these principles offer a resolution which we can affirm on reflection. There are questions which we feel sure must be answered in a certain way. For example, we are confident that religious intolerance and racial discrimination are unjust. We think that we have examined these things with care and have reached what we believe is an impartial judgment not likely to be distorted by an excessive attention to our own interests. These convictions are provisional fixed points which we presume any conception of justice must fit. But we have much less assurance as to what is the correct distribution of wealth and authority. Here we may be looking for a way to remove our doubts. We can check an interpretation of the initial situation, then, by the capacity of its principles to accommodate our firmest convictions and to provide guidance where guidance is needed.

In searching for the most favored description of this situation we work from both ends. We begin by describing it so that it represents generally shared and preferably weak conditions. We then see if these conditions are strong enough to yield a significant set of principles. If not, we look for further premises equally reasonable. But if so, and these principles match our considered convictions of justice, then so far well and good. But presumably there will be discrepancies. In this case we have a choice. We can either modify the account of the initial situation or we can revise our existing judgments, for even the judgments we take provisionally as fixed points are liable to revision. By going back and forth, sometimes altering the conditions of the contractual circumstances, at others withdrawing our judgments and conforming them to principle, I assume that eventually we shall find a description of the initial situation that both expresses reasonable conditions and yields principles which match our considered judgments duly pruned and adjusted. This state of affairs I refer to as reflective equilibrium.[4] It is an equilibrium because at last our principles and judgments coincide; and it is reflective since we know to what principles our judgments conform and the premises of their derivation. At the moment everything is in order. But this equilibrium is not necessarily stable. It is liable to be upset by further examination of the conditions which should be imposed on the contractual situation and by particular cases which may lead us to revise our judgments. Yet for the time being we have done what we can to render coherent and to justify our convictions of social justice. We have reached a conception of the original position.

. . .

Two Principles of Justice

I shall now state in a provisional form the two principles of justice that I believe would be chosen in the original position. In this section I wish to make only the most general comments, and therefore the first formulation of these principles is tentative. As we go on I shall run through several formulations and approximate step by step the final statement to be given much later. I believe that doing this allows the exposition to proceed in a natural way.

The first statement of the two principles reads as follows.

> First: each person is to have an equal right to the most extensive basic liberty compatible with a similar liberty for others.
> Second: social and economic inequalities are to be arranged so that they are both (a) reasonably expected to be to everyone's advantage, and (b) attached to positions and offices open to all.

There are two ambiguous phrases in the second principle, namely "everyone's advantage" and "open to all." . . .

By way of general comment, these principles primarily apply, as I have said, to the basic structure of society. They are to govern the assignment of rights and duties and to regulate the distribution of social and economic advantages. As their formulation suggests, these principles presuppose that the social structure can be divided into two more or less distinct parts, the first principle applying to the one, the second to the other. They distinguish between those aspects of the social system that define and secure the equal liberties of citi-

---

[4] The process of mutual adjustment of principles and considered judgments is not peculiar to moral philosophy. See Nelson Goodman, *Fact, Fiction, and Forecast* (Cambridge, Mass., Harvard University Press, 1955), pp. 65–68, for parallel remarks concerning the justification of the principles of deductive and inductive inference.

zenship and those that specify and establish social and economic inequalities. The basic liberties of citizens are, roughly speaking, political liberty (the right to vote and to be eligible for public office) together with freedom of speech and assembly; liberty of conscience and freedom of thought; freedom of the person along with the right to hold (personal) property; and freedom from arbitrary arrest and seizure as defined by the concept of the rule of law. These liberties are all required to be equal by the first principle, since citizens of a just society are to have the same basic rights.

The second principle applies, in the first approximation, to the distribution of income and wealth and to the design of organizations that make use of differences in authority and responsibility, or chains of command. While the distribution of wealth and income need not be equal, it must be to everyone's advantage, and at the same time, positions of authority and offices of command must be accessible to all. One applies the second principle by holding positions open, and then, subject to this constraint, arranges social and economic inequalities so that everyone benefits.

These principles are to be arranged in a serial order with the first principle prior to the second. This ordering means that a departure from the institutions of equal liberty required by the first principle cannot be justified by, or compensated for, by greater social and economic advantages. The distribution of wealth and income, and the hierarchies of authority, must be consistent with both the liberties of equal citizenship and equality of opportunity.

It is clear that these principles are rather specific in their content, and their acceptance rests on certain assumptions that I must eventually try to explain and justify. A theory of justice depends upon a theory of society in ways that will become evident as we proceed. For the present, it should be observed that the two principles (and this holds for all formulations) are a special case of a more general conception of justice that can be expressed as follows.

> All social values—liberty and opportunity, income and wealth, and the bases of self-respect—are to be distributed equally unless an unequal distribution of any, or all, of these values is to everyone's advantage.

Injustice, then, is simply inequalities that are not to the benefit of all. Of course, this conception is extremely vague and requires interpretation.

As a first step, suppose that the basic structure of society distributes certain primary goods, that is, things that every rational man is presumed to want. These goods normally have a use whatever a person's rational plan of life. For simplicity, assume that the chief primary goods at the disposition of society are rights and liberties, powers and opportunities, income and wealth. (Later on in Part Three the primary good of self-respect has a central place.) These are the social primary goods. Other primary goods such as health and vigor, intelligence and imagination, are natural goods; although their possession is influenced by the basic structure, they are not so directly under its control. Imagine, then, a hypothetical initial arrangement in which all the social primary goods are equally distributed: everyone has similar rights and duties, and income and wealth are evenly shared. This state of affairs provides a benchmark for judging improvements. If certain inequalities of wealth and organizational powers would make everyone better off than in this hypothetical starting situation, then they accord with the general conception.

Now it is possible, at least theoretically, that by giving up some of their fundamental liberties men are sufficiently compensated by the resulting social and economic gains. The general conception of justice imposes no restrictions on what sort of inequalities are permissible; it only requires that everyone's position be improved. We need not suppose anything so drastic as consenting to a condition of slavery. Imagine instead that men forego certain political rights when the economic returns are significant and their capacity to influence the course of policy by the exercise of these rights would be marginal in any case. It is this kind of exchange which the two principles as stated rule out; being arranged in serial order they do not permit exchanges between basic liberties and economic and social gains. The serial ordering of principles expresses an underlying preference among primary social goods. When this preference is rational so likewise is the choice of these principles in this order.

In developing justice as fairness I shall, for the most part, leave aside the general conception of justice and examine instead the special case of the two principles in serial order. The advantage of this procedure is that from the first the matter of priorities is recognized and an effort made to find principles to deal with it. One is led to attend throughout to the conditions under which the acknowledgment of the absolute weight of liberty with respect to social and economic advantages, as defined by the lexical order of the two principles, would be reasonable. Offhand, this ranking appears extreme and too special a case to be of much interest; but there is more justification for it than would appear at first sight. Or at any rate, so I shall maintain. Furthermore, the distinction between fundamental rights and liberties and economic and social benefits marks a difference among primary social goods that one should try to exploit. It suggests an important division in the social system. Of course, the distinctions drawn and the ordering proposed are bound to be at best only approximations. There are surely circumstances in which they fail. But it is essential to depict clearly the main lines of a reasonable conception of justice; and under many conditions anyway, the two principles in serial order may serve well enough. When necessary we can fall back on the more general conception.

The fact that the two principles apply to institutions has certain consequences. Several points illustrate this. First of all, the rights and liberties referred to by these principles are those which are defined by the public rules of the basic structure. Whether men are free is determined by the rights and duties established by the major institutions of society. Liberty is a certain pattern of social forms. The first principle simply requires that certain sorts of rules, those defining basic liberties, apply to everyone equally and that they allow the most extensive liberty compatible with a like liberty for all. The only reason for circumscribing the rights defining liberty and making men's freedom less extensive than it might otherwise be is that these equal rights as institutionally defined would interfere with one another.

Another thing to bear in mind is that when principles mention persons, or require that everyone gain from an inequality, the reference is to representative persons holding the various social positions, or offices, or whatever, established by the basic structure. Thus in applying the second principle I assume that it is possible to assign an expectation of well-being to representative individuals holding these positions. This expectation indicates their life prospects as viewed from their social station. In general, the expectations of representative persons depend upon the distribution of rights and duties throughout the basic structure. When this changes, expectations change. I assume, then, that expectations are connected: by raising the prospects of the representative man in one position we presumably increase or decrease the prospects of representative men in other positions. Since it applies to institutional forms, the second principle (or rather the first part of it) refers to the expectations of representative individuals. As I shall discuss below, neither principle applies to distributions of particular goods to particular individuals who may be identified by their proper names. The situation where someone is considering how to allocate certain commodities to needy persons who are known to him is not within the scope of the principles. They are meant to regulate basic institutional arrangements. We must not assume that there is much similarity from the standpoint of justice between an administrative allotment of goods to specific persons and the appropriate design of society. Our common sense intuitions for the former may be a poor guide to the latter.

Now the second principle insists that each person benefit from permissible inequalities in the basic structure. This means that it must be reasonable for each relevant representative man defined by this structure, when he views it as a going concern, to prefer his prospects with the inequality to his prospects without it. One is not allowed to justify differences in income or organizational powers on the ground that the disadvantages of those in one position are outweighed by the greater advantages of those in another. Much less can infringements of liberty be counterbalanced in this way. Applied to the basic structure, the principle of utility would have us maximize the sum of expectations of representative men (weighted by the number of persons they represent, on the classical view); and this would permit us to compensate for the losses of some by the gains of others. Instead, the two principles require that everyone benefit from economic and social inequalities. . . .

Principles for Individuals: The Principle of Fairness

In the discussion so far I have considered the principles which apply to institutions or, more exactly, to the basic structure of society. It is clear, however, that principles of another kind must also be chosen, since a complete theory of right includes principles for individuals as well.

. . .

Now the order in which principles are chosen raises a number of questions which I shall skip over. The important thing is that the various principles are to be adopted in a definite sequence and the reasons for this ordering are connected with the more difficult parts of the theory of justice. To illustrate: while it would be possible to choose many of the natural duties before those for the basic structure without changing the principles in any substantial way, the sequence in either case reflects the fact that obligations presuppose principles for social forms. And some natural duties also presuppose such principles, for example, the duty to support just institutions. For this reason it seems simpler to adopt all principles for individuals after those for the basic structure. That principles for institutions are chosen first shows the social nature of the virtue of justice, its intimate connection with social practices so often noted by idealists. When Bradley says that the individual is a bare abstraction, he can be interpreted to say, without too much distortion, that a person's obligations and duties presuppose a moral conception of institutions and therefore that the content of just institutions must be defined before the requirements for individuals can be set out.[5] And this is to say that, in most cases, the principles for obligations and duties should be settled upon after those for the basic structure.

Therefore, to establish a complete conception of right, the parties in the original position are to choose in a definite order not only a conception of justice but also principles to go with each major concept falling under the concept of right. These concepts are I assume relatively few in number and have a determinate relation to each other. Thus, in addition to principles for institutions there must be an agreement on principles for such notions as fairness and fidelity, mutual respect and beneficence as these apply to individuals, as well as on principles for the conduct of states. The intuitive idea is this: the concept of something's being right is the same as, or better, may be replaced by, the concept of its being in accordance with the principles that in the original position would be acknowledged to apply to things of its kind. I do not interpret this concept of right as providing an analysis of the meaning of the term "right" as normally used in moral contexts. It is not meant as an analysis of the concept of right in the traditional sense. Rather, the broader notion of rightness as fairness is to be understood as a replacement for existing conceptions. There is no necessity to say that sameness of meaning holds between the word "right" (and its relatives) in its ordinary use and the more elaborate locutions needed to express this ideal contractarian concept of right. For our purposes here I accept the view that a sound analysis is best understood as providing a satisfactory substitute, one that meets certain desiderata while avoiding certain obscurities and confusions. In other words, explication is elimination: we start with a concept the expression for which is somehow troublesome; but it serves certain ends that cannot be given up. An explication

---

[5] See F. H. Bradley, *Ethical Studies,* 2nd ed. (Oxford, The Clarendon Press, 1927), pp. 163–189.

achieves these ends in other ways that are relatively free of difficulty.[6] Thus if the theory of justice as fairness, or more generally of rightness as fairness, fits our considered judgments in reflective equilibrium, and if it enables us to say all that on due examination we want to say, then it provides a way of eliminating customary phrases in favor of other expressions. So understood one may think of justice as fairness and rightness as fairness as providing a definition or explication of the concepts of justice and right.

. . .

The Reasoning Leading to the Two Principles of Justice

. . .

It seems clear . . . that the two principles are at least a plausible conception of justice. The question, though, is how one is to argue for them more systematically. Now there are several things to do. One can work out their consequences for institutions and note their implications for fundamental social policy. In this way they are tested by a comparison with our considered judgments of justice. Part II is devoted to this. But one can also try to find arguments in their favor that are decisive from the standpoint of the original position. In order to see how this might be done, it is useful as a heuristic device to think of the two principles as the maximum solution to the problem of social justice. There is an analogy between the two principles and the maximin rule for choice under uncertainty.[7] This is evident from the fact that the two principles are those a person would choose for the design of a society in which his enemy is to assign him his place. The maximin rule tells us to rank alternatives by their worst possible outcomes: we are to adopt the alternative the worst outcome of which is superior to the worst outcomes of the others. The persons in the original position do not, of course, assume that their initial place in society is decided by a malevolent opponent. As I note below, they should not reason from false premises. The veil of ignorance does not violate this idea, since an absence of information is not misinformation. But that the two principles of justice would be chosen if the parties were forced to protect themselves against such a contingency explains the sense in which this conception is the maximin solution. And this analogy suggests that if the original position has been described so that it is rational for the parties to adopt the conservative attitude expressed by this rule, a conclusive argument can indeed be constructed for these prin-

---

[6] See W. V. Quine, *Word and Object* (Cambridge, Mass., M.I.T. Press, 1960), pp. 257–262, whom I follow here.

[7] An accessible discussion of this and other rules of choice under uncertainty can be found in W. J. Baumol, *Economic Theory and Operations Analysis,* 2nd ed. (Englewood Cliffs, N.J., Prentice-Hall, Inc., 1965), ch. 24. Baumol gives a geometric interpretation of these rules, including the diagram used in §13 to illustrate the difference principle. See pp. 558–562. See also R. D. Luce and Howard Raiffa, *Games and Decisions* (New York, John Wiley and Sons, Inc., 1957), ch. XIII, for a fuller account.

ciples. Clearly the maximin rule is not, in general, a suitable guide for choices under uncertainty. But it is attractive in situations marked by certain special features. My aim, then, is to show that a good case can be made for the two principles based on the fact that the original position manifests these features to the fullest possible degree, carrying them to the limit, so to speak.

. . .

Now there appear to be three chief features of situations that give plausibility to this unusual rule.[8] First, since the rule takes no account of the likelihoods of the possible circumstances, there must be some reason for sharply discounting estimates of these probabilities. Offhand, the most natural rule of choice would seem to be to compute the expectation of monetary gain for each decision and then to adopt the course of action with the highest prospect. (This expectation is defined as follows: let us suppose that g_{ij} represent the numbers in the gain-and-loss table, where i is the row index and j is the column index; and let p_j, j = 1, 2, 3, be the likelihoods of the circumstances, with $\Sigma p_j = 1$. Then the expectation for the ith decision is equal to $\Sigma p_j g_{ij}$.) Thus it must be, for example, that the situation is one in which a knowledge of likelihoods is impossible, or at best extremely insecure. In this case it is unreasonable not to be skeptical of probabilistic calculations unless there is no other way out, particularly if the decision is a fundamental one that needs to be justified to others.

The second feature that suggests the maximin rule is the following: the person choosing has a conception of the good such that he cares very little, if anything, for what he might gain above the minimum stipend that he can, in fact, be sure of by following the maximin rule. It is not worthwhile for him to take a chance for the sake of a further advantage, especially when it may turn out that he loses much that is important to him. This last provision brings in the third feature, namely, that the rejected alternatives have outcomes that one can hardly accept. The situation involves grave risks. Of course these features work most effectively in combination. The paradigm situation for following the maximin rule is when all three features are realized to the highest degree. This rule does not, then, generally apply, nor of course is it self-evident. Rather, it is a maxim, a rule of thumb, that comes into its own in special circumstances. Its application depends upon the qualitative structure of the possible gains and losses in relation to one's conception of the good, all this against a background in which it is reasonable to discount conjectural estimates of likelihoods.

. . .

Now, as I have suggested, the original position has been defined so that it is a situation in which the maximin rule applies. In order to see this, let us review briefly the nature of this situation with these three special features in mind. To begin with, the veil of ignorance excludes all but the vaguest knowledge of likelihoods. The parties have no basis for determining the probable nature of

[8] Here I borrow from William Fellner, *Probability and Profit* (Homewood, Ill., R. D. Irwin, Inc., 1965), pp. 140–142, where these features are noted.

their society, or their place in it. Thus they have strong reasons for being wary of probability calculations if any other course is open to them. They must also take in account the fact that their choice of principles should seem reasonable to others, in particular their descendants, whose rights will be deeply affected by it. There are further grounds for discounting that I shall mention as we go along. For the present it suffices to note that these considerations are strengthened by the fact that the parties know very little about the gain-and-loss table. Not only are they unable to conjecture the likelihoods of the various possible circumstances, they cannot say much about what the possible circumstances are, much less enumerate them and foresee the outcome of each alternative available. Those deciding are much more in the dark than the illustration by a numerical table suggests. It is for this reason that I have spoken of an analogy with the maximin rule.

Several kinds of arguments for the two principles of justice illustrate the second feature. Thus, if we can maintain that these principles provide a workable theory of social justice, and that they are compatible with reasonable demands of efficiency, then this conception guarantees a satisfactory minimum. There may be, on reflection, little reason for trying to do better. Thus much of the argument, especially in Part Two, is to show, by their application to the main questions of social justice, that the two principles are a satisfactory conception. These details have a philosophical purpose. Moreover, this line of thought is practically decisive if we can establish the priority of liberty, the lexical ordering of the two principles. For this priority implies that the persons in the original position have no desire to try for greater gains at the expense of the equal liberties. The minimum assured by the two principles in lexical order is not one that the parties wish to jeopardize for the sake of greater economic and social advantages. In parts of Chapters IV and IX I present the case for this ordering.

Finally, the third feature holds if we can assume that other conceptions of justice may lead to institutions that the parties would find intolerable. For example, it has sometimes been held that under some conditions the utility principle (in either form) justifies, if not slavery or serfdom, at any rate serious infractions of liberty for the sake of greater social benefits. We need not consider here the truth of this claim, or the likelihood that the requisite conditions obtain. For the moment, this contention is only to illustrate the way in which conceptions of justice may allow for outcomes which the parties may not be able to accept. And having the ready alternative of the two principles of justice which secure a satisfactory minimum, it seems unwise, if not irrational, for them to take a chance that these outcomes are not realized.

. . .

The Kantian Interpretation of Justice as Fairness

For the most part I have considered the content of the principle of equal liberty and the meaning of the priority of the rights that it defines. It seems appropriate at this point to note that there is a Kantian interpretation of the conception of justice from which this principle derives. This interpretation is based upon Kant's notion of autonomy. It is a mistake, I believe, to emphasize the place of generality and universality in Kant's ethics. That moral principles are general and universal is hardly new with him; and as we have seen these conditions do not in any case take us very far. It is impossible to construct a moral theory on so slender a basis, and therefore to limit the discussion of Kant's doctrine to these notions is to reduce it to triviality. The real force of his view lies elsewhere.[9]

For one thing, he begins with the idea that moral principles are the object of rational choice. They define the moral law that men can rationally will to govern their conduct in an ethical commonwealth. Moral philosophy becomes the study of the conception and outcome of a suitably defined rational decision. This idea has immediate consequences. For once we think of moral principles as legislation for a kingdom of ends, it is clear that these principles must not only be acceptable to all but public as well. Finally Kant supposes that this moral legislation is to be agreed to under conditions that characterize men as free and equal rational beings. The description of the original position is an attempt to interpret this conception. I do not wish to argue here for this interpretation on the basis of Kant's text. Certainly some will want to read him differently. Perhaps the remarks to follow are best taken as suggestions for relating justice as fairness to the high point of the contractarian tradition in Kant and Rousseau.

Kant held, I believe, that a person is acting autonomously when the principles of his action are chosen by him as the most adequate possible expression of his nature as a free and equal rational being. The principles he acts upon are not adopted because of his social position or natural endowments, or in view of the particular kind of society in which he lives or the specific things that he happens to want. To act on such principles is to act heteronomously. Now the veil of ignorance deprives the persons in the original position of the knowledge that would enable them to choose heteronomous principles. The parties arrive at their choice together as free and equal rational persons knowing only that those circumstances obtain which give rise to the need for principles of justice.

To be sure, the argument for these principles does add in various ways to Kant's conception. For example, it adds the feature that the principles chosen

---

[9] To be avoided at all costs is the idea that Kant's doctrine simply provides the general, or formal, elements for a utilitarian (or indeed for any other) theory. See, for example, R. M. Hare, *Freedom and Reason* (Oxford, The Clarendon Press, 1963), pp. 123f. One must not lose sight of the full scope of his view, one must take the later works into consideration. Unfortunately, there is no commentary on Kant's moral theory as a whole; perhaps it would prove impossible to write. But the standard works of H. J. Paton, *The Categorical Imperative* (Chicago, University of Chicago Press, 1948), and L. W. Beck, *A Commentary on Kant's Critique of Practical Reason* (Chicago, University of Chicago Press, 1960), and others need to be further complemented by studies of the other writings. See here M. J. Gregor's *Laws of Freedom* (Oxford, Basil Blackwell, 1963), an account of *The Metaphysics of Morals*, and J. G. Murphy's brief *Kant: The Philosophy of Right* (London, Macmillan, 1970). Beyond this, *The Critique of Judgment, Religion within the Limits of Reason,* and the political writings cannot be neglected without distorting his doctrine. For the last, see *Kant's Political Writings,* ed. Hans Reiss and trans. H. B. Nisbet (Cambridge, The University Press, 1970).

are to apply to the basic structure of society; and premises characterizing this structure are used in deriving the principles of justice. But I believe that this and other additions are natural enough and remain fairly close to Kant's doctrine, at least when all of his ethical writings are viewed together. Assuming, then, that the reasoning in favor of the principles of justice is correct, we can say that when persons act on these principles they are acting in accordance with principles that they would choose as rational and independent persons in an original position of equality. The principles of their actions do not depend upon social or natural contingencies, nor do they reflect the bias of the particulars of their plan of life or the aspirations that motivate them. By acting from these principles persons express their nature as free and equal rational beings subject to the general conditions of human life. For to express one's nature as a being of a particular kind is to act on the principles that would be chosen if this nature were the decisive determining element. Of course, the choice of the parties in the original position is subject to the restrictions of that situation. But when we knowingly act on the principles of justice in the ordinary course of events, we deliberately assume the limitations of the original position. One reason for doing this, for persons who can do so and want to, is to give expression to one's nature.

The principles of justice are also categorical imperatives in Kant's sense. For by a categorical imperative Kant understands a principle of conduct that applies to a person in virtue of his nature as a free and equal rational being. The validity of the principle does not presuppose that one has a particular desire or aim. Whereas a hypothetical imperative by contrast does assume this: it directs us to take certain steps as effective means to achieve a specific end. Whether the desire is for a particular thing, or whether it is for something more general, such as certain kinds of agreeable feelings or pleasures, the corresponding imperative is hypothetical. Its applicability depends upon one's having an aim which one need not have as a condition of being a rational human individual. The argument for the two principles of justice does not assume that the parties have particular ends, but only that they desire certain primary goods. These are things that it is rational to want whatever else one wants. Thus given human nature, wanting them is part of being rational; and while each is presumed to have some conception of the good, nothing is known about his final ends. The preference for primary goods is derived, then, from only the most general assumptions about rationality and the conditions of human life. To act from the principles of justice is to act from categorical imperatives in the sense that they apply to us whatever in particular our aims are. This simply reflects the fact that no such contingencies appear as premises in their derivation.

We may note also that the motivational assumption of mutual disinterest accords with Kant's notion of autonomy, and gives another reason for this condition. So far this assumption has been used to characterize the circumstances of justice and to provide a clear conception to guide the reasoning of the parties. We have also seen that the concept of benevolence, being a second-order notion, would not work out well. Now we can add that the assumption of mutual disinterest is to allow for freedom in the choice of a system of final ends.[10] Liberty in adopting a conception of the good is limited only by principles that are deduced from a doctrine which imposes no prior constraints on these conceptions. Presuming mutual disinterest in the original position carries out this idea. We postulate that the parties have opposing claims in a suitably general sense. If their ends were restricted in some specific way, this would appear at the outset as an arbitrary restriction on freedom. Moreover, if the parties were conceived as altruists, or as pursuing certain kinds of pleasures, then the principles chosen would apply, as far as the argument would have shown, only to persons whose freedom was restricted to choices compatible with altruism or hedonism. As the argument now runs, the principles of justice cover all persons with rational plans of life, whatever their content, and these principles represent the appropriate restrictions on freedom. Thus it is possible to say that the constraints on conceptions of the good are the result of an interpretation of the contractual situation that puts no prior limitations on what men may desire. There are a variety of reasons, then, for the motivational premise of mutual disinterest. This premise is not only a matter of realism about the circumstances of justice or a way to make the theory manageable. It also connects up with the Kantian idea of autonomy.

There is, however, a difficulty that should be clarified. It is well expressed by Sidgwick.[11] He remarks that nothing in Kant's ethics is more striking than the idea that a man realizes his true self when he acts from the moral law, whereas if he permits his actions to be determined by sensuous desires or contingent aims, he becomes subject to the law of nature. Yet in Sidgwick's opinion this idea comes to naught. It seems to him that on Kant's view the lives of the saint and the scoundrel are equally the outcome of a free choice (on the part of the noumenal self) and equally the subject of causal laws (as a phenomenal self). Kant never explains why the scoundrel does not express in a bad life his characteristic and freely chosen selfhood in the same way that a saint expresses his characteristic and freely chosen selfhood in a good one. Sidgwick's objection is decisive, I think, as long as one assumes, as Kant's exposition may seem to allow, both that the noumenal self can choose any consistent set of principles and that acting from such principles, whatever they are, is sufficient to express one's choice as that of a free and equal rational being. Kant's reply must be that though acting on any consistent set of principles could be the outcome of a decision on the part of the noumenal self, not all such action by the phenomenal self expresses this decision as that of a free and equal rational being. Thus if a person realizes his true self by expressing it in his actions, and if he desires above all else to realize this self, then he will choose to act from principles that manifest his nature as a free and equal rational being. The missing part of the argument concerns the concept of

[10] For this point I am indebted to Charles Fried.

[11] See *The Methods of Ethics*, 7th ed. (London, Macmillan, 1907), Appendix, "The Kantian Conception of Free Will" (reprinted from *Mind*, vol. 13, 1888), pp. 511–516, esp. p. 516.

expression. Kant did not show that acting from the moral law expresses our nature in identifiable ways that acting from contrary principles does not.

This defect is made good, I believe, by the conception of the original position. The essential point is that we need an argument showing which principles, if any, free and equal rational persons would choose and these principles must be applicable in practice. A definite answer to this question is required to meet Sidgwick's objection. My suggestion is that we think of the original position as the point of view from which noumenal selves see the world. The parties qua noumenal selves have complete freedom to choose whatever principles they wish; but they also have a desire to express their nature as rational and equal members of the intelligible realm with precisely this liberty to choose, that is, as beings who can look at the world in this way and express this perspective in their life as members of society. They must decide, then, which principles when consciously followed and acted upon in everyday life will best manifest this freedom in their community, most fully reveal their independence from natural contingencies and social accident. Now if the argument of the contract doctrine is correct, these principles are indeed those defining the moral law, or more exactly, the principles of justice for institutions and individuals. The description of the original position interprets the point of view of noumenal selves, of what it means to be a free and equal rational being. Our nature as such beings is displayed when we act from the principles we would choose when this nature is reflected in the conditions determining the choice. Thus men exhibit their freedom, their independence from the contingencies of nature and society, by acting in ways they would acknowledge in the original position.

Properly understood, then, the desire to act justly derives in part from the desire to express most fully what we are or can be, namely free and equal rational beings with a liberty to choose. It is for this reason, I believe, that Kant speaks of the failure to act on the moral law as giving rise to shame and not to feelings of guilt. And this is appropriate, since for him acting unjustly is acting in a manner that fails to express our nature as a free and equal rational being. Such actions therefore strike at our self-respect, our sense of our own worth, and the experience of this loss is shame. We have acted as though we belonged to a lower order, as though we were a creature whose first principles are decided by natural contingencies. Those who think of Kant's moral doctrine as one of law and guilt badly misunderstand him. Kant's main aim is to deepen and to justify Rousseau's idea that liberty is acting in accordance with a law that we give to ourselves. And this leads not to a morality of austere command but to an ethic of mutual respect and self-esteem.[12]

The original position may be viewed, then, as a procedural interpretation of Kant's conception of autonomy and the categorical imperative. The principles

[12] See B. A. O. Williams, "The Idea of Equality," in *Philosophy, Politics and Society,* Second Series, ed. Peter Laslett and W. G. Runciman (Oxford, Basil Blackwell, 1962), pp. 115f. For confirmation of this interpretation, see Kant's remarks on moral education in *The Critique of Practical Reason,* pt. II. See also Beck, *Commentary on Kant's Critique of Practical Reason,* pp. 233–236.

regulative of the kingdom of ends are those that would be chosen in this position, and the description of this situation enables us to explain the sense in which acting from these principles expresses our nature as free and equal rational persons. No longer are these notions purely transcendent and lacking explicable connections with human conduct, for the procedural conception of the original position allows us to make these ties. It is true that I have departed from Kant's views in several respects. I shall not discuss these matters here; but two points should be noted. The person's choice as a noumenal self I have assumed to be a collective one. The force of the self's being equal is that the principles chosen must be acceptable to other selves. Since all are similarly free and rational, each must have an equal say in adopting the public principles of the ethical commonwealth. This means that as noumenal selves, everyone is to consent to these principles. Unless the scoundrel's principles would be chosen, they cannot express this free choice, however much a single self might be of a mind to opt for them. Later I shall try to define a clear sense in which this unanimous agreement is best expressive of the nature of even a single self. It in no way overrides a person's interests as the collective nature of the choice might seem to imply. But I leave this aside for the present.

Secondly, I have assumed all along that the parties know that they are subject to the conditions of human life. Being in the circumstances of justice, they are situated in the world with other men who likewise face limitations of moderate scarcity and competing claims. Human freedom is to be regulated by principles chosen in the light of these natural restrictions. Thus justice as fairness is a theory of human justice and among its premises are the elementary facts about persons and their place in nature. The freedom of pure intelligences not subject to these constraints, and the freedom of God, is outside the scope of the theory. It might appear that Kant meant his doctrine to apply to all rational beings as such and therefore to God and the angels as well. Men's social situation in the world may seem to have no role in his theory in determining the first principles of justice. I do not believe that Kant held this view, but I cannot discuss this question here. It suffices to say that if I am mistaken, the Kantian interpretation of justice as fairness is less faithful to Kant's intentions than I am presently inclined to suppose.

33

Existentialism Is a Humanism

JEAN-PAUL SARTRE

Jean-Paul Sartre (1905–80) was an influential French intellectual with interests spanning philosophy, literature, and politics. His most important philosophical work is Being and Nothingness. *He also wrote a number of well-received novels and plays, including* Nausea, The Flies, *and* No Exit.

In this selection, Sartre argues that we create our own moral values. As an atheist, he denies that God is the source of moral obligations. (For a different sort of argument for this conclusion, see Plato's Euthyphro, *reading 25.) But, unlike many other moralists, Sartre also denies that moral values exist independently of God. He contends that appealing to such independent values is just a way of evading our own responsibility. In support of this, he argues that no principle can be binding on us unless we choose to adopt it. Furthermore, he contends that traditional moral theories are too vague to provide guidance. For example, before we can apply Kant's principle, "treat persons as ends rather than means" (reading 29), we must decide whether our proposed action will treat anyone as a means. In thus interpreting the principle, we are in effect making the decision. Similarly, when we ask advice, we ourselves decide the issue through our choice of adviser. Neither independent values nor "human nature" can predetermine our choices. Thus, in choosing, we create both our values and ourselves.*

WHAT IS MEANT by the term *existentialism*?

Most people who use the word would be rather embarrassed if they had to explain it, since, now that the word is all the rage, even the work of a musician or painter is being called existentialist. A gossip columnist in *Clartés* signs himself *The Existentialist,* so that by this time the word has been so stretched and has taken on so broad a meaning, that it no longer means anything at all. It seems that for want of an advance-guard doctrine analogous to surrealism, the kind of people who are eager for scandal and flurry turn to this philosophy which in other respects does not at all serve their purposes in this sphere.

Actually, it is the least scandalous, the most austere of doctrines. It is intended strictly for specialists and philosophers. Yet it can be defined easily. What complicates matters is that there are two kinds of existentialist; first, those who are Christian, among whom I would include Jaspers and Gabriel Marcel, both Catholic; and on the other hand the atheistic existentialists, among whom I class Heidegger, and then the French existentialists and myself. What they have in common is that they think that existence precedes essence, or, if you prefer, that subjectivity must be the starting point.

Just what does that mean? Let us consider some object that is manufactured, for example, a book or a paper-cutter: here is an object which has been made by an artisan whose inspiration came from a concept. He referred to the concept of what a paper-cutter is and likewise to a known method of production, which is part of the concept, something which is, by and large, a routine. Thus, the paper-cutter is at once an object produced in a certain way and, on the other hand, one having a specific use; and one can not postulate a man who produces a paper-cutter but does not know what it is used for. Therefore, let us say that, for the paper-cutter, essence—that is, the ensemble of both the production routines and the properties which enable it to be both produced and defined—precedes existence. Thus, the presence of the paper-cutter or book in front of me is determined. Therefore, we have here a technical view of the world whereby it can be said that production precedes existence.

When we conceive God as the Creator, He is generally thought of as a superior sort of artisan. Whatever doctrine we may be considering, whether one like that of Descartes or that of Leibnitz, we always grant that will more or less follows understanding or, at the very least, accompanies it, and that when God creates He knows exactly what He is creating. Thus, the concept of man in the mind of God is comparable to the concept of paper-cutter in the mind of the manufacturer, and, following certain techniques and a conception, God produces man, just as the artisan, following a definition and a technique, makes a paper-cutter. Thus, the individual man is the realization of a certain concept in the divine intelligence.

In the eighteenth century, the atheism of the *philosophes* discarded the idea of God, but not so much for the notion that essence precedes existence. To a certain extent, this idea is found everywhere; we find it in Diderot, in Voltaire, and even in Kant. Man has a human nature; this human nature, which is the concept of the human, is found in all men, which means that each man is a particular example of a universal concept, man. In Kant, the result of this universality is that the wild-man, the natural man, as well as the bourgeois, are circumscribed by the same definition and have the same basic qualities. Thus, here too the essence of man precedes the historical existence that we find in nature.

Atheistic existentialism, which I represent, is more coherent. It states that if God does not exist, there is at least one being in whom existence precedes essence, a being who exists before he can be defined by any concept, and that this being is man, or, as Heidegger says, human reality. What is meant here by saying that existence precedes essence? It means that, first of all, man exists, turns up, appears on the scene, and, only afterwards, defines himself. If man, as the existentialist conceives him, is indefinable, it is because at first he is nothing. Only afterward will he be something, and he himself will have made what he will be. Thus, there is no human nature, since there is no God to conceive it. Not only is man what he conceives himself to be, but he is also only what he wills himself to be after this thrust toward existence.

Man is nothing else but what he makes of himself. Such is the first principle of existentialism. It is also what is called subjectivity, the name we are labeled with when charges are brought against us. But what do we mean by this, if not that man has a greater dignity than a stone or table? For we mean that man first exists, that is, that man first of all is the being who hurls himself toward a future and who is conscious of imagining himself as being in the future. Man is at the start a plan which is aware of itself, rather than a patch of moss, a piece of garbage, or a cauliflower; nothing exists prior to this plan; there is nothing in heaven; man will be what he will have planned to be. Not what he will want to be. Because by the word "will" we generally mean a conscious decision, which is subsequent to what we have already made of ourselves. I may want to belong to a political party, write a book, get married; but all that is only a manifestation of an earlier, more spontaneous choice that is called "will." But if existence really does precede essence, man is responsible for what he is. Thus, existentialism's first move is to make every man aware of what he is and to make the full responsibility of his existence rest on him. And when we say that a man is responsible for himself, we do not only mean that he is responsible for his own individuality, but that he is responsible for all men.

The word subjectivism has two meanings, and our opponents play on the two. Subjectivism means, on the one hand, that an individual chooses and makes himself; and, on the other, that it is impossible for man to transcend human subjectivity. The second of these is the essential meaning of existentialism. When we say that man chooses his own self, we mean that every one of us does likewise; but we also mean by that that in making this choice he also chooses all men. In fact, in creating the man that we want to be, there is not a single one of our acts which does not at the same time create an image of man as we think he ought to be. To choose to be this or that is to affirm at the same time the value of what we choose, because we can never choose evil. We always choose the good, and nothing can be good for us without being good for all.

If, on the other hand, existence precedes essence, and if we grant that we exist and fashion our image at one and the same time, the image is valid for everybody and for our whole age. Thus, our responsibility is much greater than we might have supposed, because it involves all mankind. If I am a workingman and choose to join a Christian trade-union rather than be a communist, and if by being a member I want to show that the best thing for man is resignation, that the kingdom of man is not of this world, I am not only involving my own case—I want to be resigned for everyone. As a result, my action has involved all humanity. To take a more individual matter, if I want to marry, to have children; even if this marriage depends solely on my own circumstances or passion or wish, I am involving all humanity in monogamy and not merely myself. Therefore, I am responsible for myself and for everyone else. I am creating a certain image of man of my own choosing. In choosing myself, I choose man.

This helps us understand what the actual content is of such rather grandiloquent words as anguish, forlornness, despair. As you will see, it's all quite simple.

First, what is meant by anguish? The existentialists say at once that man is anguish. What that means is this: the man who involves himself and who realizes that he is not only the person he chooses to be, but also a lawmaker who is, at the same time, choosing all mankind as well as himself, can not help escape the feeling of his total and deep responsibility. Of course, there are many people who are not anxious; but we claim that they are hiding their anxiety, that they are fleeing from it. Certainly, many people believe that when they do something, they themselves are the only ones involved, and when someone says to them, "What if everyone acted that way?" they shrug their shoulders and answer, "Everyone doesn't act that way." But really, one should always ask himself, "What would happen if everybody looked at things that way?" There is no escaping this disturbing thought except by a kind of double-dealing. A man who lies and makes excuses for himself by saying "not everybody does that," is someone with an uneasy conscience, because the act of lying implies that a universal value is conferred upon the lie.

Anguish is evident even when it conceals itself. This is the anguish that Kierkegaard called the anguish of Abraham. You know the story: an angel has ordered Abraham to sacrifice his son; if it really were an angel who has come and said, "You are Abraham, you shall sacrifice your son," everything would be all right. But everyone might first wonder, "Is it really an angel, and am I really Abraham? What proof do I have?"

There was a madwoman who had hallucinations; someone used to speak to her on the telephone and give her orders. Her doctor asked her, "Who is it who talks to you?" She answered, "He says it's God." What proof did she really have that it was God? If an angel comes to me, what proof is there that it's an angel? And if I hear voices, what proof is there that they come from heaven and not from hell, or from the subconscious, or a pathological condition? What proves that they are addressed to me? What proof is there that I have been appointed to impose my choice and my conception of man on humanity? I'll never find any proof or sign to convince me of that. If a voice addresses me, it is always for me to decide that this is the angel's voice; if I consider that such an act is a good one, it is I who will choose to say that it is good rather than bad.

Now, I'm not being singled out as an Abraham, and yet at every moment I'm obliged to perform exemplary acts. For every man, everything happens as if all mankind had its eyes fixed on him and were guiding itself by what he does. And every man ought to say to himself, "Am I really the kind of man who has the right to act in such a way that humanity might guide itself by my actions?" And if he does not say that to himself, he is masking his anguish.

There is no question here of the kind of anguish which would lead to quietism, to inaction. It is a matter of a simple sort of anguish that anybody who has had responsibilities is familiar with. For example, when a military officer takes the responsibility for an attack and sends a certain number of men to death, he chooses to do so, and in the main he alone makes the choice.

476

Doubtless, orders come from above, but they are too broad; he interprets them, and on this interpretation depend the lives of ten or fourteen or twenty men. In making a decision he can not help having a certain anguish. All leaders know this anguish. That doesn't keep them from acting; on the contrary, it is the very condition of their action. For it implies that they envisage a number of possibilities, and when they choose one, they realize that it has value only because it is chosen. We shall see that this kind of anguish, which is the kind that existentialism describes, is explained, in addition, by a direct responsibility to the other men whom it involves. It is not a curtain separating us from action, but is part of action itself.

When we speak of forlornness, a term Heidegger was fond of, we mean only that God does not exist and that we have to face all the consequences of this. The existentialist is strongly opposed to a certain kind of secular ethics which would like to abolish God with the least possible expense. About 1880, some French teachers tried to set up a secular ethics which went something like this: God is a useless and costly hypothesis; we are discarding it; but, meanwhile, in order for there to be an ethics, a society, a civilization, it is essential that certain values be taken seriously and that they be considered as having an *a priori* existence. It must be obligatory, *a priori,* to be honest, not to lie, not to beat your wife, to have children, etc., etc. So we're going to try a little device which will make it possible to show that values exist all the same, inscribed in a heaven of ideas, though otherwise God does not exist. In other words— and this, I believe, is the tendency of everything called reformism in France— nothing will be changed if God does not exist. We shall find ourselves with the same norms of honesty, progress, and humanism, and we shall have made of God an outdated hypothesis which will peacefully die off by itself.

The existentialist, on the contrary, thinks it very distressing that God does not exist, because all possibility of finding values in a heaven of ideas disappears along with Him; there can no longer be an *a priori* Good, since there is no infinite and perfect consciousness to think it. Nowhere it is written that the Good exists, that we must be honest, that we must not lie; because the fact is we are on a plane where there are only men. Dostoevsky said, "If God didn't exist, everything would be possible." That is the very starting point of existentialism. Indeed, everything is permissible if God does not exist, and as a result man is forlorn, because neither within him nor without does he find anything to cling to. He can't start making excuses for himself.

If existence really does precede essence, there is no explaining things away by reference to a fixed and given human nature. In other words, there is no determinism, man is free, man is freedom. On the other hand, if God does not exist, we find no values or commands to turn to which legitimize our conduct. So, in the bright realm of values, we have no excuse behind us, nor justification before us. We are alone, with no excuses.

That is the idea I shall try to convey when I say that man is condemned to be free. Condemned, because he did not create himself, yet, in other respects is free; because, once thrown into the world, he is responsible for everything he does. The existentialist does not believe in the power of passion. He will never agree that a sweeping passion is a ravaging torrent which fatally leads a man to certain acts and is therefore an excuse. He thinks that man is responsible for his passion.

The existentialist does not think that man is going to help himself by finding in the world some omen by which to orient himself. Because he thinks that man will interpret the omen to suit himself. Therefore, he thinks that man, with no support and no aid, is condemned every moment to invent man. Ponge, in a very fine article, has said, "Man is the future of man." That's exactly it. But if it is taken to mean that this future is recorded in heaven, that God sees it, then it is false, because it would really no longer be a future. If it is taken to mean that, whatever a man may be, there is a future to be forged, a virgin future before him, then this remark is sound. But then we are forlorn.

To give you an example which will enable you to understand forlornness better, I shall cite the case of one of my students who came to see me under the following circumstances: his father was on bad terms with his mother, and, moreover, was inclined to be a collaborationist; his older brother had been killed in the German offensive of 1940, and the young man, with somewhat immature but generous feelings, wanted to avenge him. His mother lived alone with him, very much upset by the half-treason of her husband and the death of her older son; the boy was her only consolation.

The boy was faced with the choice of leaving England and joining the Free French Forces—that is, leaving his mother behind—or remaining with his mother and helping her to carry on. He was fully aware that the woman lived only for him and that his going-off—and perhaps his death—would plunge her into despair. He was also aware that every act that he did for his mother's sake was a sure thing, in the sense that it was helping her to carry on, whereas every effort he made toward going off and fighting was an uncertain move which might run aground and prove completely useless; for example, on his way to England he might, while passing through Spain, be detained indefinitely in a Spanish camp; he might reach England or Algiers and be stuck in an office at a desk job. As a result, he was faced with two very different kinds of action: one, concrete, immediate, but concerning only one individual; the other concerned an incomparably vaster group, a national collectivity, but for that very reason was dubious, and might be interrupted en route. And, at the same time, he was wavering between two kinds of ethics. On the one hand, an ethics of sympathy, of personal devotion; on the other hand, a broader ethics, but one whose efficacy was more dubious. He had to choose between the two.

Who could help him choose? Christian doctrine? No. Christian doctrine says, "Be charitable, love your neighbor, take the more rugged path, etc., etc." But which is the more rugged path? Whom should he love as a brother? The fighting man or his mother? Which does the greater good, the vague act of fighting in a group, or the concrete one of helping a particular human being to go on living? Who can decide *a priori*? Nobody. No book of ethics can tell him. The Kantian ethics says, "Never treat any person as a means, but as an end." Very well, if I stay with my mother, I'll treat her as an end and not as a means; but by virtue of this very fact, I'm running the risk of treating the people around me who are fighting, as means; and, conversely, if I go to join those who are fighting, I'll be treating them as an end, and, by doing that, I run the risk of treating my mother as a means.

If values are vague, and if they are always too broad for the concrete and specific case that we are considering, the only thing left for us is to trust our instincts. That's what this young man tried to do; and when I saw him, he said, "In the end, feeling is what counts. I ought to choose whichever pushes me in one direction. If I feel that I love my mother enough to sacrifice everything else for her—my desire for vengeance, for action, for adventure—then I'll stay with her. If, on the contrary, I feel that my love for my mother isn't enough, I'll leave."

But how is the value of a feeling determined? What gives his feeling for his mother value? Precisely the fact that he remained with her. I may say that I like so-and-so well enough to sacrifice a certain amount of money for him, but I may say so only if I've done it. I may say "I love my mother well enough to remain with her" if I have remained with her. The only way to determine the value of this affection is, precisely, to perform an act which confirms and defines it. But, since I require this affection to justify my act, I find myself caught in a vicious circle.

On the other hand, Gide has well said that a mock feeling and a true feeling are almost indistinguishable; to decide that I love my mother and will remain with her, or to remain with her by putting on an act, amount somewhat to the same thing. In other words, the feeling is formed by the acts one performs; so, I can not refer to it in order to act upon it. Which means that I can neither seek within myself the true condition which will impel me to act, nor apply to a system of ethics for concepts which will permit me to act. You will say, "At least, he did go to a teacher for advice." But if you seek advice from a priest, for example, you have chosen this priest; you already knew, more or less, just about what advice he was going to give you. In other words, choosing your adviser is involving yourself. The proof of this is that if you are a Christian, you will say, "Consult a priest." But some priests are collaborating, some are just marking time, some are resisting. Which to choose? If the young man chooses a priest who is resisting or collaborating, he has already decided on the kind of advice he's going to get. Therefore, in coming to see me he knew the answer I was going to give him, and I had only one answer to give: "You're free, choose, that is, invent." No general ethics can show you what is to be done; there are no omens in the world. The Catholics will reply, "But there are." Granted—but, in any case, I myself choose the meaning they have.

When I was a prisoner, I knew a rather remarkable young man who was a Jesuit. He had entered the Jesuit order in the following way: he had had a number of very bad breaks; in childhood, his father died, leaving him in poverty, and he was a scholarship student at a religious institution where he was constantly made to feel that he was being kept out of charity; then, he failed to get any of the honors and distinctions that children like; later on, at about eighteen, he bungled a love affair; finally at twenty-two, he failed in military training, a childish enough matter, but it was the last straw.

This young fellow might well have felt that he had botched everything. It was a sign of something, but of what? He might have taken refuge in bitterness or despair. But he very wisely looked upon all this as a sign that he was not made for secular triumphs, and that only the triumphs of religion, holiness, and faith were open to him. He saw the hand of God in all this, and so he entered the order. Who can help seeing that he alone decided what the sign meant?

Some other interpretation might have been drawn from this series of set-backs; for example, that he might have done better to turn carpenter or revolutionist. Therefore, he is fully responsible for the interpretation. Forlornness implies that we ourselves choose our being. Forlornness and anguish go together.

As for despair, the term has a very simple meaning. It means that we shall confine ourselves to reckoning only with what depends upon our will, or on the ensemble of probabilities which make our action possible. When we want something, we always have to reckon with probabilities. I may be counting on the arrival of a friend. The friend is coming by rail or street-car; this supposes that the train will arrive on schedule, or that the street-car will not jump the track. I am left in the realm of possibility; but possibilities are to be reckoned with only to the point where my action comports with the ensemble of these possibilities, and no further. The moment the possibilities I am considering are not rigorously involved by my action, I ought to disengage myself from them, because no God, no scheme, can adapt the world and its possibilities to my will. When Descartes said, "Conquer yourself rather than the world," he meant essentially the same thing.

The Marxists to whom I have spoken reply, "You can rely on the support of others in your action, which obviously has certain limits because you're not going to live forever. That means: rely on both what others are doing elsewhere to help you, in China, in Russia, and what they will do later on, after your death, to carry on the action and lead it to its fulfillment, which will be the revolution. You even *have* to rely upon that, otherwise you're immoral." I reply at once that I will always rely on fellow-fighters insofar as these comrades are involved with me in a common struggle, in the unity of a party or a group in which I can more or less make my weight felt; that is, one whose ranks I am in as a fighter and whose movements I am aware of at every moment. In such a situation, relying on the unity and will of the party is exactly like counting on the fact that the train will arrive on time or that the car won't jump the track. But, given that man is free and that there is no human nature for me to depend on, I can not count on men whom I do not know by relying on human goodness or man's concern for the good of society. I don't know what will become of the Russian revolution; I may make an example of it to the extent that at the present time it is apparent that the proletariat plays a part in Russia that it plays in no other nation. But I can't swear that this will inevitably lead to a triumph of the proletariat. I've got to limit myself to what I see.

Given that men are free and that tomorrow they will freely decide what man will be, I can not be sure that, after my death, fellow-fighters will carry on my work to bring it to its maximum perfection. Tomorrow, after my death, some men may decide to set up Fascism, and the others may be cowardly and muddled enough to let them do it. Fascism will then be the human reality, so much the worse for us.

Actually, things will be as man will have decided they are to be. Does that mean that I should abandon myself to quietism? No. First, I should involve myself; then, act on the old saw, "Nothing ventured, nothing gained." Nor does it mean that I shouldn't belong to a party, but rather that I shall have no illusions and shall do what I can. For example, suppose I ask myself, "Will socialization, as such, ever come about?" I know nothing about it. All I know is that I'm going to do everything in my power to bring it about. Beyond that, I can't count on anything. Quietism is the attitude of people who say, "Let others do what I can't do." The doctrine I am presenting is the very opposite of quietism, since it declares, "There is no reality except in action." Moreover, it goes further, since it adds, "Man is nothing else than his plan; he exists only to the extent that he fulfills himself; he is therefore nothing else than the ensemble of his acts, nothing else than his life."

According to this, we can understand why our doctrine horrifies certain people. Because often the only way they can bear their wretchedness is to think, "Circumstances have been against me. What I've been and done doesn't show my true worth. To be sure, I've had no great love, no great friendship, but that's because I haven't met a man or woman who was worthy. The books I've written haven't been very good because I haven't had the proper leisure. I haven't had children to devote myself to because I didn't find a man with whom I could have spent my life. So there remains within me, unused and quite viable, a host of propensities, inclinations, possibilities, that one wouldn't guess from the mere series of things I've done."

Now, for the existentialist there is really no love other than one which manifests itself in a person's being in love. There is no genius other than one which is expressed in works of art; the genius of Proust is the sum of Proust's works; the genius of Racine is his series of tragedies. Outside of that, there is nothing. Why say that Racine could have written another tragedy, when he didn't write it? A man is involved in life, leaves his impress on it, and outside of that there is nothing. To be sure, this may seem a harsh thought to someone whose life hasn't been a success. But, on the other hand, it prompts people to understand that reality alone is what counts, that dreams, expectations, and hopes warrant no more than to define a man as a disappointed dream, as miscarried hopes, as vain expectations. In other words, to define him negatively and not positively. However, when we say, "You are nothing else than your life," that does not imply that the artist will be judged solely on the basis of his works of art; a thousand other things will contribute toward summing him up. What we mean is that a man is nothing else than a series of undertakings, that he is the sum, the organization, the ensemble of the relationships which make up these undertakings.

V

VALUE AND
VALUES

THE TWO MAIN CONCEPTS of ethics are the right and the good. We ask ourselves what is right when we try to discover which acts we ought to perform. We ask ourselves what is good when we try to discover which things, or states of affairs, have value in themselves. Because many theories of right hold that our duties at least include the production of good consequences, these questions must be connected. But we cannot promote the good without knowing what it is, so the two questions remain distinct.

What *is* good in itself? Because value seems importantly connected to desire, and because everyone desires pleasure and the absence of pain, one obvious answer is "pleasant sensation." The view that pleasure, and only pleasure, has intrinsic value is defended by Jeremy Bentham in reading 34. According to Bentham, when we say that something other than pleasure is good, we mean only that it will *cause* pleasure. Even virtuous motives, which Kant took to have moral worth in themselves, are good only for this reason. But there is a difficulty here. As Robert Nozick points out in reading 35, anyone to whom pleasure alone mattered would have good reason to be connected to an "experience machine," that is, a machine that would cause him to enjoy his favorite pleasures while he floated in a tank with electrodes attached to his brain. But most of us would refuse to be attached to such a machine. Thus, what appears to matter to us is not the passive experience of pleasure, but rather the activities that *bring* us pleasure. This suggests that pleasure, in itself, is unlikely to be the only good.

Whether or not pleasure is the only good thing, a pleasurable life is obviously better than a painful one. Thus, it is clearly important to know which sorts of lives are most apt to be pleasurable. In reading 36, Epicurus argues that we maximize our pleasures not by living luxuriously, but by cultivating simple tastes that are easily satisfied. As he points out, "plain savours bring us pleasure equal to a luxurious diet, when all the pain due to want is removed; and bread and water produce the highest pleasure when one who needs them puts them to his lips." By training ourselves not to want what is expensive or hard to acquire, we lose nothing in the quality of our sensations, and gain security from frustration and disappointment.

If pleasure is not the only good thing, what other things are good? In the next two selections, we encounter two very different proposals. In reading 37, W. D. Ross disputes Bentham's claim that virtue is good only because virtuous acts tend to produce pleasure. Ross argues that even when this effect is set aside, it remains better for people to be virtuous than to be vicious. Similarly, there is intrinsic value in knowledge, and in the matching of happiness to virtue. In saying these things, Ross claims to be capturing our ordinary beliefs. But Friedrich Nietzsche disdains those beliefs. In reading 38, Nietzsche argues that the prevailing values merely codify the fears of the weak and mediocre. In his view, the highest value attaches to the emergence of a new type of person—one who is powerful, joyous, unafraid, and without the crippling inhibitions of "civilization."

Although Ross and Nietzsche hold radically different positions, they seem to agree that what has value does not depend on what people actually want. But others have sought to preserve a link between desire and the good. At the very least, what a person wants seems importantly connected to what is good *for him*. Because desires may be foolish or dangerous, there is no straightforward equivalence between what is good for someone and that person getting what he wants. But John Rawls suggests a more subtle way of connecting a person's good to his desires. In reading 39, Rawls argues that an outcome is part of someone's good if it is called for, or otherwise implicated in, the overall plan that would bring that person the highest probability of satisfying the greatest number of his most deeply held desires. This is the life plan that the agent would choose if he were fully rational and had full knowledge of the consequences of all the acts he might perform. Because different people have different combinations of desires, their "rational life plans," and therefore what is good for them, will also differ. However, as Rawls argues elsewhere (see reading 32), there are some things that it is rational to want whatever else one wants. Our range of opportunities is always increased by liberty, wealth, income, and the social bases of self-respect. Hence, these "primary goods" are part of *everyone's* good.

Is Rawls right to equate a person's good with what is called for by his rational life plan? Aspects of this suggestion are explored in the next two selections. In reading 40, Michael J. Sandel points out that for Rawls, the rational agent's "choice" of a life-plan would be based on desires that were not themselves chosen, but were simply given. The function of rationality would be merely to discover how to maximize the satisfaction of these already-given desires. Thus, there would be no rational basis upon which to criticize the desires themselves. In particular, there would be no way to argue that some desires are more central or essential to a person than others. Nor, as Vinit Haksar argues in reading 41, is it clearly coherent to speak of the choice that would be made by someone with full knowledge of all the alternatives. Where someone must choose between two different ways of life, having full knowledge of one may itself require certain tastes and preferences that preclude full knowledge of the other. For example, to understand the attractions of the worldly life, one may need tastes and preferences that would prevent one from understanding the appeal of life in a monastery. The opposite may hold as well. Given this "Dilemma of the Elusiveness of the Good," Haksar argues that we cannot substitute appeals to what well-informed people would choose for judgments about what is good for them.

Suppose, however, that something *was* part of a person's good. Would this mean that the person's having it was good in any broader sense? In particular, does one person's having a reason to want and pursue something mean that others also have a reason to want and pursue his having it? In reading 42, Thomas Nagel argues that the answer is sometimes, but not always, yes. In his view, some reasons are "agent-neutral" in that they apply even to persons who are not themselves affected or involved. For example, if A is in pain, then not only A, but also B, has a reason to want, and try to bring about, A's relief from pain. Thus, Nagel implies that we can sometimes make the transition from "X is good for A" to "X is good in itself." Although Nagel's main example involves relief from pain, he does not believe either that people want only pleasure and the absence of pain or that all agent-neutral reasons are reasons to promote what someone desires. Rather, he holds that such reasons can take a variety of forms.

Thus far, we have concentrated on views that specify what is good in abstraction from historical context. But in reading 43, Alisdair MacIntyre argues that such abstraction is impossible. In his view, we cannot make sense of our lives without regarding them as ongoing stories or narratives. This means that we must understand the traditions and social institutions in which those stories are embedded. As MacIntyre notes, even a simple activity like gardening "may be part of the history both of the cycle of household activity and of [one's] marriage, two histories which have happened to intersect." Because our lives are intelligible only as narratives, what is good for someone is what will bring his life—his story—to a satisfactory conclusion. And because each person is a citizen, son or daughter, member of a profession, and occupant of other roles, each person's "moral starting point" is a variety of "debts, inheritances, rightful expectations, and obligations" derived from those roles. To appreciate how these factors shape our good, we must overcome various dangers, temptations, and distractions. Hence, the virtues that allow us to do this—virtues that themselves vary with historical context—are also part of our good.

34

Pleasure as the Good

JEREMY BENTHAM

Jeremy Bentham (1748–1832) was a British utilitarian and legal reformer. His writings include An Introduction to the Principles of Morals and Legislation, *from which this selection is taken.*

In the selection, Bentham argues that pleasure and the absence of pain are the only things that ultimately have value. If anything else is said to be good, it is only because it promotes pleasure or prevents pain. Even agents' motives are good (or bad) only for these reasons. Other things being equal, a pleasure of longer duration or greater intensity is better than a pleasure that is shorter or less intense.

Bentham's view of the good has the virtue of simplicity. If correct, it provides a common denominator to compare the value of different states and the acts that produce them. But the view also raises questions. Do all pleasant experiences really involve a single kind of feeling? Even if they do, is the capacity to produce that feeling really all that is valuable about friendship, knowledge, and human excellence? Are even malice, envy, and cruelty good insofar as they produce the feeling? If the answers to these questions are negative, then Bentham's view will require modification.

Value of a Lot of Pleasure or Pain, How to Be Measured

I. Pleasures then, and the avoidance of pains, are the *ends* which the legislator has in view: it behoves him therefore to understand their *value*. Pleasures and pains are the *instruments* he has to work with: it behoves him therefore to understand their force, which is again, in other words, their value.

II. To a person considered *by himself*, the value of a pleasure or pain considered *by itself*, will be greater or less, according to the four following circumstances.[1]

---

[1] These circumstances have since been denominated *elements* or *dimensions* of *value* in a pleasure or a pain.

Not along after the publication of the first edition, the following memoriter verses were framed, in the view of lodging more effectually, in the memory, these points, on which the whole fabric of morals and legislation may be seen to rest:

> *Intense, long, certain, speedy, fruitful, pure*—
> Such marks in *pleasures* and in *pains* endure.
> Such pleasures seek, if *private* be thy end:
> If it be *public*, wide let them *extend*.
> Such *pains* avoid, whichever be thy view:
> If pains *must* come, let them *extend* to few.

1. Its *intensity*.
2. Its *duration*.

3. Its *certainty* or *uncertainty*.
4. Its *propinquity* or *remoteness*.

III. These are the circumstances which are to be considered in estimating a pleasure or a pain considered each of them by itself. But when the value of any pleasure or pain is considered for the purpose of estimating the tendency of any *act* by which it is produced, there are two other circumstances to be taken into the account; these are,

5. Its *fecundity*, or the chance it has of being followed by sensations of the *same* kind: that is, pleasures, if it be a pleasure: pains, if it be a pain.

6. Its *purity*, or the chance it has of *not* being followed by sensations of the *opposite* kind: that is, pains, if it be a pleasure: pleasures, if it be a pain.

These two last, however, are in strictness scarcely to be deemed properties of the pleasures or the pain itself; they are not, therefore, in strictness to be taken into the account of the value of that pleasure or that pain. They are in strictness to be deemed properties only of the act, or other event, by which such pleasure or pain has been produced; and accordingly are only to be taken into the account of the tendency of such act or such event.

IV. To a *number* of persons, with reference to each of whom the value of a pleasure or a pain is considered, it will be greater or less, according to seven circumstances: to wit, the six preceding ones; *viz.*

1. Its *intensity*.
2. Its *duration*.
3. Its *certainty* or *uncertainty*.

4. Its *propinquity* or *remoteness*.
5. Its *fecundity*.
6. Its *purity*.

And one other; to wit:

7. Its *extent;* that is, the number of persons to whom it *extends;* or (in other words) who are affected by it.

V. To take an exact account then of the general tendency of any act, by which the interests of a community are affected, proceed as follows. Begin with any one person of those whose interests seem most immediately to be affected by it: and take an account,

1. Of the value of each distinguishable *pleasure* which appears to be produced by it in the *first* instance.

2. Of the value of each *pain* which appears to be produced by it in the *first* instance.

3. Of the value of each pleasure which appears to be produced by it *after* the first. This constitutes the *fecundity* of the first *pleasure* and the *impurity* of the first *pain*.

4. Of the value of each *pain* which appears to be produced by it after the first. This constitutes the *fecundity* of the first *pain*, and the *impurity* of the first pleasure.

5. Sum up all the values of all the *pleasures* on the one side, and those of all the pains on the other. The balance, if it be on the side of pleasure, will give the *good* tendency of the act upon the whole, with respect to the interests

of that *individual* person; if on the side of pain, the *bad* tendency of it upon the whole.

6. Take an account of the *number* of persons whose interests appear to be concerned; and repeat the above process with respect to each. *Sum up* the numbers expressive of the degrees of *good* tendency, which the act has, with respect to each individual, in regard to whom the tendency of it is *good* upon the whole: do this again with respect to each individual, in regard to whom the tendency of it is *bad* upon the whole. Take the *balance;* which, if on the side of *pleasure,* will give the general *good tendency* of the act, with respect to the total number of community of individuals concerned; if on the side of pain the general *evil tendency,* with respect to the same community.

VI. It is not to be expected that this process should be strictly pursued previously to every moral judgment, or to every legislative or judicial operation. It may, however, be always kept in view: and as near as the process actually pursued on these occasions approaches to it, so near will such process approach to the character of an exact one.

VII. The same process is alike applicable to pleasure and pain in whatever shape they appear: and by whatever denomination they are distinguished: to pleasure, whether it be called *good* (which is properly the cause or instrument of pleasure), or *profit* (which is distant pleasure, or the cause or instrument of distant pleasure), or *convenience,* or *advantage, benefit, emolument, happiness,* and so forth: to pain, whether it be called *evil* (which corresponds to *good*), or *mischief,* or *inconvenience,* or *disadvantage,* or *loss,* or *unhappiness,* and so forth.

VIII. Nor is this a novel and unwarranted, any more than it is a useless theory. In all this there is nothing but what the practice of mankind, wheresoever they have a clear view of their own interest, is perfectly comformable to. An article of property, an estate in land, for instance, is valuable, on what account? On account of the pleasures of all kinds which it enables a man to produce, and what comes to the same thing, the pains of all kinds which it enables him to avert. But the value of such an article of property is universally understood to rise or fall according to the length or shortness of the time which a man has in it: the certainty or uncertainty of its coming into possession: and the nearness or remoteness of the time at which, if at all, it is to come into possession. As to the *intensity* of the pleasures which a man may derive from it, this is never thought of, because it depends upon the use which each particular person may come to make of it; which cannot be estimated till the particular pleasures he may come to derive from it, or the particular pains he may come to exclude by means of it, are brought to view. For the same reason, neither does he think of the *fecundity* or *purity* of those pleasures.

. . .

No Motives Either Constantly Good, or Constantly Bad

IX. In all this chain of motives, the principal or original link seems to be the last internal motive in prospect; it is to this that all the other motives in prospect owe their materiality; and the immediately acting motive its existence. This motive in prospect, we see, is always some pleasure, or some pain; some pleasure, which the act in question is expected to be a means of continuing or producing: some pain which it is expected to be a means of discontinuing or preventing. A motive is substantially nothing more than pleasure or pain, operating in a certain manner.

X. Now, pleasure is in *itself* a good: nay, even setting aside immunity from pain, the only good: pain is in itself an evil; and, indeed, without exception, the only evil; or else the words good and evil have no meaning. And this is alike true of every sort of pain, and of every sort of pleasure. It follows, therefore, immediately and incontestably, that *there is no such thing as any sort of motive that is in itself a bad one.*[2]

XI. It is common, however, to speak of actions as proceeding from *good* or *bad* motives: in which case the motives meant are such as are internal. The expression is far from being an accurate one; and as it is apt to occur in the consideration of almost every kind of offence, it will be requisite to settle the precise meaning of it, and observe how far it quadrates with the truth of things.

XII. With respect to goodness and badness, as it is with everything else that is not itself either pain or pleasure, so is it with motives. If they are good or bad, it is only on account of their effects: good, on account of their tendency to produce pleasure, or avert pain: bad, on account of their tendency to produce pain, or avert pleasure. Now the case is, that from one and the same motive, and from every kind of motive, may proceed actions that are good, others that are bad, and others that are indifferent. This we shall proceed to show with respect to all the different kinds of motives, as determined by the various kinds of pleasures and pains.

. . .

[2] Let a man's motive be ill-will; call it even malice, envy, cruelty; it is still a kind of pleasure that is his motive: the pleasure he takes at the thought of the pain which he sees, or expects to see, his adversary undergo. Now even this wretched pleasure, taken by itself, is good: it may be faint; it may be short: it must at any rate be impure: yet while it lasts, and before any bad consequences arrive, it is good as any other that is not more intense. See ch. iv. (Value).

35

The Experience Machine

ROBERT NOZICK

Robert Nozick (b. 1938) is Professor of Philosophy at Harvard University. His most recent book is Philosophical Explanations. *This selection is from his earlier book,* Anarchy, State and Utopia.

Here Nozick argues against the view that pleasure, and only pleasure, matters to us. If that were correct, we would have overwhelming reason to want to be hooked up to a machine that would cause all our favorite sensations. But Nozick argues that few would allow themselves to be connected to such an "experience machine." Their reasons for refusing, he speculates, would include desires to act in certain ways, desires to be certain sorts of people, and desires to be in contact with reality. But if so, then these things must matter to people for reasons that are independent of the pleasure they bring.

Although Nozick does not say so, his conclusion may have an important bearing on the view defended by Bentham in reading 34. According to Bentham, pleasure is the only good. But in the eyes of many, the fact that something matters to people is part of what makes it good. If so, and if pleasure is not all that matters to people, then pleasure is not the only good.

THERE ARE ALSO substantial puzzles when we ask what matters other than how *people's* experiences feel "from the inside." Suppose there were an experience machine that would give you any experience you desired. Super-duper neuropsychologists could stimulate your brain so that you would think and feel you were writing a great novel, or making a friend, or reading an interesting book. All the time you would be floating in a tank, with electrodes attached to your brain. Should you plug into this machine for life, prepro-gramming your life's experiences? If you are worried about missing out on desirable experiences, we can suppose that business enterprises have researched thoroughly the lives of many others. You can pick and choose from their large library or smorgasbord of such experiences, selecting your life's experiences for, say, the next two years. After two years have passed, you will have ten minutes or ten hours out of the tank, to select the experiences of your *next* two years. Of course, while in the tank you won't know that you're there; you'll think it's all actually happening. Others can also plug in to have the experiences they want, so there's no need to stay unplugged to serve them. (Ignore problems such as who will service the machines if everyone plugs in.) Would you plug in? *What else can matter to us, other than how our lives feel from the inside?* Nor should you refrain because of the few moments of distress between the moment you've decided and the moment you're plugged. What's a few moments of distress compared to a lifetime of bliss (if that's what you choose), and why feel any distress at all if your decision *is* the best one?

What does matter to us in addition to our experiences? First, we want to *do* certain things, and not just have the experience of doing them. In the case of certain experiences, it is only because first we want to do the actions that we want the experiences of doing them or thinking we've done them. (But *why* do we want to do the activities rather than merely to experience them?) A second reason for not plugging in is that we want to *be* a certain way, to be a certain sort of person. Someone floating in a tank is an indeterminate blob. There is no answer to the question of what a person is like who has long been in the tank. Is he courageous, kind, intelligent, witty, loving? It's not merely that it's difficult to tell; there's no way he is. Plugging into the machine is a kind of suicide. It will seem to some, trapped by a picture, that nothing about what we are like can matter except as it gets reflected in our experiences. But should it be surprising that what *we are* is important to us? Why should we be concerned only with how our time is filled, but not with what we are?

Thirdly, plugging into an experience machine limits us to a man-made reality, to a world no deeper or more important than that which people can construct. There is no *actual* contact with any deeper reality, though the experience of it can be simulated. Many persons desire to leave themselves open to such contact and to a plumbing of deeper significance.[1] This clarifies the intensity of the conflict over psychoactive drugs, which some view as mere local experience machines, and others view as avenues to a deeper reality; what some view as equivalent to surrender to the experience machine, others view as following one of the reasons *not* to surrender!

We learn that something matters to us in addition to experience by imagining an experience machine and then realizing that we would not use it. We can continue to imagine a sequence of machines each designed to fill lacks suggested for the earlier machines. For example, since the experience machine doesn't meet our desire to *be* a certain way, imagine a transformation machine which transforms us into whatever sort of person we'd like to be (compatible with our staying us). Surely one would not use the transformation machine to become

---

[1] Traditional religious views differ on the *point* of contact with a transcendent reality. Some say that contact yields eternal bliss or Nirvana, but they have not distinguished this sufficiently from merely a *very* long run on the experience machine. Others think it is intrinsically desirable to do the will of a higher being which created us all, though presumably no one would think this if we discovered we had been created as an object of amusement by some superpowerful child from another galaxy or dimension. Still others imagine an eventual merging with a higher reality, leaving unclear its desirability, or where that merging leaves *us*.

as one would wish, and thereupon plug into the experience machine![2] So something matters in addition to one's experiences *and* what one is like. Nor is the reason merely that one's experiences are unconnected with what one is like. For the experience machine might be limited to provide only experiences possible to the sort of person plugged in. Is it that we want to make a difference in the world? Consider then the result machine, which produces in the world any result you would produce and injects your vector input into any joint activity. We shall not pursue here the fascinating details of these or other machines. What is most disturbing about them is their living of our lives for us. Is it misguided to search for *particular* additional functions beyond the competence of machines to do for us? Perhaps what we desire is to live (an active verb) ourselves, in contact with reality. (And this, machines cannot do *for* us.) Without elaborating on the implications of this, which I believe connect surprisingly with issues about free will and causal accounts of knowledge, we need merely note the intricacy of the question of what matters *for people* other than their experiences. Until one finds a satisfactory answer, and determines that this answer does not *also* apply to animals, one cannot reasonably claim that only the felt experiences of animals limit what we may do to them.

[2] Some wouldn't use the transformation machine at all; it seems like *cheating*. But the one-time use of the transformation machine would not remove all challenges; there would still be obstacles for the new us to overcome, a new plateau from which to strive even higher. And is this plateau any the less earned or deserved than that provided by genetic endowment and early childhood environment? But if the transformation machine could be used indefinitely often, so that we could accomplish anything by pushing a button to transform ourselves into someone who could do it easily, there would remain no limits we *need* to strain against or try to transcend. Would there be anything left *to do?* Do some theological views place God outside of time because an omniscient omnipotent being couldn't fill up his days?

36

The Good Life

EPICURUS

Epicurus (341–271 B.C.) was a Greek thinker and teacher. He spent much of his life in Athens. Though few of his writings survive, the selections that follow contain the main elements of his views.

Like Bentham (reading 34), Epicurus identified the good with whatever is pleasant. In addition, he held specific views about which lives are pleasant. Such lives, he argued, are not spent at voluptuous or extravagant pursuits. These pursuits bring pain and disappointment, and so should be avoided. In their place, we should be content with simpler pleasures, notably including those of friendship. Since acquiring and maintaining these pleasures requires neither power nor wealth, they are within the grasp of everyone.

Although Epicurus's main concern was personal happiness, his views on this had implications about other topics. Of these, two warrant special mention. First, Epicurus regarded happiness as closely bound up with justice. In his view, to live a life that is truly pleasant, we must be honorable and just as well as prudent. And, second, since he viewed only sensations as good or bad, Epicurus believed that death is not to be feared. Since the dead lack sensation, their condition is not an evil.

Letter to Menoeceus

LET NO ONE when young delay to study philosophy, nor when he is old grow weary of his study. For no one can come too early or too late to secure the health of his soul. And the man who says that the age for philosophy has either not yet come or has gone by is like the man who says that the age for happiness is not yet come to him, or has passed away. Wherefore both when young and old a man must study philosophy, that as he grows old he may be young in blessings through the grateful recollection of what has been, and that in youth he may be old as well, since he will know no fear of what is to come. We must then meditate on the things that make our happiness, seeing that when that is with us we have all, but when it is absent we do all to win it.

The things which I used unceasingly to commend to you, these do and practise, considering them to be the first principles of the good life. First of all believe that god is a being immortal and blessed, even as the common idea of a god is engraved on men's minds, and do not assign to him anything alien to his immortality or illsuited to his blessedness: but believe about him everything that can uphold his blessedness and immortality. For gods there are, since the knowledge of them is by clear vision. But they are not such as the many believe them to be: for indeed they do not consistently represent them as they believe them to be. And the impious man is not he who denies the gods of the many, but he who attaches to the gods the beliefs of the many. For the statements of the many about the gods are not conceptions derived from sensation, but false suppositions, according to which the greatest misfortunes befall the wicked and the greatest blessings the good by the gift of the gods. For men being accustomed always to their own virtues welcome those like themselves, but regard all that is not of their nature as alien.

Become accustomed to the belief that death is nothing to us. For all good and evil consists in sensation, but death is deprivation of sensation. And therefore a right understanding that death is nothing to us makes the mortality of life enjoyable, not because it adds to it an infinite span of time, but because it takes away the craving for immortality. For there is nothing terrible in life for the man who has truly comprehended that there is nothing terrible in not living. So that the man speaks but idly who says that he fears death not because it will be painful when it comes, but because it is painful in anticipation. For that which gives no trouble when it comes, is but an empty pain in anticipation. So death, the most terrifying of ills, is nothing to us, since so long as we exist, death is not with us; but when death comes, then we do not exist. It does not then concern either the living or the dead, since for the former it is not, and the latter are no more.

But the many at one moment shun death as the greatest of evils, at another yearn for it as a respite from the evils in life. But the wise man neither seeks to escape life nor fears the cessation of life, for neither does life offend him nor does the absence of life seem to be any evil. And just as with food he does not seek simply the larger share and nothing else, but rather the most pleasant, so he seeks to enjoy not the longest period of time, but the most pleasant.

And he who counsels the young man to live well, but the old man to make a good end, is foolish, not merely because of the desirability of life, but also because it is the same training which teaches to live well and to die well. Yet much worse still is the man who says it is good not to be born, but

'once born make haste to pass the gates of Death'.

For if he says this from conviction why does he not pass away out of life? For it is open to him to do so, if he had firmly made up his mind to this. But if he speaks in jest, his words are idle among men who cannot receive them.

We must then bear in mind that the future is neither ours, nor yet wholly not ours, so that we may not altogether expect it as sure to come, nor abandon hope of it, as if it will certainly not come.

We must consider that of desires some are natural, others vain, and of the natural some are necessary and others merely natural; and of the necessary some are necessary for happiness, others for the repose of the body, and others for very life. The right understanding of these facts enables us to refer all choice and avoidance to the health of the body and the soul's freedom from disturbance, since this is the aim of the life of blessedness. For it is to obtain this end that we always act, namely, to avoid pain and fear. And when this is once secured for us, all the tempest of the soul is dispersed, since the living creature has not to wander as though in search of something that is missing, and to look for some other thing by which he can fulfil the good of the soul and the good of the body. For it is then that we have need of pleasure, when we feel pain owing to the absence of pleasure; but when we do not feel pain, we no longer need pleasure. And for this cause we call pleasure the beginning and end of the blessed life. For we recognize pleasure as the first good innate in us, and from pleasure we begin every act of choice and avoidance, and to pleasure we return again, using the feeling as the standard by which we judge every good.

And since pleasure is the first good and natural to us, for this very reason we do not choose every pleasure, but sometimes we pass over many pleasures, when greater discomfort accrues to us as the result of them: and similarly we think many pains better than pleasures, since a greater pleasure comes to us when we have endured pains for a long time. Every pleasure then because of its natural kinship to us is good, yet not every pleasure is to be chosen: even as every pain also is an evil, yet not all are always of a nature to be avoided. Yet by a scale of comparison and by the consideration of advantages and disadvantages we must form our judgement on all these matters. For the good on certain occasions we treat as bad, and conversely the bad as good.

And again independence of desire we think a great good—not that we may at all times enjoy but a few things, but that, if we do not possess many, we may enjoy the few in the genuine persuasion that those have the sweetest pleasure in luxury who least need it, and that all that is natural is easy to be obtained, but that which is superfluous is hard. And so plain savours bring us pleasure equal to a luxurious diet, when all the pain due to want is removed; and bread and water produce the highest pleasure, when one who needs them puts them to his lips. To grow accustomed therefore to simple and not luxurious diet gives us health to the full, and makes a man alert for the needful employments of life, and when after long intervals we approach luxuries, disposes us better towards them, and fits us to be fearless of fortune.

When, therefore, we maintain that pleasure is the end, we do not mean the pleasures of profligates and those that consist in sensuality, as is supposed by some who are either ignorant or disagree with us or do not understand, but freedom from pain in the body and from trouble in the mind. For it is not continuous drinkings and revellings, nor the satisfaction of lusts, nor the enjoyment of fish and other luxuries of the wealthy table, which produce a pleasant life, but sober reasoning, searching out the motives for all choice and avoidance, and banishing mere opinions, to which are due the greatest disturbance of the spirit.

Of all this the beginning and the greatest good is prudence. Wherefore prudence is a more precious thing even than philosophy: far from prudence are sprung all the other virtues, and it teaches us that it is not possible to live pleasantly without living prudently and honourably and justly, nor, again, to live a life of prudence, honour, and justice without living pleasantly. For the virtues are by nature bound up with the pleasant life, and the pleasant life is inseparable from them. For indeed who, think you, is a better man than he who holds reverent opinions concerning the gods, and is at all times free from fear of death, and has reasoned out the end ordained by nature? He understands that the limit of good things is easy to fulfil and easy to attain, whereas the course of ills is either short in time or slight in pain: he laughs at destiny, whom some have introduced as the mistress of all things. He thinks that with us lies the chief power in determining events, some of which happen by necessity and some by chance, and some are within our control; for while necessity cannot be called to account, he sees that chance is inconstant, but that which is in our control is subject to no master, and to it are naturally attached praise and blame. For, indeed, it were better to follow the myths about the gods than to become a slave to the destiny of the natural philosophers: for the former suggests a hope of placating the gods by worship, whereas the latter involves a necessity which knows no placation. As to chance, he does not regard it as a god as most men do (for in a god's acts there is no disorder), nor as an uncertain cause of all things: for he does not believe that good and evil are given by chance to man for the framing of a blessed life, but that opportunities for great good and great evil are afforded by it. He therefore thinks it better to be unfortunate in reasonable action than to prosper in unreason. For it is better in a man's actions that what is well chosen should fail, rather than that what is ill chosen should be successful owing to chance.

Meditate therefore on these things and things akin to them night and day by yourself, and with a companion like to yourself, and never shall you be disturbed waking or asleep, but you shall live like a god among men. For a man who lives among immortal blessings is not like to a mortal being.

Principal Doctrines

I. The blessed and immortal nature knows no trouble itself nor causes trouble to any other, so that it is never constrained by anger or favour. For all such things exist only in the weak.

II. Death is nothing to us: for that which is dissolved is without sensation; and that which lacks sensation is nothing to us.

III. The limit of quantity in pleasures is the removal of all that is painful. Wherever pleasure is present, as long as it is there, there is neither pain of body nor of mind, nor of both at once.

IV. Pain does not last continuously in the flesh, but the acutest pain is there for a very short time, and even that which just exceeds the pleasure in the flesh does not continue for many days at once. But chronic illnesses permit a predominance of pleasure over pain in the flesh.

V. It is not possible to live pleasantly without living prudently and honourably and justly, nor again to live a life of prudence, honour, and justice without living pleasantly. And the man who does not possess the pleasant life, is not living prudently and honourably and justly, and the man who does not possess the virtuous life, cannot possibly live pleasantly.

VI. To secure protection from men anything is a natural good, by which you may be able to attain this end.

VII. Some men wished to become famous and conspicuous, thinking that they would thus win for themselves safety from other men. Wherefore if the life of such men is safe, they have obtained the good which nature craves; but if it is not safe, they do not possess that for which they strove at first by the instinct of nature.

VIII. No pleasure is a bad thing in itself: but the means which produce some pleasures bring with them disturbances many times greater than the pleasures.

IX. If every pleasure could be intensified so that it lasted and influenced the whole organism or the most essential parts of our nature, pleasures would never differ from one another.

X. If the things that produce the pleasures of profligates could dispel the fears of the mind about the phenomena of the sky and death and its pains, and also teach the limits of desires and of pains, we should never have cause to blame them: for they would be filling themselves full with pleasures from every source and never have pain of body or mind, which is the evil of life.

XI. If we were not troubled by our suspicions of the phenomena of the sky and about death, fearing that it concerns us, and also by our failure to grasp the limits of pains and desires, we should have no need of natural science.

XII. A man cannot dispel his fear about the most important matters if he does not know what is the nature of the universe but suspects the truth of some mythical story. So that without natural science it is not possible to attain our pleasures unalloyed.

XIII. There is no profit in securing protection in relation to men, if things above and things beneath the earth and indeed all in the boundless universe remain matters of suspicion.

XIV. The most unalloyed source of protection from men, which is secured to some extent by a certain force of expulsion, is in fact the immunity which results from a quiet life and the retirement from the world.

XV. The wealth demanded by nature is both limited and easily procured; that demanded by idle imaginings stretches on to infinity.

XVI. In but few things chance hinders a wise man, but the greatest and most important matters reason has ordained and throughout the whole period of life does and will ordain.

XVII. The just man is most free from trouble, the unjust most full of trouble.

XVIII. The pleasure in the flesh is not increased, when once the pain due to want is removed, but is only varied: and the limit as regards pleasure in the mind is begotten by the reasoned understanding of these very pleasures and of the emotions akin to them, which used to cause the greatest fear to the mind.

XIX. Infinite time contains no greater pleasure than limited time, if one measures by reason the limits of pleasure.

XX. The flesh perceives the limits of pleasure as unlimited and unlimited time is required to supply it. But the mind, having attained a reasoned under-standing of the ultimate good of the flesh and its limits and having dissipated the fears concerning the time to come, supplies us with the complete life, and we have no further need of infinite time: but neither does the mind shun pleasure, nor, when circumstances begin to bring about the departure from life, does it approach its end as though it fell short in any way of the best life.

XXI. He who has learned the limits of life knows that that which removes the pain due to want and makes the whole of life complete is easy to obtain; so that there is no need of actions which involve competition.

XXII. We must consider both the real purpose and all the evidence of direct perception, to which we always refer the conclusions of opinion; otherwise, all will be full of doubt and confusion.

XXIII. If you fight against all sensations, you will have no standard by which to judge even those of them which you say are false.

XXIV. If you reject any single sensation and fail to distinguish between the conclusion of opinion as to the appearance awaiting confirmation and that which is actually given by the sensation or feeling, or each intuitive apprehension of the mind, you will confound all other sensations as well with the same groundless opinion, so that you will reject every standard of judgement. And if among the mental images created by your opinion you affirm both that which awaits confirmation and that which does not, you will not escape error, since you will have preserved the whole cause of doubt in every judgement between what is right and what is wrong.

XXV. If on each occasion instead of referring your actions to the end of nature, you turn to some other nearer standard when you are making a choice or an avoidance, your actions will not be consistent with your principles.

XXVI. Of desires, all that do not lead to a sense of pain, if they are not satisfied, are not necessary, but involve a craving which is easily dispelled, when the object is hard to procure or they seem likely to produce harm.

XXVII. Of all the things which wisdom acquires to produce the blessedness of the complete life, far the greatest is the possession of friendship.

XXVIII. The same conviction which has given us confidence that there is nothing terrible that lasts for ever or even for long, has also seen the protection of friendship most fully completed in the limited evils of this life.

XXIX. Among desires some are natural and necessary, some natural but not necessary, and others neither natural nor necessary, but due to idle imagination.

XXX. Wherever in the case of desires which are physical, but do not lead to a sense of pain, if they are not fulfilled, the effort is intense, such pleasures are due to idle imagination, and it is not owing to their own nature that they fail to be dispelled, but owing to the empty imaginings of the man.

XXXI. The justice which arises from nature is a pledge of mutual advantage to restrain men from harming one another and save them from being harmed.

XXXII. For all living things which have not been able to make compacts not to harm one another or be harmed, nothing ever is either just or unjust; and likewise too for all tribes of men which have been unable or unwilling to make compacts not to harm or be harmed.

XXXIII. Justice never is anything in itself, but in the dealings of men with one another in any place whatever and at any time it is a kind of compact not to harm or be harmed.

XXXIV. Injustice is not an evil in itself, but only in consequence of the fear which attaches to the apprehension of being unable to escape those appointed to punish such actions.

XXXV. It is not possible for one who acts in secret contravention of the terms of the compact not to harm or be harmed, to be confident that he will escape detection, even if at present he escapes a thousand times. For up to the time of death it cannot be certain that he will indeed escape.

XXXVI. In its general aspect justice is the same for all, for it is a kind of mutual advantage in the dealings of men with one another: but with reference to the individual peculiarities of a country or any other circumstances the same thing does not turn out to be just for all.

XXXVII. Among actions which are sanctioned as just by law, that which is proved on examination to be of advantage in the requirements of men's dealings with one another, has the guarantee of justice, whether it is the same for all or not. But if a man makes a law and it does not turn out to lead to advantage in men's dealings with each other, then it no longer has the essential nature of justice. And even if the advantage in the matter of justice shifts from one side to the other, but for a while accords with the general concept, it is none the less just for that period in the eyes of those who do not confound themselves with empty sounds but look to the actual facts.

XXXVIII. Where, provided the circumstances have not been altered, actions which were considered just, have been shown not to accord with the general concept in actual practice, then they are not just. But where, when circumstances have changed, the same actions which were sanctioned as just no longer lead to advantage, there they were just at the time when they were of advantage for the dealings of fellow-citizens with one another; but subsequently they are no longer just, when no longer of advantage.

XXXIX. The man who has best ordered the element of disquiet arising from external circumstances has made those things that he could akin to himself and the rest at least not alien: but with all to which he could not do even this, he has refrained from mixing, and has expelled from his life all which it was of advantage to treat thus.

XL. As many as possess the power to procure complete immunity from their neighbours, these also live most pleasantly with one another, since they have the most certain pledge of security, and after they have enjoyed the fullest intimacy, they do not lament the previous departure of a dead friend, as though he were to be pitied.

37

What Things Are Good?

W. D. ROSS

For biographical information about W. D. Ross, see reading 10.

In reading 31, Ross argues that we have a variety of moral duties. Here he argues that a variety of things are intrinsically good. Among the objects of value, he includes virtue, pleasure, the matching of pleasure to virtue, and knowledge. To show that each item belongs on the list, he compares imaginary states of the world that differ only by that item's presence or absence. For example, he imagines two states that differ only in quantity of pleasure. Because the state containing the greater amount of pleasure seems better, Ross concludes that pleasure is intrinsically good.

If so, then how can the pleasures of the vicious be bad? To accommodate this, Ross must complicate his theory. Instead of saying that all pleasures are good, he says that the presence of pleasure always creates a presumption *of goodness. In some cases, this presumption is outweighed by other aspects of the situation. In this respect, goodness resembles* prima facie *rightness, which provides a reason for acting that is sometimes outweighed by stronger contrary reasons.*

OUR NEXT STEP is to inquire what kinds of thing are intrinsically good. (I) The first thing for which I would claim that it is intrinsically good is virtuous disposition and action, i.e. action, or disposition to act, from any one of certain motives, of which at all events the most notable are the desire to do one's duty, the desire to bring into being something that is good, and the desire to give pleasure or save pain to others. It seems clear that we regard all such actions and dispositions as having value in themselves apart from any consequence. And if any one is inclined to doubt this and to think that, say, pleasure alone is intrinsically good, it seems to me enough to ask the question whether, of two states of the universe holding equal amounts of pleasure, we should really think no better of one in which the actions and dispositions of all the persons in it were thoroughly virtuous than of one in which they were highly vicious. To this there can be only one answer. Most hedonists would shrink from giving the plainly false answer which their theory requires, and would take refuge in saying that the question rests on a false abstraction. Since virtue, as they conceive it, is a disposition to do just the acts which will produce most pleasure, a universe full of virtuous persons would be bound, they might say, to contain more pleasure than a universe full of vicious persons. To this two answers may be made. (a) Much pleasure, and much pain, do not spring from virtuous or vicious actions at all but from the operation of natural laws. Thus even if a universe filled with virtuous persons were bound to contain more of the pleasure and less of the pain that springs from human action than a universe filled with vicious persons would, that inequality of pleasantness might easily be supposed to be precisely counteracted by, for instance, a much greater incidence of disease. The two states of affairs would then, on balance, be equally pleasant; would they be equally good? And (b) even if we could not imagine any circumstances in which two states of the universe equal in pleasantness but unequal in virtue could exist, the supposition is a legitimate one, since it is only intended to bring before us in a vivid way what is really self-evident, that virtue is good apart from its consequences.

(2) It seems at first sight equally clear that pleasure is good in itself. Some will perhaps be helped to realize this if they make the corresponding supposition to that we have just made; if they suppose two states of the universe including equal amounts of virtue but the one including also widespread and intense pleasure and the other widespread and intense pain. Here too it might be objected that the supposition is an impossible one, since virtue always tends to promote general pleasure, and vice to promote general misery. But this objection may be answered just as we have answered the corresponding objection above.

Apart from this, however, there are two ways in which even the most austere moralists and the most anti-hedonistic philosophers are apt to betray the conviction that pleasure is good in itself. (a) One is the attitude which they, like all other normal human beings, take towards kindness and towards cruelty. If the desire to give pleasure to others is approved, and the desire to inflict pain on others condemned, this seems to imply the conviction that pleasure is good and pain bad. Some may think, no doubt, that the mere thought that a certain state of affairs would be *painful* for another person is enough to account for our conviction that the desire to produce it is bad. But I am inclined to think that there is involved the further thought that a state of affairs in virtue of being painful is *prima facie* (i.e. where other considerations do not enter into the case) one that a rational spectator would not approve, i.e. is *bad*; and that similarly our attitude towards kindness involves the thought that pleasure is good. (b) The other is the insistence, which we find in the most austere moralists as in other people, on the conception of merit. If virtue deserves to be rewarded by happiness (whether or not vice also deserves to be rewarded by unhappiness), this seems at first sight to imply that happiness and unhappiness are not in themselves things indifferent, but are good and bad respectively.

Kant's view on this question is not as clear as might be wished. He points out that the Latin *bonum* covers two notions, distinguished in German as *das Gute* (the good) and *das Wohl* (well-being, i.e. pleasure or happiness); and he speaks of 'good' as being properly applied only to actions, i.e. he treats 'good' as equivalent to 'morally good', and by implication denies that pleasure (even deserved pleasure) is good. It might seem then that when he speaks of the union of virtue with the happiness it deserves as the *bonum consummatum* he is not thinking of deserved happiness as good but only as *das Wohl*, a source of satisfaction to the person who has it. But if this exhausted his meaning, he would have no right to speak of virtue, as he repeatedly does, as *das oberste Gut*; he should call it simply *das Gute*, and happiness *das Wohl*. Further, he describes the union of virtue with happiness not merely as 'the object of the desires of rational finite beings', but adds that it approves itself 'even in the judgement of an impartial reason' as 'the whole and perfect good', rather than virtue alone. And he adds that 'happiness, while it is pleasant to the possessor of it, is not of itself absolutely and in all respects good, but always presupposes morally right behaviour as its condition'; which implies that *when* that condition is fulfilled, happiness *is* good. All this seems to point to the conclusion that in the end he had to recognize that while virtue alone is morally good, deserved happiness also is not merely a source of satisfaction to its possessor, but objectively good.

But reflection on the conception of merit does not support the view that pleasure is always good in itself and pain always bad in itself. For while this conception implies the conviction that pleasure when deserved is good, and pain when undeserved bad, it also suggests strongly that pleasure when undeserved is bad and pain when deserved good.

There is also another set of facts which casts doubt on the view that pleasure is always good and pain always bad. We have a decided conviction that there are bad pleasures and (though this is less obvious) that there are good pains. We think that the pleasure taken either by the agent or by a spectator in, for instance, a lustful or cruel action is bad; and we think it a good thing that people should be pained rather than pleased by contemplating vice or misery.

Thus the view that pleasure is always good and pain always bad, while it seems to be strongly supported by some of our convictions, seems to be equally strongly opposed by others. The difficulty can, I think, be removed by ceasing to speak simply of pleasure and pain as good or bad, and by asking more carefully what it is that we mean. Consideration of the question is aided if we adopt the view (tentatively adopted already) that what is good or bad is always something properly expressed by a that-clause, i.e. an objective, or as I should prefer to call it, a *fact*. If we look at the matter thus, I think we can agree that the fact that a sentient being is in a state of pleasure is always in itself good, and the fact that a sentient being is in a state of pain always in itself bad, when this fact is not an element in a more complex fact having some other characteristic relevant to goodness or badness. And where considerations of desert or of moral good or evil do not enter, i.e. in the case of animals, the fact that a sentient being is feeling pleasure or pain is the whole fact (or the fact sufficiently described to enable us to judge of its goodness or badness), and we need not hesitate to say that the pleasure of animals is always good, and the pain of animals always bad, in itself and apart from its consequences. But when a moral being is feeling a pleasure or pain that is deserved or undeserved, or a pleasure or pain that implies a good or a bad disposition, the total fact is quite inadequately described if we say 'a sentient being is feeling pleasure, or pain'. The total fact may be that 'a sentient and moral being is feeling a pleasure that is undeserved, or that is the realization of a vicious disposition', and though the fact included in this, that 'a sentient being is feeling pleasure' would be good if it stood alone, that creates only a presumption that the total fact is good, and a presumption that is outweighed by the other element in the total fact.

Pleasure seems, indeed, to have a property analogous to that which we have previously recognized under the name of conditional or *prima facie* rightness. An act of promise-keeping has the property, not necessarily of being right but of being something that is right if the act has no other morally significant characteristic (such as that of causing much pain to another person). And similarly a state of pleasure has the property, not necessarily of being good, but of being something that is good if the state has no other characteristic that prevents it from being good. The two characteristics that may interfere with its being good are (a) that of being contrary to desert, and (b) that of being a state which is the realization of a bad disposition. Thus the pleasures of which we can say without doubt that they are good are (i) the pleasures of non-moral beings (animals), (ii) the pleasures of moral beings that are deserved and are either realizations of good moral dispositions or realizations of neutral capacities (such as the pleasures of the senses).

In so far as the goodness or badness of a particular pleasure depends on its being the realization of a virtuous or vicious disposition, this has been allowed for by our recognition of virtue as a thing good in itself. But the mere recognition of virtue as a thing good in itself, and of pleasure as a thing *prima facie* good in itself, does not do justice to the conception of merit. If we compare two imaginary states of the universe, alike in the total amounts of virtue and vice and of pleasure and pain present in the two, but in one of which the virtuous were all happy and the vicious miserable, while in the other the virtuous were miserable and the vicious happy, very few people would hesitate to say that the first was a much better state of the universe than the second. It would seem then that, besides virtue and pleasure, we must recognize (3), as a third independent good, the apportionment of pleasure and pain to the virtuous and the vicious respectively. And it is on the recognition of this as a separate good that the recognition of the duty of justice, in distinction from fidelity to promises on the one hand and from beneficence on the other, rests.

(4) It seems clear that knowledge, and in a less degree what we may for the present call 'right opinion', are states of mind good in themselves. Here too we may, if we please, help ourselves to realize the fact by supposing two states of the universe equal in respect of virtue and of pleasure and of the allocation of pleasure to the virtuous, but such that the persons in the one had a far greater understanding of the nature and laws of the universe than those in the other. Can any one doubt that the first would be a better state of the universe?

From one point of view it seems doubtful whether knowledge and right opinion, no matter what it is of or about, should be considered good. Knowledge of mere matters of fact (say of the number of stories in a building), without knowledge of their relation to other facts, might seem to be worthless; it certainly seems to be worth much less than the knowledge of general principles, or of facts as depending on general principles—what we might call insight or understanding as opposed to mere knowledge. But on reflection it seems clear that even about matters of fact right opinion is in itself a better state of mind to be in than wrong, and knowledge than right opinion.

There is another objection which may naturally be made to the view that knowledge is as such good. There are many pieces of knowledge which we in fact think it well for people *not* to have; e.g. we may think it a bad thing for a sick man to know how ill he is, or for a vicious man to know how he may most conveniently indulge his vicious tendencies. But it seems that in such cases it is not the knowledge but the consequences in the way of pain or of vicious action that we think bad.

It might perhaps be objected that knowledge is not a better state than right opinion, but merely a source of greater satisfaction to its possessor. It no doubt is a source of greater satisfaction. Curiosity is the desire to *know*, and is never really satisfied by mere opinion. Yet there are two facts which seem to show that this is not the whole truth. (*a*) While opinion recognized to be such is never thoroughly satisfactory to its possessor, there is another state of mind which is not knowledge—which may even be mistaken—yet which through lack of reflection is not distinguished from knowledge by its possessor, the state of mind which Professor Cook Wilson has called 'that of being under the impression that so-and-so is the case'.[1] Such a state of mind may be as great a source of satisfaction to its possessor as knowledge, yet we should all think it to be an inferior state of mind to knowledge. This surely points to a recognition by us that knowledge has a worth other than that of being a source of satisfaction to its possessor. (*b*) Wrong opinion, so long as its wrongness is not discovered, may be as great a source of satisfaction as right. Yet we should agree that it is an inferior state of mind, because it is to a less extent founded on knowledge and is itself a less close approximation to knowledge; which again seems to point to our recognizing knowledge as something good in itself.

Four things, then, seem to be intrinsically good—virtue, pleasure, the allocation of pleasure to the virtuous, and knowledge (and in a less degree right opinion). And I am unable to discover anything that is intrinsically good, which is not either one of these or a combination of two or more of them. And while this list of goods has been arrived at on its own merits, by reflection on what we really think to be good, it perhaps derives some support from the fact that it harmonizes with a widely accepted classification of the elements in the life of the soul. It is usual to enumerate these as cognition, feeling, and conation. Now knowledge is the ideal state of the mind, and right opinion an approximation to the ideal, on the cognitive or intellectual side; pleasure is its ideal state on the side of feeling; and virtue is its ideal state on the side of conation; while the allocation of happiness to virtue is a good which we recognize when we reflect on the ideal relation between the conative side and the side of feeling. It might of course be objected that there are or may be intrinsic goods that are

---

[1] *Statement and Inference*, i. 113.

not states of mind or relations between states of mind at all, but in this suggestion I can find no plausibility. Contemplate any imaginary universe from which you suppose mind entirely absent, and you will fail to find anything in it that you can call good in itself. That is not to say, of course, that the existence of a material universe may not be a necessary condition for the existence of many things that are good in themselves. Our knowledge and our true opinions are to a large extent about the material world, and to that extent could not exist unless it existed. Our pleasures are to a large extent derived from material objects. Virtue owes many of its opportunities to the existence of material conditions of good and material hindrances to good. But the value of material things appears to be purely instrumental, not intrinsic.

Of the three elements virtue, knowledge, and pleasure are compounded all the complex states of mind that we think good in themselves. Aesthetic enjoyment, for example, seems to be a blend of pleasure with insight into the nature of the object that inspires it. Mutual love seems to be a blend of virtuous disposition of two minds towards each other, with the knowledge which each has of the character and disposition of the other, and with the pleasure which arises from such disposition and knowledge. And a similar analysis may probably be applied to all other complex goods.

38

Beyond Morality

FRIEDRICH NIETZSCHE

The dark and cryptic writings of German philosopher Friedrich Nietzsche (1844–1900) have had a strong impact on twentieth-century intellectual movements. Nietzsche's many books include The Birth of Tragedy, Beyond Good and Evil, Thus Spake Zarathustra, *and* The Gay Science. *These works contain important discussions of aesthetics and epistemology as well as moral philosophy.*

Unlike most philosophers, Nietzsche does not present his views in the form of extended arguments. Rather, he tends to write in aphorisms—terse and often witty pronouncements. This selection brings together some of his typically provocative reflections on ethics. In it, he contends that the traditional demands of morality grow out of civilization's need to suppress our more primal impulses. When our moral standards call for benevolence and self-sacrifice, they do not reflect any authoritative requirements. Instead, they represent only the desire of the weak to protect themselves from the strong. This is especially true of the requirement proposed by the British utilitarians—to produce the greatest happiness for the greatest number. (For discussion see readings 26 and 34.) If these claims do not seem obvious, Nietzsche believes it is only because we have forgotten how morality developed.

If traditional values represent only the fears of the timid, then what, if anything, should replace them? According to Nietzsche, what is required is a "revaluation of values." He anticipates the development of a new kind of person—an "overman"—who disdains the familiar values of happiness, justice, and pity. Powerful in will and spirit, this "overman" will create new values by giving new expression to ancient instincts. In so doing, he will exemplify what is best about humanity.

From *Human, All Too Human*

38

HOW BENEFICIAL. LET us table the question, then, of whether psychological observation brings more advantage or harm upon men. What is certain is that it is necessary, for science cannot do without it. Science, however, takes as little consideration of final purposes as does nature; just as nature sometimes brings about the most useful things without having wanted to, so too true science, *which is the imitation of nature in concepts,* will sometimes, nay often, further man's benefit and welfare and achieve what is useful—but likewise *without having wanted to.* Whoever feels too wintry in the breeze of this kind of observation has perhaps too little fire in him. Let him look around meanwhile, and he will perceive diseases which require cold poultices, and men who are so "moulded" out of glowing spirit that they have great trouble in finding an atmosphere cold and biting enough for them anywhere. Moreover, as all overly earnest individuals and peoples have a need for frivolity; as others, who are overly excitable and unstable, occasionally need heavy, oppressive burdens for their health's sake; so should not *we*—the *more* intellectual men in an age that is visibly being set aflame more and more—reach for all quenching and cooling means available to remain at least as steady, harmless, and moderate as we now are and thus render service to this age at some future time as a mirror and self-reflection of itself?

39

The fable of intelligible freedom.[1] The history of those feelings, by virtue of which we consider a person responsible, the so-called moral feelings, is divided into the following main phases. At first we call particular acts good or evil without any consideration of their motives, but simply on the basis of their beneficial or harmful consequences. Soon, however, we forget the origin of these terms and imagine that the quality "good" or "evil" is inherent in the actions themselves, without consideration of their consequences; this is the same error language makes when calling the stone itself hard, the tree itself green—that is, we take the effect to be the cause. Then we assign the goodness or evil to the motives, and regard the acts themselves as morally ambiguous. We go even further and cease to give to the particular motive the predicate good or evil, but give it rather to the whole nature of a man; the motive grows out of him as a plant grows out of the earth. So we make man responsible in turn for the effects of his actions, then for his actions, then for his motives and finally for his nature. Ultimately we discover that his nature cannot be responsible either, in that it is itself an inevitable consequence, an outgrowth of the elements and influences of past and present things; that is, man cannot be made responsible for anything, neither for his nature, nor his motives, nor his actions, nor the effects of his actions. And thus we come to understand that the history of moral feelings is the history of an error, an error called "responsibility," which in turn rests on an error called "freedom of the will."

41

The unchangeable character. In the strict sense, it is not true that one's character is unchangeable; rather, this popular tenet[2] means only that during

---

[1] In ancient Greece, Plato's world of ideas—as a model for the sensual world—was referred to as the "intelligible world." "Intelligible freedom" is the pure form of freedom, the idea of freedom. See *The World as Will and Idea*, bk. 4, par. 55.—TRANS.

[2] Cf. Aristotle, *Nichomachean Ethics*, 6.13.1: "The several kinds of character are bestowed by nature," or Heraclitus: "Character is destiny."—TRANS.

a man's short lifetime the motives affecting him cannot normally cut deeply enough to destroy the imprinted writing of many millennia. If a man eighty thousand years old were conceivable, his character would in fact be absolutely variable, so that out of him little by little an abundance of different individuals would develop. The brevity of human life misleads us to many an erroneous assertion about the qualities of man.

42

Morality and the ordering of the good. The accepted hierarchy of the good, based on how a low, higher, or a most high egoism desires that thing or the other, decides today about morality or immorality. To prefer a low good (sensual pleasure, for example) to one esteemed higher (health, for example) is taken for immoral, likewise to prefer comfort to freedom. The hierarchy of the good, however, is not fixed and identical at all times. If someone prefers revenge to justice, he is moral by the standard of an earlier culture, yet by the standard of the present culture he is immoral. "Immoral" then indicates that someone has not felt, or not felt strongly enough, the higher, finer, more spiritual motives which the new culture of the time has brought with it. It indicates a backward nature, but only in degree.

The hierarchy itself is not established or changed from the point of view of morality; nevertheless an action is judged moral or immoral according to the prevailing determination.

45

Double prehistory of good and evil. The concept of good and evil has a double prehistory: namely, first of all, in the soul of the ruling clans and castes. The man who has the power to requite goodness with goodness, evil with evil, and really does practice requital by being grateful and vengeful, is called "good." The man who is unpowerful and cannot requite is taken for bad. As a good man, one belongs to the "good," a community that has a communal feeling, because all the individuals are entwined together by their feeling for requital. As a bad man, one belongs to the "bad," to a mass of abject, powerless men who have no communal feeling. The good men are a caste; the bad men are a multitude, like particles of dust. Good and bad are for a time equivalent to noble and base, master and slave. Conversely, one does not regard the enemy as evil: he can requite. In Homer, both the Trojan and the Greek are good. Not the man who inflicts harm on us, but the man who is contemptible, is bad. In the community of the good, goodness is hereditary; it is impossible for a bad man to grow out of such good soil. Should one of the good men nevertheless do something unworthy of good men, one resorts to excuses; one blames God, for example, saying that he struck the good man with blindness and madness.

Then, in the souls of oppressed, powerless men, every *other* man is taken for hostile, inconsiderate, exploitative, cruel, sly, whether he be noble or base.

509

Evil is their epithet for man, indeed for every possible living being, even, for example, for a god; "human," "divine" mean the same as "devilish," "evil." Signs of goodness, helpfulness, pity are taken anxiously for malice, the prelude to a terrible outcome, bewilderment, and deception, in short, for refined evil. With such a state of mind in the individual, a community can scarcely come about at all—or at most in the crudest form; so that wherever this concept of good and evil predominates, the downfall of individuals, their clans and races, is near at hand.

Our present morality has grown up on the ground of the *ruling* clans and castes.[3]

92

Origin of justice. Justice (fairness) originates among approximately *equal powers,* as Thucydides (in the horrifying conversation between the Athenian and Melian envoys)[4] rightly understood. When there is no clearly recognizable supreme power and a battle would lead to fruitless and mutual injury, one begins to think of reaching an understanding and negotiating the claims on both sides: the initial character of justice is *barter.* Each satisfies the other in that each gets what he values more than the other. Each man gives the other what he wants, to keep henceforth, and receives in turn what which he wishes. Thus, justice is requital and exchange on the assumption of approximately equal positions of strength. For this reason, revenge belongs initially to the realm of justice: it is an exchange. Likewise gratitude.

Justice naturally goes back to the viewpoint of an insightful self-preservation, that is, to the egoism of this consideration: "Why should I uselessly injure myself and perhaps not reach my goal anyway?"

So much about the *origin* of justice. Because men, in line with their intellectual habits, have *forgotten* the original purpose of so-called just, fair actions, and particularly because children have been taught for centuries to admire and imitate such actions, it has gradually come to appear that a just action is a selfless one. The high esteem of these actions rests upon this appearance, an esteem which, like all estimations, is also always in a state of growth: for men strive after, imitate, and reproduce with their own sacrifices that which is highly esteemed, and it grows because its worth is increased by the worth of the effort and exertion made by each individual.

How slight the morality of the world would seem without forgetfulness! A poet could say that God had stationed forgetfulness as a guardian at the door to the temple of human dignity.

[3] Cf. *On the Genealogy of Morals* (1887), first essay.—TRANS.

[4] In Bk. 5, 85–113, Thucydides recounts the surrender of Melos in 416 B.C.—TRANS.

93

The right of the weaker. If one party, a city under siege, for example, submits under certain conditions to a greater power, its reciprocal condition is that this first party can destroy itself, burn the city, and thus make the power suffer a great loss. Thus there is a kind of *equalization,* on the basis of which rights can be established. Preservation is to the enemy's advantage.

Rights exist between slaves and masters to the same extent, exactly insofar as the possession of his slave is profitable and important to the master. The *right* originally extends *as far* as the one *appears* to the other to be valuable, essential, permanent, invincible, and the like. In this regard even the weaker of the two has rights, though they are more modest. Thus the famous dictum: "unusquisque tantum juris habet, quantum potenti valet"[5] (or, more exactly, "quantum potentia valere creditur").[6]

94

The three phases of morality until now. The first sign that an animal has become human is that his behavior is no longer directed to his momentary comfort, but rather to his enduring comfort, that is, when man becomes useful, *expedient:* then for the first time the free rule of reason bursts forth. A still higher state is reached when man acts according to the principle of *honor,* by means of which he finds his place in society, submitting to commonly held feelings; that raises him high above the phase in which he is guided only by personal usefulness. Now he shows—and wants to be shown—respect; that is, he understands his advantage as dependent on his opinion of others and their opinion of him. Finally, at the highest stage of morality *until now,* he acts according to *his* standard of things and men; he himself determines for himself and others what is honorable, what is profitable. He has become the lawgiver of opinions, in accordance with the ever more refined concept of usefulness and honor. Knowledge enables him to prefer what is most useful, that is, general usefulness to personal usefulness, and the respectful recognition of what has common, enduring value to things of momentary value. He lives and acts as a collective-individual.

95

Morality of the mature individual. Until now man has taken the true sign of a moral act to be its impersonal nature; and it has been shown that in the

---

[5] "Each has as much right as his power is worth." Spinoza, *Tractatus Politicus,* vol. 2, par. 8.—TRANS.

[6] "as his power is assessed to be"—TRANS.

beginning all impersonal acts were praised and distinguished in respect to the common good. Might not a significant transformation of these views be at hand, now when we see with ever greater clarity that precisely in the most *personal* respect the common good is also greatest; so that now it is precisely the strictly personal action which corresponds to the current concept of morality (as a common profit)? To make a whole *person* of oneself and keep in mind that person's *greatest good* in everything one does—this takes us further than any pitying impulses and actions for the sake of others. To be sure, we all still suffer from too slight a regard for our own personal needs; it has been poorly developed. Let us admit that our mind has instead been forcibly diverted from it and offered in sacrifice to the state, to science, to the needy, as if it were something bad which had to be sacrificed. Now too we wish to work for our fellow men, but only insofar as we find our own highest advantage in this work; no more, no less. It depends only on what one understands by his *advantage*. The immature, undeveloped, crude individual will also understand it most crudely.

96

Mores and morality. To be moral, correct, ethical means to obey an age-old law or tradition. Whether one submits to it gladly or with difficulty makes no difference; enough that one submits. We call "good" the man who does the moral thing as if by nature, after a long history of inheritance—that is, easily, and gladly, whatever it is (he will, for example, practice revenge when that is considered moral, as in the older Greek culture). He is called good because he is good "for" something. But because, as mores changed, goodwill, pity, and the like were always felt to be "good for" something, useful, it is primarily the man of goodwill, the helpful man, who is called "good." To be evil is to be "not moral" (immoral), to practice bad habits, go against tradition, however reasonable or stupid it may be. To harm one's fellow, however, has been felt primarily as injurious in all moral codes of different times, so that when we hear the word "bad" now, we think particularly of voluntary injury to one's fellow. When men determine between moral and immoral, good and evil, the basic opposition is not "egoism" and "selflessness," but rather adherence to a tradition or law, and release from it. The *origin* of the tradition makes no difference, at least concerning good and evil, or an immanent categorical imperative; but is rather above all for the purpose of maintaining *a community*, a people. Every superstitious custom, originating in a coincidence that is interpreted falsely, forces a tradition that it is moral to follow. To release oneself from it is dangerous, even more injurious for the *community* than for the individual (because the divinity punishes the whole community for sacrilege and violation of its rights, and the individual only as a part of that community). Now, each tradition grows more venerable the farther its origin lies in the past, the more it is forgotten; the respect paid to the tradition accumulates from generation to generation; finally the origin becomes sacred and awakens awe; and thus the morality of piety is in any case much older than that morality which requires selfless acts.

From *Beyond Good and Evil*

186

The moral sentiment in Europe today is as refined, old, diverse, irritable, and subtle, as the "science of morals" that accompanies it is still young, raw, clumsy, and butterfingered—an attractive contrast that occasionally even becomes visible and incarnate in the person of a moralist. Even the term "science of morals" is much too arrogant considering what it designates, and offends *good* taste—which always prefers more modest terms.

One should own up in all strictness to what is still necessary here for a long time to come, to what alone is justified so far: to collect material, to conceptualize and arrange a vast realm of subtle feelings of value and differences of value which are alive, grow, beget, and perish—and perhaps attempts to present vividly some of the more frequent and recurring forms of such living crystallizations—all to prepare a *typology* of morals.

To be sure, so far one has not been so modest. With a stiff seriousness that inspires laughter, all our philosophers demanded something far more exalted, presumptuous, and solemn from themselves as soon as they approached the study of morality: they wanted to supply a *rational foundation* for morality— and every philosopher so far has believed that he has provided such a foundation. Morality itself, however, was accepted as "given." How remote from their clumsy pride was that task which they considered insignificant and left in dust and must—the task of description—although the subtlest fingers and senses can scarcely be subtle enough for it.

Just because our moral philosophers knew the facts of morality only very approximately in arbitrary extracts or in accidental epitomes—for example, as the morality of their environment, their class, their church, the spirit of their time, their climate and part of the world—just because they were poorly informed and not even very curious about different peoples, times, and past ages—they never laid eyes on the real problems of morality; for these emerge only when we compare *many* moralities. In all "science of morals" so far one thing was *lacking,* strange as it may sound: the problem of morality itself; what was lacking was any suspicion that there was something problematic here. What the philosophers called "a rational foundation for morality" and tried to supply was, seen in the right light, merely a scholarly variation of the common *faith* in the prevalent morality; a new means of *expression* for this faith; and thus just another fact within a particular morality; indeed, in the last analysis a kind of denial that this morality might ever be considered problematic—

certainly the very opposite of an examination, analysis, questioning, and vivisection of this very faith.

. . .

198

All these moralities that address themselves to the individual, for the sake of his "happiness," as one says—what are they but counsels for behavior in relation to the degree of *dangerousness* in which the individual lives with himself; recipes against his passions, his good and bad inclinations insofar as they have the will to power and want to play the master; little and great prudences and artifices that exude the nook odor of old nostrums and of the wisdom of old women; all of them baroque and unreasonable in form—because they address themselves to "all," because they generalize where one must not generalize. All of them speak unconditionally, take themselves for unconditional, all of them flavored with more than one grain of salt and tolerable only —at times even seductive—when they begin to smell over-spiced and dangerous, especially "of the other world." All of it is, measured intellectually, worth very little and not by a long shot "science," much less "wisdom," but rather, to say it once more, three times more, prudence, prudence, prudence, mixed with stupidity, stupidity, stupidity—whether it be that indifference and statue coldness against the hot-headed folly of the affects which the Stoics advised and administered; or that laughing-no-more and weeping-no-more of Spinoza, his so naïvely advocated destruction of the affects through their analysis and vivisection; or that tuning down of the affects to a harmless mean according to which they may be satisfied, the Aristotelianism of morals; even morality as enjoyment of the affects in a deliberate thinness and spiritualization by means of the symbolism of art, say, as music, or as love of God and of man for God's sake—for in religion the passions enjoy the rights of citizens again, assuming that—; finally even that accommodating and playful surrender to the affects, as Hafiz and Goethe taught it, that bold dropping of the reins, that spiritual-physical *licentia morum*[7] in the exceptional case of wise old owls and sots for whom it "no longer holds much danger." This, too, for the chapter "Morality as Timidity."

199

Inasmuch as at all times, as long as there have been human beings, there have also been herds of men (clans, communities, tribes, peoples, states, churches) and always a great many people who obeyed, compared with the small number of those commanding—considering, then, that nothing has been exercised and cultivated better and longer among men so far than obedience—it may fairly be assumed that the need for it is now innate in the average man, as a kind of

---

[7] Moral license.—TRANS.

formal conscience that commands: "thou shalt unconditionally do something, unconditionally not do something else," in short, "thou shalt." This need seeks to satisfy itself and to fill its form with some content. According to its strength, impatience, and tension, it seizes upon things as a rude appetite, rather indiscriminately, and accepts whatever is shouted into its ears by someone who issues commands—parents, teachers, laws, class prejudices, public opinions.

The strange limits of human development, the way it hesitates, takes so long, often turns back, and moves in circles, is due to the fact that the herd instinct of obedience is inherited best, and at the expense of the art of commanding. If we imagine this instinct progressing for once to its ultimate excesses, then those who command and are independent would eventually be lacking altogether; or they would secretly suffer from a bad conscience and would find it necessary to deceive themselves before they could command—as if they, too, merely obeyed. This state is actually encountered in Europe today: I call it the moral hypocrisy of those commanding. They know no other way to protect themselves against their bad conscience than to pose as the executors of more ancient or higher commands (of ancestors, the constitution, of right, the laws, or even of God). Or they even borrow herd maxims from the herd's way of thinking, such as "first servants of their people" or "instruments of the common weal."

On the other side, the herd man in Europe today gives himself the appearance of being the only permissible kind of man, and glorifies his attributes, which make him tame, easy to get along with, and useful to the herd, as if they were the truly human virtues: namely, public spirit, benevolence, consideration, industriousness, moderation, modesty, indulgence, and pity. In those cases, however, where one considers leaders and bellwethers indispensable, people today make one attempt after another to add together clever herd men by way of replacing commanders: all parliamentary constitutions, for example, have this origin. Nevertheless, the appearance of one who commands unconditionally strikes these herd-animal Europeans as an immense comfort and salvation from a gradually intolerable pressure, as was last attested in a major way by the effect of Napoleon's appearance. The history of Napoleon's reception is almost the history of the higher happiness attained by this whole century in its most valuable human beings and moments.

201

As long as the utility reigning in moral value judgments is solely the utility of the herd, as long as one considers only the preservation of the community, and immorality is sought exactly and exclusively in what seems dangerous to the survival of the community—there can be no morality of "neighbor love." Supposing that even then there was a constant little exercise of consideration, pity, fairness, mildness, reciprocity of assistance; supposing that even in that state of society all those drives are active that later receive the honorary designation of "virtues" and eventually almost coincide with the concept of "morality"—in that period they do not yet at all belong in the realm of moral valuations; they are still *extra-moral*. An act of pity, for example, was not considered either good or bad, moral or immoral, in the best period of the Romans; and even when it was praised, such praise was perfectly compatible with a kind of disgruntled disdain as soon as it was juxtaposed with an action that served the welfare of the whole, of the *res publica*.[8]

In the last analysis, "love of the neighbor" is always something secondary, partly conventional and arbitrary-illusory in relation to *fear of the neighbor*. After the structure of society is fixed on the whole and seems secure against external dangers, it is this fear of the neighbor that again creates new perspectives of moral valuation. Certain strong and dangerous drives, like an enterprising spirit, foolhardiness, vengefulness, craftiness, rapacity, and the lust to rule, which had so far not merely been honored insofar as they were socially useful—under different names, to be sure, from those chosen here—but had to be trained and cultivated to make them great (because one constantly needed them in view of the dangers to the whole community, against the enemies of the community), are now experienced as doubly dangerous, since the channels to divert them are lacking, and, step upon step, they are branded as immoral and abandoned to slander.

Now the opposite drives and inclinations receive moral honors; step upon step, the herd instinct draws its conclusions. How much or how little is dangerous to the community, dangerous to equality, in an opinion, in a state or affect, in a will, in a talent—that now constitutes the moral perspective: here, too, fear is again the mother of morals.

The highest and strongest drives, when they break out passionately and drive the individual far above the average and the flats of the herd conscience, wreck the self-confidence of the community, its faith in itself, and it is as if its spine snapped. Hence just these drives are branded and slandered most. High and independent spirituality, the will to stand alone, even a powerful reason are experienced as dangers; everything that elevates an individual above the herd and intimidates the neighbor is henceforth called *evil;* and the fair, modest, submissive, conforming mentality, the *mediocrity* of desires attains moral designations and honors. Eventually, under very peaceful conditions, the opportunity and necessity for educating one's feelings to severity and hardness is lacking more and more; and every severity, even in justice, begins to disturb the conscience; any high and hard nobility and self-reliance is almost felt to be an insult and arouses mistrust; the "lamb," even more the "sheep," gains in respect.

There is a point in the history of society when it becomes so pathologically soft and tender that among other things it sides even with those who harm it, criminals, and does this quite seriously and honestly. Punishing somehow seems unfair to it, and it is certain that imagining "punishment" and "being supposed to punish" hurts it, arouses fear in it. "Is it not enough to render him *undangerous?* Why still punish? Punishing itself is terrible." With this question, herd morality, the morality of timidity, draws its ultimate consequence. Supposing

---

[8] Commonwealth.—TRANS.

that one could altogether abolish danger, the reason for fear, this morality would be abolished, too, *eo ipso:* it would no longer be needed, it would no longer *consider itself* necessary.

Whoever examines the conscience of the European today will have to pull the same imperative out of a thousand moral folds and hideouts—the imperative of herd timidity: "we want that some day there should be *nothing any more to be afraid of!*" Some day—throughout Europe, the will and way to this day is now called "progress."

202

Let us immediately say once more what we have already said a hundred times, for today's ears resist such truths—*our* truths. We know well enough how insulting it sounds when anybody counts man, unadorned and without metaphor, among the animals; but it will be charged against us as almost a *guilt* that precisely for the men of "modern ideas" we constantly employ such expressions as "herd," "herd instincts," and so forth. What can be done about it? We cannot do anything else; for here exactly lies our novel insight. We have found that in all major moral judgments Europe is now of one mind, including even the countries dominated by the influence of Europe: plainly, one now *knows* in Europe what Socrates thought he did not know and what that famous old serpent once promised to teach—today one "knows" what is good and evil.

Now it must sound harsh and cannot be heard easily when we keep insisting: that which here believes it knows, that which here glorifies itself with its praises and reproaches, calling itself good, that is the instinct of the herd animal, man, which has scored a breakthrough and attained prevalence and predominance over other instincts—and this development is continuing in accordance with the growing physiological approximation and assimilation of which it is the symptom. *Morality in Europe today is herd animal morality*—in other words, as we understand it, merely *one* type of human morality beside which, before which, and after which many other types, above all *higher* moralities, are, or ought to be, possible. But this morality resists such a "possibility," such an "ought" with all its power: it says stubbornly and inexorably, "I am morality itself, and nothing besides is morality." Indeed, with the help of a religion which indulged and flattered the most sublime herd-animal desires, we have reached the point where we find even in political and social institutions an ever more visible expression of this morality: the *democratic* movement is the heir of the Christian movement.

. . .

203

. . .

Toward *new philosophers;* there is no choice; toward spirits strong and original enough to provide the stimuli for opposite valuations and to revalue and invert "eternal values"; toward forerunners, toward men of the future who in the present tie the knot and constraint that forces the will of millennia upon *new* tracks. To teach man the future of man as his *will*, as dependent on a human will, and to prepare great ventures and over-all attempts of discipline and cultivation by way of putting an end to that gruesome dominion of nonsense and accident that has so far been called "history"—the nonsense of the "greatest number" is merely its ultimate form: at some time new types of philosophers and commanders will be necessary for that, and whatever has existed on earth of concealed, terrible, and benevolent spirits, will look pale and dwarfed by comparison. It is the image of such leaders that *we* envisage: may I say this out loud, you free spirits? The conditions that one would have partly to create and partly to exploit for their genesis; the probable ways and tests that would enable a soul to grow to such a height and force that it would feel the *compulsion* for such tasks; a revaluation of values under whose new pressure and hammer a conscience would be steeled, a heart turned to bronze, in order to endure the weight of such responsibility; on the other hand, the necessity of such leaders, the frightening danger that they might fail to appear or that they might turn out badly or degenerate—these are *our* real worries and gloom—do you know that, you free spirits?—these are the heavy distant thoughts and storms that pass over the sky of *our* life.

. . .

228

May I be forgiven the discovery that all moral philosophy so far has been boring and was a soporific and that "virtue" has been impaired more for me by its *boring* advocates than by anything else, though I am not denying their general utility. It is important that as few people as possible should think about morality; hence it is *very* important that morality should not one day become interesting. But there is no reason for worry. Things still stand today as they have always stood: I see nobody in Europe who has (let alone, *promotes*) any awareness that thinking about morality could become dangerous, captious, seductive—that there might be any *calamity* involved.

Consider, for example, the indefatigable, inevitable British utilitarians, how they walk clumsily and honorably in Bentham's footsteps, walking along (a Homeric simile says it more plainly), even as he himself had already walked in the footsteps of the honorable Helvétius[9] (no, he was no dangerous person, this Helvétius, *ce sénateur Pococurante*,[10] to speak with Galiani). Not a new idea, no trace of a subtler version or twist of an old idea, not even a real history

---

[9] Claude Adrien Helvétius (1715–71) was a French philosopher whose ancestors had borne the name of Schweitzer. He was a materialist and utilitarian.—TRANS.

[10] *Poco:* little; *curante:* careful, caring; *pococurante:* easygoing.—TRANS.

of what had been thought before: altogether an *impossible* literature, unless one knows how to flavor it with some malice.

For into these moralists, too (one simply has to read them with ulterior thoughts, if one *has* to read them), that old English vice has crept which is called *cant* and consists in *moral Tartuffery;* only this time it hides in a new, scientific, form. A secret fight against a bad conscience is not lacking either, as it is only fair that a race of former Puritans will have a bad conscience whenever it tries to deal with morality scientifically. (Isn't a moral philosopher the opposite of a Puritan? Namely, insofar as he is a thinker who considers morality questionable, as calling for questions marks, in short as a problem? Should moralizing not be—immoral?)

Ultimately they all want *English* morality to be proved right—because this serves humanity best, or "the general utility," or "the happiness of the greatest number"—no, the happiness of *England*. With all their powers they want to prove to themselves that the striving for *English* happiness—I mean for comfort and fashion[11] (and at best a seat in Parliament)—is at the same time also the right way to virtue; indeed that whatever virtue has existed in the world so far must have consisted in such striving.

None of these ponderous herd animals with their unquiet consciences (who undertake to advocate the cause of egoism as the cause of the general welfare) wants to know or even sense that "the general welfare" is no ideal, no goal, no remotely intelligible concept, but only an emetic—that what is fair for one *cannot* by any means for that reason alone also be fair for others; that the demand of one morality for all is detrimental for the higher men; in short, that there is an order of rank between man and man, hence also between morality and morality. They are a modest and thoroughly mediocre type of man, these utilitarian Englishmen, and, as said above, insofar as they are boring one cannot think highly enough of their utility. They should even be *encouraged:* the following rhymes represent an effort in this direction.

> Hail, dear drudge and patient fretter!
> "More drawn out is always better,"
> Stiffness grows in head and knee,
> No enthusiast and no joker,
> Indestructibly mediocre,
> *Sans génie et sans esprit!*

From *Genealogy of Morals*

16

At this point I can no longer avoid giving a first, provisional statement of my own hypothesis concerning the origin of the "bad conscience": it may

---

[11] Nietzsche uses the English words "comfort" and "fashion."—TRANS.

sound rather strange and needs to be pondered, lived with, and slept on for a long time. I regard the bad conscience as the serious illness that man was bound to contract under the stress of the most fundamental change he ever experienced—that change which occurred when he found himself finally enclosed within the walls of society and of peace. The situation that faced sea animals when they were compelled to become land animals or perish was the same as that which faced these semi-animals, well adapted to the wilderness, to war, to prowling, to adventure: suddenly all their instincts were disvalued and "suspended." From now on they had to walk on their feet and "bear themselves" whereas hitherto they had been borne by the water: a dreadful heaviness lay upon them. They felt unable to cope with the simplest undertakings; in this new world they no longer possessed their former guides, their regulating, unconscious and infallible drives: they were reduced to thinking, inferring, reckoning, co-ordinating cause and effect, these unfortunate creatures; they were reduced to their "consciousness," their weakest and most fallible organ! I believe there has never been such a feeling of misery on earth, such a leaden discomfort—and at the same time the old instincts had not suddenly ceased to make their usual demands! Only it was hardly or rarely possible to humor them: as a rule they had to seek new and, as it were, subterranean gratifications.

All instincts that do not discharge themselves outwardly *turn inward*—this is what I call the *internalization* of man: thus it was that man first developed what was later called his "soul." The entire inner world, originally as thin as if it were stretched between two membranes, expanded and extended itself, acquired depth, breadth, and height, in the same measure as outward discharge was *inhibited*. Those fearful bulwarks with which the political organization protected itself against the old instincts of freedom—punishments belong among these bulwarks—brought about that all those instincts of wild, free, prowling man turned backward *against man himself*. Hostility, cruelty, joy in persecuting, in attacking, in change, in destruction—all this turned against the possessors of such instincts: *that* is the origin of the "bad conscience."

The man who, from lack of external enemies and resistances and forcibly confined to the oppressive narrowness and punctiliousness of custom, impatiently lacerated, persecuted, gnawed at, assaulted, and maltreated himself; this animal that rubbed itself raw against the bars of its cage as one tried to "tame" it; this deprived creature, racked with homesickness for the wild, who had to turn himself into an adventure, a torture chamber, an uncertain and dangerous wilderness—this fool, this yearning and desperate prisoner became the inventor of the "bad conscience." But thus began the gravest and uncanniest illness, from which humanity has not yet recovered, man's suffering *of man, of himself*—the result of a forcible sundering from his animal past, as it were a leap and plunge into new surroundings and conditions of existence, a declaration of war against the old instincts upon which his strength, joy, and terribleness had rested hitherto.

. . .

From *Thus Spake Zarathustra*

And Zarathustra spoke thus to the people:

"*I teach you the overman*. Man is something that shall be overcome. What have you done to overcome him?

"All beings so far have created something beyond themselves; and do you want to be the ebb of this great flood and even go back to the beasts rather than overcome man? What is the ape to man? A laughingstock or a painful embarrassment. And man shall be just that for the overman: a laughingstock or a painful embarrassment. You have made your way from worm to man, and much in you is still worm. Once you were apes, and even now, too, man is more ape than any ape.

"Whoever is the wisest among you is also a mere conflict and cross between plant and ghost. But do I bid you become ghosts or plants?

"Behold, I teach you the overman. The overman is the meaning of the earth. Let your will say: the overman *shall be* the meaning of the earth! I beseech you, my brothers, *remain faithful to the earth,* and do not believe those who speak to you of otherwordly hopes! Poison mixers are they, whether they know it or not. Despisers of life are they, decaying and poisoned themselves, of whom the earth is weary: so let them go.

"Once the sin against God was the greatest sin; but God died, and these sinners died with him. To sin against the earth is now the most dreadful thing, and to esteem the entrails of the unknowable higher than the meaning of the earth.

"Once the soul looked contemptuously upon the body, and then this contempt was the highest: she wanted the body meager, ghastly, and starved. Thus she hoped to escape it and the earth. Oh, this soul herself was still meager, ghastly, and starved: and cruelty was the lust of this soul. But you, too, my brothers, tell me: what does your body proclaim of your soul? Is not your soul poverty and filth and wretched contentment?

"Verily, a polluted stream is man. One must be a sea to be able to receive a polluted stream without becoming unclean. Behold, I teach you the overman: he is this sea; in him your great contempt can go under.

"What is the greatest experience you can have? It is the hour of the great contempt. The hour in which your happiness, too, arouses your disgust, and even your reason and your virtue.

"The hour when you say, 'What matters my happiness? It is poverty and filth and wretched contentment. But my happiness ought to justify existence itself.'

"The hour when you say, 'What matters my reason? Does it crave knowledge as the lion his food? It is poverty and filth and wretched contentment.'

"The hour when you say, 'What matters my virtue? As yet it has not made me rage. How weary I am of my good and my evil! All that is poverty and filth and wretched contentment.'

"The hour when you say, 'What matters my justice? I do not see that I am flames and fuel. But the just are flames and fuel.'

"The hour when you say, 'What matters my pity? Is not pity the cross on which he is nailed who loves man? But my pity is no crucifixion.'

"Have you yet spoken thus? Have you yet cried thus? Oh, that I might have heard you cry thus!

"Not your sin but your thrift cries to heaven; your meanness even in your sin cries to heaven.

"Where is the lightning to lick you with its tongue? Where is the frenzy with which you should be inoculated?

"Behold, I teach you the overman: he is this lightning, he is this frenzy."

. . .

"Man is a rope, tied between beast and overman—a rope over an abyss. A dangerous across, a dangerous on-the-way, a dangerous looking-back, a dangerous shuddering and stopping.

"What is great in man is that he is a bridge and not an end: what can be loved in man is that he is an *overture* and a *going under*.

. . .

39

Rational Life Plans

JOHN RAWLS

For biographical information on John Rawls, see reading 16.

In this selection, Rawls's topic is the good life. According to him, there is no single type of life that is best for everyone. Rather, for any given person, the best life is one lived in accordance with a rational plan. Very roughly, a person's rational life plan is a plan that, if followed, will afford him the highest chance of achieving the greatest number of his most important purposes. It is thus a way of allocating resources of time and energy to achieve maximal desire-satisfaction. To arrive at such a plan, a person must subject his desires to rational scrutiny. This requires clarifying both how the desires were arrived at and the degree to which they can be jointly satisfied. All in all, a rational plan is one that a person would choose if he had full imaginative knowledge of all the alternatives. Thus, the notion of hypothetical choice, so central to Rawls's conception of what is right (see reading 32), is also crucial to his conception of the good.

One important feature of desires is that they are not fixed over time. By doing something at an earlier time—say, by choosing a particular career— we may cause ourselves to form a whole new set of later desires. This raises the question of which desires to cultivate. According to Rawls, we should cultivate later desires whose satisfaction requires the possession and exercise of complex skills. This, he thinks, will raise the chances of our being happy. For a view that stands in interesting contrast, see Epicurus, reading 36. For criticism of Rawls's views about rational life plans, see Williams (reading 2) and Sandel (reading 40).

The Definition of Good for Plans of Life

TO THIS POINT I have discussed only the first stages of the definition of good in which no questions are raised about the rationality of the ends taken as given. A thing's being a good X for K is treated as equivalent to its having the properties which it is rational for K to want in an X in view of his interests and aims. Yet we often assess the rationality of a person's desires, and the definition must be extended to cover this fundamental case if it is to serve the purposes of the theory of justice. Now the basic idea at the third stage is to apply the definition of good to plans of life. The rational plan for a person determines his good. Here I adapt Royce's thought that a person may be regarded as a human life lived according to a plan. For Royce an individual says who he is by describing his purposes and causes, what he intends to do in his life.[1] If this plan is a rational one, then I shall say that the person's conception of his good is likewise rational. In his case the real and the apparent good coincide. Similarly his interests and aims are rational, and it is appropriate to take them as stopping points in making judgments that correspond to the first two stages of the definition. These suggestions are quite straightforward but unfortunately setting out the details is somewhat tedious. In order to expedite matters I shall start off with a pair of definitions and then explain and comment on them over the next several sections.

These definitions read as follows: first, a person's plan of life is rational if, and only if, (1) it is one of the plans that is consistent with the principles of rational choice when these are applied to all the relevant features of his situation, and (2) it is that plan among those meeting this condition which would be chosen by him with full deliberative rationality, that is, with full awareness of the relevant facts and after a careful consideration of the consequences.[2] (The notion of deliberative rationality is discussed in the next section.) Secondly, a person's interests and aims are rational if, and only if, they are to be encouraged and provided for by the plan that is rational for him. Note that in the first of these definitions I have implied that a rational plan is presumably but one of many possible plans that are consistent with the principles of rational choice. The reason for this complication is that these principles do not single out one plan as the best. We have instead a maximal class of plans: each member of this class is superior to all plans not included in it, but given any two plans in the class, neither is superior or inferior to the other. Thus to identify a person's rational plan, I suppose that it is that plan belonging to the maximal class which he would choose with full deliberative rationality. We criticize someone's plan, then, by showing either that it violates the principles of rational choice, or that it is not the plan that he would pursue were he to assess his prospects with care in the light of a full knowledge of his situation.

Before illustrating the principles of rational choice, I should say a few things about the rather complex notion of a rational plan. It is fundamental for the definition of good, since a rational plan of life establishes the basic point of view from which all judgments of value relating to a particular person are to

---

[1] See *The Philosophy of Loyalty,* lect. IV, sec. IV. Royce uses the notion of a plan to characterize the coherent, systematic purposes of the individual, what makes him a conscious, unified moral person. In this Royce is typical of the philosophical usage found in many of the writers cited in §61, note 2, Dewey and Perry, for example. And I shall do the same. The term is given no technical sense, nor are the structures of plans invoked to get other than obvious common sense results. These are matters I do not investigate. For a discussion of plans, see G. A. Miller, Eugene Galanter, and K. H. Pribram, *Plans and the Structure of Behavior* (New York, Henry Holt, 1960); and also Galanter's *Textbook of Elementary Psychology* (San Francisco, Holden-Day, 1966), ch. IX. The notion of a plan may prove useful in characterizing intentional action. See, for example, Alvin Goldman, *A Theory of Action* (Englewood Cliffs, N.J., Prentice-Hall, 1970), pp. 56–73, 76–80; but I do not consider this question.

[2] For simplicity I assume that there is one and only one plan that would be chosen, and not several (or many) between which the agent would be indifferent, or whatever. Thus I speak throughout of the plan that would be adopted with deliberative rationality.

be made and finally rendered consistent. Indeed, with certain qualifications we can think of a person as being happy when he is in the way of a successful execution (more or less) of a rational plan of life drawn up under (more or less) favorable conditions, and he is reasonably confident that his plan can be carried through. Someone is happy when his plans are going well, his more important aspirations being fulfilled, and he feels sure that his good fortune will endure. Since plans which it is rational to adopt vary from person to person depending upon their endowments and circumstances, and the like, different individuals find their happiness in doing different things. The gloss concerning favorable circumstances is necessary because even a rational arrangement of one's activities can be a matter of accepting the lesser evil if natural conditions are harsh and the demands of other men oppressive. The achievement of happiness in the larger sense of a happy life, or of a happy period of one's life, always presumes a degree of good fortune.

Several further points about long-term plans should be mentioned. The first relates to their time structure. A plan will, to be sure, make some provision for even the most distant future and for our death, but it becomes relatively less specific for later periods. Certain broad contingencies are insured against and general means provided for, but the details are filled in gradually as more information becomes available and our wants and needs are known with greater accuracy. Indeed, one principle of rational choice is that of postponement: if in the future we may want to do one of several things but are unsure which, then, other things equal, we are to plan now so that these alternatives are both kept open. We must not imagine that a rational plan is a detailed blueprint for action stretching over the whole course of life. It consists of a hierarchy of plans, the more specific subplans being filled in at the appropriate time.

The second point is connected with the first. The structure of a plan not only reflects the lack of specific information but it also mirrors a hierarchy of desires proceeding in similar fashion from the more to the less general. The main features of a plan encourage and secure the fulfillment of the more permanent and general aims. A rational plan must, for example, allow for the primary goods, since otherwise no plan can succeed; but the particular form that the corresponding desires will take is usually unknown in advance and can wait for the occasion. Thus while we know that over any extended period of time we shall always have desires for food and drink, it is not until the moment comes that we decide to have a meal consisting of this or that course. These decisions depend on the choices available, on the menu that the situation allows.

Thus planning is in part scheduling.[3] We try to organize our activities into a temporal sequence in which each is carried on for a certain length of time. In this way a family of interrelated desires can be satisfied in an effective and harmonious manner. The basic resources of time and energy are alloted to

---

[3] See J. D. Mabbott, "Reason and Desire," *Philosophy*, vol. 28 (1953), for a discussion of this and other points to which I am indebted.

activities in accordance with the intensity of the wants that they answer to and the contribution that they are likely to make to the fulfillment of other ends. The aim of deliberation is to find that plan which best organizes our activities and influences the formation of our subsequent wants so that our aims and interests can be fruitfully combined into one scheme of conduct. Desires that tend to interfere with other ends, or which undermine the capacity for other activities, are weeded out; whereas those that are enjoyable in themselves and support other aims as well are encouraged. A plan, then, is made up of subplans suitably arranged in a hierarchy, the broad features of the plan allowing for the more permanent aims and interests that complement one another. Since only the outlines of these aims and interests can be foreseen, the operative parts of the subplans that provide for them are finally decided upon independently as we go along. Revisions and changes at the lower levels do not usually reverberate through the entire structure. If this conception of plans is sound, we should expect that the good things in life are, roughly speaking, those activities and relationships which have a major place in rational plans. And primary goods should turn out to be those things which are generally necessary for carrying out such plans successfully whatever the particular nature of the plan and of its final ends.

These remarks are unhappily too brief. But they are intended only to prevent the more obvious misunderstandings of the notion of a rational plan, and to indicate the place of this notion in a theory of the good. I must now try to convey what is meant by the principles of rational choice. These principles are to be given by enumeration so that eventually they replace the concept of rationality. The relevant features of a person's situation are identified by these principles and the general conditions of human life to which plans must be adjusted. At this point I shall mention those aspects of rationality that are most familiar and seem least in dispute. And for the moment I shall assume that the choice situation relates to the short term. The question is how to fill in the more or less final details of a subplan to be executed over a relatively brief period of time, as when we make plans for a holiday. The larger system of desires may not be significantly affected, although of course some desires will be satisfied in this interval and others will not.

Now for short term questions anyway, certain principles seem perfectly straightforward and not in dispute. The first of these is that of effective means. Suppose that there is a particular objective that is wanted, and that all the alternatives are means to achieve it, while they are in other respects neutral. The principle holds that we are to adopt that alternative which realizes the end in the best way. More fully: given the objective, one is to achieve it with the least expenditure of means (whatever they are); or given the means, one is to fulfill the objective to the fullest possible extent. This principle is perhaps the most natural criterion of rational choice. Indeed, as we shall note later, there is some tendency to suppose that deliberation must always take this form, being regulated ultimately by a single final end. Otherwise it is thought that there is no rational way to balance a plurality of aims against one another. But this question I leave aside for the present.

526

The second principle of rational choice is that one (short-term) plan is to be preferred to another if its execution would achieve all of the desired aims of the other plan and one or more further aims in addition. Perry refers to this criterion as the principle of inclusiveness and I shall do the same.[4] Thus we are to follow the more inclusive plan if such a plan exists. To illustrate, suppose that we are planning a trip and we have to decide whether to go to Rome or Paris. It seems impossible to visit both. If on reflection it is clear that we can do everything in Paris that we want to do in Rome, and some other things as well, then we should go to Paris. Adopting this plan will realize a larger set of ends and nothing is left undone that might have been realized by the other plan. Often, however, neither plan is more inclusive than the other; each may achieve an aim which the other does not. We must invoke some other principle to make up our minds, or else subject our aims to further analysis.

A third principle we may call that of the greater likelihood. Suppose that the aims which may be achieved by two plans are roughly the same. Then it may happen that some objectives have a greater chance of being realized by one plan than the other, yet at the same time none of the remaining aims are less likely to be attained. For example, although one can perhaps do everything one wants to do in both Rome and Paris, some of the things one wishes to do seem more likely to meet with success in Paris, and for the rest it is roughly the same. If so, the principle holds that one should go to Paris. A greater likelihood of success favors a plan just as the more inclusive end does. When these principles work together the choice is as obvious as can be. Suppose that we prefer a Titian to a Tintoretto, and that the first of two lottery tickets gives the larger chance to Titian while the second assigns it to the Tintoretto. Then one must prefer the first ticket.

So far we have been considering the application of the principles of rational choice to the short-term case. I now wish to examine the other extreme in which one has to adopt a long-term plan, even a plan of life, as when we have to choose a profession or occupation. It may be thought that having to make such a decision is a task imposed only by a particular form of culture. In another society this choice might not arise. But in fact the question of what to do with our life is always there, although some societies force it upon us more obviously than others and at a different time of life. The limit decision to have no plan at all, to let things come as they may, is still theoretically a plan that may or may not be rational. Accepting the idea of a long-term plan, then, it seems clear that such a scheme is to be assessed by what it will probably lead to in each future period of time. The principle of inclusiveness in this case, therefore, runs as follows: one long-term plan is better than another for any given period (or number of periods) if it allows for the encouragement and satisfaction of all the aims and interests of the other plan and for the encouragement and satisfaction of some further aim or interest in addition. The more inclusive plan, if there is one, is to be preferred: it comprehends all the ends of the first

[4] See *General Theory of Value* (New York, Longmans, Green, 1926), pp. 645–649.

plan and at least one other end as well. If this principle is combined with that of effective means, then together they define rationality as preferring, other things equal, the greater means for realizing our aims, and the development of wider and more varied interests assuming that these aspirations can be carried through. The principle of greater likelihood supports this preference even in situations when we cannot be sure that the larger aims can be executed, provided that the chances of execution are as great as with the less comprehensive plan.

The application of the principles of effective means and the greater likelihood to the long-term case seems sound enough. But the use of the principle of inclusiveness may seem problematical. With a fixed system of ends in the short run, we assume that we already have our desires and given this fact we consider how best to satisfy them. But in long-term choice, although we do not yet have the desires which various plans will encourage, we are nevertheless directed to adopt that plan which will develop the more comprehensive interests on the assumption that these further aims can be realized. Now a person may say that since he does not have the more inclusive interests, he is not missing anything in not deciding to encourage and to satisfy them. He may hold that the possible satisfaction of desires that he can arrange never to have is an irrelevant consideration. Of course, he might also contend that the more inclusive system of interests subjects him to a greater risk of dissatisfaction; but this objection is excluded since the principle assumes that the larger pattern of ends is equally likely to be attained.

There are two considerations that seem to favor the principle of inclusiveness in the long-term case. First of all, assuming that how happy a person is depends in part upon the proportion of his aims that are achieved, the extent to which his plans are carried through, it follows that pursuing the principle of inclusiveness tends to raise this proportion and thereby enhance a person's happiness. This effect is absent only in the case where all of the aims of the less inclusive plan are already safely provided for. The other consideration is that, in accordance with the Aristotelian Principle (explained below . . .), I assume that human beings have a higher order desire to follow the principle of inclusiveness. They prefer the more comprehensive long-term plan because its execution presumably involves a more complex combination of abilities. The Aristotelian Principle states that other things equal human beings enjoy the exercise of their realized capacities (their innate or trained abilities), and that this enjoyment increases the more the capacity is realized, or the greater its complexity. A person takes pleasure in doing something as he becomes more proficient at it, and of two activities which he performs equally well, he prefers the one that calls upon the greater number of more subtle and intricate discriminations. Thus the desire to carry out the larger pattern of ends which brings into play the more finely developed talents is an aspect of the Aristotelian Principle. And this desire, along with the higher order desires to act upon other principles of rational choice, is one of the regulative ends that moves us to engage in rational deliberation and to follow its outcome.

Many things in these remarks call for further explanation. It is clear, for example, that these three principles are not in general sufficient to rank the plans open to us. Means may not be neutral, inclusive plans may not exist, the aims achieved may not be sufficiently similar, and so on. To apply these principles we view our aims as we are inclined to describe them, and more or less count the number realized by this or that plan, or estimate the likelihood of success. For this reason I shall refer to these criteria as counting principles. They do not require a further analysis or alteration of our desires, nor a judgment concerning the relative intensity of our wants. These matters I put aside for the discussion of deliberative rationality. It seems best to conclude this preliminary account by noting what seems to be reasonably clear: namely that we can choose between rational plans of life. And this means that we can choose now which desires we shall have at a later time.

One might suppose at first that this is not possible. We sometimes think that our major desires at least are fixed and that we deliberate solely about the means to satisfy them. Of course, it is obvious that deliberation leads us to have some desires that we did not have before, for example, the desire to avail ourselves of certain means that we have on reflection come to see as useful for our purposes. Furthermore, it is clear that taking thought may lead us to make a general desire more specific, as when a desire for music becomes a desire to hear a particular work. But let us suppose that, except for these sorts of exceptions, we do not choose now what to desire now. Nevertheless, we can certainly decide now to do something that we know will affect the desires that we shall have in the future. At any given time rational persons decide between plans of action in view of their situation and beliefs, all in conjunction with their present major desires and the principles of rational choice. Thus we choose between future desires in the light of our existing desires, including among these the desire to act on rational principles. When an individual decides what to be, what occupation or profession to enter say, he adopts a particular plan of life. In time his choice will lead him to acquire a definite pattern of wants and aspirations (or the lack thereof), some aspects of which are peculiar to him while others are typical of his chosen occupation or way of life. These considerations appear evident enough, and simply parallel in the case of the individual the deep effects that a choice of a conception of justice is bound to have upon the kinds of aims and interests encouraged by the basic stucture of society. Convictions about what sort of person to be are similarly involved in the acceptance of principles of justice.

Deliberative Rationality

I have already noted that the simpler principles of rational choice (the counting principles) do not suffice to order plans. Sometimes they do not apply, since there may be no inclusive plan say, or else the means are not neutral. Or it often happens that we are left with a maximal class. In these cases further rational criteria may of course be invoked, and some of these I shall discuss

below. But I shall suppose that while rational principles can focus our judgments and set up guidelines for reflection, we must finally choose for ourselves
in the sense that the choice often rests on our direct self-knowledge not only
of what things we want but also of how much we want them. Sometimes there
is no way to avoid having to assess the relative intensity of our desires. Rational
principles can help us to do this, but they cannot always determine these
estimates in a routine fashion. To be sure, there is one formal principle that
seems to provide a general answer. This is the principle to adopt that plan
which maximizes the expected net balance of satisfaction. Or to express the
criterion less hedonistically, if more loosely, one is directed to take that course
most likely to realize one's most important aims. But this principle also fails
to provide us with an explicit procedure for making up our minds. It is clearly
left to the agent himself to decide what it is that he most wants and to judge
the comparative importance of his several ends.

At this point I introduce the notion of deliberative rationality following an
idea of Sidgwick's. He characterizes a person's future good on the whole as
what he would now desire and seek if the consequences of all the various
courses of conduct open to him were, at the present point of time, accurately
foreseen by him and adequately realized in imagination. An individual's good
is the hypothetical composition of impulsive forces that results from deliberative reflection meeting certain conditions.[5] Adjusting Sidgwick's notion to the
choice of plans, we can say that the rational plan for a person is the one (among
those consistent with the counting principles and other principles of rational
choice once these are established) which he would choose with deliberative
rationality. It is the plan that would be decided upon as the outcome of careful
reflection in which the agent reviewed, in the light of all the relevant facts,
what it would be like to carry out these plans and thereby ascertained the
course of action that would best realize his more fundamental desires.

In this definition of deliberative rationality it is assumed that there are no
errors of calculation or reasoning, and that the facts are correctly assessed. I
suppose also that the agent is under no misconceptions as to what he really
wants. In most cases anyway, when he achieves his aim, he does not find that
he no longer wants it and wishes that he had done something else instead.
Moreover, the agent's knowledge of his situation and the consequences of
carrying out each plan is presumed to be accurate and complete. No relevant
circumstances are left out of account. Thus the best plan for an individual is
the one that he would adopt if he possessed full information. It is the objectively
rational plan for him and determines his real good. As things are, of course,
our knowledge of what will happen if we follow this or that plan is usually
incomplete. Often we do not know what is the rational plan for us; the most
that we can have is a reasonable belief as to where our good lies, and sometimes
we can only conjecture. But if the agent does the best that a rational person
can do with the information available to him, then the plan he follows is a

[5] See Henry Sidgwick, *The Methods of Ethics,* 7th ed. (London, Macmillan, 1907), pp. 111f.

subjectively rational plan. His choice may be an unhappy one, but if so it is because his beliefs are understandably mistaken or his knowledge insufficient, and not because he drew hasty and fallacious inferences or was confused as to what he really wanted. In this case a person is not to be faulted for any discrepancy between his apparent and his real good.

The notion of deliberative rationality is obviously highly complex, combining many elements. I shall not attempt to enumerate here all the ways in which the process of reflection may go wrong. One could if necessary classify the kinds of mistakes that can be made, the sorts of tests that the agent might apply to see if he has adequate knowledge, and so on. It should be noted, however, that a rational person will not usually continue to deliberate until he has found the best plan open to him. Often he will be content if he forms a satisfactory plan (or subplan), that is, one that meets various minimum conditions.[6] Rational deliberation is itself an activity like any other, and the extent to which one should engage in it is subject to rational decision. The formal rule is that we should deliberate up to the point where the likely benefits from improving our plan are just worth the time and effort of reflection. Once we take the costs of deliberation into account, it is unreasonable to worry about finding the best plan, the one that we would choose had we complete information. It is perfectly rational to follow a satisfactory plan when the prospective returns from further calculation and additional knowledge do not outweigh the trouble. There is even nothing irrational in an aversion to deliberation itself provided that one is prepared to accept the consequences. Goodness as rationality does not attribute any special value to the process of deciding. The importance to the agent of careful reflection will presumably vary from one individual to another. Nevertheless, a person is being irrational if his unwillingness to think about what is the best (or a satisfactory) thing to do leads him into misadventures that on consideration he would concede that he should have taken thought to avoid.

In this account of deliberative rationality I have assumed a certain competence on the part of the person deciding: he knows the general features of his wants and ends both present and future, and he is able to estimate the relative intensity of his desires, and to decide if necessary what he really wants. Moreover, he can envisage the alternatives open to him and establish a coherent ordering of them: given any two plans he can work out which one he prefers or whether he is indifferent between them, and these preferences are transitive. Once a plan is settled upon, he is able to adhere to it and he can resist present temptations and distractions that interfere with its execution. These assumptions accord with the familiar notion of rationality that I have used all along. I shall not examine here these aspects of being rational. It seems more useful to mention briefly some ways of criticizing our ends which may often help us to estimate the relative intensity of our desires. Keeping in mind that our

---

[6] On this point, see H. A. Simon, "A Behavioral Model of Rational Choice," *Quarterly Journal of Economics*, vol. 69 (1955).

overall aim is to carry out a rational plan (or subplan), it is clear that some features of desires make doing this impossible. For example, we cannot realize ends the description of which is meaningless, or contradicts well-established truths. Since π is a transcendental number, it would be pointless to try to prove that it is an algebraic number. To be sure, a mathematician in attempting to prove this proposition might discover by the way many important facts, and this achievement might redeem his efforts. But insofar as his end was to prove a falsehood, his plan would be open to criticism; and once he became aware of this, he would no longer have this aim. The same thing holds for desires that depend upon our having incorrect beliefs. It is not excluded that mistaken opinions may have a beneficial effect by enabling us to proceed with our plans, being so to speak useful illusions. Nevertheless, the desires that these beliefs support are irrational to the degree that the falsehood of these beliefs makes it impossible to execute the plan, or prevents superior plans from being adopted. (I should observe here that in the thin theory the value of knowing the facts is derived from their relation to the successful execution of rational plans. So far at least there are no grounds for attributing intrinsic value to having true beliefs.)

We may also investigate the circumstances under which we have acquired our desires and conclude that some of our aims are in various respects out of line.[7] Thus a desire may spring from excessive generalization, or arise from more or less accidental associations. This is especially likely to be so in the case of aversions developed when we are younger and do not possess enough experience and maturity to make the necessary corrections. Other wants may be inordinate, having acquired their peculiar urgency as an overreaction to a prior period of severe deprivation or anxiety. The study of these processes and their disturbing influence on the normal development of our system of desires it not our concern here. They do however suggest certain critical reflections that are important devices of deliberation. Awareness of the genesis of our wants can often make it perfectly clear to us that we really do desire certain things more than others. As some aims seem less important in the face of critical scrutiny, or even lose their appeal entirely, others may assume an assured prominence that provides sufficient grounds for choice. Of course, it is conceivable that despite the unfortunate conditions under which some of our desires and aversions have developed, they may still fit into and even greatly enhance the fulfillment of rational plans. If so, they turn out to be perfectly rational after all.

Finally, there are certain time-related principles that also can be used to select among plans. The principle of postponement I have already mentioned. It holds that, other things equal, rational plans try to keep our hands free until we have a clear view of the relevant facts. And the grounds for rejecting pure time preference we have also considered. We are to see our life as one whole, the activities of one rational subject spread out in time. Mere temporal position,

[7] For the remarks in this paragraph, I am indebted to R. B. Brandt.

or distance from the present, is not a reason for favoring one moment over another. Future aims may not be discounted solely in virtue of being future, although we may, of course, ascribe less weight to them if there are reasons for thinking that, given their relation to other things, their fulfillment is less probable. The intrinsic importance that we assign to different parts of our life should be the same at every moment of time. These values should depend upon the whole plan itself as far as we can determine it and should not be affected by the contingencies of our present perspective.

Two other principles apply to the overall shape of plans through time. One of these is that of continuity.[8] It reminds us that since a plan is a scheduled sequence of activities, earlier and later activities are bound to affect one another. The whole plan has a certain unity, a dominant theme. There is not, so to speak, a separate utility function for each period. Not only must effects between periods be taken into account, but substantial swings up and down are presumably to be avoided. A second closely related principle holds that we are to consider the advantages of rising, or at least of not significantly declining, expectations. There are various stages of life, each ideally with its own characteristic tasks and enjoyments. Other things equal, we should arrange things at the earlier stages so as to permit a happy life at the later ones. It would seem that for the most part rising expectations over time are to be preferred. If the value of an activity is assessed relative to its own period, assuming that this is possible, we might try to explain this preference by the relatively greater intensity of the pleasures of anticipation over those of memory. Even though the total sum of enjoyment is the same when enjoyments are estimated locally, increasing expectations provide a measure of contentment that makes the difference. But even leaving this element aside, the rising or at least the nondeclining plan appears preferable since later activities can often incorporate and bind together the results and enjoyments of an entire life into one coherent structure as those of a declining plan cannot.

In these remarks about the devices of deliberation and time-related principles I have tried to fill in Sidgwick's notion of a person's good. In brief, our good is determined by the plan of life that we would adopt with full deliberative rationality if the future were accurately foreseen and adequately realized in the imagination. The matters we have just discussed are connected with being rational in this sense. Here it is worth stressing that a rational plan is one that would be selected if certain conditions were fulfilled. The criterion of the good is hypothetical in a way similar to the criterion of justice. When the question arises as to whether doing something accords with our good, the answer depends upon how well it fits the plan that would be chosen with deliberative rationality.

Now one feature of a rational plan is that in carrying it out the individual does not change his mind and wish that he had done something else instead. A rational person does not come to feel an aversion for the foreseen conse-

---

[8] This name is taken from Jan Tinbergen, "Optimum Savings and Utility Maximization over Time," *Econometrica*, vol. 28 (1960).

quences so great that he regrets following the plan he has adopted. The absence of this sort of regret is not however sufficient to insure that a plan is rational. There may be another plan open to us such that were we to consider it we would find it much better. Nevertheless, if our information is accurate and our understanding of the consequences complete in relevant respects, we do not regret following a rational plan, even if it is not a good one judged absolutely. In this instance the plan is objectively rational. We may, of course, regret something else, for example, that we have to live under such unfortunate circumstances that a happy life is impossible. Conceivably we may wish that we had never been born. But we do not regret that, having been born, we followed the best plan as bad as it may be when judged by some ideal standard. A rational person may regret his pursuing a subjectively rational plan, but not because he thinks his choice is in any way open to criticism. For he does what seems best at the time, and if his beliefs later prove to be mistaken with untoward results, it is through no fault of his own. There is no cause for self-reproach. There was no way of knowing which was the best or even a better plan.

Putting these reflections together, we have the guiding principle that a rational individual is always to act so that he need never blame himself no matter how things finally transpire. Viewing himself as one continuing being over time, he can say that at each moment of his life he has done what the balance of reasons required, or at least permitted.[9] Therefore any risks he assumes must be worthwhile, so that should the worst happen that he had any reason to foresee, he can still affirm that what he did was above criticism. He does not regret his choice, at least not in the sense that he later believes that at the time it would have been more rational to have done otherwise. This principle will not certainly prevent us from taking steps that lead to misadventure. Nothing can protect us from the ambiguities and limitations of our knowledge, or guarantee that we find the best alternative open to us. Acting with deliberative rationality can only insure that our conduct is above reproach, and that we are responsible to ourselves as one person over time. We should indeed be surprised if someone said that he did not care about how he will view his present actions later any more than he cares about the affairs of other people (which is not much, let us suppose). One who rejects equally the claims of his future self and the interests of others is not only irresponsible with respect to them but in regard to his own person as well. He does not see himself as one enduring individual.

Now looked at in this way, the principle of responsibility to self resembles a principle of right: the claims of the self at different times are to be so adjusted that the self at each time can affirm the plan that has been and is being followed. The person at one time, so to speak, must not be able to complain about actions of the person at another time. This principle does not, of course, exclude the willing endurance of hardship and suffering; but it must be presently acceptable in view of the expected or achieved good. From the standpoint of the original

[9] For this and other points in this paragraph see Charles Fried, *An Anatomy of Values* (Cambridge, Harvard University Press, 1970), pp. 158–169, and Thomas Nagel, *The Possibility of Altruism* (Oxford, The Clarendon Press, 1970), esp. ch VIII.

position the relevance of responsibility to self seems clear enough. Since the notion of deliberative rationality applies there, it means that the parties cannot agree to a conception of justice if the consequences of applying it may lead to self-reproach should the least happy possibilities be realized. They should strive to be free from such regrets. And the principles of justice as fairness seem to meet this requirement better than other conceptions, as we can see from the earlier discussion of the strains of commitment.

A final observation about goodness as rationality. It may be objected that this conception implies that one should be continually planning and calculating. But this interpretation rests upon a misunderstanding. The first aim of the theory is to provide a criterion for the good of the person. This criterion is defined chiefly by reference to the rational plan that would be chosen with full deliberative rationality. The hypothetical nature of the definition must be kept in mind. A happy life is not one taken up with deciding whether to do this or that. From the definition alone very little can be said about the content of a rational plan, or the particular activities that comprise it. It is not inconceivable that an individual, or even a whole society, should achieve happiness moved entirely by spontaneous inclination. With great luck and good fortune some men might by nature just happen to hit upon the way of living that they would adopt with deliberative rationality. For the most part, though, we are not so blessed, and without taking thought and seeing ourselves as one person with a life over time, we shall almost certainly regret our course of action. Even when a person does succeed in relying on his natural impulses without misadventure, we still require a conception of his good in order to assess whether he has really been fortunate or not. He may think so, but he may be deluded; and to settle this matter, we have to examine the hypothetical choices that it would have been rational for him to make, granting due allowance for whatever benefits he may have obtained from not worrying about these things. As I noted before, the value of the activity of deciding is itself subject to rational appraisal. The efforts we should expend making decisions will depend like so much else on circumstances. Goodness as rationality leaves this question to the person and the contingencies of his situation.

40

Desire, Choice, and the Good

MICHAEL J. SANDEL

Michael J. Sandel (b. 1953) is Associate Professor of Government at Harvard University. This selection is from his book Liberalism and the Limits of Justice.

    Sandel criticizes Rawls's view of a person's good. Rawls contends in reading 39 that good lives are lives that conform to rational life plans, and that life plans are rational if persons would choose them, given full imaginative knowledge of all the alternatives. But Sandel argues that it is misleading to describe such plans as objects of even hypothetical choice. Because their aim is merely to promote the satisfaction of whatever desires people find they have, their adoption by rational persons who knew their own desires would be a matter of discovery and not of choice.

    If Sandel's target were merely Rawls's use of the word "choice," his critique would have little bite. But, in fact, his argument raises deeper issues. By focusing on the degree to which Rawls takes actual desires for granted, Sandel suggests that we might not do this. Instead of equating a person's good with the maximal satisfaction of any desires he happens to have, we might develop a different conception of the good that accepts some desires but rejects others. Needless to say, this suggestion raises difficult new questions about the standards to be used in criticizing desires.

Agency and the Role of Reflection

    WE HAVE SEEN that the choice of ends is constrained from the start by the principles of justice antecedently defined. But in order to describe Rawls' account of choice and to assess the role of reflection, if any, we need to know in greater detail how the constraint of justice makes itself felt, how exactly it enters the deliberation of the agent. Are the constraints of right somehow built into the activity of deliberation such that only just desires or conceptions of the good can arise in the first place, or does the agent form values and aims based on certain unjust desires only to suppress them in practice or set them aside once it becomes clear that they violate justice?

    At times Rawls writes as though the principles of justice shape a person's conception of the good from the start, even as the conception is formulated. 'In drawing up plans and in deciding on aspirations men are to take these constraints into account . . . [T]heir desires and aspirations are restricted from the outset by the principles of justice which specify the boundaries that men's systems of ends must respect' (31). At other times Rawls seems to favor the second account, as when he writes that in justice as fairness, persons 'implicitly agree . . . to conform their conceptions of the good to what the principles of justice require, *or at least not to press claims* which directly violate them' [emphasis added] (31).*

If it is unclear whether justice intervenes at the point I choose my life plans or only later, at the point I would pursue them, it seems clear at least that neither account introduces an element of self-reflection of the sort we are concerned with; both allow that the right does not wholly determine my good, that my conception of the good, however constrained within a certain range, still remains for me to choose. At this point Rawls introduces another set of considerations to narrow our choice, certain 'counting principles', as he describes them, which amount roughly to the basic tenets of instrumental rationality. These recommend, for example, that I choose more rather than less effective means to given ends, a more inclusive plan over a less inclusive one, the plan offering a greater rather than a lesser probability of success, and so on. Rawls acknowledges, however, that the counting principles, even when supplemented with various other principles of rational choice, 'do not suffice to order plans' (416), and that the constraints of right and of instrumental rationality taken together are not enough to lead us to a single determinate choice. Once these principles run out, we must simply choose. 'We may narrow the scope of purely preferential choice, but we cannot eliminate it altogether. . . . We eventually reach a point where we just have to decide which plan we most prefer without further guidance from principle' (552, 551).

It is at this point, according to Rawls, that our reflection must be engaged in order to determine as best we can what things we want and how much we want them, and to ascertain in the light of all the relevant facts the plan most likely to realize these desires most completely.

> I shall suppose that while rational principles can focus our judgments and set up guidelines for reflection, we must finally choose for ourselves in the sense that the choice often rests on our direct self-knowledge not only of what things we want but also of how much we want them. Sometimes there is no way to avoid having to assess the relative intensity of our desires (416). We can say that the rational plan for a person is the one (among those consistent with the counting principles and other principles of rational choice once these are established) which he would choose with deliberative rationality. It is the plan that would be decided upon as the outcome of careful reflection in which the agent reviewed, in the light of all the relevant facts, what it would be like to carry out these plans and thereby ascertained the course of action that would best realize his more fundamental desires (417).

Rawls' account of how we choose would seem to confirm the limited scope for reflection on his conception. While the plan of life or conception of the

---

* Unless otherwise noted, all page references are to John Rawls, *A Theory of Justice* (Cambridge, MA: Harvard University Press, 1971).—ED.

good most appropriate to a particular person is said to be 'the outcome of careful reflection', it is clear that the objects of this reflection are restricted to (1) the various alternative plans and their likely consequences for the realization of the agent's desires, and (2) the agent's wants and desires themselves, and their relative intensities. In neither case does reflection take as its object the self *qua* subject of desires. The reflection involved in (1), sizing up the alternatives and estimating their likely consequences, is scarcely a form of *self*-reflection at all; it looks outward rather than inward, and amounts to a kind of prudential reasoning that could in principle be carried out with equal or greater success by an outside expert who knew relatively little about the agent but a good deal about the alternatives involved and the sorts of interests and desires they typically satisfy.

The reflection involved in (2), assessing the relative intensity of desires, looks inward in a sense but not *all the way* in. It takes as its objects the contingent wants and desires and preferences of the self, but not the self *itself*. It does not extend its lights to the self standing behind the wants and desires it surveys; it cannot reach the self *qua* subject of desires. Since for Rawls the faculty of self-reflection is limited to weighing the relative intensity of existing wants and desires, the deliberation it entails cannot inquire into the identity of the agent, ('Who *am* I, really?') only into the feelings and sentiments of the agent ('What do I really *feel* like or most *prefer*?'). Because this sort of deliberation is restricted to assessing the desires of a subject whose identity is given (unreflectively) in advance, it cannot lead to self-understanding in the strong sense which enables the agent to participate in the constitution of its identity.

Although Rawls does speak briefly of 'our direct self-knowledge' of what things we want and how much we want them, 'self-knowledge' in this sense seems little more than an awareness of our immediate wants and desires. And in so far as this self-knowledge is 'direct' in the strict sense that it is given transparently to our awareness, it is difficult to imagine how anything resembling reflection or deliberation in the ordinary sense could ever take place, since we would likely know all we would need to know 'in an instant', before anything recognizably deliberative could begin. But even if 'our direct self-knowledge' permits some uncertainty for reflection to sort out, the self that is known once the uncertainty is resolved is not really the self in the strict sense distinguished throughout but merely the contingent accidents and attributes of the self.

The difference betwen the sort of reflection that attends to the desires of the agent alone and the sort that extends to the subject of desires and explores its identity corresponds in part to a distinction made by Charles Taylor in his account of human agency between the 'simple weigher' and the 'strong evaluator.' Central to both distinctions are the images of superficiality and depth. For Taylor, the 'simple weigher' is reflective in the minimal sense that he is capable of evaluating courses of action and acting out of his evaluations. But the reflection of the simple weigher lacks depth in that his evaluations are limited to the inarticulate 'feel' of the alternatives.

> Whereas for the simple weigher what is at stake is the desirability of different consummations, those defined by his *de facto* desires, for the strong evaluator reflection also examines the different possible modes of being of the agent. Whereas a reflection about what we feel like more, which is all a simple weigher can do in assessing motivations, keeps us as it were at the periphery; a reflection on the kind of beings we are takes us to the center of our existence as agents. . . . It is in this sense deeper.[1]

For Rawls, reflection 'on the kind of beings we *are*' rather than on the kind of desires we *have* is not a possibility, first because the kind of beings we are is antecedently given and not subject to revision in the light of reflection or any other form of agency, and second, because Rawls' self is conceived as barren of constituent traits, possessed only of contingent attributes held always at a certain distance, and so there is nothing *in* the self for reflection to survey or apprehend. For Rawls, the identity of the subject can never be at stake in moments of choice or deliberation (although its future aims and attributes may of course be affected), for the bounds that define it are beyond the reach of the agency—whether voluntarist or cognitive—that would contribute to its transformation.

· · ·

Agency and the Role of Choice

As we have seen, Rawls' theory of the good is voluntaristic; our fundamental aims, values, and conceptions of the good are for us to choose, and in choosing them, we exercise our agency. As Rawls describes it, once the principles of rational (i.e. instrumental) choice run out, '*We must finally choose for ourselves* in the sense that the choice often rests on our direct self-knowledge not only of what things we want but also of how much we want them. . . . *It is clearly left to the* agent himself to decide what it is that he most wants' [emphasis added] (416). Since the principles of rational choice do not specify a single best plan of life, 'a great deal remains to be *decided*. . . . We eventually reach a point where *we just have to decide* which plan we most prefer without further guidance from principle . . . . [W]e may narrow the scope of *purely preferential choice*, but we cannot eliminate it altogether. . . . *The person himself must make this decision*, taking into account the full range of his inclinations and desires, present and future' [emphasis added] (449, 551, 552, 557).

If it is clear that Rawls would describe my values and conceptions of the good as the products of choice or decision, it remains to be seen what exactly this choice consists in and how I come to make it. According to Rawls, we 'choose for ourselves *in the sense that* the choice *often rests on* our direct self-knowledge' of what we want and how much we want it. But a choice that is a choice 'in the sense that' it 'often rests on' (is determined by?) my existing

[1] Charles Taylor, "What Is Human Agency?" in *The Self: Psychological and Philosophical Issues*, ed. T. Mischel (Oxford: Oxford University Press, 1977), pp. 114–115.

wants and desires is a choice only in a peculiar sense of the word. For assuming with Rawls that the wants and desires on which my choice 'rests' are not themselves chosen but are the products of circumstance, ('We do not choose now what to desire now' (415)), such a 'choice' would involve less a voluntary act than a factual accounting of what these wants and desires really are. And once I succeed in ascertaining, by 'direct self-knowledge', this piece of psychological information, there would seem nothing left for me to *choose*. I would have still to match my wants and desires, thus ascertained, to the best available means of satisfying them, but this is a prudential question which involves no volition or exercise of will.

When Rawls writes that it is 'left to the agent himself to *decide* what it is he most wants' (416), and that 'we just have to *decide* which plans we most prefer' (551), the 'decision' the agent must make amounts to nothing more than an estimate or psychic inventory of the wants and preferences he already has, not a choice of the values he would profess or the aims he would pursue. As with the collective 'choice' or 'agreement' in the original position, such a 'decision' decides nothing except how accurately the agent has perceived something already *there*, in this case the shape and intensity of his pre-existing desires. But if this is so, then the voluntarist aspect of agency would seem to fade altogether.

To arrive at a plan of life or a conception of the good simply by heeding my existing wants and desires is to choose neither the plan nor the desires; it is simply to match the ends I already have with the best available means of satisfying them. Under such a description, my aims, values, and conceptions of the good are not the products of choice but the objects of a certain superficial introspection, just 'inward' enough to survey uncritically the motives and desires with which the accidents of my circumstance have left me; I simply know them as I feel them and seek my way as best I can to their consummation.

It might be suggested that Rawls could escape the apparent collapse of this account of agency and choice in one of two ways. The first would be to introduce the idea that persons are capable of reflecting on their desires not only in the sense of assessing their intensity but also in the sense of assessing their desirability; capable, that is, of forming second-order desires, desires whose objects are certain first-order desires.[2] I may thus want to have certain desires and not others, or regard certain sorts of desires as desirable and others less so. The fact that something was desired (and not unjust) would no longer be enough to make it good, for this would depend on the further question whether it was a desirable sort of desire or not. Once I ascertained what I (really) wanted as a matter of first-order desire, it would remain for me to assess the desirability of my desire and in this sense to affirm or reject it.

Indeed, Rawls seems vaguely to admit such a possibility when he writes that although 'we do not choose now what to desire now', we can at least 'choose now which desires we shall have at a later time . . . . We can certainly decide now to do something that we know will affect the desires we shall have in the

---

[2] Harry Frankfurt, "Freedom of the Will and the Concept of a Person," *The Journal of Philosophy* 68 (1971), pp. 5–20.

future. . . . Thus we choose between future desires in the light of our existing desires' (415).

But even if a Rawlsian agent were capable of forming desires for certain other desires, his agency would not in any meaningful sense be restored. For he would have no grounds, apart from the mere fact of his second-order desire, on which to justify or defend the desirability of one sort of desire over another. He would still have only the psychological fact of his (now, second-order) preference to appeal to and only its relative intensity to assess. Neither the intrinsic worth of a desire nor its essential connection with the identity of the agent could provide a basis for affirming it, since on Rawls' account, the worth of a desire only appears in the light of a person's good, and the identity of the agent is barren of constituent traits so that no aim or desire can be essential to it. The affirmation or rejection of desires suggested by the formation of second-order desires would on Rawls' assumptions introduce no further element of reflection or volition, for such an assessment could only reflect a slightly more complicated estimate of the relative intensity of pre-existing desires, first- and second-order desires included. The resulting conception of the good could no more be said to be chosen than one arising from first-order desires alone.

A second possible attempt to restore the coherence of choice on Rawls' conception might be to imagine a case in which the various desires of the agent, properly weighed for their respective intensities, led to a tie, and where deliberation had already taken account of all relevant preferences such that no further preferences could be introduced to break the tie. In such a case, this account might continue, the agent would have no alternative but to plump, just arbitrarily, one way or the other, without relying on any preference or desire at all. It might be suggested that a 'choice' thus independent from the influence of pre-existing wants and desires—a 'radically free choice', as it is sometimes described—would allow for the voluntarist aspect of agency seemingly unavailable when the agent is bound to 'choose' in conformity with his pre-existing wants and desires.

But Rawls rejects a wholly arbitrary form of agency that would escape the influence of pre-existing wants and desires altogether. 'The notion of radical choice . . . finds no place in justice as fairness.'[3] Unlike the principles of right, which express the autonomy of the agent and must be free from contingencies, conceptions of the good are understood to be heteronomous throughout. Where incompatible aims arise, Rawls speaks not of radically free or arbitrary choice, but instead of 'purely preferential choice', suggesting the form of (non-) agency we first considered. In any case, the notion of a purely arbitrary 'choice' governed by no considerations at all is hardly more plausible an account of voluntarist agency that a 'choice' governed wholly by predetermined preferences and desires. Neither 'purely preferential choice' nor 'purely arbitrary choice' can redeem Rawls' notion of agency in the voluntarist sense; the first confuses choice with necessity, the second with caprice. Together they reflect the limited

---

[3] John Rawls, "Kantian Constructivism in Moral Theory," *The Journal of Philosophy* 77 (1980), p. 568.

scope for reflection on Rawls' account, and the implausible account of human agency that results.

The Status of the Good

The difficulty with Rawls' theory of the good is epistemological as well as moral, and in this it recalls a problem that arose in connection with the concept of right—that of distinguishing a standard of assessment from the thing being assessed. If my fundamental values and final ends are to enable me, as surely they must, to evaluate and regulate my immediate wants and desires, these values and ends must have a sanction independent of the mere fact that I happen to hold them with a certain intensity. But if my conception of the good is simply the product of my immediate wants and desires, there is no reason to suppose that the critical standpoint it provides is any more worthy or valid than the desires it seeks to assess; as the product of those desires, it would be governed by the same contingencies.

Rawls responds to this difficulty in the case of the right by seeking in justice as fairness an Archimedean point that 'is not at the mercy, so to speak, of existing wants and interests' (261). But as we have seen, Rawls' concept of right does not extend to private morality, nor does any other instrument of detachment save the good from thoroughgoing implication in the agent's existing wants and desires. 'Purely preferential choice' is thoroughly heteronomous choice, and no person's values or conception of the good can possibly reach beyond it. As Rawls strikingly concedes, 'That we have one conception of the good rather than another is not relevant from a moral standpoint. In acquiring it we are influenced by the same sort of contingencies that lead us to rule out a knowledge of our sex and class.'[4]

The limited scope for reflection on Rawls' account, and the problematic, even impoverished theory of the good that results reveal the extent to which deontological liberalism accepts an essentially utilitarian account of the good, however its theory of right may differ. This utilitarian backround first appeared in our discussion of Dworkin's defense of affirmative action; once no individual rights were seen to be at stake, utilitarian considerations automatically prevailed. Although Dworkin defends what he calls an 'anti-utilitarian concept of right', the scope of this right is strictly (if elusively) circumscribed, such that 'the vast bulk of the laws that diminish my liberty are justified on utilitarian grounds as being in the general interest or for the general welfare.'[5] (269).

The utilitarian background to Rawls' conception most clearly appears in his references to individual moral life. Where justice as fairness rejects utilitarianism as the basis of social, or public morality, it has no apparent argument with

---

[4] John Rawls, "Fairness to Goodness," *The Philosophical Review* 84 (1975), p. 537.

[5] Ronald Dworkin, *Taking Rights Seriously* (Cambridge, MA: Harvard University Press, 1977), p. 269. For a compelling critique of Dworkin's view in this respect, see H. L. A. Hart, "Between Utility and Rights" in *The Idea of Freedom,* ed. A. Ryan (Oxford: Oxford University Press, 1979), pp. 86–89.

utilitarianism as the basis of individual, or private morality, the Kantian notion of 'duty to oneself' to the contrary. Rawls describes the utilitarian account of private morality, without discernible objection, as follows:

> A person quite properly acts, at least when others are not affected, to achieve his own greatest good, to advance his rational ends as far as possible.... [T]he principle for an individual is to advance as far as possible his own welfare, his own system of desires (23).

> To be sure, there is one formal principle that seems to provide a general answer [to an individual's choice of life plan]. This is the principle to adopt that plan which maximizes the expected net balance of satisfaction (416).

For Rawls, utilitarianism goes wrong not in conceiving the good as the satisfaction of arbitrarily-given desires undifferentiated as to worth—for justice as fairness shares in this—but only in being indifferent to the way these consummations are spread across individuals. Its mistake as he sees it is to adopt 'for society as a whole the principle of rational choice for one man', to combine 'the desires of all persons into one coherent system of desire', and to seek its overall satisfaction (26–7). In so doing, it 'fuses' or 'conflates' all persons into one, it reduces social choice to 'essentially a question of efficient administration' (as, presumably, individual choice can properly be reduced), and so fails to take seriously the distinction between persons (27, 33).

Justice as fairness seeks to remedy these shortcomings by emphasizing the distinction between persons and by insisting on the separateness of those diverse 'systems of desires' that utilitarianism conflates. But the grounds for Rawls' departure from utilitarianism in this respect are not immediately apparent. Although he seems firm in his view that to each individual human being there corresponds exactly one 'system of desires', he never says why this must be so, or what exactly a 'system of desires' consists in, or why it is wrong to conflate them. Is a 'system of desires' a set of desires *ordered* in a certain way, arranged in a hierarchy of relative worth or essential connection with the identity of the agent, or is it simply a concatenation of desires arbitrarily arrayed, distinguishable only by their relative intensity and accidental location? If it is the second, if a *system* of desires means nothing more than an arbitrary collection of desires accidentally embodied in some particular human being, then it is unclear why the integrity of such a 'system' should be taken so morally and metaphysically seriously. If desires can properly be conflated within persons, why not between persons as well?

If, on the other hand, what makes a *system* of desires is a hierarchical ordering of qualitatively distinguishable desires, then it would be no more justifiable to 'conflate' desires within a person than between persons, and what is wrong with utilitarianism would also be wrong, in this respect at least, with justice as fairness. The tendency to conflate desires, whether within persons or between them, would reflect the failure to *order* them, or to acknowledge the qualitative distinctions between them. But this failure cuts across the distinction between individual and social choice, for there is no reason to suppose that a 'system of desires' in *this* sense corresponds in all cases to the empirically-individuated person. Communities of various sorts could count as distinct 'systems of desires' in this sense, so long as they were identifiable in part by an order or structure of shared values partly constitutive of a common identity or form of life. From this point of view, the utilitarian failure to take seriously the distinction between persons would appear a mere symptom of its larger failure to take seriously the qualitative distinctions of worth between different orders of desires, a failure rooted in an impoverished account of the good which justice as fairness has been seen to share.

For a deontological doctrine such as Rawls' it might be thought that viewing the good as wholly mired in contingency, despite its implausibility generally, would have at least the redeeming advantage of making the primacy of right all the more compelling. If the good is nothing more than the indiscriminate satisfaction of arbitrarily-given preferences, regardless of worth, it is not difficult to imagine that the right (and for that matter a good many other sorts of claims) must outweigh it. But in fact the morally diminished status of the good must inevitably call into question the status of justice as well. For once it is conceded that our conceptions of the good are morally arbitrary, it becomes difficult to see why the highest of all (social) virtues should be the one that enables us to pursue these arbitrary conceptions 'as fully as circumstances permit'.

41

The Choice Criterion
of Value

VINIT HAKSAR

Vinit Haksar (b. 1937) is Reader in Philosophy at the University of Edinburgh. He is the author of Equality, Liberty, and Perfectionism, *from which this selection is taken. He has also written a number of articles on moral and social philosophy.*

In the selection, Haksar criticizes the "choice criterion of value." That criterion, given classical expression by John Stuart Mill in reading 26, asserts that one pleasure, activity, or form of life is superior to another if it is consistently chosen by persons who have knowledge of both. If successful, the choice criterion will offer a neutral standpoint from which to judge the value of different pleasures and activities.

But Haksar argues that the choice criterion cannot be applied. Though he considers several forms of the choice criterion, his central thesis is that its ideal of a neutral standpoint is unachievable. For example, until a person from a tribal background experiences life in modern industrial society, he cannot appreciate its appeal. But after exposure to it, he no longer has the innocence that is central to his previous way of life. Thus, he is never in a position to appreciate the attractions of both ways of life.

In general, Haksar believes that the choice criterion can at best show that an activity or way of life is well suited to those who already practice it. If we want to show something stronger, our endorsement must have some other basis.

EVEN IF FREE people prefer the free way of life, this may only show that the free way of life is suited to free people; but how does it follow that it is suited to non-autonomous people, for instance to people living in tribes? And if people in tribal societies (who have never observed the free way of life) insist that they want to stay on in the tribal way of life, it is not at all obvious that they are being irrational.

But do not free, autonomous people have more knowledge on which to base their decision regarding which form of life is better? Knowledge of alternative forms of life may not be a sufficient condition of a wise choice between the alternative ways of life, but it is a necessary condition. But now there is the complication that those who fulfil this necessary condition of the application of the choice criterion of value, become radically different in the process, and so what is good for such experts is not necessarily good for others, nor even good for them had they not become experts (experts being those who have acquired knowledge of different forms of life).

Some philosophers who are very impressed with problems of culture relativity, would go further and claim that in order to get knowledge of alternative cultures, we have to get this knowledge from the inside, we have to actually participate in the life-style before we can understand it fully. But one does not have to believe in such extreme culture relativity in order to be sceptical of the choice criterion of value. For let us grant, at any rate for the sake of argument, that a free man does not have to become a tribal person in order to observe what life is like for a tribal person; he could learn a lot about tribes from spending a lot of time with them, provided he is intelligent and sympathetic. But even if this is so, it is not clear how the choice criterion works impartially. For when one obtains knowledge, even as an intelligent and sympathetic onlooker, one becomes different after acquiring this knowledge from what one was before acquiring it. So the choice criterion of value is faced with a dilemma. Either the choice criterion is applied by someone who does not fully know about different forms of life, but in that case there is no free choice, and the 'choice' of one's own form of life does not reflect the superiority of one's own form of life; or the choice criterion is applied by the autonomous man who has acquired knowledge of the different forms of life between which the choice has to be made, but in that case the form of life that is chosen is not necessarily suited to non-autonomous people. So the Good for Man (in general) remains elusive—let us call this the dilemma about the elusiveness of Good.

Small acquisitions of knowledge are consistent with the personality remaining much the same. For instance, if you move from university X to university Y, you can be in a better position after you have acquired knowledge of both these universities to say which of them is more suited to you. But if a member of a tribal society, who has been leading a sheltered life, leaves his society and goes to observe an autonomous society, either he will get only a superficial picture of the autonomous society, or alternatively if he does get an intimate picture of such a society, the acquisition of this knowledge will be likely to change his tastes, character, and so forth. So if after observing the autonomous society, he says he prefers it, this may only show that the autonomous society is more suited to him after his change of personality, and it does not follow that it is more suited to men in general, or to other members of the tribal society, or would have been more suited to him before he underwent the trauma of living in the autonomous society.

Would similar considerations apply to a person who leaves a liberal society to go and observe a tribal society? Now it is part of the liberal ethos that a liberal must be allowed to choose between different forms of life; if a liberal who is exposed to a tribal form of life prefers the tribal form of life (where there are no civil liberties), then this suggests that he may be more suited to the tribal form of life. Though there is the complication that the social and other conditions that were present against which he made the choice may have been unfair. Thus it may be asserted that under normal conditions a liberal would not wish to give up his way of life for a tribal way of life; this move is similar to a move, discussed earlier in this chapter, whereby if a free man decides to become a slave this is because of the presence of abnormal conditions. The difficulty with such moves is in enabling us to explain normal conditions in a neutral, impartial way, without resorting to normative or perfectionist considerations.

In any case, in fact, at most only some liberals who have been exposed to tribal forms of life prefer the tribal form of life, while others would prefer to continue living under a liberal set-up; so it is not clear how we can decide from such considerations whether or not liberalism is more suited to man. The most that might follow is that liberalism is more suited to those who have been brought up in a liberal set-up, though even here there is, as we have seen, the problem of what to do with those liberals who prefer the tribal set-up, where there are no civil liberties.

The above-mentioned difficulties involved in the operation of the choice criterion of value need to be distinguished from a related but less forceful objection, namely the objection that the choice criterion of values involves brainwashing in the sense which implies deliberate inducements of beliefs and desires by some manipulator or manipulators. This last objection can be dealt with by ensuring that the person who observes and chooses between different forms of life does not have his beliefs or desires manipulated by any individual or set of individuals. But the objection we have mentioned cannot be dealt with so easily, for how do we prevent the person who has to choose between different forms of life from being altered by his knowledge? So we have a dilemma about the elusiveness of the good for man. On the one hand, to operate the choice criterion of value the experts have to be provided with the relevant knowledge. On the other hand, providing them with this knowledge can change their tastes and preferences, and what the experts choose as good for the experts may not be good for more primitive people. It might be suggested that the experts are better off than the primitive man and that therefore the rational thing would be to provide the primitive man also with the extra knowledge, so that the gap between what is good for the experts and what is good for others vanishes. But how can we (without resorting to perfectionist ideals) assume that the experts are better off than the primitive men? It is quite consistent to maintain that a person who leads a sheltered life in a tribal society is better off (for instance, because of greater psychological security) than are people who live in autonomous societies, even if it is the case that once he has been exposed to the autonomous forms of life, he will be worse off in his tribal set-up. Compare: it is quite consistent to maintain that non-smokers are better off than smokers, even if it is the case that once one has become habituated to smoking, one is better off smoking than being deprived of smoking.

Jonathan Glover says that in the case of those who undergo a prolonged state of withdrawal, 'The best evidence can only be provided by those who have experienced both normal life and the state of withdrawal. Since people in the withdrawn state are normally unwilling to discuss it, we must turn to those who have experienced it and then been cured. It is only because they are glad of the change that we have any right to describe it as a "cure."[1]

Now Glover's argument is probably a sound one, but it is crucial to his argument that people in the state of withdrawal do not claim to be well off, they just do not communicate, and so we have to rely on other evidence in order to make judgements about their welfare. But in the case of tribal societies many of the members of such societies are quite willing to talk and to claim that they are well off, and do not want to opt for the autonomous life. Similarly, many of those who indulge in what Mill would regard as the lower pleasures are willing to defend their form of life. That is why Mill feels the need for the expert's verdict. So we are still left with the dilemma about the elusiveness of the good for man.

Mill attempts to see which form of life is better by seeing what form of life his experts will choose. For Mill the experts must not only have knowledge of different forms of life (for otherwise how can they rationally say that one form of life is better than another?); they must also be equally susceptible to different forms of life. Presumably, this last requirement is there because Mill wants to compare different forms of life from an impartial standpoint; if a person is more susceptible to the higher forms of life, then his choice of the higher forms of life may just reflect his temperament, and the experiment will be biased against lower forms of life. Now Mill's requirements do not solve the problem about the elusiveness of the good for man. It is not at all easy to see how we decide when this requirement about equal susceptibility has been satisfied. And to the extent that we appear able to operate his test of equal susceptibility, we would get involved in strange forms of arguments. Suppose it is the case that homosexuals think that homosexuality is the best form of sexual life, heterosexuals think that heterosexuality is the best form of sexual life and bisexuals think that bisexuality is the best form of sexual life. Now in this example bisexuals satisfy the equal susceptibility requirement better than the others do, and so it would follow from Mill's theory that what they choose, namely bisexuality, is the best form of the sexual life for man. But this is an absurd argument. One fallacy in this argument is that since bisexuals satisfy the equal susceptibility requirement better than the others do, they are in the relevant respects rather different from the others; what is good for the former is not necessarily good for the latter; even if bisexuality is suitable for those who are equally susceptible to homosexuality and heterosexuality, it does not follow that bisexuality is suitable for those who do not satisfy the equal susceptibility test. Such non-perfectionist attempts to find the Good for Man (in general) appear doomed to fail!

Mill also mentions the requirement that of two pleasures, 'if there be one to which all or almost all who have experience of both give decided preference, irrespective of any feeling of moral obligation to prefer it, that is the more

---

[1] *Responsibility* (London, 1970), p. 124.

desirable pleasure'.[2] Now the reason why he does not allow feelings of moral obligation to be used in the application of the choice criterion of value, is that he wants to avoid biases. If people prefer a certain pleasure because of a moral feeling, then their preference may reflect their moral training, and if they had different moral training, their preferences might have been different. So to admit moral feelings would make the test subjective. Nor would Mill, without circularity, have allowed the correct or objective moral feelings to determine the preferences of the experts. For his expert test was meant to provide the test of morality and so it could not presuppose the correctness of any particular moral feeling.

Now though precautions such as not letting moral feelings affect the deliberations of the experts seem necessary for the working of the choice criterion of value, they are not sufficient to ensure fairness. To be fair between different forms of life requires a choice from some sort of neutral value-free standpoint, but such an idea is not a coherent one. Later, I shall criticize the idea that autonomous choices are somehow neutral between different forms of life and therefore can be used to operate the choice criterion of value.

There are several versions of the choice criterion of value. Here are two of them. First, there is what I shall call the hypothetical choice criterion of value (or of justice) according to which to find out what is valuable (or just) we have to appeal to what a hypothetical observer (or agent) would choose. Secondly, there is what I shall call the categorical choice criterion of value, according to which in order to find out what is valuable we have to allow people in real life freely to choose between different forms of life. The best form of life will emerge from the open and fair competition between the different forms of life; the undeserving ones will become extinct.

Now this distinction between hypothetical and categorical choice criterion is of some importance in understanding problems of liberalism, as well as in understanding the views of quite a few political philosophers. Many of the sophisticated contractarian philosophers, such as Rousseau and Rawls, appeal to a hypothetical choice criterion of value. Rousseau appeals to the hypothetical choice criterion of value in his rejection of slavery (see the quotation from him given earlier in this chapter). When Mill (as interpreted by Rawls)[3] suggests that the best form of life will emerge from open and fair competition between different forms of life, he is appealing to the categorical choice criterion of value. Rawls, like Mill, uses the categorical choice criterion of value in order to find out the Good.[4] But, unlike Mill, he uses the hypothetical choice criterion to construct a well-ordered society,[5] which provides a fair background against which the categorical choice criterion of Mill's can operate. Later we shall see that Rawls uses two versions of the hypothetical choice criterion.

---

[2] *Utilitarianism,* chapter II, para. 5.

[3] 'Fairness to Goodness,' *The Philosophical Review* 84 (1975), section 6.

[4] Ibid.

[5] *A Theory of Justice* (Cambridge, MA, 1971), section 3, and 'Fairness to Goodness', section 6.

There is another equally important distinction. This is the distinction between applying the choice criterion of value to ultimate values, and applying it at the non-ultimate level. If you presuppose some values and then operate the choice criterion of value, you are operating it at a non-ultimate level. If, however, you do not presuppose any values, and yet apply the choice criterion of value, then you are applying it at an ultimate level, you are using it to try to establish ultimate values. Now if the choice criterion of value enables us to establish ultimate values, then it can successfully bypass perfectionist considerations. But for reasons given in this chapter the choice criterion of value (whether in its categorical or its hypothetical version) cannot be applied at the ultimate level; at best it can be applied at the non-ultimate level.

That the categorical choice criterion cannot be applied at the ultimate level can be seen from the following considerations. When we set up a fair system for the categorical choice criterion to operate, the system itself cannot without circularity be justified by an appeal to the choice criterion. This point can be illustrated by a reference to Rawls. Rawls says that his well-ordered society sets a fair background for the operation of Mill's choice criterion of value.[6] Now it would be circular if Rawls were to try to justify his well-ordered society by appealing to Mill's choice criterion of value (and indeed earlier we saw he gets in danger of circularity when he uses the Aristotelian principle to construct his well-ordered society). Probably Rawls would try to get out of such a circle, by claiming that the well-ordered society is justified by an appeal to a hypothetical choice criterion, and not by an appeal to a categorical choice criterion such as Mill's. The principles of fairness that help to construct the well-ordered society set the stage for the operation of Mill's categorical choice criterion, are the principles that would be chosen by people in the original position; since the original position is a fiction, the choice of the principles of fairness is hypothetical; Rawls refers to what people would choose *if* they were in the original position. But hypothetical choices, too, if they are to carry the weight that they have to in Rawls's system, must be made against a fair background (otherwise, why should anyone pay heed to such choices?), and so we are still left with the problem of how to construct a fair background against which the parties in the original position must choose. If we try to answer this last problem by appealing to what people would choose we would get involved in a circle or a regress. Rawls himself seems to avoid such difficulties by appealing to our intuitions. Thus he rightly realizes that the contractarian model can be set up in different ways, with different constraints, and that the choices that the parties in the original position make could vary with the way in which the model has been set up. He then has to face the problem of why we should set up the model in one way rather than another. To answer such a problem Rawls is driven to appeal to our intuitions. That way of constructing the model is best which gives the best fit with our intuitions in reflective equilibrium. Our intuitions help to set up a fair background against which the parties in the

---

[6] 'Fairness to Goodness', p. 579.

original position can make their choices. So the choice criterion of value would here be used at a non-ultimate level; it would presuppose (at least provisionally) the values revealed by our intuitions.

Rawls would admit that the categorical choice criterion does operate against the background of a well-ordered society, and so it does presuppose what is Right and Just. Now if one uses values in a broad sense to include not only the Good but also the Right (and Just), then it follows that the categorical choice criterion presupposes the value of Right or Just, and is designed only to find out the Good. But does it even succeed in telling us how to find out the Good? Does it not presuppose some substantial idea of the Good in order to work? Later in this chapter it will be argued that it does, and that the categorical choice criterion at best can only tell us what is valuable if it already assumes certain substantial ideas of Good.

Rawls appeals to a hypothetical choice criterion (for instance, when he tells us what the parties in the original position would choose), but he also appeals to a categorical choice criterion; he appeals to the latter somewhat in the way that Mill and Hart do. Rawls believes that if a form of life deserves to survive, it must survive in open and fair competition against rival forms of life;[7] if it does not survive under such conditions its demise is not to be lamented. Here his position is similar to Mill's, who believes that a civilized community should not impose its way of life on a barbaric community by force: 'If civilization has got the better of barbarism when barbarism had the world to itself, it is too much to profess to be afraid lest barbarism, . . . should revive and conquer civilization. A civilization that can thus succumb to its vanquished enemy must first have become so degenerate . . . [that] the sooner such a civilization receives notice to quit the better.'[8] Here Mill is talking about one community not imposing its way of life upon another, but it is clear from his writings that he believed that within the same society also the state should not protect civilized forms of life by barring other forms of life (as long as the latter are not harming other people they should be allowed to co-exist with the civilized forms of life). Indeed, it has been argued that Mill's choice criterion of value requires a liberal society in order to work; for the choice to be a criterion (or evidence) of value, it must be a choice under conditions of liberty.

There is a similar idea in Hart who considers Burke's 'wisdom of the ages' argument, according to which 'the social institutions which have slowly been developed in the course of any society's history represent an accommodation to the needs of that society which is always likely to be more satisfactory to the mass of its members than any ideal scheme of social life which individuals would invent or any legislator could impose.' Hart thinks that such an argument could only work if the social institutions have developed as a result of the 'free, though no doubt unconscious adaption of men to the conditions of their lives. To use coercion to maintain the moral *status quo* at any point in a

---

[7] 'Fairness to Goodness', p. 549.

[8] Mill, *On Liberty*, chapter IV, last para.

society's history would be artificially to arrest the process which gives social institutions their value.'[9]

The Mill-Hart-Rawls view can be contrasted with that of Rousseau, for instance. Rousseau used a weaker criterion and implied that if the legislators freely banned a practice for several generations, this would tend to show that the practice was worth banning.[10] He believed in a weak version of the categorical choice criterion of value; he wanted the legislators to choose a form of life freely or under conditions of liberty, but unlike Mill, Rawls, and Hart, who believe in a stronger version of the categorical choice criterion of value, he did not think it necessary that virtuous forms of life should be made legally to co-exist with their rivals. The legislators on Rousseau's views could freely ban a form of life that they thought was a rival to the virtuous form of life. On the stronger version of the categorical choice criterion of value, the law should allow open and fair competition between rival forms of life; the different forms of life were allowed (by the law) to be practised. On the weaker version of the choice criterion of value, there is freedom to discuss the pros and cons of various forms of life; but that is weaker than the freedom to practice different forms of life.

Briefly, and roughly, the difference between the weak and the strong version of the categorical choice criterion of value can be characterized as follows: the former requires freedom of discussion, whereas the latter requires in addition to freedom of discussion, freedom to practice the rival forms of life. Now the strong version of the categorical choice principle cannot be used to defend all values, for the reasons given in this chapter. At the political level, the strong version of the categorical choice principle cannot be applied to the constitution which sets the fair background for the operation of the categorical principle (in its strong version). There is normally no room for two competing constitutions to co-exist simultaneously in the same state, applying to the same area. It may be that in some transitional situations it is not clear which constitution is binding; it is not clear whether the old constitution still applies or whether the new one has taken over; and for a time we may have two constitutions, both competing with each other for acceptance. But once one of them is accepted, the other one does not apply. It would be strange to argue that we should not have only one constitution, on the grounds that we must carry out experiments in living with several constitutions.

Now we can see a mistake that Hart makes in his discussion of 'the wisdom of the ages' argument. The 'wisdom of the ages' argument can work if the citizens, or at least the wise among them, are allowed to have considerable influence on how the laws and institutions should be adapted to the needs of society. Without such influence, there is no reason to think that the current institutions and laws incorporate the wisdom of the ages. If you have a history of tyrants ruling the country, tyrants who take no heed of the prevalent wis-

---

[9] *Law, Liberty and Morality* (London, 1963), p. 75.

[10] *The Social Contract*, Book III, chapter XI.

dom, there is no reason to think that our current laws and institutions, however old they are, represent the wisdom of the ages. Free discussion too (at any rate among the wise) is probably essential if the citizens' judgements are to be informed and wise. But such requirements are weaker than the requirements that Hart (mistakenly) thinks are essential for the working of the 'wisdom of the ages' argument. For as we have seen, Hart not only insists on freedom of discussion, but freedom to practice different forms of life. The point is not that Hart may not be right in insisting on the legal freedom to practice different forms of life, but rather that such legal freedom is not necessary for the 'wisdom of the ages' argument to work. One could quite consistently side with Devlin in the Devlin-Hart controversy[11] about the enforcement of morality and yet believe in the 'wisdom of the ages' argument.

Indeed, if Hart's strong version of liberalism were essential for the 'wisdom of the ages' argument to work, it would follow that the basic constitution of the country, even though it has been amended from time to time, in response to the prevailing wisdom of the time, could not incorporate the wisdom of the ages. For a society can only have one constitution at a time. And while people can freely discuss the pros and cons of rival constitutions, they cannot allow rival forms of constitution to legally co-exist, simultaneously. If you think (as I do) that it makes sense to say that a country's constitution incorporates the wisdom of the ages (for instance, because the constitution has been adapted from time to time in response to wise and informed criticisms), then you cannot agree with the view that the 'wisdom of the ages' argument *only* works when a law or an institution has been competing with its rivals.

All the liberals are involved in the problem of having to justify their ground-rules, the framework of justice within which different forms of life can flourish. Rawls's principles of justice have been disputed by other thinkers, even by fellow-liberals such as Hart. And Rawls himself admits that people can disagree about what principles of justice can be derived from his contractarian experiment. Again Mill lays down certain ground-rules that all ways of life must satisfy if they are to be permitted by law to compete with other forms of life. Thus he too would not allow infanticide to be legally permissible on the grounds that it was a valuable experiment in living, without which people could not reach a rational decision about the best form of life. His ground-rules were provided by his harm principle: 'the only purpose for which power can be rightfully exercised over any member of a civilized community, against his will, is to prevent harm to others.'[12]

Now people disagree about the correct formulation of the harm principle.[13] Even liberals cannot agree on what the ground-rules should be. We have seen that the strong version of the categorical choice criterion does not apply to the

---

[11] See Hart, *Law, Liberty and Morality,* and P. Devlin, *The Enforcement of Morals* (London, 1965).

[12] Mill, *On Liberty,* chapter I, para. 9.

[13] See J. Feinberg, *Social Philosophy* (Englewood Cliffs, 1973).

ground-rules; and since the question of what the ground-rules are, is contro-versial, how do we identify the sphere where it is legitimate to operate the strong version of the categorical choice criterion of value? Compare the fol-lowing suggestions:

1. Those who want to beat their wives should be allowed to do so. Then we shall have experiments in living that will enable us to decide whether wife-beating is a superior form of life to non-wife-beating. If the practice of non-wife-beating deserves to survive, it must survive in open compe-tition with the practice of wife-beating.
2. Parents who want to kill their infants should be allowed to do so. Then we shall have experiments in living that will enable us to decide whether infanticide is a superior form of life to non-infanticide. If the practice of non-infanticide deserves to survive, it must survive in open competition with the practice of infanticide.
3. Women who want abortions should be allowed to have them. Then we shall have experiments in living that will enable us to decide whether abortion is a superior form of life to non-abortion.
4. Those who eat meat and have animals killed should be allowed to do so. Then we shall have experiments in living that will enable us to decide whether these forms of life are superior. If vegetarianism deserves to survive, it must survive in open competition with meat eating.
5. Collectivist and individualist ways of life should be allowed to openly compete with each other. If collectivist ways of life deserve to survive, they must be able to survive in open competition with rival forms of life.
6. We must have experiments in living in different forms of education and the upbringing of children. Some schools should concentrate on the 'higher' forms of art, culture, and so forth; other centres should concentrate on the charms of pornography, polymorphous perversity (as recommended by Marcuse), masturbation competitions, and so forth. The best form of life can emerge from such open competition between different forms of life.

It is obvious that liberals such as Rawls and Mill will not allow practices such as 1 and 2. 'Experiments in living', like other desirable activities, have to be carried out within certain moral constraints. We have no business to sacrifice the welfare of individual women in order to find out whether the practice of wife-beating is suited to the human race, or in order to prevent the view that wife-beating is wrong from becoming a dead dogma. But what some liberals do not realize is that similar moral constraints may be operative in the case of practices such as, for instance, 3, 4, 5, and 6. No doubt if some people are vegetarians while others are meat eaters, we can learn an enormous amount about the value or non-value for human beings of eating meat; for instance, we can compare the health of meat-eaters with that of vegetarians, and try to discover whether eating meat is associated with certain illnesses, and whether lack of meat is associated with certain other illnesses, or deficiencies. But those who believe in animal rights will insist that such experiments in living are subject to moral constraints, that animal rights must not be sacrificed lightly for the sake of other desirable goals.

Again, experiments in different forms of education may well lead to many desirable ends, but such experiments are subject to moral constraints. For instance, the interests of children who get less desirable forms of education must not be sacrificed, merely because such experiments will help us to discover the best form of education. Human beings have just one life, and if an individual child is ruined by a bad education, it is not sufficient compensation for him to be told that other children in the future will benefit from the experiments that were conducted with him. He must not be treated merely as a guinea-pig. Rawls says (with considerable plausibility) that the important thing is to be fair to individuals, not to ways of life.[14] I suggest that an unnoticed but important corollary of this view is that we must not be unfair to some individuals in order to be fair to different forms of life; for instance, we must not sacrifice the interests of children by sending some of them to hippie schools in order to be fair to the hippie way of life! So this important point about being fair to individuals rather than to ways of life, is not so helpful to a person such as Rawls who wants to argue for equal liberties to the various ways of life!

There are of course other hazards in pursuing 'experiments in living'. Even from a consequentialist viewpoint, too many options can lead to neurosis, instability, and insecurity, and some people may well be much better off in an environment where they were less burdened with the agonies of choice. But here I have stressed the moral constraints or the ground-rules that must constrain our pursuit of liberal practice such as 'experiments in living'. The point about the agonies and burdens of choice makes one wonder whether it is worthwhile preferring a liberal to a non-liberal society. But even if we go in for a liberal society, we shall be limited by the kind of considerations just stressed, as well as by the undesirable effects of too many choices (for even if we opt for a liberal society, there can be enormous variations in how many options we allow).

The view that the categorical choice criterion of value cannot serve as a criterion for what is ultimately good can be reinforced by the following considerations. Barry makes some important remarks about fairness of contests, which in my opinion have serious implications for the categorical choice criteria of value, though Barry himself does not work out these implications. Barry rightly points out that the idea of a contest is to test the competitors for the possession of some quality or qualities, and he suggests that one 'can define fairness in a contest as that which makes it more likely that the competitor with the greater amount of the quality which is being tested will win'.[15] This gives us a rough idea of how to apply fairness to cases of boxing matches, intellectual exminations, and so forth; if the desired quality is intellectual effort, we will have one kind of examination, if the desired quality is to test

---

[14] 'Fairness to Goodness'.

[15] Brian Barry, *Political Argument* (London, 1965), p. 304.

intellectual ability, we shall have another kind of examination. But now when liberals like Rawls talk of fair competition between different forms of life, how can they specify the desired qualities that they are seeking for in such a contest, without presupposing some substantial idea of the Good?

It is true the aim of the categorical choice criterion of good is to discover the most suitable form of life. But this does not tell us anything sufficiently specific about the desirable qualities that we should look for in the 'contestants'. Compare: suppose examiners are told to set out an examination that is suitable for the students; this would not be a sufficiently precise guide to the examiners as to what constitutes a fair examination. On the Rawlsian liberal view we are in the dark about the Good; and yet we see that without presupposing some substantial ideas of the Good we cannot arrange a fair contest between different forms of life and so we cannot operate the categorical choice criterion of value. Perhaps the way out of this circle would be to assert that the categorical choice criterion has a more modest role; it does not tell us about what is ultimately good; but assuming certain values, it can help us to find out which forms of life are unsuited to human beings under certain conditions. Thus suppose under certain conditions the dominant form of life cannot survive in open competition with fringe forms of life; in that case it may be that such a form of life is not suited to human beings under those conditions.

In fact Rawls does appeal to certain ideals of the person,[16] and these along with his principles of justice help him to set up his well-ordered society. The well-ordered society is set up from the point of view of the original position, which is meant to be a neutral and fair standpoint. And Rawls would claim that the well-ordered society would set a fair background within which different forms of life can compete. But this does not get us out of the difficulties in the way of setting up a fair contest between different forms of life, without presupposing substantial ideas of the Good. Rawls's well-ordered society cannot be set up without appealing to perfectionist ideals; for instance, we have seen that the view that autonomous life is essential to human well being is a kind of perfectionism; and the view that animal interests count for less than human interests commits us to perfectionism in the strong sense. Moreover, the most the well-ordered society does is to tell us which forms of life should not be allowed to compete for our allegiance. For instance, the well-ordered society would rule out forms of life, such as fascism, which violate the principles of justice. But the well-ordered society does not tell us how to arrange fair competition between those forms of life that are eligible to compete with each other for our allegiance. What constitutes fair competition between forms of life that encourage polymorphous perversity, and the forms of life that encourage a more puritanical upbringing? What constitutes fair competition between the mystic way of life and the materialistic form of life? How much influence should each form of life have in the upbringing of children? Should we go by some kind of numerical weighting, so that those ways of life with 90 percent

---

[16] *A Theory of Justice*, p. 262.

support in the population are encouraged in 90 per cent of the schools, while a fringe form of life which has a following among 0.01 per cent of the population, gets 0.01 per cent of the schools. But this may be 'unfair' to the fringe form of life. For the fact that only 0.01 per cent of the population believe in the fringe form of life may be a reflection of the raw deal that such a form of life has received in the past, so how can we get a fair starting-point? How can Rawls argue that if a form of life disappears in open competition with rival forms of life, 'then its passing is not to be regretted'?[17]

One of the important problems facing the categorical choice criterion (in its more ambitious version) is that this criterion only works (if it works at all) in the case of autonomous and knowledgeable individuals. If heteronomous (or ignorant) individuals prefer a form of life, such a preference may just reflect their conditioning, and cannot be taken as evidence of the suitability of that form of life for human beings in general. For the choice criterion to work, the choice has to be by individuals who are autonomous and knowledgeable about different ways of life; that is why Mill resorted to his expert criterion (according to which that form of life is best which the experts prefer rather than what the people at large prefer). Now children are not autonomous creatures and so the choice criterion of value will not work with children. Nor will it work with the bulk of grown-up people who are not experts. The fact that many prejudiced grown-ups reject a form of life does not imply that that form of life was not a good one.

To operate the hypothetical choice criterion, we do not have to create or operate a system where experts (who are autonomous agents with competence to choose between different forms of life) choose between different forms of life. Similarly, the original position (as described by Rawls) does not have to exist; it could suffice that we simulate it. But to operate the categorical choice criterion we have to actually create and operate an actual society that is full of experts. But how do we do that? By force or by liberal means? Certainly we cannot rely upon just finding a society that is full of experts, for if we examined any existing society only a small minority would be experts. So how can we operate the categorical choice criterion? And unless we can operate this criterion how can we argue that because a way of life was rejected by our society, therefore it deserved to be rejected. For it may be that the decision to reject it reflects the ignorance of the masses.

There are certain forms of life, such as the highest form of mysticism, that require enormous cultivation and discipline. All or almost all who have experienced the highest forms of mysticism, prefer the mystical form of life to our ordinary materialistic way of life. If we use Mill's experts' test of value, the experts being those who have experienced the different forms of life that are being compared, the test would, if anything, show that the mystical forms of life are superior. Yet such superior forms of life may well disappear in a liberal–democratic society where the experts are in a minority. The bulk of

[17] 'Fairness to Goodness', p. 549.

the population, being ignorant (since they have never experienced the charms of such a form of life), may be put off by the discipline and hard work required in the initial stages. It may happen that as the experts in this sphere die out, they are not replaced. Suppose their children are educated in schools that are devoted to more materialistic ways of life, or suppose that with increasing urbanization people do not grow up in an atmosphere that is congenial to the development of the mystical personality. Now if, because of some such conditions, the masses in a liberal society reject the mystical form of life, would a Rawlsian be right in inferring that such forms of life deserved to become extinct, 'that their passing is not to be regretted'? The mystical form of life has been used here only as an illustration. Similar points could be made about other forms of life that are, as Mill would say, like tender plants and require cultivation.

There is the added problem that even the experts' choice is not an unbiased one. Even if the individual is an autonomous agent, which way he chooses will be influenced to some extent (even though it is not determined) by the way he was brought up. So we have a dilemma. The categorical choice criterion cannot work in the case of children for they are immature and non-autonomous. Yet by the time one is an autonomous individual one has already acquired preferences in favour of certain ways of life. Thus most autonomous individuals in our society would reject the life of polymorphous perversity. But had they been brought up by people who were more sympathetic to the life of polymorphous perversity, they might now, consistently with retaining their autonomy, have preferred the life of polymorphous perversity.

The autonomous man differs from the heteronomous man in not automatically accepting the way of life that he has been brought up in. He reflects upon the customary way of life and compares it with the alternatives. But even the autonomous man does not choose his final aims in a vacuum. Which way of life he will choose after reflection will depend at best partly upon the way he was brought up, and upon the prevailing social conditions. His choices depend not only upon knowledge of the alternative life-styles, but also upon his emotions and his imagination. And his emotions and imagination may depend at least partly upon the way he was brought up, upon the kind of schools he went to, his home life, and so forth. Suppose people have been brought up in rural surroundings congenial to mysticism, in the company of mystical gurus and mystical music and so forth. If a person has been brought up in such surroundings when he was young, when he grows up he may autonomously reject alternative ways of life; even after the pros and cons of alternative life-styles have been pointed out to him, he may genuinely prefer the mystical way of life. Yet it is quite possible that had the same individual been brought up in a different way and in a different setting his autonomous preferences when he grew up would have been quite different. Thus, had he been brought up in an urban, materialistic culture it may be that his capacity for the mystical form of life would have been destroyed, and as a grown-up he would autonomously reject the mystical form of life.

Even if we assume liberal-democratic forms of government, which forms of life will flourish will depend at least partly upon such factors as the amount of urbanization and industrialization. So how do we decide what is a fair starting-point? A rural setting or an industrial setting?

Perhaps the most that one might argue is that *assuming* certain values x, y, z (for instance, the values of an industrialized, materialist society), if certain forms of life do not survive in a liberal society which is dominated by values x, y, and z, then such forms of life are not suitable. But of course if we abandon the assumption that the dominant values of a society are good, then the mere fact that a form of life does not survive in that society would not show that such a form of life did not deserve to survive.

There is also an element of truth in the view that the dominant form of life should be able to survive in open competition against rival forms of life, and that if it cannot survive in such open competition, then it does not deserve to survive. But it does not follow from this that if, say, a non-dominant form of life does not survive in open competition, it did not deserve to survive. It might be that the fringe form of life, unlike the dominant form of life, did not have a chance to assert itself. The element of truth in the categorical choice criterion of value cannot enable it to bypass perfectionist considerations.

42

Value

THOMAS NAGEL

For biographical information about Thomas Nagel, see reading 30.

In this selection, Nagel discusses one version of the question of whether values are objective. In his view, an objective value is one that provides reasons for acting that do not depend on anyone's particular situation or perspective. These reasons can be recognized even by persons who are not interested parties. Although Nagel warns that we must not "elevate personal tastes and prejudices into cosmic views," his position is that there are objective values that provide all persons with reasons for acting. For example, the awfulness of physical pain is a reason for even nonsufferers to want it to disappear. Just as my pain is a reason for me to take an aspirin, so too is it a reason for you to want me to take an aspirin.

The view that values are objective has been criticized by many philosophers, among them Gilbert Harman and J. L. Mackie (readings 13 and 14). However, Nagel tries to show that arguments like theirs are inconclusive. In addition, he draws several interesting distinctions between different types of objective values. On these and other matters, his views require, and reward, careful study.

1. Whether values can be objective depends on whether an interpretation of objectivity can be found that allows us to advance our knowledge of what to do, what to want, and what things provide reasons for and against action. Last week I argued that the physical conception of objectivity was not able to provide an understanding of the mind, but that another conception was available which allowed external understanding of at least some *aspects* of mental phenomena. A still different conception is required to make sense of the objectivity of values, for values are neither physical nor mental. And even if we find a conception, it must be applied with care. Not all values are likely to prove to be objective in any sense.

Let me say in advance that my discussion of values and reasons in this lecture and the next will be quite general. I shall be talking largely about what determines whether something has value, or whether someone has a reason to do or want something. I shall say nothing about how we pass from the identification of values and reasons to a conclusion as to what should be *done*. That is of course what makes reasons important; but I shall just assume that values do often provide the basis for such conclusions, without trying to describe even in outline how the full process of practical reasoning works. I am concerned here only with the general question, whether values have an objective foundation at all.

In general, as I said last time, objectivity is advanced when we step back, detach from our earlier point of view toward something, and arrive at a new view of the whole that is formed by including ourselves and our earlier viewpoint in what is to be understood.

In theoretical reasoning this is done by forming a new conception of reality that includes ourselves as components. This involves an alteration, or at least an extension, of our beliefs. Whether the effort to detach will actually result in an increase of understanding depends on the creative capacity to form objective ideas which is called into action when we add ourselves to the world and start over.

In the sphere of values or practical reasoning, the problem is somewhat different. As in the theoretical case, in order to pursue objectivity we must take up a new, comprehensive viewpoint after stepping back and including our former perspective in what is to be understood. But in this case the new viewpoint will be *not* a new set of *beliefs,* but a new, or extended, set of *values.* If objectivity means anything here, it will mean that when we detach from our individual perspective and the values and reasons that seem acceptable from within it, we can sometimes arrive at a new conception which may endorse some of the original reasons but will reject some as subjective appearances and add others. This is what is usually meant by an objective, disinterested view of a practical question.

The basic step of placing ourselves and our attitudes within the world to be considered is familiar, but the form of the result—a new set of values, reasons, and motives—is different. In order to discover whether there are any objective values or reasons we must try to arrive at *normative* judgments, with *motivational content,* from an impersonal standpoint: a standpoint outside of our lives. We cannot use a *non-normative* criterion of objectivity: for *if* any values are objective, they are objective *values*, not objective anything else.

2. There are many opinions about whether what we have reason to do or want can be determined from a detached standpoint toward ourselves and the world. They range all the way from the view that objectivity has *no* place in this domain except what is inherited from the objectivity of those theoretical and factual elements that play a role in practical reasoning, to the view that objectivity applies here, but with a nihilistic result: i.e., that nothing is objectively right or wrong because objectively nothing matters. In between are many positive objectifying views which claim to get some definite results from a detached standpoint. Each of them is criticized by adherents of opposing views either for trying to force too much into a single objective framework or for according too much or too little respect to divergent subjective points of view.

Here as elsewhere there is a direct connection between the goal of objectivity and the belief in *realism.* The most basic idea of practical objectivity is arrived at by a practical analogue of the rejection of solipsism or idealism in the theoretical domain. Just as realism about the facts leads us to seek a detached point of view from which reality can be discerned and appearance corrected, so realism about values leads us to seek a detached point of view from which it will be possible to correct inclination and to discern what we really should do, or want. Practical objectivity means that practical reason can be understood and even engaged in by the objective self.

This assumption, though powerful, is not yet an ethical position. It merely marks the place which an ethical position will occupy if we can make any sense of the subject. It says that the world of reasons, including my reasons, does not exist only from my point of view. I am in a world whose properties are to a certain extent independent of what I think, and if I have reasons to act it is because the person who I am has those reasons, in virtue of his condition and circumstances. One would expect those reasons to be understandable from outside. Here as elsewhere objectivity is a form of understanding not necessarily available for all of reality. But it is reasonable at least to look for such understanding over as wide an area as possible.

3. It is important not to lose sight of the dangers of *false* objectification, which too easily elevate personal tastes and prejudices into cosmic values. But initially, at least, it is natural to look for some objective account of those reasons that appear from one's own point of view.

In fact those reasons usually present themselves with some pretensions of objectivity to begin with, just as perceptual appearances do. When two things look the same size to me, they look at least initially as if they *are* the same size. And when I want to take aspirin because it will cure my headache, I believe at least initially that this *is* a reason for me to take aspirin, that it can be recognized as a reason from outside, and that if I failed to take it into account, that would be a mistake, and others could recognize this.

The ordinary process of deliberation, aimed at finding out what I have reason to do, assumes that the question has an answer. And in difficult cases especially, deliberation is often accompanied by the belief that I may not *arrive* at that answer. I do not assume that the correct answer is just whatever will result or has resulted from consistent application of deliberative methods—even assuming perfect information about the facts. In deliberation we are trying to arrive at conclusions that are correct in virtue of something *independent* of our arriving at them. If we arrive at a conclusion, we believe that it would have been correct even if we *hadn't* arrived at it. And we can also acknowledge that we might be *wrong*, since the process of reasoning doesn't guarantee the correctness of the result. So the pursuit of an objective account of practical reasons has its basis in the realist claims of ordinary practical reasoning. In accordance with pretheoretical judgment we adopt the working hypothesis that there are reasons which may diverge from actual motivation even under conditions of perfect information—as reality can diverge from appearance—and then consider what form these reasons take. I shall say more about the general issue of realism later on. But first I want to concentrate on the process of thought by which, against a realist background, one might try to arrive at objective conclusions about reasons for action. In other words, if there really are values, how is objective knowledge of them possible?

In this inquiry no particular hypothesis occupies a privileged position, and it is certain that some of our starting points will be abandoned as we proceed. However, one condition on reasons obviously presents itself for consideration: a condition of generality. This is the condition that if something provides a reason for a particular individual to do something, then there is a general form of that reason which applies to anyone else in comparable circumstances. What count as comparable circumstances depends on the general form of the reason. This condition is not tautological. It is a rather strong condition which may be false, or true only for some kinds of reasons. But the search for generality is a natural beginning.

4. There is more than one type of generality, and no reason to assume that a single form will apply to every kind of reason or value. In fact I think that the choice among types of generality defines some of the central issues of contemporary moral theory.

One respect in which reasons may vary is in their *breadth*. A general principle may apply to everyone but be quite specific in content, and it is an open question to what extent narrower principles of practical reasons (don't lie; develop your talents) can be subsumed under broader ones (don't hurt others; consider your long-term interests), or even at the limit under a single widest principle from which all the rest derive. Reasons may be general, in other words, without forming a unified system that always provides a method for arriving at determinate conclusions about what one should do.

A second respect in which reasons vary is in their *relativity to the agent,* the person for whom they are reasons. The distinction between reasons that are relative to the agent and reasons that are not is an extremely important one. I shall follow Derek Parfit in using the terms 'agent-relative' and 'agent-neutral' to mark this distinction. (Formerly I used the terms 'subjective' and 'objective,' but those terms are here reserved for other purposes.)

If a reason can be given a general form which does *not* include an essential reference to the person to whom it applies, it is an *agent-neutral* reason. For example, if it is a reason for *anyone* to do or want something that it would reduce the amount of wretchedness in the world, then that is an agent-neutral reason.

If on the other hand the general form of a reason *does* include an essential reference to the person to whom it applies, it is an *agent-relative* reason. For example, if it is a reason for anyone to do or want something that it would be in *his* interest, then that is an agent-relative reason. In such a case, if something were in Jones's interest but contrary to Smith's, Jones would have reason to want it to happen and Smith would have the *same* reason to want it *not* to happen. (Both agent-relative and agent-neutral reasons are objective, since both can be understood from outside the viewpoint of the individual who has them.)

A third way in which reasons may vary is in their degree of externality, or independence of the interests of sentient beings. Most of the apparent reasons that initially present themselves to us are intimately connected with interests and desires, our own or those of others, and often with experiential satisfaction. But it is conceivable that some of these interests give evidence that their objects have intrinsic value independent of the satisfaction that anyone may derive from them or of the fact that anyone wants them—independent even of the existence of beings who can take an interest in them. I shall call a reason *internal* if it depends on the existence of an interest or desire in someone, and *external* if it does not. External reasons were believed to exist by Plato, and more recently by G. E. Moore, who believed that aesthetic value provided candidates for this kind of externality.

These three types of variation cut across one another. Formally, a reason may be narrow, external, and agent-relative (don't eat pork, keep your promises), or broad, internal, and agent-neutral (promote happiness), or internal and agent-relative (promote your own happiness). There may be other significant dimensions of variation. I want to concentrate on these because they locate the main controversies about what ethics is. Reasons and values that can be described in these terms provide the material for objective judgments. If one looks at human action and its conditions from outside and considers whether some normative principles are plausible, these are the forms they will take.

The actual *acceptance* of a general normative judgment will have motivational implications, for it will commit you under some circumstances to the acceptance of reasons to want and do things *yourself.*

This is most clear when the objective judgment is that something has *agent-neutral* value. That means *anyone* has reason to want it to happen—*and that includes someone considering the world in detachment from the perspective of any particular person within it.* Such a judgment has motivational content even before it is brought back down to the particular perspective of the individual who has accepted it objectively.

Agent-relative reasons are different. An objective judgment that some kind of thing has *agent-relative* value commits us only to believing that someone has reason to want and pursue it if it is related to him in the right way (being in *his* interest, for example). Someone who accepts this judgment is not committed to wanting it to *be the case* that people in general are influenced by such reasons. The judgment commits him to wanting something only when its implications are drawn *for the individual person he happens to be.* With regard to others, the content of the objective judgment concerns only what *they* should do or want.

I believe that judgments of both these kinds, as well as others, are evoked from us when we take up an objective standpoint. And I believe such judgments can be just as true and compelling as objective factual judgments about the real world that contains us.

5. When we take the step to objectivity in practical reasoning by detaching from our own point of view, the question we must ask ourselves is this: What reasons for action can be said to apply to people when we regard them from a standpoint detached from the values of any particular person?

The simplest answer, and one that some people would give, is "None." But that is not the only option. The suggested classification of types of generality provides a range of alternative hypotheses. It also provides some flexibility of response, for with regard to any reason that may appear to a particular individual to exist subjectively, the corresponding objective judgment may be that it does not exist at all, or that it corresponds to an agent-neutral, external value, or anything in between.

The choice among these hypotheses, plus others not yet imagined, is difficult, and there is no general method of making it any more than there is a general method of selecting the most plausible objective account of the facts on the basis of the appearances. The only 'method,' here or elsewhere, is to try to generate hypotheses and then to consider which of them seems most reasonable, in light of everything else one is fairly confident of.

This is not quite empty, for it means at least that logic alone can settle nothing. We do *not* have to be shown that the denial of some kind of objective values is *self-contradictory* in order to be reasonably led to accept their existence. There is no constraint to pick the weakest or narrowest or most economical principle consistent with the initial data that arise from individual perspectives. Our admission of reasons beyond these is determined *not* by logical entailment, but by what we cannot help believing, or at least finding most plausible among the alternatives.

In this respect it is no different from anything else: theoretical knowledge does not arise by deductive inference from the appearances either. The main difference is that our objective thinking about practical reasons is very primitive, and has difficulty taking even the first step. Philosophical skepticism and idealism about values are much more popular than their metaphysical counterparts. Nevertheless I believe they are no more correct. I shall argue that although no *single* objective principle of practical reason like egoism or utilitarianism covers everything, the acceptance of some objective values is unavoidable—not because the alternative is inconsistent but because it is not *credible*. Someone who, as in Hume's example, prefers the destruction of the whole world to the scratching of his finger, may not be involved in a *contradiction* or in any false *expectations,* but he is unreasonable nonetheless (to put it mildly), and anyone else not in the grip of an overly narrow conception of what reasoning is would regard his preference as objectively wrong.

6. But even if it is unreasonable to deny that anyone ever objectively has a reason to do anything, it is not easy to find positive objective principles that *are* reasonable. I am going to attempt to defend a few in the rest of this lecture and the next. But I want to acknowledge in advance that it is not easy to follow

the objectifying impulse without distorting individual life and personal relations. We want to be able to understand and accept the way we live from outside, but it may not always follow that we should control our lives from inside by the terms of that external understanding. Often the objective viewpoint will not be suitable as a replacement for the subjective, but will coexist with it, setting a standard with which the subjective is constrained not to clash. In deciding what to do, for example, we should not reach a result different from what we could decide objectively that that *person* should do—but we need not arrive at the result in the same way from the two standpoints.

Sometimes, also, the objective standpoint will allow us to judge how people should *be* or should *live,* without permitting us to translate this into a judgment about what they have *reasons* to do. For in some respects it is better to live and act not for reasons, but because we cannot help it. This is especially true of close personal relations. Here the objective standpoint cannot be brought into the perspective of *action* without destroying precisely what it affirms the value of. Nevertheless the possibility of this objective affirmation is important. We should be *able* to view our lives from outside without extreme dissociation or distaste, and the extent to which we should live without *considering* the objective point of view or even any reasons *at all* is itself *determined* largely from that point of view.

It is also possible that some idiosyncratic individual grounds of action, or the values of strange communities, will prove objectively inaccessible. To take an example in our midst: I don't think that people who want to be able to run twenty-six miles without stopping are irrational, but their reasons can be understood only from the perspective of a value system that is completely alien to me, and will I hope remain so. A correct objective view will have to allow for such pockets of unassimilable subjectivity, which need not clash with objective principles but won't be affirmed by them either. Many aspects of personal taste will come in this category, if, as I think, they cannot all be brought under a general hedonistic principle.

But the most difficult and interesting problems of accommodation appear where objectivity *can* be employed as a standard, but we have to decide *how.* Some of the problems are these: To what extent should an objective view admit *external* values? To what extent should it admit *internal* but *agent-neutral* values? To what extent should the reasons to respect the interests of *others* take an *agent-relative* form? To what extent is it legitimate for each person to give priority to his own interests? These are all questions about the proper form of generality for different kinds of practical reasoning, and the proper relation between objective principles and the deliberations of individual agents. I shall return to some of them later, but there is a great deal that I shall not get to.

I shall not, for example, discuss the question of external values, i.e., values which may be *revealed* to us by the attractiveness of certain things, but whose existence is independent of the existence of any interests or desires. I am not sure whether there are any such values, though the objectifying tendency produces a strong impulse to believe that there are, especially in aesthetics where the object of interest is external and the interest seems perpetually capable of criticism in light of further attention to the object.

What I shall discuss is the proper form of *internal* values or reasons—those which depend on interests or desires. They can be objectified in more than one way, and I believe different forms of objectification are appropriate for different cases.

7. I plan to take up some of these complications in the next lecture. Let me begin, however, with a case for which I think the solution is simple: that of pleasure and pain. I am not an ethical hedonist, but I think pleasure and pain are very important, and they have a kind of neutrality that makes them fit easily into ethical thinking—unlike preferences or desires, for example, which I shall discuss later on.

I mean the kinds of pleasure and pain that do not depend on activities or desires which *themselves* raise questions of justification and value. Many pleasures and pains are just sensory experiences in relation to which we are fairly passive, but toward which we feel involuntary desire or aversion. Almost everyone takes the avoidance of his own pain and the promotion of his own pleasure as subjective reasons for action in a fairly simple way; they are not backed up by any further reasons. On the other hand if someone pursues pain or avoids pleasure, these idiosyncracies usually *are* backed up by further reasons, like guilt or sexual masochism. The question is, what sort of general value, if any, ought to be assigned to pleasure and pain when we consider these facts from an objective standpoint?

It seems to me that the least plausible hypothesis is the zero position, that pleasure and pain have no value of any kind that can be objectively recognized. That would mean that looking at it from outside, you couldn't even say that someone had a reason not to put his hand on a hot stove. Try looking at it from the outside and see whether you can manage to withhold that judgment.

But I want to leave this position aside, because what really interests me is the choice between two other hypotheses, both of which admit that people have reason to avoid their own pain and pursue their own pleasure. They are the fairly obvious general hypotheses formed by assigning (a) agent-relative or (b) agent-neutral value to those experiences. If the avoidance of pain has only agent-relative value, then people have reason to avoid their own pain, but not to avoid the pain of others (unless other kinds of reasons come into play). If the avoidance of pain has agent-neutral value as well, then *anyone* has a reason to want *any* pain to stop, whether or not it is his. From an objective standpoint, which of these hypotheses is more plausible? Is the value of sensory pleasure and pain agent-relative or agent-neutral?

I believe it is agent-neutral, at least in part. That is, I believe pleasure is a good thing and pain is a bad thing, and that the most reasonable objective principle which admits that each of us has reason to pursue his own pleasure and avoid his own pain will acknowledge that these are not the only reasons present. This is a normative claim. Unreasonable, as I have said, does not mean inconsistent.

In arguing for this claim, I am somewhat handicapped by the fact that I find it self-evident. It is therefore difficult for me to find something still more certain with which to back it up. But I shall try to say what is wrong with rejecting it, and with the reasons that may lie behind its rejection. What would it be to really *accept* the alternative hypothesis that pleasure and pain are not impersonally good or bad? If I accept this hypothesis, assuming at the same time that each person has reason to seek pleasure and avoid pain for *himself,* then when I regard the matter objectively the result is very peculiar. I will have to believe that I have a reason to take aspirin for a headache, but that there *is no reason* for me to *have* an aspirin. And I will have to believe the same about anyone else. From an objective standpoint I must judge that everyone has reason to pursue a type of result that is *impersonally valueless,* that has value only to *him.*

This needs to be explained. If agent-neutral reasons are not ruled out of consideration from the start (and one would need reasons for that), why do we not have evidence of them here? The avoidance of pain is not an individual project, expressing the agent's personal values. The desire to make pain stop is simply *evoked* in the person who feels it. He may decide for various reasons not to stop it, but in the first instance he doesn't have to *decide* to want it to stop: he just does. He wants it to go away because it's *bad*: it is not *made* bad by his deciding that he wants it to go away. And I believe that when we think about it objectively, concentrating on what pain is *like,* and ask ourselves whether it is (a) not bad at all, (b) bad only for its possessor, or (c) bad *period,* the third answer is the one that needs to be argued *against,* not the one that needs to be argued *for.* The philosophical problem here is to get rid of the obstacles to the admission of the obvious. But first they have to be identified.

Consider how *strange* is the question posed by someone who wants a justification for altruism about such a basic matter as this. Suppose he and some other people have been admitted to a hospital with severe burns after being rescued from a fire. "I understand how *my* pain provides *me* with a reason to take an analgesic," he says, "and I understand how my groaning neighbor's pain gives *him* a reason to take an analgesic; but how does *his* pain give *me* any reason to want him to be given an analgesic? How can *his* pain give *me* or anyone else looking at it from outside a reason?"

This question is *crazy.* As an expression of puzzlement, it has that characteristic philosophical craziness which indicates that something very fundamental has gone wrong. This shows up in the fact that the *answer* to the question is *obvious,* so obvious that to ask the question is obviously a philosophical act. The answer is that pain is *awful.* The pain of the man groaning in the next bed is just as awful as yours. That's your reason to want him to have an analgesic.

Yet to many philosophers, when they think about the matter theoretically, this answer seems not to be available. The pain of the person in the next bed is thought to need major external help before it can provide me with a reason for wanting or doing anything: otherwise it can't get its hooks into me. Since most of these people are perfectly aware of the force such considerations actually have for them, justifications of some kind are usually found. But they take the form of working *outward* from the desires and interests of the individual for whom reasons are being sought. The burden of proof is thought always to be on the claim that he has reason to care about anything that is not *already* an object of his interest.

These justifications are unnecessary. They plainly falsify the real nature of the case. My reason for wanting my neighbor's pain to cease is just that it's awful, and I know it.

8. What is responsible for this demand for justification with its special flavor of philosophical madness? I believe it is something rather deep, which doesn't surface in the ordinary course of life: an inappropriate sense of the burden of proof. Basically, we are being asked for a demonstration of the *possibility* of real impersonal values, on the assumption that they are *not* possible unless such a general proof can be given.

But I think this is wrong. We can already *conceive* of such a possibility, and once we take the step of thinking about what reality, if any, there is in the domain of practical reason, it becomes a possibility we are bound to consider, that we cannot help considering. If there really are *reasons*, not just motivational pushes and pulls, and if agent-neutral reasons are among the kinds we can conceive of, then it becomes an obvious possibility that physical pain is simply bad: that even from an impersonal standpoint there is reason to want it to stop. When we view the matter objectively, this is one of the general positions that naturally suggests itself.

And once this is seen as a *possibility*, it becomes difficult *not* to accept it. It becomes a hypothesis that has to be *dislodged* by anyone who wishes to claim, for example, that all reasons are agent-relative. The question is, what are the alternatives, once we take up the objective standpoint? We must think *something*. If there is room in the realistic conception of reasons for agent-neutral values, then it is unnatural *not* to ascribe agent-neutral badness to burn pains. That is the natural conclusion from the fact that anyone who has a burn pain and is therefore closest to it wants acutely to be rid of it, and requires no indoctrination or training to want this. This evidence does not *entail* that burn pains are impersonally bad. It is logically conceivable that there is nothing bad about them at all, or that they provide only agent-relative reasons to their possessors to want them to go away. But to take such hypotheses seriously we would need justifications of a kind that seem totally unavailable in this case.

What could possibly show us that acute physical pain, which everyone finds horrible, is in reality not impersonally bad at all, so that except from the point of view of the sufferer it doesn't in itself matter? Only a very remarkable and farfetched picture of the value of a cosmic order beyond our immediate grasp, in which pain played an essential part which made it good or at least neutral— or else a demonstration that there can *be* no agent-neutral values. But I take it that neither of these is available: the first because the Problem of Evil has not been solved, the second because the absence of a logical demonstration that there *are* agent-neutral values is not a demonstration that there are *not* agent-neutral values.

My position is this. No demonstration is necessary in order to allow us to *consider* the possibility of agent-neutral reasons: the possibility simply *occurs* to us once we take up an objective stance. And there is no mystery about how an individual could have a reason to want something independently of its relation to his particular interests or point of view, because beings like ourselves are not *limited* to the particular point of view that goes with their personal position inside the world. They are also, as I have put it earlier, *objective selves*: they cannot *help* forming an objective conception of the world with themselves in it; they cannot help trying to arrive at judgments of *value* from that standpoint; they cannot help asking whether, from that standpoint, in abstraction from who in the world they are, they have any reason to want anything to be the case or not—any reason to want anything to happen or not.

Agent-neutral reasons do not have to find a miraculous source in our personal lives, because we are not *merely* personal beings: we are also importantly and essentially viewers of the world *from nowhere within it*—and in this capacity we remain open to judgments of value, both general and particular. The possibility of agent-neutral values is evident as soon as we begin to think from this standpoint about the reality of any reasons whatever. If we acknowledge the possibility of realism, then we cannot rule out agent-neutral values in advance.

Realism is therefore the fundamental issue. If there really are values and reasons, then it should be possible to expand our understanding of them by objective investigation, and there is no reason to rule out the natural and compelling objective judgment that pain is impersonally bad and pleasure impersonally good. So let me turn now to the abstract issue of realism about values.

9. Like the presumption that things exist in an external world, the presumption that there are real values and reasons can be defeated in individual cases, if a purely subjective account of the appearances is more plausible. And like the presumption of an external world, its complete falsity is not self-contradictory. The reality of values, agent-neutral or otherwise, is not *entailed* by the totality of appearances any more than the reality of a physical universe is. But if either of them is recognized as a possibility, then its reality in detail can be confirmed by appearances, at least to the extent of being rendered more plausible than the alternatives. So a lot depends on whether the possibility of realism is admitted in the first place.

It is very difficult to argue for such a possibility. Sometimes there will be arguments against it, which one can try to refute. Berkeley's argument against the conceivability of a world independent of experience is an example. But what is the result when such an argument is refuted? Is the possibility in a stronger position? I believe so: in general, there is no way to prove the possibility of realism; one can only refute impossibility arguments, and the more often one does this the more confidence one may have in the realist alternative. So to consider the merits of an admission of realism about value, we have to consider the reasons against it. I shall discuss three. They have been picked for their apparent capacity to convince people.

The first argument depends on the question-begging assumption that if values are real, they must be real objects of some other kind. John Mackie, for example, in his recent book *Ethics,* denies the objectivity of values by saying that they are not part of the fabric of the world, and that if they were, they would have to be "entities or qualities or relations of a very strange sort, utterly different from anything else in the universe."[1] Apparently he has a very definite picture of what the universe is like, and assumes that realism about value would require crowding it with extra entities, qualities, or relations—things like Platonic Forms or Moore's non-natural qualities. But this assumption is not correct. The impersonal badness of pain is not some mysterious further property that all pains have, but just the fact that there is reason for anyone capable of viewing the world objectively to want it to *stop,* whether it is his or someone else's. The view that values are real is not the view that they are real occult entities or properties, but that they are real *values*: that our claims about value and about what people have reason to do may be *true* or *false* independently of our beliefs and inclinations. No *other* kinds of truths are involved. Indeed, no other kinds of truths *could* imply the reality of values.[2]

The second argument I want to consider is not, like the first, based on a misinterpretation of moral objectivity. Instead, it tries to represent the unreality of values as an objective *discovery.* The argument is that if claims of value have to be objectively correct or incorrect, and if they are not reducible to any *other* kind of objective claim, then we can just *see* that all positive value claims must be false. Nothing has any objective value, because objectively nothing matters at all. If we push the claims of objective detachment to their logical conclusion, and survey the world from a standpoint completely detached from all interests, we discover that there is *nothing*—no values left of any kind: things can be said to matter at all only to individuals within the world. The result is objective nihilism.

I don't deny that the objective standpoint tempts one in this direction. But I believe this can seem like the required conclusion only if one makes the

---

[1] J. L. Mackie, *Ethics* (Harmondsworth, Middlesex: Penguin Books, 1977), p. 38.

[2] In discussion, Mackie claimed that I had misrepresented him, and that his disbelief in the reality of values and reasons does not depend on the assumption that to be real they must be strange *entities* or *properties.* As he says in his book, it applies directly to reasons themselves. For whatever they are they are not needed to explain anything that happens, and there is consequently no reason to believe in their existence. But I would reply that this raises the same issue. It begs the question to assume that *explanatory* necessity is the test of reality in this area. The claim that certain reasons exist is a normative claim, not a claim about the best explanation of anything. To assume that only what has to be included in the best explanatory picture of the world is real, is to assume that there are no irreducibly normative truths.

There is much more to be said on both sides of this issue, and I hope I have not misrepresented Mackie in this short footnote.

mistake of assuming that objective judgments of value must emerge from the detached standpoint *alone*. It is true that with nothing to go on but a conception of the world from nowhere, one would have no way of telling whether anything had value. But an objective view has more to go on, for its data include the appearance of value to individuals with particular perspectives, including oneself. In this respect practical reason is no different from anything else. Starting from a pure idea of a possible reality and a very impure set of appearances, we try to fill in the idea of reality so as to make some partial sense of the appearances, using objectivity as a method. To find out what the world is like from outside we have to approach it from within: it is no wonder that the same is true for ethics. And indeed, when we take up the objective standpoint, the problem is not that values seem to disappear but that there seem to be too many of them, coming from every life and drowning out those that arise from our own. It is just as easy to form desires from an objective standpoint as it is to form beliefs. Probably easier. Like beliefs, these desires and evaluations must be criticized and justified partly in *terms* of the appearances. But they are not just further appearances, any more than the beliefs about the world which arise from an impersonal standpoint are just further appearances.

The third type of argument against the objective reality of values is an empirical argument. It is also perhaps the most common. It is intended not to rule out the possibility of real values from the start, but rather to demonstrate that even if their *possibility* is admitted, we have no reason to believe that there are any. The claim is that if we consider the wide cultural variation in normative beliefs, the importance of social pressure and other psychological influences to their formation, and the difficulty of settling moral disagreements, it becomes highly implausible that they are anything but pure appearances.

Anyone offering this argument must admit that not every psychological factor in the explanation of an appearance shows that the appearance corresponds to nothing real. Visual capacities and elaborate training play a part in explaining the physicist's perception of a cloud-chamber track, or a student's coming to believe a proposition of geometry, but the path of the particle and the truth of the proposition also play an essential part in these explanations. So far as I know, no one has produced a general account of the kinds of psychological explanation that discredit an appearance. But some skeptics about ethics feel that because of the way we acquire moral beliefs and other impressions of value, there are grounds for confidence that no real, objective values play a part in the explanation.

I find the popularity of this argument surprising. The fact that morality is socially inculcated and that there is radical disagreement about it across cultures, over time, and even within cultures at a time is a poor reason to conclude that values have no objective reality. Even where there is truth, it is not always easy to discover. Other areas of knowledge are taught by social pressure, many truths as well as falsehoods are believed without rational grounds, and there is wide disagreement about scientific and social facts, especially where strong interests are involved which will be affected by different answers to a disputed question. This last factor is present throughout ethics to a uniquely high degree: it is an area in which one would expect extreme variation of belief and radical disagreement however objectively real the subject actually was. For comparably motivated disagreements about matters of fact, one has to go to the heliocentric theory, the theory of evolution, the Dreyfus case, the Hiss case, and the genetic contribution to racial differences in I.Q.

Although the methods of ethical reasoning are rather primitive, the degree to which agreement can be achieved and social prejudices transcended in the face of strong pressures suggests that something real is being investigated, and that part of the explanation of the appearances, both at simple and at complex levels, is that we perceive, often inaccurately, that certain reasons for action exist, and go on to infer, often erroneously, the general form of the principles that best accounts for those reasons.

The controlling conception that supports these efforts at understanding, in ethics as in science, is realism, or the possibility of realism. Without being sure that we will find one, we look for an account of what reasons there really are, an account that can be objectively understood.

I have not discussed all the possible arguments against realism about values, but I have tried to give general reasons for skepticism about such arguments. It seems to me that they tend to be supported by a narrow preconception of what there *is,* and that this is essentially question-begging.

· · ·

43

The Virtues, the Unity of a Human Life, and the Concept of a Tradition

ALISDAIR MacINTYRE

Alisdair MacIntyre (b. 1929) has taught philosophy at a number of colleges and universities, and is currently Professor of Philosophy at Vanderbilt. His books include A Short History of Ethics, Secularization and Moral Change, Against the Self-Images of the Age, *and, most recently,* After Virtue.

In this selection, taken from After Virtue, *MacIntyre traces the moral importance of the concept of narrative. While many philosophers have concentrated on isolated actions, MacIntyre argues that such actions are intelligible only as parts of the larger stories that agents tell about themselves. To understand these stories, we must appreciate both the agents' intentions and the concepts that those intentions presuppose. We must also appreciate that each storyteller is himself a character in the stories of others. So central is our status as protagonists of narratives that personal identity itself must be understood in these terms.*

What bearing does all of this have on morality? According to MacIntyre, there are a number of connections. If the unity of a life depends on its narrative structure, then a person's good is the way he "might live out that unity and bring it to completion." (For an interesting contrast, compare Rawls's view, developed in reading 39, that a person's good is determined by his rational life plan.) More generally, the "good for man" is whatever the goods of all individual persons have in common. And the virtues are dispositions that, among other things, enable us to pursue the quest for the good. Since the good is illuminated by the notion of narrative, and narratives in turn are illuminated by traditions and social practices, the good must also have a social and historical dimension. Thus, views like Kant's, which regard morality as ahistorical (see reading 29), are bound to fail.

ANY CONTEMPORARY ATTEMPT to envisage each human life as a whole, as a unity, whose character provides the virtues with an adequate *telos* encounters two different kinds of obstacle, one social and one philosophical. The social obstacles derive from the way in which modernity partitions each human life into a variety of segments, each with its own norms and modes of behaviour.

So work is divided from leisure, private life from public, the corporate from the personal. So both childhood and old age have been wrenched away from the rest of human life and made over into distinct realms. And all these separations have been achieved so that it is the distinctiveness of each and not the unity of the life of the individual who passes through those parts in terms of which we are taught to think and to feel.

The philosophical obstacles derive from two distinct tendencies, one chiefly, though not only, domesticated in analytical philosophy and one at home in both sociological theory and in existentialism. The former is the tendency to think atomistically about human action and to analyse complex actions and transactions in terms of simple components. Hence the recurrence in more than one context of the notion of 'a basic action'. That particular actions derive their character as parts of larger wholes is a point of view alien to our dominant ways of thinking and yet one which it is necessary at least to consider if we are to begin to understand how a life may be more than a sequence of individual actions and episodes.

Equally the unity of a human life becomes invisible to us when a sharp separation is made either between the individual and the roles that he or she plays—a separation characteristic not only of Sartre's existentialism, but also of the sociological theory of Ralf Dahrendorf—or between the different role- and quasi-role—enactments of an individual life so that life comes to appear as nothing but a series of unconnected episodes—a liquidation of the self characteristic, as I noticed earlier, of Goffman's sociological theory. I already also suggested in Chapter 3 that both the Sartrian and the Goffmanesque conceptions of selfhood are highly characteristic of the modes of thought and practice of modernity. It is perhaps therefore unsurprising to realise that the self as thus conceived cannot be envisaged as a bearer of the Aristotelian virtues.

For a self separated from its roles in the Sartrian mode loses that arena of social relationships in which the Aristotelian virtues function if they function at all. The patterns of a virtuous life would fall under those condemnations of conventionality which Sartre put into the mouth of Antoine Roquentin in *La Nausée* and which he uttered in his own person in *L'Etre et le néant*. Indeed the self's refusal of the inauthenticity of conventionalised social relationships becomes what integrity is diminished into in Sartre's account.

At the same time the liquidation of the self into a set of demarcated areas of role-playing allows no scope for the exercise of dispositions which could genuinely be accounted virtues in any sense remotely Aristotelian. For a virtue is not a disposition that makes for success only in some one particular type of situation. What are spoken of as the virtues of a good committee man or of a good administrator or of a gambler or a pool hustler are professional skills professionally deployed in those situations where they can be effective, not virtues. Someone who genuinely possesses a virtue can be expected to manifest it in very different types of situation, many of them situations where the practice of a virtue cannot be expected to be effective in the way that we expect a professional skill to be. Hector exhibited one and the same courage in his parting from Andromache and on the battlefield with Achilles; Eleanor Marx exhibited one and the same compassion in her relationship with her father, in her work with trade unionists and in her entanglement with Aveling. And the unity of a virtue in someone's life is intelligible only as a characteristic of a unitary life, a life that can be conceived and evaluated as a whole. Hence just as in the discussion of the changes in and fragmentation of morality which accompanied the rise of modernity in the earlier parts of this book, each stage in the emergence of the characteristically modern views of the moral judgment was accompanied by a corresponding stage in the emergence of the character-istically modern conceptions of selfhood; so now, in defining the particular pre-modern concept of the virtues with which I have been preoccupied, it has become necessary to say something of the concomitant concept of selfhood, a concept of a self whose unity resides in the unity of a narrative which links birth to life to death as narrative beginning to middle to end.

Such a conception of the self is perhaps less unfamiliar than it may appear at first sight. Just because it has played a key part in the cultures which are historically the predecessors of our own, it would not be surprising if it turned out to be still an unacknowledged presence in many of our ways of thinking and acting. Hence it is not inappropriate to begin by scrutinising some of our most taken-for-granted, but clearly correct conceptual insights about human actions and selfhood in order to show how natural it is to think of the self in a narrative mode.

It is a conceptual commonplace, both for philosophers and for ordinary agents, that one and the same segment of human behaviour may be correctly characterised in a number of different ways. To the question 'What is he doing?' the answers may with equal truth and appropriateness be 'Digging', 'Garden-ing', 'Taking exercise', 'Preparing for winter' or 'Pleasing his wife'. Some of these answers will characterise the agent's intentions, others unintended con-sequences of his actions, and of these unintended consequences some may be such that the agent is aware of them and others not. What is important to notice immediately is that any answer to the questions of how we are to under-stand or to explain a given segment of behaviour will presuppose some prior answer to the question of how these different correct answers to the question 'What is he doing?' are related to each other. For if someone's primary inten-tion is to put the garden in order before the winter and it is only incidentally the case that in so doing he is taking exercise and pleasing his wife, we have one type of behaviour to be explained; but if the agent's primary intention is to please his wife by taking exercise, we have quite another type of behaviour to be explained and we will have to look in a different direction for under-standing and explanation.

In the first place the episode has been situated in an annual cycle of domestic activity, and the behaviour embodies an intention which presupposes a partic-ular type of household-cum-garden setting with the peculiar narrative history of that setting in which this segment of behaviour now becomes an episode. In the second instance the episode has been situated in the narrative history of a marriage, a very different, even if related, social setting. We cannot, that is to say, characterise behaviour independently of intentions, and we cannot characterise intentions independently of the settings which make those intentions intelligible both to agents themselves and to others.

I use the word 'setting' here as a relatively inclusive term. A social setting may be an institution, it may be what I have called a practice, or it may be a milieu of some other human kind. But it is central to the notion of a setting as I am going to understand it that a setting has a history, a history within which the histories of individual agents not only are, but have to be, situated, just because without the setting and its changes through time the history of the individual agent and his changes through time will be unintelligible. Of course one and the same piece of behaviour may belong to more than one setting. There are at least two different ways in which this may be so.

In my earlier example the agent's activity may be part of the history both of the cycle of household activity and of his marriage, two histories which have happened to intersect. The household may have its own history stretching back through hundreds of years, as do the histories of some European farms, where the farm has had a life of its own, even though different families have in different periods inhabited it; and the marriage will certainly have its own history, a history which itself presupposes that a particular point has been reached in the history of the institution of marriage. If we are to relate some particular segment of behaviour in any precise way to an agent's intentions and thus to the settings which that agent inhabits, we shall have to understand in a precise way how the variety of correct characterisations of the agent's behaviour relate to each other first by identifying which characteristics refer us to an intention and which do not and then by classifying further the items in both categories.

Where intentions are concerned, we need to know which intention or intentions were primary, that is to say, of which it is the case that, had the agent intended otherwise, he would not have performed that action. Thus if we know that a man is gardening with the self-avowed purposes of healthful exercise and of pleasing his wife, we do not yet know how to understand what he is doing until we know the answer to such questions as whether he would continue gardening if he continued to believe that gardening was healthful exercise, but discovered that his gardening no longer pleased his wife, *and* whether he would continue gardening, if he ceased to believe that gardening was healthful exercise, but continued to believe that it pleased his wife, *and* whether he would continue gardening if he changed his beliefs on both points. That is to say, we need to know both what certain of his beliefs are and which of them are causally effective; and, that is to say, we need to know whether certain contrary-to-fact hypothetical statements are true or false. And until we know this, we shall not know how to characterise correctly what the agent is doing.

Consider another equally trivial example of a set of compatibly correct answers to the question 'What is he doing?' 'Writing a sentence'; 'Finishing his book'; 'Contributing to the debate on the theory of action'; 'Trying to get tenure'. Here the intentions can be ordered in terms of the stretch of time to which reference is made. Each of the shorter-term intentions is, and can only be made, intelligible by reference to some longer-term intentions; and the characterisation of the behaviour in terms of the longer-term intentions can only be correct if some of the characterisations in terms of shorter-term intentions are also correct. Hence the behaviour is only characterised adequately when we know what the longer and longest-term intentions invoked are and how the shorter-term intentions are related to the longer. Once again we are involved in writing a narrative history.

Intentions thus need to be ordered both causally and temporally and both orderings will make references to settings, references already made obliquely by such elementary terms as 'gardening', 'wife', 'book' and 'tenure'. Moreover the correct identification of the agent's beliefs will be an essential constituent of this task; failure at this point would mean failure in the whole enterprise. . . .

Consider what the argument so far implies about the interrelationships of the intentional, the social and the historical. We identify a particular action only by invoking two kinds of context, implicitly if not explicitly. We place the agent's intentions, I have suggested, in causal and temporal order with reference to their role in his or her history; and we also place them with reference to their role in the history of the setting or settings to which they belong. In doing this, in determining what causal efficacy the agent's intentions had in one or more directions, and how his short-term intentions succeeded or failed to be constitutive of long-term intentions, we ourselves write a further part of these histories. Narrative history of a certain kind turns out to be the basic and essential genre for the characterisation of human actions.

It is important to be clear how different the standpoint presupposed by the argument so far is from that of those analytical philosophers who have constructed accounts of human actions which make central the notion of 'a' human action. A course of human events is then seen as a complex sequence of individual actions, and a natural question is: How do we individuate human actions? Now there are contexts in which such notions are at home. In the recipes of a cookery book for instance actions are individuated in just the way that some analytical philosophers have supposed to be possible of all actions. 'Take six eggs. Then break them into a bowl. Add flour, salt, sugar, etc.' But the point about such sequences is that each element in them is intelligible as an action only as a-possible-element-in-a-sequence. Moreover even such a sequence requires a context to be intelligible. If in the middle of my lecture on Kant's ethics I suddenly broke six eggs into a bowl and added flour and sugar, proceeding all the while with my Kantian exegesis, I have *not,* simply in virtue of the fact that I was following a sequence prescribed by Fanny Farmer, performed an intelligible action.

. . .

The most familiar type of context in and by reference to which speech-acts and purposes are rendered intelligible is the conversation. Conversation is so all-pervasive a feature of the human world that it tends to escape philosophical attention. Yet remove conversation from human life and what would be left? Consider then what is involved in following a conversation and finding it intelligible or unintelligible. (To find a conversation intelligible is not the same as to understand it; for a conversation which I overhear may be intelligible, but I may fail to understand it.) If I listen to a conversation between two other people my ability to grasp the thread of the conversation will involve an ability to bring it under some one out of a set of descriptions in which the degree and kind of coherence in the conversation is brought out: 'a drunken, rambling quarrel', 'a serious intellectual disagreement', 'a tragic misunderstanding of each other', 'a comic, even farcical misconstrual of each other's motives', 'a penetrating interchange of views', 'a struggle to dominate each other', 'a trivial exchange of gossip.'

The use of words such as 'tragic', 'comic', and 'farcical' is not marginal to such evaluations. We allocate conversations to genres, just as we do literary narratives. Indeed a conversation is a dramatic work, even if a very short one, in which the participants are not only the actors, but also the joint authors, working out in agreement or disagreement the mode of their production. For it is not just that conversations belong to genres in just the way that plays and novels do; but they have beginnings, middles and endings just as do literary works. They embody reversals and recognitions; they move towards and away from climaxes. There may within a longer conversation be digressions and subplots, indeed digressions within digressions and subplots within subplots.

But if this is true of conversations, it is true also *mutatis mutandis* of battles, chess games, courtships, philosophy seminars, families at the dinner table, businessmen negotiating contracts—that is, of human transactions in general. For conversation, understood widely enough, is the form of human transactions in general. Conversational behaviour is not a special sort or aspect of human behaviour, even though the forms of language-using and of human life are such that the deeds of others speak for them as much as do their words. For that is possible only because they are the deeds of those who have words.

I am presenting both conversations in particular then and human actions in general as enacted narratives. Narrative is not the work of poets, dramatists and novelists reflecting upon events which had no narrative order before one was imposed by the singer or the writer; narrative form is neither disguise nor decoration. Barbara Hardy has written that 'we dream in narrative, daydream in narrative, remember, anticipate, hope, despair, believe, doubt, plan, revise, criticise, construct, gossip, learn, hate and love by narrative' in arguing the same point.[1]

At the beginning of this chapter I argued that in successfully identifying and understanding what someone else is doing we always move towards placing a particular episode in the context of a set of narrative histories, histories both of the individuals concerned and of the settings in which they act and suffer. It is now becoming clear that we render the actions of others intelligible in this way because action itself has a basically historical character. It is because we all live out narratives in our lives and because we understand our own lives

---

[1] Barbara Hardy, "Towards a Poetics of Fiction: An Approach Through Narrative," *Novel* 2 (1968), p. 5.

in terms of the narratives that we live out that the form of narrative is appropriate for understanding the actions of others. Stories are lived before they are told—except in the case of fiction.

This has of course been denied in recent debates. Louis O. Mink, quarrelling with Barbara Hardy's view, has asserted: 'Stories are not lived but told. Life has no beginnings, middles, or ends; there are meetings, but the start of an affair belongs to the story we tell ourselves later, and there are partings, but final partings only in the story. There are hopes, plans, battles and ideas, but only in retrospective stories are hopes unfulfilled, plans miscarried, battles decisive, and ideas seminal. Only in the story is it America which Columbus discovers and only in the story is the kingdom lost for want of a nail.'[2]

What are we to say to this? Certainly we must agree that it is only retrospectively that hopes can be characterised as unfulfilled or battles as decisive and so on. But we so characterise them in life as much as in art. And to someone who says that in life there are no endings, or that final partings take place only in stories, one is tempted to reply, 'But have you never heard of death?' Homer did not have to tell the tale of Hector before Andromache could lament unfulfilled hope and final parting. There are countless Hectors and countless Andromaches whose lives embodied the form of their Homeric namesakes, but who never came to the attention of any poet. What is true is that in taking an event as a beginning or an ending we bestow a significance upon it which may be debatable. Did the Roman republic end with the death of Julius Caesar, or at Philippi, or with the founding of the principate? The answer is surely that, like Charles II, it was a long time a-dying; but this answer implies the reality of its ending as much as do any of the former. There is a crucial sense in which the principate of Augustus, or the taking of the oath in the tennis court, or the decision to construct an atomic bomb at Los Alamos constitute beginnings, the peace of 404 B.C., the abolition of the Scottish Parliament and the battle of Waterloo equally constitute endings; while there are many events which are both endings and beginnings.

As with beginnings, middles and endings, so also with genres and with the phenomenon of embedding. Consider the question of to what genre the life of Thomas Becket belongs, a question which has to be asked and answered before we can decide how it is to be written. (On Mink's paradoxical view this question could not be asked until *after* the life had been written.) In some of the medieval versions, Thomas's career is presented in terms of the canons of medieval hagiography. In the Icelandic *Thomas Saga* he is presented as a saga hero. In Dom David Knowles's modern biography the story is a tragedy, the tragic relationship of Thomas and Henry II, each of whom satisfies Aristotle's demand that the hero be a great man with a fatal flaw. Now it clearly makes sense to ask who is right, if anyone: the monk William of Canterbury, the author of the saga, or the Cambridge Regius Professor Emeritus? The answer

[2] Louis O. Mink, "History and Fiction as Modes of Comprehension," *New Literary History,* 1 (1970), pp. 557–58.

appears to be clearly the last. The true genre of the life is neither hagiography nor saga, but tragedy. So of such modern narrative subjects as the life of Trotsky or that of Lenin, of the history of the Soviet Communist Party or the American presidency, we may also ask: To what genre does their history belong? And this is the same question as: What type of account of their history will be both true and intelligible?

. . .

I spoke earlier of the agent as not only an actor, but an author. Now I must emphasize that what the agent is able to do and say intelligibly as an actor is deeply affected by the fact that we are never more (and sometimes less) than the co-authors of our own narratives. Only in fantasy do we live what story we please. In life, as both Aristotle and Engels noted, we are always under certain constraints. We enter upon a stage which we did not design and we find ourselves part of an action that was not of our making. Each of us being a main character in his own drama plays subordinate parts in the dramas of others, and each drama constrains the others. In my drama, perhaps, I am Hamlet or Iago or at least the swineherd who may yet become a prince, but to you I am only A Gentleman or at best Second Murderer, while you are my Polonius or my Gravedigger, but your own hero. Each of our dramas exerts constraints on each other's, making the whole different from the parts, but still dramatic.

It is considerations as complex as these which are involved in making the notion of intelligibility the conceptual connecting link between the notion of action and that of narrative. Once we have understood its importance the claim that the concept of an action is secondary to that of an intelligible action will perhaps appear less bizarre and so too will the claim that the notion of 'an' action, while of the highest practical importance, is always a potentially misleading abstraction. An action is a moment in a possible or actual history or in a number of such histories. The notion of a history is as fundamental a notion as the notion of an action. Each requires the other. . . .

A central thesis then begins to emerge: man is in his actions and practice, as well as in his fictions, essentially a story-telling animal. He is not essentially, but becomes through his history, a teller of stories that aspire to truth. But the key question for men is not about their own authorship; I can only answer the question 'What am I to do?' if I can answer the prior question 'Of what story or stories do I find myself a part?' We enter human society, that is, with one or more imputed characters—roles into which we have been drafted—and we have to learn what they are in order to be able to understand how others respond to us and how our responses to them are apt to be construed. It is through hearing stories about wicked stepmothers, lost children, good but misguided kings, wolves that suckle twin boys, youngest sons who receive no inheritance but must make their own way in the world and eldest sons who waste their inheritance on riotous living and go into exile to live with the swine, that children learn or mislearn both what a child and what a parent is, what the cast of characters may be in the drama into which they have been born and what the ways of the world are. Deprive children of stories and you

581

leave them unscripted, anxious stutterers in their actions as in their words. Hence there is no way to give us an understanding of any society, including our own, except through the stock of stories which constitute its initial dramatic resources. Mythology, in its original sense, is at the heart of things. Vico was right and so was Joyce. And so too of course is that moral tradition from heroic society to its medieval heirs according to which the telling of stories has a key part in educating us into the virtues.

I suggested earlier that 'an' action is always an episode in a possible history: I would now like to make a related suggestion about another concept, that of personal identity. Derek Parfit and others have recently drawn our attention to the contrast between the criteria of strict identity, which is an all-or-nothing matter (*either* the Tichborne claimant *is* the last Tichborne heir; *either* all the properties of the last heir belong to the claimant *or* the claimant is not the heir—Leibniz's Law applies) and the psychological continuities of personality which are a matter of more or less. (Am I the same man at fifty as I was at forty in respect of memory, intellectual powers, critical responses? More or less.) But what is crucial to human beings as characters in enacted narratives is that, possessing only the resources of psychological continuity, we have to be able to respond to the imputation of strict identity. I am forever whatever I have been at any time for others—and I may at any time be called upon to answer for it—no matter how changed I may be now. There is no way of *founding* my identity—or lack of it—on the psychological continuity or discontinuity of the self. The self inhabits a character whose unity is given as the unity of a character. Once again there is a crucial disagreement with empiricist or analytical philosophers on the one hand and with existentialists on the other.

Empiricists, such as Locke or Hume, tried to give an account of personal identity solely in terms of psychological states or events. Analytical philosophers, in so many ways their heirs as well as their critics, have wrestled with the connection between those states and events and strict identity understood in terms of Leibniz's Law. Both have failed to see that a background has been omitted, the lack of which makes the problems insoluble. That background is provided by the concept of a story and of that kind of unity of character which a story requires. Just as a history is not a sequence of actions, but the concept of an action is that of a moment in an actual or possible history abstracted for some purpose from that history, so the characters in a history are not a collection of persons, but the concept of a person is that of a character abstracted from a history.

What the narrative concept of selfhood requires is thus twofold. On the one hand, I am what I may justifiably be taken by others to be in the course of living out a story that runs from my birth to my death; I am the *subject* of a history that is my own and no one else's, that has its own peculiar meaning. When someone complains—as do some of those who attempt or commit suicide—that his or her life is meaningless, he or she is often and perhaps characteristically complaining that the narrative of their life has become unintelligible to them, that it lacks any point, any movement towards a climax or a *telos.* Hence the point of doing any one thing rather than another at crucial junctures in their lives seems to such a person to have been lost.

To be the subject of a narrative that runs from one's birth to one's death is, I remarked earlier, to be accountable for the actions and experiences which compose a narratable life. It is, that is, to be open to being asked to give a certain kind of account of what one did or what happened to one or what one witnessed at any earlier point in one's life the time at which the question is posed. Of course someone may have forgotten or suffered brain damage or simply not attended sufficiently at the relevant times to be able to give the relevant account. But to say of someone under some one description ('The prisoner of the Chateau d'If') that he is the same person as someone characterised quite differently ('The Count of Monte Cristo') is precisely to say that it makes sense to ask him to give an intelligible narrative account enabling us to understand how he could at different times and different places be one and the same person and yet be so differently characterised. Thus personal identity is just that identity presupposed by the unity of the character which the unity of a narrative requires. Without such unity there would not be subjects of whom stories could be told.

The other aspect of narrative selfhood is correlative: I am not only accountable, I am one who can always ask others for an account, who can put others to the question. I am part of their story, as they are part of mine. The narrative of any one life is part of an interlocking set of narratives. Moreover this asking for and giving of accounts itself plays an important part in constituting narratives. Asking you what you did and why, saying what I did and why, pondering the differences between your account of what I did and my account of what I did, and *vice versa,* these are essential constituents of all but the very simplest and barest of narratives. Thus without the accountability of the self those trains of events that constitute all but the simplest and barest of narratives could not occur; and without that same accountability narratives would lack that continuity required to make both them and the actions that constitute them intelligible.

It is important to notice that I am not arguing that the concepts of narrative or of intelligibility or of accountability are *more* fundamental than that of personal identity. The concepts of narrative, intelligibility and accountability presuppose the applicability of the concept of personal identity, just as it presupposes their applicability and just as indeed each of these three presupposes the applicability of the two others. The relationship is one of mutual presupposition. It does follow of course that all attempts to elucidate the notion of personal identity independently of and in isolation from the notions of narrative, intelligibility and accountability are bound to fail. As all such attempts have.

It is now possible to return to the question from which this enquiry into the nature of human action and identity started: In what does the unity of an individual life consist? The answer is that its unity is the unity of a narrative embodied in a single life. To ask 'What is the good for me?' is to ask how best I might live out that unity and bring it to completion. To ask 'What is the good for man?' is to ask what all answers to the former question must have in common. But now it is important to emphasise that it is the systematic asking of these two questions and the attempt to answer them in deed as well as in word which provide the moral life with its unity. The unity of a human life is the unity of a narrative quest. Quests sometimes fail, are frustrated, abandoned or dissipated into distractions; and human lives may in all these ways also fail. But the only criteria for success or failure in a human life as a whole are the criteria of success or failure in a narrated or to-be-narrated quest. A quest for what?

Two key features of the medieval conception of a quest need to be recalled. The first is that without some at least partly determinate conception of the final *telos* there could not be any beginning to a quest. Some conception of the good for man is required. Whence is such a conception to be drawn? Precisely from those questions which led us to attempt to transcend that limited conception of the virtues which is available in and through practices. It is in looking for a conception of *the* good which will enable us to order other goods, for a conception of *the* good which will enable us to extend our understanding of the purpose and content of the virtues, 'or a conception of *the* good which will enable us to understand the place of in egrity and constancy in life, that we initially define the kind of life which is a quest for the good. But secondly it is clear the medieval conception of a quest is not at all that of a search for something already adequately characterised, as miners search for gold or geologists for oil. It is in the course of the quest and only through encountering and coping with the various particular harms, dangers, temptations and distractions which provide any quest with its episodes and incidents that the goal of the quest is finally to be understood. A quest is always an education both as to the character of that which is sought and in self-knowledge.

The virtues therefore are to be understood as those dispositions which will not only sustain practices and enable us to achieve the goods internal to practices, but which will also sustain us in the relevant kind of quest for the good, by enabling us to overcome the harms, dangers, temptations and distractions which we encounter, and which will furnish us with increasing self-knowledge and increasing knowledge of the good. The catalogue of the virtues will therefore include the virtues required to sustain the kind of households and the kind of political communities in which men and women can seek for the good together and the virtues necessary for philosophical enquiry about the character of the good. We have then arrived at a provisional conclusion about the good life for man: the good life for man is the life spent in seeking for the good life for man, and the virtues necessary for the seeking are those which will enable us to understand what more and what else the good life for man is. We have also completed the second stage in our account of the virtues, by situating them in relation to the good life for man and not only in relation to practices. But our enquiry requires a third stage.

For I am never able to seek for the good or exercise the virtues only *qua* individual. This is partly because what it is to live the good life concretely varies from circumstance to circumstance even when it is one and the same conception of the good life and one and the same set of virtues which are being embodied in a human life. What the good life is for a fifth-century Athenian general will not be the same as what it was for a medieval nun or a seventeenth-century farmer. But it is not just that different individuals live in different social circumstances; it is also that we all approach our own circumstances as bearers of a particular social identity. I am someone's son or daughter, someone else's cousin or uncle; I am a citizen of this or that city, a member of this or that guild or profession; I belong to this clan, that tribe, this nation. Hence what is good for me has to be the good for one who inhabits these roles. As such, I inherit from the past of my family, my city, my tribe, my nation, a variety of debts, inheritances, rightful expectations and obligations. These constitute the given of my life, my moral starting point. This is in part what gives my life its own moral particularity.

This thought is likely to appear alien and even surprising from the standpoint of modern individualism. From the standpoint of individualism I am what I myself choose to be. I can always, if I wish to, put in question what are taken to be the merely contingent social features of my existence. I may biologically be my father's son; but I cannot be held responsible for what he did unless I choose implicitly or explicitly to assume such responsibility. I may legally be a citizen of a certain country; but I cannot be held responsible for what my country does or has done unless I choose implicitly or explicitly to assume such responsibility. Such individualism is expressed by those modern Americans who deny any responsibility for the effects of slavery upon black Americans, saying 'I never owned any slaves'. It is more subtly the standpoint of those other modern Americans who accept a nicely calculated responsibility for such effects measured precisely by the benefits they themselves as individuals have indirectly received from slavery. In both cases 'being an American' is not in itself taken to be part of the moral identity of the individual. And of course there is nothing peculiar to modern Americans in this attitude: the Englishman who says, 'I never did any wrong to Ireland; why bring up that old history as though it had something to do with me?' or the young German who believes that being born after 1945 means that what Nazis did to Jews has no moral relevance to his relationship to his Jewish contemporaries, exhibit the same attitude, that according to which the self is detachable from its social and historical roles and statuses. And the self so detached is of course a self very much at home in either Sartre's or Goffman's perspective, a self that can have no history. The contrast with the narrative view of the self is clear. For the story of my life is always embedded in the story of those communities from which I derive my identity. I am born with a past; and to try to cut myself off from that past, in the individualist mode, is to deform my present relationships. The possession of an historical identity and the possession of a social identity coincide. Notice that rebellion against my identity is always one possible mode of expressing it.

Notice also that the fact that the self has to find its moral identity in and through its membership in communities such as those of the family, the neighbourhood, the city and the tribe does not entail that the self has to accept the moral *limitations* of the particularity of those forms of community. Without those moral particularities to begin from there would never be anywhere to begin; but it is in moving forward from such particularity that the search for the good, for the universal, consists. Yet particularity can never be simply left behind or obliterated. The notion of escaping from it into a realm of entirely universal maxims which belong to man as such, whether in its eighteenth-century Kantian form or in the presentation of some modern analytical moral philosophies, is an illusion and an illusion with painful consequences. When men and women identify what are in fact their partial and particular causes too easily and too completely with the cause of some universal principle, they usually behave worse than they would otherwise do.

What I am, therefore, is in key part what I inherit, a specific past that is present to some degree in my present. I find myself part of a history and that is generally to say, whether I like it or not, whether I recognise it or not, one of the bearers of a tradition. It was important when I characterised the concept of a practice to notice that practices always have histories and that at any given moment what a practice is depends on a mode of understanding it which has been transmitted often through many generations. And thus, insofar as the virtues sustain the relationships required for practices, they have to sustain relationships to the past—and to the future—as well as in the present. But the traditions through which particular practices are transmitted and reshaped never exist in isolation for larger social traditions. What constitutes such traditions?

We are apt to be misled here by the ideological uses to which the concept of a tradition has been put by conservative political theorists. Characteristically such theorists have followed Burke in contrasting tradition with reason and the stability of tradition with conflict. Both contrasts obfuscate. For all reasoning takes place within the context of some traditional mode of thought, transcending through criticism and invention the limitations of what had hitherto been reasoned in that tradition; this is as true of modern physics as of medieval logic. Moreover when a tradition is in good order it is always partially constituted by an argument about the goods the pursuit of which gives to that tradition its particular point and purpose.

So when an institution—a university, say, or a farm, or a hospital—is the bearer of a tradition of practice or practices, its common life will be partly, but in a centrally important way, constituted by a continuous argument as to what a university is and ought to be or what good farming is or what good medicine is. Traditions, when vital, embody continuities of conflict. Indeed when a tradition becomes Burkean, it is always dying or dead.

The individualism of modernity could of course find no use for the notion of tradition within its own conceptual scheme except as an adversary notion; it therefore all to willingly abandoned it to the Burkeans, who, faithful to Burke's own allegiance, tried to combine adherence in politics to a conception of tradition which would vindicate the oligarchical revolution of property of 1688 and adherence in economics to the doctrine and institutions of the free market. The theoretical incoherence of this mismatch did not deprive it of ideological usefulness. But the outcome has been that modern conservatives are for the most part engaged in conserving only older rather than later versions of liberal individualism. Their own core doctrine is as liberal and as individualist as that of self-avowed liberals.

A living tradition then is an historically extended, socially embodied argument, and an argument precisely in part about the goods which constitute that tradition. Within a tradition the pursuit of goods extends through generations, sometimes through many generations. Hence the individual's search for his or her good is generally and characteristically conducted within a context defined by those traditions of which the individual's life is a part, and this is true both of those goods which are internal to practices and of the goods of a single life. Once again the narrative phenomenon of embedding is crucial: the history of a practice in our time is generally and characteristically embedded in and made intelligible in terms of the larger and longer history of the tradition through which the practice in its present form was conveyed to us; the history of each of our own lives is generally and characteristically embedded in and made intelligible in terms of the larger and longer histories of a number of traditions. I have to say 'generally and characteristically' rather than 'always', for traditions decay, disintegrate and disappear. What then sustains and strengthens traditions? What weakens and destroys them?

The answer in key part is: the exercise or the lack of exercise of the relevant virtues. The virtues find their point and purpose not only in sustaining those relationships necessary if the variety of goods internal to practices are to be achieved and not only in sustaining the form of an individual life in which that individual may seek out his or her good as the good of his or her whole life, but also in sustaining those traditions which provide both practices and individual lives with their necessary historical context. Lack of justice, lack of truthfulness, lack of courage, lack of the relevant intellectual virtues—these corrupt traditions, just as they do those institutions and practices which derive their life from the traditions of which they are the contemporary embodiments. To recognise this is of course also to recognise the existence of an additional virtue, one whose importance is perhaps most obvious when it is least present, the virtue of having an adequate sense of the traditions to which one belongs or which confront one. This virtue is not to be confused with any form of conservative antiquarianism; I am not praising those who choose the conventional conservative role of *laudator temporis acti*. It is rather the case that an adequate sense of tradition manifests itself in a grasp of those future possibilities which the past has made available to the present. Living traditions, just because they continue a not-yet-completed narrative, confront a future whose determinate and determinable character, so far as it possesses any, derives from the past.

In practical reasoning the possession of this virtue is not manifested so much in the knowledge of a set of generalisations or maxims which may provide our practical inferences with major premises; its presence or absence rather appears on the kind of capacity for judgment which the agent possesses in knowing how to select among the relevant stack of maxims and how to apply them in particular situations. Cardinal Pole possessed it, Mary Tudor did not; Montrose possessed it, Charles I did not. What Cardinal Pole and the Marquis of Montrose possessed were in fact those virtues which enable their possessors to pursue both their own good and the good of the tradition of which they are the bearers even in situations defined by the necessity of tragic, dilemmatic choice. Such choices, understood in the context of the tradition of the virtues, are very different from those which face the modern adherents of rival and incommensurable moral premises in the debates about which I wrote in Chapter 2. Wherein does the difference lie?

It has often been suggested—by J. L. Austin, for example—that *either* we can admit the existence of rival and contingently incompatible goods which make incompatible claims to our practical allegiance *or* we can believe in some determinate conception of *the* good life for man, but that these are mutually exclusive alternatives. No one can consistently hold both these views. What this contention is blind to is that there may be better or worse ways for individuals to live through the tragic confrontation of good with good. And that to know what the good life for man is may require knowing what are the better and what are the worse ways of living in and through such situations. Nothing *a priori* rules out this possibility; and this suggests that within a view such as Austin's there is concealed an unacknowledged empirical premise about the character of tragic situations.

One way in which the choice between rival goods in a tragic situation differs from the modern choice between incommensurable moral premises is that *both* of the alternative courses of action which confront the individual have to be recognised as leading to some authentic and substantial good. By choosing one I do nothing to diminish or derogate from the claims upon me of the other; and therefore, whatever I do, I shall have left undone what I ought to have done. The tragic protagonist, unlike the moral agent as depicted by Sartre or Hare, is not choosing between allegiance to one moral principle rather than another, nor is he or she deciding upon some principle of priority between moral principles. Hence the 'ought' involved has a different meaning and force from that of the 'ought' in moral principles understood in a modern way. For the tragic protagonist cannot do everything that he or she ought to do. This 'ought', unlike Kant's, does not imply 'can'. Moreover any attempt to map the logic of such 'ought' assertions on to some modal calculus so as to produce a version of deontic logic has to fail.[3]

Yet it is clear that the moral task of the tragic protagonist may be performed better or worse, independently of the choice between alternatives that he or she makes—*ex hypothesi* he or she has no *right* choice to make. The tragic protagonist may behave heroically or unheroically, generously or ungenerously, gracefully or gracelessly, prudently or imprudently. To perform his or her task better rather than worse will be to do both what is better for him or her *qua*

---

[3] See, from a very different point of view, Bas C. Van Fraasen, "Values and the Heart's Command," *The Journal of Philosophy,* 70 (1973), pp. 5–19.

individual or *qua* parent or child or *qua* citizen or member of a profession, or perhaps *qua* some or all of these. The existence of tragic dilemmas casts no doubt upon and provides no counter-examples to the thesis that assertions of the form 'To do this in this way would be better for X and/or for his or her family, city or profession' are susceptible of objective truth and falsity, any more than the existence of alternative and contingently incompatible forms of medical treatment casts doubt on the thesis that assertions of the form 'To undergo this medical treatment in this way would be better for X and/or his or her family' are susceptible of objective truth and falsity.[4]

The presupposition of this objectivity is of course that we can understand the notion of 'good for X' and cognate notions in terms of some conception of the unity of X's life. What is better or worse for X depends upon the character of that intelligible narrative which provides X's life with its unity. Unsurprisingly it is the lack of any such unifying conception of a human life which underlies modern denials of the factual character of moral judgments and more especially of those judgments which ascribe virtues or vices to individuals.

---

[4] See, from a different point of view, the illuminating discussion in Samuel Guttenplan, "Moral Realism and Moral Dilemmas," *Proceedings of the Aristotelian Society* (1979–80), pp. 61–81.

VI
APPLICATIONS

MORAL THEORY and real-life problems intersect in several ways. By bringing our theories to bear on actual problems, we draw out the theories' full implications. By pitting competing principles against one another, we learn their strengths and weaknesses. By attending to the complexities of the actual world, we notice new theoretical issues that we might otherwise overlook. And, conversely, by drawing on our theoretical findings, we gain new insight into how we ought to act.

Thus, consider first the problem of famine. Millions around the world are malnourished or starving, and millions more will surely die if population levels keep increasing. Those of us who live comfortably can influence these events. We can make contributions to famine relief, work toward a lowering of the birth rate, or support egalitarian policies that would enable the very poor to buy more food. We can also do nothing, and simply let events take their course. Where do our responsibilities lie? What proportion of our time, energy, and wealth, if any, are we obligated to devote to preventing starvation? And upon what principles do our obligations rest?

The view that these obligations extend quite far is defended, from different perspectives, by Peter Singer and Onora O'Neill (readings 44 and 45). Singer's argument appeals to the principle that when we can prevent something very bad from happening without sacrificing anything of comparable importance, we morally ought to do so. Because this principle says nothing about obligations to promote positive happiness, it differs from the principle of utility.

However, like utilitarianism, it makes a person's obligations depend on the consequences of the acts open to him. By contrast, Onora O'Neill derives an obligation to take steps to prevent famine from a universal right not to be killed. Although not trying to prevent famine may seem very different from killing—the first seems merely passive, the second active—O'Neill argues that the difference is illusory in many cases. Because her argument appeals to obligations associated with rights, it does not tie what agents ought to do to the overall consequences of the acts available to them. Thus, it is deontological rather than consequentialist.

Because obligations to prevent famine deaths have been defended from both main normative perspectives, those obligations may seem uncontroversial. But Charles Fried argues in reading 46 that the issue is not this simple. If we were obligated to consider all the unintended consequences of our acts, such as the deaths from hunger that will predictably result from our economic decisions, then we would have no room to exercise personal discretion. Our particularity as agents would be lost in a sea of unintended consequences, each of which would be equally our responsibility. According to Fried, this means that no form of consequentialism can capture the whole moral truth. It also means that any viable deontological theory must restrict its absolute prohibitions to the *intentional* infliction of harm or death. Hence, those whose actions lead to unintended famine deaths violate no absolute prohibitions. If their actions are wrong—as they still may be—the reasons must lie elsewhere.

The problem of famine raises questions about the difference between causing and merely allowing a result—between killing and merely "letting die"—and about the nature and extent of the right to life. In the next two readings, both issues recur in other contexts. In reading 47, Judith Thomson takes up the controversial issue of abortion. Although the most obvious question here is whether an embryo or fetus should be considered a person with a right to life, Thomson does not address that question. Rather, she argues that even if we grant that fetuses are persons, it does not follow that abortion is impermissible. Although all persons have a right to life, Thomson argues that this right does not include a right to use whatever necessary to sustain one's life. In particular, a person has no right to use what he needs to survive if another has a prior right to control that thing. Because Thomson believes that women do have a prior right to control the use of their bodies, she concludes that a fetus has no right to remain in a woman's body until it is born. Hence, expelling it, and thus causing its death, does not violate a fetus's right to life.

As Thomson concedes, aborting a fetus is most naturally described as killing it. But there are related cases in which persons are not killed, but are merely allowed to die. For example, when an infant is born with multiple birth defects, its parents may refuse to authorize an operation that would save its life while leaving it badly handicapped. According to some, the decision to let such an infant die need not be wrong, but a decision to kill the infant (say, by lethal injection) is always wrong. In reading 48, James Rachels contests this claim. Rachels acknowledges that the motives of persons who kill others are often bad, while the motives of those who let others die, such as doctors who refuse to prolong the suffering of the terminally ill, are often good. But he argues that when we set such differences in motive aside, we find that killing *in itself* is no worse than letting die. Moreover, a quick death by painless injection is better than a lingering, painful one. Thus, Rachels concludes that killing is often preferable to letting die.

In the readings examined so far, the conflict between consequentialism and deontology has lurked in the background. In the next three readings, that conflict occupies center stage. In reading 49, R. M. Hare defends consequentialism in general, and utilitarianism in particular, by drawing out their implications concerning slavery. Although critics argue that utilitarians must condone slavery when it brings better consequences than its alternatives, Hare contends that a utility-maximizing slave system is not a realistic possibility. When we try to fill in the details, we find that the laws of psychology and other features of the human situation would almost always prevent a slave system from maximizing utility. Hence, a moral education aimed at promoting utility in the world as it is must include psychological conditioning that leads people to find all slavery repugnant. According to Hare, it is this utilitarian conditioning, and not an intuitive awareness that slavery is inherently evil, that accounts for the near-universal abhorrence of the practice. And similar conditioning accounts for all other intuitions that specific types of acts or practices are inherently wrong.

Thomas Nagel and Michael Walzer both contest this diagnosis. In reading 50, Nagel argues that the moral limits on what may be done in wars—even just wars—cannot be understood in utilitarian terms. The prohibitions against attacking noncombatants and using weapons such as poison gas are not just indirect ways of maximizing happiness or minimizing suffering. Rather, these prohibitions reflect the fact that even hostile activity places us in a certain relationship to our victims, and that we therefore ought never to treat those persons in ways that we could not justify to them. Because Nagel acknowledges that we may need to violate such prohibitions when the stakes are high enough, he concludes that the world may "[confront] a previously innocent person with a choice between morally abominable courses of action, and leave him no way to escape with his honor."

This theme is developed further by Michael Walzer. Although Walzer's topic in reading 51 is politics rather than war, he agrees that persons sometimes *should* do what is wrong in order to bring good results. For example, a superior candidate for public office may have to compromise his principles if he is to be elected or put his program into effect. As Walzer notices, this need to get one's hands dirty raises a whole new set of questions about the agent's subsequent attitude. Should the successful politician simply be content to accept his moral defilement? Should he be perpetually wracked with guilt about it? Or should he pay some form of determinate penalty? If so, what is that penalty, and who should exact it?

The issues raised by politics, war, and medicine are problems of real life; but, for most of us, they are not problems of everyday life. For most people, the activities of work, travel, and recreation seldom pit utility against absolute prohibitions, and even less often pose dilemmas of life and death. But although we seldom must decide whether, or whom, to kill or seriously harm, we very often face decisions about imposing *risks* of injury or death. Whenever we drive, smoke in public, or fail to clear our sidewalk of snow, we impose some level of risk on others. Indeed, there are few, if any, activities that involve absolutely no risk. Thus, a pervasive question of everyday life is what levels of risk we are entitled to impose. In our last selection (reading 52), Charles Fried attempts to answer this question. He argues that we are entitled to impose whatever level of risk any rational person would accept from all others in return for the opportunity to impose similar risks *on* all others while pursuing his own projects and goals. Like other obligations, our obligation to limit the risks imposed by our acts are grounded in reciprocity. In saying this, Fried extends and deepens a familiar deontological line of argument. How a consequentialist might address the same problem is left for further thought.

44

Famine, Affluence, and Morality

PETER SINGER

For biographical information on Peter Singer, see reading 19.

In this selection, Singer discusses the moral status of providing food to persons who are starving. Many people believe that while it is praiseworthy and charitable to help the destitute, the affluent have no moral obligation to do so. However, Singer challenges this way of distinguishing charity from obligation. His argument rests on the principle that "if it is in our power to prevent something bad from happening, without thereby sacrificing any thing of comparable moral importance, we ought, morally, to do it." If we accept this principle, Singer argues, then we ought to forgo many of the luxuries we currently enjoy so that we may prevent others from starving. In Singer's view, the fact that the starving live in far-off lands and that others could help them as easily as we could are not good reasons for withholding aid.

Quite obviously, the success of Singer's argument depends on the acceptability of his central premise. Although most utilitarians would accept it, many deontologists would not. On various accounts, the obligation not to cause harm is more stringent or far-reaching, or leaves the agent less discretion in its application, than the obligation to take positive steps to prevent harm. Whether this distinction has a rational basis, or whether it is merely an excuse for nonaction, are questions left for further consideration.

As I WRITE THIS, in November 1971, people are dying in East Bengal from lack of food, shelter, and medical care. The suffering and death that are occurring there now are not inevitable, not unavoidable in any fatalistic sense of the term. Constant poverty, a cyclone, and a civil war have turned at least nine million people into destitute refugees; nevertheless, it is not beyond the capacity of the richer nations to give enough assistance to reduce any further suffering to very small proportions. The decisions and actions of human beings can prevent this kind of suffering. Unfortunately, human beings have not made the necessary decisions. At the individual level, people have, with very few exceptions, not responded to the situation in any significant way. Generally speaking, people have not given large sums to relief funds; they have not written to their parliamentary representatives demanding increased government assistance; they have not demonstrated in the streets, held symbolic fasts, or done anything else directed toward providing the refugees with the means to satisfy their essential needs. At the government level, no government has given the sort of massive aid that would enable the refugees to survive for more than a few days. Britain, for instance, has given rather more than most countries. It has, to date, given £14,750,000. For comparative purposes, Britain's share of the nonrecoverable development costs of the Anglo-French Concorde project is already in excess of £275,000,000, and on present estimates will reach £440,000,000. The implication is that the British government values a supersonic transport more than thirty times as highly as it values the lives of the nine million refugees. Australia is another country which, on a per capita basis, is well up in the "aid to Bengal" table. Australia's aid, however, amounts to less than one-twelfth of the cost of Sydney's new opera house. The total amount given, from all sources, now stands at about £65,000,000. The estimated cost of keeping the refugees alive for one year is £464,000,000. Most of the refugees have now been in the camps for more than six months. The World Bank has said that India needs a minimum of £300,000,000 in assistance from other countries before the end of the year. It seems obvious that assistance on this scale will not be forthcoming. India will be forced to choose between letting the refugees starve or diverting funds from her own development program, which will mean that more of her own people will starve in the future.[1]

These are the essential facts about the present situation in Bengal. So far as it concerns us here, there is nothing unique about this situation except its magnitude. The Bengal emergency is just the latest and most acute of a series of major emergencies in various parts of the world, arising both from natural and from man-made causes. There are also many parts of the world in which people die from malnutrition and lack of food independent of any special emergency. I take Bengal as my example only because it is the present concern, and because the size of the problem has ensured that it has been given adequate publicity. Neither individuals nor governments can claim to be unaware of what is happening there.

What are the moral implications of a situation like this? In what follows, I shall argue that the way people in relatively affluent countries react to a situation like that in Bengal cannot be justified; indeed, the whole way we look at moral issues—our moral conceptual scheme—needs to be altered, and with it, the way of life that has come to be taken for granted in our society.

In arguing for this conclusion I will not, of course, claim to be morally neutral. I shall, however, try to argue for the moral position that I take, so that anyone who accepts certain assumptions, to be made explicit, will, I hope, accept my conclusion.

I begin with the assumption that suffering and death from lack of food, shelter, and medical care are bad. I think most people will agree about this, although one may reach the same view by different routes. I shall not argue

---

[1] There was also a third possibility: that India would go to war to enable the refugees to return to their lands. Since I wrote this paper, India has taken this way out. The situation is no longer that described above, but this does not affect my argument, as the next paragraph indicates.

for this view. People can hold all sorts of eccentric positions, and perhaps from some of them it would not follow that death by starvation is in itself bad. It is difficult, perhaps impossible, to refute such positions, and so for brevity I will henceforth take this assumption as accepted. Those who disagree need read no further.

My next point is this: if it is in our power to prevent something bad from happening, without thereby sacrificing anything of comparable moral importance, we ought, morally, to do it. By "without sacrificing anything of comparable moral importance" I mean without causing anything else comparably bad to happen, or doing something that is wrong in itself, or failing to promote some moral good, comparable in significance to the bad thing that we can prevent. This principle seems almost as uncontroversial as the last one. It requires us only to prevent what is bad, and not to promote what is good, and it requires this of us only when we can do it without sacrificing anything that is, from the moral point of view, comparably important. I could even, as far as the application of my argument to the Bengal emergency is concerned, qualify the point so as to make it: if it is in our power to prevent something very bad from happening, without thereby sacrificing anything morally significant, we ought, morally, to do it. An application of this principle would be as follows: if I am walking past a shallow pond and see a child drowning in it, I ought to wade in and pull the child out. This will mean getting my clothes muddy, but this is insignificant, while the death of the child would presumably be a very bad thing.

The uncontroversial appearance of the principle just stated is deceptive. If it were acted upon, even in its qualified form, our lives, our society, and our world would be fundamentally changed. For the principle takes, firstly, no account of proximity or distance. It makes no moral difference whether the person I can help is a neighbor's child ten yards from me or a Bengali whose name I shall never know, ten thousand miles away. Secondly, the principle makes no distinction between cases in which I am the only person who could possibly do anything and cases in which I am just one among millions in the same position.

I do not think I need to say much in defense of the refusal to take proximity and distance into account. The fact that a person is physically near to us, so that we have personal contact with him, may make it more likely that we *shall* assist him, but this does not show that we *ought* to help him rather than another who happens to be further away. If we accept any principle of impartiality, universalizability, equality, or whatever, we cannot discriminate against someone merely because he is far away from us (or we are far away from him). Admittedly, it is possible that we are in a better position to judge what needs to be done to help a person near to us than one far away, and perhaps also to provide the assistance we judge to be necessary. If this were the case, it would be a reason for helping those near to us first. This may once have been a justification for being more concerned with the poor in one's own town than with famine victims in India. Unfortunately for those who like to keep their moral responsibilities limited, instant communication and swift transportation have changed the situation. From the moral point of view, the development of the world into a "global village" has made an important, though still unrecognized, difference to our moral situation. Expert observers and supervisors, sent out by famine relief organizations or permanently stationed in famine-prone areas, can direct our aid to a refugee in Bengal almost as effectively as we could get it to someone in our own block. There would seem, therefore, to be no possible justification for discriminating on geographical grounds.

There may be a greater need to defend the second implication of my principle—that the fact that there are millions of other people in the same position, in respect to the Bengali refugees, as I am, does not make the situation significantly different from a situation in which I am the only person who can prevent something very bad from occurring. Again, of course, I admit that there is a psychological difference between the cases; one feels less guilty about doing nothing if one can point to others, similarly placed, who have also done nothing. Yet this can make no real difference to our moral obligations.[2] Should I consider that I am less obliged to pull the drowning child out of the pond if on looking around I see other people, no further away than I am, who have also noticed the child but are doing nothing? One has only to ask this question to see the absurdity of the view that numbers lessen obligation. It is a view that is an ideal excuse for inactivity; unfortunately most of the major evils— poverty, overpopulation, pollution—are problems in which everyone is almost equally involved.

The view that numbers do make a difference can be made plausible if stated in this way: if everyone in circumstances like mine gave £5 to the Bengal Relief Fund, there would be enough to provide food, shelter, and medical care for the refugees; there is no reason why I should give more than anyone else in the same circumstances as I am; therefore I have no obligation to give more than £5. Each premise in this argument is true, and the argument looks sound. It may convince us, unless we notice that it is based on a hypothetical premise, although the conclusion is not stated hypothetically. The argument would be sound if the conclusion were: if everyone in circumstances like mine were to give £5, I would have no obligation to give more than £5. If the conclusion were so stated, however, it would be obvious that the argument has no bearing on a situation in which it is not the case that everyone else gives £5. This, of course, is the actual situation. It is more or less certain that not everyone in circumstances like mine will give £5. So there will not be enough to provide the needed food, shelter, and medical care. Therefore by giving more than £5 I will prevent more suffering than I would if I gave just £5.

---

[2] In view of the special sense philosophers often give to the term, I should say that I use "obligation" simply as the abstract noun derived from "ought," so that "I have an obligation to" means no more, and no less, than "I ought to." This usage is in accordance with the definition of "ought" given by the *Shorter Oxford English Dictionary:* "the general verb to express duty or obligation." I do not think any issue of substance hangs on the way the term is used; sentences in which I use "obligation" could all be rewritten, although somewhat clumsily, as sentences in which a clause containing "ought" replaces the term "obligation."

It might be thought that this argument has an absurd consequence. Since the situation appears to be that very few people are likely to give substantial amounts, it follows that I and everyone else in similar circumstances ought to give as much as possible, that is, at least up to the point at which by giving more one would begin to cause serious suffering for oneself and one's dependents—perhaps even beyond this point to the point of marginal utility, at which by giving more one would cause oneself and one's dependents as much suffering as one would prevent in Bengal. If everyone does this, however, there will be more than can be used for the benefit of the refugees, and some of the sacrifice will have been unnecessary. Thus, if everyone does what he ought to do, the result will not be as good as it would be if everyone did a little less than he ought to do, or if only some do all that they ought to do.

The paradox here arises only if we assume that the actions in question—sending money to the relief funds—are performed more or less simultaneously, and are also unexpected. For if it is to be expected that everyone is going to contribute something, then clearly each is not obliged to give as much as he would have been obliged to had others not been giving too. And if everyone is not acting more or less simultaneously, then those giving later will know how much more is needed, and will have no obligation to give more than is necessary to reach this amount. To say this is not to deny the principle that people in the same circumstances have the same obligations, but to point out that the fact that others have given, or may be expected to give, is a relevant circumstance: those giving after it has become known that many others are giving and those giving before are not in the same circumstances. So the seemingly absurd consequence of the principle I have put forward can occur only if people are in error about the actual circumstances—that is, if they think they are giving when others are not, but in fact they are giving when others are. The result of everyone doing what he really ought to do cannot be worse than the result of everyone doing less than he ought to do, although the result of everyone doing what he reasonably believes he ought to do could be.

If my argument so far has been sound, neither our distance from a preventable evil nor the number of other people who, in respect to that evil, are in the same situation as we are, lessens our obligation to mitigate or prevent that evil. I shall therefore take as established the principle I asserted earlier. As I have already said, I need to assert it only in its qualified form: if it is in our power to prevent something very bad from happening, without thereby sacrificing anything else morally significant, we ought, morally, to do it.

The outcome of this argument is that our traditional moral categories are upset. The traditional distinction between duty and charity cannot be drawn, or at least, not in the place we normally draw it. Giving money to the Bengal Relief Fund is regarded as an act of charity in our society. The bodies which collect money are known as "charities." These organizations see themselves in this way—if you send them a check, you will be thanked for your "generosity." Because giving money is regarded as an act of charity, it is not thought that there is anything wrong with not giving. The charitable man may be praised, but the man who is not charitable is not condemned. People do not feel in any way ashamed or guilty about spending money on new clothes or a new car instead of giving it to famine relief. (Indeed, the alternative does not occur to them.) This way of looking at the matter cannot be justified. When we buy new clothes not to keep ourselves warm but to look "well-dressed" we are not providing for any important need. We would not be sacrificing anything significant if we were to continue to wear our old clothes, and give the money to famine relief. By doing so, we would be preventing another person from starving. It follows from what I have said earlier that we ought to give money away, rather than spend it on clothes which we do not need to keep us warm. To do so is not charitable, or generous. Nor is it the kind of act which philosophers and theologians have called "supererogatory"—an act which it would be good to do, but not wrong not to do. On the contrary, we ought to give the money away, and it is wrong not to do so.

I am not maintaining that there are no acts which are charitable, or that there are no acts which it would be good to do but not wrong not to do. It may be possible to redraw the distinction between duty and charity in some other place. All I am arguing here is that the present way of drawing the distinction, which makes it an act of charity for a man living at the level of affluence which most people in the "developed nations" enjoy to give money to save someone else from starvation, cannot be supported. It is beyond the scope of my argument to consider whether the distinction should be redrawn or abolished altogether. There would be many other possible ways of drawing the distinction—for instance, one might decide that it is good to make other people as happy as possible but not wrong not to do so.

Despite the limited nature of the revision in our moral conceptual scheme which I am proposing, the revision would, given the extent of both affluence and famine in the world today, have radical implications. These implications may lead to further objections, distinct from those I have already considered. I shall discuss two of these.

One objection to the position I have taken might be simply that it is too drastic a revision of our moral scheme. People do not ordinarily judge in the way I have suggested they should. Most people reserve their moral condemnation for those who violate some moral norm, such as the norm against taking another person's property. They do not condemn those who indulge in luxury instead of giving to famine relief. But given that I did not set out to present a morally neutral description of the way people make moral judgments, the way people do in fact judge has nothing to do with the validity of my conclusion. My conclusion follows from the principle which I advanced earlier, and unless that principle is rejected, or the arguments shown to be unsound, I think the conclusion must stand, however strange it appears.

It might, nevertheless, be interesting to consider why our society, and most other societies, do judge differently from the way I have suggested they should. In a well-known article, J. O. Urmson suggests that the imperatives of duty, which tell us what we must do, as distinct from what it would be good to do but not wrong not to do, function so as to prohibit behavior that is intolerable if men are to live together in society.[3] This may explain the origin and continued existence of the present division between acts of duty and acts of charity. Moral attitudes are shaped by the needs of society, and no doubt society needs people who will observe the rules that make social existence tolerable. From the point of view of a particular society, it is essential to prevent violations of norms against killing, stealing, and so on. It is quite inessential, however, to help people outside one's own society.

If this is an explanation of our common distinction between duty and supererogation, however, it is not a justification of it. The moral point of view requires us to look beyond the interests of our own society. Previously, as I have already mentioned, this may hardly have been feasible, but it is quite feasible now. From the moral point of view, the prevention of the starvation of millions of people outside our society must be considered at least as pressing as the upholding of property norms within our society.

It has been argued by some writers, among them Sidgwick and Urmson, that we need to have a basic moral code which is not too far beyond the capacities of the ordinary man, for otherwise there will be a general breakdown of compliance with the moral code. Crudely stated, this argument suggests that if we tell people that they ought to refrain from murder and give everything they do not really need to famine relief, they will do neither, whereas if we tell them that they ought to refrain from murder and that it is good to give to famine relief but not wrong not to do so, they will at least refrain from murder. The issue here is: Where should we draw the line between conduct that is required and conduct that is good although not required, so as to get the best possible result? This would seem to be an empirical question, although a very difficult one. One objection to the Sidgwick-Urmson line of argument is that it takes insufficient account of the effect that moral standards can have on the decisions we make. Given a society in which a wealthy man who gives five percent of his income to famine-relief is regarded as most generous, it is not surprising that a proposal that we all ought to give away half our incomes will be thought to be absurdly unrealistic. In a society which held that no man should have more than enough while others have less than they need, such a proposal might seem narrowminded. What it is possible for a man to do and what he is likely to do are both, I think, very greatly influenced by what people around him are doing and expecting him to do. In any case, the possibility that by spreading the idea that we ought to be doing very much more than we are to relieve famine we shall bring about a general breakdown of moral behavior seems remote. If the stakes are an end to widespread starvation, it is worth the risk. Finally, it should be emphasized that these considerations are relevant only to the issue of what we should require from others, and not to what we ourselves ought to do.

---

[3] J. O. Urmson, "Saints and Heroes," in *Essays in Moral Philosophy*, ed. Abraham I. Melden (Seattle and London, 1958), p. 214. For a related but significantly different view see also Henry Sidgwick, *The Methods of Ethics*, 7th edn. (London, 1907), pp. 220–221, 492–493.

The second objection to my attack on the present distinction between duty and charity is one which has from time to time been made against utilitarianism. It follows from some forms of utilitarian theory that we all ought, morally, to be working full time to increase the balance of happiness over misery. The position I have taken here would not lead to this conclusion in all circumstances, for if there were no bad occurrences that we could prevent without sacrificing something of comparable moral importance, my argument would have no application. Given the present conditions in many parts of the world, however, it does follow from my argument that we ought, morally, to be working full time to relieve great suffering of the sort that occurs as a result of famine or other disasters. Of course, mitigating circumstances can be adduced—for instance, that if we wear ourselves out through overwork, we shall be less effective than we would otherwise have been. Nevertheless, when all considerations of this sort have been taken into account, the conclusion remains: we ought to be preventing as much suffering as we can without sacrificing something else of comparable moral importance. This conclusion is one which we may be reluctant to face. I cannot see, though, why it should be regarded as a criticism of the position for which I have argued, rather than a criticism of our ordinary standards of behavior. Since most people are self-interested to some degree, very few of us are likely to do everything that we ought to do. It would, however, hardly be honest to take this as evidence that it is not the case that we ought to do it.

It may still be thought that my conclusions are so wildly out of line with what everyone else thinks and has always thought that there must be something wrong with the argument somewhere. In order to show that my conclusions, while certainly contrary to contemporary Western moral standards, would not have seemed so extraordinary at other times and in other places, I would like to quote a passage from a writer not normally thought of as a way-out radical, Thomas Aquinas.

> Now, according to the natural order instituted by divine providence, material goods are provided for the satisfaction of human needs. Therefore the division and appropriation of property, which proceeds from human law, must not hinder the satisfaction of man's necessity from such goods. Equally, whatever a man has in superabundance is owed, of natural right, to the poor for their sustenance. So Ambrosius says, and it is also to be found in the *Decretum Gratiani:* "The bread which you withhold belongs to the hungry; the clothing you shut away, to the naked; and the money you bury in the earth is the redemption and freedom of the penniless."[4]

I now want to consider a number of points, more practical than philosophical, which are relevant to the application of the moral conclusion we have reached. These points challenge not the idea that we ought to be doing all we

[4] *Summa Theologica*, II–II, Question 66, Article 7, in *Aquinas, Selected Political Writings*, ed. A. P. d'Entreves, trans. J. G. Dawson (Oxford, 1948), p. 171.

can to prevent starvation, but the idea that giving away a great deal of money is the best means to this end.

It is sometimes said that overseas aid should be a government responsibility, and that therefore one ought not to give to privately run charities. Giving privately, it is said, allows the government and the noncontributing members of society to escape their responsibilities.

This argument seems to assume that the more people there are who give to privately organized famine relief funds, the less likely it is that the government will take over full responsibility for such aid. This assumption is unsupported, and does not strike me as at all plausible. The opposite view—that if no one gives voluntarily, a government will assume that its citizens are uninterested in famine relief and would not wish to be forced into giving aid—seems more plausible. In any case, unless there were a definite probability that by refusing to give one would be helping to bring about massive government assistance, people who do refuse to make voluntary contributions are refusing to prevent a certain amount of suffering without being able to point to any tangible beneficial consequence of their refusal. So the onus of showing how their refusal will bring about government action is on those who refuse to give.

I do not, of course, want to dispute the contention that governments of affluent nations should be giving many times the amount of genuine, no-strings-attached aid that they are giving now. I agree, too, that giving privately is not enough, and that we ought to be campaigning actively for entirely new standards for both public and private contributions to famine relief. Indeed, I would sympathize with someone who thought that campaigning was more important than giving oneself, although I doubt whether preaching what one does not practice would be very effective. Unfortunately, for many people the idea that "it's the government's responsibility" is a reason for not giving which does not appear to entail any political action either.

Another, more serious reason for not giving to famine relief funds is that until there is effective population control, relieving famine merely postpones starvation. If we save the Bengal refugees now, others, perhaps the children of these refugees, will face starvation in a few years' time. In support of this, one may cite the now well-known facts about the population explosion and the relatively limited scope for expanded production.

This point, like the previous one, is an argument against relieving suffering that is happening now, because of a belief about what might happen in the future; it is unlike the previous point in that very good evidence can be adduced in support of this belief about the future. I will not go into the evidence here. I accept that the earth cannot support indefinitely a population rising at the present rate. This certainly poses a problem for anyone who thinks it important to prevent famine. Again, however, one could accept the argument without drawing the conclusion that it absolves one from any obligation to do anything to prevent famine. The conclusion that should be drawn is that the best means of preventing famine, in the long run, is population control. It would then follow from the position reached earlier that one ought to be doing all one can to promote population control (unless one held that all forms of population control were wrong in themselves, or would have significantly bad consequences). Since there are organizations working specifically for population control, one would then support them rather than more orthodox methods of preventing famine.

A third point raised by the conclusion reached earlier relates to the question of just how much we all ought to be giving away. One possibility, which has already been mentioned, is that we ought to give until we reach the level of marginal utility—that is, the level at which, by giving more, I would cause as much suffering to myself or my dependents as I would relieve by my gift. This would mean, of course, that one would reduce oneself to very near the material circumstances of a Bengali refugee. It will be recalled that earlier I put forward both a strong and a moderate version of the principle of preventing bad occurrences. The strong version, which required us to prevent bad things from happening unless in doing so we would be sacrificing something of comparable moral significance, does seem to require reducing ourselves to the level of marginal utility. I should also say that the strong version seems to me to be the correct one. I proposed the more moderate version—that we should prevent bad occurrences unless, to do so, we had to sacrifice something morally significant—only in order to show that even on this surely undeniable principle a great change in our way of life is required. On the more moderate principle, it may not follow that we ought to reduce ourselves to the level of marginal utility, for one might hold that to reduce oneself and one's family to this level is to cause something significantly bad to happen. Whether this is so I shall not discuss, since, as I have said, I can see no good reason for holding the moderate version of the principle rather than the strong version. Even if we accepted the principle only in its moderate form, however, it should be clear that we would have to give away enough to ensure that the consumer society, dependent as it is on people spending on trivia rather than giving to famine relief, would slow down and perhaps disappear entirely. There are several reasons why this would be desirable in itself. The value and necessity of economic growth are now being questioned not only by conservationists, but by economists as well.[5] There is no doubt, too, that the consumer society has had a distorting effect on the goals and purposes of its members. Yet looking at the matter purely from the point of view of overseas aid, there must be a limit to the extent to which we should deliberately slow down our economy; for it might be the case that if we gave away, say, forty percent of our Gross National Product, we would slow down the economy so much that in absolute terms we would be giving less than if we gave twenty-five percent of the much larger GNP that we would have if we limited our contribution to this smaller percentage.

I mention this only as an indication of the sort of a factor that one would have to take into account in working out an ideal. Since Western societies

---

[5] See, for instance, John Kenneth Galbraith, *The New Industrial State* (Boston, 1967); and E. J. Mishan, *The Costs of Economic Growth* (London, 1967).

generally consider one percent of the GNP an acceptable level for overseas aid, the matter is entirely academic. Nor does it affect the question of how much an individual should give in a society in which very few are giving substantial amounts.

It is sometimes said, though less often now than it used to be, that philosophers have no special role to play in public affairs, since most public issues depend primarily on an assessment of facts. On questions of fact, it is said, philosophers as such have no special expertise, and so it has been possible to engage in philosophy without committing oneself to any position on major public issues. No doubt there are some issues of social policy and foreign policy about which it can truly be said that a really expert assessment of the facts is required before taking sides or acting, but the issue of famine is surely not one of these. The facts about the existence of suffering are beyond dispute. Nor, I think, is it disputed that we can do something about it, either through orthodox methods of famine relief or through population control or both. This is therefore an issue on which philosophers are competent to take a position. The issue is one which faces everyone who has more money than he needs to support himself and his dependents, or who is in a position to take some sort of politicial action. These categories must include practically every teacher and student of philosophy in the universities of the Western world. If philosophy is to deal with matters that are relevant to both teachers and students, this is an issue that philosophers should discuss.

Discussion, though, is not enough. What is the point of relating philosophy to public (and personal) affairs if we do not take our conclusions seriously? In this instance, taking our conclusion seriously means acting upon it. The philosopher will not find it any easier than anyone else to alter his attitudes and way of life to the extent that, if I am right, is involved in doing everything that we ought to be doing. At the very least, though, one can make a start. The philosopher who does so will have to sacrifice some of the benefits of the consumer society, but he can find compensation in the satisfaction of a way of life in which theory and practice, if not yet in harmony, are at least coming together.

45

Lifeboat Earth

ONORA O'NEILL

Onora O'Neill (b. 1941) teaches philosophy at the University of Essex in England. She is the author of Acting on Principle *and, more recently,* Faces of Hunger: An Essay on Poverty, Justice, and Development. *She has also written various articles in ethics and political philosophy.*

Like Peter Singer (reading 44), O'Neill argues that we are morally obligated to try to prevent people in distant lands from starving to death. However, unlike Singer, she does not rely on any premise about our obligations to promote or prevent particular sorts of consequences. Rather, she derives the obligation to prevent famine deaths from a universal right not to be killed.

At first glance, this may seem unpromising. If someone merely goes about his business, how can he violate anyone's right not to be killed? But O'Neill notes that we may violate rights not to be killed even though we do not act alone, and even when death is not immediate. Furthermore, we may do so even when we do not intend to cause death and when we do not know whom our actions will kill. Putting all this together, she contends that many apparently innocent acts do violate rights not to be killed. For example, we violate such rights when we invest in companies whose policies reduce the resources of persons already close to starving, and thus inevitably kill some such persons.

IF IN THE fairly near future millions of people die of starvation, will those who survive be in any way to blame for those deaths? Is there anything which people ought to do now, and from now on, if they are to be able to avoid responsibility for unjustifiable deaths in famine years? I shall argue from the assumption that persons have a right not to be killed unjustifiably to the claim that we have a duty to try to prevent and postpone famine deaths. A corollary of this claim is that if we do nothing we shall bear some blame for some deaths.

Justifiable Killing

I shall assume that persons have a right not to be killed and a corresponding duty not to kill. I shall make no assumptions about the other rights persons may have. In particular, I shall not assume that persons have a right not to be allowed to die by those who could prevent it or a duty to prevent others' deaths whenever they could do so. Nor will I assume that persons lack this right.

Even if persons have no rights other than a right not to be killed, this right can justifiably be overridden in certain circumstances. Not all killings are unjustifiable. I shall be particularly concerned with two sorts of circumstances in which the right not to be killed is justifiably overridden. The first of these is the case of unavoidable killings; the second is the case of self-defense.

Unavoidable killings occur in situations where a person doing some act causes some death or deaths which he could not avoid. Often such deaths will be unavoidable because of the killer's ignorance of some relevant circumstance at the time of his decision to act. If B is driving a train, and A blunders onto the track and is either unnoticed by B or noticed too late for B to stop the train, and B kills A, then B could not have avoided killing A, given his decision to drive the train. Another sort of case of unavoidable killing occurs when B could avoid killing A or could avoid killing C, but cannot avoid killing one of the two. For example, if B is the carrier of a highly contagious and invariably fatal illness, he might find himself so placed that he cannot avoid meeting and so killing either A or C, though he can choose which of them to meet. In this case the unavoidability of B's killing someone is not relative to some prior decision B made. The cases of unavoidable killings with which I want to deal here are of the latter sort, and I shall argue that in such cases B kills justifiably if certain further conditions are met.

A killing may also be justifiable if it is undertaken in self-defense. I shall not argue here that persons have a right of self-defense which is independent of their right not to be killed, but rather that a minimal right of self-defense is a corollary of a right not to be killed. Hence the notion of self-defense on which I shall rely is in some ways different from, and narrower than, other interpretations of the right of self-defense. I shall also assume that if A has a right to defend himself against B, then third parties ought to defend A's right. If we take seriously the right not to be killed and its corollaries, then we ought to enforce others' rights not to be killed.

The right of self-defense which is a corollary of the right not to be killed is a right to take action to prevent killings. If I have a right not to be killed then I have a right to prevent others from endangering my life, though I may endanger their lives in so doing only if that is the only available way to prevent the danger to my own life. Similarly if another has the right not to be killed then I should, if possible, do something to prevent others from endangering his life, but I may endanger their lives in so doing only if that is the only available way to prevent the danger to his life. This duty to defend others is *not* a general duty of beneficence but a very restricted duty to enforce others' rights not to be killed.

The right to self-defense so construed is quite narrow. It includes no right of action against those who, though they cause or are likely to cause us harm, clearly do not endanger our lives. (However, specific cases are often unclear. The shopkeeper who shoots a person who holds him up with a toy gun was not endangered, but it may have been very reasonable of him to suppose that he was endangered.) And it includes no right to greater than minimal preventive action against a person who endangers one's life. If B is chasing A with a gun, and *A* could save his life either by closing a bullet-proof door or by shooting *B*, then if people have only a right not to be killed and a minimal corollary right of self-defense, *A* would have no right to shoot *B*. (Again, such cases are often unclear—*A* may not know that the door is bullet-proof or not think of it or may simply reason that shooting *B* is a better guarantee of prevention.) A right of proportionate self-defense which might justify *A* in shooting *B*, even were it clear that closing the door would have been enough to prevent *B*, is not a corollary of the right not to be killed. Perhaps a right of proportionate retaliation might be justified by some claim such as that aggressors lose certain rights, but I shall take no position on this issue.

In one respect the narrow right of self-defense, which is the corollary of a right not to be killed, is more extensive than some other interpretations of the right of self-defense. For it is a right to take action against others who endanger our lives whether or not they do so intentionally. *A*'s right not to be killed entitles him to take action not only against aggressors but also against those "innocent threats"[1] who endanger lives without being aggressors. If *B* is likely to cause *A*'s death inadvertently or involuntarily, then *A* has, if he has a right not to be killed, a right to take whatever steps are necessary to prevent *B* from doing so, provided that these do not infringe *B*'s right not to be killed unnecessarily. If *B* approaches *A* with a highly contagious and invariably lethal illness, then *A* may try to prevent *B* from getting near him even if *B* knows nothing about the danger he brings. If other means fail, *A* may kill *B* in self-defense, even though *B* was no aggressor.

This construal of the right of self-defense severs the link between aggression and self-defense. When we defend ourselves against innocent threats there is no aggressor, only somebody who endangers life. But it would be misleading to call this right a right of self-preservation. For self-preservation is commonly construed (as by Locke) as including a right to subsistence, and so a right to engage in a large variety of activities whether or not anybody endangers us. But the right which is the corollary of the right not to be killed is a right only to prevent others from endangering our lives, whether or not they intend to do so, and to do so with minimal danger to their lives. Only if one takes a Hobbesian view of human nature and sees others' acts as always completely threatening will the rights of self-defense and self-preservation tend to merge and everything done to maintain life be done to prevent its destruction. Without Hobbesian assumptions the contexts where the minimal right of self-defense can be invoked are fairly special, yet not, I shall argue, rare.

There may be various other circumstances in which persons' rights not to be killed may be overridden. Perhaps, for example, we may justifiably kill those who consent to us doing so. I shall take no position on whether persons can

---

[1] Cf. Robert Nozick, *Anarchy State and Utopia* (New York, 1974), p. 34. Nozick defines an innocent threat as "someone who is innocently a causal agent in a process such that he would be an aggressor had he chosen to become such an agent."

608

waive their rights not to be killed or on any further situations in which killings might be justifiable.

Justifiable Killings on Lifeboats

The time has come to start imagining lurid situations, which is the standard operating procedure for this type of discussion. I shall begin by looking at some sorts of killings which might occur on a lifeboat and shall consider the sort of justifications which they might be given.

Let us imagine six survivors on a lifeboat. There are two possible levels of provisions:

(1) Provisions are on all reasonable calculations sufficient to last until rescue. Either the boat is near land, or it is amply provisioned or it has gear for distilling water, catching fish, etc.
(2) Provisions are on all reasonable calculations unlikely to be sufficient for all six to survive until rescue.

We can call situation (1) *the well-equipped lifeboat situation*; situation (2) *the under-equipped lifeboat situation*. There may, of course, be cases where the six survivors are unsure which situation they are in, but for simplicity I shall disregard those here.

On a well-equipped lifeboat it is possible for all to survive until rescue. No killing could be justified as unavoidable, and if someone is killed, then the justification could only be self-defense in special situations. Consider the following examples:

(1A) On a well-equipped lifeboat with six persons, *A* threatens to jettison the fresh water, without which some or all would not survive till rescue. *A* may be either hostile or deranged. *B* reasons with *A*, but when this fails, shoots him. *B* can appeal to his own and the others' right of self-defense to justify the killing. "It was him or us," he may reasonably say, "for he would have placed us in an under-equipped lifeboat situation." He may say this both when *A* acts to harm the others and when *A* acts as an innocent threat.
(1B) On a well-equipped lifeboat with six persons, *B, C, D, E,* and *F* decide to withhold food from *A*, who consequently dies. In this case they cannot appeal to self-defense—for all could have survived. Nor can they claim that they merely let *A* die—"We didn't *do* anything"—for *A* would not otherwise have died. This was not a case of violating the problematic right not to be allowed to die but of violating the right not to be killed, and the violation is without justification of self-defense or of unavoidability.

On an under-equipped lifeboat it is not possible for all to survive until rescue. Some deaths are unavoidable, but sometimes there is no particular person whose death is unavoidable. Consider the following examples:

(2A) On an under-equipped lifeboat with six persons, *A* is very ill and needs extra water, which is already scarce. The others decide not to let him have any water, and *A* dies of thirst. If *A* drinks, then not all will survive. On the other hand it is clear that *A* was killed rather than allowed to die. If he had received water he might have survived. Though some death was unavoidable, *A*'s was not and selecting him as the victim requires justification.

(2B) On an under-equipped lifeboat with six persons, water is so scarce that only four can survive (perhaps the distillation unit is designed for supplying four people). But who should go without? Suppose two are chosen to go without, either by lot or by some other method, and consequently die. The others cannot claim that all they did was to allow the two who were deprived of water to die—for these two might otherwise have been among the survivors. Nobody had a greater right to be a survivor, but given that not all could survive, those who did not survive were killed justifiably if the method by which they were chosen was fair. (Of course, a lot needs to be said about what would make a selection procedure fair.)

(2C) The same situation as in (2B) holds, but the two who are not to drink ask to be shot to ease their deaths. Again the survivors cannot claim that they did not kill but at most that they killed justifiably. Whether they did so is not affected by their shooting rather than dehydrating the victims, but only by the unavoidability of some deaths and the fairness of procedures for selecting victims.

(2D) Again the basic situation is as in (2B). But the two who are not to drink rebel. The others shoot them and so keep control of the water. Here it is all too clear that those who died were killed, but they too may have been justifiably killed. Whether the survivors kill justifiably depends neither on the method of killing nor on the victims' cooperation, except insofar as cooperation is relevant to the fairness of selection procedures.

Lifeboat situations do not occur very frequently. We are not often confronted starkly with the choice between killing or being killed by the application of a decision to distribute scarce rations in a certain way. Yet this is becoming the situation of the human species on this globe. The current metaphor "spaceship Earth" suggests more drama and less danger; if we are feeling sober about the situation, "lifeboat Earth" may be more suggestive.

Some may object to the metaphor "lifeboat Earth." A lifeboat is small; all aboard have equal claims to be there and to share equally in the provisions. Whereas the earth is vast and while all may have equal rights to be there, some also have property rights which give them special rights to consume, while others do not. The starving millions are far away and have no right to what is owned by affluent individuals or nations, even if it could prevent their deaths. If they did, it will be said, this is a violation at most of their right not to be allowed to die. And this I have not established or assumed.

I think that this could reasonably have been said in times past. The poverty and consequent deaths of far-off persons was something which the affluent might perhaps have done something to prevent, but which they had (often) done nothing to bring about. Hence they had not violated the right not to be killed of those living far off. But the economic and technological interdependence of today alters this situation.[2] Sometimes deaths are produced by some persons or groups of persons in distant, usually affluent, nations. Sometimes such persons and groups of persons violate not only some persons' alleged right not to be allowed to die but also their more fundamental right not to be killed.

We tend to imagine violations of the right not to be killed in terms of the killings so frequently discussed in the United States today: confrontations between individuals where one directly, violently, and intentionally brings about the other's death. As the lifeboat situations have shown, there are other ways in which we can kill one another. In any case, we do not restrict our vision to the typical mugger or murderer context. B may violate A's right not to be killed even when

(a) B does not act alone.
(b) A's death is not immediate.
(c) It is not certain whether A or another will die in consequence of B's action.
(d) B does not intend A's death.

The following set of examples illustrates these points about killings:

(aa) A is beaten by a gang consisting of B, C, D, etc. No one assailant single-handedly killed him, yet his right not to be killed was violated by all who took part.
(bb) A is poisoned slowly by daily doses. The final dose, like earlier ones, was not, by itself, lethal. But the poisoner still violated A's right not to be killed.
(cc) B plays Russian roulette with A, C, D, E, F, and G, firing a revolver at each once, when he knows that one firing in six will be lethal. If A is shot and dies, then B has violated his right not to be killed.
(dd) Henry II asks who will rid him of the turbulent priest, and his supporters kill Becket. It is reasonably clear that Henry did not intend Becket's death, even though he in part brought it about, as he later admitted.

---

[2] Cf. Peter Singer, "Famine, Affluence, and Morality," *Philosophy & Public Affairs* I, no. 3 (Spring 1972): 229–243, 232. [Reprinted in this volume, reading 44.] I am in agreement with many of the points which Singer makes, but am interested in arguing that we must have some famine policy from a much weaker set of premises. Singer uses some consequentialist premises: starvation is bad; we ought to prevent bad things when we can do so without worse consequences; hence we ought to prevent starvation whether it is nearby or far off and whether others are doing so or not. The argument of this article does not depend on a particular theory about the grounds of obligation, but should be a corollary of any nonbizarre ethical theory which has any room for a notion of rights.

These explications of the right not to be killed are not too controversial taken individually, and I would suggest that their conjunction is also uncontroversial. Even when *A*'s death is the result of the acts of many persons and is not an immediate consequence of their deeds, nor even a certain consequence, and is not intended by them, *A*'s right not to be killed may be violated.

First Class versus Steerage on Lifeboat Earth

If we imagine a lifeboat in which special quarters are provided for the (recently) first-class passengers, and on which the food and water for all passengers are stowed in those quarters, then we have a fair, if crude, model of the present human situation on lifeboat Earth. For even on the assumption that there is at present sufficient for all to survive, some have control over the means of survival and so, indirectly, over others' survival. Sometimes the exercise of control can lead, even on a well-equipped lifeboat, to the starvation and death of some of those who lack control. On an ill-equipped lifeboat some must die in any case and, as we have already seen, though some of these deaths may be killings, some of them may be justifiable killings. Corresponding situations can, do, and will arise on lifeboat Earth, and it is to these that we should turn our attention, covering both the presumed present situation of global sufficiency of the means of survival and the expected future situation of global insufficiency.

Sufficiency Situations

Aboard a well-equipped lifeboat any distribution of food and water which leads to a death is a killing and not just a case of permitting a death. For the acts of those who distribute the food and water are the causes of a death which would not have occurred had those agents either had no causal influence or done other acts. By contrast, a person whom they leave in the water to drown is merely allowed to die, for his death would have taken place (other things being equal) had those agents had no causal influence, though it could have been prevented had they rescued him.[3] The distinction between killing and allowing to die, as here construed, does not depend on any claims about the other rights of persons who are killed. The death of the shortchanged passenger of example (1B) violated his property rights as well as his right not to be killed, but the reason the death was classifiable as a killing depended on the part which the acts of the other passengers had in causing it. If we suppose that a stowaway on a lifeboat has no right to food and water and is denied them, then clearly his property rights have not been violated. Even so, by the above definitions he is killed rather than allowed to die. For if the other passengers

---

[3] This way of distinguishing killing from allowing to die does not rely on distinguishing "negative" from "positive" acts. Such attempts seem unpromising since any act has multiple descriptions of which some will be negative and others positive. If a clear distinction is to be made between killing and letting die, it must hinge on the *difference* which an act makes for a person's survival, rather than on the description under which the agent acts.

had either had no causal influence or done otherwise, his death would not have occurred. Their actions—in this case distributing food only to those entitled to it—caused the stowaway's death. Their acts would be justifiable only if property rights can sometimes override the right not to be killed.

Many would claim that the situation on lifeboat Earth is not analogous to that on ordinary lifeboats, since it is not evident that we all have a claim, let alone an equal claim, on the earth's resources. Perhaps some of us are stowaways. I shall not here assume that we do all have some claim on the earth's resources, even though I think it plausible to suppose that we do. I shall assume that even if persons have unequal property rights and some people own nothing, it does not follow that B's exercise of his property rights can override A's right not to be killed.[4] Where our activities lead to others' deaths which would not have occurred had we either done something else or had no causal influence, no claim that the activities were within our economic rights would suffice to show that we did not kill.

It is not far-fetched to think that at present the economic activity of some groups of persons leads to others' deaths. I shall choose a couple of examples of the sort of activity which can do so, but I do not think that these examples do more than begin a list of cases of killing by economic activities. Neither of these examples depends on questioning the existence of unequal property rights; they assume only that such rights do not override a right not to be killed. Neither example is one for which it is plausible to think that the killing could be justified as undertaken in self-defense.

Case one might be called the *foreign investment* situation. A group of investors may form a company which invests abroad—perhaps in a plantation or in a mine—and so manage their affairs that a high level of profits is repatriated, while the wages for the laborers are so minimal that their survival rate is lowered, that is, their expectation of life is lower than it might have been had the company not invested there. In such a case the investors and company management do not act alone, do not cause immediate deaths, and do not know in advance who will die; it is also likely that they intend no deaths. But by their involvement in the economy of an underdeveloped area they cannot claim, as can another company which has no investments there, they they are "doing nothing." On the contrary, they are setting the policies which determine the living standards which determine the survival rate. When persons die because of the lowered standard of living established by a firm or a number of firms which dominate a local economy and either limit persons to employment on their terms or lower the other prospects for employment by damaging traditional economic structures, and these firms could either pay higher wages or

---

[4] The point may appear rather arbitrary, given that I have not rested my case on one theory of the grounds of obligation. But I believe that almost any such theory will show a right not to be killed to override a property right. Perhaps this is why Locke's theory can seem so odd—in moving from a right of self-preservation to a justification of unequal property rights, he finds himself gradually having to reinterpret all rights as property rights, thus coming to see us as the owners of our persons.

stay out of the area altogether, then those who establish these policies are violating some persons' rights not to be killed. Foreign investment which *raises* living standards, even to a still abysmal level, could not be held to kill, for it causes no additional deaths, unless there are special circumstances, as in the following example.

Even when a company investing in an underdeveloped country establishes high wages and benefits and raises the expectation of life for its workers, it often manages to combine these payments with high profitability only by having achieved a tax-exempt status. In such cases the company is being subsidized by the general tax revenue of the underdeveloped economy. It makes no contribution to the infrastructure—e.g. roads and harbors and airports—from which it benefits. In this way many underdeveloped economies have come to include developed enclaves whose development is achieved in part at the expense of the poorer majority.[5] In such cases, government and company policy combine to produce a high wage sector at the expense of a low wage sector; in consequence, some of the persons in the low wage sector, who would not otherwise have died, may die; these persons, whoever they may be, are killed and not merely allowed to die. Such killings may sometimes be justifiable—perhaps, if they are outnumbered by lives saved through having a developed sector—but they are killings nonetheless, since the victims might have survived if not burdened by transfer payments to the developed sector.

But, one may say, the management of such a corporation and its investors should be distinguished more sharply. Even if the management may choose a level of wages, and consequently of survival, the investors usually know nothing of this. But the investors, even if ignorant, are responsible for company policy. They may often fail to exercise control, but by law they have control. They choose to invest in a company with certain foreign investments; they profit from it; they can, and others cannot, affect company policy in fundamental ways. To be sure the investors are not murderers—they do not intend to bring about the deaths of any persons; nor do the company managers usually intend any of the deaths company policies cause. Even so, investors and management acting together with the sorts of results just described do violate some persons' rights not to be killed and usually cannot justify such killings either as required for self-defense or as unavoidable.

Case two, where even under sufficiency conditions some persons' economic activities result in the deaths of other persons, might be called the *commodity pricing* case. Underdeveloped countries often depend heavily on the price level of a few commodities. So a sharp drop in the world price of coffee or sugar or cocoa may spell ruin and lowered survival rates for whole regions. Yet such drops in price levels are not in all cases due to factors beyond human control. Where they are the result of action by investors, brokers, or government agen-

---

[5] Cf. P. A. Baron, *The Political Economy of Growth* (New York, 1957), especially chap. 5, "On the Roots of Backwardness"; or A. G. Frank, *Capitalism and Underdevelopment in Latin America* (New York, 1967). Both works argue that underdeveloped economies are among the products of developed ones.

cies, these persons and bodies are choosing policies which will kill some people. Once again, to be sure, the killing is not single-handed, it is not instantaneous, the killers cannot foresee exactly who will die, and they may not intend anybody to die.

Because of the economic interdependence of different countries, deaths can also be caused by rises in the prices of various commodities. For example, the present near-famine in the Sahelian region of Africa and in the Indian subcontinent is attributed by agronomists partly to climatic shifts and partly to the increased prices of oil and hence of fertilizer, wheat, and other grains.

> The recent doubling in international prices of essential foodstuffs will, of necessity, be reflected in higher death rates among the world's lowest income groups, who lack the income to increase their food expenditures proportionately, but live on diets near the subsistence level to begin with.[6]

Of course, not all of those who die will be killed. Those who die of drought will merely be allowed to die, and some of those who die because less has been grown with less fertilizer will also die because of forces beyond the control of any human agency. But to the extent that the raising of oil prices is an achievement of Arab diplomacy and oil company management rather than a windfall, the consequent deaths are killings. Some of them may perhaps be justifiable killings (perhaps if outnumbered by lives saved within the Arab world by industrialization), but killings nonetheless.

Even on a sufficiently equipped earth some persons are killed by others' distribution decisions. The causal chains leading to death-producing distributions are often extremely complex. Where they can be perceived with reasonable clarity we ought, if we take seriously the right not to be killed and seek not merely to avoid killing others but to prevent third parties from doing so, to support policies which reduce deaths. For example—and these are only examples—we should support certain sorts of aid policies rather than others; we should oppose certain sorts of foreign investment; we should oppose certain sorts of commodity speculation, and perhaps support certain sorts of price support agreements for some commodities (e.g. those which try to maintain high prices for products on whose sale poverty stricken economies depend).

If we take the view that we have no duty to enforce the rights of others, then we cannot draw so general a conclusion about our duty to support various economic policies which might avoid some unjustifiable killings. But we might still find that we should take action of certain sorts either because our own lives are threatened by certain economic activities of others or because our own economic activities threaten others' lives. Only if we knew that we were not part of any system of activities causing unjustifiable deaths could we have no duties to support policies which seek to avoid such deaths. Modern eco-

[6] Lester R. Brown and Erik P. Eckholm, "The Empty Breadbasket," *Ceres* (F.A.O. Review on Development), March–April 1974, p. 59. See also N. Borlaug and R. Ewell, "The Shrinking Margin," in the same issue.

nomic causal chains are so complex that it is likely that only those who are economically isolated and self-sufficient could know that they are part of no such systems of activities. Persons who believe that they are involved in some death-producing activities will have some of the same duties as those who think they have a duty to enforce others' rights not to be killed.

Scarcity Situations

The last section showed that sometimes, even in sufficiency situations, some might be killed by the way in which others arranged the distribution of the means of subsistence. Of far more importance in the long run is the true lifeboat situation—the situation of scarcity. We face a situation in which not everyone who is born can live out the normal span of human life and, further, in which we must expect today's normal life-span to be shortened. The date at which serious scarcity will begin is not generally agreed upon, but even the more optimistic prophets place it no more than decades away.[7] Its arrival will depend on factors such as the rate of technological invention and innovation, especially in agriculture and pollution control, and the success of programs to limit human fertility.

Such predictions may be viewed as exonerating us from complicity in famine deaths. If famine is inevitable, then—while we may have to choose whom to save—the deaths of those whom we do not or cannot save cannot be seen as killings for which we bear any responsibility. For these deaths would have occurred even if we had no causal influence. The decisions to be made may be excruciatingly difficult, but at least we can comfort ourselves that we did not produce or contribute to the famine.

However, this comforting view of famine predictions neglects the fact that these predictions are contingent upon certain assumptions about what people will do in the prefamine period. Famine is said to be inevitable *if* people do not curb their fertility, alter their consumption patterns, and avoid pollution and consequent ecological catastrophes. It is the policies of the present which will produce, defer, or avoid famine. Hence if famine comes, the deaths that occur will be results of decisions made earlier. Only if we take no part in systems of activities which lead to famine situations can we view ourselves as choosing whom to save rather than whom to kill when famine comes. In an economically interdependent world there are few people who can look on the approach of famine as a natural disaster from which they may kindly rescue some, but for whose arrival they bear no responsibility. We cannot stoically regard particular famine deaths as unavoidable if we have contributed to the emergence and extent of famine.

[7] For discussions of the time and extent of famine see, for example, P. R. Ehrlich, *The Population Bomb*, rev. ed. (New York, 1971); R. L. Heilbroner, *An Inquiry into the Human Prospect* (New York, 1974); *Scientific American*, September 1974, especially R. Freedman and B. Berelson, "The Human Population"; P. Demeny, "The Populations of the Underdeveloped Countries"; R. Revelle, "Food and Population."

If we bear some responsibility for the advent of famine, then any decision on distributing the risk of famine is a decision whom to kill. Even a decision to rely on natural selection as a famine policy is choosing a policy for killing— for under a different famine policy different persons might have survived, and under different prefamine policies there might have been no famine or a less severe famine. The choice of a particular famine policy may be justifiable on the grounds that once we have let it get to that point there is not enough to go around, and somebody must go, as on an ill-equipped lifeboat. Even so, the famine policy chosen will not be a policy of saving some but not all persons from an unavoidable predicament.

Persons cannot, of course, make famine policies individually. Famine and prefamine policies are and will be made by governments individually and collectively and perhaps also by some voluntary organizations. It may even prove politically impossible to have a coherent famine or prefamine policy for the whole world; if so, we shall have to settle for partial and piecemeal policies. But each person who is in a position to support or oppose such policies, whether global or local, has to decide which to support and which to oppose. Even for individual persons, inaction and inattention are often a decision—a decision to support the famine and prefamine policies, which are the status quo whether or not they are "hands off" policies. There are large numbers of ways in which private citizens may affect such policies. They do so in supporting or opposing legislation affecting aid and foreign investment, in supporting or opposing certain sorts of charities or groups such as Zero Population Growth, in promoting or opposing ecologically conservative technology and lifestyles. Hence we have individually the onus of avoiding killing. For even though we

(a) do not kill single-handedly those who die of famine
(b) do not kill instantaneously those who die of famine
(c) do not know which individuals will die as the result of the prefamine and famine policies we support (unless we support something like a genocidal famine policy)
(d) do not intend any famine deaths

we nonetheless kill and do not merely allow to die. For as the result of our actions in concert with others, some will die who might have survived had we either acted otherwise or had no causal influence.

Famine Policies and Prefamine Policies

Various principles can be suggested on which famine and prefamine policies might reasonably be based. I shall list some of these, more with the aim of setting out the range of possible decisions than with the aim of stating a justification for selecting some people for survival. One very general policy might be that of adopting whichever more specific policies will lead to the fewest deaths. An example would be going along with the consequences of natural selection in the way in which the allocation of medical care in situations of great shortage does, that is, the criteria for relief would be a high chance of survival if relief is given and a low chance otherwise—the worst risks would be abandoned. (This decision is analogous to picking the ill man as the victim on the lifeboat in 2A.) However, the policy of minimizing deaths is indeterminate, unless a certain time horizon is specified. For the policies which maximize survival in the short run—e.g. preventive medicine and minimal living standards—may also maximize population increase and lead to greater ultimate catastrophe.[8]

Another general policy would be to try to find further grounds which can justify overriding a person's right not to be killed. Famine policies adopted on these grounds might permit others to kill those who will forgo their right not to be killed (voluntary euthanasia, including healthy would-be suicides) or to kill those whom others find dependent and exceptionally burdensome, e.g. the unwanted sick or aged or unborn or newborn (involuntary euthanasia, abortion, and infanticide). Such policies might be justified by claims that the right not to be killed may be overridden in famine situations if the owner of the right consents or if securing the right is exceptionally burdensome.

Any combination of such policies is a policy of killing some and protecting others. Those who are killed may not have their right not to be killed violated without reason; those who set and support famine policies and prefamine policies will not be able to claim that they do not kill, but if they reason carefully they may be able to claim that they do not do so without justification.

From this vantage point it can be seen why it is not relevant to restrict the right of self-defense to a right to defend oneself against those who threaten one's life but do not do so innocently. Such a restriction may make a great difference to one's view of abortion in cases where the mother's life is threatened, but it does not make much difference when famine is the issue. Those who might be chosen as likely victims of any famine policy will probably be innocent of contributing to the famine, or at least no more guilty than others; hence the innocence of the victims is an insufficient ground for rejecting a policy. Indeed it is hard to point a finger at the guilty in famine situations. Are they the hoarders of grain? The parents of large families? Inefficient farmers? Our own generation?

In a sense we are all innocent threats to one another's safety in scarcity situations, for the bread one person eats might save another's life. If there were fewer people competing for resources, commodity prices would fall and starvation deaths be reduced. Hence famine deaths in scarcity situations might be justified on grounds of the minimal right of self-defense as well as on grounds of the unavoidability of some deaths and the reasonableness of the policies for selecting victims. For each famine death leaves fewer survivors competing for whatever resources there are, and the most endangered among the survivors might have died—had not others done so. So a policy which kills some may

---

[8] See *Scientific American*, September 1974, especially A. J. Coale, "The History of the Human Population."

be justified on the grounds that the most endangered survivors could have been defended in no other way.

Global scarcity is not here yet. But its imminence has certain implications for today. If all persons have a right not to be killed and a corollary duty not to kill others, then we are bound to adopt prefamine policies which ensure that famine is postponed as long as possible and is minimized. And a duty to try to postpone the advent and minimize the severity of famine is a duty on the one hand to minimize the number of persons there will be and on the other to maximize the means of subsistence.[9] For if we do not adopt prefamine policies with these aims we shall have to adopt more drastic famine policies sooner.

So if we take the right not to be killed seriously, we should consider and support not only some famine policy for future use but also a population and resources policy for present use. There has been a certain amount of philosophical discussion of population policies.[10] From the point of view of the present argument it has two defects. First, it is for the most part conducted within a utilitarian framework and focuses on problems such as the different population policies required by maximizing the total and the average utility of a population. Secondly this literature tends to look at a scarcity of resources as affecting the quality of lives but not their very possibility. It is more concerned with the question, How many people should we add? than with the question, How few people could we lose? There are, of course, many interesting questions about population policies which are not relevant to famine. But here I shall consider only population and resource policies determined on the principle of postponing and minimizing famine, for these are policies which might be based on the claim that persons have a right not to be killed, so that we have a duty to avoid or postpone situations in which we shall have to override this right.

Such population policies might, depending upon judgments about the likely degree of scarcity, range from the mild to the draconian. I list some examples. A mild population policy might emphasize family planning, perhaps moving in the direction of fiscal incentives or measures which stress not people's rights but their duties to control their bodies. Even a mild policy would require a lot both in terms of invention (e.g. the development of contraceptives suitable for use in poverty-stricken conditions) and innovation (e.g. social policies which reduce the incentives and pressures to have a large family).[11] More draconian policies would enforce population limitation—for example, by mandatory

---

[9] The failure of "right to life" groups to pursue these goals seriously casts doubt upon their commitment to the preservation of human lives. Why are they active in so few of the contexts where human lives are endangered?

[10] For example, J. C. C. Smart, *An Outline of a System of Utilitarian Ethics* (Melbourne, 1961), pp. 18, 44ff.; Jan Narveson, "Moral Problems of Population," *Monist* 57 (1973): 62–86; "Utilitarianism and New Generations," *Mind* 76 (1967): 62–72.

[11] Cf. Mahmood Mamdani, *The Myth of Population Control* (New York, 1972), for evidence that high fertility can be based on rational choice rather than ignorance or incompetence.

sterilization after a certain number of children were born or by reducing public health expenditures in places with high net reproduction rates to prevent death rates from declining until birth rates do so. A policy of completely eliminating all further births (e.g. by universal sterilization) is also one which would meet the requirement of postponing famine, since extinct species do not suffer famine. I have not in this argument used any premises which show that a complete elimination of births would be wrong, but other premises might give reasons for thinking that it is wrong to enforce sterilization or better to have some persons rather than no persons. In any case the political aspects of introducing famine policies make it likely that this most austere of population policies would not be considered.

There is a corresponding range of resource policies. At the milder end are the various conservation and pollution control measures now being practiced or discussed. At the tougher end of the spectrum are complete rationing of energy and materials consumption. If the aim of a resources policy is to avoid killing those who are born, and adequate policy may require both invention (e.g. solar energy technology and better waste retrieval techniques) and innovation (e.g. introducing new technology in such a way that its benefits are not quickly absorbed by increasing population, as has happened with the green revolution in some places).

At all events, if we think that people have a right not to be killed, we cannot fail to face up to its long range implications. This one right by itself provides ground for activism on many fronts. In scarcity situations which we help produce, the defeasibility of the right not to be killed is important, for there cannot be any absolute duty not to kill persons in such situations but only a commitment to kill only for reasons. Such a commitment requires consideration of the condition or quality of life which is to qualify for survival. Moral philosophers are reluctant to face up to this problem; soon it will be staring us in the face.

46

Intention, Harm, and Personal Discretion

CHARLES FRIED

Charles Fried (b. 1935) is Carter Professor of General Jurisprudence at Harvard University. His works include An Anatomy of Values, Medical Experimentation, *and* Contract as Promise. *This selection is from his book,* Right and Wrong.

In this reading, Fried's topic is the basis of the categorical prohibition against physically harming others. He argues that this prohibition is rooted in the notion of respect for persons. (For the classic statement of this idea, see reading 29, by Immanuel Kant.) Because persons are embodied creatures, Fried argues that respect for them demands that they not be physically harmed. But because persons are agents, they must also determine their own destinies. Persons would not have room for choice if they were always obligated to avoid causing any harm to others. Thus, some limit to the obligation not to cause harm must be found. Because the harms we cause intentionally "are invested with our persons in a way that concomitants are not," Fried concludes that the categorical prohibition against harming others rules out only intentional *harm.*

This has implications regarding our obligations toward famine victims. In reading 45, Onora O'Neill argues that even persons who unintentionally contribute to famine deaths may violate the victims' rights not to be killed. Although Fried does not explicitly discuss rights, his argument tells against this. If only intentional acts violate categorical prohibitions, then the unintended consequences of acts cannot do so. Although Fried does acknowledge duties to contribute to famine relief, he insists that these "allow for weighing and calculation . . . as the abstract norm does not."

IN THIS CHAPTER I examine one crucial categorical norm: that it is wrong to do physical harm to an innocent person. Now, physical harm is not the only or necessarily the worst kind of injury. A man's liberty to speak his mind or travel freely may be more important to him than security against some sorts of harm, as may be his property or his reputation. Certain violations of these other interests may also be wrong, just as wrong as doing physical harm. I shall not offer accounts of all such wrongs. I suppose that arguments analogous to those I give regarding harm and lying are available in other cases. I claim only that the norm forbidding physical harm has priority, at least in the exposition of a theory of right and wrong.

By physical harm I mean an impingement upon the body which either causes pain or impairs functioning. Thus a sharp, painful blow which, however, neither cuts nor bruises would constitute harm. So also would a laceration of the skin, since any break in the skin impairs the functioning of that tissue. On the other hand, to cut hair or a fingernail or to paint the skin with some nontoxic substance might constitute an offense to dignity but would not stand as a physical harm. This definition covers a wide range of consequences. It covers everything from killing to pinching and thus raises an important theoretical question. Can it be that pinching has the same moral quality as killing? I shall offer very little in the way of enlightenment regarding the morality of pinching, although if one takes physical harms further along the line of seriousness—maiming, blinding, or even temporary infliction of severe pain—I have no difficulty concluding that, in all of these cases, the formal nature of the moral judgment, the categorical prohibition, is the same. These are harms we must not intend to inflict, and consideration of consequences as such cannot outweigh that judgment. As we shall see, there are excuses and justifications for killing, and so there must be also for maiming and the infliction of pain. Nor is there any reason to insist that just because all instances along this gamut have the same formal structure (being the subjects of categorical prohibitions), the excusing and justifying conditions must therefore also be the same. There may, after all, also be an absolute prohibition against engaging in sex for pay, but that would not mean that the excuses and justifications for so doing would be the same as those offered for killing.

It is interesting, however, that the judgment may well run out at the lower end of the scale, that even absolute notions recognize a concept of triviality. There does indeed seem to be something absurd about wheeling out the heavy moral artillery to deal with pinching. A prohibition may be categorical, but the boundaries of that concept may be susceptible of judgments of degree, at least to the extent that one must recognize the trivial and the absurd. But it does not follow from the proposition that there is no absolute prohibition against pinching, in view of the triviality of the harm, that therefore the prohibition against intentionally killing an innocent person is also a matter of degree, also is not absolute. And even as to killing, I do not know how to answer the person who asks me whether I would be willing to kill an innocent person to save the whole of humanity from excruciating suffering and death. There are boundaries to each of these concepts, and the concepts themselves often become blurred, indeterminate, subject to judgments of prudence at those boundaries. We can accept this without at all concluding that therefore the concepts have no central core, or that they are subject throughout to judgments of degree.

In explicating this norm, I shall show how the concept of intention introduced in the previous chapter is appropriate to specify and make practicable the judgments that a particular kind of act, harming an innocent person, is wrong. Whatever may be the problems about intention in other contexts, intention as the mode of application clearly complements the substantive content of the norm. That intentional physical harm (choosing the harm of another as one's end or as the means to one's end) should be the subject of this norm also works to explain the logic of the norm, its categorical force. The two elements, intention and doing harm, may be seen as picturing a relation between a moral agent and the object of his agency, a relation which is inconsistent with the basic notion of respect for persons. And that inconsistency explains why the prohibition is categorical. The absolute norm is grounded in the importance to us of our physical integrity and in the special evil of a relation established between people in which one person exercises his peculiarly human efficacy to attack another's physical integrity. It is just because the person of the victim is threatened by the person of the actor that the relation has a special moral significance. From the victim's perspective, to be hurt by a natural force or by accident is different from being the object of an intentional attack, even though the actual injury may be identical. The intention makes for the offense.

Directness and Particularity

Consider these two cases:

III. Plunging a dagger into someone's heart.
IV. Revaluing your currency with the foreseeable result that your country's wheat crop will be more expensive and less readily available for famine relief and the further foreseeable result that some persons weakened by hunger in distant lands will die.

It is our intuitive response that without some very special and narrowly drawn justification, the conduct in case III is wrong, while the moral quality of the conduct in case IV depends on a wide variety of considerations: the purpose of the revaluation, the likely response of other countries, the history behind the move, the background of international practice, and so on. In short, it seems natural to bring the first of these cases within the ambit of the categorical norm "Do no harm." The conduct in the second case, however, must inevitably be subjected to some form of consequentialist analysis. Now, the consequentialist would argue that so must case III, that no plausible ground can exist for determining the moral quality of the act in case IV by weighing the good accomplished against the concomitant harm while refusing to have the judgment in case III depend on exactly the same kind of weighing. If that is what we must do in case IV, then—it is claimed—this is all we can *ever* do.

The Person and Disintegrating Universality

If we could not distinguish between cases III and IV, if we could not say that directly harming was wrong in some special way, if we had to weigh and balance all the consequences to see if stabbing an innocent person to death was wrong, then our whole position as free moral agents, our status as persons, would be grievously undermined. (I shall specify what I mean by directness in due course.) The connection between the concept of personality and the special moral quality of directly caused harm is based on the (metaphysical) fact that persons, the ultimate object of moral judgments, are particular entities, and more precisely particular *bodies*. This is not a necessary truth, and fanciful suppositions may be adduced to show how the concept of the person might cut across physical boundaries in some other way. But these notions are only possible in a world where choice and reflection emanate from entities other than the kinds of physical entities that actually exist.[1]

Now, if the person is to remain at the center of moral judgment, this link to the concrete must be maintained by the very form of our moral norms. We must avoid what I shall call disintegrating universality. The concept of personality, of individuality, is after all, a precarious one. Why is the particular embodied unit of the individual the primitive, the primary unit? Why are not larger or smaller units the significant ones? Why not the species, for instance? Why not some abstract idea, some conception, the universe as a whole? The more abstract our notions of value become, the more universal they are, the more the significance of the individual person is threatened. This significance of the individual person can only be asserted by the assertion of concrete particularity, by the assertion of particular contingent differences which may not make any difference in terms which can be generalized or derived from some more basic principle, but which are nevertheless the terms of the concrete particularity of individual human existence. This point is illustrated by the contrast to utilitarianism, which in its uncompromising universality deprives all individual differences, and thus the individual himself, of moral significance. Utilitarianism posits that it is the sum total of happiness that counts, and how happiness is distributed among persons is a secondary, an instrumental matter. So also an ethic of excellence, which makes the advancement of knowledge or of the arts the primary criterion of the good, is ultimately indifferent to the human actors who are the contingent vehicles of these excellences. In such systems, a moral agent must view not only his own happiness or excellences as being adventitiously and irrelevantly his own (he is like a trustee with whom these values are deposited because they must be deposited somewhere), but even his capacities, dispositions, tastes, and pleasures are just the raw materials out of which this abstract value is to be fabricated.

The contrasting view gives content to the notion that it is the individual person who is the ultimate entity of value, so that even a person's happiness is only important because it is that person's happiness. Happiness is not a kind of undifferentiated abstract plasma waiting to be attached to a particular person but the aim and outcome of individual *choice*, the success of the self in realizing its own values through its choices and efficacy. Accordingly, the maintenance of the integrity of the individual as the locus of valuation and choice is more important than the abstractions of happiness, pleasure, or excellence. These latter are, after all, rather the *objects* of individual valuation. And if the primacy of the individual is to be maintained, if it is individuality, personality, which is the point of departure of ethical judgments, then the "irrelevantly" particular must be allowed significance.

The integrity of the person as the center of moral choice and judgment

---

[1] This argument has the odd entailment of making my basically Kantian thesis about the importance of persons and about the moral norms which express that importance depend on what Kant would call contingent facts. I regard this as Kant's problem, not mine, and also I see in this an explanation of why the categorical norms I offer are much more material than those Kant proposes.

requires that we find room for the inescapably particular in personality, that we avoid disintegrating universality. The absolute norm "Do no harm" expresses this centrality of the person on both ends of the relation: it gives special prominence to the physical person as the object (victim) of the relation, and it makes the person as agent both more responsible for what he does directly or intentionally and less responsible for what merely comes about as a side effect of his purposes. If, as consequentialism holds, we were indeed equally morally responsible for an infinite radiation of concentric circles originating from the center point of some action, then while it might look as if we were enlarging the scope of human responsibility and thus the significance of personality, the enlargement would be greater than we could support. For to be responsible equally for everything is to have the moral possibility of choice, of discretion, of creative concretization of one's free self wholly preempted by the potential radiations of all the infinite alternatives for choice. Total undifferentiated responsibility is the correlative of the morally overwhelming, undifferentiated plasma of happiness or pleasure.

Direct Harm

It is a natural point of departure for any containment and highlighting of personal responsibility to give special prominence to that which we accomplish by touching, that which is accomplished by our physical bodies. Our ethical constructs attach a peculiar importance to that which is done directly, immediately, because it is through such actions that we first learn about our capacities and our efficacy. As we touch and produce results in the world by touching, we learn that we are able to produce results and that we as individuals are different from the results we produce. It is by touching that the notions of acting and efficacy develop in us. It is by touching that we learn that we are different from the world, that we become acquainted with our identity, and that we become acquainted with our capacity for causal efficacy. Willard Quine has suggested this same intuitive connection between touching and cause: "Of these two wayward idioms, the causal and the dispositional, the causal is the simpler and the more fundamental. It may have had its prehistoric beginnings in man's sense of effort as in pushing. The imparting of energy still seems to be the central idea. The transfer of momentum from one billiard ball to another is persistently cited as a paradigm case of causality in terms of the flow of energy."[2] To be sure, an objection might be raised that in stabbing, it is the

---

[2] *The Roots of Reference* (LaSalle, Ill.: Open Court, 1973), p. 5. A possible linguistic recognition of the special nature of certain ways of bringing about results in the world, those ways that are more direct, is found in the fact that transitive verbs like "melt," "break," "kill," "shatter" have a different grammatical functioning from the terms some might suppose to be their equivalents, "cause to melt," "cause to break," "cause to die." For instance, "one can cause an event by doing something at a time distinct from the time of the event. But if you melt something, then you melt it when it melts . . . [Thus] (20), but not (21), is well-formed.

"(20) John caused Bill to die on Sunday by stabbing him on Saturday.

"(21) John killed Bill on Sunday by stabbing him on Saturday" (J. A. Fodor, "Three Reasons for not Deriving 'Kill' from 'Cause to Die,'" *Linguistic Inquiry* [1970]: 433).

knife, not the hand, that makes the contact. And what of dropping a stone on somebody or running him over in a truck? The idea of direct harm is approximate and intuitive, which does not matter since it is indeed only a springboard to the concept of *intentional* harm—and intentional harm can work in very remote and indirect ways. For the moment, suffice it to say that the dagger appears quite naturally as an extension of the hand. So might the stone or even the truck appear as extensions of the person, as extensions of direct physical efficacy. The limits are vague and to a degree conventional.

Physical harm inflicted directly, personally as it were—in the language of the classical Roman law, *damnum corpore corpori datum*—provides a paradigm for the kind of relation between persons which is the subject of the categorical prohibition. And, though the discussion has been concerned so far explicitly only with one side, the agent's side, of the relation encompassed by the norm "Do no harm," the argument is symmetric. The same factors, which identify the importance of the particular embodied person for the purpose of anchoring the causal chain of responsibility in the immediate and direct *production* of results, operate as well to bind the person of the victim with peculiar closeness to what he *suffers* in his physical person.

The Analogy to Benefit

A man's life is full of particular affections and concerns. He loves his children, is fond of his friends, is moved by the suffering of a particular person, even a stranger. In Part III, I consider at length decisions to benefit particular persons rather than some abstract, impersonal mass of persons. I anticipate that discussion briefly now because the claim of a special right to benefit those who are close to us is symmetrical with the claim that direct harm, harm to those close to us, is absolutely wrong. Now, I believe that to condemn any preference for particular persons as morally invalid, to require us to treat all human beings with strict impartiality, would leave the very concept of human welfare with a remarkably poor content: there would be no room for concern based just on the fact of relationships with others. To the extent that personal concern is grounded in, say, affection or friendship, such concern would imply an improper preference, a departure from impartiality. The individual would become a kind of dimensionless locus of his own hedonistic and self-centered pleasures on the one hand and a source of completely generalized concern for all the other such loci on the other. Such total impartiality conflicts with a sense of one's own individuality. Indeed, it is but another version of what I have called the reduction of disintegrating universality. A full account of just how much impartiality we must show in benefiting others will depend on a theory of rights and of justice. Here I assert only that the maintenance of a properly rich and articulated moral life must allow us to maintain some reserve for relations with particular persons. But those persons can be the subject of our particular concern only if we have somehow made contact with their concrete, particular features.

The argument for a right to benefit specially certain identified persons (as opposed to humanity in general) is not directly translatable into an argument condemning with special stringency the harming of an identified person in a direct and immediate way. The natural obverse of the benefit argument would seem to be the case of treachery, where one harms those who trust him or to whom one has a special obligation. But that is not at all the paradigm of direct, personal harm. Rather, a direct attack upon anyone, even a stranger, is the baseline of that primitive wrong. And thus the point of departure is a point on the spectrum which in respect to *benefit* seems a most attenuated form of relationship: "mere" propinquity. Now, propinquity is indeed a necessary condition, a natural precursor, of personal relations. We cannot enter into personal relations with those with whom we have not come into contact. (Affinities contracted by correspondence or telephone are, after all, parasitic on the paradigm of a friend as someone we have encountered personally.) But even though propinquity is such a natural precursor of relations of special care, it does not follow that something especially *bad* arises out of what might be considered a mere refusal to take up the invitation to deeper involvement that propinquity offers. When we refuse aid to the stranger in our path, this is not obviously *worse* than refusing aid to some unknown, unseen, random stranger who may need our help as much. And if one can decline the invitation to enter into a relation of benefit with a particular stranger, how does the case of benefit help to show why plunging a knife into a stranger bears a greater burden of justification than increasing the level of radiation only so much as will doom one additional person of the world's population to death by cancer?

The distinction between benefit and harm arises in this way: If everyone who passed us by in a crowded street had a claim to our special *and positive* concern, a claim to be specially benefited, then little would be left over for those undoubted and strong cases—affection, kinship—in which a special claim to benefit seems justified. Nor would the problem be significantly less severe if we limited the strangers' claims to those strangers who asked for our help. The intrusion on our ability to limit and control the numbers and identities of those who have a privileged call on our help could be as bad in the latter case as in the former. If propinquity were recognized as a sufficient, not just a necessary condition for special relations of benefit, then the particular would indeed soon all but disappear in the general after all. But these problems are not with us in respect to harm. *It is not the victim who chooses the agent, but the agent who chooses the victim.* The agent retains control of his circle of concern; it cannot engulf. In direct harm, the agent focuses on the victim, knowing that his actions will impinge directly on him. It is the agent who makes the victim an issue and who must therefore take account of his particularity.

Thus some choice, some special circumstance, must single out the face in the crowd to whom the agent will stand bound by the special bond—for if he stood specially bound by everyone he met, in the end there would be no special bond to anyone. In the case of benefit, something has to reach out to particularize the beneficiary of the relation other than the general fact—applicable across too indefinite a range—of a susceptibility to benefit. If a stranger can say to me, "You might have benefited me," I can always reply, "No more than countless other persons." In harm this problem does not exist. The conscious, volitional infliction of harm directly by my person upon the person of the victim *ipso facto* sufficiently particularizes the victim. I cannot in general and always say, "If I had not harmed you, I would have harmed someone else," for usually it is open to me to harm no one at all.[3]

Now, I do insist that the direct impingement be conscious, a volitional gesture. If I harm you directly but inadvertently—through carelessness or even against my will, as when pushed—this may or may not create a relation such that I am to be blamed, must apologize or try to make it up to you, but I have not made a conscious decision to inflict harm on your person by my person. It is that decision which is the subject of the absolute norm "Do no harm." And it is from that decision that I shall now build out to deal with the issue of intentional but possibly indirect harm.

From Directness to Intention

Directness is invoked to limit and make practicable the norm "Do no harm." I have argued that without some limitation it is not possible to conceive of the norm as expressing a categorical wrong: we would be forced either to have recourse to consequentialist weighing or to risk paralysis, obsession and contradiction. Stabbing someone or running him down are cases of direct harm proscribed—unless excused or justified—by the absolute norm. But really there is no great problem about such cases of direct harm if the harm is caused knowingly and as a result of deliberate action. We do not get into the difficulties about intended means and side effects in these cases of direct harm. Recall the question from the first chapter, whether a distinction could be made between shooting a guard to assure a prisoner's escape and dynamiting a hole in a prison wall knowing that this would also kill the guard stationed on top of the wall. Or consider the distinction between deliberate bombing of civilian areas as part of a campaign of terror and bombing of a military target, causing civilian casualities. In the first case of each pair the absolute norm applies, because the deaths are intended means, not mere side effects. Intention, not directness, provides the distinction in such cases. And this is plain if we consider a case in which there is no hint of directness, as when I send my victim's mother poisoned chocolates which I expect her to serve to him. The intention is sufficient to invoke the categorical prohibition, and directness is not necessary. Direct harm deals with both too easy and too limited a range of cases. The complexities encountered in cases of more remote harming scarcely arise

---

[3] I put to one side the case in which, unless one directly harms X, he will harm Y, as where a trolley driver approaching a junction has a choice between running down several persons on one or another of the two alternative tracks. See Judith J. Thompson, "Killing, Letting Die, and the Trolley Problem," *Monist*, April 1976.

where the harm is direct.[4] The effects we produce directly are generally the first steps in a planned chain of causality radiating out from our persons. The problems about unwanted reverberations, the "mere" side effects, begin further out, after the causal sequence has left the range of our immediate person. It is to those more classically troubling cases that I now turn.

The more remote cases are, of course, crucial. Man's technical progress from the spear to the radio-actuated Mars lander epitomizes the history of his attempt to extend his efficacy in precisely targeted projects beyond the range of his own body. So, just as the concept of directness gathers its moral force from its connection with the primitive fact of personal efficacy, the concept of intention corresponds to the equally human phenomenon of planned and contrived *distant* efficacy. Direct efficacy may be the first experience of efficacy, but as intelligence is essentially human, so the mastery of increasingly complex causal processes is of the essence of intelligent agency. The *person* may be invested at first in direct efficacy, but his *intelligence* is invested in his remote projects and his person invests his intelligence. Thus planned results are the natural extension of direct results, and intention of directness.

If you would grasp the fundamentality of intelligent purposive action, consider the difference between two states of affairs, both removed from the physical and temporal proximity of the person and both equally beneficial to his ultimate goals and situation. One comes about without any intervention on his part, though he well knows that processes lead to the result. The other he brings about: he considers what he wants, he takes stock of the resources at his command and of the laws by which events unfold, he charts the course and then acts, setting the whole thing in motion. In both cases there is the result and there is the desire, but in the second there is purposive action, plan, intention. The two cases are basically different courses of events. Initiating one is the intimate, personal fact of immediate action, direct efficacy. But that is not all. Intelligence, foresight, the channel dug for events by our minds in imagination, carries that first intimate thrust forward and invests the final results with the same personal attachment as was present at the outset.

This is not an argument, it is a picture, a picture of what it is to be a human being in the world of events. And it is according to this picture that we can see why means are different from concomitants. For means are part of our plans and thus are invested with our persons in a way that concomitants are not. The means we choose are the steps along a way we have mapped out in advance. Concomitants just happen; they belong to the domain of naturally occurring processes in which we might intervene if we choose. And of course we are sometimes responsible for what just happens, but really no more responsible for what happens as a concomitant of our plans than we are for what just

---

[4] It is hard to imagine how an agent might knowingly and directly harm another but not as a means to his end. Well, I suppose the case might arise. For example, I am running very fast along a railroad platform and there you are standing in front of me. If I stop or try to get around you I might miss my train, so, because I don't stop, I knock you under a train passing on the other track. I did not knock you off the platform as a means to my end. I just kept running irrespective of whether you were there or not. I have done it directly. The case is unusual.

happens because we choose not to act at all or to concern ourselves with other things. Directness is the kernel of personal investment from which we set out. From it, the world of events takes two courses: (1) the course of events in which we are, through plan and purpose, equally as invested as in the outset and (2) those sequences of events which radiate out from the starting point in the infinite concentric circles of mere causality. If we were responsible in the fullest measure for the second, then disintegrating universality would be upon us. If we were *not* responsible for the first, then the power of our reach would to that crucial extent be truncated. The special responsibility we bear for our projects is an appropriate recognition of our special involvement in those projects.

Thus the considerations explaining the absolute characters of the norm "Do no harm" in the case of *direct* harm must be generalized to the case of *intentional* harm. Direct harm describes a wrongful relation between two particular persons, just because it so intimately involves their particularity. Intended harm is wrong for closely analogous reasons. The harm, of course, on the victim's side of the relation is the same, but my account of the significance of intention shows why the agent's personal investment in his fellow's harm is just as great as if he produced it directly. It was the agent's very plan to bring about that harm; he formed a project in his mind and included the victim's harm in that project. Thus the intended injury is a result of personal agency, while in the case of a side effect or accident the injury is the product of natural causality (even if some human actions appear in the causal chain). Another person, who after all has the same capacity for reflection and the same concern to maintain his integrity, his person, as I do, has chosen to make my body, my person, a means to some end of his own.

None of this should be understood to excuse the evil of moral callousness, of disregard of the harm which our projects produce as a side effect, or of the harm which we might by some affirmative effect have avoided. I agree that our increased capacity to produce (or avoid) distant harm extends the range of our moral responsibility for all of those results. Starving populations in distant lands are our concern. Nothing I say here should be taken to deny this. I argue for a complex, not for a myopic sense of responsibility. The absolute norm forbids direct or intentional harm, but it does not excuse all other harms. The norm does not, however, forbid those harms absolutely. (As I have argued, it could not coherently do so.) There are duties of concern and beneficence toward all human beings, but they are not absolute. They allow for weighing and calculation—inevitably—as the absolute norm does not. Often these are impersonal duties to abstract persons and so they can be fulfilled in abstract ways—through governments, institutions, and the like. As we see next, very little can override the absolute norm "Do no harm," but the duty to care for abstract humanity may be overcome in many ways. Finally, there can be no doubt that my argument for an absolute prohibition of direct or intentional harm must operate to some extent at the expense of the interest of all those others who do not come into this specially stringent circle of concern. For there must be instances where only by doing intentional harm could I ward off greater harm from perhaps many others. And still I must do no harm.

47

A Defense of Abortion[1]

JUDITH JARVIS THOMSON

Judith Jarvis Thomson is Professor of Philosophy at M.I.T. She is the author of Acts and Other Events, *and of many well-known articles on rights and other topics in ethics and social philosophy.*

In this selection, Thomson discusses the morality of abortion. Although much debate has centered on the question of whether fetuses are persons, Thomson simply assumes, for purposes of argument, that they are. Even so, she contends, it does not follow that aborting a fetus is wrong. Although all persons have a right to life, this does not mean that they have a right to be provided with everything necessary to sustain life. To drive this home, Thomson imagines a person who awakes to find that a sick violinist has been attached to his kidneys while he slept. Even though the violinist will die if detached, Thomson maintains that he has no right not to be detached. Since each person has a prior right to the use of his or her own body, nobody else can have a right to the use of that body.

Does this mean that abortion is always justified? Interestingly, Thomson does not say this. For one thing, she seems to acknowledge that a woman's degree of care in trying to avoid pregnancy may be relevant. For another, she notes that even if an abortion would violate no one's rights, there may be other reasons not to have one. For example, it would be "indecent" to have a late abortion to avoid postponing a trip abroad. For related discussion of types of moral reasons, see Charles Fried's treatment of categorical and noncategorical norms in reading 46.

MOST OPPOSITION TO abortion relies on the premise that the fetus is a human being, a person, from the moment of conception. The premise is argued for, but, as I think, not well. Take, for example, the most common argument. We are asked to notice that the development of a human being from conception through birth into childhood is continuous; then it is said that to draw a line, to choose a point in this development and say "before this point the thing is not a person, after this point it is a person" is to make an arbitrary choice, a choice for which in the nature of things no good reason can be given. It is concluded that the fetus is, or anyway that we had better say it is, a person from the moment of conception. But this conclusion does not follow. Similar things might be said about the development of an acorn into an oak tree, and

---

[1] I am very much indebted to James Thomson for discussion, criticism, and many helpful suggestions.

it does not follow that acorns are oak trees, or that we had better say they are. Arguments of this form are sometimes called "slippery slope arguments"—the phrase is perhaps self-explanatory—and it is dismaying that opponents of abortion rely on them so heavily and uncritically.

I am inclined to agree, however, that the prospects for "drawing a line" in the development of the fetus look dim. I am inclined to think also that we shall probably have to agree that the fetus has already become a human person well before birth. Indeed, it comes as a surprise when one first learns how early in its life it begins to acquire human characteristics. By the tenth week, for example, it already has a face, arms and legs, fingers and toes; it has internal organs, and brain activity is detectable.[2] On the other hand, I think that the premise is false, that the fetus is not a person from the moment of conception. A newly fertilized ovum, a newly implanted clump of cells, is no more a person than an acorn is an oak tree. But I shall not discuss any of this. For it seems to me to be of great interest to ask what happens if, for the sake of argument, we allow the premise. How, precisely, are we supposed to get from there to the conclusion that abortion is morally impermissible? Opponents of abortion commonly spend most of their time establishing that the fetus is a person, and hardly any time explaining the step from there to the impermissibility of abortion. Perhaps they think the step too simple and obvious to require much comment. Or perhaps instead they are simply being economical in argument. Many of those who defend abortion rely on the premise that the fetus is not a person, but only a bit of tissue that will become a person at birth; and why pay out more arguments than you have to? Whatever the explanation, I suggest that the step they take is neither easy nor obvious, that it calls for closer examination than it is commonly given, and that when we do give it this closer examination we shall feel inclined to reject it.

I propose then, that we grant that the fetus is a person from the moment of conception. How does the argument go from here? Something like this, I take it. Every person has a right to life. So the fetus has a right to life. No doubt the mother has a right to decide what shall happen in and to her body; everyone would grant that. But surely a person's right to life is stronger and more stringent than the mother's right to decide what happens in and to her body, and so outweighs it. So the fetus may not be killed; an abortion may not be performed.

It sounds plausible. But now let me ask you to imagine this. You wake up in the morning and find yourself back to back in bed with an unconscious violinist. A famous unconscious violinist. He has been found to have a fatal kidney ailment, and the Society of Music Lovers has canvassed all the available medical records and found that you alone have the right blood type to help. They have therefore kidnapped you, and last night the violinist's circulatory

---

[2] Daniel Callahan, *Abortion: Law, Choice and Morality* (New York, 1970), p. 373. This book gives a fascinating survey of the available information on abortion. The Jewish tradition is surveyed in David M. Feldman, *Birth Control in Jewish Law* (New York, 1968), Part 5, the Catholic tradition in John T. Noonan, Jr., "An Almost Absolute Value in History," in *The Morality of Abortion*, ed. John T. Noonan, Jr. (Cambridge, Mass., 1970).

system was plugged into yours, so that your kidneys can be used to extract poisons from his blood as well as your own. The director of the hospital now tells you, "Look, we're sorry the Society of Music Lovers did this to you—we would never have permitted it if we had known. But still, they did it, and the violinist now is plugged into you. To unplug you would be to kill him. But never mind, it's only for nine months. By then he will have recovered from his ailment, and can safely be unplugged from you." Is it morally incumbent on you to accede to this situation? No doubt it would be very nice of you if you did, a great kindness. But do you *have* to accede to it? What if it were not nine months, but nine years? Or longer still? What if the director of the hospital says, "Tough luck, I agree, but you've now got to stay in bed, with the violinist plugged into you, for the rest of your life. Because remember this. All persons have a right to life, and violinists are persons. Granted you have a right to decide what happens in and to your body, but a person's right to life outweighs your right to decide what happens in and to your body. So you cannot ever be unplugged from him." I imagine you would regard this as outrageous, which suggests that something really is wrong with that plausible-sounding argument I mentioned a moment ago.

In this case, of course, you were kidnapped; you didn't volunteer for the operation that plugged the violinist into your kidneys. Can those who oppose abortion on the ground I mentioned make an exception for a pregnancy due to rape? Certainly. They can say that persons have a right to life only if they didn't come into existence because of rape; or they can say that all persons have a right to life, but that some have less of a right to life than others, in particular, that those who came into existence because of rape have less. But these statements have a rather unpleasant sound. Surely the question of whether you have a right to life at all, or how much of it you have, shouldn't turn on the question of whether or not you are the product of a rape. And in fact the people who oppose abortion on the ground I mentioned do not make this distinction, and hence do not make an exception in case of rape.

Nor do they make an exception for a case in which the mother has to spend the nine months of her pregnancy in bed. They would agree that would be a great pity, and hard on the mother; but all the same, all persons have a right to life, the fetus is a person, and so on. I suspect, in fact, that they would not make an exception for a case in which, miraculously enough, the pregnancy went on for nine years, or even the rest of the mother's life.

Some won't even make an exception for a case in which continuation of the pregnancy is likely to shorten the mother's life; they regard abortion as impermissible even to save the mother's life. Such cases are nowadays very rare, and many opponents of abortion do not accept this extreme view. All the same, it is a good place to begin: a number of points of interest come out in respect to it.

1. Let us call the view that abortion is impermissible even to save the mother's life "the extreme view." I want to suggest first that it does not issue from the argument I mentioned earlier without the addition of some fairly powerful premises. Suppose a woman has become pregnant, and now learns that she

has a cardiac condition such that she will die if she carries the baby to term. What may be done for her? The fetus, being a person, has a right to life, but as the mother is a person too, so has she a right to life. Presumably they have an equal right to life. How is it supposed to come out that an abortion may not be performed? If mother and child have an equal right to life, shouldn't we perhaps flip a coin? Or should we add to the mother's right to life her right to decide what happens in and to her body, which everybody seems to be ready to grant—the sum of her rights now outweighing the fetus' right to life?

The most familiar argument here is the following. We are told that performing the abortion would be directly killing[3] the child, whereas doing nothing would not be killing the mother, but only letting her die. Moreover, in killing the child, one would be killing an innocent person, for the child has committed no crime, and is not aiming at his mother's death. And then there are a variety of ways in which this might be continued. (1) But as directly killing an innocent person is always and absolutely impermissible, an abortion may not be performed. Or, (2) as directly killing an innocent person is murder, and murder is always and absolutely impermissible, an abortion may not be performed.[4] Or, (3) as one's duty to refrain from directly killing an innocent person is more stringent than one's duty to keep a person from dying, an abortion may not be performed. Or, (4) if one's only options are directly killing an innocent person or letting a person die, one must prefer letting the person die, and thus an abortion may not be performed.[5]

Some people seem to have thought that these are not further premises which must be added if the conclusion is to be reached, but that they follow from the very fact that an innocent person has a right to life.[6] But this seems to me to be a mistake, and perhaps the simplest way to show this is to bring out that while we must certainly grant that innocent persons have a right to life, the

---

[3] The term "direct" in the arguments I refer to is a technical one. Roughly, what is meant by "direct killing" is either killing as an end in itself, or killing as a means to some end, for example, the end of saving someone else's life. See note 6, below, for an example of its use.

[4] Cf. *Encyclical Letter of Pope Pius XI on Christian Marriage,* St. Paul Editions (Boston, n.d.), p. 32: "however much we may pity the mother whose health and even life is gravely imperiled in the performance of the duty allotted to her by nature, nevertheless what could ever be a sufficient reason for excusing in any way the direct murder of the innocent? This is precisely what we are dealing with here." Noonan (*The Morality of Abortion,* p. 43) reads this as follows: "What cause can ever avail to excuse in any way the direct killing of the innocent? For it is a question of that."

[5] The thesis in (4) is in an interesting way weaker than those in (1), (2), and (3): they rule out abortion even in cases in which both mother *and* child will die if the abortion is not performed. By contrast, one who held the view expressed in (4) could consistently say that one needn't prefer letting two persons die to killing one.

[6] Cf. the following passage from Pius XII, *Address to the Italian Catholic Society of Midwives:* "The baby in the maternal breast has the right to life immediately from God.—Hence there is no man, no human authority, no science, no medical, eugenic, social, economic or moral 'indication' which can establish or grant a valid juridical ground for a direct deliberate disposition of an innocent human life, that is a dispositon which looks to its destruction either as an end or as a means to another end perhaps in itself not illicit.—The baby, still not born, is a man in the same degree and for the same reason as the mother" (quoted in Noonan, *The Morality of Abortion,* p. 45).

theses in (1) through (4) are all false. Take (2), for example. If directly killing an innocent person is murder, and thus is impermissible, then the mother's directly killing the innocent person inside her is murder, and thus is impermissible. But it cannot seriously be thought to be murder if the mother performs an abortion on herself to save her life. It cannot seriously be said that she *must* refrain, that she *must* sit passively by and wait for her death. Let us look again at the case of you and the violinist. There you are, in bed with the violinist, and the director of the hospital says to you, "It's all most distressing, and I deeply sympathize, but you see this is putting an additional strain on your kidneys, and you'll be dead within the month. But you *have* to stay where you are all the same. Because unplugging you would be directly killing an innocent violinist, and that's murder, and that's impermissible." If anything in the world is true, it is that you do not commit murder, you do not do what is impermissible, if you reach around to your back and unplug yourself from that violinist to save your life.

The main focus of attention in writings on abortion has been on what a third party may or may not do in answer to a request from a woman for an abortion. This is in a way understandable. Things being as they are, there isn't much a woman can safely do to abort herself. So the question asked is what a third party may do, and what the mother may do, if it is mentioned at all, is deduced, almost as an afterthought, from what it is concluded that third parties may do. But it seems to me that to treat the matter in this way is to refuse to grant to the mother that very status of person which is so firmly insisted on for the fetus. For we cannot simply read off what a person may do from what the third party may do. Suppose you find yourself trapped in a tiny house with a growing child. I mean a very tiny house, and a rapidly growing child—you are already up against the wall of the house and in a few minutes you'll be crushed to death. The child on the other hand won't be crushed to death; if nothing is done to stop him from growing he'll be hurt, but in the end he'll simply burst open the house and walk out a free man. Now I could well understand it if a bystander were to say, "There's nothing we can do for you. We cannot choose between your life and his, we cannot be the ones to decide who is to live, we cannot intervene." But it cannot be concluded that you too can do nothing, that you cannot attack it to save your life. However innocent the child may be, you do not have to wait passively while it crushes you to death. Perhaps a pregnant woman is vaguely felt to have the status of house, to which we don't allow the right of self-defense. But if the woman houses the child, it should be remembered that she is a person who houses it.

I should perhaps stop to say explicitly that I am not claiming that people have a right to do anything whatever to save their lives. I think, rather, that there are drastic limits to the right of self-defense. If someone threatens you with death unless you torture someone else to death, I think you have not the right, even to save your life, to do so. But the case under consideration here is very different. In our case there are only two people involved, one whose life is threatened, and one who threatens it. Both are innocent: the one who is threatened is not threatened because of any fault, the one who threatens does

not threaten because of any fault. For this reason we may feel that we bystand-
ers cannot intervene. But the person threatened can.

In sum, a woman surely can defend her life against the threat to it posed by
the unborn child, even if doing so involves its death. And this shows not merely
that the theses in (1) through (4) are false; it shows also that the extreme view
of abortion is false, and so we need not canvass any other possible ways of
arriving at it from the argument I mentioned at the outset.

2. The extreme view could of course be weakened to say that while abortion
is permissible to save the mother's life, it may not be performed by a third
party, but only by the mother herself. But this cannot be right either. For what
we have to keep in mind is that the mother and the unborn child are not like
two tenants in a small house which has, by an unfortunate mistake, been rented
to both: the mother *owns* the house. The fact that she does adds to the offen-
siveness of deducing that the mother can do nothing from the supposition that
third parties can do nothing. But it does more than this: it casts a bright light
on the supposition that third parties can do nothing. Certainly it lets us see
that a third party who says "I cannot choose between you" is fooling himself
if he thinks this is impartiality. If Jones has found and fastened on a certain
coat, which he needs to keep him from freezing, but which Smith also needs
to keep him from freezing, then it is not impartiality that says "I cannot choose
between you" when Smith owns the coat. Women have said again and again
"This body is *my* body!" and they have reason to feel angry, reason to feel
that it has been like shouting into the wind. Smith, after all, is hardly likely
to bless us if we say to him, "Of course it's your coat, anybody would grant
that it is. But no one may choose between you and Jones who is to have it."

We should really ask what it is that says "no one may choose" in the face
of the fact that the body that houses the child is the mother's body. It may be
simply a failure to appreciate this fact. But it may be something more interesting, namely the sense that one has a right to refuse to lay hands on people,
even where it would be just and fair to do so, even where justice seems to
require that somebody do so. Thus justice might call for somebody to get
Smith's coat back from Jones, and yet you have a right to refuse to be the one
to lay hands on Jones, a right to refuse to do physical violence to him. This, I
think, must be granted. But when what should be said is not "no one may
choose," but only "*I* cannot choose," and indeed not even this, but "*I* will not
act," leaving it opoen that somebody else can or should, and in particular that
anyone in a position of authority, with the job of securing people's rights, both
can and should. So this is no difficulty. I have not been arguing that any given
third party must accede to the mother's request that he perform an abortion
to save her life, but only that he may.

I suppose that in some views of human life the mother's body is only on
loan to her, the loan not being one which gives her any prior claim to it. One
who held this view might well think it impartiality to say "I cannot choose."
But I shall simply ignore this possibility. My own view is that if a human being
has any just, prior claim to anything at all, he has a just, prior claim to his
own body. And perhaps this needn't be argued for here anyway, since, as I

mentioned, the arguments against abortion we are looking at do grant that the woman has a right to decide what happens in and to her body.

But although they do grant it, I have tried to show that they do not take seriously what is done in granting it. I suggest the same thing will reappear even more clearly when we turn away from cases in which the mother's life is at stake, and attend, as I propose we now do, to the vastly more common cases in which a woman wants an abortion for some less weighty reason than preserving her own life.

3. Where the mother's life is not at stake, the argument I mentioned at the outset seems to have a much stronger pull. "Everyone has a right to life, so the unborn person has a right to life." And isn't the child's right to life weightier than anything other than the mother's own right to life, which she might put forward as ground for an abortion?

This argument treats the right to life as if it were unproblematic. It is not, and this seems to me to be precisely the source of the mistake.

For we should now, at long last, ask what it comes to, to have a right to lfe. In some views having a right to life includes having a right to be given at least the bare minimum one needs for continued life. But suppose that what in fact *is* the bare minimum a man needs for continued life is something he has no right at all to be given? If I am sick unto death, and the only thing that will save my life is the touch of Henry Fonda's cool hand on my fevered brow, then all the same, I have no right to be given the touch of Henry Fonda's cool hand on my fevered brow. It would be frightfully nice of him to fly in from the West Coast to provide it. It would be less nice, though no doubt well meant, if my friends flew out to the West Coast and carried Henry Fonda back with them. But I have no right at all against anybody that he should do this for me. Or again, to return to the story I told earlier, the fact that for continued life that violinist needs the continued use of your kidneys does not establish that he has a right to be given the continued use of your kidneys. He certainly has no right against you that *you* should give him continued use of your kidneys. For nobody has any right to use your kidneys unless you give him such a right; and nobody has the right against you that you shall give him this right—if you do allow him to go on using your kidneys, this is a kindness on your part, and not something he can claim from you as his due. Nor has he any right against anybody else that *they* should give him continued use of your kidneys. Certainly he had no right against the Society of Music Lovers that they should plug him into you in the first place. And if you now start to unplug yourself, having learned that you will otherwise have to spend nine years in bed with him, there is nobody in the world who must try to prevent you, in order to see to it that he is given something he has a right to be given.

Some people are rather stricter about the right to life. In their view, it does not include the right to be given anything, but amounts to, and only to, the right not to be killed by anybody. But here a related difficulty arises. If everybody is to refrain from killing that violinist, then everybody must refrain from doing a great many different sorts of things. Everybody must refrain from slitting his throat, everybody must refrain from shooting him—and everybody must refrain from unplugging you from him. But does he have a right against everybody that they shall refrain from unplugging you from him? To refrain from doing this is to allow him to continue to use your kidneys. It could be argued that he has a right against us that *we* should allow him to continue to use your kidneys. That is, while he had no right against us that we should give him the use of your kidneys, it might be argued that he anyway has a right against us that we shall not now intervene and deprive him of the use of your kidneys. I shall come back to third-party interventions later. But certainly the violinist has no right against you that *you* shall allow him to continue to use your kidneys. As I said, if you do allow him to use them, it is a kindness on your part, and not something you owe him.

The difficulty I point to here is not peculiar to the right to life. It reappears in connection with all the other natural rights; and it is something which an adequate account of rights must deal with. For present purposes it is enough just to draw attention to it. But I would stress that I am not arguing that people do not have a right to life—quite to the contrary, it seems to me that the primary control we must place on the acceptability of an account of rights is that it should turn out in that account to be a truth that all persons have a right to life. I am arguing only that having a right to life does not guarantee having either a right to be given the use of or a right to be allowed continued use of another person's body—even if one needs it for life itself. So the right to life will not serve the opponents of abortion in the very simple and clear way in which they seem to have thought it would.

4. There is another way to bring out the difficulty. In the most ordinary sort of case, to deprive someone of what he has a right to is to treat him unjustly. Suppose a boy and his small brother are jointly given a box of chocolates for Christmas. If the older boy takes the box and refuses to give his brother any of the chocolates, he is unjust to him, for the brother has been given a right to half of them. But suppose that, having learned that otherwise it means nine years in bed with that violinist, you unplug yourself from him. You surely are not being unjust to him, for you gave him no right to use your kidneys, and no one else can have given him any such right. But we have to notice that in unplugging yourself, you are killing him; and violinists, like everybody else, have a right to life, and thus in the view we were considering just now, the right not to be killed. So here you do what he supposedly has a right you shall not do, but you do not act unjustly to him in doing it.

The emendation which may be made at this point is this: the right to life consists not in the right not to be killed, but rather in the right not to be killed unjustly. This runs a risk of circularity, but never mind: it would enable us to square the fact that the violinist has a right to life with the fact that you do not act unjustly toward him in unplugging yourself, thereby killing him. For if you do not kill him unjustly, you do not violate his right to life, and so it is no wonder you do him no injustice.

But if this emendation is accepted, the gap in the argument against abortions stares us plainly in the face: it is by no means enough to show that the fetus is a person, and to remind us that all persons have a right to life—we need to be shown also that killing the fetus violates its right to life, i.e., that abortion is unjust killing. And is it?

I suppose we may take it as a datum that in a case of pregnancy due to rape the mother has not given the unborn person a right to the use of her body for food and shelter. Indeed, in what pregnancy could it be supposed that the mother has given the unborn person such a right? It is not as if there were unborn persons drifting about the world, to whom a woman who wants a child says "I invite you in."

But it might be argued that there are other ways one can have acquired a right to the use of another person's body than by having been invited to use it by that person. Suppose a woman voluntarily indulges in intercourse, knowing of the chance it will issue in pregnancy, and then she does become pregnant; is she not in part responsible for the presence, in fact the very existence, of the unborn person inside her? No doubt she did not invite it in. But doesn't her partial responsibility for its being there itself give it a right to the use of her body?[7] If so, then her aborting it would be more like the boy's taking away the chocolates, and less like your unplugging yourself from the violinist— doing so would be depriving it of what it does have a right to, and thus would be doing it an injustice.

And then, too, it might be asked whether or not she can kill it even to save her own life: If she voluntarily called it into existence, how can she now kill it, even in self-defense?

The first thing to be said about this is that it is something new. Opponents of abortion have been so concerned to make out the independence of the fetus, in order to establish that it has a right to life, just as its mother does, that they have tended to overlook the possible support they might gain from making out that the fetus is *dependent* on the mother, in order to establish that she has a special kind of responsibility for it, a responsibility that gives it rights against her which are not possessed by any independent person—such as an ailing violinist who is a stranger to her.

On the other hand, this argument would give the unborn person a right to its mother's body only if her pregnancy resulted from a voluntary act, under-taken in full knowledge of the chance a pregnancy might result from it. It would leave out entirely the unborn person whose existence is due to rape. Pending the availability of some further argument, then, we would be left with the conclusion that unborn persons whose existence is due to rape have no right to the use of their mothers' bodies, and thus that aborting them is not depriving them of anything they have a right to and hence is not unjust killing.

And we should also notice that it is not at all plain that this argument really does go even as far as it purports to. For there are cases and cases, and the details make a difference. If the room is stuffy, and I therefore open a window to air it, and a burglar climbs in, it would be absurd to say, "Ah, now he can

---

[7] The need for a discussion of this argument was brought home to me by members of the Society for Ethical and Legal Philosophy, to whom this paper was originally presented.

stay, she's given him a right to the use of her house—for she is partially responsible for his presence there, having voluntarily done what enabled him to get in, in full knowledge that there are such things as burglars, and that burglars burgle." It would be still more absurd to say this if I had had bars installed outside my windows, precisely to prevent burglars from getting in, and a burglar got in only because of a defect in the bars. It remains equally absurd if we imagine it is not a burglar who climbs in, but an innocent person who blunders or falls in. Again, suppose it were like this: people-seeds drift about in the air like pollen, and if you open your windows, one may drift in and take root in your carpets or upholstery. You don't want children, so you fix up your windows with fine mesh screens, the very best you can buy. As can happen, however, and on very, very rare occasions does happen, one of the screens is defective; and a seed drifts in and takes root. Does the person-plant who now develops have a right to the use of your house? Surely not—despite the fact that you voluntarily opened your windows, you knowingly kept carpets and upholstered furniture, and you knew that screens were sometimes defective. Someone may argue that you are responsible for its rooting, that it does have a right to your house, because after all you *could* have lived out your life with bare floors and furniture, or with sealed windows and doors. But this won't do—for by the same token anyone can avoid a pregnancy due to rape by having a hysterectomy, or anyway by never leaving home without a (reliable!) army.

It seems to me that the argument we are looking at can establish at most that there are *some* cases in which the unborn person has a right to the use of its mother's body, and therefore *some* cases in which abortion is unjust killing. There is room for much discussion and argument as to precisely which, if any. But I think we should sidestep this issue and leave it open, for at any rate the argument certainly does not establish that all abortion is unjust killing.

5. There is room for yet another argument here, however. We surely must all grant that there may be cases in which it would be morally indecent to detach a person from your body at the cost of his life. Suppose you learn that what the violinist needs is not nine years of your life, but only one hour: all you need do to save his life is to spend one hour in that bed with him. Suppose also that letting him use your kidneys for that one hour would not affect your health in the slightest. Admittedly you were kidnapped. Admittedly you did not give anyone permission to plug him into you. Nevertheless it seems to me plain you *ought* to allow him to use your kidneys for that hour—it would be indecent to refuse.

Again, suppose pregnancy lasted only an hour, and constituted no threat to life or health. And suppose that a woman becomes pregnant as a result of rape. Admittedly she did not voluntarily do anything to bring about the existence of a child. Admittedly she did nothing at all which would give the unborn person a right to the use of her body. All the same it might well be said, as in the newly emended violinist story, that she *ought* to allow it to remain for that hour—that it would be indecent in her to refuse.

Now some people are inclined to use the term "right" in such a way that it follows from the fact that you ought to allow a person to use your body for the hour he needs, that he has a right to use your body for the hour he needs, even though he has not been given that right by any person or act. They may say that it follows also that if you refuse, you act unjustly toward him. This use of the term is perhaps so common that it cannot be called wrong; nevertheless it seems to me to be an unfortunate loosening of what we would do better to keep a tight rein on. Suppose that box of chocolates I mentioned earlier had not been given to both boys jointly, but was given only to the older boy. There he sits, stolidly eating his way through the box, his small brother watching enviously. Here we are likely to say "You ought not to be so mean. You ought to give your brother some of those chocolates." My own view is that it just does not follow from the truth of this that the brother has any right to any of the chocolates. If the boy refuses to give his brother any, he is greedy, stingy, callous—but not unjust. I suppose that the people I have in mind will say it does follow that the brother has a right to some of the chocolates, and thus that the boy does act unjustly if he refuses to give his brother any. But the effect of saying this to obscure what we should keep distinct, namely the difference between the boy's refusal in this case and the boy's refusal in the earlier case, in which the box was given to both boys jointly, and in which the small brother thus had what was from any point of view clear title to half.

A further objection to so using the term "right" that from the fact that A ought to do a thing for B, it follows that B has a right against A that A do it for him, is that is going to make the question of whether or not a man has a right to a thing turn on how easy it is to provide him with it; and this seems not merely unfortunate, but morally unacceptable. Take the case of Henry Fonda again. I said earlier that I had no right to the touch of his cool hand on my fevered brow, even though I needed it to save my life. I said it would be frightfully nice of him to fly in from the West Coast to provide me with it, but that I had no right against him that he should do so. But suppose he isn't on the West Coast. Suppose he has only to walk across the room, place a hand briefly on my brow—and lo, my life is saved. Then surely he ought to do it, it would be indecent to refuse. Is it to be said "Ah, well, it follows that in this case she has a right to the touch of his hand on her brow, and so it would be an injustice in him to refuse"? So that I have a right to it when it is easy for him to provide it, though no right when it's hard? It's rather a shocking idea that anyone's rights should fade away and disappear as it gets harder and harder to accord them to him.

So my own view is that even though you ought to let the violinist use your kidneys for the one hour he needs, we should not conclude that he has a right to do so—we should say that if you refuse, you are, like the boy who owns all the chocolates and will give none away, self-centered and callous, indecent in fact, but not unjust. And similarly, that even supposing a case in which a woman pregnant due to rape ought to allow the unborn person to use her body for the hour he needs, we should not conclude that he has a right to do so; we should conclude that she is self-centered, callous, indecent, but not unjust, if she refuses. The complaints are no less grave; they are just different. However, there is no need to insist on this point. If anyone does wish to deduce "he has a right" from "you ought," then all the same he must surely grant that there are cases in which it is not morally required of you that you allow that violinist to use your kidneys, and in which he does not have a right to use them, and in which you do not do him an injustice if you refuse. And so also for mother and unborn child. Except in such cases as the unborn person has a right to demand it—and we were leaving open the possibility that there may be such cases—nobody is morally *required* to make large sacrifices, of health, of all other interests and concerns, of all other duties and commitments, for nine years, or even for nine months, in order to keep another person alive.

6. We have in fact to distinguish between two kinds of Samaritan: the Good Samaritan and what we might call the Minimally Decent Samaritan. The story of the Good Samaritan, you will remember, goes like this:

> A certain man went down from Jerusalem to Jericho, and fell among thieves, which stripped him of his raiment, and wounded him, and departed, leaving him half dead.
>
> And by chance there came down a certain priest that way; and when he saw him, he passed by on the other side.
>
> And likewise a Levite, when he was at the place, came and looked on him, and passed by on the other side.
>
> But a certain Samaritan, as he journeyed, came where he was; and when he saw him he had compassion on him.
>
> And went to him, and bound up his wounds, pouring in oil and wine, and set him on his own beast, and brought him to an inn, and took care of him.
>
> And on the morrow, when he departed, he took out two pence, and gave them to the host, and said unto him, "Take care of him; and whatsoever thou spendest more, when I come again, I will repay thee."
>
> (Luke 10:30-35)

The Good Samaritan went out of his way, at some cost to himself, to help one in need of it. We are not told what the options were, that is, whether or not the priest and the Levite could have helped by doing less than the Good Samaritan did, but assuming they could have, then the fact they did nothing at all shows they were not even Minimally Decent Samaritans, not because they were not Samaritans, but because they were not even minimally decent.

These things are a matter of degree, of course, but there is a difference, and it comes out perhaps most clearly in the story of Kitty Genovese, who, as you will remember, was murdered while thirty-eight people watched or listened, and did nothing at all to help her. A Good Samaritan would have rushed out to give direct assistance against the murderer. Or perhaps we had better allow that it would have been a Splendid Samaritan who did this, on the ground that it would have involved a risk of death for himself. But the thirty-eight not only did not do this, they did not even trouble to pick up a phone to call the police. Minimally Decent Samaritanism would call for doing at least that, and their not having done it was monstrous.

After telling the story of the Good Samaritan, Jesus said "Go, and do thou likewise." Perhaps he meant that we are morally required to act as the Good

Samaritan did. Perhaps he was urging people to do more than is morally required of them. At all events it seems plain that it was not morally required of any of the thirty-eight that he rush out to give direct assistance at the risk of his own life, and that it is not morally required of anyone that he give long stretches of his life—nine years or nine months—to sustaining the life of a person who has no special right (we were leaving open the possibility of this) to demand it.

Indeed, with one rather striking class of exceptions, no one in any country in the world is *legally* required to do anywhere near as much as this for anyone else. The class of exceptions is obvious. My main concern here is not the state of the law in respect to abortion, but it is worth drawing attention to the fact that in no state in this country is any man compelled by law to be even a Minimally Decent Samaritan to any person; there is no law under which charges could be brought against the thirty-eight who stood by while Kitty Genovese died. By contrast, in most states in this country women are compelled by law to be not merely Minimally Decent Samaritans, but Good Samaritans to unborn persons inside them. This doesn't by itself settle anything one way or the other, because it may well be argued that there should be laws in this country—as there are in many European countries—compelling at least Minimally Decent Samaritanism.[8] But it does show that there is a gross injustice in the existing state of the law. And it shows also that the groups currently working against liberalization of abortion laws, in fact working toward having it declared unconstitutional for a state to permit abortion, had better start working for the adoption of Good Samaritan laws generally, or earn the charge that they are acting in bad faith.

I should think, myself, that Minimally Decent Samaritan laws would be one thing, Good Samaritan laws quite another, and in fact highly improper. But we are not here concerned with the law. What we should ask is not whether anybody should be compelled by law to be a Good Samaritan, but whether we must accede to a situation in which somebody is being compelled—by nature, perhaps—to be a Good Samaritan. We have, in other words, to look now at third-party interventions. I have been arguing that no person is morally required to make large sacrifices to sustain the life of another who has no right to demand them, and this even where the sacrifices do not include life itself; we are not morally required to be Good Samaritans or anyway Very Good Samaritans to one another. But what if a man cannot extricate himself from such a situation? What if he appeals to us to extricate him? It seems to me plain that there are cases in which we can, cases in which a Good Samaritan would extricate him. There you are, you were kidnapped, and nine years in bed with that violinist lie ahead of you. You have your own life to lead. You are sorry, but you simply cannot see giving up so much of your life to the sustaining of his. You cannot extricate yourself, and ask us to do so. I should have thought

---

[8] For a discussion of the difficulties involved, and a survey of the European experience with such laws, see *The Good Samaritan and the Law,* ed. James M. Ratcliffe (New York, 1966).

that—in light of his having no right to the use of your body—it was obvious that we do not have to accede to your being forced to give up so much. We can do what you ask. There is no injustice to the violinist in our doing so.

7. Following the lead of the opponents of abortion, I have throughout been speaking of the fetus merely as a person, and what I have been asking is whether or not the argument we began with, which proceeds only from the fetus' being a person, really does establish its conclusion. I have argued that it does not.

But of course there are arguments and arguments, and it may be said that I have simply fastened on the wrong one. It may be said that what is important is not merely the fact that the fetus is a person, but that it is a person for whom the woman has a special kind of responsibility issuing from the fact that she is its mother. And it might be argued that all my analogies are therefore irrelevant—for you do not have that special kind of responsiblity for that violinist, Henry Fonda does not have that special kind of responsibility for me. And our attention might be drawn to the fact that men and women both *are* compelled by law to provide support for their children.

I have in effect dealt (briefly) with this argument in section 4 above; but a (still briefer) recapitulation now may be in order. Surely we do not have any such "special responsibility" for a person unless we have assumed it, explicitly or implicitly. If a set of parents do not try to prevent pregnancy, do not obtain an abortion, and then at the time of birth of the child do not put it out for adoption, but rather take it home with them, then they have assumed responsibility for it, they have given it rights, and they cannot *now* withdraw support from it at the cost of its life because they now find it difficult to go on providing for it. But if they have taken all reasonable precautions against having a child, they do not simply by virtue of their biological relationship to the child who comes into existence have a special responsibility for it. They may wish to assume responsibility for it, or they may not wish to. And I am suggesting that if assuming responsibility for it would require large sacrifices, then they may refuse. A Good Samaritan would not refuse—or anyway, a Splendid Samaritan, if the sacrifices that had to be made were enormous. But then so would a Good Samaritan assume responsibility for that violinist; so would Henry Fonda, if he is a Good Samaritan, fly in from the West Coast and assume responsibility for me.

8. My argument will be found unsatisfactory on two counts by many of those who want to regard abortion as morally permissible. First, while I do argue that abortion is not impermissible, I do not argue that it is always permissible. There may well be cases in which carrying the child to term requires only Minimally Decent Samaritanism of the mother, and this is a standard we must not fall below. I am inclined to think it a merit of my account precisely that it does *not* give a general yes or a general no. It allows for and supports our sense that, for example, a sick and desperately frightened fourteen-year-old schoolgirl, pregnant due to rape, may *of course* choose abortion, and that any law which rules this out is an insane law. And it also allows for and supports our sense that in other cases resort to abortion is even positively indecent. It would be indecent in the woman to request an abortion, and indecent in a

doctor to perform it, if she is in her seventh month, and wants the abortion just to avoid the nuisance of postponing a trip abroad. The very fact that the arguments I have been drawing attention to treat all cases of abortion, or even all cases of abortion in which the mother's life is not at stake, as morally on a par ought to have made them suspect at the outset.

Secondly, while I am arguing for the permissibility of abortion in some cases, I am not arguing for the right to secure the death of the unborn child. It is easy to confuse these two things in that up to a certain point in the life of the fetus it is not able to survive outside the mother's body; hence removing it from her body guarantees its death. But they are importantly different. I have argued that you are not morally required to spend nine months in bed, sustaining the life of that violinist; but to say this is by no means to say that if, when you unplug yourself, there is a miracle and he survives, you then have a right to turn round and slit his throat. You may detach yourself even if this costs him his life; you have no right to be guaranteed his death, by some other means, if unplugging yourself does not kill him. There are some people who will feel dissatisfied by this feature of my argument. A woman may be utterly devastated by the thought of a child, a bit of herself, put out for adoption and never seen or heard of again. She may therefore want not merely that the child be detached from her, but more, that it die. Some opponents of abortion are inclined to regard this as beneath contempt—thereby showing insensitivity to what is surely a powerful source of despair. All the same, I agree that the desire for the child's death is not one which anybody may gratify, should it turn out to be possible to detach the child alive.

At this place, however, it should be remembered that we have only been pretending throughout that the fetus is a human being from the moment of conception. A very early abortion is surely not the killing of a person, and so is not dealt with by anything I have said here.

48

Active and Passive Euthanasia

JAMES RACHELS

James Rachels (b. 1941) teaches philosophy at the University of Alabama at Birmingham. He is the author of many articles on ethics.

In this selection, Rachels's topic is the distinction between killing and merely "letting die." This distinction is hard to draw precisely—for an interesting attempt, see the discussion by Onora O'Neill in reading 45. However, many believe that some version of the disinction is morally significant. For example, many doctors might withhold life-sustaining treatment from suffering and terminally ill patients, but would not kill the same patients.

Rachels argues that such an attitude is indefensible. To show this, he compares two cases in which a child drowns in a bathtub while his uncle is present. The cases are alike except that in one the uncle holds the child under water, while in the other he merely does not come to the rescue when the child falls. Since Rachels believes that the uncle acts equally badly in both cases, he concludes that killing in itself is no worse than letting die. Moreover, he notes that killing a suffering patient is often more humane than "letting nature take its course." For this reason, he argues that active euthanasia is often preferable to passive euthanasia.

THE DISTINCTION BETWEEN active and passive euthanasia is thought to be crucial for medical ethics. The idea is that it is permissible, at least in some cases, to withhold treatment and allow a patient to die, but it is never permissible to take any direct action designed to kill the patient. This doctrine seems to be accepted by most doctors, and it is endorsed in a statement adopted by the House of Delegates of the American Medical Association on December 4, 1973:

> The intentional termination of the life of one human being by another—mercy killing—is contrary to that for which the medical profession stands and is contrary to the policy of the American Medical Association.
>
> The cessation of the employment of extraordinary means to prolong the life of the body when there is irrefutable evidence that biological death is imminent is the decision of the patient and/or his immediate family. The advice and judgment of the physician should be freely available to the patient and/or his immediate family.

However, a strong case can be made against this doctrine. In what follows I will set out some of the relevant arguments, and urge doctors to reconsider their views on this matter.

To begin with a familiar type of situation, a patient who is dying of incurable cancer of the throat is in terrible pain, which can no longer be satisfactorily alleviated. He is certain to die within a few days, even if present treatment is continued, but he does not want to go on living for those days since the pain is unbearable. So he asks the doctor for an end to it, and his family joins in the request.

Suppose the doctor agrees to withhold treatment, as the conventional doctrine says he may. The justification for his doing so is that the patient is in terrible agony, and since he is going to die anyway, it would be wrong to prolong his suffering needlessly. But now notice this. If one simply withholds treatment it may take the patient longer to die, and so he may suffer more than he would if more direct action were taken and a lethal injection given. This fact provides strong reason for thinking that, once the initial decision not to prolong his agony has been made, active euthanasia is actually preferable to passive euthanasia, rather than the reverse. To say otherwise is to endorse the option that leads to more suffering rather than less, and is contrary to the humanitarian impulse that prompts the decision not to prolong his life in the first place.

Part of my point is that the process of being "allowed to die" can be relatively slow and painful, whereas being given a lethal injection is relatively quick and painless. Let me give a different sort of example. In the United States about one in 600 babies is born with Down's syndrome. Most of these babies are otherwise healthy—that is, with only the usual pediatric care, they will proceed to an otherwise normal infancy. Some, however, are born with congenital defects such as intestinal obstructions that require operations if they are to live. Sometimes, the parents and the doctor will decide not to operate, and let the infant die. Anthony Shaw describes what happens then:

> . . . When surgery is denied [the doctor] must try to keep the infant from suffering while natural forces sap the baby's life away. As a surgeon whose natural inclination is to use the scalpel to fight off death, standing by and watching a salvageable baby die is the most emotionally exhausting experience I know. It is easy at a conference, in a theoretical discussion, to decide that such infants should be allowed to die. It is altogether different to stand by in the nursery and watch as dehydration and infection wither a tiny being over hours and days. This is a terrible ordeal for me and the hospital staff—much more so than for the parents who never set foot in the nursery.[1]

I can understand why some people are opposed to all euthanasia, and insist that such infants must be allowed to live. I think I can also understand why

---

[1] A. Shaw, "Doctor, Do We Have a Choice?" *The New York Times Magazine*, January 30, 1972, p. 54.

other people favor destroying these babies quickly and painlessly. But why should anyone favor letting "dehydration and infection wither a tiny being over hours and days"? The doctrine that says that a baby may be allowed to dehydrate and wither, but may not be given an injection that would end its life without suffering, seems so patently cruel as to require no further refutation. The strong language is not intended to offend, but only to put the point in the clearest possible way.

My second argument is that the conventional doctrine leads to decisions concerning life and death made on irrelevant grounds.

Consider again the case of the infants with Down's syndrome who need operations for congenital defects unrelated to the syndrome to live. Sometimes, there is no operation, and the baby dies, but when there is no such defect, the baby lives on. Now, an operation such as that to remove an intestinal obstruction is not prohibitively difficult. The reason why such operations are not performed in these cases is, clearly, that the child has Down's syndrome and the parents and doctor judge that because of that fact it is better for the child to die.

But notice that this situation is absurd, no matter what view one takes of the lives and potentials of such babies. If the life of such an infant is worth preserving, what does it matter if it needs a simple operation? Or, if one thinks it better that such a baby should not live on, what difference does it make that it happens to have an unobstructed intestinal tract? In either case, the matter of life and death is being decided on irrelevant grounds. It is the Down's syndrome, and not the intestines, that is the issue. The matter should be decided, if at all, on that basis, and not be allowed to depend on the essentially irrelevant question of whether the intestinal tract is blocked.

What makes this situation possible, of course, is the idea that when there is an intestinal blockage, one can "let the baby die," but when there is no such defect there is nothing that can be done, for one must not "kill" it. The fact that this idea leads to such results as deciding life or death on irrelevant grounds is another good reason why the doctrine should be rejected.

One reason why so many people think that there is an important moral difference between active and passive euthanasia is that they think killing someone is morally worse than letting someone die. But is it? Is killing, in itself, worse than letting die? To investigate this issue, two cases may be considered that are exactly alike except that one involves killing whereas the other involves letting someone die. Then, it can be asked whether this difference makes any difference to the moral assessments. It is important that the cases be exactly alike, except for this one difference, since otherwise one cannot be confident that it is this difference and not some other that accounts for any variation in the assessments of the two cases. So, let us consider this pair of cases:

In the first, Smith stands to gain a large inheritance if anything should happen to his six-year-old cousin. One evening while the child is taking his bath, Smith sneaks into the bathroom and drowns the child, and then arranges things so that it will look like an accident.

In the second, Jones also stands to gain if anything should happen to his six-year-old cousin. Like Smith, Jones sneaks in planning to drown the child in his bath. However, just as he enters the bathroom Jones sees the child slip and hit his head, and fall face down in the water. Jones is delighted; he stands by, ready to push the child's head back under if it is necessary, but it is not necessary. With only a little thrashing about, the child drowns all by himself, "accidentally," as Jones watches and does nothing.

Now Smith killed the child, whereas Jones "merely" let the child die. That is the only difference between them. Did either man behave better, from a moral point of view? If the difference between killing and letting die were in itself a morally important matter, one should say that Jones's behavior was less reprehensible than Smith's. But does one really want to say that? I think not. In the first place, both men acted from the same motive, personal gain, and both had exactly the same end in view when they acted. It may be inferred from Smith's conduct that he is a bad man, although that judgment may be withdrawn or modified if certain further facts are learned about him—for example, that he is mentally deranged. But would not the very same thing be inferred about Jones from his conduct? And would not the same further considerations also be relevant to any modification of this judgment? Moreover, suppose Jones pleaded, in his own defense, "After all, I didn't do anything except just stand there and watch the child drown. I didn't kill him; I only let him die." Again, if letting die were in itself less bad than killing, this defense should have at least some weight. But it does not. Such a "defense" can only be regarded as a grotesque perversion of moral reasoning. Morally speaking, it is no defense at all.

Now, it may be pointed out, quite properly, that the cases of euthanasia with which doctors are concerned are not like this at all. They do not involve personal gain or the destruction of normal healthy children. Doctors are concerned only with cases in which the patient's life is of no further use to him, or in which the patient's life has become or will soon become a terrible burden. However, the point is the same in these cases: the bare difference between killing and letting die does not, in itself, make a moral difference. If a doctor lets a patient die, for humane reasons, he is in the same moral position as if he had given the patient a lethal injection for humane reasons. If his decision was wrong—or, for example, the patient's illness was in fact curable—the decision would be equally regrettable no matter which method was used to carry it out. And if the doctor's decision was the right one, the method used is not in itself important.

The AMA policy statement isolates the crucial issue very well; the crucial issue is "the intentional termination of the life of one human being by another." But after identifying this issue, and forbidding "mercy killing," the statement goes on to deny that the cessation of treatment is the intentional termination of a life. This is where the mistake comes in, for what is the cessation of treatment, in these circumstances, if it is not "the intentional termination of the life of one human being by another"? Of course it is exactly that, and if it were not, there would be no point to it.

Many people will find this judgment hard to accept. One reason, I think, is that it is very easy to conflate the question of whether killing is, in itself, worse than letting die, with the very different question of whether most actual cases of killing are more reprehensible than most actual cases of letting die. Most actual cases of killing are clearly terrible (think, for example, of all the murders reported in the newspapers), and one hears of such cases every day. On the other hand, one hardly ever hears of a case of letting die, except for the actions of doctors who are motivated by humanitarian reasons. So one learns to think of killing in a much worse light than of letting die. But this does not mean that there is something about killing that makes it in itself worse than letting die, for it is not the bare difference between killing and letting die that makes the difference in these cases. Rather, the other factors—the murderer's motive of personal gain, for example, contrasted with the doctor's humanitarian motivation—account for different reactions to the different cases.

I have argued that killing is not in itself any worse than letting die; if my contention is right, it follows that active euthanasia is not any worse than passive euthanasia. What arguments can be given on the other side? The most common, I believe, is the following:

"The important difference between active and passive euthanasia is that, in passive euthanasia, the doctor does not do anything to bring about the patient's death. The doctor does nothing, and the patient dies of whatever ills already afflict him. In active euthanasia, however, the doctor does something to bring about the patient's death: he kills him. The doctor who gives the patient with cancer a lethal injection has himself caused his patient's death; whereas if he merely ceases treatment, the cancer is the cause of the death."

A number of points need to be made here. The first is that it is not exactly correct to say that in passive euthanasia the doctor does nothing, for he does do one thing that is very important: he lets the patient die. "Letting someone die" is certainly different, in some respects, from other types of action—mainly in that it is a kind of action that one may perform by way of not performing certain other actions. For example, one may let a patient die by way of not giving medication, just as one may insult someone by way of not shaking his hand. But for any purpose of moral assessment, it is a type of action nonetheless. The decision to let a patient die is subject to moral appraisal in the same way that a decision to kill him would be subject to moral appraisal: it may be assessed as wise or unwise, compassionate or sadistic, right or wrong. If a doctor deliberately let a patient die who was suffering from a routinely curable illness, the doctor would certainly be to blame for what he had done, just as he would be to blame if he had needlessly killed the patient. Charges against him would then be appropriate. If so, it would be no defense at all for him to insist that he didn't "do anything." He would have done something very serious indeed, for he let his patient die.

Fixing the cause of death may be very important from a legal point of view, for it may determine whether criminal charges are brought against the doctor. But I do not think that this notion can be used to show a moral difference between active and passive euthanasia. The reason why it is considered bad to be the cause of someone's death is that death is regarded as a great evil—and so it is. However, if it has been decided that euthanasia—even passive euthanasia—is desirable in a given case, it has also been decided that in this instance death is no greater an evil than the patient's continued existence. And if this is true, the usual reason for not wanting to be the cause of someone's death simply does not apply.

Finally, doctors may think that all of this is only of academic interest—the sort of thing that philosophers may worry about but that has no practical bearing on their own work. After all, doctors must be concerned about the legal consequences of what they do, and active euthanasia is clearly forbidden by the law. But even so, doctors should also be concerned with the fact that the law is forcing upon them a moral doctrine that may well be indefensible, and has a considerable effect on their practices. Of course, most doctors are not now in the position of being coerced in this matter, for they do not regard themselves as merely going along with what the law requires. Rather, in statements such as the AMA policy statement that I have quoted, they are endorsing this doctrine as a central point of medical ethics. In that statement, active euthanasia is condemned not merely as illegal but as "contrary to that for which the medical profession stands," whereas passive euthanasia is approved. However, the preceding considerations suggest that there is really no moral difference between the two, considered in themselves (there may be important moral differences in some cases in their *consequences,* but, as I pointed out, these differences may make active euthanasia, and not passive euthanasia, the morally preferable option). So, whereas doctors may have to discriminate between active and passive euthanasia to satisfy the law, they should not do any more than that. In particular, they should not give the distinction any added authority and weight by writing it into official statements of medical ethics.

49

What Is Wrong With Slavery

R. M. HARE

For biographical information on R. M. Hare, see reading 22.

In this selection, Hare invokes the utility principle to evaluate the practice of slavery. Slavery is morally important, not because anyone seriously recommends it, but because it is often thought to be an embarrassment to utilitarians. As critics note, we can imagine cases in which tolerating slavery would maximize utility. Because slavery still seems wrong, the critics conclude that utilitarianism has unacceptable implications.

But Hare rejects this conclusion. To show that it does not follow, he asks why we feel that slavery is wrong. The answer, he contends, is itself provided by utilitarianism. In most if not all actual situations, slavery has brought far more misery than happiness. Realizing this, we have internalized principles that strongly condemn slavery. Since these principles were designed to apply in the actual world, it does not matter that they fail to fit unrealistic imaginary cases. But, given what we know about people and the ways they would react to slavery, all cases in which slavery maximizes utility are unrealistic. Thus, such cases do not damage utilitarianism.

NEARLY EVERYBODY WOULD agree that slavery is wrong; and I can say this perhaps with greater feeling than most, having in a manner of speaking *been* a slave. However, there are dangers in just taking for granted that something is wrong; for we may then assume that it is obvious that it is wrong and indeed obvious why it is wrong; and this leads to a prevalence of very bad arguments with quite silly conclusions, all based on the so-called absolute value of human freedom. If we could see more clearly what *is* valuable about freedom, and why it is valuable, then we might be protected against the rhetoric of those who, the moment anything happens that is disadvantageous or distasteful to them, start complaining loudly about some supposed infringement of their liberty, without telling us why it is wrong that they should be prevented from doing what they would like to do. It may well *be* wrong in many such cases; but until we have some way of judging when it is and when it is not, we shall be at the mercy of every kind of demagogy.

This is but one example of the widespread abuse of the appeal to human rights. We may even be tempted to think that our politics would be more healthy if rights had never been heard of; but that would be going too far. It is the unthinking appeal to ill-defined rights, unsupported by argument, that does the harm. There is no doubt that arguments justifying some of these appeals are possible; but since the forms of such arguments are seldom understood even by philosophers, it is not surprising that many quite unjustified claims of this sort go unquestioned, and thus in the end bring any sort of appeal to human rights into disrepute. It is a tragedy that this happens, because there really are rights that ought to be defended with all the devotion we can command. Things are being done the world over which can properly be condemned as infringements of human rights; but so long as rights are used so loosely as an all-purpose political weapon, often in support of very questionable causes, our protests against such infringements will be deprived of most of their force.

Another hazard of the appeal to rights is that it is seldom that such an appeal by one side cannot be countered with an appeal to some conflicting right by the opposite side. The controversies which led finally to the abolition of slavery provide an excellent example of this, with one side appealing to rights of liberty and the other to rights of property. But we do not have to go so far back in history to find examples of this sort of thing. We have only to think of the disputes about distributive justice between the defenders of equality and of individual liberty; or of similar arguments about education. I have written about both these disputes elsewhere, in the attempt to substitute for intuitions some more solid basis for argument.[1] I have the same general motive in raising the topic of slavery, and also a more particular motive. Being a utilitarian, I need to be able to answer the following attack frequently advanced by opponents of utilitarianism. It is often said that utilitarianism must be an objectionable creed because it could in certain circumstances condone or even commend slavery, given that circumstances can be envisaged in which utility would be maximized by preserving a slave-owning society and not abolishing slavery. The objectors thus seek to smear utilitarians with the taint of all the atrocious things that were done by slave-traders and slave-owners. The objection, as I hope to show, does not stand up; but in order to see through this rhetoric we shall have to achieve a quite deep understanding of some rather difficult issues in moral philosophy; and this, too, adds to the importance and interest of the topic.

First, we have to ask what this thing, slavery, is, about whose wrongness we are arguing. As soon as we ask this question we see at once, if we have any knowledge of history, that it is, in common use, an extremely ill-defined concept. Even if we leave out of account such admittedly extended uses as 'wage-slave' in the writings of Marxists, it is clear that the word 'slave' and its near-equivalents such as 'servus' and 'doulos' have meant slightly different things in different cultures; for slavery is, primarily, a *legal* status, defined by the

---

[1] 'Justice and Equality', in J. Arthur and W. H. Shaw, eds., *Justice and Economic Distribution* (Englewood Cliffs: Prentice-Hall, 1978); 'Opportunity for What?: Some Remarks on Current Disputes about Equality in Education', *Oxford Review of Education* 3 (1977).

disabilities or the liabilities which are imposed by the law on those called slaves; and obviously these may vary from one jurisdiction to another. Familiar logical difficulties arise about how we are to decide, of a word in a foreign language, that it means the same as the English word 'slave.' Do the relevant laws in the country where the language is spoken have to be identical with those which held in English-speaking countries before slavery was abolished? Obviously not; because it would be impossible for them to be identical with the laws of all such countries at all periods, since these did not remain the same. Probably we have a rough idea of the kind of laws which have to hold in a country before we can say that that country has an institution properly called 'slavery'; but it is pretty rough.

It would be possible to pursue at some length, with the aid of legal, historical and anthropological books on slavery in different cultures and jurisdictions, the different shades of meaning of the word 'slave'. But since my purpose is philosophical, I shall limit myself to asking what is essential to the notion of slavery in common use. The essential features are, I think, to be divided under two heads: slavery is, first, a *status* in society, and secondly, a *relation* to a master. The slave is so called first of all because he occupies a certain place in society, lacking certain rights and privileges secured by the law to others, and subject to certain liabilities from which others are free. And secondly, he is the slave *of* another person or body (which might be the state itself). The first head is not enough to distinguish slavery from other legal disabilities; for example the lowest castes in some societies are as lacking in legal rights as slaves in some others, or more so, but are not called slaves because they are not the slaves *of* anybody.

The *status* of a slave was defined quite early by the Greeks in terms of four freedoms which the slave lacks. These are: a legally recognized position in the community, conferring a right of access to the courts; protection from illegal seizure and detention and other personal violence; the privilege of going where he wants to go; and that of working as he pleases. The first three of these features are present in a manumission document from Macedonia dated about 235 B.C.; the last is added in the series of manumission documents from Delphi which begins about thirty years later.[2] The state could to some extent regulate by law the treatment of slaves without making us want to stop calling them slaves, so that the last three features are a bit wobbly at the edges. But we are seeking only a rough characterization of slavery, and shall have to put up with this indefiniteness of the concept.

The *relation* of the slave to a master is also to some extent indefinite. It might seem that we could tie it up tight by saying that a slave has to be the *property* of an *owner*; but a moment's reflection will show what unsafe ground this is. So-called property-owners do not need to be reminded that legal restrictions upon the use and enjoyment of property can become so onerous as to make it almost a joke to call it property at all. I am referring not only to such recent

[2] See W. L. Westermann, *The Slave Systems of Greek and Roman Antiquity* (Philadelphia: American Philosophical Society, 1955), p. 35.

654

inventions as zoning and other planning laws (though actually they are not so recent, having been anticipated even in ancient times), and to rent acts, building regulations, clean air acts and the like, but also to the ancient restrictions placed by the common law on uses of one's property which might be offensive to one's neighbours. In relation to slavery, it is also instructive to think of the cruelty-to-animals legislation which now rightly forbids one to do what one likes to one's own dog or cow which one has legally purchased. Legislation of just this kind was passed in the days before abolition, and was even to some extent enforced, though not always effectively. The laws forbidding the slave trade were, of course, the outstanding example of such legislation preventing people from doing what they wanted with their own property.

However, as before, we are seeking only a general and rough characterization of slavery, and shall therefore have to put up with the open texture of the concept of property. This, like slavery itself, is defined by the particular rights and obligations which are conferred or imposed by a particular legal system, and these may vary from one such system to another. It will be enough to have a general idea of what would stop us calling a person the slave of another— how far the law would have to go in assigning rights to slaves before we stopped using that word of them. I have gone into these difficulties in such detail as space has allowed only because I am now going on to describe, for the purposes of our moral discussion, certain conditions of life about which I shall invite the reader's judgment, and I do not want anybody to say that what I am describing *is* not really slavery. The case I shall sketch is admittedly to some extent fantastic; and this, as we shall later see, is very important when we come to assess the philosophical arguments that have been based on similar cases. But although it is extremely unlikely that what I describe should actually occur, I wish to maintain that *if* it occurred, we should still call it slavery, so that *if* imaginary cases are allowed to be brought into the arguments, this case will have to be admitted.

It may be helpful if, before leaving the question of what slavery is, I list a few conditions of life which have to be *distinguished* from slavery proper. The first of these is *serfdom* (a term which, like 'slavery' itself, has a wide range of meaning). A serf is normally tied, not directly to a master, but to a certain area of land; the rights to his services pass with the land if it changes hands. This very distinction, however, separates the English villein in gross, who approximates to a slave although enjoying certain legal rights, from the villein regardant, whose serfdom arises through his feudal tenure of land. Those who unsuccessfully tried to persuade Lord Mansfield in Sommersett's case that slavery could exist in England attempted to show that the defendant was a villein in gross.[3] Secondly, one is not a slave merely because one belongs to a *caste* which has an inferior legal status, even if it has pretty well no rights; as I have said, the slave has to be the slave *of* some owner. Thirdly, slavery has to be distinguished from *indenture*, which is a form of contract. Apprentices

[3] Summing up for defence and judgement of Lord Mansfield in Sommersett's case, King's Bench, 12 George III, 1771-1772, *Howell's State Trials* 20, pp. 1 ff.

in former times, and football players even now, are bound by contract, entered into by themselves or, in the case of children, by their parents, to serve employers for a fixed term under fixed conditions, which were in some cases extremely harsh (so that the actual sufferings of indentured people could be a bad as those of slaves).[4] The difference lies in the voluntariness of the contract and in its fixed term. We must note however that in some societies (Athens before Solon for example) one could *choose* to become a slave by selling one's person to escape debt;[5] and it might be possible to sell one's children as well, as the Greeks sometimes did, so that even the heritability of the slave status does not serve to make definite the rather fuzzy boundary between slavery and indenture.

We ought perhaps to notice two other conditions which approximate to slavery but are not called slavery. The first is compulsory *military* or *naval service* and, indeed, other forced labour. The impressed sailors of Nelson's navy no doubt endured conditions as bad as many slaves; Dr. Johnson remarked that nobody would choose to be a sailor if he had the alternative of being put in prison.[6] But they were not called slaves, because their status as free men was only in abeyance and returned to them on discharge. By contrast, the galley slaves of the Mediterranean powers in earlier times really were slaves. Secondly, although the term 'penal servitude' was once in use, *imprisonment* for crime is not usually called slavery. This is another fuzzy boundary, because in ancient times it was possible for a person to lose his rights as a citizen and become a slave by sentence of a court for some crime;[7] though when something very like this happened recently in South Africa, it was not *called* slavery, officially.[8] Again, prisoners of war and other captives and bondsmen are not always called slaves, however grim their conditions, although in ancient times capture in war was a way of becoming a slave, if one was not fortunate enough to be ransomed.[9] I have myself, as a prisoner of war, worked on the Burma railway in conditions not *at the time* distinguishable from slavery; but because my status was temporary I can claim to have been a slave only 'in a manner of speaking'.

I shall put my philosophical argument, to which we have now come, in terms of an imaginary example, to which I shall give as much verisimilitude as I can. It will be seen, however, that quite unreal assumptions have to be made in order to get the example going—and this is very important for the argument

[4] See O. Patterson, *The Sociology of Slavery* (London: MacGibbon and Kee, 1967), p. 74; A. Sampson, *Drum* (London: Collins, 1956), chap. 3.

[5] See Westermann, *Slave Systems*, p. 4.

[6] Boswell, *Life of Johnson*, ed. G. B. Hill and L. F. Powell (Oxford: Oxford University Press, 1934), vol. 1, p. 348, 16 March 1759.

[7] See Westermann, *Slave Systems*, p. 81. In pre-revolutionary France one could be sentenced to the galleys.

[8] See Sampson, *Drum*, p. 241.

[9] See Westermann, *Slave Systems*, pp. 2, 5-7, 29.

between the utilitarians and their opponents. It must also be noted that to play its role in the argument the example will have to meet certain requirements. It is intended as a fleshed-out substitute for the rather jejune examples often to be found in anti-utilitarian writers. To serve its purpose it will have to be a case in which to abolish slavery really and clearly would diminish utility. This means, first, that the slavery to be abolished must really be slavery, and, secondly, that it must have a total utility clearly, but not enormously, greater than the total utility of the kind of regime which would be, in that situation, a practical alternative to slavery.

If it were not *clearly* greater, utilitarians could argue that, since all judgements of this sort are only probable, caution would require them to stick to a well-tried principle favouring liberty, the principle itself being justified on utilitarian grounds (see below); and thus the example would cease to divide them from their opponents, and would become inapposite.

If, on the other hand, the utility of slavery were *enormously* greater, anti-utilitarians might complain that their own view was being made too strong; for many anti-utilitarians are pluralists and hold that among the principles of morality a principle requiring beneficence is to be included. Therefore, if the advantages of retaining slavery are made sufficiently great, a non-utilitarian with a principle of beneficence in his repertory could agree that it ought to be retained—that is, that *in this case* the principle of beneficence has greater weight than that favouring liberty. Thus there would again be no difference, in this case, between the verdicts of the utilitarians and their opponents, and the example would be inapposite.

There is also another dimension in which the example has to be carefully placed. An anti-utilitarian might claim that the example I shall give makes the difference between the conditions of the slaves and those of the free in the supposed society too small, and the number of slaves too great. If, he might claim, I had made the number of slaves small and the difference between the miseries of the slaves and the pleasures of the slave-owners much greater, then the society might have the same total utility as mine (that is, greater than that of the free society with which I compare it), but it would be less plausible for me to maintain that if such a comparison had to be made in real life, we ought to follow the utilitarians and prefer the slave society.[10]

I cannot yet answer this objection without anticipating my argument; I shall merely indicate briefly how I would answer it. The answer is that the objection rests on an appeal to our ordinary intuitions; but that these are designed to deal with ordinary cases. They give no reliable guide to what we ought to say in highly unusual cases. But, further, the case desiderated is never likely to

---

[10] I am grateful to the Editors for pressing this objection. I deal with it only so far as it concerns slavery such as might occur in the world as we know it. Brave New World situations in which people are conditioned from birth to be obedient slaves and given disagreeable or dangerous tasks require separate treatment which is beyond the scope of this paper, though anti-utilitarian arguments based on them meet the same defence, namely the requirement to assess realistically what the consequences of such practises would actually be.

occur. How could it come about that the existence of a small number of slaves was necessary in order to preserve the happiness of the rest? I find it impossible to think of any technological factors (say, in agriculture or in transport by land or sea) which would make the preservation of slavery for a small class necessary to satisfy the interests of the majority. It is quite true that in the past there have been *large* slave populations supporting the higher standard of living of *small* minorities. But in that case it is hard to argue that slavery has more utility than its abolition, if the difference in happiness between slaves and slave-owners is great. Yet if, in order to produce a case in which the retention of slavery really would be optimal, we reduce the number of slaves relative to slave-owners, it becomes hard to say how the existence of this relatively small number of slaves is necessary for the happiness of the large number of free men. What on earth are the slaves doing that could not be more efficiently done by paid labour? And is not the abolition (perhaps not too abrupt) of slavery likely to promote those very technical changes which are necessary to enable the society to do without it?

The crux of the matter, as we shall see, is that in order to use an appeal to our ordinary intuitions as an argument, the opponents of utilitarianism have to produce cases which are not too far removed from the sort of cases with which our intuitions are designed to deal, namely the ordinary run of cases. If the cases they use fall outside this class, then the fact that our common intuitions give a different verdict from utilitarianism has no bearing on the argument; our intuitions could well be wrong about such cases, and be none the worse for that, because they will never have to deal with them in practise.

We may also notice, while we are sifting possible examples, that cases of *individual* slave-owners who are kind to their slaves will not do. The issue is one of whether slavery as an institution protected by law should be preserved; and if it is preserved, though there may be individuals who do not take advantage of it to maltreat their slaves, there will no doubt be many others who do.

Let us imagine, then, that the battle of Waterloo, that 'damned nice thing, the nearest run thing you ever saw in your life',[11] as Wellington called it, went differently from the way it actually did go, in two respects. The first was that the British and Prussians lost the battle; the last attack of the French Guard proved too much for them, the Guard's morale having been restored by Napoleon who in person led the advance instead of handing it over to Ney. But secondly, having exposed himself to fire as Wellington habitually did, but lacking Wellington's amazing good fortune, Napoleon was struck by a cannon ball and killed instantly. This so disorganized the French, who had no other commanders of such ability, that Wellington was able to rally his forces and conduct one of those holding operations at which he was so adept, basing himself on the Channel ports and their intricate surrounding waterways; the result was a cross between the Lines of Torres Vedras and the trench warfare of the

[11] For references, see E. Longford, *Wellington: The Years of the Sword* (London: Weidenfeld and Nicholson, 1969), p. 489.

first World War. After a year or two of this, with Napoleon out of the way and the war party discredited in England, liberal (that is, neither revolutionary nor reactionary) regimes came into power in both countries, and the Congress of Vienna reconvened in a very different spirit, with the French represented on equal terms.

We have to consider these events only as they affected two adjacent islands in the Caribbean which I am going to call Juba and Camaica. I need not relate what happened in the rest of the world, because the combined European powers could at that time command absolute supremacy at sea, and the Caribbean could therefore be effectively isolated from world politics by the agreement which they reached to take that area out of the imperial war game. All naval and other forces were withdrawn from it except for a couple of bases on small islands for the suppression of the slave trade, which, in keeping with their liberal principles, the parties agreed to prohibit (those that had not already done so). The islands were declared independent and their white inhabitants, very naturally, all departed in a hurry, leaving the government in the hands of local black leaders, some of whom were of the calibre of Toussaint l'Ouverture and others of whom were very much the reverse.

On Juba, a former Spanish colony, at the end of the colonial period there had been formed, under pressure of military need, a militia composed of slaves under white officers, with conditions of service much preferable to those of the plantation slaves, and forming a kind of elite. The senior serjeant-major of this force found himself, after the white officers fled, in a position of unassailable power, and, being a man of great political intelligence and ability, shaped the new regime in a way that made Juba the envy of its neighbours.

What he did was to retain the institution of slavery but to remedy its evils. The plantations were split up into smaller units, still under overseers, responsible to the state instead of to the former owners. The slaves were given rights to improved conditions of work; the wage they had already received as a concession in colonial times was secured to them and increased; all cruel punishents were prohibited. However, it is still right to call them slaves, because the state retained the power to direct their labour and their place of residence and to enforce these directions by sanctions no more severe than are customary in countries without slavery, such as fines and imprisonment. The Juban government, influenced by early communist ideas (though Marx had not yet come on the scene) kept the plantations in its own hands; but private persons were also allowed to own a limited number of slaves under conditions at least as protective to the slaves as on the state-owned plantations.

The island became very prosperous, and the slaves in it enjoyed a life far preferable in every way to that of the free inhabitants of the neighbouring island of Camaica. In Camaica there had been no such focus of power in the early days. The slaves threw off their bonds and each seized what land he could get hold of. Though law and order were restored after a fashion, and democracy of a sort prevailed, the economy was chaotic, and this, coupled with a population explosion, led to widespread starvation and misery. Camaica lacked what Juba had: a government with the will *and the instrument, in the shape of the institution of slavery,* to control the economy and the population, and so make its slave-citizens, as I said, the envy of their neighbours. The flood of people in fishing boats seeking to emigrate from free Camaica and insinuate themselves as slaves into the plantations of Juba became so great that the Juban government had to employ large numbers of coastguards (slaves of course) to stop it.

That, perhaps, will do for our imaginary example. Now for the philosophical argument. It is commonly alleged that utilitarianism could condone or commend slavery. In the situation described, utility would have been lessened and not increased if the Juban government had abolished slavery and if as a result the economy of Juba had deteriorated to the level of that of Camaica. So, it might be argued, a utilitarian would have had to oppose the abolition. But everyone agrees, it might be held, that slavery is wrong; so the utilitarians are convicted of maintaining a thesis which has consequences repugnant to universally accepted moral convictions.

What could they reply to this attack? There are, basically, two lines they could take. These lines are not incompatible but complementary; indeed, the defence of utilitarianism could be put in the form of a dilemma. Either the defender of utilitarianism is allowed to question the imagined facts of the example, or he is not. First let us suppose that he is not. He might then try, as a first move, saying that in the situation *as portrayed* it would indeed be wrong to abolish slavery. If the argument descends to details, the anti-utilitarians may be permitted to insert any amount of extra details (barring the actual abolition of slavery itself) in order to make sure that its retention really does maximize utility. But then the utilitarian sticks to his guns and maintains that in that case it *would* be wrong to abolish slavery, and that, further, most ordinary people, if they could be got to consider the case on its merits and not allow their judgement to be confused by association with more detestable forms of slavery, would agree with this verdict. The principle of liberty which forbids slavery is a prima facie principle admitting of exceptions, and this imaginary case is one of the exceptions. If the utilitarians could sustain this line of defence, they would win the case; but perhaps not everyone would agree that it is sustainable.

So let us allow the utilitarian another slightly more sophisticated move, still staying, however, perched on the first horn of the dilemma. He might admit that not everyone would agree on the merits of this case, but explain this by pointing to the fantastic and unusual nature of the case, which, he might claim, would be unlikely to occur in real life. *If* he is not allowed to question the facts of the case, he has to admit that abolition would be wrong; but ordinary people, he might say, cannot see this because the principles of political and social morality which we have all of us *now* absorbed (as contrasted with our eighteenth-century ancestors), and with which we are deeply imbued, prevent us from considering the case on its merits. The principles are framed to cope with the cases of slavery which actually occur (all of which are to a greater or less degree harmful). Though they are the best principles for us to have when confronting the actual world, they give the wrong answer when presented with this fantastic case. But all the same, the world being as it is, we should be morally worse people if we did not have these principles; for then we might be tempted, whether through ignorance or by self-interest, to condone slavery in cases in which, though actually harmful, it could be colourably represented as being beneficial. Suppose, it might be argued, that an example of this sort had been used in anti-abolitionist writings in, say, 1830 or thereabouts. Might it not have persuaded many people that slavery *could* be an admirable thing, and thus have secured their votes against abolition; and would this not have been very harmful? For the miseries caused by the *actual* institution of slavery in the Caribbean and elsewhere were so great that it was desirable from a utilitarian point of view that people should hold and act on moral convictions which condemned slavery as such and without qualification, because this would lead them to vote for its abolition.

If utilitarians take this slightly more sophisticated line, they are left saying at one and the same time that it would have been wrong to abolish slavery in the imagined circumstances, *and* that it is a good thing that nearly everyone, if asked about it, would say that it was right. Is this paradoxical? Not, I think, to anybody who understands the realities of the human situation. What resolves the paradox is that the example *is* imaginary and that therefore people are not going to have to pronounce, as a practical issue, on what the laws of Juba are to be. In deciding what principles it is good that people have, it is not necessary or even desirable to take into account such imaginary cases. It does not really matter, from a practical point of view, what judgements people reach about imaginary cases, provided that this does not have an adverse effect upon their judgements about real cases. From a practical point of view, the principles which it is best for them to have are those which will lead them to make the highest proportion of right decisions in actual cases where their decisions make a difference to what happens—weighted, of course, for the importance of the cases, that is, the amount of difference the decisions make to the resulting good or harm.

It is therefore perfectly acceptable that we should at one and the same time feel a strong moral conviction that even the Juban slave system, however beneficial, is wrong, *and* confess, when we reflect on the features of this imagined system, that we cannot see anything specifically wrong about it, but rather a great deal to commend. This is bound to be the experience of anybody who has acquired the sort of moral convictions that one ought to acquire, and at the same time is able to reflect rationally on the features of some unusual imagined situation. I have myself constantly had this experience when confronted with the sort of anti-utilitarian examples which are the stock-in-trade of philosophers like Bernard Williams. One is led to think, on reflection, that *if* such cases were to occur, one ought to do what is for the best in the circumstances (as even Williams himself appears to contemplate in one of his cases);[12]

---

[12] See Williams, 'A Critique of Utilitarianism', in J. J. C. Smart and B. Williams, *Utilitarianism: For and Against* (Cambridge: Cambridge University Press, 1973), p. 99.

but one is bound also to find this conclusion repugnant to one's deepest convictions; if it is not, one's convictions are not the best convictions one could have.

Against this, it might be objected that if one's deep moral convictions yield the wrong answer even in imaginary or unusual cases, they are *not* the best one could have. Could we not succeed, it might be asked, in inculcating into ourselves convictions of a more accommodating sort? Could we not, that is to say, absorb principles which had written into them either exceptions to deal with awkward cases like that in my example, or even provision for writing in exceptions ad hoc when the awkward cases arose? Up to a point this is a sensible suggestion; but beyond that point (a point which will vary with the temperament of the person whose principles they are to be) it becomes psychologically unsound. There are some simple souls, no doubt, who really cannot keep themselves in the straight and narrow way unless they cling fanatically and in the face of what most of us would call reason to extremely simple and narrow principles. And there are others who manage to have very complicated principles with many exceptions written into them (only 'written' is the wrong word, because the principles of such people defy formulation). Most of us come somewhere in between. It is also possible to have fairly simple principles but to attach to them a rubric which allows us to depart from them, either when one conflicts with another in a particular case, or where the case is such an unusual one that we find ourselves doubting whether the principles were designed to deal with it. In these cases we may apply utilitarian reasoning directly; but it is most unwise to do this in more normal cases, for those are precisely the cases (the great majority) which our principles *are* designed to deal with, since they were chosen to give the best results in the general run of cases. In normal cases, therefore, we are more likely to achieve the right decision (even from the utilitarian point of view) by sticking to these principles than by engaging in utilitarian reasoning about the particular case, wih all its temptations to special pleading.

I have dealt with these issues at length elsewhere.[13] Here all I need to say is that there is a psychological limit to the complexity and to the flexibility of the moral principles that we can wisely seek to build deeply, as moral convictions, into our character; and the person who tries to go beyond this limit will end up as (what he will be called) an unprincipled person, and will not in fact do the best he could with his life, even by the test of utility. This may explain why I would always vote for the abolition of slavery, even though I can admit that cases could be *imagined* in which slavery would do more good than harm, and even though I am a utilitarian.

So much, then, for the first horn of the dilemma. Before we come to the second horn, on which the utilitarian is allowed to object to his opponents' argument

---

[13] See my 'Ethical Theory and Utilitarianism', in H. D. Lewis, ed., *Contemporary British Philosophy* 4 (London: Allen and Unwin, 1976), and the references given there.

on the ground that their example would not in the actual world be realized, I wish to make a methodological remark which may help us to find our bearings in this rather complex dispute. Utilitarianism, like any other theory of moral reasoning that gets anywhere near adequacy, consists of two parts, one formal and one substantial. The formal part is no more than a rephrasing of the requirement that moral prescriptions be universalizable: this has the consequence that equal interests of all are to be given equal weight in our reasoning: everybody to count for one and nobody for more than one. One should not expect such a formal requirement to generate, by itself, any substantial conclusions even about the actual world, let alone about all logically possible worlds. But there is also a substantial element in the theory. This is contributed by factual beliefs about what interests people in the real world actually have (which depends on what they actually want or like or dislike, and on what they would want or like or dislike under given conditions); and also about the actual effects on these interests of different actions in the real world. Given the truth of these beliefs, we can reason morally and shall come to certain moral conclusions. But the conclusions are not generated by the formal part of the theory alone.

Utilitarianism therefore, unlike some other theories, is *exposed* to the facts. The utilitarian cannot reason a priori that *whatever* the facts about the world and human nature, slavery is wrong. He has to show that it is wrong by showing, through a study of history and other factual observation, that slavery does have the effects (namely the production of misery) which make it wrong. This, though it may at first sight appear a weakness in the doctrine, is in fact its strength. A doctrine, like some kinds of intuitionism, according to which we can think up examples as fantastic as we please and the doctrine will still come up with the same old answers, is really showing that it has lost contact with the actual world with which the intuitions it relies on were designed to cope. Intuitionists think they can face the world armed with nothing but their inbred intuitions; utilitarians know that they have to look at what actually goes on in the world and see if the intuitions are really the best ones to have in that sort of world.

I come now to the second horn of the dilemma, on which the utilitarian is allowed to say, 'Your example won't do: it would never happen that way'. He may admit that Waterloo and the Congress of Vienna could have turned out differently—after all it was a damned nice thing, and high commanders were in those days often killed on the battlefield (it was really a miracle that Wellington was not), and there were liberal movements in both countries. But when we come to the Caribbean, things begin to look shakier. Is it really likely that there would have been such a contrast between the economies of Juba and Camaica? I do not believe that the influence of particular national leaders is ever so powerful, or that such perfectly wise leaders are ever forthcoming. And I do not believe that in the Caribbean or anywhere else a system of nationalized slavery could be made to run so smoothly. I should, rather, expect the system to deteriorate very rapidly. I base these expectations on general beliefs about human nature, and in particular upon the belief that people in the power of other people will be exploited, whatever the good intentions of those who founded the system.

Alternatively, if there really had been leaders of such amazing statesmanship, could they not have done better by abolishing slavery and substituting a free but disciplined society? In the example, they gave the slaves some legal rights; what was to prevent them giving others, such as the right to change residences and jobs, subject of course to an overall system of land-use and economic planning such as exists in many free countries? Did the retention of *slavery* in particular contribute very much to the prosperity of Juba that could not have been achieved by other means? And likewise, need the government of Camaica have been so incompetent? Could it not without reintroducing slavery, have kept the economy on the rails by such controls as are compatible with a free society? In short, did not the optimum solution lie somewhere *between* the systems adopted in Juba and Camaica, but on the free side of the boundary between slavery and liberty?

These factual speculations, however, are rather more superficial than I can be content with. The facts that it is really important to draw attention to are rather deep facts about human nature which must always, or nearly always, make slavery an intolerable condition.[14] I have mentioned already a fact about slave ownership: that ordinary, even good, human beings will nearly always exploit those over whom they have absolute power. We have only to read the actual history of slavery in all centuries and cultures to see that. There is also the effect on the characters of the exploiters themselves. I had this brought home to me recently when, staying in Jamaica, I happened to pick up a history book[15] written there at the very beginning of the nineteenth century, before abolition, whose writer had added at the end an appendix giving his views on the abolition controversy, which was then at its height. Although obviously a kindly man with liberal leanings, he argues against abolition; and one of his arguments struck me very forcibly. He argues that although slavery can be a cruel fate, things are much better in Jamaica now: there is actually a law that a slave on a plantation may not be given more than thirty-six lashes by the foreman without running him up in front of the overseer. The contrast between the niceness of the man and what he says here does perhaps more than any philosophical argument to make the point that our moral principles have to be designed for human nature as it is.

The most fundamental point is one about the human nature of the slave which makes ownership by another more intolerable for him than for, say, a horse (not that we should condone cruelty to horses). Men are different from other animals in that they can look a long way ahead, and therefore can become an object of deterrent punishment. Other animals, we may suppose, can only

[14] For the effects of slavery on slaves and slave-owners, see O. Patterson, *Sociology of Slavery*; and S. M. Elkins, *Slavery* (Chicago: University of Chicago Press, 1959).

[15] R. C. Dallas, *The History of the Maroons* (London: Longman and Rees, 1803; reprinted by Frank Cass, 1968). I have not been able to obtain the book again to verify this reference.

be the object of Skinnerian reinforcement and Pavlovian conditioning. These methods carry with them, no doubt, their own possibilities of cruelty; but they fall short of the peculiar cruelty of human slavery. One can utter to a man threats of punishment in the quite distant future which he can understand. A piece of human property, therefore, unlike a piece of inanimate property or even a brute animal in a man's possession, can be subjected to a sort of terror from which other kinds of property are immune; and, human owners being what they are, many will inevitably take advantage of this fact. That is the reason for the atrocious punishments that have usually been inflicted on slaves; there would have been no point in inflicting them on animals. A slave is the only being that is *both* able to be held responsible in this way, *and* has no escape from, or even redress against, the power that this ability to threaten confers upon his oppressor. If he were a free citizen, he would have rights which would restrain the exercise of the threat; if he were a horse or a piece of furniture, the threat would be valueless to his owner because it would not be understood. By being subjected to the threat of legal and other punishment, but at the same time deprived of legal defences against its abuse (since he has no say in what the laws are to be, nor much ability to avail himself of such laws as there are) the slave becomes, or is likely to become if his master is an ordinary human, the most miserable of all creatures.

No doubt there are other facts I could have adduced. But I will end by reiterating the general point I have been trying to illustrate. The wrongness of slavery, like the wrongness of anything else, has to be shown in the world as it actually is. We can do this by first reaching an understanding of the meaning of this and the other moral words, which brings with it certain rules of moral reasoning, as I have tried to show in other places.[16] One of the most important of these rules is a formal requirement reflected in the Golden Rule: the requirement that what we say we ought to do to others we have to be able to say ought to be done to ourselves were we in precisely their situation with their interests. And this leads to a way of moral reasoning (utilitarianism) which treats the equal interests of all as having equal weight. Then we have to apply this reasoning to the world as it actually is, which will mean ascertaining what will actually be the result of adopting certain principles and policies, and how this will actually impinge upon the interests of ourselves and others. Only so can we achieve a morality suited for use in real life; and nobody who goes through this reasoning in real life will adopt principles which permit slavery, because of the miseries which in real life it causes. Utilitarianism can thus show what is wrong with slavery; and so far as I can see it is the kind of moral reasoning best able to show this, as opposed to merely *protesting* that slavery is wrong.

---

[16] See fn. 13 above, and my *Freedom and Reason* (Oxford: Oxford University Press, 1963), especially chap. 6.

This is a revised version of a lecture given in 1978 in the Underwood Memorial Series, Wesleyan University, Middletown, Connecticut.

50

War and Massacre[1]

THOMAS NAGEL

For biographical information on Thomas Nagel, see reading 30.

Nagel's topic in this reading is the rules of war, which have been widely taken to forbid such acts as the use of poison gas, the bombing of population centers, and attacks on medical personnel. If killing soldiers in other ways is permitted, what justifies these prohibitions? For utilitarians, the answer can only lie in the proscribed actions' consequences. But Nagel argues that the answer goes deeper. Even in the conduct of hostilities, he argues, some acts are absolutely forbidden.

What distinguishes acceptable from unacceptable hostile behavior? According to Nagel, even objects of hostility must be treated as persons. This means, first, that violence must be directed only against those who actually pose a threat. Attacks on noncombatants are unjustified even if tactically effective. And, second, even attacks on combatants must be directed at the threat they pose. Weapons that cause more pain or damage than necessary—napalm, dum-dum bullets, poison—are not sufficiently relevant to be permissible.

Two further aspects of Nagel's position warrant mention. First, he observes that we sometimes cannot avoid causing death to one or another innocent person. To square this with the prohibitions he is discussing, Nagel suggests that "what absolutism forbids is doing certain things to people, rather than bringing about certain results." While developing this suggestion, Nagel considers, but does not adopt, Charles Fried's claim that categorical prohibitions apply only to intended outcomes (see reading 46). Second, Nagel notes that the costs of observing the prohibitions are sometimes unacceptably high. According to some theories, such as that of W. D. Ross (reading 31), the duty to avoid unacceptable costs may override the prohibitions. But Nagel sees another possibility. In these cases, he suggests, there may simply be no right answer. We may be guilty whatever we do.

FROM THE APATHETIC reaction to atrocities committed in Vietnam by the United States and its allies, one may conclude that moral restrictions on the conduct of war command almost as little sympathy among the general public as they do among those charged with the formation of U.S. military

---

[1] This paper grew out of discussions at the Society for Ethical and Legal Philosophy, and I am indebted to my fellow members for their help.

policy. Even when restrictions on the conduct of warfare are defended, it is usually on legal grounds alone: their moral basis is often poorly understood. I wish to argue that certain restrictions are neither arbitrary nor merely conventional, and that their validity does not depend simply on their usefulness. There is, in other words, a moral basis for the rules of war, even though the conventions now officially in force are far from giving it perfect expression.

I

No elaborate moral theory is required to account for what is wrong in cases like the Mylai massacre, since it did not serve, and was not intended to serve, any strategic purpose. Moreover, if the participation of the United States in the Indo-Chinese war is entirely wrong to begin with, then that engagement is incapable of providing a justification for *any* measures taken in its pursuit— not only for the measures which are atrocities in every war, however just its aims.

But this war has revealed attitudes of a more general kind, that influenced the conduct of earlier wars as well. After it has ended, we shall still be faced with the problem of how warfare may be conducted, and the attitudes that have resulted in the specific conduct of this war will not have disappeared. Moreover, similar problems can arise in wars or rebellions fought for very different reasons, and against very different opponents. It is not easy to keep a firm grip on the idea of what is not permissible in warfare, because while some military actions are obvious atrocities, other cases are more difficult to assess, and the general principles underlying these judgments remain obscure. Such obscurity can lead to the abandonment of sound intuitions in favor of criteria whose rationale may be more obvious. If such a tendency is to be resisted, it will require a better understanding of the restrictions than we now have.

I propose to discuss the most general moral problem raised by the conduct of warfare: the problem of means and ends. In one view, there are limits on what may be done even in the service of an end worth pursuing—and even when adherence to the restriction may be very costly. A person who acknowledges the force of such restrictions can find himself in acute moral dilemmas. He may believe, for example, that by torturing a prisoner he can obtain information necessary to prevent a disaster, or that by obliterating one village with bombs he can halt a campaign of terrorism. If he believes that the gains from a certain measure will clearly outweigh its costs, yet still suspects that he ought not to adopt it, then he is in a dilemma produced by the conflict between two disparate categories of moral reason: categories that may be called *utilitarian* and *absolutist*.

Utilitarianism gives primacy to a concern with what will *happen*. Absolutism gives primacy to a concern with what one is *doing*. The conflict between them arises because the alternatives we face are rarely just choices between *total outcomes*: they are also choices between alternative pathways or measures to be taken. When one of the choices is to do terrible things to another person, the problem is altered fundamentally; it is no longer merely a question of which outcome would be worse.

Few of us are completely immune to either of these types of moral intuition, though in some people, either naturally or for doctrinal reasons, one type will be dominant and the other suppressed or weak. But it is perfectly possible to feel the force of both types of reason very strongly; in that case the moral dilemma in certain situations of crisis will be acute, and it may appear that every possible course of action or inaction is unacceptable for one reason or another.

II

Although it is this dilemma that I propose to explore, most of the discussion will be devoted to its absolutist component. The utilitarian component is straightforward by comparison, and has a natural appeal to anyone who is not a complete skeptic about ethics. Utilitarianism says that one should try, either individually or through institutions, to maximize good and minimize evil (the definition of these categories need not enter into the schematic formulation of the view), and that if faced with the possibility of preventing a great evil by producing a lesser, one should choose the lesser evil. There are certainly problems about the formulation of utilitarianism, and much has been written about it, but its intent is morally transparent. Nevertheless, despite the addition of various refinements, it continues to leave large portions of ethics unaccounted for. I do not suggest that some form of absolutism can account for them all, only that an examination of absolutism will lead us to see the complexity, and perhaps the incoherence, of our moral ideas.

Utilitarianism certainly justifies *some* restrictions on the conduct of warfare. There are strong utilitarian reasons for adhering to any limitation which seems natural to most people—particularly if the limitation is widely accepted already. An exceptional measure which seems to be justified by its results in a particular conflict may create a precedent with disastrous long-term effects.[2] It may even be argued that war involves violence on such a scale that it is never justified on utilitarian grounds—the consequences of refusing to go to war will never be as bad as the war itself would be, even if atrocities were not committed. Or in a more sophisticated vein it might be claimed that a uniform policy of never resorting to military force would do less harm in the long run, if followed consistently, than a policy of deciding each case on utilitarian grounds (even though on occasion particular applications of the pacifist policy might have worse results than a specific utilitarian decision). But I shall not consider these

---

[2] Straightforward considerations of national interest often tend in the same direction: the inadvisability of using nuclear weapons seems to be overdetermined in this way.

arguments, for my concern is with reasons of a different kind, which may remain when reasons of utility and interest fail.[3]

In the final analysis, I believe that the dilemma cannot always be resolved. While not every conflict between absolutism and utilitarianism creates an insoluble dilemma, and while it is certainly right to adhere to absolutist restrictions unless the utilitarian considerations favoring violation are overpoweringly weighty and extremely certain—nevertheless, when that special condition is met, it may become impossible to adhere to an absolutist position. What I shall offer, therefore, is a somewhat qualified defense of absolutism. I believe it underlies a valid and fundamental type of moral judgment—which cannot be reduced to or overridden by other principles. And while there may be other principles just as fundamental, it is particularly important not to lose confidence in our absolutist intuitions, for they are often the only barrier before the abyss of utilitarian apologetics for large-scale murder.

III

One absolutist position that creates no problems of interpretation is pacifism: the view that one may not kill another person under any circumstances, no matter what good would be achieved or evil averted thereby. The type of absolutist position that I am going to discuss is different. Pacifism draws the conflict with utilitarian considerations very starkly. But there are other views according to which violence may be undertaken, even on a large scale, in a clearly just cause, so long as certain absolute restrictions on the character and direction of that violence are observed. The line is drawn somewhat closer to the bone, but it exists.

The philosopher who has done most to advance contemporary philosophical discussion of such a view, and to explain it to those unfamiliar with its extensive treatment in Roman Catholic moral theology, is G. E. M. Anscombe. In 1958 Miss Anscombe published a pamphlet entitled *Mr. Truman's Degree*,[4] on the occasion of the award by Oxford University of an honorary doctorate to Harry Truman. The pamphlet explained why she had opposed the decision to award that degree, recounted the story of her unsuccessful opposition, and offered

---

[3] These reasons, moreover, have special importance in that they are available even to one who denies the appropriateness of utilitarian considerations in international matters. He may acknowledge limitations on what may be done to the soldiers and civilians of other countries in pursuit of his nation's military objectives, while denying that one country should in general consider the interests of nationals of other countries in determining its policies.

[4] (Privately printed.) See also her essay "War and Murder," in *Nuclear Weapons and Christian Conscience*, ed. Walter Stein (London, 1963). The present paper is much indebted to these two essays throughout. These and related subjects are extensively treated by Paul Ramsey in *The Just War* (New York, 1968). Among recent writings that bear on the moral problem are Jonathan Bennett, "Whatever the Consequences, *Analysis* 26, no. 3 (1966): 83–102; and Philippa Foot, "The Problem of Abortion and the Doctrine of the Double Effect," *The Oxford Review* 5 (1967): 5–15. Miss Anscombe's replies are "A Note on Mr. Bennett," *Analysis* 26, no. 3 (1966): 208, and "Who is Wronged?" *The Oxford Review* 5 (1967): 16–17.

some reflections on the history of Truman's decision to drop atom bombs on Hiroshima and Nagasaki, and on the difference between murder and allowable killing in warfare. She pointed out that the policy of deliberately killing large numbers of civilians either as a means or as an end in itself did not originate with Truman, and was common practice among all parties during World War II for some time before Hiroshima. The Allied area bombings of German cities by conventional explosives included raids which killed more civilians than did the atomic attacks; the same is true of certain fire-bomb raids on Japan.

The policy of attacking the civilian population in order to induce an enemy to surrender, or to damage his morale, seems to have been widely accepted in the civilized world, and seems to be accepted still, at least if the stakes are high enough. It gives evidence of a moral conviction that the deliberate killing of noncombatants—women, children, old people—is permissible if enough can be gained by it. This follows from the more general position that any means can in principle be justified if it leads to a sufficiently worthy end. Such an attitude is evident not only in the more spectacular current weapons systems but also in the day-to-day conduct of the nonglobal war in Indochina: the indiscriminate destructiveness of antipersonnel weapons, napalm, and aerial bombardment; cruelty to prisoners; massive relocation of civilians; destruction of crops; and so forth. An absolutist position opposes to this the view that certain acts cannot be justified no matter what the consequences. Among those acts is murder—the deliberate killing of the harmless: civilians, prisoners of war, and medical personnel.

In the present war such measures are sometimes said to be regrettable, but they are generally defended by reference to military necessity and the importance of the long-term consequences of success or failure in the war. I shall pass over the inadequacy of this consequentialist defense in its own terms. (That is the dominant form of moral criticism of the war, for it is part of what people mean when they ask, "Is it worth it?") I am concerned rather to account for the inappropriateness of offering any defense of that kind for such actions.

Many people feel, without being able to say much more about it, that something has gone seriously wrong when certain measures are admitted into consideration in the first place. The fundamental mistake is made there, rather than at the point where the overall benefit of some monstrous measure is judged to outweigh its disadvantages, and it is adopted. An account of absolutism might help us to understand this. If it is not allowable to *do* certain things, such as killing unarmed prisoners or civilians, then no argument about what will happen if one doesn't do them can show that doing them would be all right.

Absolutism does not, of course, require one to ignore the consequences of one's acts. It operates as a limitation on utilitarian reasoning, not as a substitute for it. An absolutist can be expected to try to maximize good and minimize evil, so long as this does not require him to transgress an absolute prohibition like that against murder. But when such a conflict occurs, the prohibition takes complete precedence over any consideration of consequences. Some of the results of this view are clear enough. It requires us to forgo certain potentially useful military measures, such as the slaughter of hostages and prisoners or indiscriminate attempts to reduce the enemy civilian population by starvation, epidemic infectious diseases like anthrax and bubonic plague, or mass incineration. It means that we cannot deliberate on whether such measures are justified by the fact that they will avert still greater evils, for as intentional measures they cannot be justified in terms of any consequences whatever.

Someone unfamiliar with the events of this century might imagine that utilitarian arguments, or arguments of national interest, would suffice to deter measures of this sort. But it has become evident that such considerations are insufficient to prevent the adoption and employment of enormous antipopulation weapons once their use is considered a serious moral possibility. The same is true of the piecemeal wiping out of rural civilian populations in airborne antiguerrilla warfare. Once the door is opened to calculations of utility and national interest, the usual speculations about the future of freedom, peace, and economic prosperity can be brought to bear to ease the consciences of those responsible for a certain number of charred babies.

For this reason alone it is important to decide what is wrong with the frame of mind which allows such arguments to begin. But it is also important to understand absolutism in the cases where it genuinely conflicts with utility. Despite its appeal, it is a paradoxical position, for it can require that one refrain from choosing the lesser of two evils when that is the only choice one has. And it is additionally paradoxical because, unlike pacifism, it permits one to do horrible things to people in some circumstances but not in others.

IV

Before going on to say what, if anything, lies behind the position, there remain a few relatively technical matters which are best discussed at this point.

First, it is important to specify as clearly as possible the kind of thing to which absolutist prohibitions can apply. We must take seriously the proviso that they concern what we deliberately do to people. There could not, for example, without incoherence, be an absolute prohibition against *bringing about* the death of an innocent person. For one may find oneself in a situation in which, no matter what one does, some innocent people will die as a result. I do not mean just that there are cases in which someone will die no matter what one does, because one is not in a position to affect the outcome one way or the other. That, it is to be hoped, is one's relation to the deaths of most innocent people. I have in mind, rather, a case in which someone is bound to die, but who it is will depend on what one does. Sometimes these situations have natural causes, as when too few resources (medicine, lifeboats) are available to rescue everyone threatened with a certain catastrophe. Sometimes the situations are man-made, as when the only way to control a campaign of terrorism is to employ terrorist tactics against the community from which it has arisen. Whatever one does in cases such as these, some innocent people will die as a result. If the absolutist prohibition forbade doing what would result in the deaths of innocent people, it would have the consequence that in such cases nothing one could do would be morally permissible.

This problem is avoided, however, because what absolutism forbids is *doing* certain things to people, rather than bringing about certain *results*. Not everything that happens to others as a result of what one does is something that one has *done* to them. Catholic moral theology seeks to make this distinction precise in a doctrine known as the law of double effect, which asserts that there is a morally relevant distinction between bringing about the death of an innocent person deliberately, either as an end in itself or as a means, and bringing it about as a side effect of something else one does deliberately. In the latter case, even if the outcome is foreseen, it is not murder, and does not fall under the absolute prohibition, though of course it may still be wrong for other reasons (reasons of utility, for example). Briefly, the principle states that one is sometimes permitted knowingly to bring about as a side effect of one's actions something which it would be absolutely impermissible to bring about deliberately as an end or as a means. In application to war or revolution, the law of double effect permits a certain amount of civilian carnage as a side effect of bombing munitions plants or attacking enemy soldiers. And even this is permissible only if the cost is not too great to be justified by one's objectives.

However, despite its importance and its usefulness in accounting for certain plausible moral judgments, I do not believe that the law of double effect is a generally applicable test for the consequences of an absolutist position. Its own application is not always clear, so that it introduces uncertainty where there need not be uncertainty.

In Indochina, for example, there is a great deal of aerial bombardment, strafing, spraying of napalm, and employment of pellet- or needle-spraying antipersonnel weapons against rural villages in which guerrillas are suspected to be hiding, or from which small-arms fire has been received. The majority of those killed and wounded in these aerial attacks are reported to be women and children, even when some combatants are caught as well. However, the government regards these civilian casualties as a regrettable side effect of what is a legitimate attack against an armed enemy.

It might be thought easy to dismiss this as sophistry: if one bombs, burns, or strafes a village containing a hundred people, twenty of whom one believes to be guerrillas, so that by killing most of them one will be statistically likely to kill most of the guerrillas, then isn't one's attack on the group of one hundred a *means* of destroying the guerrillas, pure and simple? If one makes no attempt to discriminate between guerrillas and civilians, as is impossible in an aerial attack on a small village, then one cannot regard as a mere side effect the deaths of those in the group that one would not have bothered to kill if more selective means had been available.

The difficulty is that this argument depends on one particular description of the act, and the reply might be that the means used against the guerrillas is not: killing everybody in the village—but rather: obliteration bombing of the *area* in which the twenty guerrillas are known to be located. If there are civil-ians in the area as well, they will be killed as a side effect of such action.[5]

Because of casuistical problems like this, I prefer to stay with the original, unanalyzed distinction between what one does to people and what merely happens to them as a result of what one does. The law of double effect provides an approximation to that distinction in many cases, and perhaps it can be sharpened to the point where it does better than that. Certainly the original distinction itself needs clarification, particularly since some of the things we do to people involve things happening to them as a result of other things we do. In a case like the one discussed, however, it is clear that by bombing the village one slaughters and maims the civilians in it. Whereas by giving the only available medicine to one of two sufferers from a disease, one does not kill the other, even if he dies as a result.

The second technical point to take up concerns a possible misinterpretation of this feature of the position. The absolutist focus on actions rather than outcomes does not merely introduce a new, outstanding item into the catalogue of evils. That is, it does not say that the worst thing in the world is the deliberate murder of an innocent person. For if that were all, then one could presumably justify one such murder on the ground that it would prevent several others, or ten thousand on the ground that they would prevent a hundred thousand more. That is a familiar argument. But if this is allowable, then there is no absolute prohibition against murder after all. Absolutism requires that we *avoid* murder at all costs, not that we *prevent* it at all costs.[6]

Finally, let me remark on a frequent criticism of absolutism that depends on a misunderstanding. It is sometimes suggested that such prohibitions depend on a kind of moral self-interest, a primary obligation to preserve one's own moral purity, to keep one's hands clean no matter what happens to the rest of the world. If this were the position, it might be exposed to the charge of self-indulgence. After all, what gives one man a right to put a purity of his soul or the cleanness of his hands above the lives or welfare of large numbers of other people? It might be argued that a public servant like Truman has no right to put himself first in that way; therefore if he is convinced that the alternatives would be worse, he must give the order to drop the bombs, and take the burden of those deaths on himself, as he must do other distasteful things for the general good.

But there are two confusions behind the view that moral self-interest under-lies moral absolutism. First, it is a confusion to suggest that the need to preserve one's moral purity might be the *source* of an obligation. For if by committing murder one sacrifices one's moral purity or integrity, that can only be because there is *already* something wrong with murder. The general reason against

---

[5] This counterargument was suggested by Rogers Albritton.

[6] Someone might of course acknowledge the *moral relevance* of the distinction between deliberate and nondeliberate killing, without being an absolutist. That is, he might believe simply that it was *worse* to bring about a death deliberately than as a secondary effect. But that would be merely a special assignment of value, and not an absolute prohibition.

committing murder cannot therefore be merely that it makes one an immoral person. Secondly, the notion that one might sacrifice one's moral integrity justifiably, in the service of a sufficiently worthy end, is an incoherent notion. For if one were justified in making such a sacrifice (or even morally required to make it), then one would not be sacrificing one's moral integrity by adopting that course: one would be preserving it.

Moral absolutism is not unique among moral theories in requiring each person to do what will preserve his own moral purity in all circumstances. This is equally true of utilitarianism, or of any other theory which distinguishes between right and wrong. Any theory which defines the right course of action in various circumstances and asserts that one should adopt that course, ipso facto asserts that one should do what will preserve one's moral purity, simply because the right course of action *is* what will preserve one's moral purity in those circumstances. Of course utilitarianism does not assert that this is *why* one should adopt that course, but we have seen that the same is true of absolutism.

V

It is easier to dispose of false explanations of absolutism than to produce a true one. A positive account of the matter must begin with the observation that war, conflict, and aggression are relations between persons. The view that it can be wrong to consider merely the overall effect of one's actions on the general welfare comes into prominence when those actions involve relations with others. A man's acts usually affect more people than he deals with directly, and those effects must naturally be considered in his decisions. But if there are special principles governing the manner in which he should *treat* people, that will require special attention to the particular persons toward whom the act is directed, rather than just to its total effect.

Absolutist restrictions in warfare appear to be of two types: restrictions on the class of persons at whom aggression or violence may be directed and restrictions on the manner of attack, given that the object falls within that class. These can be combined, however, under the principle that hostile treatment of any person must be justified in terms of something *about that person* which makes the treatment appropriate. Hostility is a personal relation, and it must be suited to its target. One consequence of this condition will be that certain persons may not be subjected to hostile treatment in war at all, since nothing about them justifies such treatment. Others will be proper objects of hostility only in certain circumstances, or when they are engaged in certain pursuits. And the appropriate manner and extent of hostile treatment will depend on what is justified by the particular case.

A coherent view of this type will hold that extremely hostile behavior toward another is compatible with treating him as a person—even perhaps as an end in himself. This is possible only if one has not automatically stopped treating him as a person as soon as one starts to fight with him. If hostile, aggressive, or combative treatment of others always violated the condition that they be treated as human beings, it would be difficult to make further distinctions on that score *within* the class of hostile actions. That point of view, on the level of international relations, leads to the position that if complete pacifism is not accepted, no holds need be barred at all, and we may slaughter and massacre to our hearts' content, if it seems advisable. Such a position is often expressed in discussions of war crimes.

But the fact is that ordinary people do not believe this about conflicts, physical or otherwise, between individuals, and there is no more reason why it should be true of conflicts between nations. There seems to be a perfectly natural conception of the distinction between fighting clean and fighting dirty. To fight dirty is to direct one's hostility or aggression not at its proper object, but at a peripheral target which may be more vulnerable, and through which the proper object can be attacked indirectly. This applies in a fist fight, an election campaign, a duel, or a philosophical argument. If the concept is general enough to apply to all these matters, it should apply to war—both to the conduct of individual soldiers and to the conduct of nations.

Suppose that you are a candidate for public office, convinced that the election of your opponent would be a disaster, that he is an unscrupulous demagogue who will serve a narrow range of interests and seriously infringe the rights of those who disagree with him; and suppose you are convinced that you cannot defeat him by conventional means. Now imagine that various unconventional means present themselves as possibilities: you possess information about his sex life which would scandalize the electorate if made public; or you learn that his wife is an alcoholic or that in his youth he was associated for a brief period with a proscribed political party, and you believe that this information could be used to blackmail him into withdrawing his candidacy; or you can have a team of your supporters flatten the tires of a crucial subset of his supporters on election day; or you are in a position to stuff the ballot boxes; or, more simply, you can have him assassinated. What is wrong with these methods, given that they will achieve an overwhelmingly desirable result?

There are, of course, many things wrong with them: some are against the law; some infringe the procedures of an electoral process to which you are presumably committed by taking part in it; very importantly, some may backfire, and it is in the interest of all political candidates to adhere to an unspoken agreement not to allow certain personal matters to intrude into a campaign. But that is not all. We have in addition the feeling that these measures, these methods of attack are *irrelevant* to the issue between you and your opponent, that in taking them up you would not be directing yourself to that which makes him an object of your opposition. You would be directing your attack not at the true target of your hostility, but at peripheral targets that happen to be vulnerable.

The same is true of a fight or argument outside the framework of any system of regulations or law. In an altercation with a taxi driver over an excessive fare, it is inappropriate to taunt him about his accent, flatten one of his tires, or smear chewing gum on his windshield; and it remains inappropriate even if he casts aspersions on your race, politics, or religion, or dumps the contents of your suitcase into the street.[7]

The importance of such restrictions may vary with the seriousness of the case; and what is unjustifiable in one case may be justified in a more extreme one. But they all derive from a single principle: that hostility or aggression should be directed at its true object. This means both that it should be directed at the person or persons who provoke it and that it should aim more specifically at what is provocative about them. The second condition will determine what form the hostility may appropriately take.

It is evident that some idea of the relation in which one should stand to other people underlies this principle, but the idea is difficult to state. I believe it is roughly this: whatever one does to another person intentionally must be aimed at him as a subject, with the intention that he receive it as a subject. It should manifest an attitude to *him* rather than just to the situation, and he should be able to recognize it and identify himself as its object. The procedures by which such an attitude is manifested need not be addressed to the person directly. Surgery, for example, is not a form of personal confrontation but part of a medical treatment that can be offered to a patient face to face and received by him as a response to his needs and the natural outcome of an attitude toward *him*.

Hostile treatment, unlike surgery, is already addressed *to* a person, and does not take its interpersonal meaning from a wider context. But hostile acts can serve as the expression or implementation of only a limited range of attitudes to the person who is attacked. Those attitudes in turn have as objects certain real or presumed characteristics or activities of the person which are thought to justify them. When this background is absent, hostile or aggressive behavior can no longer be intended for the reception of the victim as a subject. Instead it takes on the character of a purely bureaucratic operation. This occurs when one attacks someone who is not the true object of one's hostility—the true object may be someone else, who can be attacked through the victim; or one may not be manifesting a hostile attitude toward anyone, but merely using the easiest available path to some desired goal. One finds oneself not facing or addressing the victim at all, but operating on him—without the larger context of personal interaction that surrounds a surgical operation.

If absolutism is to defend its claim to priority over considerations of utility, it must hold that the maintenance of a direct interpersonal response to the people one deals with is a requirement which no advantages can justify one in abandoning. The requirement is absolute only if it rules out any calculation of what would justify its violation. I have said earlier that there may be circumstances so extreme that they render an absolutist position untenable. One may

---

[7] Why, on the other hand, does it seem appropriate, rather than irrelevant, to punch someone in the mouth if he insults you? The answer is that in our culture it is an insult to punch someone in the mouth, and not just an injury. This reveals, by the way, a perfectly unobjectionable sense in which convention may play a part in determining exactly what falls under an absolutist restriction and what does not. I am indebted to Robert Fogelin for this point.

find then that one has no choice but to do something terrible. Nevertheless, even in such cases absolutism retains its force in that one cannot claim *justification* for the violation. It does not become *all right*.

As a tentative effort to explain this, let me try to connect absolutist limitations with the possibility of justifying *to the victim* what is being done to him. If one abandons a person in the course of rescuing several others from a fire or a sinking ship, one *could* say to him, "You understand, I have to leave you to save the others." Similarly, if one subjects an unwilling child to a painful surgical procedure, one can say to him, "If you could understand, you would realize that I am doing this to help you." One could *even* say, as one bayonets an enemy soldier, "It's either you or me." But one cannot really say while torturing a prisoner, "You understand, I have to pull out your fingernails because it is absolutely essential that we have the names of your confederates"; nor can one say to the victims of Hiroshima, "You understand, we have to incinerate you to provide the Japanese government with an incentive to surrender."

This does not take us very far, of course, since a utilitarian would presumably be willing to offer justifications of the latter sort to his victims, in cases where he thought they were sufficient. They are really justifications to the world at large, which the victim, as a reasonable man, would be expected to appreciate. However, there seems to me something wrong with this view, for it ignores the possibility that to treat someone else horribly puts you in a special relation to him, which may have to be defended in terms of other features of your relation to him. The suggestion needs much more development; but it may help us to understand how there may be requirements which are absolute in the sense that there can be no justification for violating them. If the justification for what one did to another person had to be such that it could be offered to him specifically, rather than just to the world at large, that would be a significant source of restraint.

If the account is to be deepened, I would hope for some results along the following lines. Absolutism is associated with a view of oneself as a small being interacting with others in a large world. The justifications it requires are primarily interpersonal. Utilitarianism is associated with a view of oneself as a benevolent bureaucrat distributing such benefits as one can control to countless other beings, with whom one may have various relations or none. The justifications it requires are primarily administrative. The argument between the two moral attitudes may depend on the relative priority of these two conceptions.[8]

VI

Some of the restrictions on methods of warfare which have been adhered to from time to time are to be explained by the mutual interests of the involved

---

[8] Finally, I should mention a different possibility, suggested by Robert Nozick: that there is a strong general presumption against benefiting from the calamity of another, whether or not it has been deliberately inflicted for that or any other reason. This broader principle may well lend its force to the absolutist position.

parties: restrictions on weaponry, treatment of prisoners, etc. But that is not all there is to it. The conditions of directness and relevance which I have argued apply to relations of conflict and aggression apply to war as well. I have said that there are two types of absolutist restrictions on the conduct of war: those that limit the legitimate targets of hostility and those that limit its character, even when the target is acceptable. I shall say something about each of these. As will become clear, the principle I have sketched does not yield an unambiguous answer in every case.

First let us see how it implies that attacks on some people are allowed, but not attacks on others. It may seem paradoxical to assert that to fire a machine gun at someone who is throwing hand grenades at your emplacement is to treat him as a human being. Yet the relation with him is direct and straightforward.[9] The attack is aimed specifically against the threat presented by a dangerous adversary, and not against a peripheral target through which he happens to be vulnerable but which has nothing to do with that threat. For example, you might stop him by machine-gunning his wife and children, who are standing nearby, thus distracting him from his aim of blowing you up and enabling you to capture him. But if his wife and children are not threatening your life, that would be to treat them as means with a vengeance.

This, however, is just Hiroshima on a smaller scale. One objection to weapons of mass annihilation—nuclear, thermonuclear, biological, or chemical— is that their indiscriminateness disqualifies them as direct instruments for the expression of hostile relations. In attacking the civilian population, one treats neither the military enemy nor the civilians with that minimal respect which is owed to them as human beings. This is clearly true of the direct attack on people who present no threat at all. But it is also true of the character of the attack on those who *are* threatening you, viz., the government and military forces of the enemy. Your aggression is directed against an area of vulnerability quite distinct from any threat presented by them which you may be justified in meeting. You are taking aim at them through the mundane life and survival of their countrymen, instead of aiming at the destruction of their military capacity. And of course it does not require hydrogen bombs to commit such crimes.

This way of looking at the matter also helps us to understand the importance of the distinction between combatants and noncombatants, and the irrelevance of much of the criticism offered against it intelligibility and moral significance. According to an absolutist position, deliberate killing of the innocent is murder, and in warfare the role of the innocent is filled by noncombatants. This has been thought to raise two sorts of problems: first, the widely imagined difficulty of making a division, in modern warfare, between combatants and noncombatants; second, problems deriving from the connotation of the word "innocence."

---

[9] It has been remarked that according to my view, shooting at someone establishes an I-thou relationship.

Let me take up the latter question first.[10] In the absolutist position, the operative notion of innocence is not moral innocence and it is not opposed to moral guilt. If it were, then we would be justified in killing a wicked but noncombatant hairdresser in an enemy city who supported the evil policies of his government, and unjustified in killing a morally pure conscript who was driving a tank toward us with the profoundest regrets and nothing but love in his heart. But moral innocence has very little to do with it, for in the definition of murder "innocent" means "currently harmless," and it is opposed not to "guilty' but to "doing harm." It should be noted that such an analysis has the consequence that in war we may often be justified in killing people who do not deserve to die, and unjustified in killing people who do deserve to die, if anyone does.

So we must distinguish between combatants from noncombatants on the basis of their immediate threat or harmfulness. I do not claim that the line is a sharp one, but it is not so difficult as is often supposed to place individuals on one side of it or the other. Children are not combatants even though they may join the armed forces if they are allowed to grow up. Women are not combatants just because they bear children or offer comfort to the soldiers. More problematic are the supporting personnel, whether in or out of uniform, from drivers of munitions trucks and army cooks to civilian munitions workers and farmers. I believe they can be plausibly classified by applying the condition that the prosecution of conflict must direct itself to the cause of danger, and not to what is peripheral. The threat presented by an army and its members does not consist merely in the fact that they are men, but in the fact that they are armed and are using their arms in the pursuit of certain objectives. Contributions to their arms and logistics are contributions to this threat; contributions to their mere existence as men are not. It is therefore wrong to direct an attack against those who merely serve the combatants' needs as human beings, such as farmers and food suppliers, even though survival as a human being is a necessary condition of efficient functioning as a soldier.

This brings us to the second group of restrictions: those that limit what may be done even to combatants. These limits are harder to explain clearly. Some of them may be arbitrary or conventional, and some may have to be derived from other sources; but I believe that the condition of directness and relevance in hostile relations accounts for them to a considerable extent.

Consider first a case which involves both a protected class of noncombatants and a restriction on the measures that may be used against combatants. One provision of the rules of war which is universally recognized, though it seems to be turning into a dead letter in Vietnam, is the special status of medical personnel and the wounded in warfare. It might be more efficient to shoot medical officers on sight and to let the enemy wounded die rather than be patched up to fight another day. But someone with medical insignia is supposed to be left alone and permitted to tend and retrieve the wounded. I believe this

---

[10] What I say on this subject derives from Anscombe.

is because medical attention is a species of attention to completely general human needs, not specifically the needs of a combat soldier, and our conflict with the soldier is not with his existence as a human being.

By extending the application of this idea, one can justify prohibitions against certain particularly cruel weapons: starvation, poisoning, infectious diseases (supposing they could be inflicted on combatants only), weapons designed to maim or disfigure or torture the opponent rather than merely to stop him. It is not, I think, mere casuistry to claim that such weapons attack the men, not the soldiers. The effect of dum-dum bullets, for example, is much more extended than necessary to cope with the combat situation in which they are used. They abandon any attempt to discriminate in their effects between the combatant and the human being. For this reason the use of flamethrowers and napalm is an atrocity in all circumstances that I can imagine, whoever the target may be. Burns are both extremely painful and extremely disfiguring—far more than any other category of wound. That this well-known fact plays no (inhibiting) part in the determination of U.S. weapons policy suggests that moral sensitivity among public officials has not increased markedly since the Spanish Inquisition.[11]

Finally, the same condition of appropriateness to the true object of hostility should limit the scope of attacks on an enemy country: its economy, agriculture, transportation system, and so forth. Even if the parties to a military conflict are considered to be not armies or governments but entire nations (which is usually a grave error), that does not justify one nation in warring against every aspect or element of another nation. That is not justified in a conflict between individuals, and nations are even more complex than individuals, so the same reasons apply. Like a human being, a nation is engaged in countless other pursuits while waging war, and it is not in those respects that it is an enemy.

The burden of the argument has been that absolutism about murder has a foundation in principles governing all one's relations to other persons, whether

---

[11] Beyond this I feel uncertain. Ordinary bullets, after all, can cause death, and nothing is more permanent than that. I am not at all sure why we are justified in trying to kill those who are trying to kill us (rather than merely in trying to stop them with force which may also result in their deaths). It is often argued that incapacitating gases are a relatively humane weapon (when not used, as in Vietnam, merely to make people easier to shoot). Perhaps the legitimacy of restrictions against them must depend on the dangers of escalation, and the great utility of maintaining *any* conventional category of restriction so long as nations are willing to adhere to it.

Let me make clear that I do not regard my argument as a defense of the moral immutability of the Hague and Geneva Conventions. Rather, I believe that they rest partly on a moral foundation, and that modifications of them should also be assessed on moral grounds.

But even this connection with the actual laws of war is not essential to my claims about what is permissible and what is not. Since completing this paper I have read an essay by Richard Wasserstrom entitled "The Laws of War" (forthcoming in *The Monist*), which argues that the existing laws and conventions do not even attempt to embody a decent moral position: that their provisions have been determined by other interests, that they are in fact immoral in substance, and that it is a grave mistake to refer to them as standards in forming moral judgments about warfare. This possibility deserves serious consideration, and I am not sure what to say about it, but it does not affect my view of the moral issues.

aggressive or amiable, and that these principles, and that absolutism, apply to warfare as well, with the result that certain measures are impermissible no matter what the consequences.[12] I do not mean to romanticize war. It is sufficiently utopian to suggest that when nations conflict they might rise to the level of limited barbarity that typically characterizes violent conflict between individuals, rather than wallowing in the moral pit where they appear to have settled, surrounded by enormous arsenals.

VII

Having described the elements of the absolutist position, we must now return to the conflict between it and utilitarianism. Even if certain types of dirty tactics become acceptable when the stakes are high enough, the most serious of the prohibited acts, like murder and torture, are not just supposed to require unusually strong justification. They are supposed *never* to be done, because no quantity of resulting benefit is thought capable of *justifying* such treatment of a person.

The fact remains that when an absolutist knows or believes that the utilitarian cost of refusing to adopt a prohibited course will be very high, he may hold to his refusal to adopt it, but he will find it difficult to feel that a moral dilemma has been satisfactorily resolved. The same may be true of someone who rejects an absolutist requirement and adopts instead the course yielding the most acceptable consequences. In either case, it is possible to feel that one has acted for reasons insufficient to justify violation of the opposing principle. In situations of deadly conflict, particularly where a weaker party is threatened with annihilation or enslavement by a stronger one, the argument for resorting to atrocities can be powerful, and the dilemma acute.

There may exist principles, not yet codified, which would enable us to resolve such dilemmas. But then again there may not. We must face the pessimistic alternative that these two forms of moral intuition are not capable of being brought together into a single, coherent moral system, and that the world can present us with situations in which there is no honorable or moral course for a man to take, no course free of guilt and responsibility for evil.

The idea of a moral blind alley is a perfectly intelligible one. It is possible to get into such a situation by one's own fault, and people do it all the time. If, for example, one makes two incompatible promises or commitments—becomes engaged to two people, for example—then there is no course one can take which is not wrong, for one must break one's promise to at least one of them. Making a clean breast of the whole thing will not be enough to remove one's

---

[12] It is possible to draw a more radical conclusion, which I shall not pursue here. Perhaps the technology and organization of modern war are such as to make it impossible to wage as an acceptable form of interpersonal or even international hostility. Perhaps it is too impersonal and large-scale for that. If so, then absolutism would in practice imply pacifism, given the present state of things. On the other hand, I am skeptical about the unstated assumption that a technology dictates its own use.

reprehensibility. The existence of such cases is not morally disturbing, however, because we feel that the situation was not unavoidable: one had to do something wrong in the first place to get into it. But what if the world itself, or someone else's actions, could face a previously innocent person with a choice between morally abominable courses of action, and leave him no way to escape with his honor? Our intuitions rebel at the idea, for we feel that the constructibility of such a case must show a contradiction in our moral views. But it is not in itself a contradiction to say that someone can do X or not do X, and that for him to take either course would be wrong. It merely contradicts the supposition that *ought* implies *can*—since presumably one ought to refrain from what is wrong, and in such a case it is impossible to do so.[13] Given the limitations on human action, it is naïve to suppose that there is a solution to every moral problem with which the world can face us. We have always known that the world is a bad place. It appears that it may be an evil place as well.

---

[13] This was first pointed out to me by Christopher Boorse.

51

Political Action: The Problem of Dirty Hands[1]

MICHAEL WALZER

Michael Walzer (b. 1935) is a Senior Fellow at the Institute for Advanced Study in Princeton, New Jersey. Previously he taught government at Harvard University. His books include Obligations, Just and Unjust Wars, Radical Principles, *and* Spheres of Justice.

In this reading Walzer takes up a variant of the problem raised by Thomas Nagel in reading 50. Nagel observes that in war, soldiers sometimes must choose between violating moral prohibitions and failing to prevent great disasters. Similarly, Walzer notes that politicians often must choose between using morally unsavory tactics (say, for example, making deals with corrupt bosses) and failing to implement worthwhile policies. Because implementing worthwhile policies is the aim of the best people who enter politics, such people must, as Machiavelli puts it, "learn not to be good." But how can this be?

One answer is given by utilitarianism. According to many utilitarians, moral prohibitions have no absolute force. Rather, they are guidelines as to what generally maximizes utility. If the prohibitions seem absolute, it is because utility is served by our tendency to feel guilty when we violate them. (For pertinent discussion, see reading 26, by Mill, and reading 49, by Hare.)

But Walzer rejects all such suggestions. According to him, the decent politician may not simply dismiss the prohibitions he violates. Instead, he must acknowledge these even while he transgresses against them. This requires not only that he feel guilt, but also that he pay some more public penalty. Yet this raises a further problem. Since successful politicians receive power and honor rather than punishment, how is the penalty to be exacted?

IN AN EARLIER issue of *Philosophy & Public Affairs* there appeared a symposium on the rules of war which was actually (or at least more importantly) a symposium on another topic.[2] The actual topic was whether or not

[1] An earlier version of this paper was read at the annual meeting of the Conference for the Study of Political Thought in New York, April 1971. I am indebted to Charles Taylor, who served as commentator at that time and encouraged me to think that its arguments might be right.

[2] *Philosophy & Public Affairs* 1, no. 2 (Winter 1971/72): Thomas Nagel, "War and Massacre," pp. 123–144 [reprinted in this volume, reading 50]; R. B. Brandt, "Utilitarianism and the Rules of War," pp. 145–165; and R. M. Hare, "Rules of War and Moral Reasoning," pp. 166–181.

a man can ever face, or ever has to face, a moral dilemma, a situation where he must choose between two courses of action both of which it would be wrong for him to undertake. Thomas Nagel worriedly suggested that this could happen and that it did happen whenever someone was forced to choose between upholding an important moral principle and avoiding some looming disaster.[3] R. B. Brandt argued that it could not possibly happen, for there were guidelines we might follow and calculations we might go through which would necessarily yield the conclusion that one or the other course of action was the right one to undertake in the circumstances (or that it did not matter which we undertook). R. M. Hare explained how it was that someone might wrongly suppose that he was faced with a moral dilemma: sometimes, he suggested, the precepts and principles of an ordinary man, the products of his moral education, come into conflict with injunctions developed at a higher level of moral discourse. But this conflict is, or ought to be, resolved at the higher level; there is no real dilemma.

I am not sure that Hare's explanation is at all comforting, but the question is important even if no such explanation is possible, perhaps especially so if this is the case. The argument relates not only to the coherence and harmony of the moral universe, but also to the relative ease or difficulty—or impossibility—of living a moral life. It is not, therefore, merely a philosopher's question. If such a dilemma can arise, whether frequently or very rarely, any of us might one day face it. Indeed, many men have faced it, or think they have, especially men involved in political activity or war. The dilemma, exactly as Nagel describes it, is frequently discussed in the literature of political action—in novels and plays dealing with politics and in the work of theorists too.

In modern times the dilemma appears most often as the problem of "dirty hands," and it is typically stated by the Communist leader Hoerderer in Sartre's play of that name: "I have dirty hands right up to the elbows. I've plunged them in filth and blood. Do you think you can govern innocently?"[4] My own answer is no, I don't think I could govern innocently; nor do most of us believe that those who govern us are innocent—as I shall argue below—even the best of them. But this does not mean that it isn't possible to do the right thing while governing. It means that a particular act of government (in a political party or in the state) may be exactly the right thing to do in utilitarian terms and yet leave the man who does it guilty of a moral wrong. The innocent man, afterwards, is no longer innocent. If on the other hand he remains innocent, chooses, that is, the "absolutist" side of Nagel's dilemma, he not only fails to do the right thing (in utilitarian terms), he may also fail to measure up to the

[3] For Nagel's description of a possible "moral blind alley," see "War and Massacre," pp. 142–144. Bernard Williams has made a similar suggestion, though without quite acknowledging it as his own: "many people can recognize the thought that a certain course of action is, indeed, the best thing to do on the whole in the circumstances, but that doing it involves doing something wrong" (*Morality: An Introduction to Ethics* [New York, 1972], p. 93).

[4] Jean-Paul Sartre, *Dirty Hands,* in *No Exit and Three Other Plays,* trans. Lionel Abel (New York, n.d.), p. 224.

duties of his office (which imposes on him a considerable responsibility for consequences and outcomes). Most often, of course, political leaders accept the utilitarian calculation; they try to measure up. One might offer a number of sardonic comments on this fact, the most obvious being that by the calculations they usually make they demonstrate the great virtues of the "absolutist" position. Nevertheless, we would not want to be governed by men who consistently adopted that position.

The notion of dirty hands derives from an effort to refuse "absolutism" without denying the reality of the moral dilemma. Though this may appear to utilitarian philosophers to pile confusion upon confusion, I propose to take it very seriously. For the literature I shall examine is the work of serious and often wise men, and it reflects, though it may also have helped to shape, popular thinking about politics. It is important to pay attention to that too. I shall do so without assuming, as Hare suggests one might, that everyday moral and political discourse constitutes a distinct level of argument, where content is largely a matter of pedagogic expediency.[5] If popular views are resistant (as they are) to utilitarianism, there may be something to learn from that and not merely something to explain about it.

<h1 style="text-align:center">I</h1>

Let me begin, then, with a piece of conventional wisdom to the effect that politicians are a good deal worse, morally worse, than the rest of us (it is the wisdom of the rest of us). Without either endorsing it or pretending to disbelieve it, I am going to expound this convention. For it suggests that the dilemma of dirty hands is a central feature of political life, that it arises not merely as an occasional crisis in the career of this or that unlucky politician but systematically and frequently.

Why is the politician singled out? Isn't he like the other entrepreneurs in an open society, who hustle, lie, intrigue, wear masks, smile and are villains? He is not, no doubt for many reasons, three of which I need to consider. First of all, the politician claims to play a different part than other entrepreneurs. He doesn't merely cater to our interests; he acts on our behalf, even in our name. He has purposes in mind, causes and projects that require the support and redound to the benefit, not of each of us individually, but of all of us together. He hustles lies, and intrigues *for us*—or so he claims. Perhaps he is right, or at least sincere, but we suspect that he acts for himself also. Indeed, he cannot serve us without serving himself, for success brings him power and glory, the greatest rewards that men can win from their fellows. The competition for these two is fierce; the risks are often great, but the temptations are greater. We imagine ourselves succumbing. Why should our representatives act differently? Even if they would like to act differently, they probably can not: for

---

[5] Hare, "Rules of War and Moral Reasoning," pp. 173–178, esp. p. 174: "the simple principles of the deontologist . . . have their place at the level of character-formation (moral education and self-education)."

other men are all too ready to hustle and lie for power and glory, and it is the others who set the terms of the competition. Hustling and lying are necessary because power and glory are so desirable—that is, so widely desired. And so the men who act for us and in our name are necessarily hustlers and liars.

Politicians are also thought to be worse than the rest of us because they rule over us, and the pleasures of ruling are much greater than the pleasures of being ruled. The successful politician becomes the visible architect of our restraint. He taxes us, licenses us, forbids and permits us, directs us to this or that distant goal—all for our greater good. Moreover, he takes chances for our greater good that put us, or some of us, in danger. Sometimes he puts himself in danger too, but politics, after all, is his adventure. It is not always ours. There are undoubtedly times when it is good or necessary to direct the affairs of other people and to put them in danger. But we are a little frightened of the man who seeks, ordinarily and every day, the power to do so. And the fear is reasonable enough. The politician has, or pretends to have, a kind of confidence in his own judgment that the rest of us know to be presumptuous in any man.

The presumption is especially great because the victorious politician uses violence and the threat of violence—not only against foreign nations in our defense but also against us, and again ostensibly for our greater good. This is a point emphasized and perhaps overemphasized by Max Weber in his essay "Politics as a Vocation."[6] It has not, so far as I can tell, played an overt or obvious part in the development of the convention I am examining. The stock figure is the lying, not the murderous, politician—though the murderer lurks in the background, appearing most often in the form of the revolutionary or terrorist, very rarely as an ordinary magistrate or official. Nevertheless, the sheer weight of official violence in human history does suggest the kind of power to which politicians aspire, the kind of power they want to wield, and it may point to the roots of our half-conscious dislike and unease. The men who act for us and in our name are often killers, or seem to become killers too quickly and too easily.

Knowing all this or most of it, good and decent people still enter political life, aiming at some specific reform or seeking a general reformation. They are then required to learn the lesson Machiavelli first set out to teach: "how not to be good."[7] Some of them are incapable of learning; many more profess to be incapable. But they will not succeed unless they learn, for they have joined the terrible competition for power and glory; they have chosen to work and struggle as Machiavelli says, among "so many who are not good." They can do no good themselves unless they win the struggle, which they are unlikely to do unless they are willing and able to use the necessary means. So we are

---

[6] In *From Max Weber: Essays in Sociology,* trans. and ed. Hans H. Gerth and C. Wright Mills (New York, 1946), pp. 77–128.

[7] See *The Prince,* chap. XV; cf. *The Discourses,* bk. I, chaps. IX and XVIII. I quote from the Modern Library edition of the two works (New York, 1950), p. 57.

suspicious even of the best of winners. It is not a sign of our perversity if we think them only more clever than the rest. They have not won, after all, because they were good, or not only because of that, but also because they were not good. No one succeeds in politics without getting his hands dirty. This is conventional wisdom again, and again I don't mean to insist that it is true without qualification. I repeat it only to disclose the moral dilemma inherent in the convention. For sometimes it is right to try to succeed, and then it must also be right to get one's hands dirty. But one's hands get dirty from doing what it is wrong to do. And how can it be wrong to do what is right? Or, how can we get our hands dirty by doing what we ought to do?

II

It will be best to turn quickly to some examples. I have chosen two, one relating to the struggle for power and one to its exercise. I should stress that in both these cases the men who face the dilemma of dirty hands have in an important sense chosen to do so; the cases tell us nothing about what it would be like, so to speak, to fall into the dilemma; nor shall I say anything about that here. Politicians often argue that they have no right to keep their hands clean, and that may well be true of them, but it is not so clearly true of the rest of us. Probably we do have a right to avoid, if we possibly can, those positions in which we might be forced to do terrible things. This might be regarded as the moral equivalent of our legal right not to incriminate ourselves. Good men will be in no hurry to surrender it, though there are reasons for doing so sometimes, and among these are or might be the reasons good men have for entering politics. But let us imagine a politician who does not agree to that: he wants to do good only by doing good, or at least he is certain that he can stop short of the most corrupting and brutal uses of political power. Very quickly that certainty is tested. What do we think of him then?

He wants to win the election, someone says, but he doesn't want to get his hands dirty. This is meant as a disparagement, even though it also means that the man being criticized is the sort of man who will not lie, cheat, bargain behind the backs of his supporters, shout absurdities at public meetings, or manipulate other men and women. Assuming that this particular election ought to be won, it is clear, I think, that the disparagement is justified. If the candidate didn't want to get his hands dirty, he should have stayed at home; if he can't stand the heat, he should get out of the kitchen, and so on. His decision to run was a commitment (to all of us who think the election important) to try to win, that is, to do within rational limits whatever is necessary to win. But the candidate is a moral man. He has principles and a history of adherence to those principles. That is why we are supporting him. Perhaps when he refuses to dirty his hands, he is simply insisting on being the sort of man he is. And isn't that the sort of man we want?

Let us look more closely at this case. In order to win the election the candidate must make a deal with a dishonest ward boss, involving the granting of contracts for school construction over the next four years. Should he make the deal? Well, at least he shouldn't be surprised by the offer, most of us would probably say (a conventional piece of sarcasm). And he should accept it or not, depending on exactly what is at stake in the election. But that is not the candidate's view. He is extremely reluctant even to consider the deal, puts off his aides when they remind him of it, refuses to calculate its possible effects upon the campaign. Now, if he is acting this way because the very thought of bargaining with that particular ward boss makes him feel unclean, his reluctance isn't very interesting. His feelings by themselves are not important. But he may also have reasons for his reluctance. He may know, for example, that some of his supporters support him precisely because they believe he is a good man, and this means to them a man who won't make such deals. Or he may doubt his own motives for considering the deal, wondering whether it is the political campaign or his own candidacy that makes the bargain at all tempting. Or he may believe that if he makes deals of this sort now he may not be able later on to achieve those ends that make the campaign worthwhile, and he may not feel entitled to take such risks with a future that is not only his own future. Or he may simply think that the deal is dishonest and therefore wrong, corrupting not only himself but all those human relations in which he is involved.

Because he has scruples of this sort, we know him to be a good man. But we view the campaign in a certain light, estimate its importance in a certain way, and hope that he will overcome his scruples and make the deal. It is important to stress that we don't want just *anyone* to make the deal; we want *him* to make it, precisely because he has scruples about it. We know he is doing right when he makes the deal because he knows he is doing wrong. I don't mean merely that he will feel badly or even very badly after he makes the deal. If he is the good man I am imagining him to be, he will feel guilty, that is, he will believe himself to be guilty. That is what it means to have dirty hands.

All this may become clearer if we look at a more dramatic example, for we are, perhaps, a little blasé about political deals and disinclined to worry much about the man who makes one. So consider a politician who has seized upon a national crisis—a prolonged colonial war—to reach for power. He and his friends win office pledged to decolonization and peace; they are honestly committed to both, though not without some sense of the advantages of the commitment. In any case, they have no responsibility for the war; they have steadfastly opposed it. Immediately, the politician goes off to the colonial capital to open negotiations with the rebels. But the capital is in the grip of a terrorist campaign, and the first decision the new leader faces is this: he is asked to authorize the torture of a captured rebel leader who knows or probably knows the location of a number of bombs hidden in apartment buildings around the city, set to go off within the next twenty-four hours. He orders the man tortured, convinced that he must do so for the sake of the people who might otherwise die in the explosions—even though he believes that torture is wrong, indeed abominable, not just sometimes, but always.[8] He had expressed this belief often and angrily during his own campaign; the rest of us took it as a sign of his goodness. How should we regard him now? (How should he regard himself?)

Once again, it does not seem enough to say that he should feel very badly. But why not? Why shouldn't he have feelings like those of St. Augustine's melancholy soldier, who understood both that his war was just and that killing, even in a just war, is a terrible thing to do?[9] The difference is that Augustine did not believe that it was wrong to kill in a just war; it was just sad, or the sort of thing a good man would be saddened by. But he might have thought it wrong to torture in a just war, and later Catholic theorists have certainly thought it wrong. Moreover, the politician I am imagining thinks it wrong, as do many of us who supported him. Surely we have a right to expect more than melancholy from him now. When he ordered the prisoner tortured, he committed a moral crime and he accepted a moral burden. Now he is a guilty man. His willingness to acknowledge and bear (and perhaps to repent and do penance for) his guilt is evidence, and it is the only evidence he can offer us, both that he is not too good for politics and that he is good enough. Here is the moral politician: it is by his dirty hands that we know him. If he were a moral man and nothing else, his hands would not be dirty; if he were a politician and nothing else, he would pretend that they were clean.

III

Machiavelli's argument about the need to learn how not to be good clearly implies that there acts known to be bad quite apart from the immediate circumstances in which they are performed or not performed. He points to a distinct set of political methods and stratagems which good men must study (by reading his books), not only because their use does not come naturally, but also because they are explicitly condemned by the moral teachings good men accept—and whose acceptance serves in turn to mark men as good. These methods may be condemned because they are thought contrary to divine law or to the order of nature or to our moral sense, or because in prescribing the law to ourselves we have individually or collectively prohibited them. Machiavelli does not commit himself on such issues, and I shall not do so either if I

---

[8] I leave aside the question of whether the prisoner is himself responsible for the terrorist campaign. Perhaps he opposed it in meetings of the rebel organization. In any case, whether he deserves to be punished or not, he does not deserve to be tortured.

[9] Other writers argued that Christians must never kill, even in a just war; and there was also an intermediate position which suggests the origins of the idea of dirty hands. Thus Basil The Great (Bishop of Caesarea in the fourth century A.D.): "Killing in war was differentiated by our fathers from murder . . . nevertheless, perhaps it would be well that those whose hands are unclean abstain from communion for three years." Here dirty hands are a kind of impurity or unworthiness, which is not the same as guilt, though closely related to it. For a general survey of these and other Christian views, see Roland H. Bainton, *Christian Attitudes Toward War and Peace* (New York, 1960), esp. chaps. 5–7.

can avoid it. The effects of these different views are, at least in one crucial sense, the same. They take out of our hands the constant business of attaching moral labels to such Machiavellian methods as deceit and betrayal. Such methods are simply bad. They are the sort of thing that good men avoid, at least until they have learned how not to be good.

Now, if there is no such class of actions, there is no dilemma of dirty hands, and the Machiavellian teaching loses what Machiavelli surely intended it to have, its disturbing and paradoxical character. He can then be understood to be saying that political actors must sometimes overcome their moral inhibitions, but not that they must sometimes commit crimes. I take it that utilitarian philosophers also want to make the first of these statements and to deny the second. From their point of view, the candidate who makes a corrupt deal and the official who authorizes the torture of a prisoner must be described as good men (given the cases as I have specified them), who ought, perhaps, to be honored for making the right decision when it was a hard decision to make. There are three ways of developing this argument. First, it might be said that every political choice ought to be made solely in terms of its particular and immediate circumstances—in terms, that is, of the reasonable alternatives, available knowledge, likely consequences, and so on. Then the good man will face difficult choices (when his knowledge of options and outcomes is radically uncertain), but it cannot happen that he will face a moral dilemma. Indeed, if he always makes decisions in this way, and has been taught from childhood to do so, he will never have to overcome his inhibitions, whatever he does, for how could he have acquired inhibitions? Assuming further that he weighs the alternatives and calculates the consequences seriously and in good faith, he cannot commit a crime, though he can certainly make a mistake, even a very serious mistake. Even when he lies and tortures, his hands will be clean, for he has done what he should do as best he can, standing alone in a moment of time, forced to choose.

This is in some ways an attractive description of moral decision-making, but it is also a very improbable one. For while any one of us may stand alone, and so on, when we make this or that decision, we are not isolated or solitary in our moral lives. Moral life is a social phenomenon, and it is constituted at least in part by rules, the knowing of which (and perhaps the making of which) we share with our fellows. The experience of coming up against these rules, challenging their prohibitions, and explaining ourselves to other men and women is so common and so obviously important that no account of moral decision-making can possibly fail to come to grips with it. Hence the second utilitarian argument: such rules do indeed exist, but they are not really prohibitions of wrongful actions (though they do, perhaps for pedagogic reasons, have that form). They are moral guidelines, summaries of previous calculations. They ease our choices in ordinary cases, for we can simply follow their injunctions and do what has been found useful in the past; in exceptional cases they serve as signals warning us against doing too quickly or without the most careful calculations what has not been found useful in the past. But they do no more than that; they have no other purpose, and so it cannot be the case that it is or even might be a crime to override them.[10] Nor is it necessary to feel guilty when one does so. Once again, if it is right to break the rule in some hard case, after conscientiously worrying about it, the man who acts (especially if he knows that many of his fellows would simply worry rather than act) may properly feel pride in his achievement.

But this view, it seems to me, captures the reality of our moral life no better than the last. It may well be right to say that moral rules ought to have the character of guidelines, but it seems that in fact they do not. Or at least, we defend ourselves when we break the rules as if they had some status entirely independent of their previous utility (and we rarely feel proud of ourselves). The defenses we normally offer are not simply justifications; they are also excuses. Now, as Austin says, these two can *seem* to come very close together—indeed, I shall suggest that they can appear side by side in the same sentence—but they are conceptually distinct, differentiated in this crucial respect: an excuse is typically an admission of fault; a justification is typically a denial of fault and an assertion of innocence.[11] Consider a well-known defense from Shakespeare's *Hamlet* that has often reappeared in political literature: "I must be cruel only to be kind."[12] The words are spoken on an occasion when Hamlet is actually being cruel to his mother. I will leave aside the possibility that she deserves to hear (to be forced to listen to) every harsh word he utters, for Hamlet himself makes no such claim—and if she did indeed deserve that, his words might not be cruel or he might not be cruel for speaking them. "I must be cruel" contains the excuse, since it both admits a fault and suggests that Hamlet has no choice but to commit it. He is doing what he has to do; he can't help himself (given the ghost's command, the rotten state of Denmark, and so on). The rest of the sentence is a justification, for it suggests that Hamlet intends and expects kindness to be the outcome of his actions—we must assume that he means greater kindness, kindness to the right persons, or some such. It is not, however, so complete a justification that Hamlet is able to say that he is not *really* being cruel. "Cruel" and "kind" have exactly the same status; they both follow the verb "to be," and so they perfectly reveal the moral dilemma.[13]

When rules are overridden, we do not talk or act as if they had been set aside, canceled, or annulled. They still stand and have this much effect at least:

---

[10] Brandt's rules do not appear to be of the sort that can be overridden—except perhaps by a soldier who decides that he just *won't* kill any more civilians, no matter what cause is served—since all they require is careful calculation. But I take it that rules of a different sort, which have the form of ordinary injunctions and prohibitions, can and often do figure in what is called "rule-utilitarianism."

[11] J. L. Austin, "A Plea for Excuses," in *Philosophical Papers*, ed. J. O. Urmson and G. J. Warnock (Oxford, 1961), pp. 123–152.

[12] *Hamlet* 3.4.178.

[13] Compare the following lines from Bertold Brecht's poem "To Posterity": "Alas, we/ Who wished to lay the foundations of kindness/ Could not ourselves be kind . . ." (*Selected Poems*, trans. H. R. Hays [New York, 1969], p. 177). This is more of an excuse, less of a justification (the poem is an *apologia*).

that we know we have done something wrong even if what we have done was also the best thing to do on the whole in the circumstances.[14] Or at least we feel that way, and this feeling is itself a crucial feature of our moral life. Hence the third utilitarian argument, which recognizes the usefulness of guilt and seeks to explain it. There are, it appears, good reasons for "overvaluing" as well as for overriding the rules. For the consequences might be very bad indeed if the rules were overridden every time the moral calculation seemed to go against them. It is probably best if most men do not calculate too nicely, but simply follow the rules; they are less likely to make mistakes that way, all in all. And so a good man (or at least an ordinary good man) will respect the rules rather more than he would if he thought them merely guidelines, and he will feel guilty when he overrides them. Indeed, if he did not feel guilty, "he would not be such a good man."[15] It is by his feelings that we know him. Because of those feelings he will never be in a hurry to override the rules, but will wait until there is no choice, acting only to avoid consequences that are both imminent and almost certainly disastrous.

The obvious difficulty with this argument is that the feeling whose usefulness is being explained is most unlikely to be felt by someone who is convinced only of its usefulness. He breaks a utilitarian rule (guideline), let us say, for good utilitarian reasons: but can he then feel guilty, also for good utilitarian reasons, when he has no reason for believing that he *is* guilty? Imagine a moral philosopher expounding the third argument to a man who actually does feel guilty or to the sort of man who is likely to feel guilty. Either the man won't accept the utilitarian explanation as an account of his feeling about the rules (probably the best outcome from a utilitarian point of view) or he will accept it and then cease to feel that (useful) feeling. But I do not want to exclude the possibility of a kind of superstitious anxiety, the possibility, that is, that some men will continue to feel guilty even after they have been taught, and have agreed, that they cannot possibly *be* guilty. It is best to say only that the more fully they accept the utilitarian account, the less likely they are to feel that (useful) feeling. The utilitarian account is not at all useful, then, if political actors accept it, and that may help us to understand why it plays, as Hare has pointed out, so small a part in our moral education.[16]

---

[14] Robert Nozick discusses some of the possible effects of overriding a rule in his "Moral Complications and Moral Structures," *Natural Law Forum* 13 (1968): 34–35 and notes. Nozick suggests that what may remain after one has broken a rule (for good reasons) is a "duty to make reparations." He does not call this "guilt," though the two notions are closely connected.

[15] Hare, "Rules of War and Moral Reasoning," p. 179.

[16] There is another possible utilitarian position, suggested in Maurice Merleau-Ponty's *Humanism and Terror*, trans. John O'Neill (Boston, 1970). According to this view, the agony and the guilt feelings experienced by the man who makes a "dirty hands" decision derive from his radical uncertainty about the actual outcome. Perhaps the awful thing he is doing will be done in vain; the results he hopes for won't occur; the only outcome will be the pain he has caused or the deceit he has fostered. Then (and only then) he will indeed have committed a crime. On the other hand, if the expected good does come, then (and only then) he can abandon his guilt feelings; he can say, and the rest of us must agree, that he is justified. This is a kind of delayed utilitarianism, where justification is a matter of actual and not at all of predicted outcomes. It

IV

One further comment on the third argument: it is worth stressing that to feel guilty is to suffer, and that the men whose guilt feelings are here called useful are themselves innocent according to the utilitarian account. So we seem to have come upon another case where the suffering of the innocent is permitted and even encouraged by utilitarian calculation.[17] But surely an innocent man who has done something painful or hard (but justified) should be helped to avoid or escape the sense of guilt; he might reasonably expect the assistance of his fellow men, even of moral philosophers, at such a time. On the other hand, if we intuitively think it true of some other man that he *should* feel guilty, then we ought to be able to specify the nature of his guilt (and if he is a good man, win his agreement). I think I can construct a case which, with only small variation, highlights what is different in these two situations.

Consider the common practice of distributing rifles loaded with blanks to some of the members of a firing squad. The individual men are not told whether their own weapons are lethal, and so though all of them look like executioners to the victim in front of them, none of them know whether they are really executioners or not. The purpose of this stratagem is to relieve each man of the sense that he is a killer. It can hardly relieve him of whatever moral responsibility he incurs by serving on a firing squad, and that is not its purpose, for the execution is not thought to be (and let us grant this to be the case) an immoral or wrongful act. But the inhibition against killing another human being is so strong that even if the men believe that what they are doing is right, they will still feel guilty. Uncertainty as to their actual role apparently reduces the intensity of these feelings. If this is so, the stratagem is perfectly justifiable, and one can only rejoice in every case where it succeeds—for every success subtracts one from the number of innocent men who suffer.

But we would feel differently, I think, if we imagine a man who believes (and let us assume here that we believe also) either that capital punishment is wrong or that this particular victim is innocent, but who nevertheless agrees to participate in the firing squad for some overriding political or moral reason—I won't try to suggest what that reason might be. If he is comforted by

---

is not implausible to imagine a political actor anxiously awaiting the "verdict of history." But suppose the verdict is in his favor (assuming that there is a *final* verdict or a statute of limitations on possible verdicts): he will surely feel relieved—more so, no doubt, than the rest of us. I can see no reason, however, why he should think himself justified, if he is a good man and knows that what he did was wrong. Perhaps the victims of his crime, seeing the happy result, will absolve him, but history has no powers of absolution. Indeed, history is more likely to play tricks on our moral judgment. Predicted outcomes are at least thought to follow from our own acts (this is the prediction), but actual outcomes almost certainly have a multitude of causes, the combination of which may well be fortuitous. Merleau-Ponty stresses the risks of political decision-making so heavily that he turns politics into a gamble with time and circumstance. But the anxiety of the gambler is of no great moral interest. Nor is it much of a barrier, as Merleau-Ponty's book makes all too clear, to the commission of the most terrible crimes.

[17] Cf. the cases suggested by David Ross, *The Right and the Good.* (Oxford, 1930), pp. 56–57, and E. F. Carritt, *Ethical and Political Thinking* (Oxford, 1947), p. 65.

the trick with the rifles, then we can be reasonably certain that his opposition to capital punishment or his belief in the victim's innocence is not morally serious. And if it is serious, he will not merely feel guilty, he will know that he is guilty (and we will know it too), though he may also believe (and we may agree) that he has good reasons for incurring the guilt. Our guilt feelings can be tricked away when they are isolated from our moral beliefs, as in the first case, but not when they are allied with them, as in the second. The beliefs themselves and the rules which are believed in can only be *overridden,* a painful process which forces a man to weigh the wrong he is willing to do in order to do right, and which leaves pain behind, and should do so, even after the decision has been made.

V

That is the dilemma of dirty hands as it has been experienced by political actors and written about in the literature of political action. I don't want to argue that it is only a political dilemma. No doubt we can get our hands dirty in private life also, and sometimes, no doubt, we should. But the issue is posed most dramatically in politics for the three reasons that make political life the kind of life it is, because we claim to act for others but also serve ourselves, rule over others, and use violence against them. It is easy to get one's hands dirty in politics and it is often right to do so. But it is not easy to teach a good man how not to be good, nor is it easy to explain such a man to himself once he has committed whatever crimes are required of him. At least, it is not easy once we have agreed to use the word "crimes" and to live with (because we have no choice) the dilemma of dirty hands. Still, the agreement is common enough, and on its basis there have developed three broad traditions of explanation, three ways of thinking about dirty hands, which derive in some very general fashion from neoclassical, Protestant, and Catholic perspectives on politics and morality. I want to try to say something very briefly about each of them, or rather about a representative example of each of them, for each seems to me partly right. But I don't think I can put together the compound view that might be wholly right.

The first tradition is best represented by Machiavelli, the first man, so far as I know, to state the paradox that I am examining. The good man who aims to found or reform a republic must, Machiavelli tells us, do terrible things to reach his goal. Like Romulus, he must murder his brother; like Numa, he must lie to the people. Sometimes, however, "when the act accuses, the result excuses."[18] This sentence from *The Discourses* is often taken to mean that the politician's deceit and cruelty are justified by the good results he brings about. But if they were justified, it wouldn't be necessary to learn what Machiavelli claims to teach: how not to be good. It would only be necessary to learn how to be good in a new, more difficult, perhaps roundabout way. That is not

[18] *The Discourses,* bk. I, chap. IX (p. 139).

Machiavelli's argument. His political judgments are indeed consequentialist in character, but not his moral judgments. We know whether cruelty is used well or badly by its effects over time. But that it is bad to use cruelty we know in some other way. The deceitful and cruel politician is excused (if he succeeds) only in the sense that the rest of us come to agree that the results were "worth it" or, more likely, that we simply forget his crimes when we praise his success.

It is important to stress Machiavelli's own commitment to the existence of moral standards. His paradox depends upon that commitment as it depends upon the general stability of the standards—which he upholds in his consistent use of words like good and bad.[19] If he wants the standards to be disregarded by good men more often than they are, he has nothing with which to replace them and no other way of recognizing the good men except by their allegiance to those same standards. It is exceedingly rare, he writes, that a good man is willing to employ bad means to become prince.[20] Machiavelli's purpose is to persuade such a person to make the attempt, and he holds out the supreme political rewards, power and glory, to the man who does so and succeeds. The good man is not rewarded (or excused), however, merely for his willingness to get his hands dirty. He must do bad things well. There is no reward for doing bad things badly, though they are done with the best of intentions. And so political action necessarily involves taking a risk. But it should be clear that what is risked is not personal goodness—*that is thrown away*—but power and glory. If the politician succeeds, he is a hero; eternal praise is the supreme reward for not being good.

What the penalties are for not being good, Machiavelli doesn't say, and it is probably for this reason above all that his moral sensitivity has so often been questioned. He is suspect not because he tells political actors they must get their hands dirty, but because he does not specify the state of mind appropriate to a man with dirty hands. A Machiavellian hero has no inwardness. What he thinks of himself we don't know. I would guess, along with most other readers of Machiavelli, that he basks in his glory. But then it is difficult to account for the strength of his original reluctance to learn how not to be good. In any case, he is the sort of man who is unlikely to keep a diary and so we cannot find out what he thinks. Yet we do want to know; above all, we want a record of his anguish. That is a sign of our own conscientiousness and of the impact on us of the second tradition of thought that I want to examine, in which personal anguish sometimes seems the only acceptable excuse for political crimes.

The second tradition is best represented, I think, by Max Weber, who outlines its essential features with great power at the very end of his essay "Politics as a Vocation." For Weber, the good man with dirty hands is a hero still, but he is tragic hero. In part, his tragedy is that though politics is his vocation, he has not been called by God and so cannot be justified by Him. Weber's hero

---

[19] For a very different view of Machiavelli, see Isaiah Berlin, "The Question of Machiavelli," *The New York Review of Books,* 4 November 1971.

[20] *The Discourses,* bk. I, chap. XVIII (p. 171).

is alone in a world that seems to belong to Satan, and his vocation is entirely his own choice. He still wants what Christian magistrates have always wanted, both to do good in the world and to save his soul, but now these two ends have come into sharp contradiction. They are contradictory because of the necessity for violence in a world where God has not instituted the sword. The politician takes the sword himself, and only by doing so does he measure up to his vocation. With full consciousness of what he is doing, he does bad in order to do good, and surrenders his soul. He "lets himself in," Weber says, "for the diabolic forces lurking in all violence." Perhaps Machiavelli also meant to suggest that his hero surrenders salvation in exchange for glory, but he does not explicitly say so. Weber is absolutely clear: "the genius or demon of politics lives in an inner tension with the god of love . . . [which] can at any time lead to an irreconcilable conflict."[21] His politician views this conflict when it comes with a tough realism, never pretends that it might be solved by compromise, chooses politics once again, and turns decisively away from love. Weber writes about this choice with a passionate high-mindedness that makes a concern for one's soul seem no more elevated than a concern for one's flesh. Yet the reader never doubts that his mature, superbly trained, relentless, objective, responsible, and disciplined political leader is also a suffering servant. His choices are hard and painful, and he pays the price not only while making them but forever after. A man doesn't lose his soul one day and find it the next.

The difficulties with this view will be clear to anyone who has ever met a suffering servant. Here is a man who lies, intrigues, sends other men to their death—and suffers. He does what he must do with a heavy heart. None of us can know, he tells us, how much it costs him to do his duty. Indeed, we cannot, for he himself fixes the price he pays. And that is the trouble with this view of political crime. We suspect the suffering servant of either masochism or hypocrisy or both, and while we are often wrong, we are not always wrong. Weber attempts to resolve the problem of dirty hands entirely within the confines of the individual conscience, but I am inclined to think that this is neither possible nor desirable. The self-awareness of the tragic hero is obviously of great value. We want the politician to have an inner life at least something like that which Weber describes. But sometimes the hero's suffering needs to be socially expressed (for like punishment, it confirms and reinforces our sense that certain acts are wrong). And equally important, it sometimes needs to be socially limited. We don't want to be ruled by men who have lost their souls. A politician with dirty hands needs a soul, and it is best for us all if he has some hope of personal salvation, however that is conceived. It is not the case that when he does bad in order to do good he surrenders himself forever to the demon of politics. He

---

[21] "Politics as a Vocation," pp. 125–126. But sometimes a political leader does choose the "absolutist" side of the conflict, and Weber writes (p. 127) that it is "immensely moving when a *mature* man . . . aware of a responsibility for the consequences of his conduct . . . reaches a point where he says: 'Here I stand; I can do no other.' " Unfortunately, he does not suggest just where that point is or even where it might be.

commits a determinate crime, and he must pay a determinate penalty. When he has done so, his hands will be clean again, or as clean as human hands can ever be. So the Catholic Church has always taught, and this teaching is central to the third tradition that I want to examine.

Once again I will take a latter-day and a lapsed representative of the tradition and consider Albert Camus' *The Just Assassins*. The heroes of this play are terrorists at work in nineteenth-century Russia. The dirt on their hands is human blood. And yet Camus' admiration for them, he tells us, is complete. We consent to being criminals, one of them says, but there is nothing with which anyone can reproach us. Here is the dilemma of dirty hands in a new form. The heroes are innocent criminals, just assassins, because, having killed, they are prepared to die—*and will die*. Only their execution, by the same despotic authorities they are attacking, will complete the action in which they are engaged: dying, they need make no excuses. That is the end of their guilt and pain. The execution is not so much punishment as self-punishment and expiation. On the scaffold they wash their hands clean and, unlike the suffering servant, they die happy.

Now the argument of the play when presented in so radically simplified a form may seem a little bizarre, and perhaps it is marred by the moral extremism of Camus' politics. "Political action has limits," he says in a preface to the volume containing *The Just Assassins*, "and there is no good and just action but what recognizes those limits and if it must go beyond them, at least accepts death."[22] I am less interested here in the violence of that "at least"—what else does he have in mind?—than in the sensible doctrine that it exaggerates. That doctrine might best be described by an analogy: just assassination, I want to suggest, is like civil disobedience. In both men violate a set of rules, go beyond a moral or legal limit, in order to do what they believe they should do. At the same time, they acknowledge their responsibility for the violation by accepting punishment or doing penance. But there is also a difference between the two, which has to do with the difference between law and morality. In most cases of civil disobedience the laws of the state are broken for moral reasons, and the state provides the punishment. In most cases of dirty hands moral rules are broken for reasons of state, and no one provides the punishment. There is rarely a Czarist executioner waiting in the wings for politicians with dirty hands, even the most deserving among them. Moral rules are not usually enforced against the sort of actor I am considering, largely because he acts in an official capacity. If they were enforced, dirty hands would be no problem. We would simply honor the man who did bad in order to do good, and at the same time we would punish him. We would honor him for the good he has done, and we would punish him for the bad he has done. We would punish him, that is, for the same reasons we punish anyone else; it is not my purpose here to defend

[22] *Caligula and Three Other Plays* (New York, 1958), p. x. (The preface is translated by Justin O'Brian, the plays by Stuart Gilbert.)

any particular view of punishment. In any case, there seems no way to establish or enforce the punishment. Short of the priest and the confessional, there are no authorities to whom we might entrust the task.

I am nevertheless inclined to think Camus' view the most attractive of the three, if only because it requires us at least to imagine a punishment or a penance that fits the crime and so to examine closely the nature of the crime. The others do not require that. Once he has launched his career, the crimes of Machiavelli's prince seem subject only to prudential control. And the crimes of Weber's tragic hero are limited only by *his* capacity for suffering and not, as they should be, by *our* capacity for suffering. In neither case is there any explicit reference back to the moral code, once it has, at great personal cost to be sure, been set aside. The question posed by Sartre's Hoerderer (whom I suspect of being a suffering servant) is rhetorical, and the answer is obvious (I have already given it), but the characteristic sweep of both is disturbing. Since it is concerned only with those crimes that ought to be committed, the dilemma of dirty hands seems to exclude questions of degree. Wanton or excessive cruelty is not at issue, any more than is cruelty directed at bad ends. But political action is so uncertain that politicians necessarily take moral as well as political risks, committing crimes that they only think ought to be committed. They override the rules without ever being certain that they have found the best way to the results they hope to achieve, and we don't want them to do that too quickly or too often. So it is important that the moral stakes be very high—which is to say, that the rules be rightly valued. That, I suppose, is the reason for Camus' extremism. Without the executioner, however, there is no one to set the stakes or maintain the values except ourselves, and probably no way to do either except through philosophic reiteration and political activity.

"We shall not abolish lying by refusing to tell lies," says Hoerderer, "but by using every means at hand to abolish social classes."[23] I suspect we shall not abolish lying at all, but we might see to it that fewer lies were told if we contrived to deny power and glory to the greatest liars—except, of course, in the case of those lucky few whose extraordinary achievements make us forget the lies they told. If Hoerderer succeeds in abolishing social classes, perhaps he will join the lucky few. Meanwhile, he lies, manipulates, and kills, and we must make sure he pays the price. We won't be able to do that, however, without getting our own hands dirty, and then we must find some way of paying the price ourselves.

[23] *Dirty Hands*, p. 223.

52

Imposing Risks
Upon Others

CHARLES FRIED

For biographical information on Charles Fried, see reading 46.

In this selection, Fried addresses a little-discussed but very important moral problem. When philosophers ask how we ought to act, they often make the simplifying assumption that we know exactly how our behavior will affect others. But most often, we know no such thing. Instead, we generally know only that each available act will impose some risk of harm upon others. Thus, there is a question about the levels of risk we may legitimately impose.

At first glance, the answer may seem to be "the lowest possible levels." But Fried does not say this. Instead, he argues that just as each rational person takes some avoidable risks in pursuit of his own ends, so too is it rational to accept a principle that allows each person to impose some avoidable risks on others. By agreeing to this, and so subjecting ourselves to risks imposed by others, we would increase our ability to pursue our own purposes. Thus, "we are justified in imposing that degree of risk on others which we would all agree to so that we would have the maximum degree of freedom to pursue our ends and exercise our capacities."

But this principle must be applied with some care. According to Fried, it does not imply that all persons may impose the same degree of risk on all others regardless of context. For example, a Sunday driver may not impose as much risk as the driver of a fire truck on call. Nor may we subject others to risks as great as those to which we are willing to subject ourselves. For related discussion, see both Fried's own treatment of personal discretion in reading 46 and the form of Kantianism developed by Rawls in reading 32.

The General Theorem

EVERY CHOICE A person makes has some effect on the risks of death he confronts; so also it has some effects on the risks confronted by others. What moral considerations govern choices involving the risk of death for others? The general theorem advanced in this section is built on the proposition that the justifications for imposing this risk on others are analogous to those governing the rationality of imposing the risk on oneself. Evidently the pursuit of ends other than the prolongation of life involves a sacrifice of that single end, both for oneself and others. Perhaps one may imagine some persons single-mindedly devoted to prolonging the lives of others (never mind for the moment how the benefits of their devotion would be distributed), but, unless the rest would then be bent on other pursuits, we would have a collective version of the madness of the life plan whose sole purpose is to prolong life. One might say that just as it is rational to use up our lives, so it is moral to use up each other's lives. The question is, on what basis do we use up each other's lives. In putting the issue in this form I intend to conflate problems of act and omission, right to act and liberty to forbear from acting, since these distinctions must be derived from and justified by more general principles. I consider it an open question, therefore, not only whether I am morally justified in doing that which endangers another, but also whether I am morally justified in ever pursuing some end other than that which will actively contribute to the greatest prolongation of another's life.

. . .

Summarizing, then, the general theorem which I put forward for consideration is that persons are justified in imposing risks of death upon each other by reference to the principle of equal right, that is the principle of morality. This would mean that all persons may impose risks of death upon each other for the ends and to the extent that all other persons may do so. This, then, would be a special case of the Kantian principle of right, that a person is entitled to the fullest amount of freedom compatible with a like freedom for all other persons according to general laws. Applied to this situation the Kantian principle would mean a person has the fullest freedom to impose risk of death upon others compatible with an equal right on the part of others to impose risks of death upon him according to universal laws.

What does it mean to have this kind of a moral right to impose risks of death upon others? Roughly, it means that the necessity for action, for the pursuit of ends and the exercise of capacities, requires a certain freedom to impose risk of death on others, and that we are justified in imposing that degree of risk on others which we would all agree to so that we would have the maximum degree of freedom to pursue our ends and exercise our capacities. . . .

The argument for this is as follows. Impositions of all sorts on other persons are morally justified because any rational person would agree to permit such impositions upon himself as a price for his freedom of action, provided that the imposition he was permitting to others assured him the maximum degree of freedom compatible with universal laws to impose upon others in the pursuit of his own ends. If a person knows that he and all other persons would accept for themselves in the pursuit of their own ends a certain degree and kind of risk of death in particular circumstances, then it is rational to assume that those persons would allow others to impose that degree of risk of death upon them when the others are engaged upon those certain ends. In this way each person's impositions on others in the pursuit of those ends would be justified. Moreover, were a man to withhold the title to other persons to impose the risk of death upon him in the pursuit of those specified ends, he would not have that same title to impose on them, and therefore would be restricted in the pursuit of his own ends and capacities.

Now this argument does suggest an equality of a sort between the right to impose the risk of death on others and the willingness to accept the risk of death for one's self. Through the principle of equal right this equation is perfectly appropriate. By granting the right of others to impose upon him, he does, of course, increase his own risk of death. However, he grants this right and increases this risk of death as a way of purchasing, as it were, the right to pursue his ends and capacities, and in so doing to impose risks upon others. Presumably he would purchase this right only where the ends and capacities justify accepting a certain level of risk. The only trick is that he accepts the level of risk of death in the pursuit of his ends and capacities not directly, but by granting to others a title to impose this risk upon him. Once again, it must be emphasized that this argument will only work if some rough equation of the trade-offs of all rational persons can be made.

This, then, is the general theorem, and the arguments for it. The next step in our discussion will be to consider how the arguments made in the previous chapter about a rational person's trade-off function in respect to risk of death would work to specify a principle of equal right in respect to risk of death.

The Concept of the Risk Pool

In Chapter Ten, there was put forward the concept of the risk budget, by which a rational person determines the allocation of risks in his life plan. The largest part of the actual determinations in the risk budget cannot be specified beforehand—they are intuitive judgments about the level of risk appropriate to discrete actions such as crossing a street or climbing a ladder. It was possible to be more concrete about the relation of such discrete actions to general classes of ends, and about the concept of a class of ends itself. This in turn permitted some more concrete judgments about discrete actions: that substitutability and postponability did not mean that no risk was rational. Moreover, as ends became less substitutable and postponable, or as a discrete end tended to absorb the whole of a general end or capacity, a higher level of risk was appropriate. Finally, this apportionment of risks to ends through time was related to the changing pattern of ends in a life plan for a life cycle. In this section these notions must be transferred to the interpersonal level.

The most obvious correlate to the notion developed in Chapter Ten is the notion of reasonableness, as embodied in the law of negligence. By that notion a person is held to have acted negligently, to have been at fault, when he has caused an injury or loss to another by taking an unreasonable risk; and this means that given the ends for which he was acting, he imposed a greater degree of risk on others than was justified. Negligence, then, is a function of these two variables, the significance of the end and the degree of risk; this is quite clear in the law.

. . .

Although the appeal to intuition in the law by the very vague concept of reasonableness has the same form as the appeal to rationality, it must be shown what the general aim of this vague concept is. In the intrapersonal case, the degree of risk was measured against the seriousness of the end pursued. In the interpersonal case the situation will be somewhat more complex, because person A may be pursuing a serious end and impose risks on person B who at that time is pursuing a trivial end. For instance, a fire engine may be going to a fire traveling the same road as someone driving on a Sunday outing. The concept of reasonableness in negligence law would hold that the Sunday driver could not complain if the fire company imposed a higher risk on him than he was entitled to impose on the fire company. If we consider the justification for imposing risks on others set forth in the first section of this chapter, it will appear why this is perfectly appropriate. On the assumption that each individual in society has a risk budget having at least the same very general contents and constraints, then, it has been argued, it is a corollary concept that it is rational to take risks in order to pursue one's own ends and that it is justified to impose the risks on others and accept the imposition of risks from others in the mutual pursuit of ends.

This general theorem does not entail any need for a correspondence at any particular time between the risk imposed and the end pursued. That is, there is nothing in this concept to require that a risk of a certain level may be imposed on others only when those others are themselves imposing risks of that level. Rather, the general notion of a lifetime risk budget would suggest that at various times risks of various degrees will be imposed for ends of varying degrees of seriousness, and if those risks have ends roughly corresponding to each other the liberty of all will be maximized if the risks may be properly imposed and accepted. Applying this to the Sunday driver and fire engine, the point would be that although the Sunday driver's house may not be the house that is on fire at the moment, his house might have been on fire at some other time or may be on fire in the future, or some other significant corresponding risk may be appropriate at some time, and this makes the imposition upon him of this serious risk appropriate. Nor would it be correct for him to argue that he is entitled to impose the same degree of risk on the fire company when he is out on his Sunday drive that they are entitled to impose on him as they go to a fire, since he is not at that point pursuing an end which in his risk budget, or the risk budget of a rational person, has a degree of risk attached to it of that seriousness.

The notion that emerges I would characterize by the concept of the risk pool which is the interpersonal correlate of the risk budget. This notion holds that all persons by virtue of their interactions contribute, as it were, to a common pool of risks which they may impose upon each other, and on which they may draw when pursuing ends of the appropriate degree of seriousness. Now the case of the Sunday driver and the fireman indicates some problem in that one may argue that an actor may simply decide to draw very heavily on his contribution to the risk pool in respect to an end which other actors might consider quite trifling. There are several reasons why this kind of strict "consumer sovereignty" is not followed out in the law. The most obvious reason is administrative: by judging the seriousness of the occasion in terms of generally accepted estimates, there is some control over whether an individual is in fact withdrawing more than his share from the risk pool. If an individual were indeed allowed to allocate whatever degree of risk he wished to whatever end he wished, the problem of determining what balance he was maintaining in the risk pool would be intolerable. The correlate in morality of this legal administrative argument is the notion that not only should persons be fair—and the risk pool is an aspect of fairness—but also that it is important that persons have a degree of confidence that others are being fair. This confidence could scarcely be maintained if persons could draw on their balance in the risk pool ad lib.

There are, no doubt, also paternalistic reasons for denying this kind of full consumer sovereignty. By such reasons the unwillingness to allow a person to assign to a particular end any degree of seriousness that he wishes is related to a judgment that to exceed certain limits would be so irrational that society should not go along with that assignment, and thus, however indirectly, society puts a degree of pressure on the individual not to take what are conceived of as irrational risks. To be sure, the individual can (except in extreme cases) avoid this pressure if he takes the risk himself and does not impose it on others. That is to say, a person may take foolish risks in respect to his own safety, and society often will not interfere.

Finally, in addition to administrative and paternalistic reasons against full consumer sovereignty relative to the risk pool there is a complex reason about the coordination of activities. The point is that by assuming that persons' risk budgets are similar, we each know what to expect from each other and we each know approximately what kind of risks will be imposed upon us in various situations. If persons were allowed to impose wildly anomalous degrees of risk for anomalous ends, even though their total withdrawal from the risk pool was not excessive, this kind of coordination of expectations would be considerably impaired. In a sense this might be urged simply as a reason for saying that a person taking a high risk for an anomalous end imposes even higher risk on others than might have at first appeared, and reduces his balance in the risk pool by a correspondingly higher amount than might have first appeared. The point is strong enough made even in that way, but I believe that the importance of coordination and the importance of allowing persons to form some notion of what risks might be imposed upon them in certain situations, so that they might plan whether or not to get into those situations, makes the imposition of a degree of uniformity of judgments particularly pressing. However, whether this argument ends up giving determinative weight to this degree of uniformity or only a very great weight, to be traded off against other values, I cannot say.

Ordinary and Grave Risks

The concept of the rational risk budget allows for a number of cases where certain ends will loom so large as to justify the actor in taking very high risks

703

of his own death to attain them. Does the concept of the risk pool mean that one is justified in imposing on others whatever risk we would be rational in accepting ourselves? Is there no difference between the imposition of a risk on another, and the acceptance of a risk for oneself? I have not shown that as a purely formal matter the general theorem is inconsistent with a notion of the risk pool by which persons may never impose a risk of more than a certain magnitude upon each other, though they may accept much larger risks for themselves. I have only shown the necessity of some pooling of risk at some level.

What reasons would all rational persons have for preferring a principle which places a lower limit on the degree of risk they are willing to have imposed on them by others—and therefore may impose on others—than on the degree of risk they will impose on themselves? In answering this, it should be recalled that in the individual risk budget high risks become more appropriate as they are necessary to more significant ends and capacities. Now if the right to impose risks on others were truly symmetrical with the risk budget, then as a person approached the point of critical need for his own purposes, he would be entitled to sacrifice not only his own life but that of another person. There are a number of reasons why this symmetry is unacceptable, but they all derive from the single point that sacrificing another for one's own purposes must be viewed as different from sacrificing oneself.

In sacrificing myself for some grave end of my own I am using up my own life in a way that I choose; that choice is a manifestation of my life plan and of my commitment to it. As such it is also a manifestation of my self-respect, for that concept might well be specified in terms of the seriousness with which I take my own ends. In short, because my ends are important to my life plan, in a sense because I *am* my system of ends, it is rational for me to use up my life for those ends. Does it follow that therefore I can use up another person's life? The argument why it might follow is that by acknowledging this right in myself I acknowledge a similar right in others, and by acknowledging this right in others I use up my life indirectly—that is I open myself up to its being used up—for a purpose of my own. But when I stand prepared to sacrifice my own life, I do it when *I* choose, and in specific conjunction with a crucial aspect of my life plan. If another person does this to me, the sacrifice will have no specific connection with some crucial end or capacity of mine. I may well be cut off in an entirely random way, relative to my life plan, and the only comfort would be that I had lost a gamble which I had made in order to allow myself to impose at some point greatly on others. Thus while the grave risks I would take for myself will be tied specifically to a crucial end, the grave risks imposed on me would be random over my life cycle.

This, I would suggest, is a result we should not accept. Rather we should accept a certain lesser freedom in accomplishing our ends (a lesser freedom, that is, to impose on others) in return for a greater security that we will not be exposed to grave risks by others at random points in our life cycle. This more cautious principle allows me to retain a greater measure of control over my life. It allows me to limit the grave risks to which I am exposed to cases where crucial ends are at stake.

This same point can be made another way. By denying myself the right to impose grave risks on another I am showing him respect; I am forgoing an advantage of my own because I cannot know that I shall not cut him off at a particularly inopportune point in his life cycle. (If I know that I shall, the argument is even stronger.) This is, of course, the exact complement of the point made above about my self-respect.

What is presented here can only be an argument of degree. It cannot be allowed to prove too much. It cannot be allowed to prove that we may not impose and should not accept the mutual imposition of some degree of risk. This would make all action impossible. What is being argued is that there is a certain level of risk—let us call it the ordinary or background level of risk— which is necessary to allow ordinary activity to take place. Moreover, within this there may be some modulations: not every legitimate activity will justify the same level of risk. This ordinary level is mutually imposed and accepted. Beyond this ordinary level one may accept risks for ends of his own, but may only exceptionally impose them on another, unless that other also accepts the risk as part of what might be considered a joint venture.

. . .

Obligations

There are cases in which the past history of the situation is generally thought to make a difference, varying the level of risk one may impose on others. Ordinary prudence and care require that a person be prepared and willing to stop short—say within 100 feet of first seeing a hazard—if by so doing he can avoid death or injury to another person. Let it be conceded also that a person need not in general take an action sacrificing his own life in order to avert a grave risk to another. Now let us imagine the case where A loads his truck with heavy steel pipe in such a way that if he stops short it will shift forward and is very likely to crush him in the driver's cab. A, thus laden, sees B drive out of a side road into his path. If A stops short he will avoid hitting and perhaps killing B, but he will also risk being killed by the pipe stacked in his truck. It would seem that A had the right to impose no more than a certain level of risk on others in venturing out on the highway in pursuit of his ends. If he stays within that level and there is an accident—something goes wrong— he is not at fault. If he stays within that level and something goes wrong, he need not sacrifice his life to avoid taking the life of another person who is involved in the encounter. But since he ventured out bearing this particularly heavy and dangerous burden he forfeits that right.

This argument makes the rightfulness of A's conduct depend on choices made and risks taken on some distinct, earlier occasion. We can see this if we contrast A's situation with that of C, a hitchhiker who is a passenger in the cab of A's truck. C is not constrained to risk his life to save B. If A in a fit of cowardice had leapt from the cab leaving C at the controls, we feel that C would be justified in not stopping short. Yet at the moment of the crucial option—to stop or not to stop—the choice of risks presented to A or to C would be exactly the same. This must show that A's prior action in loading the truck in some way obligated him to drive so as to avert danger to persons in B's position, even at the risk of his own life. It is this obligation that I wish to explore.

Let us consider the most obvious case of an obligation. This is a case where I have promised to some person that I will accept a certain rather high risk to save him if he should get into peril, in return for his agreement to do the same for me. If circumstances turn out so that I am called upon to risk my life to save that person, one would say that here is an obligation to take the higher level of risk than would otherwise be required. It is the past history which creates the obligation here.[1]

As we have seen, the obligation of promises is simply one sort of obligation. The general obligation of fairness, which is the obligation to do one's part in compliance with a scheme which one has voluntarily entered, or from which one voluntarily has derived benefits, is the more general case. And this more general obligation of fairness will apply in respect to the question of accepting and imposing risks as well. Even if there have been no explicit promises, therefore, if a person involves himself in a situation where persons accept and impose levels of risk upon each other on the understanding that others will abide by the limits set by these levels, then there is an obligation to do one's part when one's turn comes to accept burdens.

Applying this to the truck case, we may say that a person who ventures out on the highway is taking advantage of a general societal scheme in terms of which persons accept and impose levels of risks of a certain sort on each other. It is one's obligation to stay within those levels. But the driver of the truck can only do so by applying the brakes and risking being crushed by the pipe with which he has loaded his truck. If the lives of the people in a car with which he might come into a collision are at stake there would seem to be no excusing circumstance, and his obligation would be to make that sacrifice. In general we might say that the person has no right to excuse himself from the performance of an obligation because he himself has for his own purposes made the performance of that obligation more onerous than it need have been. Indeed, we may specify the concept of the risk pool further by recognizing that liberty is maximized if persons are allowed to do things such as loading their trucks in the way the driver in our hypothetical case has done, provided only that if

---

[1] A standard gambit in dealing with this sort of a moral problem is to treat the security of promises in the future as one of the forward-looking considerations which bind me to keep my promise. But that gambit can be readily blocked by further positing a situation in which my failure to keep my promise will not become known. It should be readily apparent that this is simply a standard case of the moral requirement that one fulfill obligations of fairness, of which obligations under a promise are an example, even though no utility maximizing considerations would compel us to do so. The structure of this argument is fully developed in Part One. We have here nothing more than a special case in which the burden we must take up in fulfillment of our obligation is a burden which involves the acceptance of risk.

an emergency arises they are willing to accept the consequences of their action and not shift them on to others. The driver of the truck who refuses to stop short, arguing that it is unreasonable to make him sacrifice his life, is in the position of somebody who voluntarily determines that he will not insure his house against fire, because he prefers to save the premium and use it in some other way, and then claims when a fire occurs that the fire has cost him so much money that he should be compensated by the insurance company anyway.

In all these situations we must consider not only the last moment of choice but the context, the history of the circumstances, since these might create an obligation to act in a certain way and may determine what that obligation is. And this conclusion requires us to revise to some extent the argument in the preceding section which held that the past history is irrelevant.[2]

These arguments lead to a rather surprising conclusion. Let us posit that the reasonable level of risk in driving is a function simply of speed. And let us posit further that the rate of speed corresponding to reasonable care in the risk pool is 50 miles an hour. Suppose that last week I drove for a time at 75 miles an hour without mishap. One might suppose that the fact that the risk did not eventuate should make that bit of misconduct irrelevant; I should not have to drive less than 50 miles an hour during the next week in order to "make up" for it.

Consider, however, that if I plan my driving for two weeks, driving one week at 75 miles an hour and the other week at 50 miles an hour, then my plan of conduct is in the aggregate gravely more risky than that of a person who plans to drive 50 miles an hour during both weeks. And if I plan to drive one week at 75 miles an hour and the second week at 25 miles an hour my conduct may be about as risky as a person who drives at a steady 50 miles an hour. But if I drive during the first week at 75 miles an hour and nothing happens (or something does happen and I pay), is not the only question before us, how risky should my conduct be in the next week? And is not the only rational answer that I should drive at 50 miles an hour, no more no less?

The answer to this last question is no. If I made an explicit bargain with the other members of the public that I will drive 75 miles an hour one week and 25 miles the next, then surely if I get through the first week I should not be able to go back on my bargain. To do so would be to withdraw more than my share from the risk pool. Now one would be tempted to say that the only

---

[2] The complex bearing of the past history of an event on our present rights in effecting withdrawals from the risk pool is well illustrated by legal doctrines and distinctions. The person who has himself created the hard choice between his own life and that of another will in law only be able to defend his taking of the other life if he did not create that situation improperly or on the assumption that he would take the consequences. An assailant who initiates a deadly attack on another cannot then hide behind the defense of self-defense if his victim in defending himself threatens the assailant's life. A driver who has negligently proceeded to cross the tracks when he should have seen an approaching train cannot complain if the engineer will not endanger the safety of his passengers by stopping abruptly to avoid a collision. Persons who employ dangerous instrumentalities (such as railroad engines or escalators) have a special obligation to come to the aid of persons injured by those instrumentalities even though it is conceded that they were free of fault in respect to the accident.

question would be what risks will I impose in the future. One would be tempted to say that risks in the past are like dreams from which we have awakened; they have no further reality. But we can see that this argument for escaping from one's obligation to drive at 25 miles an hour the second week is really the same thing exactly as an argument on the part of a person, who is called upon to fulfill a promise, that utility would be maximized overall if now that his turn has come to fulfill his promise, he did not do so. Such conduct would be unfair, and if generalized disastrous. Nor at this stage should we be impressed by the argument that the unfair, undutiful conduct may not in fact be an example to others, may not in fact be generalized, for that is beside the point.

This point may be illustrated by another example. Let us imagine that parking spaces are rationed by the use of parking meters. If I come to a meter and find I have no change, perhaps I should still be allowed to park there. This is equivalent to driving 75 miles an hour during the first week. But should it be open to me to argue that when I next have the chance I can simply forget about the money that I would have put into the meter? Should I not on some future occasion put twice as much into a meter? Or should I not accept a system of sanctions by which I pay a reasonable fine which is nevertheless a very large multiple of the money I would have put into the meter, on the assumption that the cost of the fine discounted by the probability of my being tagged is about the equivalent of the money I would have paid? Surely if every time it was inconvenient to put money into a parking meter there were no consequences at all in the future, the scheme for rationing parking spaces by parking meters would break down. Further, my obligation to the scheme is an obligation of fairness, so that I must make my contribution regardless of the probabilities that my delinquency will or will not in fact contribute to its breakdown.

Is the situation as to risks truly analogous to this example? Might it not be argued that in the case where I park at the meter and do not pay I have (let us assume there is a genuine scarcity of parking spaces) deprived somebody else of the convenience of parking at that meter, but where I have driven 75 miles per hour during the course of the week and injured nobody it would seem that no harm has been done, no costs imposed on others. It seems somewhat metaphysical to equate the palpable disutility of being deprived of a parking space to the disutility of having been subjected to a risk. And yet the equivalence is there, and must be taken seriously. If a large number of drivers drive on alternate weeks 50 and 75 miles an hour the highways will be a good deal less safe, and there will be an appreciably larger number of accidents than if all drivers drove 75 miles an hour and 25 miles an hour on alternate weeks.

It would seem then that we have here a rather different principle for decisions under uncertainty when we consider the interpersonal case than when we consider decisions under uncertainty where an individual is making choices only for himself. If a person acts unreasonably in relation to his own personal risk budget, but gets away with it, it does not make any sense to insist that he has an obligation to "pay back" in the future. At most what he must do in reflecting on his past deviations is to assure himself that it was, indeed, a deviation and not in fact the assertion of a rival risk budget in a rival life plan.

But once he is assured that his conduct was truly an anomaly, that he will be true to his risk budget, it is hard to see what sense there could be in his imposing on himself a penalty in the future. Yet such penalties in the future because of past conduct are just what we have argued for in respect to the interpersonal case under the concept of the risk pool. The closest one can come to such an argument for the intrapersonal case is the argument of self-discipline.

Should the argument be allowed to lead to the conclusion that the person who drove particularly carefully last week is entitled to drive more heedlessly of the safety of others the next week? And more generally, should we conclude that the risk pool furnishes a certain stake for each participant in the pool upon which he might draw as he chooses so long as he does not exceed the total amount of his share? Some objections to an analogous notion have already been adduced: in particular it was pointed out that such a principle would in practice be utterly unadministerable. The agrument from administrative convenience is not, I should say, an insubstantial or merely legalistic one. The fairness of a scheme depends on the confidence the participants have that others are abiding by it, and an unadministerable scheme would be unstable because it could not create that confidence. Obligations of the risk pool arise out of the principle of fairness, and persons are not as clearly bound by fairness to schemes which are easily evaded and difficult to administer.

It must be recognized that these objections must overcome the argument that where possible a person should be able to arrange his withdrawals from the risk pool in any way he likes. It is not clear that they do overcome the argument. After all that argument has working for it the presumption in favor of liberty. But it is our intuition that a person who has been more careful than necessary in the past is *not* thereby entitled to impose greater risks on others, even apart from problems of administration. And we feel this even though we may come to agree that a person who has been careless in the past is thereby obliged to make a kind of restitution by being particularly careful for a time in the future. This asymmetry, I would suggest, is an aspect of the principle about the special status of grave risks. The point has been made that the concept of the risk pool puts a ceiling on the risks we may properly impose on others which is lower than the ceiling on the risks we would be willing to take ourselves. This agrument might be extended to the issue before us now. By allowing the past to vary the social risk ceiling only in one direction, we say that no matter how careful we have been in the past, we may not on any particular occasion deliberately withdraw more than a certain amount from the pool. In less abstract terms this would mean that we may not deliberately confront others with a grave risk of death so long as we have any choice in the matter.[3]

---

[3] This argument should not, of course, be taken to state too much. It should not be taken to state that where there is a small risk r of a grave risk q, and the product of r and q is a risk of reasonable proportions, we may not take the risk $r \cdot q$ where, should r occur, we would be powerless to turn back. Rather, the argument states at most that once r has occurred and we can turn back from confronting risk q we should do so. Imagine that I have sent a salesman on

a trip in a one-engine plane in summer to the south. I know there is a certain chance of his being killed by a tornado, and yet all things considered this may not be an unreasonable risk. If I learn as he is underway that there are twisters in his vicinity, I should warn him to turn back. But if the twisters develop and there is nothing I can do, then I should be blameless. Indeed one of the factors that leads us to characterize the original decision as reasonable is the assurance that, in the class of case where I can instruct him to turn back, I will do so, thereby reducing the ex ante total risk involved in the decision. But if I can do nothing subsequently, the potential partitioning of the risks is irrelevant. What one might well ask, however, is whether it is permissible to create deliberately the situation where one cannot turn aside from the grave risk q, in order to save the possible additional resources? If one may not so bind the situation deliberately in advance, and if one is not entitled to be less careful later because one has been more careful in the past, is not all incentive gone to be specially careful? If I am right about this asymmetry of the bearing of past history, then instances of extra care in the past are like gifts: one need not make them, but once made we cannot demand payment after all.

continued from page ii

THE JOURNAL OF PHILOSOPHY   For "Moral Education and Indoctrination," by George Sher and William J. Bennett; reprinted from *The Journal of Philosophy,* LXXXI:11 (November 1982) by permission; for "The Alleged Moral Repugnance of Acting From Duty," by Marcia Baron; reprinted from *The Journal of Philosophy,* LXXXI:4 (April 1984) by permission; for "Moral Saints," by Susan Wolf; reprinted from *The Journal of Philosophy,* LXXIX:8 (August 1979) by permission.

MACMILLAN PUBLISHING COMPANY   For "Morality and Rationality," by Immanuel Kant, reprinted with permission of Macmillan Publishing Company from *Foundations of the Metaphysics of Morals,* translated by Lewis White Beck. Copyright 1959 by Macmillan Publishing Company.

NEW ENGLAND JOURNAL OF MEDICINE   For "Active and Passive Euthanasia," by James Rachels; reprinted from *New England Journal of Medicine.* Vol. 292, pp. 78–80, 1975. Copyright 1975 Massachusetts Medical Society.

OXFORD UNIVERSITY PRESS   For "Ethics and Observation," from *The Nature of Morality: An Introduction to Ethics,* by Gilbert Harman. Copyright © 1977 by Oxford University Press, Inc. Reprinted by permission. For "The Good Life," by Epicurus, from *Epicurus: The Extant Remains,* translated by Cyril Bailey, 1926; for "The Choice Criterion of Value," from *Equality, Liberty, and Perfectionism* by Vinit Haksar, 1979; for "Freedom and Reason," from *Freedom and Reason,* by R. M. Hare, 1963; for "Our Intuitive Knowledge of Right and Wrong," from *Foundations and Ethics,* by W. D. Ross, 1939; for "What Makes Right Acts Right?" and "What Things Are Good?" from *The Right and the Good,* by W. D. Ross, 1930. All reprinted by permission of Oxford University Press.

PENGUIN BOOKS   For "The Subjectivity of Value," from *Ethics* by J. L. Mackie. Copyright © J. L. Mackie, 1977. Reprinted by permission of Penguin Books Ltd.

PHILOSOPHICAL LIBRARY   For "Existentialism Is a Humanism," from *Existentialism and Human Emotions* by Jean-Paul Sartre; reprinted by permission of Philosophical Library.

PHILOSOPHICAL REVIEW   For "Skepticism About Weakness of Will," by Gary Watson, from *The Philosophical Review,* vol. 86, no. 3 (July 1977), pp. 316–39; for "Outline of a Decision Procedure for Ethics," by John Rawls, from *The Philosophical Review,* vol. 60 (1951), pp. 177–97; for "Morality as a System of Hypothetical Imperatives," by Philippa Foot, from *The Philosophical Review,* vol. 81, no. 3 (1972), pp. 305–16. All reprinted by permission.

PRINCETON UNIVERSITY PRESS   For "What Is Wrong with Slavery," by R. M. Hare, from *Philosophy & Public Affairs* 8, no. 2 (Winter 1979). Copyright © 1979 by R. M. Hare. Reprinted by permission of the author and Princeton University Press; for "War and Massacre," by Thomas Nagel, from *Philosophy & Public Affairs* 1, no. 2 (Winter 1972). Copyright © 1972 by Princeton University Press. Reprinted with permission of Princeton University Press; for "Lifeboat Earth," by Onora O'Neill, from *Philosophy & Public Affairs* 4, no. 3 (Spring 1975). Copyright © 1975 by Princeton University Press. Reprinted with permission of Princeton University Press; for "Famine, Affluence, and Morality," by Peter Singer, from *Philosophy & Public Affairs* 1, no. 3 (Spring 1972). Copyright © 1972 by Princeton University Press; for "A Defense of Abortion," by Judith Jarvis Thomson, from *Philosophy & Public Affairs* 1, no. 1 (Fall 1971). Copyright © 1971 by Princeton University Press. Reprinted with permission of Princeton University Press; for "Political Action: The Problem of Dirty Hands," by Michael Walzer, from *Philosophy & Public Affairs* 2, no. 2 (Winter 1973). Copyright © 1973 by Princeton University Press. Reprinted with permission of Princeton University Press.

RANDOM HOUSE   For "Beyond Morality," by Friedrich Nietzsche, from *Genealogy of Morals,* translated by Walter Kaufmann and R. J. Hollingdale, and *Beyond Good and Evil,* translated by Walter Kaufmann. Reprinted by permission.

ROWMAN & ALLANHELD   For "Moral Explanations," by Nicholas L. Sturgeon, in David Copp and David Zimmerman, eds., *Morality, Reason and Truth: New Essays on the Foundations of Ethics* (Totowa, N.J.: Rowman & Allanheld, © 1984), pp. 49–73. Reprinted by permission.

UNIVERSITY OF CALIFORNIA   For "Persons, Character, and Morality," by Bernard Williams, in *The Identities of Persons,* Amelie Oksenberg Rorty, ed. © 1976 The Regents of the University of California, used by permission of the University of California Press.

UNIVERSITY OF NEBRASKA PRESS   For "Beyond Morality," by Friedrich Nietzsche. Reprinted from *Human, All Too Human,* by Friedrich Nietzsche, translated by Marion Faber, with Stephen Lehmann, by permission of the University of Nebraska Press. Copyright 1984 by the University of Nebraska Press.

UNIVERSITY OF NOTRE DAME PRESS   For "The Virtues, the Unity of a Human Life, and the Concept of a Tradition," by Alisdair MacIntyre. Reprinted with permission from *After Virtue,* Second Edition, by Alisdair MacIntyre, 1984, University of Notre Dame Press, Notre Dame, IN 46556.

UNIVERSITY OF UTAH PRESS   For "Value," by Thomas Nagel, from *The Tanner Lectures on Human Values,* vol. 1. Printed with permission of The Tanner Lectures on Human Values, a Corporation, University of Utah, Salt Lake City, Utah. Copyright 1980 The Tanner Lectures on Human Values, a Corporation. Published 1980 University of Utah Press, Salt Lake City, and Cambridge University Press, Cambridge, England.

GEORGE ALLEN & UNWIN LTD.   For "The Nature of Moral Virtue," by Aristotle, translated by J. A. K. Thomson, from *The Ethics of Aristotle.* Reprinted by permission.

VIKING PENGUIN   For "Beyond Morality," by Friedrich Nietzsche, from "Thus Spake Zarathustra," from *The Portable Nietzsche,* translated by Walter Kaufmann. Edited by Walter Kaufmann. Copyright 1954 by The Viking Press, Inc. Copyright renewed © 1982 by Viking Penguin, Inc. Reprinted by permission of Viking Penguin, Inc.

WADSWORTH PUBLISHING COMPANY   For "Psychological Egoism," by Joel Feinberg, from *Reason and Responsibility* by Joel Feinberg (4th ed.) © 1965 by Dickenson Publishing Company, Inc. Reprinted by permission of Wadsworth, Inc., Belmont, CA 94002; for "Ethical Relativism," by Paul Taylor, from *Principles of Ethics: An Introduction* by Paul W. Taylor. © 1975 by Dickenson Publishing Company, Inc. Reprinted by permission of Wadsworth, Inc. Belmont, CA 94002.

WAYNE STATE UNIVERSITY PRESS   For "Toward a Credible Form of Utilitarianism," by Richard Brandt, reprinted from *Morality and the Language of Conduct,* 1963, pp. 107–40, by Richard Brandt, by permission of the Wayne State University Press.

A 6
B 7
C 8
D 9
E 0
F 1
G 2
H 3
I 4
J 5